An Illustrated
Dictionary of Jewelry

HAROLD NEWMAN

An Illustrated
Dictionary of Jewelry

2,530 entries, including definitions of
jewels, gemstones, materials, processes,
and styles, and entries on principal
designers and makers, from antiquity
to the present day

685 illustrations, 16 in colour

THAMES AND HUDSON

To the memory of my father

Text filmset in Singapore by Graphic Consultants International Pte Ltd.
Printed in Japan by Dai Nippon Printing Company Limited.

Preface

The first problem, when compiling a dictionary of jewelry, is to decide how to define the term 'jewelry', and how far a strict definition can justifiably be extended in order to make the book, within its limited space, of greatest use to readers. Basically, jewelry includes any decorative article that is made of metal, gemstones and/or hard organic material of high quality, contrived with artistry or superior craftsmanship, and intended to be worn on a person (such as a necklace, bracelet, ear-rings or brooch), including certain such articles that are functional as well as decorative (e.g. cuff links, buckles, tie clip). A slight extension can reasonably go beyond such movable jewelry and include articles that are sewn on a garment, e.g. a hat ornament (enseigne), decorative buttons, and jewelled dress ornaments.

On the other hand, there are a number of articles, similarly made, that are not worn but are carried by a person and that, even though highly ornamental, serve primarily a utilitarian purpose. Such articles are usually classified as objects of vertu rather than as jewelry. They include such carried objects as a snuff box, scent bottle, vanity case, and lipstick case, as well as objects with an essential part artistically decorated and often jewelled, such as a sword hilt, handle of a walking stick, frame of a handbag. They also include decorative accessories and ornaments that normally rest on a table or in a cabinet, such as a jewelled casket, hand mirror, or ring stand, as well as Fabergé Easter eggs and flower ornaments and large carved gemstones. All of such objects of vertu are beyond the scope of this book. Also excluded are spectacles and other vision aids, however ornamentally decorated, as well as such utilitarian objects as gold pens and pencils, cigarette holders and lighters, and lady's fans, even those enamelled and jewelled.

But in order to make this book as comprehensive about articles of, or very closely related to, jewelry as is reasonable possible within the available space, a few borderline objects have been included. Although watches are excluded as primarily within the field of horology, some ornamental watch cases are included, as well as wrist watches, lapel watches, and pendant watches. For the same reason, some articles of royal regalia (usually called 'Crown Jewels') are included, such as a few representative and important royal crowns, orbs, etc., as well as a few typical badges and collars of orders of knighthood or of guilds.

However, some articles that are worn by a person and are prized for their decorative appeal fall beyond the scope of jewelry when they are primarily in the field of costume; that applies especially to many objects worn ornamentally or ritualistically by primitive people, such as some carved or even jewelled head-dresses. But even here some exceptions have been made so as to include gold and jewelled articles of the pre-Columbian Indians and the contemporary Indians of the United States.

The range of objects having been established for present purposes, the limitations of time and space must be fixed. The use of jewelry for personal adornment dates back to millennia before the Christian era, and as each period has had some influence on the later styles and techniques, no limitation of time can justifiably be imposed on a comprehensive dictionary, and the oft-repeated phrase 'through the ages' must again be accepted here.

As to the geographical area to be embraced, difficult questions again arise, mainly because in some regions, especially black Africa and the islands of the south Pacific, the demarcation between jewelry, costume, and ritual is at times imperceptible. For example, in what category is a beaded waist ornament or a carved mask, both fabricated ornamentally and at times with great skill, but worn primarily for reasons other than personal adornment? Such objects are generally considered to be within the field of ethnology, and often the name of such articles varies according to the region or even the tribe, thus making definitions here impracticable. Also, the materials are often not of a nature that would be regarded by the Western world as precious, such as tusks, bones, teeth, seeds, feathers, and other such *objets trouvés*. So, however personal and decorative these may be, they will generally be excluded here from the term 'jewelry', as well as other ethnological objects from tribal cultures of black Africa and Pacific islands, except, however, those gold articles (e.g. Ashanti jewelry) made by methods or with decoration similar to those which this dictionary includes generally (such as granulated gold, filigree, *repoussé* work, enamelling, etc.) and also carved ivory personal ornaments (such as Benin bracelets and some Eskimo amulets).

It may seem to some readers superfluous to define here such familiar objects as a bracelet, necklace, finger ring, etc., but their inclusion as entries provides pegs on which to hang cross-references to various types of such articles. Indeed, the maximum usefulness of this book lies in the extensive use of cross-references (which are printed in SMALL CAPITALS). By this method each entry could be confined to essentials, duplication could be avoided, and a cue could be given for finding related subjects, whether a term more basic than a word defined or some specific example.

Another problem relates to gemstones and the extent that various varieties should be defined and technical details relating to them should be included. Although gemstones are normally (especially when uncut or unset) exhibited in a gemmological collection rather than in a collection of jewelry, they have always been so important an element of jewelry that the most important ones must be included here. However, the range of gemstones is so broad that those included here are only those frequently found set in jewelry; the many others can be readily studied in treatises on gemstones, or seen in mineralogical collections. But over fifty famous gemstones – although not all are worn as jewelry today – are described, especially to relate briefly their interesting histories.

However, this is a book primarily about jewelry and not gemmology or crystallology, so technical terms relating to gemstones are omitted, such as their chemical composition, specific gravity, refractive index, etc. as well as the structure of crystals and their physical characteristics, such as single or double refraction, colour dispersion, etc.

It certainly is not intended that this book should be a manual for makers of jewelry, amateur or professional. However, some processes of production (e.g. those for making synthetic gemstones) and some methods of decoration (e.g. *champlevé* and *cloisonné* enamelling) are briefly described in order to enable the reader better to understand how the finished product has been achieved; but the details of the processes are intentionally omitted. Likewise, the tools used by jewellers to make metal settings are omitted, as well as the highly technical apparatuses used to test gemstones and pearls, e.g. spectroscopes, refractometers, endoscopes, lauegrams, etc.

Although definitions here extend beyond the length of brief definitions such as are found in academic dictionaries, so as to include some historical background or reference to related topics, it must be emphasized that this is not an encyclopaedia of jewelry, and so there has generally been no attempt to trace through the centuries the historical or stylistic development of particular articles of jewelry.

Brief biographical data are given for some outstanding individuals and firms of the past and present who are well regarded in the jewelry world, but not their lifetime details.

Many important and meritorious jewellers of the past - whether individuals or firms - are not included, but their omission is not intended as a critical judgment of their work, rather it is due to limitations of space here.

Contemporary individual designers of jewelry are so numerous world-wide (especially in recent decades when in many cases the functions of designer and maker are combined) and opinions and tastes differ so widely in appraising the quality of their work, that it has been deemed prudent to omit entries for those born after 1950, thus avoiding what might be regarded as personal preferences among those still establishing their reputations. The same approach has been applied to present-day jewelry firms; hence only a few that are universally recognized are included.

Summarizing all of the above considerations, the author, when deciding on the entries and illustrations to be included in this book, has had to be selective and to be guided by what was considered by him to be of most interest and usefulness to the readership of a book of convenient size. In short, the book is planned to assist owners and buyers of jewelry, be they amateurs or connoisseurs, and also dealers and museum curators, as well as those having merely an aesthetic interest in jewelry, by defining the terms and listing the names that they are more likely to encounter and by providing them with photographic illustrations of significant types and examples of jewelry in various museums and collections that are not readily available for their viewing.

When preparing a book of this type and scope, it is normal, indeed inevitable, to draw on the writings and knowledge of predecessors and contemporaries, whether they be authors of earlier glossaries, of treatises on jewelry of various types, periods or regions, or of relevant magazine articles. However, no bibliography is included here, as the literature of jewelry is too vast, and much of it is in books in foreign languages not available to or readily understandable by the average English-speaking reader, and besides, many books on jewelry already do include extensive bibliographics. But in many instances a reference is made, at the end of an entry, to a source book or magazine article that discusses authoritatively the particular subject or that includes an exceptionally large number of related illustrations. I gratefully acknowledge my indebtedness to all such prior writers.

Appreciation is expressed to the many museums that have made available photographs of their pieces with permission to reproduce them, named in each case in the caption. To those museums that have supplied a large number of photographs, special thanks are due. These include:

Birmingham	City Museums and Art Gallery
Budapest	Hungarian National Museum
London	British Museum
	Museum of Mankind
	Victoria & Albert Museum
	Wallace Collection
Munich	Residenz Museum
New York	Metropolitan Museum of Art
	Museum of the American Indian
Oxford	Ashmolean Museum
Pforzheim	Schmuckmuseum
Stockholm	Statens Historiska Museum
	Nordiska Museum
Taranto	Museo Nazionale
Vienna	Kunsthistorisches Museum
Washington, DC	National Gallery of Art
	Smithsonian Institution

I am also grateful to Her Majesty the Queen for granting her gracious permission to reproduce photographs of several pieces of the Crown Jewels and the Royal Collection. Several photographs have been reproduced with the permission of the Controller of Her Majesty's Stationery Office (HMSO).

Thanks are extended to a number of jewelry firms that have generously supplied photographs of pieces owned or handled by them, especially Wartski, London, and S. J. Philips Ltd, London. Appreciation is also expressed to the London and New York offices of Sotheby's and Christie's for photographs supplied by them.

I wish particularly to express my thanks to Shirley Bury, Deputy Keeper of Metalwork and Jewelry at the Victoria & Albert Museum, and my appreciation to several persons expert in their fields who have read the portions of the manuscript in their realms. These include Dr Reynold Higgins, retired Keeper of Greek and Roman Antiquities at the British Museum, as to pre-Christian jewelry; Anna Somers-Cocks, Assistant Keeper of Metalwork and Jewelry at the Victoria & Albert Museum, as to Christian-era jewelry, including that of the Renaissance and modern periods; Elizabeth Carmichael, Keeper of South American and Central American Jewelry at the Museum of Mankind, London, as to pre-Columbian jewelry; Susan Stronge, of the Indian Department at the Victoria & Albert Museum, as to Indian jewelry; and E. A. Jobbins, Keeper of Minerals and Gemstones at the Institute of Geological Studies, London, as to matters relating to gemstones. I also thank Barbara Cartlidge, of Electrum Gallery, London, for assistance regarding some designer-makers of contemporary jewelry. Their assistance has been extremely helpful, but in all cases the responsibility for the entries is solely mine.

Finally, I wish to express my gratitude to my wife Wendy, without whose constant encouragement and frequent invaluable suggestions and comments this book (and my prior dictionaries), in the words of the well-worn cliché, but truly, 'could not have been written'.

H. N.

London 1981

Dictionary of Jewelry

Alphabetization of entries in the dictionary is by the word-by-word method: thus 'Ark Locket' precedes 'Arkansas diamond'. Cross-references to related subjects, where more information can be found, are indicated by SMALL CAPITALS. Initial capitals are used in entry headings to denote a particular jewel: thus the 'Darnley Ring' is the ring given to Lord Darnley, whereas 'Celtic brooch' refers to any of a number of brooches made by the Celts. Birth/death dates are given in parentheses: dates between commas indicate reigns.

Illustrations in black and white will as a rule be found on the same page as the relevant entry or on the facing page, though a few appear on adjacent pages owing to considerations of space. The following abbreviations are used in the captions: D. = diameter; H. = height; L. = length; W. = width.

The colour plates listed below illustrate the following entries:

A

AA Pendant. A gold MONOGRAM PENDANT with enamelling and set with TABLE CUT diamonds forming the monogram AA, and having superimposed a crown set with rubies. It is thought to have been a wedding gift in 1546 to Anna (daughter of Christian II of Denmark) from the future Elector Augustus I of Saxony — the monogram combining their respective initials — and to have been designed by Matthias Zündt and made in a workshop in either Augsburg or Munich. It has been recently suggested that the occasion for the gift was more likely in 1553 when Augustus succeeded to the title as Elector, thus giving a later date to the piece. The pendant is still preserved in the Green Vault (Grünes Gewölbe), Dresden.

abalone pearl. A variety of salt-water pearl produced by the abalone (or ear-shell). The pearls are usually small, but have high-quality NACRE and striking colours, such as green, yellow, and blue. The bowl-like shell of the abalone is valuable for making mother-of-pearl buttons and for inlays. *See* MOLLUSC SHELL.

abbot's ring. A type of finger ring worn by an abbot. Such rings were usually of gold, set with a single gemstone, and worn on the third finger of the right hand. In England in medieval times they were supposed to be surrendered to the Crown on the death of the owner (*see* BISHOP'S RING). An abbess also was permitted to wear a ring of this type until the practice was banned by Pope Gregory XIII in 1572; thereafter an abbess wore only her NUN'S RING.

Abingdon Brooch. The same as the MILTON BROOCH.

abraxas stone. A gem engraved with (1) the mystical word *abraxas* or *abrasax*, composed of seven Greek letters which, converted to numerals, totalled 365, the number of heavens of the Gnostic sect; or (2) the figure of Abraxas, a deity worshipped by the Gnostics, usually represented with the head of a cock or a lion, a human body, and legs in the form of serpents, and bearing a whip and a shield. The Gnostic cult emerged in the 2nd century AD and was still current in the 3rd. After the engraved stones had lost their symbolic significance they were worn either as an AMULET or as a TALISMAN. *See* GNOSTIC SEALS.

Achaemenian jewelry. Articles of jewelry, including finger rings, earrings, anklets, and bracelets, attributed to the period of the Achaemenid dynasty, founded by Cyrus the Great, in Persia (*c.* 559–330 BC). Such articles were made of gold, sometimes with FILIGREE decoration and sometimes set with coloured gemstones. A frequent decorative motif was an animal-head, comparable to those found on ANIMAL-HEAD BRACELETS of the Classical and Hellenistic periods.

achroite. An uncommon variety of TOURMALINE that is colourless.

acrostic jewelry. Various articles of jewelry decorated with gemstones set in a row or a circle, the initials of the names of the stones forming a word or name, e.g. (1) two bracelets that belonged to Josephine de Beauharnais (1763–1814), later Napoleon's empress, are set with stones whose initials form the Christian names of her two children, Eugène and Hortense; (2) a gold pencil-holder made by CARL FABERGÉ *c.* 1913, set with gemstones of which the initials spell the Russian Christian name of the owner; and (3) a ring or brooch with gemstones whose initials spell 'dear' or 'dearest', or a

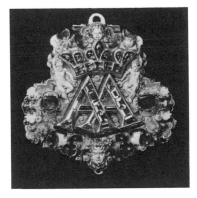

AA Pendant. Gold monogram pendant with inset gemstones. Probably German, *c.*1546–53. Staatliche Kunstsammlungen, Dresden.

Achaemenian jewelry. Gold ear-rings, 6th/5th century BC. W. 6 cm. Schmuckmuseum, Pforzheim, Germany.

female name, or sometimes a day of the week. The French term for such a ring is *bague hiéroglyphique*. *See* HARLEQUIN RING.

acrylic jewelry. Articles of CONTEMPORARY JEWELRY made with a PLASTIC material that is used in sheet, rod or liquid resin form. The material can be moulded when heated, or cut into various shapes, and has a glossy or matt appearance and wide colour range. It has been used in jewelry mainly since *c.* 1970, especially by such DESIGNER-MAKERS as DAVID WATKINS, CLAUS BURY, and SUSANNA HERON (Great Britain), and FRITZ MAIERHOFER (Austria). It is sometimes used in conjunction with gold, and is often made in bands of various colours.

acus. (1) The pin of a FIBULA or a brooch that is either an extension of the piece itself or is attached by a hinge. (2) A needle or pin used in Roman days for fastening the hair.

adamant. An ancient name for a diamond, derived from the Greek *adamas* (unconquerable). Owing to an early misconception that the word was derived from the Latin *adamare* (to be attracted to), it was formerly applied to a loadstone or magnet, which led to the belief that a diamond has magnetic power.

adamantine. (1) The type of LUSTRE shown by a diamond and certain other heavy gemstones. (2) Extremely hard, as a diamond.

adder stone. A stone, highly absorbent, that was formerly believed to be efficacious in drawing out poison, as from the bite of a snake. Such stones were set in finger rings and worn as an AMULET. Also called 'serpent stone'. *See* DRACONITES.

Adolphus, Gustavus, Pendant. A silver pendant in the form of a sarcophagus containing a small wooden figure of Gustavus Adolphus II (King of Sweden, 1611-32) commemorating him after his army defeated Wallenstein at the Battle of Lützen in 1632, in which he died. Other pendants, some of enamelled gold, also commemorated the event. *See* MEMENTO MORI.

Adriatic jewelry. Articles of jewelry made during the 16th/17th centuries in Italy along the Adriatic coast and on the neighbouring Greek islands. The pieces, often decorated with CLOISONNÉ enamelling, included SHIP PENDANTS and crescent-shaped ear-rings.

adularescence. The effect in a MOONSTONE, when cut EN CABOCHON, of a pronounced SHEEN, appearing in the form of a shimmering white light, sometimes with a bluish tinge. It is due to the reflection of light from fine lamellae of orthoclase and albite FELDSPAR. The effect is also seen in ADULARIA (from which it takes its name) and in LABRADORITE (there called 'labradorescence'). *See* AVENTURESCENCE; SCHILLER.

adularia. A variety of orthoclase FELDSPAR found in colourless crystals. It exhibits the effect known as ADULARESCENCE, named after the stone, which is itself named after the Adular Alps in Switzerland, a range that does not now include the St Gotthard region where the stone was first found.

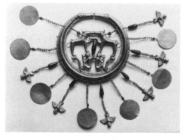

Aegina Treasure. Gold ear-ring with double-headed snake encircling monkeys and greyhounds, with suspended discs and owls. Minoan, 17th century BC. W. (hoop) 6.5 cm. British Museum, London.

Aegina Treasure. A TREASURE of MINOAN JEWELRY, usually attributed to the 17th century BC, that has been said to have been found in a Mycenaean tomb on the island of Aegina, near Athens, but that is now considered to be of Cretan origin, plundered in the 19th century from a burial enclosure at Mallia. The gold articles include necklaces, pendants, ear-rings, hairpins, and diadems, some with beads of CORNELIAN, AMETHYST, and LAPIS LAZULI. Some of the pieces show Egyptian influence. The treasure was acquired in 1892 by the British Museum.

aegirine. A mineral that is intensely green and related to JADEITE; it is also related to acmite, but its crystals have blunt ends rather than pointed. It is sometimes CHATOYANT when cut EN CABOCHON.

African emerald. A local misnomer for green fluorspar found in south-west Africa.

African jade. A local misnomer for green GROSSULAR. Also called 'Transvaal jade'.

African (West) jewelry. Articles of jewelry, especially objects made of gold or ivory, from the region of west Africa extending along the Atlantic from the Ivory Coast to Nigeria, including (1) ivory BENIN JEWELRY from southern Nigeria, as well as that of the Ife and Esie tribes of Nigeria; (2) gold ASHANTI JEWELRY from the central Gold Coast (now Ghana); and (3) Baoulé jewelry of gold and ivory from the Ivory Coast. In earlier times gold was generally reserved for sovereigns and their retinue, but gold articles were made also for the ruling classes and religious leaders. In the regions there were gold supplies and artisans who made jewelry of a high standard.

agate. A variety of CHALCEDONY (QUARTZ) that has a variegated colour, the natural colours being (1) in intercalated bands distinctly marked from each other (called 'banded agate'), the difference in the bands being due to degrees of transparency and colour and to INCLUSIONS of milky layers alternating with layers of QUARTZ, JASPER, CORNELIAN, ONYX, SARDONYX, or SARD (*see* STRIPED AGATE; EYE AGATE; OWL'S-EYE AGATE; FORTIFICATION AGATE; RUIN AGATE); or (2) in cloud-like, moss-like, or dendritic form, due to coloured inclusions or DENDRITES, as in MOSS AGATE (MOCHA AGATE), CLOUD AGATE, FEATHER AGATE, and MOSQUITO AGATE. Most banded agate is artificially coloured; the process, for black or brown and white stones, involves steeping in a solution of honey or sugar, then soaking in sulphuric acid and applying heat so that the carbon is released and enters the absorbent parts, colouring them blackish. This is an acceptable practice if the colour is fast and the trade description correct. Agate was used extensively in Egypt and Rome, in ornamental pieces and in jewelry such as beads and brooches; in the Middle Ages it was worn as an AMULET or TALISMAN. *See* CORNELIAN AGATE; IRIS AGATE; JASPER AGATE; OPAL AGATE; TURRITELLA AGATE.

agate. Portrait cameo of Shah Jehan carved by European lapidary at Mughal court, *c.* 1630-40. W. 2 cm. Victoria & Albert Museum, London.

agate jasper. The same as JASPER AGATE.

agate opal. The same as OPAL AGATE.

agatized coral. A variety of fossilized CORAL which is partly replaced by CHALCEDONY. It is made into jewelry in CABOCHON form, and is sometimes dyed pink or blue.

aggry (aggri) bead. A type of bead made by cutting obliquely a varicoloured glass cane (a glass rod made of several fused adjacent rods of different colours), resulting in a zigzag pattern. Such beads are of ancient manufacture and have been found buried in the Gold Coast (now Ghana).

aglet. A tapering ornament of gold, silver or other metal that was worn on a garment or sometimes a hat, either tied by a short ribbon or sewn on; some were enamelled or jewelled. They were usually worn in pairs or in larger numbers from 12 to 36, and were movable from one garment to another. Aglets were popular in England before and during the Elizabethan period, some having been used on head-dresses of Henry VIII. They were also worn in Germany, Bohemia, France, and Spain. *See* DRESS ORNAMENT.

Agnus Dei. Gold pendant set with diamonds, garnets, and pearls. Hungarian, 17th century. Victoria & Albert Museum, London.

Agnus Dei. A jewel depicting the Lamb of God as the emblem of Christ. The lamb often appears having a circular nimbus around its head and with a Latin cross and with a banner or a staff bearing a MALTESE CROSS. It has been used on several types of pendants and TALISMANS, e.g.: (1) On a pendant, with the figure IN THE ROUND, enamelled or jewelled or engraved (*see* DEVIZES PENDANT). (2) As a talisman, in the form of a circular case, often of silver gilt, bearing on the front a representation of the Agnus Dei in NIELLO or in REPOUSSÉ work, and sometimes with a corded edge. Such cases enclosed a roundel of wax bearing a stamped impression of the Agnus Dei, made from the wax of a paschal candle blessed at Rome by the Pope in the first year of his pontificate and each seventh year thereafter. They were distributed in Europe to the faithful in the 14th/15th centuries. Some of the cases have a cover of transparent HORN on the front and back. A 15th-century example from Germany bears the name of Pope Urban VI, 1378–89. A bronze die for stamping the wax, made in Italy in the 14th century, is in the British Museum. (3) A so-called 'Agnus Dei pendant', worn by peasants of Norway and Sweden during the 18th century, in the form of a large coin hanging from a NECK CHAIN and having suspended from the coin several smaller coins (with ornamental pieces in turn suspended from the latter), and often having cheap hanging ornaments in lieu of missing coins. Such pieces, without any representation of the Agnus Dei, are said to be derived from earlier pilgrims' talismans that did bear such a representation.

agraf(f)e. A clasp or fastener for a cloak, in the form of a hook sewn on one side of the garment, to be attached to a loop or ring sewn on the other side.

aigrette. A gold or silver hat ornament or hair ornament to support a feather, or made in the form of a jewelled feather or sometimes a brooch supporting a jewelled feather. Shaped like an egret plume (hence the name), it was often almost entirely set with small gemstones, and sometimes also enamelled; it might be further adorned with light, vibrating, vertical metal stalks. A slide or a vertical pin was occasionally provided, enabling the ornament to be worn in the hair or attached to a head-dress. Aigrettes were in use from the 17th century until the late 18th, and again in the late 19th and early 20th centuries. *See* TREMBLANT; GIKA OF NADIR SHAH.

aigrette. Gold tremblant aigrette with diamonds. English, 18th century. Courtesy of Wartski, London.

aiguillette (French, from *aiguille*, needle). A brooch or ear-ring decorated with a series of cascading gemstones of diminishing size, terminating in a thin, tapering, pointed stone. The style is known as EN PAMPILLES.

Ajjul Hoard. A HOARD, including articles of gold and silver jewelry, found at Tell el-Ajjul, near Gaza, in Israel, by Sir Flinders Petrie (1853–1942), and suggested by him to have been concealed by a local jeweller pending melting for remodelling. The articles (pendants, ear-rings, AMULETS in the form of a fly, and TOGGLES) include examples of Bronze Age Canaanite art, in which Egyptian motifs are blended with local traditions. The decoration of some pieces is in GRANULATED GOLD. *See* ASTARTE PENDANT; FLY JEWELRY; CENOTAPH, TREASURE OF THE.

ajouré work. An OPENWORK pattern, e.g. one formed by cutting holes in a metal sheet. *See* JOUR, À; OPUS INTERRASILE.

akabar. *See* KING CORAL.

Akbar Shah Diamond. A famous Indian diamond formerly owned by the Great Mogul of India, Akbar Shah (1542-1605), and once having engraved on it, by order of his grandson and successor, Shah Jehan, the Arabic inscriptions translated as 'Shah Akbar, Shah of the World, 1028' (an incorrect date) and 'To the Lord of Two Worlds, Shah Jehan, 1039', the Hegira dates corresponding to AD 1618 and 1629. The stone is said to have been taken to Persia by Nadir Shah when he sacked Delhi in 1739, but it disappeared until 1866, when it reappeared in Constantinople, called then the 'Shepherd Stone'. It was recognized by the inscriptions and was bought by George Blogg, a London merchant, who had it recut in London into a pear-shaped stone, reducing its weight from 116 old carats to 71¾ old carats and destroying the inscriptions. In 1867 it was sold to the Gaekwar of Baroda, after which date nothing is known of it. For other engraved diamonds, *see* ENGRAVED GEMSTONES.

ajouré work. Gold plaque depicting king making offering to a god. Egyptian, *c.* 1795 BC. W. 3 cm. British Museum, London.

alalite. A variety of DIOPSIDE that is light green.

Alaska diamond. A local misnomer for ROCK CRYSTAL.

Albert, Gilbert (1930-   ). A leading Swiss DESIGNER-MAKER of jewelry. He has designed jewelled WATCH-CASES, being Chief Designer for the firm Patek Philippe from 1954 and later for Omega. In 1962 he opened his own workshop in Geneva, and in 1965 was the first modern artist ever to have a one-man show at Goldsmiths Hall in London. He has specialized in abstract gold jewelry and has, since 1964, to enhance the overall effect, incorporated in the design fragments of METEORITES and other objects of little intrinsic value; among such pieces are necklaces in the form of loose nets.

Albert chain. A gold or silver WATCH CHAIN of a broad class of chains characterized by having a swivel on at least one end and by being worn usually across a man's waistcoat from pocket to pocket, threaded through a waistcoat buttonhole, or more often secured to it by a short attached bar. Such chains are made in a great variety of types, with many styles and groupings of the links; they include mass-produced, machine-made chains of standardized forms and nomenclature (e.g. CURB CHAIN, FETTER CHAIN, TRACE CHAIN), as well as hand-made chains of original design. Usually a watch was worn at one end and a key, WATCH KEY, SEAL, FAUSSE MONTRE, sovereign case or other article on the other end. Such chains, named after Prince Albert, Consort of Queen Victoria, were popular from the mid-19th century, and they are still often used by men when wearing a waistcoat. Sometimes a version of the Albert chain was worn by women, in which case it was more ornate and often composed of two strands, having inserted at the centre a gold ornamental section.

Alençon diamond. A misnomer for a type of brilliant smoky QUARTZ found at Alençon, in France. Such stones were used on the NORMAN CROSS. The French term is *pierre d'Alençon*.

Aleppo stone. The same as EYE AGATE. It was so called on account of the power attributed to it in the Orient of curing a sore known as an 'Aleppo boil'.

alexandrite. A variety of CHRYSOBERYL. Due to the presence of oxide of CHROMIUM, it appears dull grass-green by daylight (which is rich in blue rays), but by electric light it appears yellowish or reddish-yellow, and by soft candle-light (which is rich in red rays) it appears reddish. It is highly dichroic. Its original source was near Ekaterinburg, in the Ural Mountains of Russia. The stone was discovered there in 1830, the year Alexander II came of age; hence it was named after him. The variety now found in Sri Lanka (formerly Ceylon) changes from dark olive-green to brownish-red; it is larger than that of Russia (which is bluer) but less valuable. The stone is imitated by SYNTHETIC SPINEL and in great quantities by SYNTHETIC CORUNDUM (both incorrectly marketed as SYNTHETIC ALEXANDRITE); these are produced so as to show the changing colours. *See* ANDALUSITE.

Alfred Jewel. A renowned Anglo-Saxon pear-shaped object whose central ornament, set on a gold plate, is a CLOISONNÉ enamel portrait covered by a bevelled plate of ROCK CRYSTAL and surrounded by a gold, sloping, openwork rim that terminates in a socket containing a cross-rivet to secure it to a shaft. The portrait is of a half-length male figure holding in each hand a SCEPTRE or wand with a floral head. In the openwork around the rim there is, in gold letters, the Saxon inscription 'AELFRED MEC HEHT GEWYRCAN' ('Alfred ordered me to be made'), thought to refer to King Alfred, 871–901. The lower part, in GRANULATED GOLD, is in the form of a boar's head, from whose snout projects the hollow socket. The portrait, against a dark-blue ground, is in green, brown, and white. On the reverse is a flat, gold plate bearing elaborate engraved foliage and scale decoration. The piece is probably of late-9th-century workmanship, possibly by a Winchester or Glastonbury jeweller, or a European attached to the royal court. It was found in 1693 at Newton Park, three miles from the Isle of Athelney, Somerset, where Alfred had fled from the Danes in 878 and is said to have hidden or lost the jewel. It was presented to the Ashmolean Museum, Oxford, in 1718 by Thomas Palmer. There has been much speculation as to the purpose of the jewel, whether the head of a sceptre, the jewel of a crown, or the tip of an *aestel* (a pointer for indicating the lines of a manuscript, possibly the same one to which was attached the MINSTER LOVEL JEWEL. The figure has been variously ascribed to Christ, the Pope, Alfred, or a saint, but is possibly an allegorical representation of Sight. Copies have been made, with the portrait printed on paper covered by glass. *See* J. R. Kirk, *The Alfred and Minster Lovel Jewels* (1948).

Alhstan Ring. A gold Saxon finger ring, whose hoop is in the form of four small roundels (decorated with birds and monsters) alternating with

Albert, Gilbert. Gold pendant watch concealed under lid with baroque pearls. By Patek Philippe, Geneva.

Alfred Jewel (side view below). Gold with *cloisonné* portrait. Probably 9th century. H. 6.3 cm. Ashmolean Museum, Oxford.

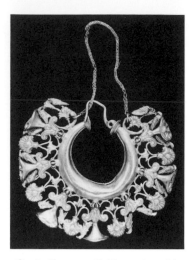

Aliseda Treasure. Gold ear-ring with granulation. 7th/6th centuries BC. Museo Arqueológico Nacional, Madrid.

Ålleberg Collar (detail below). Gold with filigree and granulation. Norway, 6th century. Statens Historiska Museum, Stockholm.

four LOZENGE-shaped ornaments, all decorated in NIELLO. The roundels are inscribed with the letters A LH ST A (the last followed by a runic N), being the name of the presumed owner, Bishop Alhstan of Sherborne (824–67). It was found probably in 1753 at Llys-faen, in Caernarvonshire (now Gwynedd), Wales, and is in the Victoria & Albert Museum, London. *See* ETHELSWITH RING; ETHELWULF RING.

Aliseda Treasure. A TREASURE found in 1920 in the village of La Aliseda, near Cáceres, Spain, that included gold articles decorated with GRANULATED GOLD and FILIGREE in openwork designs, attributed to Phoenician–Punic sources, of the 7th/6th centuries BC. Much of it is now in the Museo Arqueológico Nacional in Madrid. *See* PHOENICIAN JEWELRY.

Ålleberg Collar. A gold, circular, rigid COLLAR made in two hinged sections, each of three concentric tubes completely decorated with adjacent rings, FILIGREE work, and GRANULATED GOLD. One section is composed of hollow tubes, the other of solid rods, with the ends of the latter fitting into the former to make a circle when the piece is closed. The space between the tubes is further decorated with small animals and faces cut from gold plates. It is from Scandinavia, from the Migration period of the 6th century, before the coming of the Vikings, and was found at Ålleberg, in Sweden. A similar collar, but with five circular tubes, was found at Fårjestaden, Öland, Sweden.

allegorical subjects. Symbolic subjects used decoratively in jewelry and portrayed by figures often identifiable by traditional attributes accompanying them, e.g. 'Justice and Peace' and 'Prudence and Simplicity' (both depicted on pendants inspired by woodcuts by JOST AM-MAN), 'The Five Senses' (*see* FULLER BROOCH), and 'Charity' (*see* CHARITY PENDANT).

alloy. A mixture of two or more compatible metals (or sometimes a metal and a non-metal, e.g. steel, an alloy of iron and carbon), made by being fused into each other to form a homogeneous mass, the resultant new metal usually being harder, more durable and more fusible than the components but less malleable and of a different colour. Non-compatible metals (e.g. nickel and silver) cannot be alloyed because they will not dissolve into each other. Some alloys are formed by nature (e.g. ELECTRUM), but most are man-made to increase strength or workability, or to alter colour, e.g. a base metal mixed with a precious metal. Alloys made of various metals and in various proportions to meet different industrial needs are made by refiners and sold to makers of jewelry, e.g. gold and silver SOLDER.

Alma chain. A type of CHAIN composed of broad links having a ribbed surface.

almandine. A variety of GARNET that is transparent and commonly deep crimson with tinges of purple. Its colour may resemble that of RUBY. It is cut in several forms; when cut EN CABOCHON (usually as hollow cabochon to lighten the colour), it is called CARBUNCLE. Some stones are shaped in India by TUMBLING, and sometimes now are faceted. The main sources are Sri Lanka (formerly Ceylon), Fort Wrangel in Alaska, and India. An alternative name is 'almandite'. A sub-variety has INCLUSIONS of NEEDLES of foreign substances, which sometimes form a weak 4-pointed or 6-pointed star (*see* ASTERISM); such stones are called 'star almandine'. *See* ALMANDINE SPINEL; RHODOLITE.

almandine spinel. A misnomer for purple-red varieties of SPINEL (ALMANDINE being a variety of GARNET) which resemble the almandine in colour.

almandite. (1) The same as ALMANDINE. (2) A misnomer for SYNTHETIC SPINEL, which sometimes resembles the almandine (almandite).

Altenstetter, David (d. 1617). A goldsmith from Colmar who settled in Augsburg and became a Master Goldsmith in 1583. In 1610 he was invited to Prague by Rudolf II to become Court Jeweller, and worked there until his death. His work often featured BASSE TAILLE enamelling, and some pieces made by his workshop are decorated with birds, fruit, and flowers.

aluminium (in the United States, **aluminum**). A bluish silver-white metal that is very light, very malleable, ductile, and resistant to OXIDATION. The metal was originally called by Sir Humphry Davy 'alumium'; the name was changed soon after to 'aluminum', but was then made 'aluminium' in England to conform to the names of other elements such as 'barium'. In the early decades after its discovery it was more highly prized than gold, and was used in some jewelry made for Empress Eugénie, some articles being displayed at the Great Exhibition of 1851 in London. It is now used in jewelry only for COSTUME JEWELRY and JUNK JEWELRY, some such pieces being given a coloured finish since the introduction of anodizing.

amalgam. An ALLOY of GOLD or SILVER with mercury that can be applied to the surface of a base metal (or porcelain) and when it is fired to a point when the mercury vaporizes, a gold residue will be left. This is the classical method of GILDING metals, known as 'fire gilding' or 'mercury gilding'.

Amaryl. A trade-name for a variety of SYNTHETIC CORUNDUM that is light green. The name is said to have been suggested by the colour of the leaves of *Amaryllis belladonna*, the South African belladonna lily.

Amazon jade. A misnomer for the green variety of AMAZONSTONE that has a slight resemblance to JADE.

amazonstone (or **amazonite**). A variety of FELDSPAR of the microcline series; its colour ranges from vivid green to blue-green and when turned in the light it sometimes appears to have been sprinkled with stardust. It is opaque, with a pearly SHEEN and may show ADULARESCENCE. Amazonstone is never faceted but cut EN CABOCHON: it is used in finger rings and as beads. The name is derived from the Amazon, perhaps as some specimens have been found in Minas Gerais, Brazil. It is sometimes called by the misnomer 'Amazon jade'.

amber. An amorphous translucent or opaque fossilized natural resin from an extinct variety of pine tree (*Pinus succinifera*) submerged under the sea some 60,000,000 years ago. It is light in weight, warm to the touch, very brittle, and electrified when rubbed. Its colour covers a wide range, usually from pale yellow and honey to reddish-brown, brown, red, and almost black; but some is whitish (*see* BONE AMBER). Some pieces show two colours, and these have sometimes been cut as CAMEOS. The best-quality amber is clear, but some is cloudy (*see* BASTARD AMBER), some pieces include 'stress marks' giving a crackled appearance, and some rare specimens contain embedded insects or other organic or inorganic material trapped in prehistoric times. Amber is soft but tough, hence often intricately carved (especially in China) and sometimes faceted. It has been used mainly for articles with a smooth and polished surface, e.g. beads, finger rings, and bracelets. Many such pieces have been made in Tibet, Mongolia, and Ethiopia (the amber having been transported there); amber was also used for such pieces in England during the Celtic and Victorian eras. It has been used as a TALISMAN and as an ornament in jewelry since the Bronze Age; it was also so used by the ancient Greeks, Romans, Etruscans, Phoenicians, Persians, Byzantines, Vikings, Celts, Saxons, Chinese, and Japanese, and then again in the 19th century in Russia and the Baltic states. Amber is of two main varieties: (1) sea amber (SUCCINITE), pieces of which are washed up along certain shores, especially the Baltic Sea near Kaliningrad, and also along the shores of eastern England and the Netherlands (from the Lower Tertiary beds buried beneath the North Sea); and (2) pit amber, mined from Oligocene deposits in Burma (called BURMITE). Other sources are Sicily (called SIMETITE), Romania (called ROUMANITE), Danzig (called GEDANITE), and Mexico. Amber boiled in suitable oils changes from opaque to clear and also in colour. In modern times it has been used for tobacco-pipe stems and for cigar- and cigarette-holders. Various substitutes have been developed in recent years; *see* AMBROID; COPAL; KAURI GUM. Imitations have also been made using PLASTIC; these are distinguishable by their greater specific gravity, by the fact that in a strong brine solution they sink while amber would float, and by amber's characteristic smell when heated. Amber has also been imitated in GLASS, sometimes with faked inserted insects. Amber has no connection with AMBERGRIS. The German term for amber is *Bernstein*, the French *ambre*. *See* G. C. Williamson, *The Book of Amber* (1932); Rosa Hunger, *The Magic of Amber* (1977).

amber opal. A variety of OPAL that is brownish coloured, due to the presence of iron oxide.

ambergris. A waxy substance (having no relationship with AMBER) that is found floating in the Indian Ocean and other tropical waters, believed to be the secretion of the sperm whale. Its colour is white, grey, yellow or black, often variegated. Ambergris is used mainly as a fixative for prefumery, and rarely employed in jewelry. A few known examples include figures carved in ambergris (one built over a silver core) by Dutch jewellers of the Mannerist period; one is a pendant with a group depicting Charity with three children, formerly in the Morgan Collection and now in the Metropolitan Museum of Art, New York, and a similar piece is in the Walters Art Gallery, Baltimore.

amberine. A variety of MOSS AGATE that is yellowish-green.

amblygonite. A mineral that produces crystals suitable as gemstones. They are colourless ranging to shades of pale yellow. It is brittle but is cut with FACETS or EN CABOCHON. The name is derived from the Greek *amblygonios* (obtuse-angled), after the angle in which it cleaves.

ambroid (or **amberoid**). A substance made, in the manner of a RECONSTRUCTED STONE, by heating small pieces of true amber and fusing them under pressure. It closely resembles natural amber in appearance and physical properties, but is distinguishable by its embedded, elongated bubbles and by the visible fusion lines. Also sometimes called 'pressed amber'.

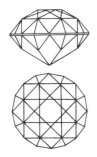

American brilliant cut
side and top views

American brilliant cut. A modification of the BRILLIANT CUT of a diamond in which the width of the TABLE is reduced so as to be only one-third of the width of the stone, and the height of the CROWN is increased to be about two-thirds that of the PAVILION. The number of BEZEL FACETS on the crown is increased by adding a row of 8 small facets abutting the table, making a total of 40 facets on the crown, in addition to the table. The style of the cut was developed by Henry D. Morse and other American cutters, and the angles of the facets were confirmed in 1919 by Marcel Tolkowsky (a mathematician who published a treatise on the correct manner of cutting a brilliant) as the 'ideal cut', most effective to maximize the BRILLIANCE at some cost of lost weight; but *see* EUROPEAN BRILLIANT CUT.

American Indian jewelry. *See* INDIAN (UNITED STATES) JEWELRY; PRE-COLUMBIAN JEWELRY.

American jade. A misnomer for CALIFORNITE.

American ruby. A misnomer for PYROPE GARNET.

American setting. A type of SETTING for a diamond or other transparent gemstone that has a high MOUNT and is pierced À JOUR.

amethyst. A variety of QUARTZ that is transparent and CRYSTALLINE, usually deep purple to pale bluish-violet; the hues are sometimes mingled in the same stone, owing to irregular colour zoning, and some show patches of yellow. Other colours are reddish-mauve (Siberian stones), reddish-violet (Uruguayan stones) or grey-mauve (Mexican stones). When natural amethysts (not the variety from Madagascar) are heated, the colour changes to pale yellow (sometimes then mistaken for CITRINE, but distinguishable by its dichroism); when the heat is increased, it changes to dark yellow or reddish-brown and, when increased further, to milky white. Some Brazilian amethysts when heated change colour to green (*see* GREENED AMETHYST; PRASIOLITE). Specimens containing INCLUSIONS of goethite or other fibrous minerals are polished as CAT'S-EYES. Amethysts have been set in globular or pear-shaped PENDANTS and as pierced BEADS for necklaces and ear-drops. Some large stones have been embellished by having set into them a design of small diamonds. *See* AMETHYST QUARTZ; STAR AMETHYST; CAIRNGORM; SARK STONE.

amethyst quartz. A variety of AMETHYST that is banded with INCLUSIONS of MILKY QUARTZ or AGATE.

amethystine. A variety of QUARTZ or GLASS with patches of purple or violet colour.

Amherst Brooch. A COMPOSITE BROOCH of which the front is gold, decorated with FILIGREE work and with CLOISONS forming cells of step, quatrefoil and triangular form, and the back is of silver set with a central garnet. The cells were set with garnets, now missing, over chequered gold foil. Four of the eight triangular cells are set with green glass. Between the two parts a white substance is now visible where the brooch was damaged as a result of being dropped in 1859 by Lord Amherst, the then owner. It resembles the KINGSTON BROOCH, but is greatly inferior in quality of workmanship. The brooch is Anglo-Saxon, of the early 7th century, and was found many years ago in a grave in Kent. It is sometimes called the 'Sarre II Brooch' to distinguish it from the SARRE DISC BROOCH in the British Museum. *See* MONKTON BROOCH.

Amherst Brooch. Composite gold and silver brooch with filigree work; garnets missing. Anglo-Saxon, 7th century. W. 5.5 cm. Ashmolean Museum, Oxford.

Amman, Jost (1539-91). A woodcut illustrator whose designs have been said to have inspired several pieces of gold enamelled jewelry. Born in Zurich, the brother of a goldsmith, he settled in 1560 in Nuremberg, where he became attached to VIRGIL SOLIS and, upon the latter's death in 1562, completed some of his engraving work, thereafter continuing as an illustrator. In 1577 he left Zurich to return to Nuremberg. He produced two notable books (one titled *Ein neuw Thierbuch*) that were published in Frankfurt in 1569 and 1578, with drawings of figures of horseback couples, angels, animals and ALLEGORICAL SUBJECTS; some have been identified with jewelled and enamelled gold pendants depicting such figures IN THE ROUND. These pendants have been said to have been executed by unidentified German jewellers at Munich, Augsburg, and Nuremberg in the second half of the 16th century, though one probably by GIOVANNI BATTISTA SCOLARI (*see* SLEIGH-RIDE PENDANT). *See* Yvonne Hackenbroch, 'Renaissance Pendants after Designs by Jost Amman', in *Connoisseur*, September 1965, p. 58.

ammonite. A variety of mollusc that existed 150,000,000 years ago and whose shell was in the form of a flat, snail-like spiral with interior compartments. The fossil, polished to reveal the interior structure, was sometimes mounted, *c.* 1850, in gold, silver or jet, and worn as a brooch or pendant, especially those found in abundance in Dorset, England, and some western regions of the United States.

amulet. Coral set in gold mount. Italian, 16th century. H. 7.5 cm. Kunstgewerbemuseum, Cologne.

amorphous. Without any CRYSTALLINE structure, e.g. OPAL and GLASS. *See* MASSIVE.

amulet. An object (such as a brooch, finger ring, bracelet, reliquary or pendant) or a gemstone believed to have special supernatural qualities and worn primarily for its supposed ability to ward off evil, witchcraft or illness, but sometimes to bring good fortune. Such pieces often bore an inscription, e.g. the names of the Magi (*see* THREE KINGS)) or a symbol. In China, as early as the Shang-Yin Dynasty (*c.* 1766-1122 BC), a large variety of JADE AMULETS were made in the form of carved animals and pendants. Early Egyptian examples were made of glass, *c.* 1375 BC, and were often in the form of an actual or mythological animal. Etruscan amulets were decorated with various symbols and later Roman ones are known, often enclosed in a BULLA in the form of a finger ring. They were also worn in Europe throughout the Middle Ages and the 16th century. *See* CHARM; TALISMAN; DEITY AMULET; HAND AMULET; HIGA; TAU CROSS; MAGICAL JEWELRY.

amulet box. A small container in the form of a box with a cover and an attachment for a suspensory cord. Such boxes were worn in Tibet for protection, especially when travelling. They contained a stamped plaque with Buddhist images or wood-block printed charms on paper or cloth, or charms of grains or pebbles. One example from the 18th century is said to

amulet box. Gold set with turquoises. Tibetan, 18th century. W. 5.1 cm. British Museum, London.

amulet case. Gold with openings backed with garnets. Gandhara, Afghanistan, 2nd/3rd centuries. L. 7.3 cm. British Museum, London.

have been worn on the pigtail of an official's servant. *See* AMULET; AMULET CASE.

amulet case. A hollow container in which was kept an AMULET. Examples made in Persia from the 2nd century to the 11th were cylindrical or of polygonal section, about 2.5 to 7.5 cm long, having top loops for suspension rings so that it could be hung by a cord; some were made of gold or silver, decorated with REPOUSSÉ work, sometimes having shaped openwork set with gemstones and open ends closed by a cap. A Phoenician example, 7th/6th century BC, has, above a hollow cylinder, a zoomorphic figure decorated with GRANULATED GOLD and CLOISONS. *See* AMULET BOX; CYLINDRICAL AMULET CASE.

amygdaloid. Almond-shaped, hence the name from the Greek *amygdale* (almond), such as some beads and engraved gems of MINOAN JEWELRY and MYCENAEAN JEWELRY.

anatase. A gemstone that may be transparent and brownish (cut with FACETS) or opaque and blue (cut EN CABOCHON). The name is derived from the Greek *anatasis* (stretching out), referring to the length of the crystals. Also called OCTAHEDRITE.

andalusite. A mineral that, when translucent and green or reddish-green, is used as a gemstone. It is found in other colours, e.g. grey, and reddish- to yellowish-brown. It has strong dichroism which causes it to show green when viewed in one direction, but brownish-red in another, thus resembling ALEXANDRITE, except that the green colour is not affected by artificial light. Andalusite with streaky INCLUSIONS shows CHATOYANCY and is cut EN CABOCHON; when translucent it is faceted. It was first found in Andalusia. *See* CHIASTOLITE.

Andamooka Opal. A WHITE OPAL in the form of an oval CABOCHON weighing 203 carats and having brilliant fire. It was cut from a stone weighing rough 170 grams (6 oz) that was found in 1949 at Andamooka, South Australia. When presented in March 1954 to Queen Elizabeth II by the government of South Australia, it was set in a palladium necklet with two other white opals and 180 diamonds.

animal-head bracelet. Gold penannular bracelet with ram's-head terminals. 5th century BC. British Museum, London.

andradite. A common variety of GARNET that is found in several colours, e.g. green, yellow, red, brown, and black, some of which are sub-varieties with special names: DEMANTOID (green), MELANITE (black), and TOPAZOLITE (yellow). It was named after J. B. de Andrade e Silva (1763-1838), a Portuguese mineralogist.

Anglo-Saxon jewelry. Articles of jewelry made in Britain between the Roman Occupation and the Norman Conquest (i.e. 5th century to 1066), during which period races of Germanic origin invaded and settled, mainly in East Anglia, Mercia, Wessex, Northumbria, and Kent. The jewelry of the period, especially the SUTTON HOO TREASURE, has been recovered mainly from burial sites. It is usually made of gold, silver or bronze, ornamented (with great technical skill) with FILIGREE or GRANULATED GOLD and inlaid with garnets and coloured glass, or with enamelling. The pieces were intended mainly as personal ornaments for the women, and included a great variety of brooches, PINS, FIBULAE, CROSSES, BRACTEATES, and finger rings, but also elaborate BELT BUCKLES, SWORD HARNESSES, etc.; the most famous piece is the ALFRED JEWEL. The decoration is characterized by a lack of naturalism, with no accurate portrayals of human or animal figures, and the patterns are usually abstract interlaced designs or with distorted animal forms. The designs were influenced by Scandinavian and Germanic art. *See* Ronald Jessup, *Anglo-Saxon Jewellery* (1974). [*Plate I*]

animal-head bracelet. Gold with lion's-head terminals and shank of metal strip with convex outer surface. 4th/3rd centuries BC. Museo Nazionale, Taranto, Italy.

animal-head bracelet. A type of bracelet that is a rigid PENANNULAR ring (sometimes with the terminals touching or overlapping), having both terminals in the form of a head, IN THE ROUND, of an animal (e.g. bull, lion, ram, snake). Such bracelets were made in ACHAEMENIAN JEWELRY and in the jewelry of the Classical and Hellenistic periods, *c.* 500 BC-AD 300. The SHANKS were made in a number of forms, e.g. (a) a solid metal circular rod; (b) wire coiled around a core; (c) a hollow tube made of tightly twisted rope-like wire strands; (d) a flat metal strip, sometimes metal bar of square or rectangular section, forming a rod with sharp edges (called a 'bar twist'); (g) a twisted metal bar of cruciform section, with a convex outer surface; (e) a twisted flat metal strip; (f) a twisted forming a rod with smooth edges (called a 'flange twist'). Some rare examples have the terminals in the form of complete animals. A modern replica in traditional form was made, probably by Pasquale Novissimo, for Carlo Giuliano (*see* GIULIANO FAMILY), *c.* 1880, with FILIGREE and GRANULATED GOLD.

animal-head bracelet. Gold with overlapping shank having ram's-head terminals and twisted shank. 4th/3rd centuries BC. Museo Nazionale, Taranto, Italy.

animal-head brooch. A type of brooch that is penannular and that has the terminals in the form of a head of an animal. Such brooches were of bronze, with enamelling usually either in CHAMPLEVÉ or MILLEFIORI style. The most common decorations on the terminals are the stylized palmette, the spherical triangle (the central gap left by three touching spheres), and the spiral. The brooches are Celtic and were made from the second half of the 2nd century AD to the middle of the 5th. It has been said that they are modelled on a 2nd-century North British penannular bangle. *See* Howard Kilbride-Jones, *Zoomorphic Penannular Brooches* (1980).

animal-head ear-ring. A type of EAR-RING that is of tapering PENANNULAR form and that has one terminal, as the larger end, in the form of the head of an animal or sometimes a female human head, or a dolphin. Some examples have, instead of a solid SHANK, a shank made of twisted hollow tube or of wire twisted to form a coil. There is usually a hook at the tapered terminal, to be attached to a loop at the animal's mouth. Some examples have beads threaded along the hoop. Such ear-rings, usually made of gold, were widely used in the eastern Mediterranean region, having been developed in the 2nd century BC in Egypt, Syria, and Cyprus, and continued in Roman times until the 1st century AD.

animal-head bracelet. Bronze with chamois terminals. Luristan, 7th century BC. Courtesy of Carola van Ham, Kunsthaus am Museum, Cologne.

animal-head necklace. A type of NECKLACE made as a CHAIN, loose-linked or corded, having terminals in the form of animal heads, usually a lion's head, similar to the ANIMAL-HEAD BRACELETS and ANIMAL-HEAD EAR-RINGS. A variation was made with beads or set gemstones instead of links. Such pieces are known as types of HELLENISTIC JEWELRY.

animal jewelry. Articles of jewelry whose principal decorative motif is the figure or painting of an animal. Many PENDANTS, BROOCHES, ENSEIGNES, etc., have been so decorated with animals, such as a dog (talbot), monkey, dromedary, lion, camel, elephant, lizard (*see* LIZARD JEWELRY), bird (*see* BIRD JEWELRY), dolphin (*see* DOLPHIN JEWELRY), fly (*see* FLY JEWELRY), frog (*see* FROG JEWELRY), butterfly, cock, etc. Pendants of SUMERIAN JEWELRY are known in the form of a bull and a goat. Jewelry in the Victorian era was often made with such animal motifs. *See* BAROQUE PEARL JEWEL.

animal-head ear-rings. Gold with lion's-head terminal; twisted tube shank. 4th century BC. Museo Nazionale, Taranto, Italy.

ankh. An Egyptian symbol of life, in the form of a TAU CROSS with a loop resting on the transverse arm. It combines the male and female symbols of Osiris and Isis and is found held in the hand of certain deities depicted on some TUTANKHAMUN JEWELRY and other objects from Egypt. Also known as the 'Key of Life' and the *crux ansata*.

anklet. A ring, chain, band or other ornamental form worn around the ankle. Also called an 'ankle ring'. Such pieces were worn by women in Egypt, Greece, and Rome. Examples from India and the Far East are broad and highly ornamented, with suspended discs and bells.

Anne of Brittany's Ruby. A polished but irregular ruby weighing 105 carats, now in the Louvre, Paris.

anodyne necklace. A necklace that was used as a charm against illness or pain (especially by babies when teething) in the 18th century. The name is from 'anodyne', a medicine that allays pain.

annular. In the form of an unbroken ring or circle. *See* PENANNULAR.

antigorite. One variety of SERPENTINE that is soft, very pale grey to green or brownish-green, sometimes with LAMELLAR inclusions. A source is the Valle d'Antigorio, in Piedmont, Italy. It resembles JADE and is sometimes confused with it.

anklet. Silver. Ajmer, India, 19th century. Victoria & Albert Museum, London.

Antilles pearl. A pearly piece cut from the shell of the sea-snail and sometimes used as a small pearl. It has a nacreous top surface and a yellowish non-nacreous underside. Also called 'oil pearl'.

antique cut. *See* CUSHION CUT.

Antwerp, John of (fl. *c*. 1515-50). An Antwerp goldsmith and jeweller whose family name was Van der Gow, but who was usually called John (or Hans) of Andwarpe. He settled in London *c*. 1515, remaining until his death, and was employed extensively by Thomas Cromwell, Earl of Essex (1485-1540), and by Henry VIII to make and repair jewelry. He was a very close friend of HANS HOLBEIN THE YOUNGER, whose jewelry designs he executed. *See* L. Cust, 'John of Antwerp', in *Burlington Magazine*, February 1906, p. 356.

Antwerp rose cut. The same as the BRABANT ROSE CUT.

anulus pronubus (Latin). Literally, betrothal ring. The finger ring used by the Romans as a BETROTHAL RING. It was given by the man as a pledge to his betrothed.

Apache tear. A variety of OBSIDIAN found in tear-like form. Some examples when cut are greyish and are occasionally CHATOYANT. They are found as pebbles in south-west regions of the United States, and were named after a supposed resemblance to the tears of Apache squaws.

apatite. A mineral that occasionally produces some crystals that are used as gemstones. It is soft and brittle, and therefore seldom used in jewelry. The colours are varied, including light blue, mauve, yellow, green, and blue. It resembles TOURMALINE but can be readily distinguished. Varieties are ASPARAGUS STONE and MOROXITE. A green, CHATOYANT variety, known as 'apatite cat's-eye', is found in Brazil. A number of other countries also provide sources for apatite.

appliqué (French, from *appliquer*, to put on). A type of decoration made by affixing a design of one material to a base of another, e.g. a design in lacquer attached to metalwork.

apron. A large dress ornament worn by a woman over her garments, usually in the form of network hanging from the waist. Examples from Tibet, dating from the 19th century, were made from pieces of carved human bones.

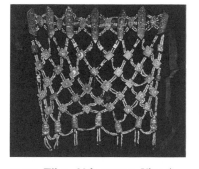

apron. Tibet, 19th century. Victoria & Albert Museum, London.

apron-stage pendant. A type of pendant having a protruding area (comparable to the apron stage of a theatre, i.e. the stage extending out in front of the proscenium arch) upon which is a group of figures in ÉMAIL EN RONDE BOSSE in front of an enamelled backdrop. Such pendants, of unknown origin, have been ascribed to the 16th century.

aquamarine. A variety of BERYL that is transparent and of various shades of blue and blue-green; almost all of the specimens of the preferable sky-blue colour are (since 1920) the result of HEAT TREATMENT applied to greenish or yellow-brown beryls. The stones are dichroic, and are usually cut as a BRILLIANT or STEP CUT. They resemble the EMERALD (the chemical composition is identical, as is the hexagonal crystal form) but the stones are paler and, being less rare, are much less valuable. They also resemble euclase and blue TOPAZ, from all of which (as well as from glass imitations and SYNTHETIC GEMSTONES) they can readily be distinguished. There are many sources, but Brazil has produced the finest and some very large specimens, e.g. one found in 1919 weighing 110.2 kg. (243 lb). Some ancient aquamarines were engraved with portraits, e.g. one with a portrait of Julia, daughter of the Roman Emperor Titus. The synthetic stone resembling aquamarine is the blue SYNTHETIC SPINEL. *See* EVYAN AQUAMARINE.

aquamarine chrysolite. An undesirable and unnecessary misnomer for a BERYL that is greenish-yellow.

aquamarine topaz. A variety of TOPAZ the colour of which shades toward green. The name is undesirable and unnecessary.

arabesque. A form of decoration of intricately interlaced motifs which in Islamic art was often geometric or angular, and in Renaissance art was composed of flowing curved lines and fanciful intertwining of swags of foliage, fruit, scrolls, and part-foliate figures, being derived from GROTESQUES (*grotteschi*) based on Nero's frescoes and often found on Italian maiolica. The style was imported into Europe in the late 15th century and was much used in the 16th century as decoration in all the applied arts. It was a popular form of Moorish decoration, its Spanish version excluding close representations of animal or human figures, those being found there in the work of Christian artists. In 19th-century England such designs were often termed 'Moresques'. Arabesque decoration is found on some jewelry, especially that of the Renaissance, such as the designs of VIRGIL SOLIS.

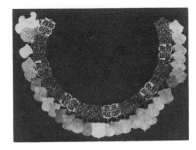

archer's collar. Silver collar with shields of successive wearers. Netherlands, *c.* 1419. W. 62 cm. Wallace Collection, London.

archaeological jewelry. Articles of jewelry made in the 19th century, inspired by the Etruscan archaeological discoveries, and especially such pieces made by PIO FORTUNATO CASTELLANI and Carlo Giuliano (*see* GIULIANO FAMILY), the latter while employed in London by ROBERT PHILLIPS. Such jewelry was also made by JOHN BROGDEN.

archer's collar. A type of LIVERY COLLAR that was the insigne of office of an ancient guild of archers. An example is that of the Netherlands Archers' Shooting Guild, known as the 'Collier du Roi de l'Arc'; it is composed of twelve silver hinged plaques, alternating in design, and having suspended from it the shields of the successive wearers from 1419 to 1826.

archer's pendant. A type of pendant awarded in the Middle Ages to an archer as a marksmanship prize. Archers were formed into companies emulating the orders of knighthood, and winners in competitions were awarded a chain from which was suspended such a pendant, usually in the form of a POPINJAY or the figure of St Sebastian, the patron saint of archers. They were popular in northern Germany, Holland, and Scandinavia.

archer's thumb ring. A type of finger ring worn by an archer so that, when properly used, the flight of the arrow is swifter and more accurate. Such a ring has a projection on one side of the hoop behind which the bow-string is hitched before the arrow is drawn. They have been used for over 2000 years, examples being known from China in the 5th century BC, and later ones from Greece in the 14th century and India in the 17th and 18th centuries. They vary somewhat in form, and many are made of JADE, some being inlaid with gold and set with gemstones.

architectural style. A sculptural style of decoration, suggestive of medieval church architecture, usually found on a PENDANT, in which the piece is in the form of a tabernacle (a canopied niche framed by columns or pilasters supporting an entablature) in which are one or more figures. Such pieces are usually of gold, decorated with polychrome enamelling and square-cut gemstones, and having the figures IN THE ROUND. The pendants are usually of fanciful, irregular shape, but occasionally are circular. Designs for such jewelry were made by ERASMUS HORNICK in Nuremberg in the 1560s. The style is sometimes called '*style cathédrale*' or 'tabernacle style'. *See* CHARITY PENDANT.

Arcot Diamonds. Two pear-shaped diamonds, perfectly matched, weighing together 57.35 carats. They were among five diamonds presented in 1777 by the Nawab of Arcot, in Madras, India, to Queen Charlotte, consort of George III. Upon her death they were sold by the Crown Jewellers, Rundell & Bridge (*see* RUNDELL, BRIDGE & RUNDELL) and in 1837 were bought by the Marquess of Westminster. They were remounted in 1930 and set in a TIARA (sold in 1959 at Sotheby's, London, to HARRY WINSTON), and are reportedly now privately owned in Texas.

Arizona ruby. A local misnomer for a ruby-coloured PYROPE.

Arizona spinel. A local misnomer for a red or green variety of GARNET.

Ark Locket. A gold LOCKET related to the ARMADA JEWEL. On one side is a hinged lid bearing a similar depiction of the Ark carved in low relief on

Ark Locket. Gold with mother-of-pearl medallion, and rubies. English, late 16th century. Museo Poldi-Pezzoli, Milan.

Armada Jewel. Front of locket with cast gold portrait of Elizabeth I, and (far right) portrait of Elizabeth I within locket. Probably English, 1588. Victoria & Albert Museum, London.

Armada Jewel. Back of locket with enamelled depiction of the Ark.

armilla. Arm ornament. Gilt copper with Crucifixion scene in *champlevé* enamel. Mosan or Rhenish, *c.* 1165. 11.5 x 13 x 4.5 cm. Courtesy of Sotheby's, London.

a mother-of-pearl medallion, encircled by the same motto as on the Armada Jewel. The motto is enamelled on a white ground and surrounded by a band of table-cut rubies within a smooth-edged oval frame which is enamelled in translucent red and green with opaque white; above the frame is an ornamental suspensory ring. On the other side is an oval space for a miniature portrait, encircled by a Latin inscription, 'Per tot discrimina rerum'. The locket has been attributed to an English goldsmith, *c.* 1600. *See* JAMES I JEWELRY.

Arkansas diamond. (1) A local misnomer for ROCK CRYSTAL. (2) Any real diamond found in Arkansas, the state producing more diamonds than any other of the United States; diamonds were found in 1906 near Murfreesboro in four pipes, one of which has been called 'The Crater of Diamonds', where the public are permitted to search upon payment of a small daily fee. (3) A diamond, called the 'Arkansas Diamond', discovered on a farm near Searcy, Arkansas, in 1926, and bought by TIFFANY & CO., which still displays it in the rough, weighing 27.21 carats. Other diamonds found in Arkansas include the UNCLE SAM DIAMOND and at least seven others each weighing rough over 3 carats.

Armada (Heneage) Jewel. A gold LOCKET made probably in England, late in 1588, to commemorate the victory of England over the Spanish Armada in July and August of that year. On the front under a convex glass is a profile bust portrait (from the Garter Badge of 1585) of Elizabeth I in cast gold on a blue translucent enamel ground, within a separated frame of openwork enamelled in blue, with motifs in green and red, and set with 4 table-cut diamonds and 4 table-cut rubies; at the top is a trefoil suspensory ornament. The back of the locket is enamelled with an Ark (symbolic of the English Church) securely floating on a stormy sea and beneath a shower from a cloud, with an encircling motto 'Saevas tranquilla per undas' ('Tranquil through stormy seas'), the motto from the Naval Medal of 1588. Within the locket is a miniature portrait of Elizabeth, perhaps by NICHOLAS HILLIARD, dated 1580, later retouched. The inside of the lid is enamelled with the Tudor rose within a wreath and a Latin laudatory inscription from the Phoenix Badge of 1574. The piece is said to have been a gift by the Queen to Sir Thomas Heneage (d. 1595), of Copt Hall, Essex, for services as Treasurer at the time of the Armada; hence it is sometimes called the 'Heneage Jewel'. It was kept in the Heneage family until July 1902 when it was sold at Christie's, London, for £5,250 to the Pierpont Morgan Collection, which in 1935 sold it to Lord Wakefield, who donated it to the Victoria & Albert Museum. *See* ARK LOCKET.

armilla (or **armill**). An archaeological term used to designate an ARMLET, or sometimes a bracelet, usually one worn by royalty. Such pieces were worn in ancient times in the Orient and the Near East as emblems of sovereignty, and continued to be used later, especially by the Germanic peoples from the 7th century. In England they have been long used, but as part of the coronation REGALIA only since 1100. Among outstanding examples are: (1) One from the von Hirsch Collection sold at Sotheby's, London, on 22 June 1978, for £1,100,000 plus 10%. It is a curved band of gilt copper decorated in CHAMPLEVÉ enamel, with a scene showing the Crucifixion with other figures, all in brilliant colours and with accenting in NIELLO. It has been attributed to a Mosan or Rhenish source, c. 1165, either Godefroid de Claire or a Mosan enameller in whose workshop NICOLAS OF VERDUN was trained. Together with a companion piece in the Louvre depicting the Resurrection, it is thought to have been part of the Imperial Regalia of Frederick I (Barbarossa), 1152–90, and to have been presented to him by the Russian Prince Andrei Bogoliubski (1111–74), whose embassy visited the Imperial Court at Aachen in 1165. It was later given to the cathedral at Vladimir, near Moscow, and remained in Russia until c. 1933, having been in the Hermitage Museum from 1917. (2) Two pairs among the British CROWN JEWELS: one, of enamelled gold, made for the coronation of Charles II but not used, and another presented by the Commonwealth to Elizabeth II upon her coronation in 1953.

armillary ring. *See* ASTRONOMICAL RING.

armlet. An ornament worn on the upper arm, made in various materials, forms, and styles in different regions and cultures. Some worn in Egypt during the XVIIIth Dynasty (c. 1552–1296 BC) were hollow bands of gold sheet beaten into a circular shape, the ends soldered, and the join sealed with another strip. In India in the Mughal period (1526–1857) the armlet (called a BAZU BAND) worn by men (the Emperor and nobility) consisted of a gold ornament (sometimes three-sectioned) attached at both ends to a long, encircling, silken cord. *See* ARMILLA; BANGLE; BRACELET; OXUS ARMLET; SPIRAL ARMLET; SUSSEX ARM-RING.

Art Deco. A decorative style that originated in France in the 1920s and 1930s in protest against the ART NOUVEAU style and later art movements, and that was popularized in the United States. Scorned by many in its early period, it reacquired some popularity in the 1960s and 1970s. The style emphasized abstract designs and geometric patterns. Examples are found in many branches of the decorative arts, including jewelry. The name is derived from 'L' Exposition Internationale des Arts Décoratifs et Industriels Modernes', held in Paris in 1925. *See* Bevis Hillier, *Art Deco* (1968); T. Walters, *Art Deco* (1973). *See* GEOMETRIC STYLE.

Art Nouveau. The style of decoration current in the 1890s and early 1900s, the name being derived from a gallery for interior decoration opened by Samuel Bing in Paris in 1896, called the 'Maison de l'Art Nouveau'. It was introduced in England c. 1890, mainly as a product of the movement started by William Morris and the Pre-Raphaelites, which spread to the Continent and America. It came to an end with the outbreak of World War I. The same style in Germany was called *Jugendstil*, after a magazine called *Die Jugend* (Youth), and in Italy *Floreale* or *Stile Liberty* (after the London store that featured it). Applicable to all the decorative arts, it was adapted to jewelry in England and on the Continent. The style resulted from a revolt against the rigid styles of the previously mass-produced wares and a philosophy that sought to revive the craft movement and aestheticism in art. It featured free-flowing, curving lines with asymmetrical natural motifs, such as intertwining floral patterns, butterflies and dragonflies, and ethereal, human, female faces, greatly influenced by Japanese art. It used gemstones to emphasize their beauty, preferring pearls and CABOCHON opals and moonstones rather than faceted stones, and employed colourful enamelling. The pieces include pendants, necklaces, and elaborate HAIR ORNAMENTS. Eventually its own extravagances led to its demise, c. 1910–14. Among its leading exponents in France were RENÉ LALIQUE, MAISON VEVER, GEORGES FOUQUET, and LUCIEN GAILLARD, in Belgium Philippe Wolfers (*see* WOLFERS FRÈRES), and in Vienna Josef Hoffmann (1870–1955). In England the leaders were CHARLES R. ASHBEE and HENRY WILSON, and in Scotland Charles Rennie Mackintosh. *See* Graham Hughes, *Art Nouveau Jewellery* (1966).   [*Plate II*]

articulated. Having movable parts, e.g. a brooch or pendant in the form of a fish made with joined sections that permit movement in a swimming manner, or a SNAKE BRACELET (or necklace) having a body made of

armlet. Gold set with emeralds. 4th century AD. W. 15 cm. Römisch-Germanisches Museum, Cologne.

Art Deco. Bracelet; crystal, platinum, sapphires. René Boivin, Paris, c. 1925. Schmuckmuseum, Pforzheim, Germany.

Art Nouveau. Pendant with crystal head set in silver with baroque pearl. René Lalique. L. 9.8 cm. Gulbenkian Foundation, Lisbon.

articulated. Pendant in form of articulated fish. Kunsthistorisches Museum, Vienna.

Ashanti jewelry. Gold discs, with repoussé work and chasing. Victoria & Albert Museum, London.

Ashbee, C.R. Silver pendant with pearls. Art Nouveau style. English, *c.* 1900. Victoria & Albert Museum, London.

flexible sections. *See* ARTICULATED BRACELET; FISH JEWELRY; MIXTEC JEWELRY; TOR ABBEY JEWEL.

articulated bracelet. A rigid, circular bracelet or BANGLE made with one section that opens on a hinge to permit it to be placed on the wrist.

artificial pearl. *See* IMITATION PEARL.

artist-designer. A painter or sculptor who also made designs for jewelry, to be executed by professional craftsmen and jewellers, such as HANS HOLBEIN THE YOUNGER and ALBRECHT DÜRER. Among those of the 20th century are Georges Braque, Salvador Dali, Jean Arp, Jean Cocteau, André Derain, Jean Dubuffet, Max Ernst, Alberto Giacometti, Pablo Picasso, Man Ray, and Yves Tanguy. *See* DESIGNER; DESIGNER-MAKER.

Ashanti jewelry. Articles of jewelry made in the kingdom of Ashanti, in central Gold Coast (now part of Ghana) in West Africa during the 18th/19th centuries. Similar jewelry was also made in the neighbouring regions of the Anyi and Baoulé, but it is all usually grouped as 'Akan' ware, as Akan is the common language of the three regions. Many articles were made of the abundant local supply of gold, but its wearing was restricted to the king and high dignitaries; all gold dust acquired privately could be made into jewelry only with the king's consent and by controlled artisans. Much was made by skilful use of the CIRE PERDUE process, which had been introduced possibly as early as the 13th century. Pieces were elaborately decorated with REPOUSSÉ work and CHASING. Some articles were made by the application of gold FOIL over a wooden core. The articles included discs worn as official insignia, and also PECTORALS (*akrafokonmu*), bracelets, finger rings, TOE RINGS, and TALISMANS, some decorated with zoomorphic subjects IN THE ROUND.

Ashbee, Charles Robert (1863-1942). An English designer of jewelry who was an important figure in the promotion of the ART NOUVEAU style in England. Having been an architect and goldsmith, he became in the 1880s interested in jewelry and a leader of the Arts and Crafts Movement. In 1888 he founded the Guild and School of Handicraft in London but in 1895 the school closed; in 1898 he registered the mark of the Guild of Handicraft which in 1902 moved to Chipping Campden, Gloucestershire, but closed in 1908. In 1912 he published *Silverware and Jewellery*. His jewelry designs, which were executed by the Guild, were mainly for articles of silver ornamented with such inexpensive translucent gemstones as turquoise, moonstone, and opal, and also with BLISTER PEARLS, often using flowers and a peacock as his motifs. His influence was important in developing Art Nouveau jewelry, especially at Liberty & Co., and at the Wiener Werkstätte. His marks were C R A from 1896, and after 1898 G O H Ltd.

asparagus stone. A variety of APATITE that is yellowish-green.

assaying. The process of testing the purity of metal in an article, e.g. ascertaining the proportion of GOLD or SILVER in relation to other metals that are constituents of the ALLOY, but without making a complete analysis. Assaying has been legally required in Great Britain since *c.* 1300 for articles of gold or silver (since 1975 for platinum). The process formerly involved rubbing with a TOUCHSTONE, but today technical procedures are used to test the scrappings of each part of an article submitted; gold is tested by cupellation, silver by the 'volumetric method', and in both cases the content must be established to the nearest 0.1%. When an article contains a metal of two different qualities (e.g. 22- and 18-carat gold), the assaying applies only to that of lower quality, and the mark ignores the metal of higher quality. Certain articles are exempted, such as pieces of a delicate nature (e.g. FILIGREE) or low monetary value, as well as pins and springs that must be of a strong metal; for CHAINS, all links are assayed but the mark is dispensed with. Assaying was done in ancient Egypt and Rome, and has been carried out on the Continent for centuries; there is no governmental assaying of jewelry in the United States.

assembled stone. *See* DOUBLET; TRIPLET.

Assur-bani-pal Bracelet. Gold with appliqué relief depicting return from the hunt. John Brogden. L. 7 cm. Victoria & Albert Museum, London.

Assur-bani-pal Bracelet. A gold, hinged, rigid bracelet with an applied decoration depicting, after an Assyrian relief, Assur-bani-pal (d. 626 BC?), King of Assyria, returning from a lion hunt. It was made by JOHN BROGDEN, *c.* 1851.

Astarte pendant. A type of gold, amuletic pendant depicting in stylized manner the nude figure of Astarte, the Canaanite goddess of fertility, beauty, and love; she was the most important Phoenician goddess, corresponding to the Greek Aphrodite. Examples are one found at Tell el-Ajjul (*see* AJJUL HOARD), now belonging to the Israel Department of Antiquities and exhibited at the Israel Museum, one belonging to the Ashmolean Museum, Oxford, and one in the British Museum.

asteria. A gemstone that exhibits ASTERISM. It is best seen in the STAR RUBY and the STAR SAPPHIRE, including the synthetic varieties. Also called a 'star stone'.

asterism. An optical phenomenon of a star-like figure that is seen in some crystals by reflected light (*see* EPIASTERISM) or transmitted light (*see* DIASTERISM). An example is the 6-ray (sometimes 4-ray, 8-ray or 12-ray) star-like figure that is observed by reflected light in some gemstones (especially the STAR RUBY and STAR SAPPHIRE) when cut EN CABOCHON in such a manner that the greatest thickness of the stone lies parallel to the vertical axis of the crystal. The effect is caused by the reflection of light from a series of microscopic fibrous inclusions or small canals lying within the crystal parallel to the prism faces and arranged in three directions that intersect, usually at angles of 60°. Such stars are also seen in some other gemstones, e.g. BERYL, ALMANDINE, STAR OPAL, ROSE QUARTZ. A stone showing asterism is known as an ASTERIA or a 'star stone'.

astronomical ring. A type of SCIENTIFIC RING composed of hoops that swivel open to form an astronomical (armillary) sphere, one or more of the hoops being inscribed with the signs of the zodiac and the planets. The skeleton sphere is formed by 2 outer hoops that swivel, and within the sphere are 2 to 4 smaller hoops that swivel on a different axis. All the inner hoops are concealed when the ring is closed. Examples of such rings were made in Germany in the 16th/17th centuries. One is mentioned as owned by Touchstone in Shakespeare's *As You Like It*. Although sometimes called an 'astrolabe ring', they are not devices for ascertaining the time.

Augustus Cameo. A CAMEO carved with a profile portrait of the Roman Emperor Augustus (63 BC–AD 14), of which there are several examples, e.g. (1) ST HILARY JEWEL; (2) a large unmounted cameo (in the British Museum) carved in three-layer SARDONYX, attributed to the gem-engraver Dioskorides, 1st century AD, with the Emperor wearing the aegis with the Gorgon's head and around his brow a golden DIADEM set with two small cameos and gemstones; the diadem is medieval (restored in the 18th century), replacing a simple fillet, and the piece was probably set originally in a pendant or a brooch.

aureole. A decorative feature in the form of a ring or an emanation of rays in oval shape that surrounds the representation of the whole body of a

Astarte pendant. Gold with repoussé and incised work, depicting face of goddess and female attributes. Canaanite, 1900 BC–1200 BC. H. 9.5 cm. Israel Department of Antiquities and Museums, Jerusalem (photo by Israel Museum).

astronomical ring. Silver four-hoop folding ring in form of an armillary sphere. Possibly German, early 17th century. Schmuckmuseum, Pforzheim, Germany.

Augustus Cameo. Sardonyx (three-layered) with head of Emperor Augustus wearing aegis with Gorgon's head. Roman, 1st century AD. W. 9.3 cm. British Museum, London.

Austrian Imperial Crown. Front view of crown made in Prague, 1602. Schatzkammer, Hofburg, Vienna.

sacred figure; also called a *mandorla* and, when having pointed ends, a *vesica piscis*. It is a type of nimbus, which term also includes a HALO.

Austrian Imperial Crown. The CROWN made for Rudolf II, King of Hungary and Bohemia, after he became Holy Roman Emperor in 1576. It is in the form of a gold circlet over which there is a single gold arch surmounted by a small cross; above this is a large, uncut, egg-shaped sapphire. Its main feature is a pair of curved, triangular, gold panels on the sides that rise to a point to form a mitre-shaped cap and that are decorated in bas-relief depicting four scenes involving Rudolf. Around the circlet are eight upright fleurs-de-lis. All parts are richly studded with gemstones and fringed with pearls. The crown was made in 1602 by Jan Vermeyen at the workshop of Rudolf at Hradschin, Prague. It was worn by the successors of Rudolf as emperor, but no one was ever crowned with it; in 1804 it was designated by Emperor Francis I as the official Austrian Imperial Crown, but it was never so worn. It is kept now in the Schatzkammer of the Hofburg at Vienna.

Austrian Yellow. The same as the FLORENTINE DIAMOND, also called the 'Tuscany Diamond'.

Austrias, Jewel of the. A jewel (known also as the *joyel rico*) that was created for the Royal Family of Austria in the early 17th century and is shown in a portrait of Margaret of Austria who was married in 1599 to Philip III of Spain. Its principal ornament is the square-cut diamond known as the *Estanque* (bought by Philip II for Isabel of Valois), below which is suspended LA PEREGRINA. The diamond was in a gold setting with flowers and fruit in relief and enamels of red, black and white. The jewel was also shown as worn by the Queen in a portrait by Velasquez.

Ave. One of the small BEADS on a ROSARY, of which there are ten grouped in each DECADE between a PATERNOSTER and a GLORIA, by which the reciting of Ave Marias is counted. *See* DECADE RING.

aventurescence. The effect of showing glittering reflections from internal plates or flakes of mica, HEMATITE, or other very small crystals, as shown by AVENTURINE QUARTZ, AVENTURINE FELDSPAR, and MOONSTONE, as well as by aventurine glass (goldstone). *See* ADULARESCENCE; SCHILLER.

aventurine feldspar. A gemstone that strongly resembles AVENTURINE QUARTZ. It appears to glow, suggesting self-illumination, with internal yellowish or reddish beams, due to reflection from INCLUSIONS of thin flakes of an iron mineral (HEMATITE or goethite) scattered within the stone. It can be distinguished from aventurine quartz by its lower HARDNESS and often by the presence of parallel striations. It is usually cut EN CABOCHON. It is also called 'sunstone'.

aventurine quartz. A variety of massive QUARTZ that is translucent or opaque, and spangled throughout with scales of mica, HEMATITE, or other flaky mineral giving a spangled appearance to a polished surface when seen by reflected light. Its colour is yellow, green, grey, or reddish-brown. Although large opaque pieces are made into vases and bowls, small specimens are cut with a flat or slightly rounded surface and made into rings and brooches. The green stones are sometimes similar in appearance to green JADE and to MALACHITE. The principal sources of green aventurine quartz (sometimes incorrectly called 'Chinese jade' or 'Indian jade') are China, Brazil, and India; it is often carved in China. *See* AVENTURESCENCE.

Averbode, Pectoral Cross of Abbot of. A gold PECTORAL CROSS made in two sections to contain a relic. It is decorated with black CHAMPLEVÉ enamel and pendent pearls; on the front there is a smaller crucifix of bright gold with the figure in ÉMAIL EN RONDE BOSSE, and on the reverse there is a coat of arms at the crossing and an inscription on the lower limb. It was made in 1562 from a design by HANS COLLAERT THE ELDER for the Abbot of Averbode, near Malines, Belgium.

awabi pearl. The Japanese name for the ABALONE PEARL.

awaw (Egyptian). A type of honorific BANGLE or ARMLET made in the form of a gold hollow band. Such bangles were made by beating into circular shape on a wooden ring a strip of thin gold sheet equal to the length of the external circumference of the proposed bangle and then soldering the two ends so as to form a three-sided hoop with the inner face open; the open inner face was then closed with a thin, gold strip that was soldered to the edges of the hoop. They were made during the XVIIIth Dynasty, *c.* 1552–1296 BC.

axe god. An article of PRE-COLUMBIAN JEWELRY shaped as though carved from an axe or celt, having the upper part carved as a low-relief, stylized, anthropomorphic figure and the lower part as a blade. Such pieces, usually made of JADEITE, have a pierced hole for suspension as a pendant and were made mainly in Costa Rica. Their average height is about 10 cm but they range from 3 to 26 cm. *See* PRE-COLUMBIAN JADE JEWELRY.

Aztec jewelry. Articles of PRE-COLUMBIAN JEWELRY made by the Aztec Indians, who came from east-central Mexico and *c.* 1325 founded Tenochtitlán (the site of present-day Mexico City), absorbed the culture of the Toltec and Maya peoples, and developed a high degree of civilization until their ruler Montezuma was conquered by the Spaniards under Hernando Cortés in 1520. Gifts to Cortés (*see* MONTEZUMA'S HEAD DRESS) included gold necklaces decorated with gemstones and gold bells, and articulated gold animals and fish; other articles made by the Aztecs included bracelets, ear-rings, and nose ornaments. Strict regulations prescribed who in the hierarchy was permitted to wear the jewelry. Few specimens survive, as an estimated 30 tons (about 30,000 kg.) of gold jewelry were melted by the Spaniards for the gold content. *See* MEXICAN JEWELRY.

azurite. A mineral that is normally opaque and azure-blue. It is misleadingly called 'blue malachite' to distinguish it from 'green malachite'. It is sometimes used in jewelry in flat-top pieces. *See* CHESSYLITE; MALACHITE.

axe-god. Translucent green jade. Costa Rica. H. 7.4 cm. American Museum of Natural History, New York. Photo courtesy of André Emmerich, New York.

B

back ornament. A type of body ornament made by the Mixtec Indians of Mexico, worn during the late post-classic Aztec period, *c.* 1200–1500. It was made of a human skull, covered with a mosaic depiction of the features made of lignite, TURQUOISE, SHELL, and PYRITES. Such pieces were worn by the men, tied on the back of the hip by a long leather thong. Funerary masks were similarly made of mosaic. *See* MIXTEC JEWELRY.

badge. An insigne of membership or office, worn since the 17th century. Early examples were sewn on the upper arm of a garment, but later ones, of various metals and made to be pinned on or suspended, were issued by Livery companies, Masonic lodges, some corporations, etc. *See* ORDER.

baguette. A gemstone (usually a diamond or an emerald) cut so that the TABLE is in the shape of a long, narrow rectangle, bordered by four FACETS each STEP CUT in the shape of an isosceles trapezoid. The name is derived from the French *baguette* (a long loaf of bread). *See* BATON.

baikalite. A dark-green variety of DIOPSIDE.

balas ruby (or **balas**). A misnomer for a variety of SPINEL that is rose-red, of a paler shade than the red of the variety called RUBY SPINEL. It can be distinguished from a RUBY, which it resembles in colour, by its single refraction and lack of dichroism. Its main source in medieval times was Badakhshan, a province in north-east Afghanistan, from which the name was derived. *See* BLACK PRINCE'S RUBY; TIMUR RUBY; CÔTE DE BRETAGNE; OEUF DE NAPLE.

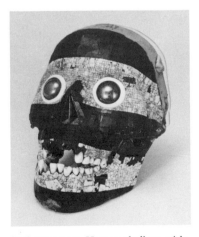

back ornament. Human skull set with mosaic of turquoise and lignite, having eyes of iron pyrites circled by white shell, and a movable jaw. Mixtec, of Aztec period. W. 14.5 cm. Museum of Mankind, London.

ball bracelet. A type of bracelet composed of one or two rows of hollow hemispheres of undecorated gold, linked together. Such bracelets were made in ROMAN JEWELRY, and are similar in style to the BALL EAR-RING.

ball catch. A device serving as a safety-catch on a jewel closed by a pin, e.g. a brooch. It is in the form of a partial circle with a central groove, having within a smaller, partially-circular tongue to which is affixed a small knob that fits into the groove and is moved forward to close the circle and fasten the catch, and backward to open it.

ball chain. A type of CHAIN composed of small metal balls joined by tiny metal connections.

ball ear-ring. A type of ear-ring in the form of a hollow hemisphere of undecorated gold to which was attached an S-shaped wire hook for fastening in the ear-lobe. Such pieces were worn in the Roman Empire in the 1st/2nd centuries AD. Some later examples have added decoration in the form of a suspended ornament with three bosses.

Ballochyle Brooch. A silver-gilt eight-pointed brooch set with a CABOCHON crystal within an engraved inscription and bearing the initials M C, with shields bearing Campbell arms and leopard heads for MacIver. It was made in Scotland, *c.* 1550, and has long been in the possession of the MacIver-Campbells of Ballochyle, Argyll.

bandeau. A type of HEAD ORNAMENT in the form of a narrow band encircling the forehead, as worn by medieval Italian women, and also in France and England in the 1840s and again in the 1920s. *See* BANDELET(TE); CHAPLET; FERRONIÈRE; FILLET.

banded opal. A variety of OPAL that has variously coloured layers of opal or of opal alternating with other minerals or MATRIX.

bandelet(te). A type of HEAD ORNAMENT in the form of a decorated small band or ribbon worn by women in the hair. Some were ornamented with pearls, AMBER, CORAL or JET. They were worn in the late 19th century. *See* BANDEAU; CHAPLET; FILLET.

bangle. A non-flexible arm ornament (circular or oval) that slips over the hand or is hinged and closed by a clasp. Such pieces have been made in many styles and sizes, with or without decoration, and of gold, silver, CORAL, AMBER, GLASS, etc. They are worn on the wrist or the lower or upper arm (sometimes several together). They have been made in many regions and in many periods, from the Middle La Tène period (300 BC–100 BC) of the Iron Age onward until today, especially in Africa and Asia. Some were made in Rome of glass, clear or variously coloured. *See* ARMLET; ARTICULATED BRACELET.

Bapst family. Several generations of Parisian jewellers who were descended from Bapst ancestors from Hall, Swabia, in southern Germany. They became prominent in Paris, making Court jewelry and producing articles made of STRASS. Jean-Melchior Bapst, who started a jewelry business in Paris in 1725, had two sons, Georges-Michel Bapst (1718–70) and Georges-Christophe Bapst (1724–84). The former left Hall in 1743 to join his uncle, Georges-Frédéric Strass (creator of strass), by whom he was ceded in 1752 the strass part of the business, and in 1755 he married Suzanne-Elisabeth Strass (1737–89), the daughter of Philippe-Jacques Strass (1693–1757), brother of Georges-Frédéric Strass. The couple's eldest son, Georges-Frédéric Bapst (1756–1826), carried on the business in strass and other jewelry, and made a jewelled sword for Louis XVI; he died without children, and left the business to his cousin, Jacques-Evrard (originally Jacob Eberhard) Bapst (1771–1841). The latter, the son of Georges-Christophe Bapst (*supra*), was brought to Paris in 1796 by his childless cousin, married in 1797 Marie-Nicole Ménière (daughter of the Parisian Court jeweller, Paul-Nicolas Ménière), and taking the name Bapst-Ménière he directed the business, becoming a Court jeweller during the Restoration, 1814–30, remodelling from 1815 to 1830 some of the jewels of the regalia of Napoleon I for Louis XVIII, and making the coronation jewelry for Charles X in 1824. His sons, Constant Bapst (1797–1853) and Charles-Frédéric Bapst (1799–1872), continued

Ballochyle Brooch. Silver gilt with crystal cabochon. Scotland, *c.* 1550. W. 14 cm, National Museum of Antiquities of Scotland, Edinburgh.

bangle. Gold. Cologne(?), mid-4th century. D. 10 cm. Römisch-Germanisches Museum, Cologne.

the business as Bapst Frères, making jewelry for Empress Eugénie, wife of
Napoleon III; they were joined by Constant Bapst's son, Alfred Bapst
(1823–79), until he withdrew to join Lucien Falize, forming the firm of
Bapst & Falize, and thereafter the brothers carried on the family business
as Bapst Frères et fils. Charles-Frédéric Bapst's sons, Jules and Paul, had
been associated with the firm of their cousin, Alfred Bapst (*supra*), until
they withdrew in 1885 and founded the firm of J. & P. Bapst, which
continued until 1930. Alfred Bapst was Court jeweller during the Second
Empire, 1852–70; upon his death, his son Germain (1853–1921) joined
Lucien Falize from 1880 to 1892, and thereafter continued alone as the
last jeweller in his family line. There was another line of the family,
descended from Jacques-Frédéric Bapst (b. 1720), a brother of Jean-
Melchior Bapst; his grandson, Frédéric Bapst (1789–1870), a nephew of
Jacques-Evrard Bapst, left Hall in 1805 and was with the Bapst firm for
over fifty years. *See* Hans Haug, 'Les Pierres de Strass', in *Cahiers de la
Céramique* (Paris), no. 23 (1961), p. 175. *See* FALIZE FAMILY.

bar brooch. A type of brooch in the form of a horizontal bar with
decoration along its length or with gemstones or a decorative motif at the
centre and gemstones at the terminals.

bar ear-ring. A type of ear-ring set with a gemstone below which was an
attached horizontal bar from which were suspended several small
pendants or pearls. Such pieces were worn during the Roman Empire
from the 2nd century AD and continued into the Byzantine period.

bar pin. A type of BROOCH having a long and narrow horizontal axis like
a bar.

barbaric jewelry. Articles of jewelry made during the Dark Ages, from *c.*
AD 410 until *c.* AD 870, when the barbarian tribes (the Visigoths,
Ostrogoths, Franks, Lombards, Anglo-Saxons) were sweeping west over
Europe and bringing with them the culture of the Orient to influence
Roman art. The styles included those brought from the Middle East and
south-east Europe, as skilfully adapted by the invaders. (*See* ANGLO-
SAXON JEWELRY; CAROLINGIAN JEWELRY; FRANKISH JEWELRY; GOTHIC
JEWELRY; MEROVINGIAN JEWELRY.) The articles were essentially colourful,
with CLOISONNÉ enamelling and inlaid coloured gemstones prominent,
but also with much metalwork in gold decorated with FILIGREE and
REPOUSSÉ work. Necklaces, FIBULAE, and finger rings were popular, often
decorated with zoomorphic motifs. Much has been found, e.g. CHILDERIC
TREASURE; GUARRAZAR TREASURE; PETROSSA TREASURE; SUTTON HOO
TREASURE.

Barbor Jewel. A pendant of oval shape surmounted by a crown, the
centre decoration being a CAMEO of SARDONYX portraying Queen

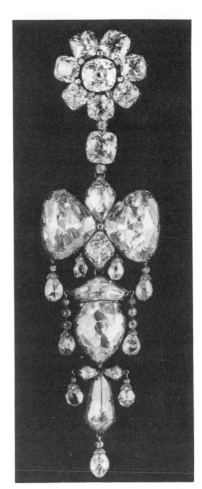

Bapst family. Brooch set with
diamonds known as 'Mazarin 17 and
18'. Alfred Bapst, 1855. Museé du
Louvre, Paris.

Barbor Jewel (front and back). Gold
pendant with cameo of sardonyx, and
enamelling and gemstones. English, *c.*
1600. Victoria & Albert Museum,
London.

Elizabeth I. The frame is gold decorated with translucent blue and green enamel on opaque white enamel, set with alternating RUBIES and TABLE CUT diamonds. Below the main part is suspended a grape-like cluster of small pearls. On the reverse is an enamelled oak tree. It is the family tradition that this jewel was ordered by William Barbor (d. 1586), who had been sentenced to be burned at the stake at Smithfield for his Protestantism, to commemorate his last-minute deliverance, brought about by the accession of Elizabeth I in 1558 upon the death of Mary Tudor. However, the tradition has been recently questioned on the ground that the style of dress shown on Elizabeth cannot date from before 1580 and that the PEAPOD style on the reverse must be from later than *c*. 1600. It was given by Barbor to his first granddaughter, who was named Elizabeth, and subsequently passed to each first-born female child to be named Elizabeth. When the last Elizabeth died unmarried, it passed into the possession of the Blencowe family by marriage some time after 1757, and was eventually bequeathed by Miss M. Blencowe, who died in 1904, to the Victoria & Albert Museum.

barion cut. A modern style of cutting a diamond that is a modification of the EMERALD CUT, intended to improve the BRILLIANCE of the square and rectangular stones while retaining maximum weight. In addition to the usual 24 FACETS plus the TABLE on the CROWN, and the 28 facets plus the CULET on the PAVILION, there are 4 half-moon facets on each side of the GIRDLE, making a total of 62 facets. It was developed by Basil Watermeyer, a cutter of Johannesburg, and named by him with his initial combined with the name of his wife Marion.

barleycorn chain. A type of TRACE CHAIN of which the links are shaped like an isosceles triangle, with the apex of one link looped around the base of the adjoining link.

baroque. A style in art and decoration that developed shortly before 1600 and remained current in Europe until the emergence of the ROCOCO style *c*. 1730. It was started in Italy, and spread to Germany, Austria, the Low Countries, and Spain and Portugal, with only a somewhat severely classical version being popular in France under Louis XIV. The style was a development of the Renaissance style (*see* RENAISSANCE JEWELRY) and is characterized by lively, curved, and exuberant forms, by vigorous movement, and by rich ornament, based on classical sources, being symmetrical as distinguished from the asymmetry of the following ROCOCO style. During the baroque period both men and women ceased to bedeck themselves with ostentatious jewelry and tended to wear quantities of pearls or of jewels with gemstones playing a larger role than the polychrome effects of enamelling. Enamelling in restrained style continued to be found on the backs of jewelry, such as lockets and watch-cases (*see* PEAPOD style), and in the 1630-80s naturalistic floral styles predominated, largely as a consequence of the botanical mania then current in Europe. Diamonds were often used following the discoveries at the Golconda and Hyderabad mines in India and the new methods of diamond cutting.

baroque pearl. A natural pearl or a CULTURED PEARL of irregular shape, formed by a PEARL OYSTER around some irregularly-shaped intrusion. Such pearls are ordinarily not suitable for modern jewelry but natural baroque pearls were featured in certain RENAISSANCE JEWELRY in pendants and brooches made in the form of a figure or animal IN THE ROUND, of which the body was such a baroque pearl; *see* BAROQUE PEARL JEWEL; HINGE PEARL; HAMMER PEARL. Probably the largest known baroque pearl, 'The Pearl of Asia', weighs 2,420 grains.

baroque pearl jewel. A type of jewel (usually a pendant, but sometimes a BROOCH) having the principal ornament in the form of a single figure or animal, IN THE ROUND and decorated in ÉMAIL EN RONDE BOSSE, of which the torso is a BAROQUE PEARL to which is added decoration of enamelling and gemstones. In the best examples the figure conformed to the shape of the pearl. The figures were usually drawn from mythology, e.g. a centaur, mermaid, triton, siren, harpy, dragon, sea serpent, hippocampus, etc., but sometimes were a bull, butterfly, cock, turkey or other animal. Often three baroque pearls were suspended from such a pendant in triangular arrangement, a large pearl in the centre flanked by two smaller ones.

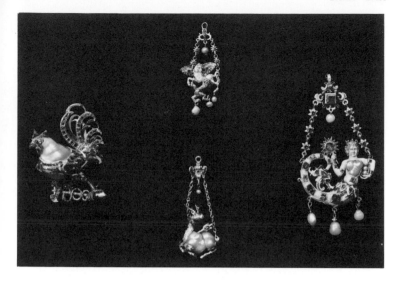

baroque pearl jewels. Gold with enamelling and gemstones. Treasure of Grand Duke of Tuscany, 2nd half of 16th century. Museo degli Argenti (Pitti Palace), Florence.

Such pieces were usually the work of German, Italian, and Spanish jewellers of the Renaissance period. *See* CANNING SIREN JEWEL; CANNING TRITON JEWEL; CENTAUR PENDANT; COCK PENDANT; DRAGON JEWELRY; EUROPA PENDANT; LIZARD JEWELRY; MERMAID PENDANT; SIREN PENDANT; TRITON PENDANT.

barrel and link chain. A type of CHAIN composed mainly of groups of links but having between each group a long, thin, cylindrical ornament.

barrel polishing. The same as TUMBLING.

barrette. *See* SLIDE.

basalt. A dark-grey to black, dense, fine-grained, volcanic rock that was used in Egyptian jewelry. It was imitated by Josiah Wedgwood in his 'black basaltes' stoneware that was used by him for making portrait MEDALLIONS; such medallions were sometimes mounted as a brooch or pendant.

basket ear-ring. A type of EAR-RING with an ornament suggestive of the shape of a basket. Such pieces were made over an extended period and in several forms. Some made in the Early Bronze Age in Britain, *c.* 2100 BC–1800 BC, are in the form of a shallow elongated basket with an overhead handle, made of half-tubular gold sheet with rounded sides and having the ear-hook rising from the centre of one side and curving toward the other side; some were decorated with beaten REPOUSSÉ work. Later examples in LANGOBARDIC JEWELRY made in the 6th and 7th centuries have been found in the valley of the Danube and in Bohemia; these examples were often in the form of a loop to which was attached a hemispherical openwork basket, on the front of which was a flat disc set with several gemstones or coloured glass beads around a central stone, and having suspended from the basket a small ring for the suspension of a pendant. Such Langobardic examples were closed by the wearer by slipping one end of the open circular loop that pierced the ear into an aperture on the other end of the loop. *See* Katherine Reynolds Brown, 'Langobardic Ear-rings', in *Connoisseur*, August 1980, p. 272.

basket ear-rings. Gold sheet hammered thin, with repoussé decoration. British, Early Bronze Age, *c.* 2100 BC–1800 BC. L. 3.2 cm. British Museum, London.

Basket-Maker necklace. A type of necklace made by the Basket Makers, who were among the earliest prehistoric inhabitants of south-western United States, *c.* 1000 BC–500 BC. Such necklaces were made of strands of yucca fibre with suspended turquoise ornaments.

basse taille (French). Literally, shallow cut. The technique of decoration by ENAMELLING on a metal base in which the design was first made in several levels by CHASING, CARVING, ENGRAVING or STAMPING (or, in later examples, by engine-turning) and then the surface was covered with

basse taille. Gold shuttle-shaped snuff box with green *basse taille* enamel decoration. Jean Joseph Bauière, mid-18th century. Courtesy of Wartski, London.

baule ear-rings. Gold with repoussé work, granulated gold, and filigree. Etruscan, 6th century BC. L. 1.9 cm. British Museum, London.

baule ear-rings. Gold with filigree and granulated gold. Etruscan, 7th/5th century BC. Victoria & Albert Museum, London.

beak bird. Translucent pale-green jade. Costa Rica. H. 6 cm. American Museum of Natural History, New York. Photo courtesy of André Emmerich, New York.

transparent or translucent coloured enamel (but without any partitions to separate the colours) that was then fused by firing. The varying depths of the depressions of the design resulted in different tones of the enamels and thus enhanced the effect of apparent INTAGLIO relief. The enamel decoration, after firing and polishing, was smooth and level with the metal surface. The metal base was usually gold or silver. The enamel was sometimes of different colours, but was most effective when of a single colour (usually blue or green). The technique is said to have originated in Italy in the late 13th/14th century, and thereafter was used elsewhere on the Continent, especially in the Rhineland and France, and in England. Sometimes called 'translucent enamelling'. *See* CHAMPLEVÉ; CLOISONNÉ; PLIQUE À JOUR; TAILLE D'ÉPARGNE.

bastard amber. A variety of AMBER that has a cloudy appearance due to many embedded air bubbles.

bastard cut gemstone. A gemstone that has a regular and symmetrical arrangement of FACETS, but departs from the recognized standard styles of cutting or has some modification of such styles. If the facets are irregular or not symmetrical, the term is 'cap cut'.

baton. A gemstone cut in the shape of a BAGUETTE but longer.

Battersea enamelled ware. Articles of jewelry and OBJECTS OF VERTU decorated in very limited number, *c.* 1753-6, with enamelling, at the factory at York House, Battersea, London, founded by Sir Stephen Theodore Janssen. The decoration was painted over transfer printing from copperplate engravings to a white enamelled ground, on a base of copper, and depicted portraits, flowers, and other motifs. The enamelled plaques were mounted in gold or gilt frames and set in bracelets, brooches, pendants, finger rings, watch-cases, and snuff boxes (but no recorded snuff bottle). Much enamelling of similar character, often attributed to Battersea, was made in the Midlands at Bilston (formerly in Staffordshire), and near Birmingham, and also by London enamellers in the 1750s. *See* R.J. Charleston, 'Battersea, Bilston . . . or Birmingham?', in *Victoria & Albert Museum Bulletin*, III, no. 1, January 1967, p. 1. *See* BILSTON ENAMELLED WARE.

baule ear-ring. A type of ear-ring of ETRUSCAN JEWELRY having a suspended ornament suggestive of the form of certain women's handbags, being made of a strip of gold bent almost to form a cylinder, and sometimes having one end closed by a circular plate, and with an overhead wire or narrow band (in the form of the handle) that passes through the lobe of the ear. Such pieces are usually decorated with REPOUSSÉ work, GRANULATED GOLD, and FILIGREE.

bayadère (French). A type of necklace composed of several strings of SEED PEARLS that are twisted together in a rope-like manner, the strings usually being of contrasting colours.

bazu band. An article of MUGHAL JEWELRY in the form of a gold ornament (sometimes three-sectioned), decorated with enamelling and gemstones, that is tied around the upper arm. *See* ARMLET.

bead. A small object, usually globular (but sometimes oblate, cylindrical, polyhedral or irregular) and generally pierced for stringing, made for personal adornment or to embellish other wares and usually used in strands. Beads have been made from earliest times and in all civilizations, being of a great variety of sizes and materials, including gold, silver or other metals, glass, porcelain, earthenware, stone, coral, jet, wood, or other organic substance, jade or gemstone. Beads have been worn or carried as ornamental objects or as TALISMANS. They have been strung in strands as a necklace, bracelet or ROSARY, or suspended from a brooch or an ear-ring.

beak bird. An article of PRE-COLUMBIAN JEWELRY in the form of a bird figure with a greatly exaggerated and stylized beak (sometimes up to 15 cm long) and having holes pierced through the neck horizontally so as to be suspended as a pendant with the beak forward. Such pieces were made usually of JADEITE, sometimes of SERPENTINE or green CHALCEDONY, in

Middle America, mainly Costa Rica and Mexico. *See* PRE-COLUMBIAN JADE JEWELRY.

bearded girdle. The GIRDLE of a diamond that shows natural fine lines on or just within it, being a form of flaw that usually results from too rapid cutting.

bearing. A thin metal collar, soldered on the interior of a COLLET, upon which a set gemstone is supported. *See* CLAW SETTING.

Beauharnais Brooch. A SPRAY BROOCH (separable into two brooches) mounted in gold and silver, composed of 22 laurel leaves set with diamonds and Burma rubies. It was made, *c.* 1804–9, by Ouizille Lemoine, 7 Rue Duphot, Paris, and was in the collection of Empress Josephine, first wife of Napoleon. It became the property of Prince Eugène de Beauharnais (her son by her first marriage), Viceroy of Italy and the future Duke of Leuchtenberg, from whom it descended to the Dukes of Leuchtenberg de Beauharnais, in whose family it remained until *c.* 1955.

Bedouin jewelry. Articles of jewelry made and worn by the Bedouin tribes in Saudi Arabia. The jewelry is almost always of silver, frequently set with TURQUOISE, sometimes with stones of reddish colour. The pieces have distinctive forms and styles, with ornamentation frequently of chains, beads, bells and such local objects as Koran cases. Typical examples include: *Iqd*, a necklace with suspended pendants or charm cases (*hirz*); finger rings having the bezel in the form of a flower, with a central red-stone pistil surrounded by six turquoise petals; *kaqf*, a glove-like piece with an attached ring for each finger, a bracelet, and an ornament for the back of the hand, all connected by chains; and nose rings. In the different regions of the country there are indigenous variations of style. *See* Heather Colyer Ross, *Bedouin Jewellery of Saudi Arabia* (Stacey International, 1978).

beetle jewelry. (1) Articles of jewelry made of an actual South American dried beetle, featuring the green iridescent colour of the wings. The shell is tough so that the beetle can be mounted in brooches and pendants. The wing cases (the outer pair of stiff wings that cover the inner pair when folded) are sometimes strung as a necklace. (2) Beads of gilded metal made in China in the form of a beetle, enamelled in various colours to simulate beetle wings. *See* SCARAB.

belcher chain. A type of TRACE CHAIN of which the links, made of D-section wire, are broad and of equal length.

belcher ring. A type of ring with a wide hoop through which a scarf is passed. Called now a 'scarf ring'.

belcher setting. A style of SETTING for securing a stone in a finger ring, the stone being secured by prongs or claws that are cut into the SHANK of the ring so that the stone, when set, does not extend above the circumference of the shank. *See* GYPSY SETTING.

belemnite. The FOSSIL remains of the posterior inner shell of certain extinct squids, being cylindrical and tapering to a point at one extremity and with a conical cavity at the other end. Pieces of it are sometimes mounted in jewelry, polished or unpolished. The name is derived from the Greek *belemnon* (dart). Also called 'thunderstone', based on a belief that they were hurled down to earth as thunderbolts in a storm.

Bella, La. A large HYACINTH, 416 carats, that was bought in 1687 by Leopold I, Holy Roman Emperor, 1658–1705, from the Hungarian family of Humanay and is set to form the breast of a gold and enamelled Imperial double eagle with crown. It is now in the Schatzkammer of the Hofburg, Vienna.

belt buckle. A type of BUCKLE for fastening a belt, early examples being attached at one of its ends to the belt (or to a BUCKLE PLATE) and having a tongue at the other end that fastens through a hole in the other end of the belt. Some examples of ANGLO-SAXON JEWELRY are massive and made of

Beauharnais Brooch. Composite spray brooch with diamonds and rubies, Paris, *c.* 1804–9. L. 17 cm. Courtesy of Wartski, London.

Bedouin jewelry. Silver *Iqd* (necklace). Saudi Arabia. Courtesy of Heather Colyer Ross, London.

belt buckle. Gold with zoomorphic design in filigree on repoussé base, and with granulated gold and *cloisonné* inlay of garnets. Anglo-Saxon, *c.* 700. L. 9.9 cm. British Museum, London.

gold, decorated in RIBBON STYLE, or with zoomorphic filigree motifs; such buckles were the main article of male jewelry in the late 6th and early 7th centuries, and were used to clasp a broad belt worn around the waist or hips. *See* BELT SLIDE.

belt clasp. A type of belt fastener, sometimes in the form of a bronze rectangular plaque, with a hook attached to the reverse.

belt hook. A type of BELT BUCKLE having a stud on its back that fastened a hook to one end of the belt and having a ring or loop at the other end of the belt that was placed over the hook. Such articles were a main item of ornament in China. The early examples were rather unornamented casting but later, in the 4th/1st centuries BC, they were elaborately decorated, some being made of gilt bronze or JADE. *See* BELT CLASP.

belt pendant. An article of RENAISSANCE JEWELRY in three-dimensional form with openwork decoration. Such pieces, made in Vienna, *c.* 1590-1600, are often decorated with drops of seed pearls or projecting scroll ornaments.

belt plaque. An ornamental plaque that was used to fasten a belt. Examples from the Ordos region of China, near Mongolia, from the 3rd/2nd centuries BC, are often of silver, in the form of animals (e.g. a kneeling horse, a stylized kneeling tiger) with features in low relief. Later Chinese examples, 7th/8th centuries AD, are a series of rectangular plaques joined to make a belt, each carved in low relief, with the backs pierced at the corners for attachment to a leather belt.

belt slide. A type of BELT BUCKLE that has a raised vertical bar at the rear of an open frame, the bar being sewn to one end of a belt, which then functions by passing the other end of the belt under the frame and over the bar so as to secure the belt by tension.

Benin armlet. A type of cylindrical ARMLET, 11-13 cm long, made of IVORY in the 16th century (*see* BENIN JEWELRY). Such pieces were decorated with intricate carving, sometimes inlaid with brass. Rare examples were made of two cylinders that interlocked.

Benin jewelry. Articles of jewelry made, mainly in the 16th century, in Benin (an ancient kingdom of West Africa, which became the Benin Province of south Nigeria in 1914). Many objects were made entirely of IVORY, some being carved from whole tusks; items of ivory jewelry were also made, including carved armlets (*see* BENIN ARMLET), pendants, and bracelets. Some necklaces were made of CORAL and CORNELIAN beads. The styles were indigenous but became influenced by Portuguese importations. The ivory work was done by artisans organized into guilds controlled by the king, for whose court the articles were exclusively made. Other Benin objects worn ornamentally were hip masks and belt masks made of bronze. There was little use of gold. *See* IKHOKO; AFRICAN (WEST) JEWELRY.

benoîton (French). A type of CHAIN, made of several strands of gold or silver links or of beads, such as was worn descending from a lady's evening coiffure and festooned across her bosom, or sometimes descending from a bonnet or velvet head-band. It was worn *c.* 1865-7 and was named after the comedy by the French dramatist Victorien Sardou, *La Famille Benoîton*, then popular in Paris.

Beresford Hope Cross. A PECTORAL CROSS made of two pure-gold cruciform parts set into a hinged silver-gilt frame of later workmanship than the crosses, so that the piece formed a RELIQUARY. The entire surfaces of the crosses are decorated with translucent CLOISONNÉ enamel, one with a full-length figure of the Virgin surrounded by portraits of four saints, and the other with Christ on the cross between bust portraits of the Virgin and St John. The cross is from the 8th/9th century, Byzantine or Italian. It was acquired by the Victoria & Albert Museum from the collector Beresford Hope.

Berghem, Ludwig van (Louis de Berquen or **Berchem).** A diamond-cutter from Bruges, Belgium, who was under the patronage of Jacques

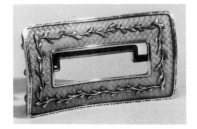

belt slide. Gold with *guilloché* decoration. Fabergé, *c.* 1900. Courtesy of Wartski, London.

Benin jewelry. Ivory armlet depicting king and royal attributes. 16th century. L. 11.2 cm. Museum of Mankind, London.

Beresford Hope Cross (front and back). *Cloisonné* enamel on gold, mounted on two-part hinged silver gilt cross. Byzantine or Italian, 8th/9th centuries. H. 8 cm. Victoria & Albert Museum, London.

Coeur (*c*.1395–1456), the noted French financier from Bourges. He is traditionally said (based on the writings in 1661 of his descendant Robert de Berchem) to have improved the surface reflection of diamonds by increasing the number of facets; but it is now recognized that there were numerous skilled lapidaries in Paris during the late 14th century who might also have done such cutting. It has been stated that the cut diamond of the THREE BROTHERS JEWEL was the first diamond cut by him; however, the cutting of a diamond in half had been previously accomplished.

Berlin iron jewelry. Articles of jewelry of cast iron, often in delicate openwork patterns, made principally in Germany during the early 19th century (often called 'Berlin iron'). The earliest factory for such ware in Berlin was the Royal Berlin Factory founded in 1804, making many varieties of iron goods, but it had operated previously in Silesia. In 1806, when Napoleon captured Berlin, the casts were taken to Paris where production is presumed, based on the style and decoration of some surviving pieces, to have continued for several years. The bulk of iron jewelry produced in Berlin was made *c*. 1813–15, when, owing to the scarcity of gold and silver as a result of the Napoleonic and later wars, a campaign was conducted to collect such metal from the populace. This led to the State offering to give simple iron finger rings and other iron articles to women who, to assist the war effort, exchanged valuable jewelry; the pieces bore such inscriptions as 'Gold gab ich für Eisen' ('I gave gold for iron'), and on the reverse a portrait of Frederick William III (1770–1840) of Prussia. Iron crosses were also given to those awarded by Prussia the Order of the Iron Cross, founded in 1813 (and renewed in 1870, 1895, and 1914). Iron jewelry included brooches, necklaces, bracelets, fans, GOTHIC CROSSES, COMBS, and PARURES, occasionally set with MEDALLIONS such as those made by Wedgwood in JASPER and by James Tassie (*see* TASSIE MEDALLION). Most examples of such iron jewelry are lacquered black, and some rare ones have gold decoration. Some pieces were made of iron mesh of very fine strands of wire; these have been thought to have been made in Silesia in the late 18th century. The pieces are generally not marked, so the place of origin is almost impossible to determine, but occasional examples bear the stamped name of the manufacturer, e.g. Geiss, Berlin, or Lehmann, Berlin, or Schott, Ilsenburg-am-Harts. During the Napoleonic period, the motifs were mainly neo-classical, but later they were less austere and more naturalistic, and, *c*. 1830–50, were of Gothic Revival style. The production continued until the fashion ended towards the close of the century. *See* Anne Clifford, *Cut-Steel and Berlin Iron Jewellery* (1971). *See* WIREWORK MESH JEWELRY; CUT STEEL JEWELRY; PARURE.

Berlin iron jewelry. Pectoral cross. Kenwood (Hull Grundy Collection), London.

berthe (French). A large, collar-shaped necklace composed of a network of gemstones, sometimes embellished with suspended pearls or drop-shaped gemstones.

beryl. A mineral that includes several varieties of gemstones, especially EMERALD and AQUAMARINE, but also several varieties of pale colours (owing to the presence of impurities), known as 'yellow beryl' (HELIODOR) and 'pink beryl' (MORGANITE) and by colour prefixes (e.g. 'orange beryl', 'green beryl', etc.). When pure, or nearly so, it is colourless (called GOSHENITE). Beryl has reasonable HARDNESS, exhibits double refraction and is dichroic; it is unaltered by exposure to artificial light. Some specimens are CHATOYANT (showing a CAT'S-EYE) and some show a star. The opaque variety, which occurs in tremendous crystals weighing up to several tons, is not used for gemstones, but gem quality crystals have been found of very large size (over 2,000 carats). Beryls resemble some other gemstones but can be distinguished by several methods.

beryl glass. A type of GLASS that is the result of fusing BERYL so that it is no longer CRYSTALLINE but AMORPHOUS. It is variously coloured by metallic oxides and is faceted, and so is sometimes used in jewelry in imitation of coloured gemstones, but is readily distinguishable.

betrothal jewel. A JEWEL in form and decoration appropriate for a gift upon a betrothal. A typical example is a brooch decorated with a betrothed couple in enamelled gold, standing together in a garden, the piece ornamented with pearls and gemstones; it is attributed to the Netherlands, *c.* 1430–40. Various articles, e.g. a gold BELT BUCKLE, sometimes bore an inscription indicating the nature of the gift.

betrothal ring. A type of finger ring of no generally standardized form that is given by a man to his fiancée as a token of betrothal, usually called today an ENGAGEMENT RING. Such rings have been used since Roman times (called *anulus pronubus*), when they were originally made of iron (a gold ring was generally forbidden) and without any gemstone; but later gold rings were so used, bearing appropriate amatory inscriptions, as well as motifs such as a lover's-knot (*see* LOVER'S-KNOT RING) or clasped hands (*see* FEDE RING) and set with gemstones. When more significance became attached to a betrothal, the ring became known as an engagement ring, and it was also used as a WEDDING RING, without any special change in form or style. Other forms of finger rings may have been used as a betrothal ring, e.g. GIMMEL (GEMEL) RING and PUZZLE RING.

bezel. (1) Originally, and still strictly, the top metal rim or setting edge of a finger ring that is usually extended to surround the cavity which holds the stone or other ornament. In modern usage, it is often loosely applied to all or part of the SETTING of the ring, including the set gemstone, or other ornament in lieu of a stone, e.g. the seal of a SIGNET RING. The French term is *chaton*. (2) The former name for 4 of the LOZENGE-shaped FACETS on the CROWN of a BRILLIANT, all having their apex touching the GIRDLE and extending up to touch the TABLE. The 4 bezels (also formerly called 'templets'), alternating with 4 similar adjacent QUOINS (LOZENGES), were usually considered together as a group of 8 templets, the only difference being their orientation to the stone and the direction and sequence in which they were ground. All such lozenge-shaped facets are now each called a KITE FACET or MAIN FACET. The bezels are the first facets to be ground after the table. Bezel facets in varying shapes and numbers are on some stones of other cuts. (3) The metal rim on the front of a WATCH CASE in which the crystal is set. (4) The metal rim or band around the top of a box, such as a snuff box, upon which the lid rests. (5) The part of a cut gemstone that is above the GIRDLE, now more properly called the CROWN.

bezoar stone. A solid concretion found in the alimentary organs of certain ruminant animals (especially the bezoar goat) and formerly supposed to have curative powers, particularly against poisoning, hence taken internally in powdered form. The whole stone was also worn as an AMULET, sometimes mounted in gold or silver jewelry, to be worn as an antidote against poisoning, first in Persia and later in the 13th to 17th centuries in Spain and other countries of Europe until its efficacy was disproved. Some silver spherical containers, divided midway, and with exteriors decorated with silver-gilt overlaid openwork, perhaps English of the 17th century, have been said possibly to be such amulets.

Biblical gemstones. A number of gemstones that are mentioned in the Bible, albeit sometimes by a name different from the name accepted today, e.g., in Exodus xxviii, sardius (meaning SARD), TOPAZ, CARBUNCLE, EMERALD, SAPPHIRE, DIAMOND, JACINTH, AGATE, AMETHYST, BERYL, ONYX, and JASPER, all being stones set in the breastplate of Aaron, the High Priest.

Biblical subjects. Subjects based on people or events from the Bible. Such subjects from the New Testament are found on many articles of jewelry, e.g. Christ, the Virgin Mary, the Annunciation, or the Birth of Christ, as well as St Peter, St Paul, and St John the Evangelist. *See* WOMAN OF SAMARIA ENSEIGNE. Examples from the Old Testament are less frequent, but some pieces depict Cain and Abel, Noah (*see* NOAH CAMEO), Joseph (*see* JOSEPH-IN-THE-WELL PENDANT), King Solomon, and Moses.

biconical bead. A type of bead in the form of two cones joined at the bases, the base angles being acute or obtuse. Some are truncated at both apexes and have flat ends, and sometimes the beads are ribbed. Such beads are found among ancient Sumerian and early Egyptian and Greek jewelry.

bijouterie. The French term for jewelry in general composed of GOLD and gemstones, and whose decorative effect is based mainly on design and craftsmanship. *See* JOAILLERIE; ORFÈVRERIE.

billiment (or **habilliment**). An ornament or band, often jewelled, that decorated a feminine head-dress in medieval times; specifically, the row of jewels that bordered the front of a hooded or gable head-dress, such as worn in England in the 16th century, e.g. as shown in portraits of Anne Boleyn. Such ornaments were sometimes made in two or three pieces, worn separately or together.

Billy and Charley. The name given to objects of a large group of 19th-century jewelry FORGERIES, including particularly some PILGRIM BADGES, made at Tower Hill, London, by two illiterate mud-rakers, known as Billy and Charley, who claimed that the medals made of cock-metal and sold by them, had been found during an excavation near the Thames. Specimens are preserved at the Cuming Museum, London.

Bilston enamelled ware. Articles of jewelry and OBJECTS OF VERTU embodying small plaques decorated with ENAMELLING, usually on copper, that were made at several factories at Bilston, West Midlands (formerly in Staffordshire). The enamelled plaques were mounted in gold or silver frames and set in bracelets, brooches, clasps, buttons, etc. The first factory was started in 1749 by Benjamin Bickley, who transferred it to Samuel Yardley; the last factory to make such ware closed in 1831. The motifs included landscapes, flowers, exotic birds, etc., painted in ROCOCO style. Much enamelware formerly attributed to Battersea was made at Bilston, where such work was done long after the Battersea factory closed. *See* BATTERSEA ENAMELLED WARE.

bird fibula. A type of FIBULA of MEROVINGIAN JEWELRY made in the shape of the profile of a hook-beaked bird. Several known examples, some found at Cologne, are made of gold completely decorated with CLOISONNÉ INLAY of GARNETS (some cells with PÂTE DE VERRE). Such pieces were worn from the early 6th century by Merovingian women in addition to a pair of larger fibulae.

bird jewelry. Articles of jewelry whose principal decorative motif is a representation of a bird. Such motifs have been used in many periods and cultures, and include the parrot (*see* PARROT JEWELRY), pelican (*see* PELICAN JEWELRY); DOVE (*see also* SAINT-ESPRIT), eagle (*see* EAGLE PENDANT; GISELA BROOCH), vulture (*see* KING VULTURE PENDANT), humming bird (*see* HUMMING-BIRD JEWELRY), phoenix (*see* PHOENIX JEWELRY), POPINJAY, and owl. For some examples in EGYPTIAN JEWELRY, *see* MENET BIRD; TUTANKHAMUN FALCON PECTORAL; TUTANKHAMUN VULTURE COLLAR; HAWK JEWEL. Some jewels of Anglo-Saxon and German origin depict a bird, sometimes set with gemstones; the motif is often found also in RENAISSANCE JEWELRY. *See* BAROQUE PEARL JEWEL; BEAK BIRD; BIRD FIBULA.

birthstone. A gemstone designated by custom, religious tradition, and superstition as being related to the month of one's birth. Pagan legends,

bird fibula. Gold with *cloisonné* inlay of garnets. Merovingian, 1st half of 6th century. L. 3.6 cm. Römisch-Germanisches Museum, Cologne.

bird jewelry. Brooch in form of swallow. *Plique à jour* wings, with diamonds and sapphires. Courtesy of Wartski, London.

mingled with Christian and Jewish traditions, led to the association of certain stones with different months. In the 18th century the relationship of stones with months was popularized but it was based mainly on the colours of the stones. Owing to the fact that several stones have the same colours, confusion resulted, so that in 1937 the National Association of Goldsmiths of Great Britain established a uniform list (with some alternatives for the more costly stones) and this list has been recognized throughout the British Commonwealth and the United States as follows:

January	garnet
February	amethyst
March	aquamarine (bloodstone)
April	diamond (rock crystal)
May	emerald (chrysoprase)
June	pearl (moonstone)
July	ruby (cornelian or onyx)
August	peridot (sardonyx)
September	sapphire (lapis lazuli)
October	opal (tourmaline)
November	topaz (citrine)
December	turquoise

bishop's (or **episcopal**) **ring.** A type of finger ring worn by a bishop upon his consecration and sometimes thereafter, except during the celebration of the Mass (*see* PONTIFICAL RING). The form is not specified, but the Synod of Milan in the 7th century decreed that such rings should be of pure gold and set with an unengraved gem, hence early examples bear only a rough stone as found. The usual stone in England is a sapphire, somtimes an amethyst. Such a ring was originally worn on the right hand, but more recently on the third finger of the left. Only one such ring is worn, but formerly several other rings were worn by bishops, on fingers and thumb and sometimes more than one on a finger (and occasionally over a glove). Each bishop's ring was made for a particular bishop and was sometimes interred with him; but, although it was customary for a bishop to be buried wearing a ring, it was not always his consecration ring, hence many rings found in tombs of bishops are not a 'bishop's ring'. From the 13th century an abbot was accorded the right to a ring similar to a bishop's ring. From the time of Edward I every bishop's ring and ABBOT'S RING was supposed to be surrendered to the Crown, as a 'mortuary' (death duty), but this seems not to have been rigidly enforced, especially as to the pontifical ring, and sometimes a less valuable substitute was surrendered or was interred with a deceased bishop.

Bismarck Sapphire. A deep-blue SAPPHIRE from Sri Lanka (formerly Ceylon) that weighs 98.6 carats and is now mounted in a pendant set with small diamonds and sapphires, suspended from a diamond necklace. It was donated by Countess Mona Bismarck to the Smithsonian Institution, Washington, DC.

Biwa pearl. A variety of non-nucleated CULTURED PEARL produced since World War II by means of the fresh-water mussel (*Hyriopsis schlegeli*) in Lake Biwa, Honshu, Japan. Owing to the internal anatomy of the mussel, a solid foreign nucleus cannot readily be inserted, so that a small piece of mantle tissue (which later disappears) from another mussel is inserted in each of ten to twenty incisions in the mantle of the host mussel, which then, in about 1 to 2 years, produces the pearls. They are brown or salmon-coloured, and seldom spherical; they are bleached to a bright white. The process is repeated in some mussels, producing larger and darker BAROQUE PEARLS. Comparable non-nucleated cultured pearls have also been produced since 1958 in Australia by using a large variety of PEARL OYSTER (*Pinctada maxima*).

black amber. (1) A misnomer for JET. (2) Amber stained black.

black diamond. (1) A misnomer for HEMATITE. (2) A so-called 'black diamond' that is of gun-metal colour and usually found in Brazil; but an example is known from India (*see* BLACK ORLOV DIAMOND) and another possibly from Zaire, formerly the Belgian Congo (*see* BLACK STAR OF AFRICA). (3) The same as carbonado, a type of industrial diamond.

black moonstone. A misnomer for a dark LABRADORITE with a bluish play of colour.

black onyx. A misnomer for CHALCEDONY dyed black and used as a substitute for JET, especially in the 1920–30s.

black opal. A variety of PRECIOUS OPAL that is almost opaque and of which the background colour is deep blue to dark grey or black (very rare). It contains tiny iridescent opal spheres that cause a play of colours as a result of diffraction of light. It is one of the most valuable varieties, discovered in 1905 in Australia in the Lightning Ridge mine. Imitations are known in which the dark background has been produced by immersing a poor opal or OPAL MATRIX in a sugar solution and then in sulphuric acid. *See* OPAL DOUBLET; DEVONSHIRE OPAL; PRINCE HARLEQUIN OPAL.

Black Orlov (Orloff) Diamond. A gun-metal-colour, cushion-cut, Indian diamond, weighing 67.50 carats, that is said once to have been in a 19th-century shrine near Pondicherry, India (hence sometimes known as the 'Eye of Brahma Diamond'), and owned in the 18th century by the Russian Princess Nadia Vygin-Orlov. It was acquired by Charles F. Winson Gems, Inc., a New York diamond dealer, which exhibited it at the Museum of Natural History, London, in 1951 and in Johannesburg in 1967; it was sold privately in July 1979.

black pearl. A pearl of blackish gun-metal colour, one of the most valuable varieties.

Black Prince's Ruby. A large red SPINEL (sometimes called a BALAS RUBY) that was once regarded as a RUBY. It is now set in the diamond-encrusted CROSS FORMÉE above the CULLINAN II DIAMOND ('The Second Star of Africa') on the front of the British IMPERIAL STATE CROWN. The stone has never been cut, merely polished, and so is of irregular shape, almost 5 cm long. It was once pierced to be worn as a pendant, but the hole is now filled with a small ruby. The stone was first mentioned as being owned by Abu Said, King of Granada, and seized, upon his being murdered, by Pedro the Cruel, King of Castile, who gave it as a tribute to Edward, the Black Prince, son of Edward III of England, after his aid in the victory at the Battle of Najera in Spain in 1367. It was brought to England and worn in the coronet of the helmet of Henry V at the Battle of Agincourt (1415) and by Richard III at Bosworth (1485), and was later added to the CROWN JEWELS by Henry VIII. It was sold during the Commonwealth for a trifling sum, but after the Restoration was returned to the Crown. It was set in the crown worn by Charles II and in that worn by Mary II, and then restored to the crown of Charles II by George II. It was later transferred to the present Imperial State Crown.

black spot. A small spot of black made by a pitch-like paint that is found on the CULET (or FOIL) of most 18th-century PASTE stones, as well as on some early diamonds and other gemstones. Its purpose has not been determined, but it is said to have been intended to simulate the dark spot that seems to be on the culet of a BRILLIANT CUT diamond when viewed through the TABLE. It is not a proof of antiquity, as it may have been applied to a piece at a late date; and its absence is not conclusive as to a late date, as a spot may have worn off.

Black Star of Africa. A so-called BLACK DIAMOND of 202 carats, found in Zaire (formerly the Belgian Congo); it has been said to be the largest coloured diamond in the world. It was exhibited with Belgian stones in Tokyo in 1971.

blackamoor. The figure of a young male Negro or black African depicted (in jewelry) in a head or bust, usually made of black ONYX or black-dyed CHALCEDONY ('black onyx'). Such pieces were made as a CAMEO or as an ornament IN THE ROUND to decorate a pendant, brooch, hatpin or the SHANK of a SEAL. They were, and still are, a speciality of Venice, but such cameos, of male or female heads, were also produced elsewhere in the 16th to 18th centuries. *See* GRESLEY JEWEL.

blemish. A marriage of the surface of a gemstone, as distinguished from a FLAW, which is an internal imperfection. *See* CHIP.

blister pearl. A type of pearl (often hollow and irregular) that is cut away from being attached to the nacreous interior of the shell of a PEARL OYSTER, and hence having a non-nacreous, flat underside. It is formed (1) when a foreign body (e.g. a grain of sand) has entered the shell and become cemented as an excrescence to the inside of the shell between it and the MANTLE, causing an irritation that is covered by secreted NACRE except where it is attached; or (2) when a parasite bores its way into the shell and the oyster forms a protective deposit around the entrance. Such pearls are irregularly shaped or somewhat hemispherical. When used in jewelry, the non-nacreous underside is placed in a SETTING so as to be concealed. Also called a 'chicot pearl' or 'wart pearl'. *See* TURTLE-BACK PEARL.

bloodstone. A MASSIVE variety of CHALCEDONY that is a green PLASMA speckled with red spots resembling blood (due to oxidizing of the green). It has been used as a stone for a SEAL, and also in the Middle Ages as an AMULET to prevent loss of blood. The red spots on some stones have been utilized on some CAMEOS to indicate drops of blood on carved figures of Christ, especially in Italy in the 16th century. The stone is also called HELIOTROPE and bloodstone jasper, and has sometimes been miscalled HEMATITE, probably because the German word *Blutstein* refers to hematite. *See* MAGICAL STONE.

bloomed gold. A type of TEXTURED GOLD with its natural surface given a matt finish, but sometimes immersed in acid to produce a very lightly pitted effect. It is used sometimes to provide contrast on the unenamelled surface of some pieces decorated in BASSE TAILLE style.

Blue Diamond of the Crown. A blue diamond that is said to be the blue diamond that was found in the Kollur Mine, near Golconda, in southern India, weighing $112^3/16$ old carats and INDIAN CUT, and that was bought in 1642 by Jean-Baptiste Tavernier (*see* TAVERNIER DIAMONDS) and sold by him in 1669 to Louis XIV. Then known as the 'French Blue' or the 'Tavernier Blue', it was recut in 1673, by Sieur Pitau, into a triangular or heart-shaped BRILLIANT weighing $67^1/8$ old carats and officially renamed the 'Blue Diamond of the Crown'. It was worn by the Marquise de Montespan, by Louis XIV, who had it set as a pendant, and also by Louis XV after 1749 when it was mounted in a GOLDEN FLEECE jewel with the CÔTE DE BRETAGNE. It was later worn by Louis XVI and by Marie Antoinette and others of the Court. The diamond was listed in French inventories until stolen in 1792 from the Garde Meuble, and is not known to have been recovered. One story is that the jewel was taken by a thief to London, broken up, and the diamond recut into two or three stones. It is now believed, based on colour and quality, that the largest resulting stone (44.52 carats) is the HOPE DIAMOND, and it has been suggested (but contradicted) that two other stones that resulted were the 'Brunswick I' (13.75 carats), that once belonged to the Duke of Brunswick and was sold at Geneva in 1874, and the 'Brunswick II' (6.5 carats), also then sold at Geneva (both of unknown whereabouts today).

blue gold. A bluish ALLOY of GOLD, made with 25% arsenic or iron. It is very seldom used in jewelry but is occasionally used in GOLD À QUATRE COULEURS.

Blue Heart Diamond. An INDIAN CUT deep-blue diamond weighing 112.50 carats rough that was sold by Jean-Baptiste Tavernier to Louis XIV. It was recut in 1673 as a heart-shaped stone weighing 31 carats. Louis XVI inherited it and it was worn by Marie Antoinette. It was among the diamonds stolen from the Garde Meuble in 1792. After a period of unknown whereabouts, it was bought in 1911 by CARTIER in Paris and was sold in Buenos Aires. In 1953 the diamond was owned by VAN CLEEF & ARPELS of Paris, who sold it, rebought it, and in 1960 sold it again.

blue moonstone. (1) A variety of MOONSTONE that is blue. (2) A misnomer for CHALCEDONY that has been stained blue by DYEING.

blue pearl. A variety of pearl that is lead-greyish, owing to a thin crust over a layer of conchiolin near the surface, or a dark kernel rich in conchiolin.

blue-white diamond. A diamond that, strictly, is classified as a JAGER, but commonly and incorrectly means any diamond that is colourless or shows only a trace of blue. In Great Britain and the United States it is prohibited to apply the term to any stone that shows in daylight any colour other than a trace of blue, and the American Gem Society forbids its use altogether, owing to former abuse which sometimes applied it even to stones with a trace of yellow.

boat ear-ring. A type of ear-ring, the lower rim of which curves upward so as to have a crescent or boat-shaped form, sometimes flat but occasionally cylindrical, tapering upward to the points where it joins the wire loop that passes through the ear-lobe. Such ear-rings, made in the Middle East, are found among BYZANTINE JEWELRY and ROMAN JEWELRY. Some examples are decorated with suspended ornaments.

bodkin. A HAIR PIN, so called during the Renaissance when they were made of gold or silver and richly decorated with gemstones. These developed into the later AIGRETTE.

boat ear-rings. Roman, 2nd/3rd centuries AD. W. 2 cm. National Trust, Waddesdon Manor, Aylesbury, Buckinghamshire.

bogwood. The wood of trees preserved in peat marshes, mainly oak, in Eire. It is of shiny ebony colour, and has been used in the Victorian era, as a cheap substitute for JET, for inexpensive MOURNING JEWELRY, being carved and sometimes set with Irish PEARLS.

Bohemian diamond. A local misnomer for ROCK CRYSTAL.

Bohemian ruby. A local misnomer for PYROPE, and for reddish or rose-coloured QUARTZ.

boîte de senteur (French). A type of box used frequently from the 17th century to contain scented spices and perfumes, originally to counteract offensive odours and supposedly to protect against infection, and later to emit a pleasant scent. Such articles were called in England a POMANDER, scent ball or MUSK BALL. Some were divided internally into compartments, called cells or *loculi*.

boat ear-rings. Gold with bird designs and *opus interrasile*. Byzantine, 6th century. Victoria & Albert Museum, London.

bola (United States Indian). A length of thin, braided leather with decorative silver tips on each end, worn around the neck and having a sliding ornament (a TOGGLE) that is raised upward when worn to achieve the effect of a string necktie. The sliding ornament is of various forms, sometimes a NAJA and sometimes a silver disc inlaid with turquoise. It is worn mainly by men in western United States. It was perhaps named after the Gaucho hurling weapon, called a *bola*, in the form of a leather thong with a ball on each end.

bolt fibula. A type of FIBULA (unlike the usual SAFETY-PIN FIBULA) composed of two elements: one consists of 3 or 4 horizontal thin tubes curving downward to one end, with the tubes joined together by a transverse plate to which is hinged a similar plate, and having long pins attached to the outer tubes; the second element consists of similar tubes, but bent toward the other end. To fasten a garment, the pins are pushed through the garment and then into the tubes of the second element. All four plates are decorated with encrusted animal figures. Such pieces are Etruscan, 7th century BC.

bolt fibula. Gold. Etruscan, 7th century BC. L. (closed) 12.1 cm. British Museum, London.

bolt ring. A small, ring-shaped device for affixing a pendant to a chain, fastening a necklace, or some other such purpose. It is hollow or partly hollow, enclosing a curved tongue that may be drawn back by a small projecting knob to expose an opening in the ring, which is closed by the pressure of an internal steel spring. There is attached a tiny loop to join the ring permanently to one end of the chain, etc. Also called a 'revolver catch'.

bone. A hard material from the skeleton of most vertebrate species, but the variety mainly used in jewelry is the compact bone from such animals as the wild boar and wild hog, or the horns of stags. It is used principally for inexpensive jewelry, except when sometimes stained and carved in imitation of IVORY. In primitive jewelry it has been carved and used for beads, finger rings, brooches, pins, hair pins, etc. Carved bone was used for Minoan SEALS and for beads for ROSARIES in the Middle Ages in

Boscobel Oak Locket. Gold with enamelling. English, *c*. 1660. H. 6.3 cm. Victoria & Albert Museum, London.

Boucheron. Platinum necklace with diamonds. Courtesy of Boucheron, Paris and London.

Europe. Examples exist in ANGLO-SAXON JEWELRY in the form of buckles, finger rings and brooches. Bone is slightly heavier than ivory and of about the same HARDNESS; it is readily distinguishable by microscopic examination. Today it is imitated by PLASTIC.

bone amber. A variety of AMBER that is opaque and includes a mass of closely-spaced, air-filled cavities that result in a cloudy whitish appearance. Also called 'osseous amber'.

bone turquoise. The same as ODONTOLITE.

book cover. A hinged covering for a small book, usually a devotional one, made of gold, silver, bronze or other metal and decorated with pierced work, chasing, enamelling, and sometimes gemstones. Some had a suspensory ring so that they could be carried on a CHATELAINE or from the girdle (*see* GIRDLE BOOK). An example in enamelled gold (now in the Victoria & Albert Museum) was once attributed to BENVENUTO CELLINI, another in gold (now in the British Museum) to GEORGE HERIOT of Edinburgh, and some were made of carved BOXWOOD in Germany during the 16th century.

bootlace fringe. A type of ornamentation on some 19th-century jewelry in the form of a fringe, each strand of which is suggestive of the crimped end of a bootlace (shoestring).

bornite. A mineral that is pinkish-silver, but when it tarnishes becomes iridescent in shades of red and blue, and so is called 'peacock ore'. It is used in jewelry for CABOCHONS that tarnish to desirable peacock colours. It was named after Ignatius von Born (1742-91), an Austrian mineralogist. Also called 'variegated copper ore'.

Borre style. A Viking style of decoration used in the 9th/10th centuries, named after a burial site at Borre, Norway. It has three main motifs: a ring-chain pattern, a backward-looking animal, and a lion-like beast. It was used generally in Scandinavia and also in Russia. *See* VIKING JEWELRY.

Boscobel Oak Locket. A copper-gilt LOCKET that contains a miniature portrait of Major William Carlos, who hid with Charles II in the Boscobel Oak when the latter was fleeing the country after his defeat by Cromwell at Worcester in 1651. On the front is an engraved depiction of them hiding in the oak-tree, and on the back are the engraved arms and motto granted to Carlos after the escape. Inside the locket is an inscribed poem to Carlos.

Boucheron. A leading French jewelry firm, founded in 1858 in the Palais Royal, Paris, by Frédéric Boucheron (1830-1902) and now having its main establishment at 26 Place Vendôme, Paris, with branches in London and elsewhere. Frédéric Boucheron was succeeded by his son Louis (1874-1959), in turn succeeded by his son Gérard (b. 1910), whose son Alain (b. 1948) is now active in the business. The London office, established in 1907, is at 180 New Bond St. In 1960 the firm, at the request of the Shah of Iran, set up in Tehran the display of the Royal Jewelry Collection. Boucheron is noted as a specialist in gems as well as a designer of luxury and medium-priced jewelry.

bouchon de carafe (French). A type of ear-ring having a suspended diamond so large that it was called a 'decanter stopper'. The style was introduced in France *c*. 1870 by the courtesan La Païva.

boule (from the French word for 'ball'). An embryonic SYNTHETIC GEMSTONE produced as a single-crystal drop from fused alumina by the flame fusion process of the VERNEUIL FURNACE. It was originally made in a somewhat pear-shaped form but was later nearly cylindrical. The boule is smooth and has no crystal faces, but the internal structure (except for curved striae instead of straight lines), HARDNESS, specific gravity, refractive index, double refraction, and dichroism are almost identical with the natural gemstone that is simulated. When the boule has grown and cooled it usually divides itself in half, but it can be split longitudinally, by a blow, into symmetrical halves. Commercial boules weigh up to about 300 carats, and most are colourless (many being used as bearings for watches, etc.), but coloured boules, for use in making synthetic gemstones, are produced by use of various metallic oxides. Some boules may contain trapped air bubbles.

Boulton, Matthew (1728–1809). A leading manufacturer of metal objects, having inherited in 1759 a metal business in Birmingham and later expanding it greatly and adding factories in Sheffield and Wolverhampton. He made articles of jewelry in Sheffield plate and cut steel (*see* CUT STEEL JEWELRY), as well as vast quantities of BUTTONS, but is best known, in the art world, for the many mounts that his Soho factory, owned with John Fothergill, made of ORMOLU for objects of fine porcelain. *See* H. W. Dickinson, *Matthew Boulton* (1937).

bouquet pendant. A type of pendant in the form of a bouquet of flowers, sometimes standing in a vase. One German example, *c.* 1620–30, has the flowers made of silver decorated with ÉMAIL EN RONDE BOSSE and set with emeralds; four flowers are on coiled-spring stems so that they vibrate.

bouquet pendant. Silver with *émail en ronde bosse* and emeralds. German, *c.* 1620–30. Museum für Kunst und Gewerbe, Hamburg.

Bourguet, Jean (fl. 1700–23). A Parisian goldsmith who made jewelry set with gemstones but is best known for his design book, *Livre de Taille d'Épargne*, which includes designs for enamelling and contemporary motifs. *See* TAILLE D'ÉPARGNE.

bouton pearl. A type of natural pearl or CULTURED PEARL that is flat on one side, or bun-shaped. It is formed when the incomplete pearl becomes attached to the inside of the shell and hence has grown, by subsequent deposits of NACRE, round on one side but flat on the other. Such pearls are used in ear-rings, finger rings, and cuff links, and are sometimes CHINESE DRILLED. Also called 'button pearl'.

bow. The upper part of a FIBULA that covers the pin (ACUS). The bow on some fibulae was enclosed within a glass leech-shaped tube (or a 'runner' in the form of a half-section of such a tube). Others were decorated with relief figures or ornamentation.

bow fibula. Silver gilt. Gotland, Sweden, 8th century. L. 16 cm. Statens Historiska Museum, Stockholm.

bow fibula. A type of FIBULA having a high arched BOW, related to the Celtic Iron Age and Roman SAFETY-PIN FIBULA, but showing in its decoration the influence of Scandinavian and eastern European sources. There are several variations, such as the CROSSBOW FIBULA, CRUCIFORM FIBULA, SMALL-LONG FIBULA, and SQUARE-HEADED FIBULA.

bow-knot brooch. A type of brooch in the form of a single or double bow-knot, usually set with gemstones and often having suspended a pendent PEARL. They were made in France, England, the Netherlands, and Spain from the second half of the 17th century. Some were enamelled on the front, and especially on the back, in the style of GILLES LÉGARÉ. *See* LOVER'S-KNOT RING; SÉVIGNÉ.

bow-tie. A dark shape, somewhat resembling a bow-tie, that is seen through the TABLE of some diamonds cut as a MARQUISE or cut oval or pear-shaped.

bow-knot brooch. Gold enamelled with pearls and gemstones. Netherlands, 3rd quarter of 17th century. L. 9.5 cm. Rijksmuseum, Amsterdam.

bowenite. A variety of SERPENTINE that is hard and pale grey to cream and pale green. It resembles NEPHRITE (JADE) but is softer and more sectile. It is named after G. T. Bowen who first analysed it. It is used for carved ornaments and jewelry. Carved pieces exported from China are sometimes incorrectly called 'new jade'. Also miscalled 'serpentine jade'.

box brooch. A type of Viking brooch of drum-shape, made with a circular gold plaque on a cylindrical bronze frame. The top and sides are heavily decorated with GRANULATED GOLD and FILIGREE, and sometimes there are silver rims and attached plates with NIELLO decoration. Such brooches were made in Gotland, Sweden, in the 11th century; an outstanding example is the Mårtens brooch in the British Museum. *See* VIKING JEWELRY.

box ear-ring. The same as BAULE EAR-RING.

box setting. A style of SETTING a gemstone in a finger ring, the stone being set in a square or rectangular metal frame and held in place by

bow-knot brooch. Gold with diamonds in openwork *pavé* setting. Fabergé. Courtesy of Wartski, London.

box brooch. Bronze with silver plates decorated with niello and with gold filigree and granulated gold. Gotland, Sweden, 11th century. W. 7.6 cm. Statens Historiska Museum, Stockholm.

boxwood. Carved pendant. French, dated 1577. Wallace Collection, London.

bracelet. Gold; 4 links representing in relief the seasons, 4 with 13 table-cut diamonds representing weeks; enamelled interior in style of Jacques Callot. Danish (?), c. 1640. L. 19.3 cm. Royal Collection, Rosenborg Castle, Copenhagen.

bending the top edge of the metal over the edge of the stone to secure it. A variation, using a circular tube to hold the stone, is called a COLLET SETTING. *See* RUB-OVER SETTING; OPEN SETTING.

box snap. A type of fastener for a bracelet, necklace, etc., that is in the form of a small box on each end of the piece, one being hollow and having a slot and the other a flat, doubled-over metal tongue that fits compressed into the slot and expands within the box to fasten the two ends; attached to the tongue is a small thumbpiece that must be depressed to open the fastening. Such fasteners are found on expensive jewelry.

boxwood. A very close-grained, tough, hard, and heavy wood of the box family. Its colour is light yellow, light brown or white. Because of its fine grain and hardness, it is very suitable for wood carving and engraving, e.g. for some beads or a NUT on a ROSARY, or as a pendant. Some BOOK COVERS for a small prayer-book were made of carved boxwood. *See* DEVONSHIRE ROSARY.

Brabant rose cut. The style of cutting a diamond that is a modification of the standard ROSE CUT (DUTCH ROSE CUT) stone so that the stone is flatter. It may have the same 24 FACETS, cut in 2 rows with 6 triangular facets in the upper row and 18 triangular facets in the lower, but it usually has only 12 facets, also cut in 2 rows, with 6 triangular facets in the upper row forming a low hexagonal pyramid and 6 isosceles-trapezoidal facets in the lower row. Thus it is a 12-sided or 6-sided stone. Also called the 'Antwerp rose cut'.

Brabant rose cut
side view

bracelet. An ornament worn on the wrist or forearm as a flexible band or series of links, in contrast to a BANGLE, which is rigid. Such ornaments have been worn by men as well as women from earliest times (made of BONE, CORAL or IVORY, as well as of metal) and in primitive as well as civilized societies. In the West they are worn mainly by women, but in the East they are still worn by men. Occasionally they are worn on both arms, and two or more at the same time. Bracelets were worn by the Egyptians, the Greeks, and the Romans, sometimes set with gemstones and coins, and were popular articles of ETRUSCAN JEWELRY and ANGLO-SAXON JEWELRY. They were used less often in the Middle Ages and the Renaissance, owing to the long sleeves then worn, but their use was revived in the 18th and 19th centuries, many pieces being made with CAMEOS and MEDALLIONS, and in the Victorian era they were a part of MOURNING JEWELRY, often in the form of HAIR JEWELRY. Later, and until today, luxurious examples have been lavishly set with gemstones, but they occur in a multitude of styles and price ranges, including COSTUME JEWELRY and JUNK JEWELRY. They have often formed a unit of a PARURE. Some bracelets have been made in PENANNULAR form (*see* ANIMAL-HEAD BRACELET; SNAKE BRACELET) and some in the form of a long continuous coil of gold band. *See* ANKLET; ARMLET; CADENAS; CHARM BRACELET; CUFF BRACELET; EXPANDABLE BRACELET; HALF-HOOP BRACELET; ID BRACELET; JARRETIÈRE; LINK BRACELET; SLAVE BRACELET; WATCH BRACELET.

bractea. A thin disc of precious metal. Such pieces, pierced with holes to be attached to a garment, were used in ancient Greece. Multiple examples are decorated by EMBOSSING, a number of specimens being stamped with the same die. They were used singly or in groups as designs or borders. In Greece, they were also used as burial ornaments to save the expense of more costly objects and also to minimize the risk of subsequent tomb pilfering. *See* BRACTEATE.

bracteate. A type of pendant in the form of a disc of thin, beaten gold with stamped decoration based on Roman coin and medallion prototypes, surrounded by a wide band, sometimes ornamented with FILIGREE and GRANULATED GOLD, and having at the top a horizontal cylindrical attachment for suspension from a woman's necklace. They frequently depict human or zoomorphic subjects. The decoration was stamped with a die and so often several examples are known from the same die. They had their origin in Scandinavian countries in the 6th/8th centuries and reached England (where they have been found in Anglo-Saxon graves) directly or via Germany. *See* BRACTEA; ENKOLPION; GOTLANDIC BRACTEATE; VIKING JEWELRY.

Braganza Stone. A large gemstone reputed to have been found in 1740 in Minas Gerais, Brazil, and to have weighed rough 1,640 metric carats. It was formerly said to have been a diamond, but is now considered to have been a colourless TOPAZ. It was claimed by the King of Portugal, and was worn by King John VI, 1816–26, as a suspended rough stone. Its present whereabouts is unknown.

Brandebourg (French). A type of CLASP used in France in the 17th century in the form of a frog-fastener decorated with diamonds, sometimes worn on a bodice in a vertical group of diminishing sizes.

brass. An ALLOY of COPPER and zinc, in varying proportions. It is used in making gilding metal but otherwise not often in jewelry except in some COSTUME JEWELRY and BUTTONS. *See* ORMOLU; TOMBAC.

Brazilian chrysolite. A local misnomer for a green variety of CHRYSO-BERYL, and also sometimes for a green variety of TOURMALINE.

Brazilian emerald. A local misnomer for a green variety of TOURMALINE found in Brazil. The name is especially misleading since emeralds have been found in Brazil, and so should be discarded.

Brazilian peridot. A local misnomer for a yellowish-green variety of TOURMALINE.

Brazilian ruby. A local misnomer for a red TOPAZ found occasionally in Brazil.

Brazilian sapphire. A local misnomer for a transparent blue variety of TOURMALINE found in Brazil.

Brazilian topaz. A jewellers' name sometimes applied to yellow TOPAZ, as distinguished from yellow quartz (CITRINE) or sometimes applied as a misnomer to citrine.

brazilianite. A gemstone that is slightly greenish-yellow, transparent to translucent. It was first described in 1945 and was found in Minas Gerais, Brazil, hence its name. Clear stones are faceted, cloudy ones are cut EN CABOCHON.

break facets. A former collective name for the 8 SKILL FACETS and the 8 CROSS FACETS above the GIRDLE on the CROWN of a BRILLIANT, and now called 'upper girdle facets'. Also formerly sometimes called 'halves' or 'half facets'.

breast chain. A type of long CHAIN worn as an ornament extending over the breast and back, usually composed of many ornamental discs or beads, and having 2 large discs, 1 to hang on the front and 1 on the back. One Byzantine example, made in Egypt in the 6th century, is composed of 4 chains of equal length, each made of 23 gold discs, and all connected to the 2 large discs, so that 2 of the chains rest on each shoulder, in the manner of such chains seen on some Romano-Egyptian terracotta figures.

breast ornament. *See* PECTORAL.

breccia. A rock composed of angular fragments of minerals or rocks cemented together. Some examples are made of fragments of the same variety of a gemstone, e.g. brecciated JASPER or brecciated AGATE. Pieces made of different layers of colours were often carved as a CAMEO, e.g. the FLORA OF PISTRUCCI.

breloque. A small charm, often in the form of a statuette, that is worn on a WATCH CHAIN or a CHATELAINE. Examples were made of porcelain at Chelsea and Derby. They have a small suspensory ring, but have no seal affixed. *See* WATCH-CHARM.

bridal crown. A type of CROWN worn by a bride at the wedding ceremony. Its precursor was the CHAPLET worn by an unmarried girl. Such crowns were used from the 15th century in Germany, and the custom was extended in Scandinavia to the wearing by the bride of a

bracteate. Gold pendant with stamped decoration. Probably Gotland, Sweden, 6th century. W. 3.6 cm. British Museum, London.

breast chain. Four gold chains attached to two discs. Byzantine, 6th century. L. 73.4 cm. British Museum, London.

bridal crown. Silver gilt with glass stones. Hallmark of Hans Persson Berg, Vimmerby, Sweden, *c.* 1662–1700. H. 11.5 cm. Nordiska Museum, Stockholm.

BRIDAL PARURE decorated with glass stones. The crowns were generally of silver, sometimes set with ROCK CRYSTAL. They were usually owned by the church and lent to the bride. *See* SØLJE.

bridal parure. A suite (PARURE) of JEWELRY worn by a bride at the wedding ceremony, usually owned by the church or local authorities and lent for the occasion. It would include a BRIDAL CROWN and usually also a brooch, ear-rings, and sometimes a SÉVIGNÉ, GIRANDOLE, and pendants. Such suites have been so used in Scandinavian countries since the 15th century and the custom has continued to modern times, although some pieces now used are set with ROCK CRYSTAL instead of diamonds.

bright cut. A style of decoration on metal achieved by cutting sharply into the metal at an angle and with short strokes, then highly burnishing to create a bright effect in comparison with the surrounding area. If not highly polished, it is called 'dull cut'.

brilliance. The radiant brightness of a transparent gemstone (especially a diamond) resulting from the refraction and reflection of light rays entering it. The greater the refraction and the less the loss of light through the bottom of a faceted gemstone (enhanced by expert FACETING), the greater the brilliance of the stone.

brilliant. A diamond that is BRILLIANT CUT. If properly proportioned and FACETED, light cannot escape at the bottom but is reflected inside the stone and back out through the CROWN.

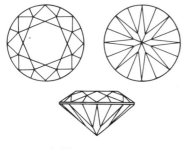

brilliant cut (modern)
top, bottom, and side views

brilliant cut. The style of cutting a diamond (or other transparent gemstone) as a BRILLIANT in a prescribed manner with many FACETS of different shapes and sizes so as to increase its BRILLIANCE by minimizing the amount of light that escapes at the bottom of the stone. The basic brilliant-cut stone (usually circular but sometimes oval) is in the form of 2 octagonal pyramids juxtaposed base to base, the upper one being truncated near its apex (forming the large TABLE) and the lower one truncated very near its apex (forming the very small CULET). The line where the pyramids meet is the GIRDLE, above which is the CROWN (rows of sloping facets extending up to and including the table) and below which is the PAVILION (rows of sloping facets extending down to and including the culet). The facets along both sides of the girdle are triangular and are now collectively called GIRDLE FACETS; those that extend upward from the girdle are called 'upper girdle facets' and those that extend downward 'lower girdle facets'. The large LOZENGE-shaped facets that extend upward from the girdle to the crown are called KITE FACETS or MAIN FACETS, and those that extend downward from the girdle to the culet (or the point, if there is no culet) are called PAVILION FACETS. The small triangular facets that extend upward to the table from the kite facets are called STAR FACETS. The ordinary brilliant (sometimes called a 'full-cut brilliant') has, in addition to the table and the culet, 56 facets, of which 32 are above the girdle (8 star facets, 8 kite facets, and 16 upper girdle facets) and 24 below (16 lower girdle facets and 8 pavilion facets), with sometimes 8 additional small facets around the culet. The angle between the crown facets and the girdle must be (to produce the most brilliance) between 35° and 40°, and that between the pavilion facets and the girdle must be 40°. The 'double brilliant' (usually a stone weighing over 10 carats) has 40 facets above the girdle, 32 below; and the 'half-brilliant' has 16 above and 12 to 16 below. The depth of the crown is about 35–40% of that of the pavilion, the diameter of the table is about 55% of that of the girdle, and the culet is small (or not present in some modern stones). If the pavilion is too shallow or too deep, too much light is lost through the bottom of the stone. The original brilliant cut, said to have been invented by VINCENZO PERUZZI, largely superseded the former ROSE CUT style. There are many variations of the standard brilliant cut. *See* AMERICAN BRILLIANT CUT; CAIRO STAR CUT; EIGHT CUT (single cut); ENGLISH SQUARE CUT; EUROPEAN BRILLIANT CUT; JUBILEE CUT; KING CUT; MAGNA CUT; MARQUISE CUT; MAZARIN CUT; OLD MINE CUT; PERUZZI CUT; ROYAL CUT; ROYAL 144 CUT; STAR CUT; SWISS CUT; VICTORIAN CUT; ZIRCON CUT. *See also* BRIOLETTE; PENDELOQUE CUT.

briolette. A diamond (or other transparent gemstone) cut in a style that is an elongated modification of the DOUBLE ROSE CUT, being without a

TABLE or a CULET, and being drop-shaped with a pointed apex and rounded bottom. There are three varieties of cutting: (1) the entire surface is cut in small, triangular FACETS in 4 to 7 horizontal rows, those meeting at the apex being elongated; (2) the form is that of two many-faceted pyramids joined at their bases and forming a GIRDLE dividing the CROWN from the smaller PAVILION, and having the facets above the girdle elongated, with those adjacent to the girdle being triangular and those above them that meet at the apex being LOZENGE-shaped, and with the facets below the girdle being shorter, similarly triangular, and the lower ones lozenge-shaped; or (3) similarly formed as joined many-faceted pyramids, but having above the girdle 2 rows of facets in the shape of elongated triangles and below the girdle 2 rows of smaller triangular facets. Such stones are sometimes pierced along the length (to be suspended in an ear-ring) or across the top (to be suspended in a pendant). *See* BRIOLETTE OF INDIA.

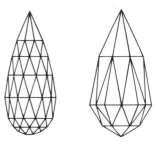

briolette (types 1 and 2)
side views

Briolette of India. A large diamond cut as a BRIOLETTE and weighing 90.38 carats. By tradition, it is the oldest diamond on record. The alleged first owner was Eleanor of Aquitaine (1122?-1204), who may have acquired it in Asia Minor when on the Second Crusade (1146-9) with her then husband, Louis VII of France. She is said to have given it to Richard, Coeur de Lion, who took it on the Third Crusade and probably used it as ransom when imprisoned in Austria. It next appeared when Henry II of France (1519-59) gave it to Diane de Poitiers, and is shown in many portraits of her. It then disappeared until 1950 when an Indian maharajah sold it to HARRY WINSTON. He resold it to Mrs I. W. Killam, but bought it back from her estate ten years later. It was still owned by him in 1970 when it was shown at the Diamond Dinner in New York but was resold in Europe in 1971.

Bristol diamond. A local misnomer for ROCK CRYSTAL or colourless QUARTZ that is found in England in the Clifton limestone near Bristol, and known in the 17th and 18th centuries as a 'Bristow'. It has also been called 'Bristol gem' or 'Bristol stone'.

brittle. Easily fractured by a blow or snapped, as distinguished from 'fragile', meaning merely easily broken. Brittleness of a stone does not correspond with its HARDNESS. The converse of brittleness is TOUGHNESS.

briolette. Ear-rings with suspended briolette sapphires. Courtesy of Christie's, New York.

Brogden, John (fl. 1842-85). A London jeweller and goldsmith whose work was mainly in antique styles, including especially some with Egyptian and Assyrian motifs, influenced by the work of FORTUNATO PIO CASTELLANI. He became in the 1840s a member of the firm of Watherston and Brogden in Covent Garden but from 1860 worked independently until the 1880s. His best-known piece is the ASSUR-BANI-PAL BRACELET. He also made some pieces with mounted tiger's claws (*see* TIGER'S-CLAW JEWELRY) and vulture's claws, as well as pieces of ARCHAEOLOGICAL JEWELRY.

bronze. An ALLOY of COPPER (about 97%) and tin, sometimes with small proportions of other elements added, e.g. SILVER, zinc, ALUMINIUM, LEAD or phosphorus. It corrodes quickly, but is excellent for CASTING. Bronze has been used often as primitive jewelry since the Bronze Age, for pins and brooches. It was used along with GOLD as the only metals employed in early European jewelry. Bronze was used for jewelry in Britain in the Celtic period, and examples have been found of bracelets, brooches, buckles, pins, and TORCS, some gilded and some enamelled in CHAMPLEVÉ manner; in the Romano-British period most jewelry was made of bronze, generally gilded. It was used extensively during the Renaissance in Italy and France, but not often for jewelry, and even less so in recent years. *See* GILT BRONZE; ORMOLU.

Brogden, John. Ear-rings; tiger's claws in gold mounts. London, *c.* 1860. Courtesy of Wartski, London.

brooch. An ornamental clasp having an attached pin for affixing it to a garment, hat, hood, turban or sleeve, as a fastener or as a decorative piece. The body of the brooch may be of many forms, e.g. a disc, ring, PENANNULAR ring, heart, flower, bow-knot, or any fantasy shape. The brooch evolved originally from the FIBULA of safety-pin form, and that term is sometimes loosely applied to any form of ancient brooch. A modern brooch usually has at the back a PIN (ACUS) and a catch (sometimes a form of safety-catch to prevent its being lost). Brooches have been made of many sizes and have been decorated with ENAMELLING, ENGRAVING, GEMSTONES, etc., and sometimes embellished with a suspended pearl, tassel, small pendant, etc. Formerly worn by men and women, they are now only for women. For various types, *see* BAR BROOCH; BOW-KNOT BROOCH; CATHERINE WHEEL BROOCH; CELTIC BROOCH; CLUSTER BROOCH; CRESCENT BROOCH; CRUCIFORM BROOCH; DISC BROOCH; LUCKEN-BOOTH BROOCH; MARZABOTTO BROOCH; PELICAN BROOCH; PIN BROOCH; PLAQUE BROOCH; QUOIT BROOCH; RING BROOCH; SAUCER BROOCH; STAR BROOCH; SUNBURST; THISTLE BROOCH; TRISKELION BROOCH; WHEEL BROOCH. For some named brooches, *see* CANTERBURY COIN BROOCH; CASTELLANI BROOCH; CUXTON BROOCH; FAVERSHAM BROOCH; GLENLYON BROOCH; HUNTERSTON BROOCH; KING'S SCHOOL, CANTERBURY, BROOCH; LOCH BUY BROOCH; LONDESBOROUGH BROOCH; SARRE DISC BROOCH; SARRE QUOIT BROOCH; STRICKLAND BROOCH; SUTTON BROOCH; TARA BROOCH.

Brosamer, Hans (*c*. 1480-1554). A German designer of jewelry who published, *c*. 1545-8, a pattern book with woodcuts of pendants set with gemstones, including some pendants that were WHISTLES.

Browning Rings. Two finger rings worn by the Brownings: (1) A gold ring with oval BEZEL engraved 'Ba', behind which is a circular panel of glass under which a hair was presumably kept when worn by Robert Browning (1812-89); on the inside of the hoop is the inscription 'God bless you June 29, 1861'. (2) A silver-gilt ring with octagonal bezel set with an amethyst INTAGLIO inscribed 'E B B', for Elizabeth Barrett Browning (1806-61).

Browning Rings. Gold finger rings worn by Robert and Elizabeth Barrett Browning. English, 1846-61. W. 1.9 and 1.5 cm. British Museum, London.

brushed gold. A type of TEXTURED GOLD having a matt finish produced by means of a wire brush revolving on a lathe.

bruting. The process of roughly shaping a diamond (or other transparent gemstone), after splitting the rough stone by CLEAVING or SAWING, so as to establish its desired fundamental somewhat rounded shape and surface before FACETING. The operation is done by vigorously rubbing one diamond against another, both being mounted in a holder (called a 'dop'), the one to be shaped being fastened on the axis of a cutting bench that causes the stone to revolve at speed in a vertical direction, and the other held in a dop-stick by the diamond-cutter (bruter) and rubbed against the revolving stone so as to remove any sharp edges and points. This operation was formerly carried out by hand, but now it is done by a mechanically-operated lathe. The term is derived from the French *brutage*, and the process is sometimes referred to as 'grinding' or 'shaping'.

Bry, Theodore de (1528-98). A designer of jewelry born at Liège who emigrated to Frankfurt with his sons Johann Theodore and Johann Israel; he worked there from 1570 to 1598 except for 3 years in England in 1586-9. Their designs featured the use of white enamel on a black ground, depicting scrollwork with fruit, flowers, grotesques, and animals in the MORESQUE SILHOUETTE STYLE. He specialized in making engravings with which to decorate knife handles, clasps, buckles, etc.

buffer-terminal torc. Gold. (Knot of unknown purpose.) La Tène Iron Age, 4th/1st centuries BC. W. 15.1 cm. British Museum, London.

buckle. A fastener (sometimes used merely as an ornament) for a belt, girdle, etc. (and formerly for the kneeband of breeches) that is attached at one of its ends to the buckle and secured by the buckle's pointed tongue, which passes through a hole near the other end. The buckle was developed in England in the late 17th century, where it was first used to replace shoe-laces. Later buckles, of various sizes and styles, were used for other purposes, and sometimes were attached as an ornament to a ribbon (throatlet) worn around a woman's neck. The buckle is usually in the form of a rectangular or curved frame that has a horizontal tongue attached to one side or to a vertical bar across the centre of the buckle; the tongue is long enough to rest its tip on the opposite side of the buckle. There are sometimes two or more tongues, or a single tongue may be forked so as to have two points. The buckle is attached to the belt, etc., by having one end of the belt folded and sewn to, or riveted around, the vertical bar. Buckles have been used since Roman times, made of gold, silver or other metal (sometimes covered with fabric); some have been decorated with MARCASITE, CUT STEEL, JET, PASTE or other material, and expensive ones have been set with gemstones. A buckle is also used as a fastener or an ornament on some shoes (*see* SHOE BUCKLE) or on a wristband. *See* BELT BUCKLE; BUCKLE PLATE; CLASP.

buckle plate. A metal attachment to the back end of a BUCKLE on which one end of the belt is attached, the purpose being to provide better wearability than if the belt were folded over the rear bar of the buckle. Such buckle plates were usually of ornamented metalwork, often with settings of jewels. *See* MORDANT.

buff-top cut. *See* CUSHION CUT.

buffer-terminal torc. A type of TORC of which the terminals are discoid ornaments attached at right angles to the main PENANNULAR hoop. Some bronze torcs from the La Tène Iron Age, *c.* 4th/1st centuries BC, have such terminals attached, and they are also present on gold torcs found at Snettisham, Norfolk, England, from the South British Late Iron Age, 1st century BC.

bugle bead. A type of glass bead in the form of an elongated, hollow cylinder, generally black, used in embroidered decoration on some ladies' dresses. Such beads were imported into England from Venice. Some were made in England at a factory established in the late 1570s at Beckley, near Rye, by Godfrey Delahay, a Frenchman, and Sebastian Orlandini, a Venetian; in 1580 the factory was bought and moved to Ratcliffe by John Smith. They were also made at a factory at Godalming, near Guildford, set up *c.* 1587 by an Italian named Luthery.

Bulgari. A leading Italian jewelry firm, located at 10 Via dei Condotti, Rome, that was founded in 1881 by Sotirio Bulgari (1857–1932), a Greek goldsmith who in 1881 emigrated to Naples. He moved to Rome and was later joined by his sons, Constantine (1889–1973) and Giorgio (1890–1966). The firm is highly reputed for its creations in luxury and exotic modern jewelry, and is now directed by Gianni, Paolo, and Nicola Bulgari (the sons of Giorgio) and Anna (daughter of Constantine).

Bulgarian jewelry. Articles of jewelry found in the region that is now Bulgaria, much of the early work being difficult to attribute as to origin or period, as some was imported from Greek centres but much was made by local Thracian goldsmiths. A large quantity of gold jewelry and other articles has been found in a great many *tumuli* where it was buried with dead nobles from the 6th to the 3rd centuries BC and even later. Skilfully made gold earrings (some PROTOME EAR-RINGS), spiral and serpent finger rings, necklaces, and pectorals are decorated with hammered designs and filigree work. Examples exist from the 6th century BC, but the finest pieces are from the 5th/3rd centuries BC, after which characteristics of Greek, Byzantine, Roman, and Persian styles appear. After the invasion by the Bulgarians in the 7th century AD, gold jewelry continued to be made, but in smaller quantity, including belt ornaments and TORCS, some decorated with enamelling, pearls and garnets, and some with Christian motifs; examples have been found from the 13th/14th centuries. *See* Venedikov, *Bulgaria's Treasures from the Past* (1966).

bulla. A small ornament, made usually of gold (sometimes of leather), and to be worn suspended from a string around the neck. Some *bullae* were worn in groups forming a necklace or sometimes a bracelet. They were made of two concave plates fastened together to make a hollow container. Etruscan examples were made as a globe or were lenticular-, heart-, or vase-shaped. They were adopted by the Romans, those of lenticular shape being worn as an AMULET by children (made of gold for children of noble families, of leather for children of freedmen), and those of other shapes (cylindrical or box-shaped, or shaped as a vase or pouch) by women as an ornament on a necklace. It has been suggested that some were made to contain a liquid scent.

bunch ring. A type of finger ring that is set with a minuscule diamond which is sometimes only partly faceted. Such rings were inexpensive and sold in bunches.

Buontalenti, Bernardo (1541–1608). A Florentine artist associated with the Medici from *c.* 1551 and later architect and stage designer for Francesco de'

bulla. Gold necklace with lenticular and heart-shaped *bullae*, and *bulla* as head of river-god. Etruscan, 4th century BC. L. 46.2 cm. British Museum, London.

bulla. Gold. Roman, 100 BC–AD 100. H. 7 cm. Ashmolean Museum, Oxford.

Buontalenti, Bernardo. Triton pendant with baroque pearl and enamelled gold. Probably by Buontalenti, late 16th century. Courtesy of Christie's, London.

Burgundian jewelry. Silver brooch with Annunication scene in *émail en ronde bosse* within acanthus wreath set with gemstones. German, late 15th century. Kunstgewerbemuseum, Cologne.

Medici and also director of his porcelain factory and lapidary works. He designed jewelry made in his workshop by Italian, French, and Dutch artisans. The suggestion has been made, based largely on similarities of some of his drawings to the designs of some BAROQUE PEARL JEWELS, that he also designed, and his workshop possibly executed, some pendants depicting a dragon, a hippocampus or a bearded triton. *See* Yvonne Hackenbroch, 'Some Florentine Jewels', in *Connoisseur*, November 1968, p. 137. *See* TRITON PENDANT.

Burgundian jewelry. A traditional 19th-century attribution for all articles of northern European jewelry of outstanding splendour and ostentatious ornamentation worn in the 14th and 15th centuries, based on a belief that the jewelry worn by the Dukes of Burgundy and their Courts surpassed in opulence the jewelry worn at the contemporary and friendly courts of France under Charles V, 1364-80, and Charles VI, 1380-1422. Renowned was the richness of the collections of Philip the Bold, 1363-1404, of John the Fearless, 1404-19, of Philip the Good, 1419-67, and of Charles the Bold, 1467-77. Jewelry was worn then more profusely for decoration than in the earlier periods, and the necklaces, brooches, medallions, and rings featured enamelled gold, carved gemstones (inspired by antique coins), cut diamonds (the POINT CUT DIAMOND and the TABLE CUT), and articles in ÉMAIL EN RONDE BOSSE. Much of the jewelry was of an ecclesiastical and devotional nature, including ornate RELIQUARIES (*see* RELIQUARY PENDANT), and also insignia of the many orders of knighthood and the related religious brotherhoods and jousting societies. *See* PORTRAIT MEDALLION; THREE BROTHERS JEWEL; WHITE ROSE JEWEL.

Burma ruby. A variety of RUBY from Burma. It may be purplish-red, and is then often termed a PIGEON'S-BLOOD RUBY.

burmite. A variety of AMBER that is found in Upper Burma, mined from Oligocene deposits in the clay soil. It is harder and denser than other varieties, and the colour is yellow to brownish or fiery red. It is used for most Chinese amber carvings, and some pieces made there are stained red.

Burne-Jones, Sir Edward (1833-98). An English artist who also designed jewelry. He was a close friend and associate of William Morris, and many of his designs show the Pre-Raphaelite influence. He made three sketch-books for jewelry, the pieces being executed by Carlo Giuliano (*see* GIULIANO FAMILY) or the Kensington firm of Child and Child. Few pieces from his designs are known to have survived.

Bury, Claus (1946-). A DESIGNER-MAKER of jewelry who was born in Hanau, Germany, studied in Pforzheim, and moved to London in 1969 where he worked for ANDREW GRIMA. His experiments in the use of acrylic led to his becoming a leading exponent of jewelry made of this material (*see* ACRYLIC JEWELRY), sometimes combined with gold. His work has been widely exhibited and there are examples in some leading museums.

butterfly. A motif often used for articles of jewelry, from the time of the Aztecs in Mexico to the ART NOUVEAU iridescent pieces of RENÉ LALIQUE, with the butterfly's wings depicted in coloured enamels or in various coloured gemstones.

butterfly clip. A device, used by Dutch goldsmiths in the Netherlands and in England, in the 16th century, for securing from the back a cast gold or a REPOUSSÉ figure to the front of a jewel, e.g. an ENSEIGNE, thus clearly defining the outline of the figure.

button. A small object used usually to fasten together two sides of a garment by being attached to one side and passed through a slit, button-hole or loop on the other side, but sometimes being only ornamental and attached to a single piece of material by a prong or by sewing, without any corresponding buttonhole. Buttons were used in ancient Greece and Rome, but were first employed generally in southern Europe in the 13th century and had become useful and fashionable by the 14th century. By the 16th/17th centuries they had come to be used almost exclusively by men and were made in highly decorative styles, including some made of gold set with gemstones or pearls, of enamelware, or of CAMEOS. Less

butterfly. Brooch set with diamonds, pear-shaped emeralds in wings, and ruby eyes. Courtesy of Wartski, London.

buttons. Steel, mother-of-pearl, glass, paste. English and French, 1785–1820. National Trust, Waddesdon Manor, Aylesbury, England.

luxurious varieties have been made of a great variety of materials, including base metals, WOOD, GLASS, AGATE, JADE, IVORY, JET, MARCASITE, cut steel (*see* CUT STEEL JEWELRY), SHELL, BONE, HORN, PORCELAIN, JASPER (with medallions by Wedgwood), PINCHBECK, lacquer, etc., as well as some of metal or cloth over a wood core and some embroidered with silk threads. Common varieties are made today of MOTHER-OF-PEARL, bone, horn, and synthetic materials. They are of many shapes (although usually circular), styles, and sizes. Some are attached by thread through two or more eyelets or by a SHANK attached to the back, or by a fixed or twisting bar (as some STUDS or collar-buttons). In England a vast trade was built up at Birmingham, the principal manufacturers in the 18th century being John Taylor and MATTHEW BOULTON. *See* Victor Houart, *Buttons* (1977).

button pearl. The same as a BOUTON PEARL.

Buxton diamond. A local misnomer for ROCK CRYSTAL found near Buxton, Derbyshire.

by(e)water (or **bye**). A classification formerly used in the colour grading of diamonds to designate a stone tinged with yellow.

Byzantine jewelry. Articles of jewelry made in Byzantium after the decline of the Roman Empire and the founding of Constantinople by Constantine I in AD 330 and until the 13th century, but mainly when Byzantine art was at its height in the 6th century. The jewelry was very ornate, with generous use of coloured gemstones, pearls and CLOISONNÉ enamelling, and with gold mounts decorated with FILIGREE and especially in OPUS INTERRASILE style. Ear-rings were worn by men and women, made with suspended gold crescents or with several pendent strings set with coloured gemstones. Other popular articles were gold pendants and finger rings. The extensive wearing of jewelry by the Court is evidenced by the portraits in the mosaics at Ravenna, a fortunate source of information in view of the ending of the custom of burying jewelry with the dead. The Byzantine influence spread from Constantinople throughout the Christian world and continued even after the conquest of Constantinople in 1204. *See* CUFF BRACELET.

Byzantine jewelry. Gold ear-ring with granulation. 6th century. H. 6 cm. Schmuckmuseum, Pforzheim, Germany.

C

cabochon. Gold brooch set with diamonds and four cabochon amethysts. Fabergé, c. 1900. Courtesy of Wartski, London.

Calder, Alexander. Gold necklace with helical ornaments. 1938. Victoria & Albert Museum, London.

Calima jewelry. Pectoral of hammered sheet gold, with added necklace. W. 36 cm. Museum of Mankind, London (photo copyright, Times Newspapers Ltd).

cabochon (from French *caboche*, knob). A stone cut with a smooth, rounded surface, with no FACETS and highly polished. Usually it is cut from an opaque or translucent stone (but some EMERALDS, AMETHYSTS, and GARNETS have been so cut), or a stone with a special optical effect (e.g. ASTERIA, OPAL, MOONSTONE). The style of cut was used in antiquity and continued until the 15th century when it began to be displaced by FACETING; but its vogue was revived in ART NOUVEAU jewelry. Cabochons are of various shapes, usually circular or oval, but sometimes rectangular or triangular. There are four basic forms: (1) the 'simple cabochon', with a dome of varying degrees of steepness and a flat base; (2) the 'double cabochon', with a dome-shaped underside that is flatter than the upper dome; (3) the 'hollow cabochon', with the interior cut away so as to make a shell-like form with increased translucency and often to have FOIL attached to the interior; and (4) the 'tallow-topped cabochon', with a shallow dome. On rare occasions a cabochon is cut with a flat surface or 'table' on the top of the dome. Among the stones that are often cut as cabochons are the CARBUNCLE (ALMANDINE), CAT'S-EYE, TIGER'S-EYE, and AMAZONITE. The stones so cut are said to be cut *en cabochon*. *See* JADEITE TRIPLET.

cacholong. A variety of COMMON OPAL that is opaque and bluish-white (with a surface like porcelain in appearance) or sometimes, if alumina is present, pale yellow. Cacholong is so porous that it will adhere to the tongue. It is highly regarded in the East.

cadenas (French). Literally, padlock. A type of bracelet having concealed, in a compartment under a hinged lid on the front, an enamelled miniature portrait. The hoop was sometimes made of curved segments or of chain.

cage. An openwork globular form that is found in MINOAN JEWELRY enclosing a spherical bead; *see* HORNET PENDANT. It derives from a similar cage-like form found on the heads of some PINS of earlier periods.

caillou du Rhin (French). Literally, pebble of the Rhine. The French term for cut ROCK CRYSTAL. Also called *pierre d'Alençon*. *See* RHINE-STONE.

cairngorm (stone). A variety of QUARTZ that is yellowish-brown to a smoky shade of yellow. It was originally found on Cairn Gorm, a mountain in the Cairngorm range in Scotland, and has been used frequently in SCOTTISH JEWELRY. The popular demand exceeds the local supply, and so it is often imitated with heat-treated varieties of Brazilian AMETHYST. The name is now discouraged, as the stones today rarely, if at all, come from the Cairngorms. Other sources are Arran (Scotland), the Swiss Alps, and Colorado.

Cairo star cut. The style of cutting a large diamond so that it has a small 6-sided TABLE that is only one-quarter of the width of the GIRDLE and has a CULET larger than the usual size; the high CROWN is composed of 6 STAR FACETS, 6 BEZEL FACETS, and 12 CROSS FACETS, the sides of the last forming the girdle, and the PAVILION is cut with 49 FACETS in a great variety of shapes and sizes so as to form a very complicated surface, plus a CULET, making a total of 74 facets.

calaite. An obsolete name for TURQUOISE.

Calder, Alexander (1898-1976). An American sculptor, born in Philadelphia, best known for his mobiles. After making objects with mechanical moving parts, he developed his special technique of mobiles dependent upon air currents and perfect balance. He began designing and making jewelry *c.* 1932, but his jewelry is mainly static. A frequent motif is a HELICAL PATTERN made of a continuous strand of coiled wire or coiled metal ribbon. His style, not requiring technical skill, has often been copied. *See* POSAMENTERIE STYLE.

calibré cut. A style of cutting a gemstone, usually of small size, in a shape, often oblong or elliptical, so that it and others so cut will fit snugly together in clusters. Stones are cut in this way to standardized measurements so as to be readily fitted into standard mounts.

californite. A compact variety of IDOCRASE (VESUVIANITE) that is olive-green or grass-green, or white with green streaks. It resembles NEPHRITE (JADE). Its name is derived from its source, California. It is sometimes miscalled 'American jade' and 'California jade'.

Calima jewelry. Articles of PRE-COLUMBIAN JEWELRY made in the Calima region of south-western Colombia (perhaps the oldest, *c.* 300 BC, in Colombia), often cut from nearly pure gold sheet metal and having hammered and REPOUSSÉ decoration, and sometimes having miniature work cast by the CIRE PERDUE process. The articles are large, and include PECTORALS (sometimes decorated with *repoussé* human faces), NOSE ORNAMENTS (sometimes with thin, dangling cylinders that vibrate), LIME DIPPERS and long pins (with ornate tops in the form of naturalistic or imaginative human or animal figures), funerary MASKS, and the 'twisted-nail' EAR ORNAMENTS made of long, tightly coiled wire, and also a so-called 'diadem' (*see* DIADEM, *Calima*).

cameo. Originally a gemstone having layers of different colours (e.g. SARDONYX and CORNELIAN) carved to show in low relief the design and background in contrasting colours. The earliest carved two-colour stones, dating from the period of SUMERIAN JEWELRY, were merely beads in CABOCHON form and sometimes stones carved in INTAGLIO for use as SEALS. Later, from the Hellenistic period in the 2nd century BC, carving was done by the Greeks (and subsequently by the Romans) to produce cameos in low relief as ornamental pieces of jewelry. The art continued to a reduced extent throughout the Middle Ages and became very popular during the Renaissance when master gem-engravers worked for prominent collectors such as Lorenzo de' Medici. Thereafter, with intervening periods of more or less fashionability, cameos have been made and mounted in articles of jewelry, e.g. brooches, pendants, and especially finger rings. The leading artist of the 19th century was TOMMASO SAULINI. In later periods cameos were also carved in other hard materials, e.g. ROCK CRYSTAL, CORAL, JET, SHELL, etc., and also moulded of JASPER earthenware in two or more colours by Josiah Wedgwood, or of glass paste by James Tassie (*see* TASSIE MEDALLION). Some were copies of classical subjects and coins, but from the Renaissance period new motifs were introduced. Some were made in CHALCEDONY with either the portrait or the background painted with gold. *See* CAMEO HABILLÉ; DOUBLE CAMEO; DOUBLET; NICOLO; PORTRAIT MEDALLION; PORTRAIT RING; SHELL CAMEO; AUGUSTUS CAMEO; EPSOM CAMEO; NOAH CAMEO.

cameo habillé (French). A type of CAMEO depicting the head of a person, carved in the stone, wearing a necklace, hair ornament or ear-rings made of small gemstones. Such pieces were made in the Victorian era.

canary stone. A variety of CORNELIAN that is yellow.

candy-twist link. A type of link in a CHAIN that is long and twisted to form spiral ridges.

cannetille (French). A type of metal decoration on jewelry in the form of thin wires making a coarse FILIGREE pattern, sometimes enhanced with a gemstone or ENAMELLING. It is named after the type of embroidery made with very fine twisted gold or silver thread. The patterns are often in the form of scrolls or rosettes made of tightly coiled wire. The style may have been derived from sources in Portugal or India where filigree work was popular, but possibly it was developed in England, where it was frequently used in the early 19th century, and it was later adopted in

cameo. Onyx pendant, Franco-Burgundian, *c.* 1400, with 17th-century enamelled gold frame. Museo degli Argenti (Pitti Palace), Florence.

cameo habillé. Black agate cameo of blackamoor with diamond hair ornament and ear-rings. English, *c.* 1850. Courtesy of Wartski, London.

cannetille. Gold pendant with *cannetille* decoration and gemstones. English, 19th century. Courtesy of Sotheby's, London.

Canning Triton Jewel. Gold pendant with baroque pearl, enamelling, ruby, and diamonds. Italian, *c.* 1580. Victoria & Albert Museum, London.

Canterbury Coin Brooch. Rings of silver wire encircling silver coin. W. 7.5 cm. Ashmolean Museum, Oxford.

Canterbury Cross. Cruciform brooch, gilded bronze with niello. Anglo-Saxon, 9th century. Royal Museum, Canterbury, England.

France. Gold articles so decorated were hand-made but when used on silver or a base metal, the pattern was made by STAMPING.

Canning Siren Jewel. A gold, enamelled, and jewelled SIREN PENDANT, the torso being composed of a BAROQUE PEARL. The siren holds in one hand what is meant to represent a mirror (in fact, made of a large diamond) as she combs her hair with a golden comb; the tail is enamelled and now lacks an original pearl drop. On the back of the tail is an enamelled inscription with the initials 'V D', presumed to be those of the unidentified Italian maker. The piece is Italian, *c.* 1580, possibly made by the same hand as the related CANNING TRITON JEWEL and has the same traditional history. It is said to have been presented, *c.* 1648, by a Medici duke to a Mughal emperor and after the Indian Mutiny of 1857-8 it was found in the Treasury of the King of Oudh at Delhi, was seized by the Indian Government, and was sold by it to Lord Canning (1812-62), Governor-General and first Viceroy of India. In 1863 it is said to have been purchased from the Canning estate by Julius Goldschmidt, of Frankfurt am Main, for Baroness Mathilde de Rothschild, also of Frankfurt. It was sold for £40,000 at Sotheby's, London, on 13 October 1970 from the estate of Arturo Lopez-Willshire (d. 1962), it is believed to a private collector in the United States.

Canning Triton Jewel. A gold, enamelled, and jewelled pendant in the form of a triton whose torso is composed of a BAROQUE PEARL (*see* BAROQUE PEARL JEWEL) and whose face and arms are of white enamel, the hair and beard being gold; his tail is enamelled in bright green and set with a row of diamonds and a large carved ruby. In his left hand he holds as a shield a mask of Medusa in green and blue, with a ruby in its mouth; in his upright right hand he flourishes a scimitar set with jewels. Three baroque pearls are suspended. It was formerly thought to be of Italian make, but is now, based on stylistic grounds, considered to be of South German origin, late 16th century, with the carved ruby in the tail and the pendent cluster of rubies and baroque pearl added later. The piece is reputed to have been given to one of the Mughal emperors by a Medici duke and brought back from India in 1862 by Lord Canning (1812-62), Governor-General and first Viceroy of India. It was inherited by the Marquess of Clanricarde, who bequeathed it to his great-nephew, the Earl of Harewood; the latter sold it in 1931 at Sotheby's, London, to Mrs Edward Harkness, of New London, Connecticut, who donated it to the Victoria & Albert Museum. A related SIREN PENDANT was also once owned by Lord Canning; *see* CANNING SIREN JEWEL.

Canterbury Coin Brooch. A circular brooch made of twelve concentric rings of silver wire, alternately beaded and twisted, framing a central silver Saxon coin encircling which is an Anglo-Saxon and Latin inscription translated as 'Wudeman made it'. On the reverse there is a small cross and the legend 'Nomine Domini'. The brooch, of Anglo-Saxon make from the second half of the 10th century, was found near Canterbury, and was donated in 1951 by E. Thurlow Leeds (d. 1955) to the Ashmolean Museum, Oxford.

Canterbury Cross. A brooch cast from light gold-coloured bronze in the form of a cross with four arms of equal length and having rounded and curled extremities. The decoration is a leaf- or vine-scroll on the arms, to each of which is attached a NIELLO triquetra in the TREWHIDDLE STYLE. The pin is missing from the fittings on the reverse. The cross was found in St George's Street in Canterbury in 1867. It is Anglo-Saxon, 9th century; many reproductions have been sold as souvenirs.

cap cut. *See* BASTARD CUT GEMSTONE.

Cape. (1) A word (short for Cape of Good Hope or Cape Province) prefixed to the names of certain gemstones to indicate the source as South Africa, but resulting in misnomers, e.g. 'Cape ruby' for PYROPE, and 'Cape emerald' and 'Cape chrysolite' for PREHNITE. (2) A diamond of yellowish tinge of several grades, as formerly classified; it was so called because early diamonds from the Cape were yellowish in contrast to stones from Brazil. *See* DIAMOND COLOURS.

Cape May diamond. A local misnomer that has been applied to ROCK CRYSTAL found near Cape May, New Jersey.

Caradosso (Ambrogio Foppa, called Caradosso; *c.* 1452– *c.* 1527; his first name was stated, in a publication of 1521–3, to be 'Cristoforo'). A famous goldsmith, medallist, and jeweller, but none of whose works is known to have survived. He was born at Mondonico near Milan, and after working in the 1490s in Milan for Ludovico Sforza 'Il Moro' (1451–1508), and in other northern Italian cities, he settled in Rome in 1505. He was employed by several Popes, making medals, gold and silver plate, and dies for coins; he made a gem-studded tiara for Pope Julius II. He also made small enamelled medallions from thin gold plate decorated with subjects from mythology modelled in high relief and enamelled. He excelled in enamelling and in engraving gemstones (including a diamond engraved in 1500). His reputation rivalled that of BENVENUTO CELLINI who praised him highly.

carat. (1) The unit of weight for a diamond or other gemstone and also for a pearl. Formerly it had various values, ranging from 0.1885 to 0.2135 grams, in different countries and at different times (so that the weights stated for some old stones must be viewed with caution), but now the International Metric Carat (since 1 April 1914 standard in Great Britain, most European countries and the United States) is 200 mg. (3.086 grains troy), or one-fifth of a gram (28 g. equalling about 1 oz). Fractional weights for metric carats are usually expressed decimally, but fractionally for old carats. The term 'carat(s)' used alone now means metric carat(s). the carat is divided into 4 GRAINS, especially in measuring the weight of pearls, and also into POINTS for measuring diamonds. (2) The measure for the FINENESS of gold and GOLD ALLOY, expressed as a number, out of 24 parts by weight, of parts of gold in the alloy, e.g. '24 carat' means pure gold, '14 carat' means 14/24ths gold in the alloy. (A carat has sometimes erroneously been stated to be 1/24th of an ounce or of a pound troy.) Most jewelry uses gold of 14 or 18 carats, 24-carat gold being used only for very fine work. In Continental marking, gold fineness is expressed as a decimal, e.g. 75% fine = 16 carat = 0.750 gold. The term 'carat' is derived from the Arabic *qirat*, a bean originally used as a measure of the weight of gold. It is sometimes spelt 'karat' in the United States when it applies to the measure of fineness of gold, to distinguish it from the term 'carat' as applied to the weight of gemstones.

caravel ear-ring. A type of ear-ring with a suspended ornament in the form of a caravel (a fully rigged sailing-ship, with a forecastle and a poop). Examples made of gold, enamelled and set with gemstones, are found in ADRIATIC JEWELRY. *See* CARAVEL PENDANT.

caravel pendant. A type of SHIP PENDANT with its suspended ornament in the form of a caravel. Such pendants were made of gold with coloured enamelling and with gold for the rigging, and were embellished with gemstones; some have figures decorated in ÉMAIL EN RONDE BOSSE. They were made in Venice, Germany, and France during the Renaissance, and comparable pieces were made in England (some with ships of different type) as well as on some Greek Islands. *See* CARAVEL EAR-RING; DRAKE PENDANT.

carbuncle. An ALMANDINE (GARNET) that is cut EN CABOCHON.

carcan(et). A CHAIN or necklace composed of ornamental gold links, usually enamelled and often set with gemstones; the links are sometimes joined in alternating patterns and occasionally separated by groups of pearls. Such pieces were worn during the 15th–17th centuries, sometimes at the base of a high collar but more often suspended around the neck and extending down to the waist. Some examples are decorated on the back of the links with enamelling in MORESQUE patterns from designs by HANS MIELICH.

cardinal's ring. A type of finger ring given to a cardinal by the Pope upon his consecration. There is no apparent prescribed form, but such rings are usually set with a SAPPHIRE. Beneath the BEZEL is the engraved coat of arms of the Pope.

carnelian. *See* CORNELIAN.

Carolingian jewelry. Articles of jewelry made during the dynasty of the

caravel ear-rings. Gold with enamelling and pearls. Island of Sifnos, Greece, early 18th century. L. 12.5 cm. Benaki Museum, Athens.

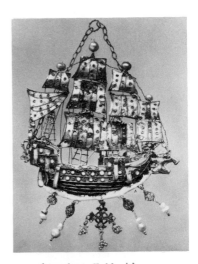

caravel pendant. Gold with enamelling and pearls. Island of Patmos, Greece, 17th century. L. 13.8 cm. Benaki Museum, Athens.

Carolingian jewelry. Ceremonial finger ring with cabochon amethyst in raised collet and filigree shoulders. Rhenish, 2nd half of 9th century. Hessiches Landesmuseum, Darmstadt.

Cartier. Necklace set with diamonds. Courtesy of Cartier & Co., London.

cascabeles. Gold finger ring with bird's beak and dangling ornaments. Mixtec, *c.* 1200-1540. Museo Nacional de Antropología, Mexico.

Frankish kings, from *c.* 751 to the reign of Charlemagne, 800-14, and thereafter under his successors until the 10th century. The style is characterized by the use of coloured gemstones, sometimes featured by being mounted in high settings and surrounded by small stones to emphasize the large central stone. During this period there was a revival of interest in Roman antiquities. The forms of the preceding MEROVINGIAN JEWELRY were influenced by Byzantine styles, as well as by decrees of Charlemagne, such as his banning the use of jewelry by the laity except royalty and the nobility; consequently, jewelry thereafter consisted mainly of religious articles made in the abbeys and Court workshops of Germany, including crosses and reliquaries. Another decree prohibited burials with jewelry, so that surviving specimens are rare, being from abbeys, cathedrals, and royal treasuries. *See* LOTHAIR, CRYSTAL OF; CHARLEMAGNE RELIQUARY; OTTONIAN JEWELRY.

carré. A STEP CUT diamond that is square.

Carthage Treasure. A TREASURE of silver plate and jewelry (including necklaces, finger rings, cameos, and intaglios) of the Early Christian Era, *c.* AD 400, found at the Hill of St Louis at Carthage in present-day Tunisia.

Cartier. A leading French jewelry firm, founded in 1847 by Louis-François Cartier (1819-1904). Its headquarters are in Paris, with branches in several major centres. The founder was joined in 1872 by his son Alfred (1836-1925), and the latter, with his eldest son, Louis (1875-1942), moved the Paris business in 1898 to its present address, 13 Rue de la Paix. In 1902 Alfred's second son, Pierre (1878-1964), opened a branch in London and in 1903 in New York City. In 1909 the London branch was taken over by·the youngest brother Jacques (1885-1942), by which time it had moved to its present address at 175 New Bond St. A group headed by Robert Hocq (1917-79) acquired fom the Cartier family the branches in Paris (1972), London (1974), and New York (1976), Hocq was Managing Director until his death when he was succeeded by his daughter, Nathalie (b. 1951), who since 1974 had headed the high-fashion jewelry department and promoted the boutique collection of jewelry known as 'Les Musts'. Originally the firm made jewelry of enamelled gold set with gemstones, which attracted a prestigious clientele, including French royalty and the future Edward VII; in recent years it has greatly expanded into new types and styles of jewelry, and is extending its world-wide operations. *See* WRIST WATCH.

Cartier Diamond. A diamond found in the Premier Mine, South Africa, in 1966, and weighing rough 240.80 carats. It was bought in 1967 by Mrs Walter Ames (sister of Walter Annenberg, former American Ambassador to the Court of St James's) from HARRY WINSTON, who had had it cut as a pear-shaped diamond weighing 69.42 carats. She sold it at auction in November 1969 at Parke-Bernet Galleries, New York City, with the understanding that the buyer could name it. It was purchased by CARTIER of New York, which immediately named it. The next day it was bought by Richard Burton for his then wife, Elizabeth Taylor, who renamed it the 'Taylor-Burton Diamond'; he soon had a duplicate cut for her in YTTRIUM-ALUMINIUM-GARNET. In 1979, the stone (having then been named the Cartier-Burton Diamond) was sold by her (then Mrs John Warner) to Lambert Bros., jewellers, of New York City, who resold it privately.

carved setting. A style of CLOSED SETTING of a gemstone in a finger ring that is similar to PAVÉ SETTING except that the depression for the stone is not cut out of the metal but is merely scooped or carved into the metal, so that the stone is covered at the back. This style was often used in the 18th century.

carving. A process of decorating metal or a gemstone by cutting into it to produce an artistic pattern. *See* CHIP-CARVING.

cascabel (pl. **cascabeles**) (Mexican). A type of ornament in the form of a small, elongated, flat-topped, and pointed bell such as was suspended in groups from some articles of MIXTEC JEWELRY and other MEXICAN JEWELRY.

Castelbolognese, Bernardi Giovanni (1495–1555). An engraver of gem-stones during the Renaissance who carved pieces depicting mythological and religious figures for Pope Clement VII, Cardinal Alexander Farnese, and the Duke of Ferrara. He was also a medallist.

Castellani, Alessandro. *See* CASTELLANI, FORTUNATO PIO.

Castellani, Fortunato Pio (1793–1865). A Roman antique dealer, goldsmith, and jeweller, renowned for seeking to revive the styles of ETRUSCAN JEWELRY. After a time in his father's jewelry workshop in Rome, 1814–15, making jewelry in the French and English traditions, he became interested during the late 1820s in Etruscan jewelry and sought to learn the method of producing its GRANULATED GOLD. He located some artisans in Umbria who were thought, incorrectly as it eventuated, to have preserved the ancient techniques and he brought them to Rome for his research. After failing to find the old secret processes, he did succeed, with his sons Alessandro (1822–83) and Augusto (1829–1914), in making simulations that became world-famous. He also produced jewelry with miniature MOSAIC work. He retired *c.* 1851 and the Casa Castellani was continued by the sons, who extended the work in ARCHAEOLOGICAL JEWELRY to include Byzantine and Carolingian styles. Augusto continued to carry on the business and later became Director of the Capitoline Museum in Rome. Alessandro, a great collector, devoted himself to workshop experimenting and to restoration of antique pieces; after a period of imprisonment, 1850–58, for political activity, he continued his research work while living in exile in Naples. Much of his Etruscan-style jewelry was acquired by the British Museum in 1872–3 and by the Villa Giulia Museum in Rome, and his Italian PEASANT JEWELRY by the Victoria & Albert Museum in 1867 and 1884. The Castellanis had for many years as their patron and adviser Michelangelo Caetani, Duke of Sermoneta (1804–83), who designed for them some pieces in antique style. They employed Carlo Giuliano (*see* GIULIANO FAMILY) as designer and as agent in London, and also employed GIACINTO MELILLO. The Castellanis made gold settings for some CAMEOS carved by TOMMASO SAULINI. Their work became very popular in England, and was extensively imitated there and in Italy, France, and the United States. Their mark is a monogram with interlaced Cs back to back. *See* Shirley Bury, 'Alessandro Castellani and the Revival of Granulation', in *Burlington Magazine*, October 1975, p. 664; Geoffrey Munn, 'Jewels of Castellani', in *Connoisseur*, February 1981, p. 126.

Castellani Brooch. A gold brooch in the form of a disc with three concentric circles decorated with varicoloured CLOISONNÉ enamel and pearls, in the centre of which is a roundel with an enamelled bust portrait of a woman wearing a similar brooch hung with three pendants. The brooch itself has at the bottom three loops, suggesting that originally it also had three pendants as on the portrait. The brooch is of unidentified place and date, but it shows Byzantine influence and has been attributed to the 7th/8th centuries, possibly from southern Italy. It was found at Canosa, Italy, and was acquired by the British Museum from ALESSANDRO CASTELLANI in 1872–3.

casting. The process of shaping metal objects by pouring molten metal into a hollow mould which has been made from a model of the desired article. In ancient times a hand-carved stone mould was used, but later a clay mould was formed around the model. These early methods (known as 'open casting') produced a solid object. Later hollow articles were made by suspending a close-fitting object within the mould so that the metal flowed between it and the walls of the mould (called 'hollow casting'). An improved method, for intricately designed pieces of jewelry, was used as early as EGYPTIAN JEWELRY and PRE-COLUMBIAN JEWELRY, known as the CIRE PERDUE process. Later methods were CUTTLEFISH CASTING, DIE CASTING, SAND CASTING and, in modern times for mass production, CENTRIFUGAL (INVESTMENT) CASTING. *See* CASTING ON.

casting on. The process of making a bimetallic article by CASTING in two steps, first casting half of the article with the metal having the higher melting point and placing the partial object in a new larger mould, and then casting the other metal in the remaining space; the parts become

Castellani. Gold brooch, copied from pair of Helios brooches in Campana Collection, Louvre, Paris. Casa Castellani. Courtesy of Wartski, London.

Castellani, Fortunato Pio. Gold strap necklace. *c.* 1870–80. Victoria & Albert Museum, London.

Castellani Brooch. Gold disc brooch with *cloisonné* enamel and pearls, enclosing enamel portrait. South Italy (?), 7th/8th centuries. W. 6 cm. British Museum, London.

catch-plate. Bronze fibula. Romano-British, 1st/2nd centuries. L. of fibula, 8.5 cm. National Museum of Antiquities of Scotland, Edinburgh.

bound by the phenomenon known as 'diffusion'. The process was used to make some rare tiny objects of MIXTEC JEWELRY.

cataseistae. Short lengths of chain that were suspended from some Byzantine crowns as insignia of sovereignty. *See* ST STEPHEN'S CROWN.

catch-plate. A metal terminal on one end of a FIBULA or side of a brooch that engages and fastens the pin (ACUS).

Catherine I Demi-parure. A partial PARURE consisting of a NECKLACE with a pendant, a brooch, and ear-rings, made of silver and set with diamonds, the main ornaments being in the form of florettes. It is reputed to have been offered by Catherine I (1684?-1727) as ransom for her husband, Peter the Great (1672-1725), after his capture at the battle of Rusen in 1711.

Catherine wheel brooch. A type of brooch in the form of a Catherine wheel, with eight or more spokes extending from the hub (named after the St Catherine torture wheel). They were made in the 18th century, often studded with gemstones, and sometimes made as a pendant suspended from a brooch.

cat's-eye. A general term for several varieties of gemstones that, when suitably cut EN CABOCHON and viewed in a certain direction and light, show CHATOYANCY resembling a moving streak of light as seen in a cat's eye. The streak is caused by reflection from parallel layers of asbestos fibre or from minute internal canals. The stones, which have a silky LUSTRE, include: (1) a variety of CHRYSOBERYL (known as CYMOPHANE); (2) a variety of greyish-yellow, brownish or grey-green QUARTZ, similarly chatoyant but inferior, having a less sharp streak and lower hardness, and which, when replacing CROCIDOLITE in a stone, is known as TIGER'S-EYE and HAWK'S-EYE; (3) a variety of TOURMALINE that has fibrous INCLUSIONS; (4) some varieties of DIOPSIDE, MOONSTONE, ANDALUSITE, APATITE, scapolite, and fibrolite (sillimanite); and (5) some of the varieties of CORUNDUM. All such stones are preferably designated as 'cat's-eye' accompanied by the name of the stone; the use of the term alone, without the name of a stone, should be restricted to designate a chrysoberyl. The stones must be cut with meticulous care so that the streak will cross the middle of the dome when light falls upon it vertically. The stones are used for beads or set in finger rings. *See* KANDY CAT'S-EYE; OPERCULUM; SHELL CAT'S-EYE.

Cellini, Benvenuto (1500-71). A renowned Florentine sculptor and goldsmith, who worked under the patronage of Pope Clement VII in Rome until 1540, when he went to France to work for Francis I until 1545, returning to Florence to work under the patronage of Cosimo de' Medici until his death. Although more famed as a sculptor, he also made gold jewelry; no known specimen has been definitely attributed to him, nevertheless much of the finest jewelry of the Renaissance has often been ascribed to him or his school. His autobiography, *Vita* (1558), translated by John Addington Symonds (1887, 5th ed. 1949, with copious notes by Sir John Pope-Hennessy), and his two treatises, *Due Trattati* (1568), translated by C. R. Ashbee (1898), describe articles that he made and the methods of jewelry-making of the period.

Celtic brooch. A brooch of various types that gradually evolved in the Celtic periods, both the pagan period and also in the later Christian period under the Hallstatt and La Tène cultures (*see* CELTIC JEWELRY). The brooches were made usually of bronze, but some of iron and a few of gold or silver. They were worn by women, as well as men, and often were made in pairs. The early examples were the SAFETY-PIN FIBULA, and later variations of the PENANNULAR PIN BROOCH. The reverse was sometimes decorated with spiral ornamentation called the TRUMPET PATTERN, used before the 11th century. Celtic brooches ceased to be made after the 13th century.

Celtic jewelry. Various articles of jewelry made by the Celts, a people who included those of (1) the pagan period of the Early Iron Age (in the 1st millennium BC), whose culture is divided into the Hallstatt culture (*c.* 750 BC–*c.* 450 BC) that was centred in and is named after Hallstatt, near

Salzburg, Austria, and the La Tène culture (c. 450 BC–1st century BC), named after a site near Lake Neuchâtel, Switzerland, that spread throughout western and central Europe, being brought to Britain c. 250 BC; and (2) the Christian ('Late Celtic') period, after the Roman invasion of western Europe, whose culture was centred in Wales, Scotland, Cornwall, and Ireland after the Roman invasion of Britain and continued until the 10th century AD in Britain and the 6th century AD in Ireland. The jewelry of the pagan period included BEADS of AMBER, JET, and GLASS, but featured metalwork, e.g. LUNULAE, BRACELETS, TORCS, and BROOCHES (the SAFETY-PIN FIBULA and the PENANNULAR PIN BROOCH) made of gold, silver, bronze, and ELECTRUM, and decorated with ENGRAVING, REPOUSSÉ work, and CHAMPLEVÉ enamelling. The engraving of the early era emphasized geometrical motifs, but in the La Tène culture it featured flowing lines, the characteristic TRUMPET PATTERN and complicated designs. The jewelry of the Christian period shows the influence of Italian and Byzantine styles; it still featured metalwork decorated in many techniques, and the pieces were mainly the BROOCH in penannular form (*see* HUNTERSTON BROOCH; TARA BROOCH) and the FINGER RING. The styles merged with that of ANGLO-SAXON JEWELRY and ceased in the early 11th century.

Celtic Revival jewelry. Articles of jewelry made in Ireland c. 1850–70 in the styles of CELTIC JEWELRY, inspired by local archaeological finds. The pieces include many BROOCHES made of gold, silver, and silver gilt, some in the style of the TARA BROOCH that was found at about that time. Some such pieces are marked with the maker's name, e.g. Waterhouse or West, of Dublin.

Cenotaph, Treasure of the. A TREASURE found by Sir Flinders Petrie (1853–1942) in a cenotaph of a local queen of the Middle Bronze Age (2200 BC–1550 BC) at Tell el-Ajjul, near Gaza, in Israel. It included gold bracelets, finger rings, ear-rings, and dress pins, some decorated with LAPIS LAZULI. *See* AJJUL HOARD.

centaur pendant. A pendant in the form of a centaur, the torso being a BAROQUE PEARL and the head, hindquarters, and legs being enamelled gold, set with gemstones and having suspended pearls. One example, with the centaur holding a bow and arrow, is set with rubies, a diamond, and a sapphire, and has been attributed to Italian make, 16th century. *See* BAROQUE PEARL JEWEL.

centipede. A type of FRACTURE within certain gemstones, e.g. MOONSTONE, in the form of a series of tiny parallel, wavy and tapering lines.

centrifugal casting. A complicated CASTING process that is a modern version of the CIRE PERDUE process; it is used for mass production of certain articles of jewelry having complex patterns. The process involves several steps: (1) a metal model made by hand is enclosed in a vulcanized rubber casing; (2) the rubber is split into halves, the model removed, and the halves are tied together, leaving a small hole; (3) molten wax is forced under pressure into the rubber casing and when the wax has cooled and hardened, the casing is removed — this process is repeated to make a number of wax models; (4) several such wax models are placed in a metal container and are covered with plaster of Paris (called an 'investment') and the wax is heated so that it runs out, leaving the investment with a number of hollow moulds; (5) the investment is placed on a centrifuge, and molten metal is forced into it by centrifugal force, so that when it is removed there are a number of metal pieces in the form of the original model. The process is also called 'investment casting'.

ceramic jewelry. Articles of jewelry made of porcelain or pottery. A variety of articles have been made of porcelain (*see* PORCELAIN JEWELRY; PARIAN JEWELRY) but pottery or glazed earthenware (FAIENCE or maiolica) is ordinarily not suitable for jewelry other than beads (but *see* EGYPTIAN FAIENCE; LUSTREWARE JEWELRY; WEDGWOOD JEWELRY).

Certosa fibula. A type of SAFETY-PIN FIBULA made with no ornamentation, being merely a wire forming an asymmetrical, slender, sharply-arched BOW and coiled to extend as the ACUS terminating in a

centaur pendant. Baroque pearl and enamelled gold set with gemstones. Italian, 16th century. W. 5.5 cm. National Gallery of Art (Widener Collection), Washington, DC.

simple CATCH-PLATE. It is so named because many have been found in the Certosa Cemetery at Bologna. They date from the 5th century BC.

Ceylon chrysolite. A local misnomer for a greenish-yellow variety of TOURMALINE.

Ceylon diamond. A local misnomer for colourless ZIRCON.

Ceylon peridot. A local misnomer for yellowish-green TOURMALINE.

Ceylon ruby. A local misnomer for ALMANDINE.

ceylonite. A variety of opaque SPINEL that contains ferrous iron and is dark green or brown to blackish. It is also called 'pleonaste'.

chain. A series of rings, links, beads or discs, usually of metal, connected with or fitted to each other. They have been made from earliest times in a great variety of styles and lengths, and used in jewelry for many purposes, e.g. NECK CHAIN, NECKLACE, BREAST CHAIN, BRACELET, FOB chain, WATCH CHAIN, ALBERT CHAIN, MUFF CHAIN. They have been made of gold or other precious metals and base metals, with the links made in various forms, e.g. circular, oval, cylindrical, irregular, flattened, etc. Links are usually made by bending a piece of wire and soldering the ends together. Heavy gold chains were popular during the Renaissance and Victorian eras. Most modern jewelry chains are machine-made, but fine ones have hand-wrought links of intricate patterns created by designers. On one end there is usually a BOLT RING for fastening an object. Many different styles of chains have special names but such names are today, in view of the multitude of current and newly-created styles of chain, being supplanted by manufacturers and jewellers by the use of design numbers. Among the specific names still occasionally being used are the ALMA CHAIN; BALL CHAIN; BARLEYCORN CHAIN; BARREL AND LINK CHAIN; BELCHER CHAIN; BENOÎTON; CHAÎNE DE FORÇAT; CORD CHAIN; CURB CHAIN; DIAMOND TRACE CHAIN; FETTER CHAIN; JASERON CHAIN; LOOP-IN-LOOP CHAIN; ROPE CHAIN; STRAP CHAIN; TRACE CHAIN. *See* also SAUTOIR. Chains of heavy character have long been used to suspend BADGES of office (as mayoral chains) or ORDERS of chivalry (*see* SS COLLAR), guilds, etc. (*see* ARCHER'S COLLAR).

chaîne de forçat (French). Literally, slave chain. A type of CHAIN made of heavy gold links that was worn by men of elegance in the mid–19th century, suspended around the neck and tucked into a pocket, securing a purse, watch or monocle. Those for women had a suspended cross. Also called a *galérienne* (galley slave).

chalcedony. The cryptocrystalline variety of QUARTZ that is usually pale blue or grey, uniform in tint, but some varieties of which have vari-coloured internal bands or markings. It is porous and so can be (and often is) stained to alter or enhance the colour. The gemstone varieties include AGATE, SARDONYX, SARD, CORNELIAN, CHRYSOPRASE, ONYX, PRASE, and many sub-varieties. It is widely imitated in coloured GLASS, sometimes in several colours blended into each other. *See* JET.

chalcedonyx. A variety of ONYX in which the bands are white or grey.

chalchuite. A variety of TURQUOISE that is blue or green.

Chalcis Hoard. A HOARD of silver jewelry and other personal ornaments that was found at the Castle of Chalcis on the Island of Euboea in Greece in the 19th century. It has been suggested that the articles were deposited between 1385 and 1470, when the island was under the control of the Venetians. The pieces include finger rings, BELT BUCKLES, and belt fittings, some decorated with FILIGREE ENAMELLING.

chameleon diamond. A yellow diamond that changes to green when exposed to sunlight (ultraviolet light) but, if heated or kept away from sunlight, reverts to yellow.

champlevé (French). Literally, a raised field. The technique of decoration by ENAMELLING in which the design was made by lines or cells cut into the metal base (by CARVING, ENGRAVING, ETCHING or STAMPING) and filled with powdered ENAMEL of various colours and then fired to fuse the enamels. In early examples, only lines of the design were incised and filled, but later more of the metal was cut away, leaving only walls of thin metal that formed the design and separated the colours, thus simulating earlier CLOISONNÉ work except that the partitions were part of the base rather than affixed to it. After firing, the surface was smoothed with pumice and polished, so that the entire surface was level. Decorating in *champlevé* enamelling was done mainly on bronze and copper, but occasionally on gold. For such pieces COUNTER-ENAMELLING was not needed as the metal used was of a thick gauge. *See* NIELLO; MOCK-CHAMPLEVÉ; TAILLE D'ÉPARGNE.

chaplet. Silver with repoussé decoration. Hanseatic, 1st half 14th century. Statens Historiska Museum, Stockholm.

chandelier ear-ring. A type of ear-ring in the form of a large gemstone in a gold setting from which are suspended three other gemstones. Such ear-rings, of ROMAN JEWELRY, are the apparent precursors of the Renaissance GIRANDOLE.

channel setting. A style of SETTING in a finger ring to secure a single row of gemstones of square shape and identical size, made of two circular bands bridged together to secure the stones between them. It is used for an ETERNITY RING.

channel work. A technique of ornamenting silver jewelry similar to ENAMEL INLAY, by which the design is cut into the silver matrix as small cells into which are cemented pieces of turquoise or other stone cut to fit the cells, and then the piece is ground and polished to provide a smooth surface. The method has been used by the Navajo Indians of south-western United States, and especially by the Zuñi Indians since the early 1940s. *See* NAVAJO JEWELRY; ZUÑI JEWELRY.

chape. The same as MORDANT.

chaplet. (1) A type of HEAD ORNAMENT in the form of a garland, wreath, or ornamented band, to be worn around the head. Chaplets of metal with REPOUSSÉ decoration or embellished with gemstones and pearls, or with an AIGRETTE, were worn by unmarried girls in the 14th–16th centuries. These were the precursors of the BRIDAL CROWN. (2) A short ROSARY, being one-third of the length of a complete rosary and composed of 55 (sometimes 59) beads.

Charity Pendant. A pendant depicting a figure group of Charity with 2 or 3 children, sometimes together with figures of her sisters Faith and Hope, and occasionally also with 2 allegorical figures or 2 music-playing *putti*. The figures, usually in ÉMAIL EN RONDE BOSSE, are set against a background in ARCHITECTURAL STYLE, decorated with enamelling and gemstones and with pendent pearls. The pieces were made in Germany and the Netherlands, *c.* 1565–1600, sometimes in the style of ERASMUS HORNICK. An example in the Waddesdon Bequest at the British Museum resembles a similar pendant at Waddesdon Manor in which the central figure personifies Astronomy. Two rare examples have the figures of Charity and 3 children carved in AMBERGRIS. *See* ROMAN CHARITY, THE; REINHOLD VASTERS.

Charity Pendant. Gold pendant with enamelled figures and gemstones, and pendent pearls. Style of Erasmus Hornick. South German, *c.* 1560-70. H. 9.4 cm. British Museum, London.

Charlemagne Crown. *See* IMPERIAL CROWN.

Charlemagne Reliquary. A RELIQUARY in the form of a double-faced circular pendant having a gold frame, slightly different on front and reverse, enclosing on the front an oval CABOCHON of blue glass (replacing the original sapphire) and on the reverse an almost circular sapphire; between the stones is a relic said to be from the True Cross. The front of the frame is set with four oval garnets alternating with four square emeralds, separated by pearls; on the reverse are garnets, emeralds, and pearls, slightly different in shape and size from those on the front. At the top is a jewelled ornament to which are attached suspensory rings. The piece was worn by Charlemagne, 800–14, who received it as a gift from Harun al-Rashid, Caliph of Baghdad, 786–809). It was found on the neck of Charlemagne when his tomb in the cathedral at Aix-la-Chapelle (Aachen) was opened by Otto III in 1166 and was preserved at the cathedral. In 1804 it was given by Bishop Berdolet (in gratitude for

Charlemagne Reliquary. Front of gold double-faced reliquary. German (?), 9th century. W. 6.5 cm. Cathedral Treasury, Rheims.

Charles I rings. Gold finger rings (one with locket) with enamelled portrait of Charles I. English, *c.* 1650. British Museum, London.

Charles V jewelry. Gold *enseigne* with enamelled portrait. Possibly French; dated 1520. Kunsthistorisches Museum, Vienna.

Napoleon's restoration of the cathedral's treasures that had been taken to Paderborn, in Westphalia) to Empress Josephine to wear at her coronation. It was kept by her after her divorce and later by Queen Hortense (wife of Louis Bonaparte), then passed to her son, Louis-Napoleon Bonaparte (Napoleon III), from whom it was inherited by his widow, Empress Eugénie (1826–1920). She kept it with her in exile but after World War I she donated it to Rheims Cathedral as recompense for its bombardment in 1914. Now displayed at the Palais du Tau, Rheims, the pendant has been attributed to German origin, early 9th century.

Charlemagne's Crown. *See* OTTO THE GREAT, CROWN OF.

Charles I jewelry. Articles of COMMEMORATIVE JEWELRY worn in England by Royalists in memory of Charles I (1600–49) after his execution. Such pieces were usually a finger ring (*see* CHARLES I RING) but also included a LOCKET or a SLIDE to be worn over a ribbon. They were usually decorated as MOURNING JEWELRY, with black enamelling and sometimes depicting a skull.

Charles I ring. A type of gold finger ring made in England, *c.* 1650, after the execution of Charles I (1600–49), bearing a miniature portrait of him, painted on vellum under crystal, or enamelled on the BEZEL, with a celestial blue ground and usually surrounded by bands of black and white. Often the hoop has an engraved laurel wreath on a black ground. A few have a concealing lid. One example portrays Charles and his consort, Henrietta Maria (1609–69), flanking a portrait of their young son, later Charles II. Some such rings (as well as similar LOCKETS and CLASPS) were presented to Loyalists by Henrietta Maria in appreciation of financial support of the Royalist cause, with the understanding that they would be redeemed when the war was ended; most, but not all, were redeemed for the amount of the loan or for an honour.

Charles V Cameo. A CAMEO of SARDONYX in 3 layers, mounted in a gold frame. It depicts a standing figure of Jupiter with an eagle at his feet. Inscribed around the edge, on a ground of red and blue enamel, are prophylactic verses of the type that are found on AMULETS, as well as the opening words of the Gospel of St John. On an appendage below the frame is a crowned escutcheon decorated with the French fleur-de-lis, the crown being inscribed to record the presentation of the piece in 1367 to the Treasury of the cathedral at Chartres by Charles V (1337–80), King of France from 1364. It is a 14th-century piece, and is now in the Bibliothèque Nationale, Paris.

Charles V jewelry. Articles of jewelry decorated with a carved or enamelled portrait of Charles V (1500–58), King of Spain (as Charles I) from 1516 and Holy Roman Emperor from 1519. A gold ENSEIGNE dated 1520 bears an enamelled portrait encircled by an inscription naming his kingdoms in Spain.

charm. (1) An object worn or carried for its supposed ability to bring good fortune or ward off evil or illness. *See* AMULET; SHAMAN'S CHARM; TALISMAN. (2) A small decorative object worn suspended from a bracelet, usually part of a collection of such pieces. Charms of this kind, of gold or gilded metal, are made in a vast number of forms, including replicas of animals, fish, musical instruments, sporting equipment, zodiacal signs, hearts, padlocks, horseshoes, and (enclosed between slices of crystal) a leaf of four-leaf clover or shamrock. They were made from the Victorian era, in both expensive jewelled form and in inexpensive materials, and are still produced and popularly worn.

charm bracelet. A type of bracelet from which are suspended a number of decorative CHARMS. They have been popular, made of gold or of inexpensive ware, throughout the 20th century, and continue to be today, as the variety of charms has greatly increased.

charm ring. A type of finger ring supposed to possess some mystic, magical or curative power. They bear appropriate inscriptions or symbols, or are set with a stone supposed to have supernatural powers (*see* 'VIRTUOUS' STONE). Such rings were usually not worn on a finger but suspended from the neck by a ribbon or chain.

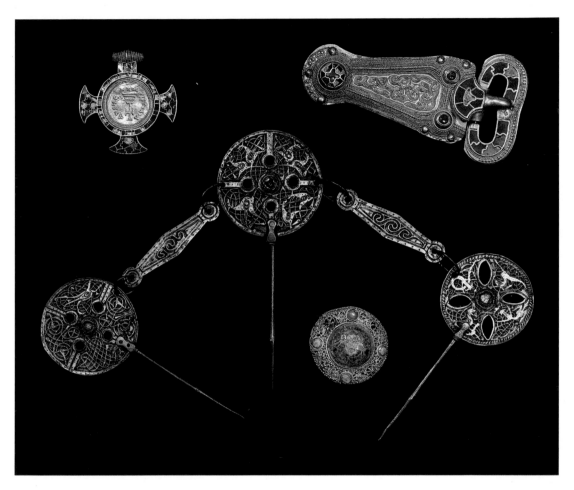

I *Anglo-Saxon jewelry*. Top left, a small cross containing a coin of the Byzantine Emperor Heraclius; top right, a buckle of gold filigree and garnets; centre, the Witham pins, a suite of three linked pins with animal motifs on the gilt bronze heads; bottom, the Dowgate Hill Brooch, an enamelled roundel encircled by an openwork band with filigree and granulated gold. British Museum, London.

II *Art Nouveau jewelry*. Left, gold brooch/pendant with *plique à jour* enamelling, diamonds, and pendent pearl. French, *c.* 1900. H. 7 cm. Top, brooch with gold face within enamelled bat-wings. Marked 'Lalique', *c.* 1900. Bottom, brooch, with mother-of-pearl cabochon within a wirework grille and with two pink pearls and a pendent baroque pearl. Marked 'B H J', probably German, *c.* 1905. W. 4 cm. Courtesy of Sotheby Belgravia, London.

chasing. The technique of decorating by handwork the front surface of metalware, by indenting it and so raising the design, without cutting into it (as in ENGRAVING), using a chasing tool and a chasing hammer. It is done either to enhance REPOUSSÉ work by sharpening the relief decoration or as independent decoration by beating down the metal to form a relief pattern. When used to make a design on a flat surface, rather than to develop relief work, it is called 'flat chasing'. It is also used to remove surface roughness resulting from use of the CIRE PERDUE process. The piece of metal being worked is laid on a bed of pitch or, for hard metal, of wood or steel. It has been done since antiquity. During the 18th century the French are said to have excelled in such work, but there are also good English examples. *See* CISELÉ.

chatelaine. An ornamental clasp worn in daytime at a woman's waist, attached to a belt or girdle, with a hook-plate from which are suspended several (usually five, but up to nine) short chains terminating with rings or SWIVEL CATCHES to which are attached various small objects for daily household use. Early examples had attached a SEAL and a WATCH; later, more articles were added, e.g. keys, watch keys, ÉTUI, POMANDER, scissors, thimble case, bodkin case, household notebook in a metal case, small purse, penknife, pin-cushion, and tape measure, as well as sometimes a GIRDLE BOOK, CAMEO, CHARM, and PENDANTS. Some chatelaines made for men were longer and were worn suspended at each thigh to conceal the openings on breeches; early examples held a watch, seals, and charms, but after *c*. 1800 they were simpler and no longer held a watch. Some chatelaines had two suspensory chains, joined at the belt by a short chain. Chatelaines were made of gold, silver, PINCHBECK, cut steel, and later polished steel, and were ornamented with enamelling, beads, beaded tassels, and sometimes MEDALLIONS of Wedgwood's JASPER; they very rarely had a gemstone. They came into use in England in the 17th century and were very popular in the 18th and 19th centuries, but *c*. 1830 declined in use as fashionable jewelry and were worn only for utilitarian purposes. *See* MACARONI.

chatelaine hook. A simplified version of a CHATELAINE, made in the form of a hook worn by a woman at the waist to suspend a watch.

Chatham emerald. A type of SYNTHETIC EMERALD developed in 1935 in the United States by C. F. Chatham of San Francisco. It should be designated 'synthetic emerald by Chatham'.

chaton. (1) The French term for a BEZEL, i.e. the ornament at the top of a finger ring and, in the case of a ring set with a gemstone, the COLLET together with the stone. (2) A faceted glass stone backed with silver FOIL.

chatoyancy. The effect in certain translucent stones, when cut EN CABOCHON and viewed in a suitable direction and light, of showing a streak of light in the interior that undulates across the curved surface as the position of the stone is changed. It is caused by bundles of interior cavities or parallel needle-shaped crystals or to fibrous INCLUSIONS. When the stone is cut en cabochon and the base is set parallel to the length of the needles, the dome serves as a convex lens and each needle is shown as a point at the apex; together they form the gleaming streak. The result is a CAT'S-EYE effect found mainly in CHRYSOBERYL and certain QUARTZ, but also in other fibrous stones. Other stones showing chatoyancy are the TOURMALINE, DIOPSIDE, MOONSTONE, ANDALUSITE, scapolite, and fibrolite. A stone showing chatoyancy is sometimes said to be 'chatoyant'; the terms are derived from the French *chat* (cat).

chatoyant. The quality in gemstones of displaying CHATOYANCY.

chatter-mark. The same as a FIRE-MARK.

Chaumet & Cie. One of the leading French jewelry firms, founded *c*. 1780 by Étienne Nitot. Its initial success came after Nitot, seeing an accident outside his shop in the Rue St Honoré, Paris, assisted the victim, who happened to be First Consul Napoleon Bonaparte. He showed his appreciation by commissioning the making of the Emperor's Coronation Crown and Sword, the tiara given to the Pope, and the jewelry worn in 1810 by Marie Louise upon her marriage to Napoleon. The firm was

chatelaine. Pinchbeck, with repoussé decoration. French or English, *c*. 1740-60. Kenwood (Hull Grundy Collection), London.

Chaumet & Cie. Neck ring and earrings of gold with white and canary diamonds and sapphires. Courtesy of Chaumet & Cie, Paris.

Chavín jewelry. Crown of embossed sheet gold. Lambayeque, Peru. H. 23.3 cm. Museum of the American Indian, Heye Foundation, New York.

Cheapside Hoard. Chains, gold with enamelling and/or gemstones, *c.* 1640. Museum of London.

appointed jewellers to Louis Philippe in 1830, and thereafter achieved international recognition. It was managed until 1815 by Étienne Regnault and his son François, then by Jean-Baptiste Fossin (1786–1848) and his son Jules (1808–69); in 1862 it was taken over by Prosper Morel until 1889, when his partner and son-in-law, Joseph Chaumet (1854–1928), who had been with the firm since 1874, became director. He was succeeded by his son Marcel, whose sons Jacques and Pierre manage the business today. The main showroom is at 12 Place Vendôme, Paris, and since 1875 there has been a London branch, now at 178 New Bond St, and recently a showroom at Riyadh, Saudi Arabia.

Chavín jewelry. Articles of PRE-COLUMBIAN JEWELRY from Peru, made during the period of the Chavín culture, *c,* 900–500 BC, when the art of working gold by hammering and soldering was already known. The few extant pieces are said to be the earliest known goldwork made in the Americas; they include 3 tall, cylindrical crowns of sheet gold decorated with REPOUSSÉ work and several pairs of EAR-SPOOLS. *See* PERUVIAN JEWELRY.

Cheapside Hoard. A HOARD of about 230 articles of early-17th-century jewelry that was found by a workman under a house in Cheapside, London, in 1912, during a demolition. It has been surmised that it was hidden *c.* 1640 as part of the stock of a jeweller. The hoard includes a great variety of articles, e.g. necklaces, bracelets, ear-rings, chains, finger rings, pendants, buttons, etc., as well as some 'holders' of unknown purpose and some engraved and faceted gemstones. The pieces are of moderate value but good craftsmanship, and their significance is mainly in showing the styles of ordinary unaltered jewelry of the period. It is now divided among the Victoria & Albert Museum, the British Museum, and the Museum of London. There is at the Museum of London an earlier Cheapside Hoard, 11th century, mainly finger rings and brooches of pewter set with paste stones. *See* 'The Cheapside Hoard of Elizabethan and Jacobean Jewelry', in *London Museum Catalogue,* no. 2 (1928).

Chelsea toys. Small objects made at the Chelsea porcelain factory, 1745–84, e.g. scent bottles, seals, bonbonnières, patch boxes, and some articles of jewelry, such as étuis and breloques. The English term was 'toy', the German (for such pieces made at Meissen) was *Galanteriewaren*. *See* G. E. Bryant, *Chelsea Porcelain Toys* (1925).

chemin de fer jewelry. A type of jewelry that was made *c.* 1861 by a French jeweller, Félix Duval, of odd pieces of iron, e.g. bolts, screws, chains etc.

chenier. A thin metal tube, usually short, to be used for making a hinge but also used in simple forms of some jewelry, e.g. a hollow bracelet, or for some SETTINGS. It can be made with varied cross-sections, e.g. round, semi-circular, oval, triangular, square or rectangular. Such cheniers can be made by a jeweller, but today they are usually bought from a dealer or a metal refiner.

cherry opal. A reddish-coloured variety of COMMON OPAL.

chessylite. AZURITE that is found at Chessy, near Lyons.

chi-rho monogram. The monogram (sometimes called the XP monogram) composed of the Greek letters *chi* and *rho,* being the first two letters of the Greek name for Christ, and used as a symbol or emblem of Him. Sometimes the letters are used apart, but more often in a monogram of three intersecting lines, sometimes enclosed within a circle, and occasionally accompanied by the Greek letters *alpha* and *omega*. It is found on articles of early Christian jewelry from a wide geographical area.

chiastolite. An opaque variety of ANDALUSITE that occurs in four-sided fusiform crystals. It is also called 'macle' from the tessellated or cruciform appearance of a cross-section in the form of a dark cross on a light background (due to the arrangement of impurities), but which varies in shape in successive sections of the crystal. The name is derived from the Greek *chiastos* (marked with a *chi,* i.e. marked diagonally). One source of the stone is Santiago de Compostela, Spain, the shrine of St James, which has led to the Christian symbolism attached to the stones and their being worn as an AMULET; the slices are polished as flat pieces or with slight convexity, and are set in finger rings or strung on a necklace. *See* CROSS STONE.

chicken-bone jade. A type of NEPHRITE (JADE) that, as a result of having been buried in the soil, loses its deep colouration and acquires an outer brown skin (in JADEITE the skin sometimes becomes bright red). Nephrite is sometimes converted, by being heated, to a yellowish-white colour, occasionally with a minutely crackled surface and patches of pink. Both are referred to as 'chicken-bone jade'. *See* TOMB JADE.

chicot pearl. The same as a BLISTER PEARL.

Childeric Treasure. A TREASURE of jewelry that was the regalia of King Childeric I (436-481), founder of the Merovingian Dynasty, who was buried with it at Tournai, in Languedoc, France. In 1653 it was discovered, being identified by a finger ring (now lost) bearing his name. It included a bracelet, a sword, and the finger ring, all inlaid with slices of GARNET or red GLASS in CLOISONNÉ INLAY style, and also about 300 gold bees for use as mantle ornaments. The treasure was placed in the Cabinet des Médailles in Paris, from which it was stolen in 1831 and thrown into the Seine, but most was recovered and is now in the Bibliothèque Nationale, Paris. *See* Abbé Cochet, *Le Tombeau de Childeric Ier* (1859). *See* BARBARIC JEWELRY.

Chilean jewelry. Articles of PRE-COLUMBIAN JEWELRY made by the Araucanian Indians in Chile, who resisted the invading Spaniards and were not subdued until the late 19th century. Examples of their jewelry included silver breast ornaments worn by the Araucanian women, decorated with pre-Columbian and colonial motifs; some such pieces were made of three or more vertically-linked ornaments, at the bottom of which was attached an embossed plaque with several suspended figures or discs. *See* SNUFF SPOON.

Chimú jewelry. Articles of PRE-COLUMBIAN JEWELRY made by the Chimú Indians, whose culture flourished, *c*. AD 1000-1500, on the desert coastal region of northern Peru (the capital being Chan Chan, near modern Trujillo), succeeding that of the Mochicas. The pieces are superior in technique and artistry to those of the Mochicas and Nazcas, reflecting new processes, especially hammering and welding gold of different colours and often decorating with gemstones precisely cut and polished. The articles included bracelets, necklaces, ear-rings, NOSE ORNAMENTS, and TWEEZERS, and also elaborate, stylized, gold funerary masks, some coloured, with anthropomorphic features and pendent gemstones, as well as gold funerary gloves. The Chimú Indians also made large gold discs (about 30 cm wide) completely decorated with REPOUSSÉ work; their purpose is not known. Each piece was unique, as repetition of a design was deemed offensive to their gods. Great quantities of Chimú jewelry were discovered in the 1930s by Brünning in the Lambayeque district of Peru. *See* PERUVIAN JEWELRY; TUMI.

Chinese cat's-eye. *See* OPERCULUM.

Chinese drilled. A style of drilling a BOUTON PEARL toward the back, crosswise, and parallel to the dome, or a DROP PEARL across the top, so that it can be sewn to a garment for best appearance.

Chinese jade. (1) A misnomer for green AVENTURINE QUARTZ, due to its resemblance to green JADE. (2) A misnomer for JADEITE which, although carved in quantity in China, is not found there.

Chinese jewelry. Articles of jewelry made in China since as early as the Shang-Yin Dynasty (*c*. 1766 BC-1122 BC). Among the earliest articles were JADE AMULETS, hair ornaments (HAIR PINS and COMBS) for women, and belt ornaments for men. BELT HOOKS of bronze were made in the Chou Dynasty (1122 BC-249 BC) and the Han Dynasty (206 BC-AD 220), the earlier ones showing the influence of western Asia; but from the T'ang Dynasty (AD 618-906) into the Ming Dynasty (1368-1644) complete belt sets were made of carved plaques of JADE and AGATE. Hair pins, of the

two-pin type, were made of undecorated massive gold during the Han and
T'ang Dynasties, but by the latter period they were of one-pin and two-
pin types, delicately and elaborately decorated. Gold, although used
earlier for some beads, became more abundantly used in the Han
Dynasty; pieces were often cast by the CIRE PERDUE process but, especially
in the T'ang Dynasty, were being made of thin sheet metal intricately
decorated with GRANULATED GOLD. During the Sung Dynasty (960–1279)
and Yüan Dynasty (1260–1368), the technique of openwork
ornamentation, used sparingly in the Han Dynasty, was developed,
especially for small plaques of cast silver and gilded bronze; pieces of
worked thin metal became increasingly used, being decorated with
animal, fish, and flower motifs that were contemporaneously being used
on porcelain. Such work was the precursor of the elaborate work done in
the Ming Dynasty (1368–1644) and Ch'ing Dynasty (1644–1912), when the
main development was the change from pierced decoration on sheets of
gold to the use of wire FILIGREE and, in the Ming period, the introduction
of gemstones in primitive settings. By the second half of the 16th century
the filigree was supplemented and sometimes replaced by the use of wire
mesh, and this style continued into the 17th and 18th centuries,
culminating in animal ornaments made solely of coiled and meshed wire.
Hair ornaments for men were made of jade or gold from the Sung to the
Ming periods, being in the form of hollow pieces to fit over and hold in
place a small bun of hair, secured by a long inserted pin (*see* HAIR
ORNAMENT). Other jewelry of the Ming period includes elaborate head-
dresses for women (such as worn from the Sung period) and BELT PLAQUES
of carved jade for men, as well as gold bracelets, ear-rings, and hair pins.
See KINGFISHER-FEATHER JEWELRY; MANDARIN NECKLACE.

chinoiserie (French). European decoration inspired by fanciful oriental
sources, particularly Chinese. *Chinoiseries* are pseudo-Chinese figures,
pagodas, monsters, and landscapes, with imaginative fantasy elements.
Introduced during the 17th century, the style was developed mainly on
enamelled porcelain and lacquer ware after *c.* 1720 and was widely used
in decoration of all kind until *c.* 1760. In England it was popular in the
Regency period. In jewelry it was not often used, but is found on some
articles made *c.* 1760 in England. The term is sometimes used broadly to
include exotic motifs inspired by scenes of Japan (*Japonaiseries*), India
(*Indienneries*) or Turkey (*Turqueries*).

chip. (1) A small piece cut or broken from a gemstone. (2) The place on a
gemstone from which such a chip has been broken. A chip of that nature
can sometimes be concealed by the manner in which the stone is set. (3) A
diamond weighing less than three-quarters of a CARAT, usually one that is
ROSE CUT or SINGLE CUT, or one cut irregularly.

chip-carving. Originally, a form of hand CARVING of wood by cutting
with a knife, but later a process of decorating metal in imitation of the
wood carving. It was practised by Roman metalworkers and later by
makers of VIKING JEWELRY and ANGLO-SAXON JEWELRY. The design was
deeply cut in the surface of metal by use of a chisel, creating facets that
emphasized the interplay of light and shade on the angled surface. *See*
EQUAL-ARMED FIBULA.

Chiriquí jewelry. Articles of PRE-COLUMBIAN JEWELRY made in the
Chiriquí region that spread across what is now the border of Costa Rica
and Panama, and which are related in style to that of those countries.
Much gold jewelry was found in 1858–60 but most was sent to London to
be melted into bullion. Until recent years most Panamanian jewelry was
referred to as 'Chiriquí'. The largest collection is in the Banco Central at
San José, Costa Rica, the bank having bought the jewelry from local
landowners on whose land it was found. *See* COSTA RICAN JEWELRY;
PANAMANIAN JEWELRY.

chlorastrolite. A variety of gemstone that is green, sometimes with white
markings and, when cut EN CABOCHON, shows star-like markings. Its
source is pebbles found along the shore of Lake Superior in the United
States. It is sometimes called 'greenstone'. The name is derived from
Greek *chloros* (green) and *astron* (star). It is related to THOMSONITE and is
sometimes embedded with it.

chloromelanite. A variety of JADEITE that is dark green to black, hence the name derived from the Greek words *chloros* (green) and *melas* (black), given to it in 1865 by A. Damour.

chlorospinel. A variety of SPINEL that contains ferric iron and is grass-green.

choker. A short narrow necklace that is worn close to a woman's throat, sometimes having an attached pendant. Examples in SUMERIAN JEWELRY consisted of adjacent triangles of gold and LAPIS LAZULI alternately inverted. *See* DOG COLLAR.

Christian amulet. An AMULET in the form of a Christian symbol, such as a CROSS or a crucifix. Some were made of silver in Sweden in the 10th century.

chromdiopside. A variety of DIOPSIDE that is transparent and chrome-green. It is fibrous and CHATOYANT when cut EN CABOCHON.

chrome tourmaline. A variety of TOURMALINE that is bright green, due to the presence of chrome.

chromium (or **chrome**). A greyish-white metal that is hard, brittle, and resistant to corrosion, and is the rust-resistant constituent of stainless steel. It is used for plating articles of COSTUME JEWELRY, providing a bright surface finish, although it peels or pits when inefficiently or thinly applied. Sometimes enamel decoration is added.

chryselephantine. Composed of, or decorated with, GOLD and IVORY. When used on Greek figures, ivory was used for the flesh, and gold, sometimes coloured, for the hair and garments. The name is derived from Greek *chrysos* (gold) and *elephas* (ivory).

chrysoberyl. A variety of gemstone that is characteristically yellow but varies from golden-yellow and brown to yellowish-green or bluish-green. Such stones are transparent and do not alter colour under varying illumination, hence are sometimes confused with SAPPHIRE. The dark-green variety is ALEXANDRITE. A colourless variety is rare, and seldom used as a gemstone. The popular variety displays good CHATOYANCY; it was formerly known as CYMOPHANE, but now is called 'chrysoberyl cat's-eye' or occasionally 'Oriental cat's-eye'. The yellowish-green variety has sometimes been confused with PERIDOT and spodumene. The transparent stones are faceted, usually MIXED CUT, but those that are cloudy or chatoyant are cut EN CABOCHON. The name is derived from Greek *chrysos* (gold). *See* HOPE CHRYSOBERYL.

chrysocolla. A MASSIVE, AMORPHOUS copper mineral of blue to green colour. It is used as a gemstone cut EN CABOCHON, and sometimes when found embedded in ROCK CRYSTAL it is cut in its MATRIX. The name is derived from Greek *chrysos* (gold) and *kolla* (glue), the word in Greek meaning 'gold solderer' because in ancient times it and related minerals were so used. *See* EILAT STONE.

chrysolite. A variety of OLIVINE that is yellowish-green. However, the name has been applied confusingly to various stones and it has been recommended that its use be discontinued; it was originally applied to any yellow stone, later it has been used as a misnomer in such compound names as 'Oriental chrysolite' (for yellow-green SAPPHIRE and yellowish-green CHRYSOBERYL), 'Brazilian chrysolite' (for pale-green chrysoberyl), 'Saxony chrysolite' (for greenish-yellow TOPAZ), 'Siberian chrysolite' (for ANDRADITE), 'Ceylon chrysolite' (for TOURMALINE), and 'aquamarine chrysolite' (for BERYL), and in the United States it has been used as a synonym for OLIVINE and PERIDOT. The stone resembles DIOPSIDE. The name is derived from Greek *chrysos* (gold) and *lithos* (stone).

chrysopal. A variety of COMMON OPAL that is light green.

chrysoprase. (1) A variety of CHALCEDONY that is apple-green, owing to the presence of nickel. It is used for beads and cut EN CABOCHON; in the Victorian era the cabochons were cut in the TALLOW-TOP style with facets around the rim. An imitation in GLASS can be detected by the presence of

Christian amulet. Silver cross (oldest known in Sweden). Uppland, Sweden, 10th century. H. 3.4 cm. Statens Historiska Museum, Stockholm.

internal bubbles. If heated, it loses water and becomes pale. The name is derived from Greek *chrysos* (gold) and *prasios* (leek-green). (2) A misnomer for AGATE stained green.

chute, à la, necklace. The classical style of necklace of pearls in the form of a single strand (about 42 cm long) of graduated pearls.

cinnamon stone. A variety of HESSONITE that is reddish-brown.

circlet. A type of HEAD ORNAMENT in the form of a complete circle worn usually above the brow and slightly tilted back, and having ornaments projecting upward and embellished with gemstones. An example is that worn by Queen Victoria, as shown in the QUEEN VICTORIA COMMESSO and in the portrait of her, dated June 1838, painted by Thomas Sully, in the Wallace Collection; the circlet was made for George IV in 1820.

cire perdue (French). Literally, lost wax. A process of CASTING metal, originally used in casting BRONZE ware, but later for much GOLD jewelry. Its use was primarily for articles of intricate design IN THE ROUND that could not readily be made by shaping the metal by chiselling, HAMMERING or ordinary methods of CASTING. The technique for a solid object involved carving a model in wax, then encasing ('investing') it in a clay, plaster or STEATITE mould, and applying heat to cause the wax to melt and run out of a hole (sprue) in the mould, after which the mould was filled under pressure with molten gold or silver (or, later, glass). In the modern technique the mould, before having the molten gold poured into it, is placed in a vacuum to force the metal into the entire space. For making a hollow object, it was necessary to insert a core inside the mould, leaving a thin surrounding space for the wax, with the core held in position by small pegs (called 'chaplets'). The method was used in ancient times by the Egyptians in the 15th/14th centuries BC. It was extensively used in Colombia (especially in QUIMBAYA JEWELRY) and in PERUVIAN JEWELRY, *c.* 500–1500, and in West Africa in ASHANTI JEWELRY of the 18th/19th centuries. Articles of ANGLO-SAXON JEWELRY were also made by this method. It is sometimes called the 'lost wax process', and a modern mass production method is called CENTRIFUGAL CASTING (or 'investment casting'). As the mould must be broken to retrieve the object, only one reproduction can be made from each wax model and from each mould.

ciselé (French). A style of decoration of metal that embraces both ENGRAVING and CHASING done on the same article, although it has been said that it was done with a non-cutting tool called a *ciselet* (a chisel). The outstanding exponent of such work was a Frenchman, Gérard Débêche, during the early Louis XV period; but the names of many noted later French *ciseleurs* are recorded, e.g. Jules Chaise (1807–70) and Honoré-Séverin Bourdoncle (1823–93).

citrine. A variety of QUARTZ that is CRYSTALLINE and usually yellow but sometimes red-brown to red-orange. It is uncommon in nature; most yellow stones sold as citrine are SMOKY QUARTZ or AMETHYST that have had the colour changed by HEAT TREATMENT. Natural citrine always shows dichroism, which is absent in heat-treated yellow quartz. The main source of citrine is Brazil, where it is often confused with yellow TOPAZ also found there, and hence the latter has locally been called 'Brazilian topaz' to distinguish it from the yellow quartz. The prefix 'Brazilian' should be discarded as confusing, and also such misnomers as 'Occidental topaz', 'Spanish topaz', and 'false topaz'. The name 'citrine' is derived from the French word *citron* (lemon), the colour that it usually exhibits.

Cividale Reliquary. A gold RELIQUARY, made as a pendant, in the form of an ivy leaf. It is decorated in CHAMPLEVÉ enamel, the hinged front with a tree and perched birds in green on a blue ground, and the reverse with a DIAPER chequered pattern having in alternate squares a fleur-de-lis on a blue ground and a double-headed eagle on a red ground. Inside there is a very small compartment for a relic. It is traditionally said, on account of the heraldic devices, that it was probably a wedding gift to Philip II of Taranto and Princess Tamara of Epirus upon their marriage in Naples in 1294, and that it was given in 1365 by Charles IV (1316–78), King of Luxembourg and Bohemia, later Holy Roman Emperor, to the Monastery of Sta Maria in Valle, near Cividale del Friuli, in north-eastern

Cividale Reliquary (front and back). Gold pendant with enamelled decoration. French, 13th/14th centuries. W. 8 cm. Museo Archeologico Nazionale, Cividale del Friuli, Italy.

Italy, then containing as a relic a particle of the True Cross. It has been suggested that its source was a French or Rhenish goldsmith at the Neapolitan Court of the Angevin rulers in Naples in the 13th century.

clam pearl. A variety of salt-water pearl that is non-nacreous and of inferior quality, produced by bivalve molluscs of several species, e.g. (1) the hard clam or quahog clam from the waters of the Atlantic coast of the United States; (2) the giant clam from tropical seas; and (3) a clam found near Singapore (*see* COCONUT PEARL). The term is sometimes incorrectly applied to the MUSSEL PEARL from the Mississippi Valley.

Clare Reliquary. A RELIQUARY in the form of a Latin cross suspended from a chain and decorated with POINTILLÉ work. It has affixed to the front a cruciform panel showing the Crucifixion, with the inscription 'INRI' in black. The cross contains fragments of wood and granite, said to be possibly from the True Cross and the Rock of Calvary. It was found in 1866 on the site of Clare Castle, Suffolk, England, and is attributed to the early 15th century.

clarity grading. The classification of polished diamonds according to their clarity (formerly called 'purity'). The top grade is variously termed, e.g. flawless, pure, clean or perfect. Next are VVS (very very small inclusions), VS (very small), SI (small inclusions) and PIQUÉ. Lower grades are sometimes called 'spotted' or 'rejections'. Grades above piqué must be determined through a lens. The term 'clean' is restricted in the United States.

clasp. A type of fastener made of two parts, usually a hook on one piece and a slot on the other. It is used to fasten a girdle or a belt, and smaller ones to fasten a BRACELET or NECKLACE, the parts being attached to opposite ends of the piece to be joined. The hook and the slot are usually placed on the back so as not to be visible. Some clasps for a belt are not attached by a slot but have a hook(s) that is fitted into a hole(s) in the other end of the belt. On some valuable jewelry there is an added safety clasp of various types that is closed after the main clasp has been fastened. *See* SAFETY CHAIN.

Classical jewelry. Articles of jewelry made in Greece during the Classical period, from the Age of Pericles, *c.* 475 BC, to 323 BC, when, after the conquests by Alexander the Great, foreign influences changed the character of Greek styles and techniques. Gold was scarce, and the jewelry emphasized workmanship of the metal, with minor use of enamelling, granulation or gemstones. The main articles were ear-rings (especially rosettes from which pendants were suspended), necklaces with pendants and beads, finger rings (some with seals), WREATHES, and bracelets (spirals and PENANNULAR hoops with ornate finials).

Classical style. The style of shaping and decorating articles during the entire period of Greek and Roman civilization, but sometimes restricted to the period of highest Greek culture, *c.* 475–323 BC (sometimes called the 'Hellenic style'). *See* CLASSICAL JEWELRY.

claw setting. A style of SETTING a gemstone in a finger ring in which the stone is held above the GIRDLE by a series of encircling, vertically projecting prongs (claws) cut into (or soldered on the outside of) the COLLET (circular, square, etc.) and that secure the stone by holding the FACETS on the CROWN. In such settings the stone rests on a BEARING (a thin metal band) that is soldered inside the collet. This type of setting was developed in the 19th century and is used mainly for transparent faceted stones, as it permits much light to enter the exposed stone. As the CULET of the stone in such a setting is exposed, the setting precludes the painting or FOILING of the culet to improve the stone's appearance. The collet is now sometimes made from an open GALLERY supplied by refiners. *See* CORONET SETTING.

clean. Applied to gemstones, having no noticeable interior FLAWS. Applied to diamonds, no INCLUSION must be visible to a trained eye when the stone is magnified 10 times. *See* CLARITY GRADING.

cleavage. (1) The property of many crystalline minerals to split readily in one or more directions along or parallel to certain planes ('cleavage

Clare Reliquary. Gold cross with attached crucifix. English, 15th century. H. 3.8 cm. Reproduced by gracious permission of Her Majesty the Queen.

planes') when subjected to a blow, and thus produce a somewhat smooth, well-defined surface rather than a CONCHOIDAL FRACTURE. Various gemstones split in different directions and with varying degrees of facility, e.g. DIAMOND (difficult) and TOPAZ and spodumene (both easy), but some show little or no trace of cleavage, e.g. TOURMALINE, CORUNDUM, GARNET etc. Cleavage is not a property by which gemstones can ordinarily be identified, but it is important in determining the procedure for CLEAVING. *See* PARTING. (2) The direction of the plane along which a stone will most readily split. (3) A rough diamond that has been cleaved from a larger stone.

cleaving. The technique for dividing a rough diamond along a CLEAVAGE plane before BRUTING and FACETING. The process involves: (1) determining that the stone should be split (i.e. not already sufficiently well shaped); (2) tracing on the stone, with ink, the indicated line of CLEAVAGE, as determined by viewing the interior through a preliminary small FACET; (3) fixing the stone with cement in a dop on a dop-stick; (4) making a small V-shaped nick ('kerf') in the right direction at the marked spot, using a smaller diamond, similarly mounted, to do so; (5) finally, placing a blunt blade in the nick and giving it a sharp blow with a mallet or a steel hammer, thus dividing the stone. This operation usually follows many hours of study, often days in the case of a large stone. *See* SAWING.

Cleopatra Bracelet. A famous bracelet made by GEORGES FOUQUET from a design by ALPHONSE MUCHA for Sarah Bernhardt (1844–1923) to wear in her role as Cleopatra. The bracelet is in the form of a gold and enamelled snake that encircles the wrist three times, with a carved OPAL winged head with RUBY eyes that rests on the top of the hand; from the mouth a thin gold chain extends to a gold finger ring also set with opals. It was exhibited in Brussels in 1965, and was last reported (1979) as being in the private collection of Michel Périnet, Paris.

Cleopatra Pendant. An elaborate gold pendant in the form of a bust of Cleopatra, the head and hand being made of carved HYACINTH(?) and set with diamonds, rubies, and emeralds, with coloured enamelling. The right hand holds at her breast a green enamelled asp. The carving is Italian, *c.* 1560; the mount is from Prague(?), *c.* 1580–90.

clip. An article of modern jewelry that resembles a brooch but has, instead of a fastening pin, a hinged support that fastens on the edge of a garment, or a hinged double-prong that can be passed through fabric. They are often made of precious metal and set with gemstones. *See* DOUBLE CLIP; EAR-CLIP.

cloak fastener. A device for fastening the two sides of a cloak, being composed of two ornamental pieces for attachment to the sides of the cloak, each having an attached small chain which hooks together as the fastener. *See* AGRAF(F)E.

cloison (French). Literally, a partition. The bent wire or thin metal strip affixed to the base metal plate in making articles of CLOISONNÉ enamel and which separates the enamels of different colours. The term has sometimes been used to refer to the spaces or cells formed by the partitions and covered with the enamel or set with CLOISONNÉ INLAY.

cloisonné (French). The technique of decoration by ENAMELLING in which a design is outlined on a metal plate with bent wire or metal strips of rectangular-section wire that are affixed edgewise to the metal base and the spaces filled in with coloured enamels that are then fused. Originally the wire or strips were held in position by SOLDERING, but in some later ware, especially Japanese, they were initially attached by an adhesive and then permanently held by the enamel itself. The technique was used in ancient times in Mycenaean, Greek, Egyptian, Byzantine, and Roman jewelry, as well as some ANGLO-SAXON JEWELRY of the 7th to 10th centuries. It has been used extensively on porcelain and metalware in China, especially during the Ming Dynasty (1368–1644) and the Ch'ing Dynasty from 1644, and also in Japan, some BEADS and snuff bottles being so decorated with intricate designs. Occasionally called 'cell enamelling'. *See* CHAMPLEVÉ; CLOISONNÉ INLAY; FILIGREE ENAMEL; PLATE INLAY; TRANSYLVANIAN ENAMEL; ALFRED JEWEL.

Cleopatra Pendant. Gold mount from Prague, *c.* 1580–90, with carved hyacinth head and hand, *c.* 1560, and diamonds, rubies, and emeralds. Schatzkammer, Residenz, Munich.

cloisonné. Gold brooch with *cloisonné* enamel from tomb of Queen Armegarde, (d. *c.* 570), excavated at St Denis. Trésor de la Basilique, St Denis, Paris.

cloisonné inlay. A type of decoration made, in the manner of CLOISONNÉ enamelware, by outlining the design on a metal base with thin wire or strips of metal (CLOISONS) and filling in the spaces with cemented slices of coloured gemstones (often GARNET) or coloured glass cut to fit the spaces and usually backed with silver or gold FOIL. The design covers the entire metal base and results in a smooth surface. It is found on EGYPTIAN JEWELRY, and later CAROLINGIAN JEWELRY, OTTONIAN JEWELRY, and still later northern Germanic and ANGLO-SAXON JEWELRY (*see* SUTTON HOO TREASURE). The French term was *verroterie cloisonnée*. *See* PLATE INLAY; ST CUTHBERT'S CROSS; KINGSTON BROOCH.

Clonmacnois Pin. A PIN BROOCH made of silver with decoration in FILIGREE, NIELLO, and white enamel. It was made in Ireland in the Christian period of the Celtic era. Its whereabouts today is unknown; a similar pin brooch, with different decoration, is in the National Museum of Ireland.

closed culet. A point, instead of a faceted flat CULET, at the bottom of the PAVILION of a cut gemstone.

closed setting. A style of SETTING a gemstone in a finger ring in which there is metal under the stone so that no part of the stone below the GIRDLE is exposed to light; the stone was set in a COLLET soldered to the hoop of the ring. This was the style of early ring settings and often the jeweller used FOIL or paint on the unexposed back of the stone to enhance its appearance. The style was used in the Renaissance, before the importance of the gemstone itself was appreciated, and the BEZEL received lavish decoration. It was superseded in the 18th century by the CUT-DOWN SETTING, but to a greater extent in the 19th century by the use of a collet made of a thin band and the development of the CLAW SETTING, the MILLEGRAIN SETTING, and later variations. Sometimes a small hole is bored in the base of a closed setting for transparent stones so that they can be cleaned. *See* CARVED SETTING; OPEN SETTING.

cloud agate. A variety of AGATE where the layers have been broken so as to show a number of round black masses having feathery edges, somewhat resembling clouds.

cluster brooch. A type of brooch in the form of a RING BROOCH but having the centre space decorated with a large central gemstone surrounded by a cluster of smaller gemstones and pearls. Such brooches were a development of the 14th century.

cluster ring. A type of finger ring embellished with several gemstones in the form of one large central stone framed by a number of smaller ones.

cluster setting. A style of SETTING a group of gemstones in a finger ring, either by several single-stone settings around a large central stone, or by one large setting with COLLETS for small single stones on a plate surrounding a central collet for a large stone.

coated stone. (1) A variety of diamond crystal having a coloured coating that is removable by cutting. (2) A gemstone that has been tinted with a colouring agent.

cobalt glass. A variety of GLASS that has been coloured bluish by cobalt oxide and is sometimes used as an imitation gemstone.

cock pendant. A pendant in the form of a cock, the body being a BAROQUE PEARL and the head and feathers being enamelled gold set with gemstones. A number of such pendants are recorded with the cock, sometimes holding a pilgrim's staff, as the motif. *See* BAROQUE PEARL JEWEL.

cocktail ring. A modern type of finger ring (so called in the mid-20th century) that is not of any prescribed form but basically is large, having an ornate shank and usually being set with a cluster or pattern of varicoloured stones in a high domed arrangement so that it could not readily be worn under a glove. The shank is usually of gold, PLATINUM or PALLADIUM, often with pierced shoulders. Some have a miniature watch

cock pendant. Baroque pearl jewel, gold with enamelling and gemstones. German (?), *c.* 1600. H. 7.5 cm. Rijksmuseum, Amsterdam.

set in the BEZEL. Such rings have been popular since the second quarter of the 20th century, and are often worn with a COCKTAIL WATCH.

cocktail watch. A type of lady's WRIST WATCH that is designed primarily to be worn as a piece of jewelry, with the watch usually concealed under a jewelled lid. Such watches are usually made of gold and set with gemstones. They have been popular since the second quarter of the 20th century, and are often worn with a COCKTAIL RING.

Coclé jewelry. Articles of PRE-COLUMBIAN JEWELRY found in the Coclé Province of Panama, north of the Canal Zone, the region being known as Parita, after an early Indian chief. The find was excavated by Samuel K. Lothrop, of the Peabody Museum of Harvard University. The articles include pendants depicting a crested alligator, embossed breastplates, hollow cast anthropomorphic figures, nose ornaments, cuff bracelets, finger rings, and necklaces composed of miniature beads. The style is often similar to that of QUIMBAYA JEWELRY of nearby Colombia. Some of the pieces were set with gemstones, including some large emeralds.

coconut pearl. A variety of CLAM PEARL from Singapore which resembles the meat of a coconut. The term is sometimes used as a misnomer for pearl-like concretions in a coconut which are valueless.

coiled ring. Bronze finger ring. W. 2.7 cm. British Museum, London.

coiled ring. A type of finger ring made in the form of a solid band coiled into three or four contiguous loops that taper at the two ends. They have been attributed to the Bronze Age, 13th century BC. Some have been found in south-eastern England, but similar rings are known from contemporary northern Europe.

coin bracelet. A type of rigid bracelet made of a gold hoop and having at the front a decorative ornament made of adjacent gold coins. An example (one of a pair found in Egypt and attributed to AD 610-40, based on the dates of the coins) includes five coins of Constantinople.

coin pendant. A type of pendant in the form of a circular band enclosing a coin. The band is usually decorated and has a suspensory ring or chains. Such pendants were sometimes worn as an AMULET, especially when the coin (e.g. a gold noble of Edward III or Edward IV) bore a motto believed to have amuletic significance. Some German examples of the 16th or 17th century enclose a coin bearing a portrait of a Bavarian or Bohemian duke; they were usually a gift to visiting dignitaries or favoured retainers. The German term is *Gnadenpfennig*. See MEDAL MEDALLION.

coin bracelet. Gold tubular hoop with 5 Byzantine coins. Constantinople or Egypt, 610-41. W. 11 cm. Dumbarton Oaks Collection (Harvard University), Washington, DC.

coin ring. A type of finger ring ornamented with a gold coin set on the BEZEL. Such rings were made in Rome during the latter years of the Empire, and often the coins depicted the head of an emperor.

coin watch. A type of luxury POCKET WATCH or WRIST WATCH that is very thin and of which the WATCH-CASE is, or is in the form of, a coin. Such pieces were fashionable from the early 19th century in France, examples being known that are set in a 100-franc gold coin. Watches of this type are still being made today with gold coins of various countries.

Colenso Diamond. A large, yellowish, nearly perfect octahedral diamond crystal that was donated by John Ruskin to the British Museum in 1887 and named by him to honour his friend, John William Colenso, first Bishop of Natal (d. 1883). It weighed 133.145 carats. It was stolen on 29 April 1965, and has never been recovered.

Collaert, Hans, the Elder (1540-1622). A designer of jewelry who worked in Antwerp and whose designs were notable for pendants departing from the styles of the Renaissance; some were executed by, or inspired adaptations by, Flemish or German jewellers. His designs, sometimes depicting mythological figures, may have been suggested by designs of ERASMUS HORNICK; some are in the Mannerist style or the MORESQUE SILHOUETTE STYLE. A pendant from one of his designs depicts a DRAGON. His reputation is based on books of engravings of his designs, made by his son, Hans Collaert the Younger, one having been published in Antwerp in 1573 by Johannes Liefrinck and two published in Antwerp by Philip Gale in 1581 and 1582. See ROMAN CHARITY, THE.

coin pendant. Pendant with gold coin (rose noble) of Edward IV within cabled border; Latin amuletic inscription. English, 15th century. W. 4.1 cm. British Museum, London.

collar. A band or other form of broad ornament worn around the neck. Some examples were made of gold in ancient times, e.g. one made in Ireland in the 7th century BC. Other types are known of VIKING JEWELRY. The oldest order whose knights were invested with a collar is the Order of the GOLDEN FLEECE, created in 1429 by Philip the Good, Duke of Burgundy; the Order of the Garter, although older, did not have its members wear a collar until Henry VIII's time. *See* NECK RING; ÅLLEBERG COLLAR; ARCHER'S COLLAR; DOG COLLAR; LIVERY COLLAR; SS COLLAR.

collar pin. A type of PIN (modern), generally similar to a safety-pin or a simple FIBULA, that is used to join both sides of the soft collar of a shirt, passing horizontally under the knot of a necktie. A piece for like purpose has, instead of a pin, a clip on each end that is slipped over the edges of the collar. Such pins are often made of gold.

collet. A circular band of metal in which a gemstone is set. *See* COLLET SETTING.

collet necklace. A type of necklace composed of a number of gemstones each set in a COLLET and all linked together without other ornamentation. Sometimes a RIVIÈRE is so made.

collet setting. A style of SETTING a stone in which the stone is fitted in a circular 'box' (made from a piece of metal tubing or from a thin metal band or 'collet'). When the upper edge is bent (rubbed) over the GIRDLE of the stone to secure it, it is known as a 'rub-over setting'. Such settings are usually for a finger ring with an opaque stone or a flawed stone (often backed with FOIL) or for a SIGNET RING; they are also used in a COLLET NECKLACE.

colloid hard-soldering. A process of SOLDERING ('hard-soldering') pieces of gold without the use of any SOLDER. The process, patented in 1933 by H. A. P. LITTLEDALE, an English chemist, involves joining the pieces with glue mixed with a copper salt (preferably a carbonate) and heating the joined piece in a reducing atmosphere (a non-oxidizing condition), then as the heat increases to 100°C. the copper salt changes to copper oxide, at 600°C. the glue changes to carbon, and at 850°C. the carbon absorbs the oxygen from the copper oxide and evaporates as carbon dioxide, and finally at 890°C. a thin layer of remaining copper melts with the gold as a brazing ALLOY and makes the join. The technique is based on the fact that when copper is heated in contact with gold the melting point of the two together is lower than when heated separately, so that the copper in the salt used to weld both the pieces and the gold both melt and unite at 890°C., whereas the gold alone would melt only at 1063°, hence the piece itself is not affected by the heat. It has been said that a similar process may have been used in some ETRUSCAN JEWELRY and PRE-COLUMBIAN JEWELRY to fix FILIGREE or to join hollow gold hemispheres or to produce GRANULATED GOLD, none of which show any evidence of the use of solder. The term 'colloid' is derived from Greek *kolla* (glue). A similar technique was used to solder silver to copper in making Sheffield plate. A simplification of the process was developed in England in 1961 by W. Haendel, which he called EUTECTIC WELDING, and also in 1974 by Michael Jackson. *See* DIFFUSION BONDING.

Colombian jewelry. Articles of PRE-COLUMBIAN JEWELRY made in Colombia (which included the neighbouring region of Panama until 1903) by the various Indian tribes whose techniques and styles differed in the various regions. The jewelry and many other objects were made of gold or TUMBAGA (a gold–copper ALLOY) from *c.* 300 BC until the conquest, *c.* 1539, of the country by the Spanish Conquistadors under Jiménez de Quesada. Among the articles that have been found are PECTORALS (often in the form of anthropomorphic figures), PENDANTS, NOSE ORNAMENTS, EAR ORNAMENTS, LABRETS, MASKS and the indigenous TUNJOS (votive figures), POPORAS (lime flasks), and EFFIGY FLASKS. The pieces were often made of thin, flat, hammered metal decorated with REPOUSSÉ work and CHASING, sometimes with threads of FALSE FILIGREE, and fine examples were made by the CIRE PERDUE process. The surviving pieces (over 5,000 are in the Museo del Oro, Bogotá) are principally the result of plundering by grave robbers or of grave excavations by archaeologists in recent years; a vast number of pieces were melted into

Colombian jewelry. Gold *tunjo* of raft with figures in ceremony of El Dorado. Muisca region. L. 18.3 cm. Museo del Oro, Bogotá.

ingots by the Conquistadors or after being taken to Spain. However, much is believed to remain in the depths of Lake Guatavita, the circular mountain lake near Bogotá into which, upon the installation of each Muisca chief (known as 'El Dorado', on account of his being completely covered with gold dust), gold offerings and emeralds were thrown from his raft into the lake, as sacrifices to the gods. *See* CALIMA JEWELRY; MUISCA JEWELRY; NARIÑO JEWELRY; POPAYÁN JEWELRY; QUIMBAYA JEWELRY; QUIMBAYA TREASURE; SINÚ JEWELRY; TAIRONA JEWELRY; TOLIMA JEWELRY; TUMACO JEWELRY; DARIEN PECTORAL; DIADEM; LIME DIPPER; LIZARD; MASK; PENIS SHEATH; SNUFF TRAY; SPACER BEAD; TWEEZER.

colour. The sensation produced on the eyes by decomposed light, referring in general parlance to the colours of the spectrum. Most natural gemstones, with the exception of the usual diamond, have colour or various colours, or shades or hues, due to the natural presence of finely dispersed particles of minerals or impurities in extremely small quantities. The same species of stone may have several colours and also several species may have similar colour, so that colour alone is the least reliable means of identifying a gemstone. The quality of colour affects the value of certain gemstones. Some stones exhibit simultaneously several colours, e.g. the OPAL. The colour of some stones can be changed or enhanced artificially (*see* DYEING; HEAT TREATMENT; TREATED DIAMOND), and SYNTHETIC GEM-STONES and ENAMELS can be coloured by the use of metallic oxides.

colouring (gemstones). The changing of the colour of a true gemstone or the imparting of colour to a synthetic gemstone, which can be done by several processes. For a true gemstone: (1) by the application of heat (*see* HEAT TREATMENT); (2) by DYEING (STAINING); (3) by FOILING; (4) by TINTING; (5) by making the stone into a DOUBLET; (6) by IRRADIATION (*see* TREATED DIAMOND). For a synthetic gemstone: by the use of a metallic oxide. *See* STAINED PEARL.

colouring (metals). The changing of the colour of a metal or giving it a coloured surface, which can be done by several processes, e.g. ENAMELLING, HEAT TREATMENT, electroplating, and chemical colouring. *See* DEPLETION GILDING.

comb. Silver, with upper section gilded. China, 10th century. W. 18.2 cm. British Museum, London.

comb. An article which, as an object of jewelry, is worn by a woman to confine the hair or as a hair ornament. Such combs are usually slightly curved, with an ornamental upper part above a single row of teeth; they are of varying widths and heights. Ornamental combs have been made of GOLD, SILVER, AMBER, CORAL, JET, BONE, TORTOISE SHELL, IVORY, HORN, etc., and have been decorated since the time of the Renaissance with GEMSTONES, PEARLS, CAMEOS, or openwork metal designs. In the 15th century, combs made of gold were crown-shaped, set with gemstones. Those worn in the 19th century were usually made to be seen from the front; the Spanish type (worn with a mantilla) is usually a back comb. Examples in ART NOUVEAU style are usually enamelled. *See* CHINESE JEWELRY.

comb fibula. A type of FIBULA having the appearance of a comb and functioning unlike the usual SAFETY-PIN FIBULA. It is composed of a central tube, ornamentally decorated, with a wire attached lengthwise along each side, and two separate comb-like pieces made of a series of adjacent bent wires; the 'combs' are sewn on opposite sides of a cloak and are fastened by being hooked over the wires on the tube. Examples made of PARCEL GILT silver are known in ETRUSCAN JEWELRY from the Early Etruscan Period, 7th century BC.

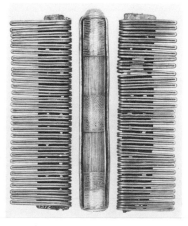

comb fibula. Silver, parcel-gilt. Etruscan, 7th century BC. L. 12.4 cm. British Museum, London.

commemorative jewelry. Articles of jewelry worn to commemorate some occasion, such as a political event, military victory or defeat, or royal marriage, coronation or death, and bearing an appropriate engraved or enamelled reference to the occasion. The most usual such piece was a COMMEMORATIVE RING. *See* MOURNING JEWELRY; CHARLES I JEWELRY; CHARLES V JEWELRY; JAMES I JEWELRY.

commemorative ring. A type of finger ring (an example of COMMEMORATIVE JEWELRY) having on the BEZEL an engraving or enamelled portrait to commemorate some occasion. Many such English rings related to the execution of Charles I (*see* CHARLES I JEWELRY), the

Restoration, and the Jacobite cause (*see* JACOBITE JEWELRY), as well as the death of persons connected with the 1745 Rebellion. French rings commemorate events such as Napoleon's escape from Elba. Some pieces made in Poland commemorate events in that country. All such rings were popular in the 18th and 19th centuries. *See* MOURNING RING; REVOLUTION RING.

commesso (Italian). Literally, joined. A rare type of Renaissance jewel, usually depicting a figure or a head, that combines in a unified composition one or more HARDSTONES carved to form a CAMEO and gold accessories, sometimes enamelled. The technique was practised by jewellers and gem-cutters in France under Henry II. In Italy, the term is applied to designs in various *pietre dure*, as in the version of *commesso* developed by OTTAVIO MISERONI. The *commesso* technique was revived by the Parisian firm of F. Dafrique which exhibited an example (*see* VICTORIA, QUEEN, COMMESSO) at the Great Exhibition of 1851. Modern jewelry similarly combining a cameo with gold has been made, e.g. by RENÉ LALIQUE. *See* Yvonne Hackenbroch, 'Commessi', in *Metropolitan Museum of Art Bulletin,* New Series, XXIV (1966), p. 13. *See* JAHANGIR PENDANT; LEDA AND THE SWAN JEWEL.

commesso. Pendant with female figure in white chalcedony on onyx background and with drapery in burnished gold. French (?), late 16th century. L. 7 cm. British Museum, London.

common opal. One of the varieties of OPAL (as contrasted with PRECIOUS OPAL), which includes CACHOLONG, GEYSERITE, MENILITE, MOSS OPAL, MILK OPAL, CHERRY OPAL, CHRYSOPAL, PRASOPAL, BANDED OPAL (OPALITE) and RESIN OPAL. It usually has a whitish background and a milky OPALESCENCE, and does not exhibit flashes of colour. It has less value as a gemstone.

compass ring. A type of finger ring used for measuring time, having a locket-type BEZEL set with a compass, around the edge of which were engraved (as on a horizontal sundial) the hours, and for which the lid served as a gnomon (or which had a hole for inserting a string as a gnomon). Such rings were made, probably in Germany, in the 16th century. *See* RING DIAL.

composite brooch. A type of BROOCH made of two plates bound together, sometimes edged with a narrow strip of beaded gold and sometimes filled with a white clay-like substance. The front plate is variously decorated with CLOISONNÉ INLAY, enamelling and gemstones, and the reverse has a pin with a catch-plate and often a safety-loop. *See* AMHERST BROOCH; KINGSTON BROOCH; MONKTON BROOCH.

composite stone. A simulation of a gemstone that is made of two or three layers of gemstone or GLASS that are cemented or fused together so as to appear as a whole natural stone. The purpose is to provide a more attractive colour or a protective top surface (as for an OPAL). *See* DOUBLET; TRIPLET. They can be distinguished from genuine stones by several tests: (1) by revealing a ring around the GIRDLE, especially when immersed in water or certain liquids and then viewed from the side; (2) by having different specific gravity; (3) by microscopic examination; or (4) by immersion in hot water or an organic solvent which will soften the cement and separate the layers. Such stones are sometimes called an 'assembled stone'. *See* SOUDÉ EMERALD.

composite suite. An article of jewelry, usually of a luxurious character, that is composed of two or three parts which can be worn assembled (e.g. as a necklace) or individually (e.g. pendants forming a brooch and a pair of EAR-CLIPS). This permits use with evening or daytime attire. A related article is the DOUBLE CLIP, which can be worn as a brooch or separated into two single clips. Another example is a set of brooches that can be assembled on a circular metal frame and a pair of small combs to form a TIARA. *See* STOMACHER.

conch pearl. A variety of salt-water PEARL produced by the univalve giant conch or queen conch (also called 'helmet conch' or 'cameo conch'). Such pearls are of inferior quality, being non-nacreous; they are usually white or pink. The shell, also white or pink, is used for carving a CAMEO. Such pearls are sometimes imitated by a bead of pink CORAL.

concha belt. Detail with silver and turquoise ornaments. Tom Bahti Indian Art Shop, Tucson, Arizona.

concha belt. A type of belt, made by the Indians in south-western United States, in the form of a wide leather band on which is affixed a row of convex discs made of carved shell or of silver inlaid with turquoise and sometimes pieces of coral or mother-of-pearl.

consecration ring. *See* BISHOP'S RING; FISHERMAN'S RING.

contemporary jewelry. Articles of jewelry made since World War II, *c.* 1945, in many countries of Europe and in the United States by people (many of the designers being primarily sculptors or painters or DESIGNER–MAKERS) who have made pieces of highly original designs and by use of various materials (*see* ACRYLIC JEWELRY) outside the range of traditional jewelry, to meet their own very personal conceptions of form and style. The range of people and forms is so wide as to make their inclusion impracticable within the scope of this book, except for a few recognized designer–makers born before 1950. *See* Ralph Turner, *Contemporary Jewelry* (1976).

Cooper, John Paul (1869-1933). An English jeweller and silversmith closely identified with the Arts and Crafts Movement. After first making boxes of silver and shagreen, he started making jewelry, principally in 1902-10, producing gold pendants, brooches, and necklaces. His workshop was in his home at Westerham, Kent. His style was influenced by his teacher and friend, HENRY WILSON, and from 1906 he developed a Japanese technique called *Mokumé* that combined silver and copper. His mark: J P C. *See* Charlotte Gere, 'The Work of John Paul Cooper', in *Connoisseur*, November 1975, p. 200.

copal. A natural RESIN from certain tropical trees of Africa, especially Tanzania and Sierra Leone, and of New Zealand, found fossilized in the ground near the trees and some 40,000,000 years old. It is used for jewelry in the same manner as AMBER, which it resembles. *See* KAURI GUM.

copaline (or **copalite**). A reddish, resinous substance, said to be probably from vegetable matter altered from having remained in earth. It is sometimes used as a substitute for COPAL or AMBER.

copper. A metallic element of reddish colour, though in its natural state it is often green, as oxidation of the surface forms verdigris. It has been used from early civilizations in making jewelry, both in its pure state and in various ALLOYS, e.g. BRONZE and BRASS, and in more recent centuries in ORMOLU, PINCHBECK, nickel silver, and gilding metal, and also to a small extent in Britannia metal, GOLD ALLOY, and SILVER ALLOY.

Coptic jewelry. Articles of jewelry made by the Copts (an ancient Egyptian sect that adhered to Christianity and resisted Islam), and articles imitative of their style that were made in the 19th and early 20th centuries. Frequently seen examples are Coptic crosses, with four equal arms and a circle at the centre, often with elaborate added ornamentation. Another example is the so-called Jimma Jala, a necklace with several ornaments containing charcoal (a type of AMULET).

coque de perle (French). Literally, pearl shell. The oval section of the central whorl of the convex outer shell of the pearly NAUTILUS. It resembles a BLISTER PEARL, being a MOTHER-OF-PEARL bubble, sometimes rather large, that is usually thin and hence it is backed with cement, but it appears to be solid unless there is a hole in the skin. Such pearls are pear-shaped or irregular, and are porcelain-white with a faint LUSTRE. They have been mounted in articles of jewelry. Also called 'eggshell pearl'.

coral. A hard, calcareous, organic substance that is the skeleton of certain polyps, small marine invertebrates that live in colonies. The variety used in jewelry (as distinguished from the stony coral in reefs of the Pacific atolls) is the *corallium nobile* (precious coral), which is compact, glyptic, and solid, without visible indentations. The colours shade from pinkish-white to pale pink (angel-skin) and ox-blood red. It is mainly used as BEADS (some seed-size) or set EN CABOCHON, or carved as a CAMEO or INTAGLIO. The principal centre for such carving has long been Torre del Greco, near Naples, but other centres are near Genoa and Leghorn, as well as now in Korea, China, and Japan. Its main sources are along the shores of the Mediterranean, but today it also comes from Japan, Hawaii, and Australia. Some coral is left in its natural tree-like stalks, being merely polished and pierced for suspension or mounted. Coral was used in ancient Egypt (especially as SCARABS) and also by the Greeks and Etruscans who engraved it as SEALS. It has been used extensively since the 14th century for beads in a ROSARY or as a CHARM (in the form of a stalk mounted at one end in a gold ring); it is still used for a baby's teething ring or rattle. It has been believed to have amuletic powers and to be a protection against spells. Coral is sometimes used as a bead to imitate a pink CONCH PEARL, but the pearl can be distinguished by its surface markings. Coral has been imitated in GLASS, dyed SHELL, and PLASTICS, but can be identified by its hardness and its effervescing when tested with an acid. *See* AGATIZED CORAL; KING CORAL.

coral (reef) limestone. A variety of limestone composed of fossilized CORAL from a coral reef. It exhibits reddish spots and streaks, and pieces of irregular shape, when polished, are used in jewelry.

cord chain. A cross-linked double LOOP-IN-LOOP CHAIN, made by a very complicated process by which 4, 6 or 8 double loop-in-loop chains are crossed and then bent upward to form a chain with 4, 6 or 8 faces, appearing to be plaited and being very flexible.

cordelière (French). A long, beaded girdle, usually worn knotted in front with the ends hanging. Such girdles, sometimes made of silver beads, were worn in the mid-19th century.

cordierite. The same as IOLITE. It was named after P. L. A. Cordier (1777–1861), a French geologist.

cornelian. A variety of CHALCEDONY that is usually flesh-red, but also ranges from yellowish-red to reddish-brown. The colour is intensified by heating. The stone is sometimes mottled by flecks of the MATRIX. It is hard and tough, and so is often carved in INTAGLIO form as a SEAL, or used as beads. The name was probably derived from the Latin *cornum* (the red cornelian cherry); the alternative name 'carnelian', sometimes used since the 15th century but less frequently today, is possibly derived from the Latin *carneus* (fleshy), on account of the flesh-red colour. *See* CANARY STONE; SARD.

cornelian agate. A variety of AGATE with alternating bands of CORNE- LIAN.

corneol. A variety of CHALCEDONY that is dyed a pink colour.

Cornish diamond. A local misnomer for ROCK CRYSTAL found in Cornwall, England.

coronal. A circlet for the head, especially worn by ladies of rank. Such jewelled pieces, known in Italian as *ghirlande,* were especially made by the goldsmith/painter Domenico del Ghirlandaio (1450–1517) for the young and newly-wedded ladies of Florence.

coronation ring. A finger ring used in the ceremony of consecration of a monarch. The earliest known English example is that of King Edgar (AD 973). Such rings of British sovereigns were sometimes worn continuously (as by Queen Elizabeth I), but more often they have been kept in the Royal Treasury except for coronations, as that used for William IV (1830) and for every later coronation except in the case of Queen Victoria. *See* ROYAL RINGS.

coronet. A small or inferior type of CROWN, especially one worn by a person of high rank but lower than a sovereign, and usually made without arches. In the United Kingdom, coronets are worn by peers and peeresses, the highest coronet being that of the Prince of Wales, which is the same as the Crown of England (*see* CROWN JEWELS, BRITISH) except that is has only one arch. Next (without arches) are those of the sons, brothers and nephews of royal blood, and after them are circlets various adorned: Duke, with 8 conventional strawberry leaves; Marquess, with 4 strawberry leaves, alternating with 4 pearls; Earl, with 8 pearled rays alternating with 8 strawberry leaves; Viscount, with 16 pearls; Baron, with 6 pearls. The coronets of the wives of peers are facsimiles of reduced size. All the foregoing coronets are now worn only at a coronation, at the moment of the crowning of the sovereign. They are worn set on a 'Cap of Estate'. *See* ST EDWARD'S CROWN.

coronet setting. A type of circular CLAW SETTING having high spires (for securing a large SOLITAIRE stone) sawn to form a small crown with the inside of the spires incised to hold the stone, and with the top of the spires bent slightly over the GIRDLE of the stone.

Cortés Ex Voto Jewel. A 16th-century enamelled, emerald-studded JEWEL depicting a lizard and suspended by two chains as a PENDANT. It has been said to be an *ex voto* offering made by a Mexican goldsmith and sent in 1528 by Hernando Cortés, conqueror of Mexico, to the Monastery of the Virgin of Guadalupe in Estremadura, Spain; it is now in Madrid. Its origin has been disputed, the contention being that any *ex voto* jewel donated by Cortés would more likely have been a gold representation of a scorpion of Mexican Indian gold and style of workmanship, rather than such a Renaissance jewel, and that the present jewel is probably a replacement. *See* Priscilla E. Muller, 'The So-called "Ex Voto of Hernán Cortés"', in *Connoisseur*, April 1968, p. 264. *See* LIZARD JEWELRY.

Cortés Ex Voto Jewel. Lizard with green enamel scales, emeralds, and ruby eyes; pendent pearls. Instituto de Valencia de Don Juan, Madrid.

corundum. A mineral (aluminium oxide) that is the hardest mineral other than the diamond; its HARDNESS on the MOHS' SCALE is 9. It is found in two varieties: (1) common corundum, which is impure, coarse, opaque and granular (known as EMERY), and used as an abrasive; and (2) transparent corundum, which includes the RUBY and the SAPPHIRE (both identical except as to colour). Corundum (seldom colourless) exhibits a wide range of colours (blue, pink, green, yellow, etc.) and such stones are properly termed sapphires preceded by the appropriate colour (designations using the names of other similar-appearing stones preceded by the word 'Oriental' being misnomers), except that the red variety is called 'ruby'. The colours in some cases are probably due to traces of metallic oxides. The cut specimens are characterized by their vitreous LUSTRE high specific gravity, weak colour dispersion, double refraction and, when coloured, dichroism, which enable them to be distinguished from other varieties of stones of similar appearance, as does microscopic examination. Some specimens show a SHEEN (SILK) and some have an interior series of minute, needle-like INCLUSIONS (FEATHERS) of RUTILE; these, when properly cut EN CABOCHON, are STAR RUBIES and STAR SAPPHIRES (*see* ASTERISM) or, when having only one ray of light, 'corundum cat's-eye'. Multicoloured stones are common, and patches of two colours are sometimes found in a stone and show an apparent blended tint. Corundum stones are cut as TABLE CUT, STEP CUT, BRILLIANT CUT, and MIXED CUT. *See* FINGERPRINT.

cosse de pois (French). *See* PEAPOD.

Costa Rican jewelry. Articles of PRE-COLUMBIAN JEWELRY made, *c.* AD 800–1500, in the Diquís and Linea Viaja regions of what is now Costa Rica and the Chiriquí region that extended from Costa Rica into Panama. The pieces are generally similar in style and workmanship to the jewelry of Panama and also show the influence of the styles of Mexico to the north and Colombia to the south. Gold, which was not abundant locally, was imported in quantity, and much gold jewelry was worn (hence the name, which means 'Rich Coast', given to the country by Columbus on his 4th voyage). The articles included gold and TUMBAGA objects cast by the CIRE PERDUE process and were sometimes in the form of a pendant depicting zoomorphic figures, e.g. the king vulture (*see* KING VULTURE PENDANT), eagle (single- and double-headed), frog, owl, crab, bat, and deer, as well as anthropomorphic figures (sometimes holding rattles, a rope or a flute). A popular object was a small gold bell that was worn attached to garments. Some pieces were made of string-cut or carved JADE. *See* CHIRIQUÍ JEWELRY; DIQUÍS JEWELRY; LINEA VIAJA JEWELRY. *See* E. K. Easby, *Pre-Columbian Jade from Costa Rica* (1968).

costume jewelry. Various articles of moderate-priced to inexpensive jewelry, originally pieces suitable for a particular type of costume but now applied to two classes of jewelry: (1) gem-set imitations, which resemble precious jewelry but are made usually of SILVER (sometimes rhodium-coated) or PINCHBECK and set with substitutes for gemstones, e.g.

III *Devonshire Parure.* Enamelled gold by C.F. Hancock, 1856, set with antique and Renaissance cameos and intaglios. Left, diadem, coronet, comb, and bandeau; centre, bracelet; right, stomacher and necklace. From 1863 chromolithograph. Devonshire Collection, Chatsworth, Bakewell, England. (Photo courtesy of *Country Life*)

IV *Giuliano family*. Top left, enamelled gold pendant with transfer enamel portrait. Carlo G., *c*. 1880. Top right, pendant, tourmalines and diamonds with enamel and pearls. Carlo G., *c*. 1880. Below left, pendant with enamel, pearls, and rubies. Carlo G., *c*. 1880. Below right, gold brooch with ancient Egyptian faience scarab. Carlo G., *c*. 1880. Centre, pendant, gold Tudor rose, Carlo and Arthur G., *c*. 1910. Courtesy of Wartski, London.

MARCASITE, PASTE or SYNTHETIC GEMSTONES; although usually the stones are cemented, some are hand-set. (2) Articles made of some base metal and imitations of gemstones, being intended as a novelty and to meet an ephemeral fashion trend. Such latter articles are today usually purchasable at various types of shops other than jewellers; although much is mass-produced, some well-designed and rather costly examples have been made for leading couturiers, such as Chanel, Christian Dior, etc. The introduction of costume jewelry occurred in the 18th century, but its development and extended use were during the 19th century, especially in England when mass-produced jewelry was made by the Birmingham factory of MATTHEW BOULTON. When such pieces are made of materials of reasonable value and designed and made with skill and artistry, they may be considered to be within the meaning of the term 'jewelry'. *See* JUNK JEWELRY; SCHMUCK.

Côte de Bretagne. A large red SPINEL (BALAS RUBY) of very unusual, irregular shape. It was owned by Henry II of France and inherited by his son and successor, Francis II, 1559–60, and thereafter pawned by Charles IX. In 1749 it was owned by Louis XV and sent by him to Jacquemin, the Court Jeweller, to be made into a jewel. Jacquemin had it carved by JACQUES QUAY who, to conceal 3 disfiguring holes, cut it into the form of the body and head of a dragon (reducing it from 206 to 105 carats), adding wings and tail in small diamonds and using topazes to form flames from its mouth; it was mounted in a jewel above the BLUE DIAMOND OF THE CROWN (set within the flames) from which was suspended a gold GOLDEN FLEECE. It was later owned by Louis XVI. After it was stolen in 1792 from the French Garde Meuble, it turned up in various hands and finally was returned to Louis XVIII. It is now in the Galerie d'Apollon at the Louvre, Paris.

cotière (French). An elaborate long CHAIN with pendant worn by ladies of the French Court during the late Renaissance. Some were made EN SUITE with a CARCANET.

counter-enamelling. The technique of ENAMELLING on metal by painting both sides of the metal with ENAMEL. It was invented toward the end of the 15th century when enamelling on gold, silver or copper was found to be unsuccessful on account of the difficulty of making enamel adhere to a thin metal plate. (It tended to curl during the process of firing, as a result of the different rates of contraction and expansion of the metal and the glass in the enamel.) The problem was solved by covering both sides of the metal with the same thickness of enamel so that, when fired, the two coats would shrink equally and secure the metal plate between them. The technique was possibly discovered by Venetians, but was extensively used at Limoges.

counterfeit. An article made or sold, with intent to deceive, as a close imitation of a contemporaneously available genuine article, being dependent for its value mainly on the material that it imitates rather than the workmanship or style. (1) Gemstones: for centuries there have been imitations of gemstones, being made of GLASS or PASTE, sometimes backed with FOIL to give a false hue, or with gelatin to make a DOUBLET, or topped with a sliver of diamond to simulate a diamond. The practice of imitating continued until medieval times and was expanded by such practices as mingling, in one piece, glass or spurious gems with PRECIOUS STONES, or mingling inferior pearls with those of quality. Sometimes stones whose colour had been changed by HEAT TREATMENT were sold as stones naturally of the same colour. Some transparent uncoloured stones of QUARTZ have been miscalled a local variety of diamond (but such stones or SYNTHETIC GEMSTONES are not regarded as counterfeits if not intended to deceive). *See* IMITATION GEMSTONE. (2) Metals: base metals have been silvered or gilded so as to imitate a precious metal (but such materials as STRASS, PINCHBECK, and SIMILOR are not regarded as counterfeits, as not intended to deceive but only to simulate). Some counterfeit articles of gold or silver have been made of sub-standard metal, which practice was sought to be eliminated by the use of the HALLMARK (difficult to apply to small articles of jewelry, especially a finger ring, and so not always successful). More pernicious counterfeiting was the making of a gold ring with a hollow SHANK or a shank filled with some composition. *See* FAKE; FORGERY; REPRODUCTION.

Croix de Saint Lô. Gilded metal and strass. Musée de Normandie, Caen, France.

Coventry Ring. A gold DEVOTIONAL RING in the form of a broad hoop, engraved on the exterior with a depiction of Christ arising from the tomb and with words describing the five wounds of Christ and on the interior with a Latin inscription including the names of the three Magi (*see* THREE KINGS), and the magic words 'ananyzapta' and 'tetragrammaton'. It was made in the first half of the 15th century and found in England, at Coventry, in 1802. It is in the British Museum.

cowrie shell. The shell of a small gastropod mollusc, found in the Indian Ocean, that was used in the Neolithic Age, *c.* 5000 BC, in necklaces and in dynastic Egypt as an AMULET against sterility (as well as later in Africa and southern Asia as a form of money). Such shells have been used in modern times in articles of jewelry and OBJECTS OF VERTU. *See* MOLLUSC SHELL; OBJETS TROUVÉS.

crackled. Having the appearance of a multitude of tiny closely-placed cracks. Some gemstones are given this appearance by being heated and then immersed in cold water, thus producing the fissures; some are cooled in dyed water that enters the fissures and imparts a colour to the stone.

cramp ring. A finger ring that was formerly believed to avert or cure cramp (epilepsy) by virtue of having been consecrated by the British sovereign, whose power was said to be derived from the unction received at the coronation. The rings were made from silver coins offered to the Church by the sovereign on Good Friday. They were of no established form, so none is recognizable today by mere viewing. The earliest reference to such Good Friday donations was to Edward II in 1323, but the hallowing of the rings is first known under Edward III, 1327–77. By Tudor times in the 16th century, such rings were much sought in Britain and on the Continent for their reputed curative effect. The hallowing of rings stopped under Henry VIII, but was revived briefly under Mary I, 1516–58, and ended finally under Elizabeth I; however, some cramp rings were still worn in England in the 19th century to ward off disease.

cramp setting. A style of SETTING a gemstone in a finger ring that is a variation of the RUB-OVER SETTING, in that the rim of the metal band is not bent over the stone but is cut to make a serrated edge and then each metal point is bent (cramped) over the stone to secure it.

cravat pin. The same as TIE PIN.

Creole ear-ring. A type of ear-ring that is in the form of a smooth, tapered hoop, circular or PENANNULAR, wide at the bottom and narrowing on both sides and toward the top. Some were set with gemstones. Such ear-rings were worn from the mid-19th century; modern versions are sometimes made as an EAR-CLIP.

crescent brooch. A type of brooch of crescent shape, made and decorated in various styles and often set with one to three rows of gemstones. Some examples have a detachable pin that could be replaced by a prong for wearing as a HAIR ORNAMENT.

crimped plate. An ornament on some articles of jewelry in the form of a very narrow, flat strip of gold crimped or goffered into ridges. It is found on some enamelled ENSEIGNES depicting pictorial subjects, said to have been made by an unknown Spanish enameller.

crocidolite. A mineral that is a variety of asbestos, lavender-blue to leek-green in colour, and fibrous. When it is silicified and infiltrates QUARTZ CAT'S-EYE, the stone is known as HAWK'S-EYE or FALCON'S-EYE if the blue colour has been retained, but if the colour has changed to golden-brown by oxidation of the iron present, the stone is known as TIGER'S-EYE. A general name for such stones is 'crocidolite quartz'.

Croix à la Jeannette (French). An article of French PEASANT JEWELRY in the form of a heart from which is suspended a cross (sometimes entwined with a serpent). The heart and cross were made of the same material, gold (for wealthy owners) or silver, or gilded or silvered metal. Sometimes the heart served as a slide (*coulant*) through which passed a chain to support the cross. They were worn, *c.* 1835, suspended from a chain or a plain black ribbon worn around the neck.

Croix de Saint Lô. An article of French PEASANT JEWELRY in the form of a cross, composed of five gemstones or of STRASS, one set in the centre and one forming each of the four limbs of the cross, the lowest being the largest, sometimes in PENDELOQUE form. The metal mount was of gold or silver, or of gilded or silvered metal. On some examples small stones were added as additional decoration. Such a cross (similar to the Croix de Rouen) differed from a CROIX À LA JEANNETTE by being made without a suspensory heart.

cross. (1) An ornamental or devotional article of jewelry in the form of an upright joined by a horizontal arm as in a T (*see* TAU CROSS), or traversed by an arm as in a Latin cross (*see* CROSS FORMÉE, MALTESE CROSS, PATRIARCHAL CROSS, GREEK CROSS), and worn suspended from a chain or necklace as a PENDANT (*see* PECTORAL CROSS; CRUCIFORM PENDANT) or as a BROOCH. Such crosses have been made of various materials, e.g. GOLD, SILVER, ROCK CRYSTAL, JET, CORAL, CUT STEEL etc. Luxurious examples have been set with, or have suspended from them, gemstones or pearls, or have been decorated with enamelling. They have been worn as a reliquary (*see* RELIQUARY CROSS; BERESFORD HOPE CROSS), and were popular everywhere in Europe as PEASANT JEWELRY, especially various types of provincial cross. The cross was also used as a design for other objects, e.g. a type of WATCH CASE. (2) The first group of FACETS ground on a diamond, being the 4 TEMPLETS on the CROWN and the 4 PAVILION FACETS on the PAVILION.

cross cut. The style of cutting a diamond (or other transparent gemstone) in a modification of the STEP CUT. It is usually used on a square or rectangular stone, cut so that each of the 4 usual four-sided FACETS surrounding the TABLE is additionally cut, rather than left flat-topped, to form 4 triangular facets meeting at an apex. Also called the 'scissors cut'.

cross facet. The former name for one of a number of relatively small triangular FACETS on the CROWN or on the PAVILION of a BRILLIANT, all abutting the GIRDLE. The 8 cross facets (formerly also called SKEW FACETS) on the crown, alternating with 8 similar adjacent facets (formerly called SKILL FACETS), and the 8 cross facets on the pavilion, alternating with 8 similar adjacent skill facets (now collectively called GIRDLE FACETS) were all usually considered together as a group of 32 cross facets, as they are all of identical shape and the only differences are their orientation to the stone and the direction and sequence in which they are ground. Also sometimes formerly called a 'break facet'. Cross facets of slightly different shapes and numbers are on some stones of different cut. *See* DUTCH ROSE CUT.

cross formée (formy). A type of CROSS having four arms of equal length, each arm being narrow at the centre and expanding in a concave, curved line toward the end, the ends being straight, unlike the indented ends of a MALTESE CROSS. Examples are on the CROWN JEWELS (BRITISH), e.g. the IMPERIAL STATE CROWN and ST EDWARD'S CROWN. Sometimes called 'cross pattée'.

Cross of Carlo de' Medici. *See* MEDICI, CARLO DE', CROSS OF.

cross pattée (paty). *See* CROSS FORMÉE.

cross rose cut. A style of cutting a diamond (or other transparent gemstone) that is a modification of the ROSE CUT. It has a flat base and no TABLE but 8 LOZENGE-shaped FACETS pointing upward and meeting at a point at the apex, these being abutted by 8 triangular facets to complete the upper portion of the stone (the CROWN), which is surrounded by 8 four-sided (isosceles-trapezoidal) facets whose lower sides form the GIRDLE.

cross stone. A type of stone that (1) is in the form of a cross, due to the twinning of the crystals (e.g. STAUROLITE), or (2) exhibits within the stone a cruciform pattern (e.g. CHIASTOLITE). Such stones were frequently worn as an AMULET.

crossbow fibula. A type of Roman FIBULA in a shape suggestive of a crossbow, having a high, arched BOW and two arms extending at right angles from one end of the bow. They were made during the 2nd and 3rd centuries, and in Britain in the late Roman period, 4th century AD.

cross. Pendant of gold mesh with enamelling and pearl drops. Signed: Carlo Giuliano. Courtesy of Christie's, New York.

cross cut
top view

cross rose cut
side view

crossbow fibula. Gold. Roman, 4th century. L. 8.2 cm. Schmuckmuseum, Pforzheim, Germany.

crossover ring. Finger ring with 2 circular cut diamonds. Courtesy of Christie's, New York.

crossover ring. A type of finger ring, the SHANK of which exceeds a full circle and is wrapped around the finger so that the two terminals overlap and lie alongside each other, each usually being set with a gemstone. Some rigid BRACELETS are similarly made.

crown. (1) A royal head-dress of sovereignty, worn by a monarch or consort. A crown, which developed from the FILLET, CIRCLET, and DIADEM, is usually circular (although some Anglo-Saxon crowns were square), has an open centre and is characterized in most cases by vertical ornaments (e.g. fleurs-de-lis) projecting upward from the rim and by two or four arches topped at the intersection by some symbolic ornament (e.g. a MONDE and cross). There are several types, depending upon the occasion for their use: (a) coronation crown, used only at the coronation; (b) state crown, worn at other state occasions; (c) personal crown, worn on lesser occasions; (d) wedding or nuptial crown, worn only at a wedding (but *see* BRIDAL CROWN); (e) VOTIVE CROWN; (f) reliquary crown, used as a reliquary on the head of a statue; and (g) FUNERARY CROWN. *See* CORONET; GUARRAZAR TREASURE; TIARA; IMPERIAL STATE CROWN; ST EDWARD'S CROWN; IRON CROWN; IMPERIAL CROWN; ST STEPHEN, CROWN OF; PAHLAVI CROWN; FARAH DIBA CROWN; and KIANI CROWN. For many examples of crowns, with their histories, legends, and photographs, *see* Lord Twining, *History of the Crown Jewels of Europe* (1960) and *European Regalia* (1967). (2) The upper part of a cut gemstone. (3) The part of a BRILLIANT above the GIRDLE. The crown usually protrudes above the SETTING. *See* BRILLIANT CUT.

Crown Jewels (British). The REGALIA of Great Britain, now displayed at the Jewel House (opened in 1967) of the Tower of London (where they have been kept since the reign of Charles II, 1660-85, except during World War II when removed to Windsor Castle), including the following principal objects: (1) ST EDWARD'S CROWN; (2) IMPERIAL STATE CROWN; (3) other crowns worn by the Royal Family, including (a) crown made for Queen Victoria, *c.* 1877; (b) Imperial Crown of India, made for the Delhi Durbar, 1911; (c) Queen Elizabeth the Queen Mother's Crown, made for the coronation in 1937 and including the KOH-I-NOOR DIAMOND; (d) Queen Mary of Modena Crown, called the Queen Consort's Crown; (4) ROYAL SCEPTRES; (5) ROYAL ORBS; (6) ARMILLAS; (7) JEWELLED STATE SWORD; and (8) ROYAL RINGS. *See* WALES'S, PRINCE OF, INVESTITURE CORONET. *See* Martin Holmes and H. D. W. Sitwell, *The English Regalia* (1972). The Crown Jewels are distinct from the jewelry owned personally by the Sovereign and members of the Royal Family. *See* Sheila Young, *The Queen's Jewellery* (1968).

Crown Jewels (Iran). The jewels of the Royal Collection of Iran, accumulated from the reign of Shah Abbas, 1587-1628, and partly recovered from Delhi by Nadir Shah in 1740, and added to by the Qajar Dynasty (*see* QAJAR JEWELRY). In 1938 the collection was placed by Reza Shah Pahlavi in the custody of the Bank Melli (National Bank of Iran), Tehran, and held by it, not as property of the Shah, but as collateral for national obligations and the currency; in 1960 custody was transferred to the Bank Markazi Iran (Central Bank of Iran) but the jewels were permitted to remain in the special vault (open to tourists) of the Bank Melli. The collection, often said to be the world's richest collection of jewels, includes, among a vast number of jewelled ornaments and unset (some uncut) gemstones, the Royal Regalia, among which are the PAHLAVI CROWN, the FARAH DIBA CROWN, the KIANI CROWN, the DARYA-I-NUR DIAMOND, the GIKA OF NADIR SHAH, the FARAH DIBA TIARA (with the NUR-UL-AIN DIAMOND), the Royal Gold Girdle (with a buckle set with an oval cabochon EMERALD weighing 175 carats), and a great number of other tiaras, ear-rings, bracelets, necklaces, finger rings, brooches (three made as birds, having a body of a BAROQUE PEARL and wings set with diamonds), etc. *See* IRANIAN DIAMONDS. *See* V. B. Meen and A. D. Tushingham, *Crown Jewels of Iran* (1968).

Crown of the Andes. A CROWN said to have been decorated with 453 EMERALDS, weighing *c.* 1,500 carats, that were confiscated from the Incas of Peru by the Spanish Conquistadors and said to have been dedicated by the Spaniards of Popayán in 1599. No definite facts are known as to its existence.

crown setting. A style of SETTING for securing a stone in a finger ring that is a variation of the GYPSY SETTING by having the metal between projecting short prongs pared down so as to create a crown-like form.

crucifix pendant. A type of pendant in the form of a crucifix. Examples have been made almost everywhere in Europe from the Middle Ages to the present time.

cruciform fibula. A type of FIBULA that is in the general form of a Latin cross, having wide, sectioned, and ornamented cross-arms and an arched BOW that extends toward the long foot. At the extremities of the cross-arms and at the top there are usually moulded knobs, and between the bow and the foot there is usually a rectangular plate or side lappets. On the back there is a catch-plate for a bilaterally coiled spring. Such pieces were usually made of cast bronze, sometimes gilded, but some were plated with silver; only rarely were they of gold or set with gemstones. The decoration was added after the piece was cast, so that the decoration varies on pieces of identical shape. Examples have been found from the Roman era, 4th century, and are known in ANGLO-SAXON JEWELRY, some having been found in regions of England, made from the 4th to the 11th centuries. They were worn as clasps on military or civil uniforms, and the type of metal and the style indicated rank. Some examples are heavily and excessively decorated; *see* FLORID CRUCIFORM FIBULA. An earlier type, from the 3rd century, often found in Germanic regions of the Roman Empire, was a precursor of the cruciform fibula and was of articulated form. The cruciform fibula has no relationship to the Christian cross, some having been found in pagan graves. Some examples, 10–18 cm long (rather than the more usual 7–8 cm), are called a 'long fibula'. *See* SMALL-LONG FIBULA.

cruciform pendant. A type of pendant made in the form of a cross, usually a Latin cross or a cross with four arms of equal length. The arms were decorated with engraved patterns or set with gemstones. A notable example is the CROSS OF CARLO DE' MEDICI. *See* CLARE RELIQUARY.

cruciform ring. A type of finger ring of which the decoration consists of five gemstones arranged in a cruciform pattern. Examples are known from painted portraits made by William Locke in 1614 showing such rings being worn and secured by a long cord or lace wound around the wrist.

crumb bead. A type of glass bead having two pieces of glass of different colours fixed to the surface. A 'flush crumb bead' has the pieces marvered flush into the surface. They were first made in the Aegean Islands, *c.* 1300 BC, and in Egypt several centuries later.

crystal. (1) A term sometimes applied to ROCK CRYSTAL. (2) A term sometimes applied to CRYSTAL GLASS. (3) A body formed by the solidification of certain elements or compounds and having a definite external form, bounded by natural plane surfaces symmetrically arranged, which is the external expression of a definite internal structure owing to atomic arrangement. Gems of greatest value are those cut from large transparent crystals, but some are from minerals composed of small crystals or without crystalline structure (*see* AMORPHOUS). Crystals are classified into seven systems according to their symmetry and also have characteristic forms (called 'crystal habit'), but the technical details of such systems and habits are beyond the scope of this book, which deals primarily with jewelry.

crystal glass. Colourless transparent GLASS that resembles ROCK CRYSTAL and is made with lead (hence often called 'lead glass'). The term has heretofore been used loosely for all fine glass, but today glass so called must contain at least 24% lead oxide (called 'half-lead') or 30% lead oxide (called 'full lead'). Such glass is the type most commonly used for high-quality glass beads and other articles of GLASS JEWELRY. *See* FLINT GLASS; LEAD GLASS.

crystal intaglio. *See* REVERSE CRYSTAL INTAGLIO.

crystal jewelry. Articles of jewelry made of ROCK CRYSTAL (natural quartz, as distinguished from lead glass sometimes called crystal), such as

crucifix pendant. Silver over wooden core, with decoration on both sides in niello. Probably Lower Rhenish, early 13th century. H. 8.8 cm. Kunstgewerbemuseum, Cologne.

cruciform fibulae. Gilt bronze. Anglo-Saxon. L. 6.4 cm. Museum of Archaeology, Cambridge University.

cuff bracelet. Gold with enamelling. Byzantine, 9th century. Archaeological Museum, Thessaloniki, Greece.

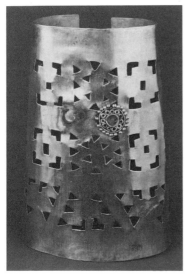

cuff bracelet. Gold cut-out pattern with 2 soldered rosettes (1 missing). Peru, Ica style, *c.* 1000-1470. H. 16 cm. Museum für Völkerkunde, West Berlin.

chains and girdles having crystal links cut in the form of spindles, acorns, and buttons, polished and faceted. Examples are known from Germany in the 16th century.

crystalline. Composed of CRYSTALS, as opposed to being AMORPHOUS.

cubic zirconia. A synthetic gemstone that is a simulant for a diamond. It has been produced since 1977 under the trade-name 'Djevalite' by Hrand Djevahirdjian, S.A., a Swiss firm, and a version has been made in the USSR called 'Phianitex'. Its colour ranges from white to light yellow and brown. Its refractive index and colour dispersion are fairly close to the diamond, but its HARDNESS is lower and its specific gravity much higher. Although very deceptive to the eye, it can be distinguished by a jeweller by several tests, e.g. observing comparative marks made by a special blue pencil or by the shape of a drop of water on its TABLE. It is sold in England under the trade-name 'Windsor Gem'.

cuff bracelet. A type of non-flexible bracelet made in the form of a wide cylindrical band tapering in one direction and having the appearance of a broad, slightly tapering cuff. Such bracelets were made, in BYZANTINE JEWELRY of the 9th century, of gold, decorated with two bands of adjacent squares separated by filigree work and enamelling to depict animal and abstract motifs. Another example, but in PENANNULAR form, was made by the Incas of the Ica culture in Peru, *c.* 1000-1470. Later examples more closely simulate a cuff, sometimes decorated so as to appear fastened with a row of buttons or with laces. Such bracelets have been made in France in the mid-18th century and also later in modern styles. The French term is *manchette*.

cuff-link. A device that is employed to join temporarily the two ends of a cuff around the wearer's wrist without overlapping the cuff ends, being inserted through two buttonholes. Such articles are made of gold, silver or other materials, in many ornamental styles, shapes and sizes; luxury examples are ornamented with gemstones, ENAMELLING, ENGRAVING, or relief decoration. They are made in several forms: (1) with a short chain or loose link connecting the head with the rear head or back-plate, being attached to each by a 'jump ring'; (2) with a back-plate of lentoid form that is joined by a fixed bar to the ornamented head; (3) with a bar fixed vertically to the head and attached to a swivel bar that slides through the buttonholes and is then twisted into a securing horizontal position; (4) with a chain that is coiled inside the head and that uncoils as the back-plate is passed through the buttonholes, to afford a variable space; (5) with two separate pieces, one having a small boss and the other a corresponding depression, so that they can be pressed together as a 'press-stud'. Some cuff-links have a decorative piece at each end that is too large to pass through a button hole; these 'double cuff-links' are joined by a detachable link with a spring-like fastener. Cuff-links are generally made in identical pairs, but some are of two different but harmonious designs. *See* DRESS SET; SLEEVE BUTTON; SLEEVE FASTENER.

culasse. The same as PAVILION.

culet. The small flat FACET at the base of a BRILLIANT, i.e. the lowest facet of the PAVILION, parallel with the TABLE. It is made to minimize splintering and is now often omitted, in which case the sharp point at the bottom is called a 'closed culet'. If larger than normal it is called an 'open culet'. The word is sometimes spelt 'culette' or 'collet'.

Cullinan Diamond. A famous diamond found on 20 January 1905 at the Premier Mine near Pretoria, South Transvaal, in South Africa. The rough stone weighed 3,106 carats (about $1\frac{1}{3}$ lb). It was sold to the Transvaal Government which presented it in 1907 to King Edward VII. He had it sent to Amsterdam to be cut by the firm of I. J. Asscher (now Asscher's Diamond Co., Ltd). It was cut in 1908 into 9 major stones, 96 small BRILLIANTS, and 9 carats of polished fragments, of which the 2 largest stones became CROWN JEWELS and the balance were given to Asscher as its fee. The total weight of the cut material was 1,063.40 carats, a yield of $34\frac{1}{4}\%$. The 9 major stones, named after Sir Thomas Cullinan, the discoverer of the mine in 1902 and the chairman of the company that then owned it, are as follows:

(I) A brilliant in PENDELOQUE form, 530.22 carats and having 74 facets, the world's largest cut diamond and called 'The Great Star of Africa'; it is now set in the head of a Royal Sceptre of the British REGALIA. (II) A brilliant CUSHION CUT stone, 317.40 carats and having 66 facets, the world's second largest cut diamond and called 'The Second Star of Africa'; it is now set in the British IMPERIAL STATE CROWN. (III) A pendeloque, 94.40 carats, set in Queen Mary's Crown, but owned by Elizabeth II and sometimes worn with IV in a pendant brooch. (IV) A square brilliant, 63.60 carats, set in the same crown but also owned by Elizabeth II and sometimes worn with III. (V) A heart-shaped stone, 18.80 carats, set in a brooch for Queen Mary. (VI) A marquise, 11.50 carats, bought by Edward VII and presented to Queen Alexandra; it is now mounted in a necklace. (VII) A marquise, 8.80 carats, set as a pendant on a diamond brooch worn by Elizabeth II. (VIII) An oblong stone, 6.80 carats, set as the centre stone of the brooch of which VII is the pendant. (IX) A pear-shaped stone, 4.39 carats, set in a finger ring formerly owned by Queen Mary and inherited by Elizabeth II.

The major stones (except I, II, and VI) were bought by the people of South Africa and presented in 1910 to Queen Mary, thus now belonging to the Royal Family. The other 96 brilliants were dispersed and the whereabouts of most are now unknown, except two, last reported as being owned by the family of General Louis Botha, first Prime Minister of the Union of South Africa, 1910-19. As the rough stone had only one cleavage face and a NAIF on only one side, it has been suggested that it may have been part of a larger crystal, but this has not been established nor any trace of the supposed other part found.

cultured pearl. A variety of pearl that is created by a mollusc in the same manner as a natural (wild) pearl except that the process is stimulated by the human insertion into the shell of a grain of sand, a bead, a piece of mantle tissue, or other irritant that becomes the nucleus of the pearl when encased in many layers of NACRE. The method was first attempted in China in the 13th century (inserting various objects into a fresh-water mussel), and again later in the 18th century in Sweden (see LINNEAN PEARL), but it was accomplished c. 1896 by Kokichi Mikimoto (1858-1954), who produced first a type of BLISTER PEARL (called a MABE PEARL) by inserting an irritant and later cutting out the nucleus of the pearl and cementing a nacreous covering over the opening. Later, c. 1915, he and others perfected the cultured spherical pearl, for which purpose native Japanese PEARL OYSTERS have since been specially cultivated; the method involved inserting into an incision in the mantle of the oyster a piece of living mantle tissue from another oyster that enclosed a mother-of-pearl bead (later the sliver of tissue was first inserted and then the bead) and covering the hole with nacreous material and returning the oyster to the sea, where it secretes nacre to enlarge the nucleus. Such cultured pearls were introduced into the London market in 1921, and the prices of cultured pearls soon greatly dropped, especially when methods of identification were developed. Recently a non-nucleated, tissue-graft, cultured pearl has been produced in Japan (see BIWA PEARL) and Australia. The smaller the nucleus of a cultured pearl in relation to the size of the final pearl, the better the quality. Many cultured pearls now come from the Far East. See IMITATION PEARL.

—— *identification.* Visual examination is seldom adequate, although some cultured pearls show a greenish tinge and certain markings on the surface. Tests of specific gravity and luminescence have been proved inconclusive. Instruments for testing are the lucidoscope, the pearl compass, and the pearl microscope (pearlometer), but the most efficient tests are by means of the endoscope or a modern X-ray test (the skiagram) or, for undrilled pearls, the lauégram; the technical details of the functioning of these are beyond the scope of this book.

—— *weighing.* The units of weight for a cultured pearl are the CARAT and the GRAIN; in Japan the momme is officially no longer sanctioned but is still in use.

cupelliform brooch. The same as a SAUCER BROOCH, being shaped like a shallow cupel or cup.

curb chain. A type of CHAIN in which the links are oval and twisted similarly, so that the chain will lie flat. There are many varieties of the basic curb chain composed of simple oval links, e.g. depending on the size

cuff-links. Gold with sunburst *guilloché* enamel and rose cut diamonds. Fabergé. Courtesy of Wartski, London.

and the closeness of the links, the 'close curb', 'medium curb', and 'open curb'. Occasionally the links are of graduated size, tapering slightly from the largest in the centre (called a 'graduated curb'). Often links of the curb chain type are combined with the elongated links of a FETTER CHAIN.

currency jewelry. Articles of jewelry, including probably certain TORCS and HAIR RINGS, used as special purpose currency rather than primarily for ornamental wear. Regarding the torcs, it has been said that they (alone or with others) were valued for the precise metal content, sometimes being embellished with gold rings to round up the weight, or trimmed down to a specific amount representing a multiple of weight used by the prehistoric Celts (*see* SNETTISHAM TORC). Some HAIR RINGS (sometimes called 'ring money'), of the Irish Late Bronze Age, *c.* 1200 BC–800 BC, may also have been so used, as well as certain so-called DRESS FASTENERS and SLEEVE FASTENERS of the 8th/7th centuries BC found in Ireland.

curvette. A type of CAMEO carved so that the background of the design is concave and the edge of the stone is at the same level as the highest part of the central design.

cushion cut. A style of CUTTING of a diamond or other gemstone with a square or rectangular shape but having rounded corners. Stones so shaped may be cut with FACETS in the usual styles. Also sometimes called 'buff-top cut' and, especially as regards SYNTHETIC STONES, 'antique cut'. *See* ORLOV DIAMOND.

cushion cut brilliant
top view

cut. The final form into which a rough gemstone is shaped, e.g. BRILLIANT CUT.

cut-corner triangle cut. A style of cutting a diamond (or other transparent stone) so that the TABLE is five-sided, with two adjacent long equal sides, two very short equal sides, and the latter two connected by a medium-length horizontal side, i.e. an isosceles-triangle with its bottom corners chamfered. When each of the five sides of a stone with such a table is bordered by a sloping trapezoidal FACET, or a descending row of such facets, the stone is STEP CUT.

cut-down setting. A style of INCRUSTATION for securing a gemstone in a finger ring in which the metal of the COLLET is raised into a band encircling the stone and strengthened at intervals by narrow vertical strips of metal. This was an early style used in the 18th century, superseding the earlier CLOSED SETTING, and requiring handwork in its making; it was in turn replaced by the open CLAW SETTING and MILLEGRAIN SETTING.

cut steel jewelry. Articles of jewelry made of steel cut as studs or 'heads', faceted and densely set to provide brilliance. They were made from the 1760s in England, mainly at Woodstock (*see* WOODSTOCK JEWELRY) and Birmingham (by MATTHEW BOULTON), and also possibly at Sheffield and Wolverhampton. Later such ware was made in France, Holland, and elsewhere in Europe, being popular until the late 19th century, and even later in Birmingham (especially that made by W. Hipkins & Co.). In France cut steel was made in the 18th century, especially after 1759 when wealthy people were asked to contribute their jewelry to the Treasury, and again in the Napoleonic era (when Napoleon gave to Marie Louise a cut steel PARURE). Cut steel was used as frames for CAMEOS and MEDALLIONS, as well as to decorate CHATELAINES, BROOCHES, BRACELETS, NECKLACES, TIARAS, BUCKLES for shoes and belts, handbag frames, quizzing glasses, SEALS, BUTTONS, and FINGER RINGS, also HAIR ORNAMENTS and COMBS. The studs were individually faceted (having up to 15 facets on some 18th-century examples but usually 5 on 19th-century pieces) and polished, then mounted (often in a PAVÉ SETTING) by riveting them, through small, closely arranged holes, to a base-plate (or several joined base-plates) so that minute rivets protruded from the back of the studs. The rivets aid in distinguishing cut steel studs from hand-set MARCASITE. No pieces are dated but approximate dates are usually determinable by the style. Some pieces were made of cut steel alone, but others combine plaques of enamel or medallions of Wedgwood JASPER. The decline of such ware started with the mass production of ribbons of cut steel in which the studs were stamped instead of being hand-made individually, and accelerated after the austerity of the post-Napoleonic period ended with the revival of use of more luxurious jewelry. An important collection of cut steel jewelry, assembled by Henri le Secq des Tournelles, and including pieces sold by the Court Jeweller Granchez in Paris, is now in the ironware collection in the former Church of St Laurent in Rouen, France. Sometimes called 'faceted steel'. *See* Anne Clifford, *Cut-Steel and Berlin Iron Jewellery* (1971).

cutting. The process and art of shaping a PRECIOUS STONE or other gemstone by severing part of it from its original form (after BRUTING) so as to enhance its brilliancy, beauty, and value. The final shapes are usually symmetrical, either in CABOCHON form or with many FACETS. Before being cut, some large stones are required to be split into smaller pieces (CLEAVING or SAWING) so as to produce a portion free of FLAWS and of such form that a desirable shape can be cut. The principal centres for cutting diamonds are Amsterdam, Antwerp, New York City, Tel Aviv, and Smolensk, and that for cutting many other gemstones is Idar-Oberstein, near Bingen, West Germany. The cutting of diamonds is said to have been started by LUDWIG VAN BERGHEM, of Bruges, in 1475. If the cutting is done imperfectly so as to result in a lack of symmetry (as in some cutting done in the East and called 'Indian cut'), it detracts from the brilliance and value of the stone. *See* DIAMOND CUTTING.

cuttlefish casting. The process of CASTING a metal article by using a mould of cuttlefish bone. The bone is cut in half lengthwise and the faces rubbed flat, then the model is placed between the two sections which are pressed firmly together so that an impression (mould) of the model is made in the soft bone. A small groove is cut in the mould so that molten metal can be poured in to make the casting; the two sections are then joined to complete the mould, and molten metal is poured in.

Cuxton Brooch. A silver DISC BROOCH with openwork decoration and bearing the inscription + AELFGIVVMEAH, believed to refer to Emma (sister of the Duke of Normandy), the first wife of Ethelred the Unready, 978–1016, and second wife of King Canute, 1016–35. It is Anglo-Saxon, 10th century, and was found at Cuxton, Kent.

cylinder seal. A type of SEAL of cylindrical form, used by rolling it on damp clay to impart a wide impression. Examples from southern Mesopotamia, from the 4th millennium BC, were made of soft stone, engraved originally with designs of animals, humans or scenes, together with an inscription identifying the owner, but later with cuneiform characters. They were worn suspended by a thong that passed through a pierced hole, but sometimes they were attached to a large TOGGLE. Later hard stones were used, e.g. CORNELIAN, QUARTZ, ROCK CRYSTAL, HEMATITE or marble. They were used *c.* 1400 BC in Egypt, but were supplanted there by the SCARAB RING. An existing example, at the British Museum, bears the seal of Darius I, King of the Persians, *c.* 500 BC.

cylindrical amulet case. A type of AMULET CASE in the form of a vertical metal cylinder with both ends everted into a funnel shape, the upper end having attached to it a small horizontal tube for a suspension cord. Such metal cases were made in Egypt in the Middle Kingdom, *c.* 2035 BC–*c.* 1668 BC, and later into the New Kingdom from *c.* 1552 BC. Other cylindrical pieces of similar shape (but not hollow, and so probably amulets rather than cases) were made of stone beads with similar metal funnel-shaped ends; these were from the Middle Kingdom, and have also been found in female burials but with no evidence of having been worn.

cymophane. A variety of CHRYSOBERYL that is opalescent and possesses superior CHATOYANCY when cut EN CABOCHON. It resembles CAT'S-EYE QUARTZ, but has greater HARDNESS, higher specific gravity and a sharper 'eye'. It is preferably called 'chrysoberyl cat's-eye'.

Cymric. The trade-name adopted in 1899 by Liberty & Co., London, for jewelry and silver articles sold by it which were designed by British designers and made by English firms, as distinguished from its imported merchandise. Some of the pieces were designed by leaders of the Arts and Crafts Movement exclusively for Liberty & Co., and many pieces were in ART NOUVEAU style, but a large number were plagiarized by competitors.

Cuxton Brooch. Silver disc brooch with openwork motif. Anglo-Saxon, 10th century. British Museum, London.

Cypriote jewelry. Gold-plated bronze spiral ear-ring with griffin-head. Cyprus, 5th century BC. W. 2.9 cm. British Museum, London.

The pieces were made mainly by Wm. Hutton & Sons, Sheffield, and W. H. Hasler & Co., Birmingham, but were not marked to show the names of the designers or makers, merely the trade-name to promote the store.

cyprine. A variety of IDOCRASE that is pale ,sky-blue or greenish-blue, owing to the presence of copper. Its name is derived from Latin *cyprius* (relating to copper), Cyprus being the ancient source of copper.

Cypriote jewelry. Articles of jewelry produced on the island of Cyprus, from *c.* 2000 BC onwards, the output being continuous and plentiful until Byzantine times. Examples have been excavated, *c.* 1896-7, in Cyprus in tombs at Enkomi (*see* ENKOMI PENDANT) and at Amathus. Before World War I some silver jewelry in Byzantine style, *c.* AD 600, was found in two find-spots at Lambousa, Cyprus, and other articles of Cypriote Byzantine jewelry have been found at Kyrenia.

cyst pearl. A type of natural pearl that is formed when the foreign body that penetrates the shell of an oyster is not a grain of sand or other inanimate object but a living parasite. The parasite does not permit itself to be cemented to the inside of the shell (which would produce a BLISTER PEARL), but is trapped in a depression of the mantle which then closes and entirely surrounds it within a sac. The mantle in the sac then secretes NACRE to surround the parasite in a series of concentric layers. Such pearls are usually spherical, but if the sac is interfered with or is too near the edge of the mantle, or if the nucleus is of irregular shape, the pearl is irregularly shaped. A pearl so formed is also called a MANTLE PEARL. *See* HEM PEARL; LIGAMENT PEARL; MUSCLE PEARL.

D

Danny Jewel. Enamelled gold ship pendant with narwhal ivory hull. English, *c.* 1560. W. 6 cm. Victoria & Albert Museum, London.

Dali jewelry. Articles of jewelry designed, in watercolour sketches, between 1953 and 1969 by Salvador Dali (1904-   ), the Spanish surrealist painter. The largest collection of such jewelry, including pieces for ordinary wear but also some large sculptural pieces with moving parts operated by a tiny electric motor, has been owned by the Owen Cheatham Foundation, New York City; 37 of these pieces were sold in January 1981 to a group associated with the Terrot Moore Museum, at Cadaques, Spain, which is reported to plan a world-wide exhibition tour.

danburite. A variety of gemstone that resembles TOPAZ and yellow QUARTZ. It is transparent and colourless or with shades of yellow or brown. It was named after Danbury, Connecticut, where it was first found. Some colourless and pink crystals have been found in Mexico.

Danny Jewel. A SHIP PENDANT in simplified form, made *c.* 1560 of a carved section of the tusk of a narwhal whale (*see* NARWHAL IVORY), mounted in gold decorated with arabesque scrolls on a black enamel ground. Suspensory chains are attached to a central enamelled rosette and the two lion's-head gold masks at the ends. The back is decorated with blue enamelling. The jewel has been owned by the Campion family of Danny, Sussex, England, and hence it is sometimes called the 'Campion Jewel'.

Darien pectoral. A type of gold PECTORAL of PRE-COLUMBIAN JEWELRY in the form of an anthropomorphic figure having spiral-ornamented upright wings beside the face, broad straight legs, flat feet, a head-dress surmounted by two hallucinogenic mushrooms (or bell-shaped objects, suggesting the humorous name sometimes applied, 'telephone gods') and usually a pair of stick-like batons or pipes held to the mouth. The forms vary considerably, some being naturalistic, others very stylized; some of the figures wear a mask, some have a head like that of an alligator or jaguar, and some have over the breast a row of cut-out birds. Although the pieces have been found mainly in the Sinú region of Colombia, bordering the Darien Isthmus (*see* SINÚ JEWELRY), they have been found in many other regions of Colombia, and exported examples or local copies are known from Panama, Costa Rica, and Yucatán, Mexico. The pieces (sometimes called 'bat gods') were made of cast gold or TUMBAGA, the height varying from 5 to 25 cm.

Darien pectoral. Cast tumbaga figure with two sticks. H. 7.2 cm. Museo del Oro, Bogotá.

Darnley Jewel. A heart-shaped gold LOCKET (also called the Lennox Jewel) richly decorated with gemstones and many enamelled emblematic figures and inscriptions. It was made in England for Lady Margaret Douglas, Countess of Lennox and mother of Henry Stuart, Lord Darnley (1545–67; second husband of Mary, Queen of Scots), in memory of her murdered husband, the Earl of Lennox (1516–71), and given by her to her grandson, later James I. Once owned by Horace Walpole, it was sold at Strawberry Hill on 11 May 1842 and bought on behalf of Queen Victoria, and is now in the Royal Collection at Windsor Castle. On the front the central feature is a CABOCHON sapphire set within a winged heart (the Douglas crest), surrounded by enamelled figures of Faith, Hope, Victory, and Truth, and surmounted by a crown set with two rubies and an emerald; both the cabochon and the crown are hinged and open to reveal symbolic enamelled motifs and mottoes, and around the edge is another inscribed legend. On the reverse are enamelled symbolic emblems (a phoenix in flames, a pelican in-her-piety, a sun in glory, a crescent moon, a crowned salamander in flames, and a reclining male), all surrounded by another legend. The locket opens, but the presumed miniature of Lennox is missing; its interior has further enamelled figures and legends. The complex symbols and inscriptions have been said to refer to relationships in the lives of Margaret Douglas and Lennox and their ambition for her grandson (the son of Darnley and Mary, Queen of Scots) to become James I of England, as he did in 1603. *See* Victoria & Albert Museum catalogue, *Princely Magnificence* (1980), pp. 57–8.

Darnley Ring. The BETROTHAL RING that was given by Mary, Queen of Scots, upon her engagement in 1565 to her cousin and second husband, Henry Stuart, Lord Darnley (1545–67). It is of gold, having on the circular BEZEL the conjoined monogram 'HM' tied with two lover's knots and on the interior of the SHANK the name 'Henri L Darnley 1565' below a crowned shield with a lion rampant. It is said to have been found at Fotheringay Castle, Northamptonshire, the place of Mary's execution, and was exhibited in 1849. Silver copies stamped from sheet metal were made before 1940 and sold in England and the United States. *See* MARY, QUEEN OF SCOTS, SIGNET RING.

Darnley Ring. Gold with engraved monogram. Victoria & Albert Museum, London.

Darya-i-Nur (Dacca) Diamond. A diamond known from a steel engraving of it when shown by the East India Company at the Great Exhibition, London, in 1851, being almost square cut and (by comparison with the KOH-I-NOOR DIAMOND, shown alongside it) estimated to weigh about 150 old carats. It was reported to have been sold later to the Nawab of Dacca (now in Bangladesh), and it is possibly the stone he offered for sale in 1955 and 1959, but its whereabouts is now unknown. *See* DARYA-I-NUR (IRAN) DIAMOND.

Darya-i-Nur (Iran) Diamond (Persian for 'Sea of Light' Diamond). The world's largest pink diamond, now in the CROWN JEWELS (IRAN) at Tehran. It is a rectangular STEP CUT table stone, pale pink, measuring 3.75 by 2.5 cm, and weighing 182 carats. It is engraved with an inscription in Persian, 'The Sultan, Sahib Qiran, Fath Ali Shah, Qajar, 1250' (the Hegira date for AD 1834, the year of Fath Ali's death). It is now mounted in a gold, rectangular frame, surmounted by a jewelled crown between two jewelled lions (called 'The Lion and the Sun'), all set with 457 diamonds and 4 rubies. In 1967 it was established by experts to be a major part of the GREAT TABLE DIAMOND (but having been damaged before 1834 and recut), the other part of which is now believed to be the NUR-UL-AIN DIAMOND. The Darya-i-Nur is said to have been in the possession of Sultan Baber (1480–1530), the first Mughal Emperor of India, from whom it (and the KOH-I-NOOR DIAMOND) descended to Mohammed Shah, and from whom they and the TAJ-I-MAH DIAMOND, after his defeat at Delhi in 1739, were taken to Persia by Nadir Shah. After the latter's assassination it passed through several owners until it reached Agha Mohammed Khan, the founder of the Qajar Dynasty, and his nephew Fath Ali Shah

Darnley (Lennox) Jewel (front and back). Heart-shaped gold pendant with 2 lockets. English, 16th century. L. 6.5 cm. At Windsor Castle. Reproduced by gracious permission of Her Majesty the Queen

decade ring. Silver. English. Merseyside County Museum, Liverpool.

(1797–1834), the predecessors of the Pahlavi Dynasty. It was seen set, together with the Taj-i-Mah, in two arm-bands worn in 1791 and seen again in the arm-bands in 1827. It was worn in a military cap by Mohammed Reza Shah Pahlavi at his coronation in 1967 and also set in a brooch and an AIGRETTE. *See* DARYA-I-NUR (DACCA) DIAMOND.

decade. Each group of ten small beads (called AVES) on a ROSARY, preceded by a large bead called a PATERNOSTER and usually followed by one called a GLORIA. *See* DECADE RING.

decade ring. A type of finger ring (sometimes called a 'rosary ring') used in counting prayers, as with a ROSARY. Such rings have around the SHANK ten projecting knobs or ridges, to correspond to the ten AVES of the DECADE on a rosary, with the BEZEL being the PATERNOSTER. Some examples have more than ten knobs (one for a Paternoster, one for a Credo), being from the 15th century when the method of counting prayers was not standardized. The bezel of the 15th century was engraved with a depiction of a saint, but from Tudor times the decoration was usually the engraved sacred monogram 'I H S', accompanied by a cross and three nails, but sometimes a crucifix. Such rings have been used from the 15th century, but mainly in the 17th and 18th centuries (particularly during the periods of Catholic persecution, being easier to conceal than a rosary), and they are still used in Spain.

Deepdene Diamond. A golden-yellow, cushion-shaped diamond, weighing 104.52 carats, which may have been a stone involved in a dispute among gemmological experts as to whether its colour had been artificially altered. It was first known as owned by Cary Bok, of Philadelphia, and named after his estate, and for many years had been on loan to the Academy of Natural Science of Philadelphia. In 1954 it was acquired by HARRY WINSTON and resold to an unidentified American. In May 1971 a diamond catalogued as the 'Deepdene' was offered for auction, by Christie's at Geneva, on behalf of a German owner, and was described as of the same colour and approximate weight as the Deepdene. Although German experts had certified it for colour, Dr E. Gübelin of Geneva warned that it had been artificially coloured. The sale was held and the diamond was bought for £190,000 by VAN CLEEF & ARPELS. Later, London experts confirmed Dr Gübelin's opinion and the sale was annulled. It has not been established whether the auctioned stone was the true Deepdene with its colour artificially improved or was a different stone artificially coloured, nor is the present ownership known.

deity amulet. A type of AMULET in the form of a deity, made in Egypt from the XXth Dynasty (*c.* 1185 BC-1070 BC) to the Ptolemaic period (3rd century BC). Some were made of gold, some of gold foil over a light core. Such amulets were small, *c.* 2.4 to 3.1 cm high.

Delau(l)ne, Étienne (Stephanus) (1518?–83?). A French designer of jewelry who did ornamental engraving in which his success was abetted by his knowledge of the needs of the goldsmith and the enameller. Born at Orléans, he moved to Paris and worked under BENVENUTO CELLINI during the latter's stay there. He became principal medallist to Henry II in 1552 and from 1556 furnished designs for the King's armour; after the death of Henry in 1559 he fled from Paris as a Huguenot refugee and moved to Strasbourg in 1572 where he thereafter did most of his work. He was in Augsburg 1574–8, where his designs influenced local goldsmiths and where he may have had a workshop. He published in Augsburg in 1578 and in Strasbourg in 1580 designs for jewelry, often for FIGURAL JEWELRY. Some of his early designs are thought to have been executed in a French royal workshop; no piece is known to have been made by him. *See* Yvonne Hackenbroch, 'Jewels and Designs after Étienne Delaune', in *Connoisseur*, May 1966, p. 83.

De Long Star Ruby. A STAR RUBY, weighing 100.32 carats, and measuring 3.8 by 2.5 cm, that was discovered in Burma in the mid-1930s. It was donated in 1938 by Mrs George Bowen de Long to the American Museum of Natural History, New York City, from which it was stolen; it was later recovered.

demantoid. A sub-variety of ANDRADITE and the most valuable of the GARNETS. The colour ranges from dark green (hence sometimes miscalled

'Uralian emerald') to yellowish-green (hence sometimes miscalled 'olivine'). It has many similarities with the diamond ('demant'), hence its name (meaning 'diamond-like'), but it has low HARDNESS, so that it is not suitable for hard wear as jewelry. The stones have INCLUSIONS of fine asbestos fibres (byssolite) that are sometimes called PONYTAILS.

dendrite. A feature in certain gemstones consisting of a branching tree-like, bushy or feather-like pattern that resembles fern or moss. It is found in the MOSS AGATE, MOSS OPAL, FEATHER AGATE, and CLOUDY AGATE. The name, also applied to a stone so marked, is from Greek *dendron* (tree).

dentalium shell. The shell of a dentalium (a genus of the tooth shell, a mollusc with a thin, pointed shell). Such dentalia shells were used as beads for necklaces as long ago as 10,000 BC-8000 BC, the Natufian Period in Israel, where plentiful examples have been found in Mount Carmel caves.

dentelle. The row of 18 triangular FACETS on a ROSE DIAMOND that extend down from the CROWN (the STAR FACETS) to meet the GIRDLE. Of the 18 facets, 6 have their base abutting the bases of the star facets, and the other 12 have their bases along the girdle.

depletion gilding. A process that was used on some articles of TUMBAGA (an ALLOY of gold and copper) to produce a gold surface. It involved applying an acid substance that brought the copper to the surface as a black scale which was then removed by repeated hammering and heating or by applying a PICKLE solution that dissolved the copper oxide. By repeating the process the surface of the article was left with a thin layer of pure gold. The process differs from electric plating in that no additional metal was added and no gold of the alloy was lost, as the gold content remained on the surface. A purpose, in addition to the decorative effect, may have been to protect against discolourization from oxidation of the copper on the surface. By sometimes treating only a part of the surface in such manner, a design could be produced in contrasting colours of pure gold and copper alloy. After such a process, the article was cleaned and burnished, not only to impart a shiny finish but also to consolidate the superficial layer of gold. The process was used by the Indians of Colombia, Peru, and Central America in making PRE-COLUMBIAN JEWELRY. A similar process has been used to produce a gold surface on pieces made of ELECTRUM. A similar result is achieved if an article of gold alloy is buried for a long period; the soil dissolves out the alloying metals from the surface, leaving pure gold, and if the object had been soldered the solder would be altered to pure gold and so would not be discernible. The basic process is also called 'surface enrichment' or, on the Continent, *'mise en couleur'*. See DIFFERENTIAL PICKLING; ENRICHED SURFACE; DEPLETION SILVERING.

depletion silvering. A process that was used on some articles made of an ALLOY of silver and copper to produce a silver surface. It involved repeatedly cold hammering and then annealing the sheet metal until the surface became more silvery after each operation, finally producing a surface appearance of pure silver. The process was used by the Colombian Indians before 1000 BC. See DEPLETION GILDING.

designer. A person who, although occasionally a maker of jewelry, is best known for published books of jewelry designs made for execution by others. Included among these are THEODORE DE BRY; HANS COLLAERT THE ELDER; ÉTIENNE DELAUNE; JACQUES ANDROUET DUCERCEAU; JEAN DUVET; ERASMUS HORNICK; GILLES LÉGARÉ; ARNOLD LULLS; DANIEL MIGNOT; CORVINIANUS SAUR; VIRGIL SOLIS; PIERRE WOEIRIOT. These are to be distinguished from the ARTIST-DESIGNERS and the DESIGNER-MAKERS.

designer-maker. A person who uses the combined skills of a designer and of a maker of jewelry by executing personally designed pieces, as contrasted with a DESIGNER or an ARTIST-DESIGNER who creates designs to be executed by others. Among the most renowned from early periods are BENVENUTO CELLINI and AMBROGIO FOPPA CARADOSSO, from the 19th century RENÉ LALIQUE, and from the 20th century JEAN SCHLUMBERGER. After the end of the period of ART NOUVEAU style, their role was largely taken over by designers in the regular employ of the large jewelry firms and who participated in the execution of the pieces. Since *c.* 1920 there have been a host of designer-makers of CONTEMPORARY JEWELRY,

deity amulets. H. 4.5 cm. Tomb of Tutankhamun. Photograph by Egyptian Expedition, Metropolitan Museum of Art, New York.

dentalium shell. Necklace of dentalia and bone found at el-Wad, Israel, from Natufian period, 10,000 BC–8000 BC. Israel Department of Antiquities and Museums, Jerusalem.

including in England JOHN DONALD, GERDA FLÖCKINGER, ANDREW GRIMA, SUSANNA HERON, LOUIS OSMAN, WENDY RAMSHAW, and DAVID THOMAS. Among the leading contemporary American designer-makers are MARY LEE HU, STANLEY LECHTZIN, and MARY ANN SCHERR.

Devizes Pendant. A gold PENDANT of square shape with three lobes across the top and one on each side and a suspensory ring. Both sides were originally enamelled, with also on the front an engraved standing figure of an archbishop and on the reverse an engraved figure of St John the Baptist with the AGNUS DEI. On each side are eight engraved tears, and along the bottom six engraved tears. A black enamelled legend, 'A mon derreyne', signifies the last moment of existence and an invocation for help. The pendant may have been a RELIQUARY or an Agnus Dei jewel. It is attributed probably to English origin of the 15th century, and was found near Devizes, Wiltshire, England, before 1848.

Devizes Pendant. Gold pendant with engraved figures and enamelled inscription. English (?), 15th century. W. 3.3 cm. British Museum, London.

Devonshire Chatelaine. An unusual type of CHATELAINE, gold and silver, with 2 belt hooks connected by a chain; from one hook hang chains to support 2 seals, 1 watch key, and 2 diamond tassels, and from the other hook hangs an open-face WATCH, the gold case of which is bordered with diamonds. On the ornament on the chatelaine is the unidentified monogram G H C and on the back of the watch an unidentified cipher. The piece is from the early 19th century and is now in the DEVONSHIRE COLLECTION.

Devonshire Collection. A renowned art collection, including articles of jewelry, kept at Chatsworth, Derbyshire, England, the country seat of the Dukes of Devonshire. In addition to the famous DEVONSHIRE PARURE, the collection includes the DEVONSHIRE EMERALD, the DEVONSHIRE OPAL, the DEVONSHIRE CHATELAINE, and the DEVONSHIRE ROSARY, and mainly the collection of ENGRAVED GEMSTONES assembled by the 2nd (1672–1729) and 6th (1790–1858) Dukes of Devonshire, both Classical and later examples, which when catalogued in 1900 numbered 560 pieces and which supplied many of the stones set in the Devonshire Parure. *See* Royal Academy Exhibition Catalogue, *Treasures from Chatsworth (The Devonshire Inheritance)* (London 1979).

Devonshire Chatelaine. Gold and silver, set with diamonds, and with diamond-set watch. Early 19th century. Devonshire Collection, Chatsworth, England.

Devonshire Emerald. A natural crystal of uncut, rich-green EMERALD, in the characteristic form of a hexagonal prism terminated by a flat, basal face and rough on the other end, having many flaws. A crack crosses a corner at the top (perhaps from a blow) and a small piece of MATRIX adheres to the base. It measures 6.5 by 5.5 by 5 cm, and weighs 1383.95 carats. It is from the Muzo mines, in Colombia, South America, and was given in 1831 by Dom Pedro I, abdicated Emperor of Brazil, 1822–31, to the 6th Duke of Devonshire. The emerald was shown in the Great Exhibition of 1851 and elsewhere, and is now in the DEVONSHIRE COLLECTION. In 1831, it was in the possession of Rundell & Bridge, Crown Jewellers, who held it for Dom Pedro after he brought it from Brazil; it is sometimes called the Dom Pedro Emerald.

Devonshire Opal. A BLACK OPAL from Lightning Ridge, in New South Wales; it has spangled coloration, is oval, and is of shallow convex shape. It weighs *c.* 100 carats, measures 2.5 cm by 5 cm, and is now in the DEVONSHIRE COLLECTION.

Devonshire Parure. A PARURE made in 1856 for the 6th Duke of Devonshire (1790–1858), to be worn by Countess Granville (wife of Lord Granville, the nephew of the Duke, who had been designated to represent Queen Victoria as the head of the British mission to Moscow) at the coronation that year of Tsar Alexander II. The parure, made in Renaissance style by C. F. Hancock (*see* HANCOCKS), consists of seven pieces, all made of openwork gold enriched with polychrome enamelling and set with 88 ancient and Renaissance CAMEOS and INTAGLIOS depicting mainly mythological characters and some Roman personages, the pieces being a CORONET, DIADEM, BANDEAU, COMB (no two of these pieces to be worn simultaneously), STOMACHER, NECKLACE, and BRACELET. The engraved gemstones had been acquired by the 2nd (1672–1729) and 6th Dukes of Devonshire. The parure was thereafter entailed as an heirloom on the Duchesses of Devonshire and is now in the DEVONSHIRE COLLECTION. *See* Diana Scarisbrick, 'Classic Gems in an English Masterpiece', in *Country Life*, 7 June 1979, p. 1796. *[Plate III]*

Devonshire Rosary. A short decade ROSARY made of carved BOXWOOD. The ten AVE beads are each divided into five roundels carved with figures of ten of the Apostles, together with sentences of the Creed, Prophets and Sibyls with relevant texts, and scenes from the Old and New Testaments. The PATERNOSTER is carved with three rows of eight roundels each, having further scenes and the two remaining Apostles, and with the name and royal arms of Henry VIII; it is hinged and has two scenes carved inside (as in a NUT). The beads hang from a cross carved on one side with a crucifix and the four Evangelists and on the other side four Doctors of the Church; it hangs from a finger ring bearing the Garter motto and a Latin inscription. The rosary is Flemish (?), *c.* 1509–26, and the designs have been attributed to HANS HOLBEIN THE YOUNGER. It was made probably for Henry VIII before his break with Rome in 1533, and later was owned by a Jesuit, Père de La Chaise (1624–1709), confessor to Louis XIV, and then by the Paris house of his Order, and in the 18th century by another Jesuit, Père Gabriel Brotier (1723–89). It was bought in the early 19th century in Paris by the 6th Duke of Devonshire, and is now in the DEVONSHIRE COLLECTION.

devotional jewelry. Various articles of jewelry associated by use and decoration with the Christian religion, although some also had decoration of a secular nature or were used for reasons of superstition or supposed magical powers. The earliest types were the SIGNET RINGS decorated with various Christian symbols or inscriptions, usually made of iron or bronze but sometimes of gold. Another early example was the RELIQUARY in the form of a pendant or a finger ring; these were worn especially in the 13th to 15th centuries. Other types of devotional jewelry of the period were the DEVOTIONAL RING, and AGNUS DEI pendant, and the pendants decorated with relief figures of saints. *See* CHI-RHO MONOGRAM; DECADE RING; DIPTYCH; ICHTHUS; IHS PENDANT; PECTORAL CROSS; PILGRIM BADGE; ROSARY; TAU CROSS.

devotional ring. A type of finger ring having a broad hoop and enamelled with a sacred monogram (*see* CHI-RHO MONOGRAM) or holy names, e.g. names of Jesus and Mary or of the THREE KINGS (MAGI) or Christian inscriptions. Such rings are mainly from the 15th century. *See* COVENTRY RING; DECADE RING; ICONOGRAPHIC RING.

diadem. An ornamented band worn around the brow of a man or woman, sometimes as a badge of sovereignty. Such pieces were made from ancient times of metal, often gold, in the form of a wreath or sometimes decorated with gemstones, pearls, and other ornaments. They were usually held in place by a long HAIR PIN. Many worn by women had attached long heavy pendent ornaments extending down over the ears and to the shoulders, and sometimes also rings or tassels suspended over the forehead and temples. Diadems, from simple forms to those lavishly decorated, were worn by the Egyptian pharaohs and their wives; *see* TUTANKHAMUN DIADEM. Greek examples varied from simple gold or silver bands to those decorated with REPOUSSÉ or STAMPED rosettes or other motifs (including the HERACLES KNOT), and later with FILIGREE work and GRANULATED GOLD. Roman diadems developed from wreaths of leaves to head-dresses anticipating the form of a CROWN. In western Europe during the Middle Ages the form was that of a CHAPLET and later of a band of

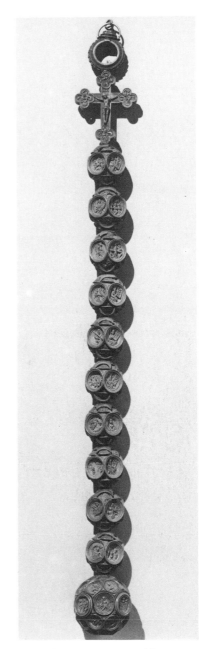

Devonshire Rosary. Carved boxwood decade rosary. Flemish (?), *c.* 1509–26. L. 58 cm. Devonshire Collection, Chatsworth, England.

diadem. Gold with enamelling and flowers set with gemstones and glass. 3rd century BC. Museo Nazionale, Taranto, Italy.

hinged plaques with enamelled and jewelled decoration. In later centuries in France and England the form approached the semi-circular and was profusely ornamented with gemstones. More recently examples were made in ART NOUVEAU style. The wearing of a diadem has not been confined to royalty or the nobility; they have also been worn by ladies of wealth or fashion on important social occasions. *See* TIARA.

—— , *Calima*. A type of head-dress, called a 'diadem', in the form of a high (*c*. 28-35 cm), flat, cut-out ornament of hammered sheet gold with decoration of an anthropomorphic face and various motifs in REPOUSSÉ work. They are chased, often have nose and ear ornaments made separately and stapled to the central face, and also often have pendent cylindrical ornaments. *See* CALIMA JEWELRY.

Diagem. A trade-name for STRONTIUM TITANATE.

diamanté (French). A colourless PASTE used for decorating inexpensive COSTUME JEWELRY or for attaching to dress material as decoration (being sold in strips ready for attaching).

Diamonair. A trade-name for a colourless SYNTHETIC 'GARNET' (YTTRIUM-ALUMINIUM-GARNET), or 'YAG', that simulates a diamond.

diamond. A PRECIOUS STONE that is pure native crystallized carbon, highly valued, especially when free from FLAWS and cut into various forms with differently shaped FACETS of variable numbers and positions (*see* DIAMOND CUTTING), and consequently showing great BRILLIANCE and prismatic colours (*see* FIRE). It is the hardest substance known, being rated 10 on the MOHS' SCALE (although hardness varies with the direction in the crystal and with the geographic source of the stone); hence it can be cut or faceted only with another diamond or diamond powder. Nevertheless, diamonds are BRITTLE. The stone is readily subject to CLEAVAGE, as was known to Indian lapidaries and rediscovered by W. H. Wollaston. It has a very high refractive index and strong colour dispersion. It is sometimes colourless or nearly so; but some diamonds have various colours in pastel shades (*see* DIAMOND COLOURS). Many diamonds fluoresce under ultraviolet rays in a range of colours. Clear and flawless diamonds are of the 'first water' (*see* WATER). The largest known faceted diamond is the CULLINAN DIAMOND (530.20 carats); the smallest weighs 0.0008 carats and has 58 facets. As for large rough diamonds, a list made in 1970 shows 24 of over 500 carats and 24 between 400 and 500 carats. The value of a diamond depends on its size (increasing rapidly when over 4 carats, but less so for very large stones), and also on the colour, freedom from flaws (*see* CLEAN), and quality of the cutting (*see* MAKE). The principal source was originally India and then Brazil (from 1728), but now it is South Africa and other countries in Africa, as well as Siberia and Venezuela. The largest producer of gem quality diamonds is De Beers Consolidated Mines, Ltd (founded in 1888 by Cecil Rhodes), which exercises control of the western world's supply and distribution, thus maintaining control of prices. SYNTHETIC DIAMONDS have been produced in very minute crystals for industrial purposes, and since 1970 some of gemstone size. Certain other SYNTHETIC GEMSTONES imitate the diamond, e.g. the white SYNTHETIC RUTILE, white SYNTHETIC SPINEL, and white SYNTHETIC SAPPHIRE. PASTE and STRASS have also been made into stones as cheap substitutes for a diamond. ROCK CRYSTAL (QUARTZ) has been given local misnomers as a diamond, e.g. ALASKA DIAMOND, BRISTOL DIAMOND, BUXTON DIAMOND, CORNISH DIAMOND, etc. ZIRCON altered by HEAT TREATMENT simulates a diamond. All of these imitations are distinguishable by their degrees of hardness and brilliance and by their refractive indices. Another deception is the diamond DOUBLET with a diamond slice cemented as a CROWN on another colourless stone. Certain types of diamonds are used exclusively for industrial purposes, e.g. the ballas, carbonado (also called 'black diamond' or 'carbon diamond'), and bo(a)art; these are used in drilling and cutting tools and as abrasives. *See* TREATED DIAMOND. *See* Eric Bruton, *Diamonds* (2nd ed., 1978).

—— *famous diamonds*. Among the most famous or the largest diamonds are the: AKBAR SHAH; ARCOT; BRIOLETTE OF INDIA; CARTIER (Taylor-Burton); COLENSO; CULLINAN; DARYA-I-NUR (DACCA and IRAN); DRESDEN DIAMONDS; EARTH STAR; ENGLISH DRESDEN; EUGÉNIE; EUGÉNIE BLUE; EUREKA; EXCELSIOR; FLAMING STAR; FLORENTINE (Austrian Yellow; Tuscany); GREAT MOGUL; GREAT TABLE; HOPE; IDOL'S EYE; IMPERIAL

diadem (Calima). Gold sheet embossed and chased. Nose and ear ornaments stapled. H. 31 cm. Museo del Oro, Bogotá.

(Victoria; Great White); IRANIAN DIAMONDS; JAHANGIR; JONKER; JUBILEE (Reitz); KOH-I-NOOR; LESOTHO DIAMONDS; LIBERATOR; LIGHT OF PEACE; MARLBOROUGH DIAMOND; MAZARIN DIAMONDS; MIRROR OF PORTUGAL; NASSAK; NEPAL; NIARCHOS; NIZAM; OPPENHEIMER (Dutoitspan); ORLOV; PIGOTT; POHL; PORTUGUESE; PREMIER ROSE (Big Rose); PRESIDENT VARGAS; RED CROSS; REGENT (Pitt); SANCY; SHAH; SHAH OF PERSIA; STAR OF AFRICA; STAR OF ARKANSAS; STAR OF EGYPT; STAR OF INDEPENDENCE; STAR OF SIERRA LEONE; STAR OF SOUTH AFRICA (Dudley); STAR OF THE EAST; STAR OF THE SOUTH; TAJ-I-MAH; TAVERNIER DIAMONDS; TIFFANY; UNCLE SAM; VICTORIA-TRANSVAAL; WILLIAMSON (Queen Elizabeth Pink); WINSTON; WITTELSBACH. For additional examples, *see Notable Diamonds of the World,* published by De Beers Consolidated Mines, Ltd (1970); Lawrence L. Copeland, *Diamonds: Famous, Notable and Unique* (1966).

diamond colour grading. There are various systems for grading diamonds by colour, varying in different countries and also varying among diamond dealers (many of whom have their own special designations). Modern methods use numerals or letters, but the traditional systems are still also used. The latter range down from pure white ('extra river', 'river'), through top-white ('top WESSELTON', 'wesselton'), off-white ('silver cape', 'top cape', 'cape', and 'dark cape') to shades of yellow and brown. A new system aimed at uniformity has recently been internationally developed. In Germany an apparatus has been developed that permits comparison of a stone with standard tints.

diamond colours. The range of colours found in natural untreated diamonds, due possibly to defects in the atomic lattice of the stone rather than to traces of minerals. Completely colourless stones are extremely rare and valuable, and most stones used in jewelry are tinged from white to bluish to shades of yellow or brown. There are various systems for grading diamonds according to colour (*see* DIAMOND COLOUR GRADING). More pronounced colours (termed 'fancy diamonds' or 'fancies') include the rarest varieties, i.e. shades of red, green, and blue, and also shades of violet, pink, canary-yellow, brown, black (gun metal). The variety sometimes called 'red diamond' is usually red-brown or rose; ruby-coloured is extremely rare. Colour is established by comparison with a set of test stones under special lighting or with an electronic apparatus that measures the light absorbed. The colour of a diamond can be artificially changed or improved by heat or irradiation (*see* TREATED DIAMOND; DEEPDENE DIAMOND). *See* BY(E)WATER; BLUE-WHITE DIAMOND; BLACK DIAMOND; CHAMELEON DIAMOND. *See* Benjamin Zucker, 'Connoisseurship in Coloured Diamonds', *Connoisseur*, December 1980, p. 252, and 'Connoisseurship in White Diamonds', *Connoisseur*, April 1981, p. 700.

diamond cutting. The process of altering the shape and surface of a diamond from its original crude form to a finished stone with FACETS selected to provide maximum BRILLIANCE and with the least waste of material. Several steps are required: (1) CLEAVING or SAWING the stone to remove any parts with FLAWS and to slice it into the desired pieces, sometimes slicing a large stone into three or more pieces that will be suitable for gems; (2) BRUTING, to give it the desired fundamental, somewhat rounded, shape; and (3) GRINDING, to make the facets. The sequence for making the facets is established. When the faceting is completed, polishing is not required (the stone having no Beilby layer), and so it receives only an acid cleaning. *See* MAKE. The first facets are made by a specialist called a 'cross-cutter', and the final ones by a 'brillandeur' in an operation called 'brillianteering'. The major diamond-cutting firms have been located in Amsterdam and Antwerp, and in recent years in New York City (*see* HARRY WINSTON), Israel (the Ramat Gan district of Tel Aviv), and Smolensk, USSR.

diamond gauge. An instrument for estimating the weight of a diamond in a SETTING, based on the fact that the various cuts of diamonds are prescribed and the dimension of the GIRDLE of a stone can be the basis for calculating its weight. There are several types of such instruments: (1) the 'stencil gauge' or 'aperture gauge', which has a series of graduated holes which are fitted over the stone until one fits the girdle, indicating its size; (2) the 'caliper gauge', which uses calipers to measure the width of the girdle and the depth of the stone, from which measurements available tables show the approximate weight for the particular cut of stone, usually a BRILLIANT CUT but sometimes also other cuts (examples are the Moe Calculator and the Leveridge Gauge); (3) the 'comparison gauge', which is composed of a series of swivelling arms at the end of each of which is a stone (e.g. a SYNTHETIC SPINEL) of known graduated size, used for comparison of size; and (4) the 'slide gauge', which has two adjustable arms to hold the stone and a circular scale with a needle that records the size as the arms are adjusted to the stone.

diamond-milling. A modern process of decorating some metal jewelry, e.g. a finger ring, which makes a pattern of sharp cuts in the metal, using a machine with a diamond-tipped tool. A great variety of patterns can be so made, including some of symmetrical form with straight or curved lines and some of apparent random form. The design has a bright finish, with no need for buffing or polishing. The process is adaptable to mass production, but can be supplemented by hand engraving.

diamond paste. A variety of PASTE made of very fine lead glass, ground, fused, cooled and polished, and used to imitate colourless gemstones, especially the diamond.

diamond point. A diamond in the form of an equilateral square pyramid, being made by splitting in half a diamond of OCTAHEDRON form, having 8 faces of equilateral triangles. The form was used in the 15th and early 16th centuries, and was sometimes called *point naïf.*

diamond-point ring. A type of finger ring having a high BEZEL set with a diamond cut as a DIAMOND POINT, or cut in OCTAHEDRON shape so that the PAVILION is within the setting and the CROWN projects above it. Such rings were used from the 15th century to the 17th, a famous example bearing the device of the Medici. Sometimes called a 'writing-diamond ring', as it was sometimes used to write, with the pointed apex, on glass.

diamond-shaped. Having 4 equal straight sides, enclosing pairs of equal and opposite acute and obtuse angles. *See* LOZENGE.

diamond trace chain. A type of TRACE CHAIN of which the wire of the links is flattened.

diaper. An ornamental pattern in the form of contiguous repetitions of one or more units of design, usually a chequered pattern of diamond- or lozenge-shaped units enclosing some decorative motif or motifs. The outline of each unit generally forms part of the outline of adjoining units so as to make an overall pattern for a ground or a border. *See* CIVIDALE RELIQUARY; ENKOMI PENDANT.

diasterism. The type of ASTERISM that is observed by transmitted light, i.e. when seen through a material (e.g. mica), in contrast to EPIASTERISM observed by reflected light.

dichroic. Having the property, as certain gemstones, of exhibiting dichroism.

dichroism. The property of double refracting coloured stones to show two or more colours according to the direction in which they are viewed by transmitted light. Dichroism is never observed in single refracting stones or in GLASS.

dichroite. The same as IOLITE.

die casting. The process of CASTING by pouring molten metal into a cut steel die, now largely replaced for mass production of jewelry by CENTRIFUGAL CASTING.

die stamping. The process of making a complete relief pattern on metal by pressure in a die made from a master model. A flat sheet of metal is enclosed in the two-part die and the pattern is made on it by the application of pressure, either by a heavy blow or by gradually tightening with a winch. The process permits the mass production of objects, such as coins, medals, etc. It is a modern adaptation of the process of manual STAMPING, and is sometimes called 'die striking'.

differential pickling. A process used to create a surface of two gilt colours on all or part of an object made of a gold ALLOY, e.g. TUMBAGA. Upon heating the object in air, a thin layer of copper oxide formed on the surface and this (after protecting, with an acid-resistant, the part not intended to be affected) was removed chemically with an acid (possibly a form of oxalic acid) made from the juice of certain plants, leaving a thin layer of pure gold on the surface over the alloy core. The process is said to have been used by a secret formula in the Tairona and Nariño regions of Colombia on some PRE-COLUMBIAN JEWELRY. It creates an effect similar to that of DEPLETION GILDING. *See* PICKLE.

diffusion bonding. A process of joining two pieces of gold, similar to the process of COLLOID HARD-SOLDERING, and said to have been used in making some articles of PRE-COLUMBIAN JEWELRY in Colombia and Ecuador. The join is barely visible, hence it is difficult to recognize whether the object was made by the CIRE PERDUE process.

Dinglinger, Johann Melchior (1664–1731). A goldsmith and jeweller born at Biberach, near Ulm, Germany, who is 1693 settled in Dresden and in 1702 was made Court Jeweller by Augustus II, Elector of Saxony. There, with his brothers, Georg Friedrich (1666–1720) and Georg Christoph (1668–1746), and his son, Johann Friedrich (1702–67), he planned and organized the Green Vault at Dresden. He created many elaborate pieces, such as jewelled AIGRETTES as adapted by himself, and contributed to the revival of the art of enamelling jewelry. *See* Erna von Watzdorf, *J. M. Dinglinger* (1962).

diopside. A mineral of which the colour ranges, owing to the presence of varying quantities of iron, from yellow to pale green to dark bottle-green, sometimes having more than one shade in the same crystal. Some specimens that have inclusions show CHATOYANCY and are cut EN CABOCHON, and some show ASTERISM with a four-pointed star. Small crystals used for gemstones are transparent and are sometimes STEP CUT. Varieties include ALALITE, BAIKALITE, CHROMDIOPSIDE, and VIOLAN(E).

dioptase. A MASSIVE mineral, found in copper mines, from which translucent, emerald-green crystals are sometimes derived. It is very soft and has strong CLEAVAGE, hence seldom used as a gemstone; but some small crystals have been EMERALD CUT, and some clusters (druses) have been set in jewelry. It has high colour dispersion, often concealed by the deep colour. It is sometimes called by the misnomer 'copper emerald'.

dipped enamelling. The technique of ENAMELLING by which a heated metal core was dipped into and covered with molten glass and shaped to a desired form. It was introduced in HELLENISTIC JEWELRY in the 3rd century BC and used mainly on pendants for ear-rings.

diptych. A picture or a carving made in two compartments that are hinged side by side, folding over each other to protect the decoration. Some, in contrast to large altar-pieces, were made small enough to be worn as a pendant. Examples made in the Middle Ages were decorated with ENAMELLING depicting religious subjects and occasionally had attached a small RELIQUARY; these were worn as personal ornaments, suspended from a girdle or a NECK CHAIN. Examples from Flanders are made of BOX-WOOD enclosing minute carvings, and some from Italy have small IVORY figures. A type in use in the Eastern Church is made of gold, silver, ivory or wood, bearing on the outside religious scenes and on the inside on one leaf the name of certain living persons and on the other the names of prominent deceased persons for whom prayers were said during the Eucharist. *See* TRIPTYCH.

Diquis jewelry. Articles of PRE-COLUMBIAN JEWELRY made by the Indians of the Diquis region of south-western Costa Rica. A speciality was an articulated pendant in anthropomorphic form with movable limbs. Some pendants have, instead of a suspensory ring, a horizontal bar across the back, attached to which was a suspensory string. *See* COSTA RICAN JEWELRY.

disc brooch. A type of BROOCH that is made in the form of a flat disc, to the back of which is attached a fastening pin. The precursors of such

Diquis jewelry. Gold male figure holding rattles. Costa Rica. H. 6 cm. New Orleans Museum of Art.

disc ear-rings. Gold with granulation and central inlay (missing). Greek, 8th century BC. W. 2.9 cm. British Museum (Elgin Collection), London.

Disruption brooch. Silver disc brooch with commemorative dates. M. Rettie, Aberdeen, 1843. W. 5 cm. National Museum of Antiquities of Scotland; Edinburgh.

djed pillar. Gold overlaid on unknown material. Bears amuletic inscription and throne name. Tomb of Tutankhamun. H. 9 cm. Photograph by Egyptian Expedition, Metropolitan Museum of Art, New York.

brooches are pieces found in cemeteries of southern Europe from the Early Iron Age, having a circular plate fitted with a hinged pin; later examples were made in Roman times, often inlaid with enamel. They were also made as ANGLO-SAXON JEWELRY, being of bronze silvered (or tinned to appear silvery) or occasionally of pewter, decorated with geometrical patterns engraved or in openwork. *See* RING BROOCH. Later and modern examples have a hinged or spring pin. *See* FULLER BROOCH; KING'S SCHOOL, CANTERBURY, BROOCH; MILTON BROOCH; SARRE DISC BROOCH; STRICKLAND BROOCH; SUTTON BROOCH.

disc ear-ring. A type of ear-ring decorated with a gold disc and GRANULATED GOLD, sometimes with a central inlay. They were made in Greece in the 8th century BC.

Disruption brooch. A silver DISC BROOCH that commemorated the founding of the Free Church of Scotland in 1843 by secession from the Church of Scotland, led by Thomas Chalmers. It has panels bearing the dates 1560, 1592, 1638, 1688, and 1843. An inscription on the back gives the reasons for the formation of the Free Church. The brooches were made by M. Rettie, jewellers of Aberdeen; they were commercial souvenirs sold to the public.

djed pillar. An Egyptian AMULET in the form of a column encircled near the top by four thin protruding bands. In antiquity it had a cult of its own, but in later years it was given various symbolic interpretations, including that of being the backbone of Osiris. One or more were placed on the neck of a deceased on the day of his funeral. Such pieces were supposed to be made of gold; that in the TUTANKHAMUN JEWELRY is gold over a core of unknown substance and is decorated with an inscription (a spell from the *Book of the Dead*) and the King's throne name.

Djevalite. The trade-name for a version of ZIRCONIUM OXIDE (*see* CUBIC ZIRCONIA) produced in Switzerland.

documentary specimens. Examples of jewelry which throw light on the history of jewelry or the identification of similar pieces, including pieces: signed by the maker or decorator (*see* MARK); bearing an informative inscription; discovered in certain TREASURES or HOARDS; descended in a family known from early times; decorated with armorial bearings; referred to in old documents.

dog collar. A wide, ornamented, jewelled NECKLACE worn tightly around a woman's throat. Such pieces were used from the 16th century but became popular in the Victorian era, when they were first in the form of a wide band of ribbon ornamented with bands of gemstones or cheaper BEADS. Later, in the 1880s, they took the form of bands of metal ornamented with rows of PEARLS, or multiple strings of ungraduated pearls, sometimes up to twelve rows and, *c.* 1900-10, had in the front an elaborate rectangular ornament (called a *plaque de cou*). Such collars were also made of JET or CORAL. The French term is *collier de chien*. *See* CHOKER.

dolphin pendant. A type of pendant in the form of a gold, enamelled, and jewelled dolphin suspended by a chain attached to its head and tail and having a male figure astride its back. Although the dolphin is sometimes depicted as a familiar benign cetacean, most such jewels depict a ferocious-looking toothed species of the genus *Delphinidae*, with the rider usually depicted as carrying a spear and a shield; hence it has been suggested that the figure is perhaps Palaemon, the sea-god who provided aid to sailors, or possibly Ariosto's Orlando astride the Orca, rather than (as has been dubiously suggested) the musician Arion of Greek legend who, thrown into the sea by mariners, was carried by a dolphin to safety on the island of Taeneros, as the latter would have been holding a lyre rather than war-like implements. Several examples and drawings of such pendants are known.

Donald, John (1928–   ). An English DESIGNER-MAKER of gold jewelry in contemporary style, who has had a workshop in London since 1961 where his craftsmen execute his designs, and also retail shops in London since 1968 and in Geneva since 1978. His work emphasizes decorative designs, recent examples combining flake goldwork and openwork patterns set with gemstones and natural baroque pearls.

Doria, Carlo. Possibly an Italian jewelry craftsman who emigrated to London in the 1850/160s and who may have made jewelry for Carlo Giuliano (*see* GIULIANO FAMILY) or for ROBERT PHILLIPS. There is no record of his having been in London and no piece is definitely identified with him. The only evidence of his existence is a statement, reported from an unidentified art magazine of the 1850s, which ascribed as the mark of Doria an ambiguous monogram on a pendant that was possibly C D back-to-back and bisected by a three-plumed device. That mark, in relief and soldered on, is found on a number of gold and silver pieces of Italian workmanship, alone or in conjunction with the mark of Phillips, and a view accepted until recently is that all such pieces were made by Doria for marketing by his employer Phillips. On the other hand, it has now been pointed out that the mark is more probably the monogram of back-to-back Ps (for Phillips Bros.) with the Prince of Wales's feathers (used by Phillips), especially as it is on a number of pieces found in Phillips's boxes, and so it has been postulated that if Doria existed he was a craftsman without known mark who, having emigrated to London in the 1850/60s as an apprentice, possibly worked for Giuliano or for Phillips. *See* Geoffrey Munn, 'Carlo Doria', in *Connoisseur*, September 1979, p. 38.

dot-repoussé. Decoration of REPOUSSÉ work made in the form of dots hammered into a sheet of metal with a punch, usually massed together to form a pattern or to depict an animal or other motif. It is found on gold articles from the Early Minoan period, 2500 BC-2000 BC.

double cameo. A CAMEO having carved relief decoration on both sides of the same stone, e.g. an Italian ONYX cameo, *c.* 1520-30, with on one side a carved bust of Hercules cut in blue stratum, and on the other side a carved bust of Omphale cut in white/brown strata, given *c.* 1530 by Emperor Charles V to Pope Clement VII (d. 1534) who gave it to the Piccolomini family (it was probably set originally as a pendant).

double clip. A type of CLIP that can be worn as an integrated BROOCH or separated into 2 individual clips. It is a type of COMPOSITE SUITE.

double-hoop finger ring. A type of finger ring in the form of 2 hoops joined side by side so as to be worn on 2 adjacent fingers, each ring having its own BEZEL. Examples were worn in the Roman era, 5th century, made of gold and set with gemstones.

double-hour-glass torc. A type of TORC of which the terminals are in the form of 2 hour-glasses joined base to base; the terminals and slotted onto the main PENANNULAR hoop. Such torcs are Celtic, from north-western Iberia, 2nd/1st century BC.

double rose cut. A style of cutting a diamond in the form of two diamonds that are ROSE CUT and placed base to base, so that it is faceted

dolphin pendant. Gold with enamelling and gemstones. Spanish, *c.* 1600. H. 5.8 cm. Courtesy of Christie's, London.

Donald, John. Brooch; nugget flake gold with lapis lazuli and diamonds. 1977. W. 5 cm. Courtesy of John Donald, London.

Doria, Carlo. Mark on jewelry attributed until recently to Carlo Doria; now said possibly to be a mark of Robert Phillips. Courtesy of Geoffrey Munn, London.

double cameo (front and back). Onyx cameos, Hercules on front, Omphale on reverse; gold mount set with diamonds and rubies. Italian, *c.* 1520-30. W. 4.5 cm. British Museum, London.

double-hour-glass torcs. Gold. Galician Castro culture, north-western Iberia, 2nd/1st centuries BC. W. 14.1 cm. British Museum, London.

dove. Reliquary of hexagonal rock crystal set in silver with glass stones and suspended silver-gilt dove. Schnütgen Museum, Cologne.

Dowgate Hill Brooch. Gold with enamelled roundel encircled by band with filigree and granulated gold. Probably German, *c.* 1000. W. 3.5 cm. British Museum, London.

as a dome on both sides. It is an old cut, found on the FLORENTINE DIAMOND and the SANCY DIAMOND. It was used in the 19th and early 20th centuries for a pendant or for ear-rings. A diamond so cut is sometimes called a 'double rosette'.

doublet. A COMPOSITE STONE made of two layers cemented or fused together and usually intended to appear as a whole natural stone. (The term is sometimes also applied to a TRIPLET, made of three layers.) There are several varieties: (1) The two layers being of the same natural stone and of like quality, being joined together by being cemented at the GIRDLE so as to appear as a larger stone (the 'true doublet'); (2) the upper layer (the CROWN) being of QUARTZ, ALMANDINE, BERYL, or other inexpensive, colourless or pale coloured, natural stone and the lower layer (the base being of coloured GLASS or PASTE to provide the colour by refraction; (3) the upper layer consisting of the stone being imitated and the lower layer an inferior stone of the same species or of a different mineral or of glass, e.g. diamond over white CORUNDUM; and (4) the upper layer being a SYNTHETIC GEMSTONE (e.g. SYNTHETIC BERYL) over a layer of the same genuine stone. A composite OPAL is sometimes made as a doublet; *see* OPAL DOUBLET. Some doublets include a pocket of coloured liquid or a piece of coloured metal FOIL. Sometimes a CAMEO is a COUNTERFEIT, made as a doublet, with the upper part being carved glass and the lower part CHALCEDONY, or with the two parts of contrasting stones. Doublets can be produced as counterfeits, to be deceptive or fraudulent, but some are made legitimately under recognized trade-names, e.g. the SMARYLL. Some doublets are superior to coloured glass IMITATION GEMSTONES; if the upper layer is a gemstone it will resist scratching when tested for HARDNESS. All such composite stones can be readily distinguished from whole natural stones; one simple test, usually effective, is immersion in water, which causes the join to be revealed by the different light refraction of the parts. *See* PIGGY-BACK DIAMOND.

dove. A decorative motif found on various articles of jewelry, especially a PENDANT or RELIQUARY PENDANT, having suspended from it a figure of a dove IN THE ROUND. It was often used as a symbol of the Holy Ghost. *See* SAINT-ESPRIT CROSS.

Dowgate Hill Brooch. A gold circular BROOCH or MORSE with a central roundel enamelled to depict a crowned, unidentified, male, full-face bust, encircled by an openwork band with FILIGREE and GRANULATED GOLD decoration and set with four PEARLS. It is probably of German origin, *c.* 1000, and was found near Dowgate Hill, in Thames St, London, in 1839. It is from the collection of Charles Roach Smith, and is sometimes called the 'Roach Smith nouch' (*see* NOUCH; OUCH). The roundel closely resembles the ALFRED JEWEL. *[Plate I]*

draconites. A fabulous variety of stone said to be from the head of a dragon and to have curative powers. Also called 'serpent stone'. *See* ADDER STONE.

dragon jewelry. Articles of jewelry whose principal decorative motif is the representation of a dragon, a fabulous animal in the form of a large winged and scaly lizard with large claws. A related piece depicted a sea-dragon, having a fish-tail instead of claws. Examples were made of JADE in China; some Renaissance examples are often in the form of a BAROQUE PEARL JEWEL with the pearl forming the body and with the head and claws (or tail) of gold with coloured enamelling and set with gemstones. The dragon was usually a decorative motif on a pendant but sometimes ornamented a TOOTHPICK.

Drake Enseigne. *See* STAR JEWEL.

Drake Jewel. A gold pendant locket on the front of which is a two-layer sardonyx CAMEO of a BLACKAMOOR, within an enamelled setting mounted with table-cut rubies and diamonds, and inside is a miniature portrait of Elizabeth I by NICHOLAS HILLIARD, with an inscription *Ano Dm 1575 Regni 20*; inside the lid of the locket is a parchment lining painted with a phoenix. Below the locket is suspended a cluster of small pearls, below which hangs a large pear-shaped pearl. The jewel was given to Sir Francis Drake, possibly on the occasion of the defeat of the Spanish Armada in

1588, but certainly before 1591 when a portrait of Drake shows him wearing the jewel. By descent in the Drake family, it is now owned by Lt. Col. Sir George Meyrick, Bart. *See* DRAKE STAR.

Drake Pendant. A SHIP PENDANT of which the hull is made of EBONY, set with a TABLE DIAMOND; the masts and rigging are of gold decorated with opaque enamelling in black, white, green, and blue, set with SEED PEARLS. Seated in the ship is an enamelled figure of Victory blowing a horn, and behind her stands an *amorino* crowning her with a wreath. Below it there is suspended a small boat enamelled in blue. The jewel is said to depict the *Golden Hind*, the ship in which Sir Francis Drake circumnavigated the world (1577–80). It was a gift from him to Queen Elizabeth I, who in turn gave it to Lord Hunsdon, of Berkeley Castle, where it is now included in the HUNSDON COLLECTION.

Drake Star. A gold HAT BADGE (or ENSEIGNE) in the form of a SUNBURST having in the centre a large foiled ruby engraved in INTAGLIO and surrounded by a circle of cabochon opals within a circle of table-cut rubies and diamonds. The reverse, covered with glass, encloses a miniature head portrait, possibly of Elizabeth I, that dates from *c.* 1585. It is associated with the DRAKE JEWEL, and has descended in the Drake family to its present owner, Lt. Col. Sir George Meyrick, Bart.

dravite. A brown variety of TOURMALINE.

Dresden Diamonds. Six Indian diamonds that are so called because they were kept in the famous Green Vault (Grünes Gewölbe) at Dresden. They are: (1) the Dresden White, square-cut and weighing 49.71 carats, bought by Augustus the Strong of Saxony (1670–1733); (2) the Dresden Green, almond-shaped, weighing 41 carats, the largest known apple-green diamond, sometimes said to have been bought by Augustus the Strong in 1743, but as he had died in 1733, the purchase must have been made by his son and successor, Frederick Augustus II, who had it set in a SHOULDER KNOT; and (3) the four Dresden Yellows, weighing 38.00, 29.25, 23.10 and 13.48 carats. All were confiscated by the Russians after World War II but in 1958 were returned to Dresden. *See* ENGLISH DRESDEN DIAMOND; SAXON DIAMONDS.

dress fastener. A type of PENANNULAR ring in the form of a swelling hoop that is wider at the middle. Such pieces are similar to the SLEEVE FASTENER that is of the same form except for larger disc or trumpet-mouth terminals. It was also made in the Irish Bronze Age, *c.* 8th/7th centuries BC. Such pieces may have been used to fasten a cloak or other heavy garment by being attached at the neck or shoulder, but it has also been suggested that they may have been CURRENCY JEWELRY.

dress ornament. A small ornament, usually set with gemstones, made to be worn with similar pieces attached to a woman's dress. Some were worn as a small group made EN SUITE (*see* ÉCHELLE) but often they were made in large numbers so as to be sewn on as a scattered overall decoration, sometimes accompanied by one larger and more ornate piece. They were popular in England and on the Continent in the 16th/17th centuries, but such objects were also made of PRE-COLUMBIAN JEWELRY in the form of discs made of TUMBAGA or GOLD. *See* AGLET.

dragon jewelry. Pendant. Gold sea-dragon with figure in *émail en ronde bosse.* From a design by Hans Collaert, Antwerp, 1582. H. 11.5 cm. Schmuckmuseum, Pforzheim, Germany.

dress ornaments. Silver set with paste. Russian, *c.* 1760. Victoria & Albert Museum, London.

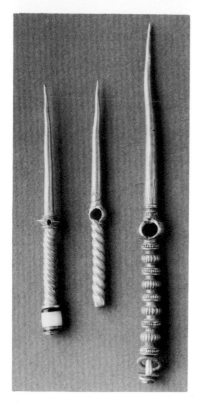

dress pins. Gold. Egyptian, from Treasure of the Cenotaph, Tell el-Ajjul, Israel, *c.* 2200 BC–1550 BC. Israel Department of Antiquities and Museums, Jerusalem.

dress pin. A long (15–20 cm), straight or tapering pin used to fasten a garment; sometimes in the form of a 'toggle-pin'. Some examples of SUMERIAN JEWELRY, *c.* 2500 BC, were made of GOLD, SILVER or ELECTRUM, in attenuated form, with one end pointed and the other ornamented with a bead of CORNELIAN or LAPIS LAZULI capped with gold. Egyptian examples from the Middle Bronze Age (*c.* 2200 BC–1550 BC), and Late Bronze Age (1550 BC–1200 BC) were divided midway by a hole from one side of which extended the attenuated smooth pin and from the other side a twisted or ornamented straight stem handle; the method of use involved passing the pin twice through the garment, and then fastening it with string tied through the hole and looped a few times around the two exposed ends. The name 'toggle-pin' was applied by Sir Flinders Petrie, the noted English archaeologist.

dress set. A set of jewelry, decorated EN SUITE, to be worn by a man with evening attire, usually including a pair of CUFF LINKS, 3 or 4 waistcoat (vest) STUDS, and 2 or 3 shirt studs. Such sets are usually made of gold or platinum, sometimes with a MOTHER-OF-PEARL or black ONYX ground, and often centred with a gemstone.

drop pearl. A type of PEARL that is drop-shaped (although often called 'pear-shaped'). Such pearls are frequently used suspended from a pendant or brooch, singly or in threes, or from an ear-ring. They are sometimes CHINESE DRILLED, to be sewn on a garment.

drum bead. A type of BEAD made in cylindrical shape, covered at both ends and having a hole pierced through the side of the cylinder for suspension. Examples in MINOAN JEWELRY (Early, Middle, and Late periods) and EGYPTIAN JEWELRY were sometimes decorated with REPOUSSÉ work in floral patterns.

Ducerceau, Jacques Androuet (1515?–85?). A jeweller and designer who was born in Paris but worked mainly in Orléans. He left about 50 models for jewelry, including pendants, brooches, clasps, and ear-rings, as well as many designs for pendants featuring cartouches with rolled and voluted frames.

Dudley Diamond. The same as the STAR OF SOUTH AFRICA.

Dujardin, François (d. 1575). A French jeweller who was recognized as a Master Jeweller in 1563, as Jeweller to the Queen Mother, Catherine de' Medici (1519–89), widow of Henry II (1519–59), in 1569, and as Goldsmith and Lapidary to her son, Charles IX, 1560–74, in 1570. He remodelled the crown jewels for the wedding in 1570 of Elisabeth of Austria and Charles IX, and other crown jewels, and created designs for some jewelry for Catherine de' Medici. Some pieces executed by him were probably designed, it has been suggested, by Olivier Codoré. Only a few jewels made by Dujardin are known to have survived. Other French jewellers of identical surname are recorded, from 1539 to 1610–43, all members of Catholic families of jewellers. *See* Yvonne Hackenbroch, 'Catherine de' Medici and her Court Jeweller, François Dujardin', in *Connoisseur*, September 1966, p. 28.

dumortierite. A variety of gemstone that is usually found in bright-blue, greenish-blue or violet fibrous masses, but a crystal variety found in Sri Lanka (formerly Ceylon) is brownish and a mauve-red variety comes from Madagascar. It has high dichroism. It was named after Vincent Eugène Dumortier (1801–76), a French palaeontologist. Crystalline material is found as INCLUSIONS in a variety of QUARTZITE called 'dumortierite quartz'.

Dunstable Swan Jewel. A gold BROOCH in the form of a swan whose plumage on its body, head, wings, and legs, is of opaque white ÉMAIL EN RONDE BOSSE. Around its neck is a gold coronet from which project six fleurs-de-lis and to which is attached a gold chain of thirty links ending in a ring. On the reverse is the original pin and clasp. The jewel is said to have been worn probably by an English person of noble or aristocratic birth whose ancestry was traced through the House of Boulogne to the Knight of the Swan of medieval romance. It has been attributed to French or English origin, mid-15th century; it was found on the site of the

Dunstable Swan Jewel. Gold jewel with white *émail en ronde bosse*; gold coronet and chain. English or French, 11th century. H. 3.2 cm. British Museum, London.

Dominican Priory at Dunstable, England, in 1965. The jewel was award-ed to the owner of the land, who sold it in 1966 at Sotheby's to the Metropolitan Museum of Art, New York, for £4,800, but after an export licence was refused it was bought by the British Museum. *See* John Cherry, 'The Dunstable Swan Jewel', in *Journal of the British Archaeological Association,* XXXII (1969), p. 38; *Burlington Magazine,* June 1968, p. 43.

duo. A modern term for a bracelet and necklace made EN SUITE.

Dürer, Albrecht (1471-1528). The German artist, born in Nuremberg, renowned for his drawings and prints, who also made designs for jewelry, probably intended to be executed by his brother Endres. The jewelry designs, many of which were used by WENCESLAS HOLLAR for making engraved jewels, often featured mythological creatures, dolphins, dragons, and mermaids, postured to conform to the shape of the article. The designs were for such articles as finger rings, buckles, clasps, brooches, and pendent WHISTLES. His work in jewelry design continued to influence the later goldsmiths of Nuremberg and Augsburg. Dürer started his career as a goldsmith, following his father, and later made woodcuts and engravings, as well as painting altar-pieces. All his jewelry designs were made before 1515 when he became a follower of Martin Luther.

Dutch metal. An ALLOY of copper and zinc (a variety of BRASS) that is beaten into thin FOIL in imitation of GOLD LEAF. It is used for gilding cheap jewelry. Also called 'Dutch gold'. *See* TOMBAC(K).

Dutch rose cut. The style of cutting a diamond (or other transparent gemstone) in the basic form of the ROSE CUT, with a flat, 12-sided base and two horizontal rows of 24 FACETS; the upper row (called the CROWN) has 6 low facets (called STAR FACETS), rising to a point, and the lower row (called the DENTELLE) has 18 facets (called CROSS FACETS), of which 6 abut the star facets and point downward and 12 in pairs are between them and are along the GIRDLE. The height of the stone is ideally equal to half of the diameter. It is used mainly for small diamonds set in jewelry that includes a larger coloured stone. Also called 'Holland rose' or 'crowned rose'.

Dutch rose cut
side view

Dutoitspan Diamond. The early name for the OPPENHEIMER DIAMOND. Two other diamonds, yellowish in colour, weighing rough 250 old carats and 127 old carats, are named, respectively, Dutoit I and Dutoit II; they were found in 1871 in the Dutoitspan Mine, at Kimberley, South Africa, and were named after Dr A. L. Dutoit, an early irrigation expert and later the head of the Geological Department of De Beers Consolidated Mines Ltd. Their whereabouts are unknown. A large number of other yellow diamonds have since been found at Dutoitspan. A yellow diamond (the largest known octahedron diamond, weighing rough 616 carats) was found in April 1974; now called the Dutoitspan Diamond, this stone is still owned uncut by De Beers Consolidated Mines Ltd and exhibited at the Kimberley Museum.

Duvet, Jean (1485-*c.* 1560). A French designer of jewelry who was a goldsmith to Francis I and Henry II. His designs were for small articles for personal use and featured flowers, foliage, and scrolls to be executed in enamelling.

dyeing. The process of artificially changing or enhancing the colour of certain coloured gemstones, especially a porous stone (e.g. AGATE), by causing a colouring chemical (or carbon) to enter the pores of the stone, or of imparting a colour to certain colourless stones, in either case sometimes enhanced by HEAT TREATMENT. Examples are: banded agate which is dyed various colours; calcite which is then termed MEXICAN JADE; CHALCEDONY which, after being dyed and heated, is CORNELIAN, or when green or blue is sometimes called 'emeraldine' or 'blue moonstone'; ONYX which is usually dyed; JASPER which dyed blue is sometimes called 'German', 'Swiss' or 'false' LAPIS LAZULI; and CHRYSOPRASE which dyed green is sometimes called 'agate'. If aniline dyes are used to produce varied colours, they will fade in sunlight. The terms 'dyeing' and STAINING are often used interchangeably.

E

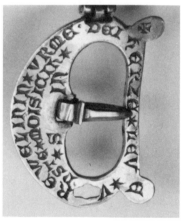

E Jewel. Gold locket. Lower Saxony, 14th century. H. 3 cm. Courtesy of Sotheby's, London.

eagle pendant. Gold or tumbaga. Costa Rica, Diquis culture. H. 3 cm. New Orleans Museum of Art.

E Jewel. A gold LETTER JEWEL that is a LOCKET made in the form of the letter E in Lombardic script. It is in two sections, hinged together at the top. The front section has on its front an applied male figure IN THE ROUND and on its reverse there is a small receptacle (perhaps for a hair); the other section, when the front is raised, reveals on its inside an amatory inscription in Middle High German script. The piece is from Lower Saxony, 14th century, and was sold from the Von Hirsch Collection at Sotheby's, London, on 22 June 1978. It resembles the FOUNDER'S JEWEL.

eagle pendant. A type of PENDANT of PRE-COLUMBIAN JEWELRY made of flat hammered and cast gold by the Indians of various cultures of Central and South America. The motif is a stylized bird facing front, with outspread wings and broad tail feathers, realistically depicted head and claws, and sometimes having a hollow body with occasionally a small enclosed bell and also inset eyes that move and rattle. The bird, usually referred to as an eagle, is of various forms, sometimes resembling somewhat a horned owl, toucan, pelican or vulture (*see* KING VULTURE PENDANT). Examples are often found in COSTA RICAN JEWELRY. *See* POPAYÁN EAGLE.

eagle stone. A type of stone, about the size of a walnut, that was thought in the Middle Ages to be carried by an eagle to her nest to facilitate egg-laying and said to have magical powers. It was worn as an AMULET.

ear-clip. A type of ear ornament (often included in the general term ear-ring) that is worn by being secured to the lobe of the ear by a hinged support. They were generally not known before the Renaissance, but an example was mentioned by Cellini. They are a prevalent type today. Also called a 'snap ear-ring'. *See* CLIP.

ear-drop. A small PENDANT worn on the ear attached, as an ear-ring, by a looped wire passed through a hole pierced in the lobe of the ear or as an EAR-CLIP or EAR-SCREW fastened or screwed to the lobe. Such pendants are usually in the form of an ornament IN THE ROUND, made in a variety of forms, e.g. as a bird, charioteer, etc., examples of which are from many sources, from Greek jewelry of the 4th century BC to Hungarian jewelry of the 19th century.

ear-flare. A type of ear ornament of MAYAN JEWELRY and OLMEC JEWELRY composed of three sections: (1) a flared ornament, with a central aperture, that was worn on the front of the ear-lobe; (2) a tubular bead that was worn through a hole in the lobe and that connected, by telescoping, the front and rear ornaments; and (3) a miniature flared ornament or a JADE bead that fitted at the back of the tube to secure it to the ear. Sometimes there was in the opening of the front flare a 'throat plate' of jade or shell, as an added ornament, and at the back of the piece, fitted in the rear section, a long tassel. *See* EAR-SPOOL.

ear-loop. A type of ear ornament that is in the form of a PENANNULAR loop that encircles most of the ear, rather than being wired through or attached to the ear-lobe. Examples made of gold, *c.* 100 BC-AD 100, sometimes have, as the ornament that hangs below the ear-lobe, a figure IN THE ROUND, similar to some examples of an EAR-DROP.

ear ornament. An ornament of various forms, styles, and sizes worn on the ear, including the EAR-CLIP, EAR-DROP, EAR-FLARE, EAR-LOOP, EAR-PLUG, EAR-RING, EAR-SCREW, EAR-SPOOL, and EAR-STUD. Examples made of PRE-COLUMBIAN JEWELRY were often of circular shape with openwork decoration in the lower half or in semi-circular shape completely decorated with openwork decoration (sometimes the decoration being

very similar to that in a similarly-shaped NOSE ORNAMENT). A type made
in INDIAN JEWELRY covered the entire ear and was so heavy that it had to
be supported by, in addition to a band encircling the ear, an attached
ornate hair pin; another type was composed of a disc over the lobe and a
heavy ornate group of pendants and tassels.

ear-pick. An instrument with a small scoop for removing wax from the
ears. Examples made of gold or silver were popular in Europe in the
Renaissance period; some were enamelled or decorated with gems, and
were worn suspended from a NECK CHAIN. Some are made with a
TOOTHPICK on the end opposite the scoop, and some have an ear-pick and
a toothpick joined by a swivel. Examples of ear-picks are recorded in the
inventories of James II of Scotland (1488), of Henry VIII (1530), and of
Elizabeth I (1573-7). Some were enclosed in WHISTLES designed by
ALBRECHT DÜRER and in a whistle said to have been owned by Anne
Boleyn. See PASFIELD JEWEL.

ear-plug. An ear ornament, sometimes in papyrus-column form (having
a flattened head, resembling an Egyptian papyrus stalk), to be inserted
into the lobe of the ear, especially to distend it. The plugs were pierced
vertically. Examples made of GLASS in Egypt during the XVIIIth and
XIXth Dynasties (c. 1552 BC–1185 BC) are of various colours, some with
opaque enclosed threads making a pattern of contrasting colours.
Somewhat different are ear-plugs made of glass in China, being either
cylindrical with one large extended head at the front end or spool-like
with flared terminals.

ear-ring. An ear ornament, worn suspended from a bent wire or thin
hoop passed through a hole pierced in the lobe of the ear or, in later
years, clipped or screwed to the lobe (called an EAR-CLIP or EAR-SCREW).
Ear-rings, worn from earliest times, have been made of gold, silver, platinum, silver gilt, etc., and in a great variety of shapes, styles, and sizes,
and with various ornamentation and pendants made of a variety of
materials, e.g. GOLD, CORAL, JADE, JET, GLASS, etc. Hellenistic examples
were often decorated with the head of an animal, siren, etc. Later Greek,
Roman, and Etruscan examples were often made as a hook with a pendant that was shaped like a crescent, boat, or figure, or with a rosette or
disc masking the hook, or in the form of a PENANNULAR ring having one
end decorated with a human or animal head. Some Anglo-Saxon examples are set with a GARNET or red glass. During the Renaissance, the
style of shorter hair led to a revival of the wearing of ear-rings, not only by
women but also, in Spain and England, by men (sometimes wearing only
one); the decoration was more elaborate and often included pendent
PEARLS (see GIRANDOLE). Thereafter ear-rings have continued to be worn,
often set with gemstones, the styles reflecting the prevalent styles of the
times. The French term is *boucle d'oreille*. See ANIMAL-HEAD EAR-RING;
BALL EAR-RING; BAR EAR-RING; BASKET EAR-RING; BAULE EAR-RING; BOAT
EAR-RING; BOUCHON DE CARAFE; CHANDELIER EAR-RING; CREOLE EAR-RING;
DISC EAR-RING; HOOP EAR-RING; LEECH EAR-RING; PROTOME EAR-RING;
SLEEPER; TOP AND DROP EAR-RING.

ear-screw. A type of ear ornament (often included in the general terms
EAR-RING or EAR-CLIP) that is worn by being secured to the lobe of the ear
by pressure. The pressure is applied by a flat-headed screw that is attached to the ornament by a loop of wire passing below the lobe.

ear-spool. A type of ear ornament of PRE-COLUMBIAN JEWELRY worn in a
large hole made in a greatly distended ear-lobe. It was made of gold or
TUMBAGA as a cylindrical tube that was inserted in the lobe and that had
affixed to the front a circular frame, often ornamented with cut-out
designs and REPOUSSÉ work. A rear section was attached telescopically to
the tubular section to secure it to the lobe. It was worn in the same manner as an EAR-FLARE. Some examples were further decorated with
suspended ornaments, sometimes in the form of a fringe of snake-like
dangles. The wearing of ear-spools by the Incas of Peru was restricted to
the adult male nobility, a custom dating back to the Chavín culture, c.
900 BC; see CHAVÍN JEWELRY.

ear-stud. A type of ear ornament composed of a front and a rear part
joined by shanks of tubular form (one larger than the other) that fit
through the ear-lobe and connect in a telescopic manner. When worn,

ear-drop. Gold winged charioteer.
Greek, 4th century BC. Museum of
Fine Arts (H. L. Pierce Fund),
Boston, Mass.

ear-drop. Gold and niello, with bird
and pearls. Hungarian, early 19th
century. H. 6 cm. Hungarian
National Museum, Budapest.

ear-flare. Jadeite. Mayan. W. 8 cm.
Museum of Mankind, London.

ear-loop. Gold. *c.* 100 BC–AD 100. Museo Nazionale, Naples.

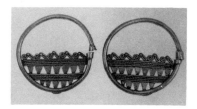

ear ornaments. Pre-Columbian. Sinú jewelry. Cast tumbaga. W. 5.9 cm. Museo del Oro, Bogotá.

ear-plug. Glass. Chinese. New Orleans Museum of Art.

only the front part is seen, and it is sometimes boss-shaped and decorated, while the rear part is flat and undecorated. Examples are recorded in EGYPTIAN JEWELRY near the end of the reign of Amenhotep III (1410 BC–1374 BC). Sometimes an elaborate ornament was suspended from the shank, as on a pair in the TUTANKHAMUN JEWELRY. Examples in ETRUSCAN JEWELRY are in the form of a disc with a rear projection for insertion in the ear-lobe. It has been suggested, on account of the very large shanks, that some examples may not have been ear ornaments but possibly a type of dress fastener.

Earth Star Diamond. A diamond of PENDELOQUE shape and cut, noted for its very unusual coffee-brown colour. It weighs 111.59 carats (cut from a 248.9-carat stone) and is said to be the largest known diamond of such colour. It was reported in October 1979 to be owned by Baumgold Bros, Inc., New York City.

ecclesiastical ring. A type of finger ring worn and used by ecclesiastical dignitaries (hence not including a so-called PAPAL RING). Such rings include an ABBOT'S RING; BISHOP'S RING; CARDINAL'S RING; FISHERMAN'S RING; PONTIFICAL RING; PRIEST'S RING.

échelle (French). Literally, a ladder or gradation. A set of three or more jewelled DRESS ORNAMENTS shaped and decorated EN SUITE but of graduated sizes, made with a metal loop on the back so as to be sewn to a woman's garment in a vertical row of diminishing size and changeable to various garments. Examples were popular in England in the Georgian period, sometimes in the form of BOW-KNOTS set with diamonds. Sometimes many matching dress ornaments of ungraduated sizes were worn to supplement the *échelles.*

Écrin de Charlemagne Finial. A JEWEL from the *Écrin de Charlemagne* (Casket of Charlemagne), which belonged to the Abbey of St Denis, where the Kings of France were crowned, but which was destroyed during the French Revolution, only the finial surviving. It is in the form of a centre oval INTAGLIO of AQUAMARINE, engraved with a profile portrait of Julia, daughter of the Roman Emperor Titus (AD 40–81), and with the name, in Greek letters, of the cutter Evodus. The intaglio is surrounded by 9 radiating channelled COLLETS in gold, each set with a SAPPHIRE cut in CABOCHON form, of which 3 on each side have an extended calyx-shaped socket set with a PEARL. The top sapphire is carved with a monogram of the Virgin and a symbolic fish. The piece is from the end of the Carolingian period, *c.* 860–70. It is now in the Cabinet des Médailles, Paris.

Ecuadorian jewelry. Articles of PRE-COLUMBIAN JEWELRY, *c.* 250 BC–AD 1500, made in Ecuador by the native Indians, especially, so far as is known today, along the northern coast, in the Esmeraldas region, near La Tolita, that extends also into Colombia; but some gold finds have also been made in the southern highlands. The pieces were made mainly of gold or TUMBAGA from hammered flat sheet metal cut out and decorated in REPOUSSÉ work or cast by the CIRE PERDUE process. Articles included some exceptionally tiny gold nose rings and LABRETS; circular copper ornaments (sometimes called 'gongs', but possibly breast ornaments), embossed with a human or puma face; minute coiled springs worn as ear ornaments; and studs of gold, emerald or turquoise worn in holes pierced in the cheek or lip. Some articles were covered with gold plating and some were made of an ALLOY of platinum and gold produced by SINTERING.

Edward VI Prayer-Book. A miniature prayer-book, the cover of which is of gold inlaid with black CHAMPLEVÉ enamel in ARABESQUE designs and having a rosette of enamel at each corner. The centre of one cover is decorated with a boss of translucent green and red enamel, of the other cover with a SHELL CAMEO. The book contains, in manuscript written on vellum, the last prayer of Edward VI, made 6 July 1553. The book is said to have been worn by Elizabeth I as a GIRDLE BOOK and to have been later owned by Lord Fitzharding. *See* BOOK COVER.

Edwardes Ruby. A RUBY weighing 167 carats. It was donated by John Ruskin in 1887 to the British Museum (Natural History) and named in honour of Major-General Sir Herbert Benjamin Edwardes (1819–68) who saved British rule in India during the years of the Indian Mutiny (Sepoy Rebellion), 1857–8.

Edwardian jewelry. Articles of jewelry popularly worn in England during the reign of Edward VII, 1901-10. They included articles lavishly decorated with gemstones, especially diamonds in very fine spindly settings, such as necklaces, collars, tiaras, and pendent ear-rings. Edwardian jewelry is no longer considered fashionable, and much of it has been broken up to reuse the gemstones.

effigy flask. An article of PRE-COLUMBIAN JEWELRY in the form of a small flask decorated on the front with the representation of a human figure and having the two sides indented to form what seems to be a handgrip. Such pieces are sometimes depicted being worn on figures made as a PECTORAL. They are examples of QUIMBAYA JEWELRY. Their use is unknown but it has been suggested that they may have contained a hallucinogenic substance used in religious rites.

egg pearl. A type of PEARL that is of ovoid shape.

egg pendant. A PENDANT in the form of a miniature egg made of gold and decorated with enamelling and gemstones, worn suspended from a necklace (known as a 'necklace egg') or a bracelet. Examples were produced by CARL FABERGÉ suggestive of his famous jewelled Easter eggs made for the Russian tsars. Some were executed by his workmaster, A. Thielemann.

Egyptian faience. A ware made in Egypt, from before 3000 BC, of ground quartz fused by the use of an alkali and covered with a glaze made of a similarly produced material, but coloured (usually green to dark blue, sometimes other colours) and finely pulverized. The term 'faience' is incorrect, since the body is not pottery and the glaze contains no tin oxide as in the case of glazed faience. Examples of such ware are the mummiform ushabti tomb figures, and also examples of jewelry, such as beads, finger-rings, necklaces, and SCARABS (*see* TUTANKHAMUN JEWELRY; UDJAT EYE). The glaze employed was an early forerunner of similar objects made of glass.

Egyptian jasper. A variety of JASPER in which the mixed colours are in zones, in contrast to RIBBON JASPER.

Egyptian jewelry. Articles of jewelry made in Egypt from about 3000 BC until the conquest by Alexander the Great in 332 BC, when Egyptian art declined and Hellenistic influences spread. The use of gold and gemstones in jewelry of high-quality workmanship prevailed from early periods, as evidenced by bracelets and amuletic figures found in tombs; the jewelry was at first worn only by the pharaohs and the court. Increased supplies of gold in the Middle Kingdom, *c.* 2035 BC-*c.* 1668 BC, led to greater use of the metal, then made into pectorals and other ornaments of openwork design decorated with coloured enamels; *see* SESOSTRIS III PECTORAL. After the decline under the Hyksos kings, the New Kingdom saw a revival of prosperity and the making of jewelry of the richest character, with polychrome decoration, as exemplified by the jewelry of the XVIIIth Dynasty (1552-1296 BC) and particularly the TUTANKHAMUN JEWELRY. The motifs of such jewelry were mainly symbols of deities, figures of animals (the vulture, hawk, asp, or cobra), or various symbols (e.g. SHEN, DJED PILLAR, URAEUS, MENET BIRD, ANKH, UDJAT EYE). Elaborate pendants, diadems, bracelets, head-dresses, pectorals, necklaces, bead collars, ear-rings, ear-studs, and anklets, as well as honorific decorations such as the SHEBU, AWAW, and fly pendant (*see* FLY JEWELRY), and also the plain EAR PLUG and PENANNULAR ear-rings, were made, often of gold, decorated with enamelling and gemstones (especially LAPIS LAZULI, TURQUOISE, CORNELIAN, and sometimes AMETHYST, as well as coloured GLASS and EGYPTIAN FAIENCE. The SCARAB was used extensively in SEALS, FINGER RINGS, and AMULETS, spreading throughout the Mediterranean region. After the XVIIIth Dynasty, Egypt declined politically and artistically and after the Persian conquest in 525 BC the arts were influenced by styles introduced by the Greeks. The jewelry throughout the centuries was made for several purposes, as personal adornment during lifetime, as amuletic jewelry, as royal regalia or honorific jewelry, and as FUNERARY JEWELRY. *See* SEREKH BEAD; SIT-HATHOR-YUNET PECTORAL.

Egyptian Revival jewelry. Articles of jewelry made *c.* 1860-70, copying the overall appearance of classical EGYPTIAN JEWELRY, but made with

ear-ring. Gold with hoop masked by plate having suspended head and jars. Etruscan, 3rd century BC. H. 10.7 cm. British Museum, London.

ear-spools. Gold, cut out and embossed. Chavín culture. Lambayeque, Peru. W. 11.5 cm. Museum of the American Indian, Heye Foundation, New York.

ear-stud. Gold with filigree and granulation. Etruscan, 6th century BC. W. 6.8 cm. British Museum, London.

effigy flask. Cast gold. Effigy flanked by handgrip base. Quimbaya culture, Colombia, c. 500–1000. H. 23.9 cm. Jan Mitchell Collection, New York.

egg pendants. Miniature necklace eggs; gold with enamelling and gemstones. Fabergé. Courtesy of Wartski, London.

gold and enamelling without using the ancient Egyptian techniques. The articles included brooches, necklaces, ear-rings, etc.

eight cut. A modification of the BRILLIANT CUT, used on small diamonds (usually under 0.05 carats) that has 17–18 FACETS: an octagonal TABLE to which abut 8 isosceles-trapezoid facets, the lower and longer sides of which form the octagonal GIRDLE, and below the girdle and abutting it (forming the PAVILION) 8 triangular facets extending down to a point (or sometimes isosceles-trapezoid facets extending down to a small CULET). The pavilion is slightly deeper than the CROWN. Also called the 'single cut' or, when cut with a circular girdle, 'rounded single cut'.

Eilat stone. A mineral that is opaque and of mottled blue and green colours, being a mixture of various minerals, including CHRYSOCOLLA, TURQUOISE, and pseudo-malachite. It is said to come from King Solomon's mines near Eilat on the Gulf of Aqaba. In Israel it is considered a gemstone and is cut EN CABOCHON or shaped by TUMBLING.

electric jewelry. A type of jewelry that was kept vibrating by means of an electric battery concealed in the wearer's clothing. Such pieces were made as a novelty in Paris in the late 19th century. Some were worn as hair ornaments. See TREMBLANT.

electroforming. The modern term for the technique formerly (and sometimes today) known as ELECTROTYPING, which involves producing a metal article by depositing, by means of an electric current, metal (gold, silver or copper) in a mould so that the article will be an exact reproduction of the model. The model is sometimes made of wax, but is often an actual antique article for which reproductions are sought. The technique was introduced in England in the 1840s, developed in the 1850s in making copies of Celtic jewelry, and then expanded to make copies of much ancient jewelry. Many examples are in the British Museum (e.g. copies of the OXUS TREASURE) and in the Victoria & Albert Museum (e.g. copies of the PETROSSA TREASURE and of many pieces of Victorian jewelry). In recent years it has been used in England by LOUIS OSMAN (see WALES'S, PRINCE OF, INVESTITURE CORONET) and in the United States by STANLEY LECHTZIN. Unlike electroplating, it does not deposit the metal on a permanent metal base, and so permits the production of relatively large articles of reasonably light weight. The mould can be reused, so that the process is practicable commercially for mass production. See HELMET.

electrotexturing. A modern modification of the technique of ELECTROTYPING which produces on the article a textured surface. Grant MacDonald, of London, is a leading English exponent of the process. It is used principally on silverware, but sometimes on pieces of jewelry.

electrotyping. The technique of making metal articles by depositing, by means of an electric current, silver or gold in a mould. It was developed in England in the 1840s by Elkington Bros. of Birmingham, as a development of the process of electroplating, and is today generally known as ELECTROFORMING. The article produced by the process is an exact reproduction of the object used as a model, and is sometimes called an 'electrotype'.

electrum. (1) A natural ALLOY of GOLD and SILVER that is pale yellow. It was used in Egypt and Asia Minor from the third millennium BC, and later in Etruria and Latium, in Italy, especially to mount articles of jewelry made of AMBER. The proportions varied; Pliny refers to 4 parts gold to 1 silver, but 3 to 2 is more usual. (2) A modern, similar, man-made alloy, sometimes called 'white gold', that is used to produce objects with a gold surface after dissolving out the surface silver by a process similar to DEPLETION GILDING.

elenchi. A pear-shaped pearl.

elephant hair. The hair of an elephant, used in Indian jewelry to make a finger ring, bracelet, etc.

elephant ivory. A variety of IVORY from the tusks (incisor teeth) of elephants. Good-quality ivory, from male and female elephants, comes from Africa (mellow in colour and resilient) and India (white and drier, yellowing with age); elephants in Sri Lanka (formerly Ceylon) are usually tuskless, in Asia only the male has tusks, and the finest ivory is said to come from Thailand (formerly Siam). The tusks have fine longitudinal canals containing a gelatinous substance that provides the high polish. In cross-section it shows intersecting arcs that resemble engine-turning on metal and ceramic ware, which distinguishes elephant ivory from all other varieties.

Elizabeth I cameo. A CAMEO depicting a profile bust portrait of Elizabeth I, usually wearing a jewelled cap and a bodice with a ruff. A large number of such cameos, set in pendants and finger rings, were made, some of which were gifts by her. Based on the style of costume, they were made after *c.* 1575. *See* BARBOR JEWEL; WILD JEWEL.

Elizabeth I portrait ring. A type of PORTRAIT RING set with a gemstone carved with a profile bust portrait of Elizabeth I. The most famous is the ESSEX RING. Another, with both the exterior and interior of the hoop and the back of the BEZEL decorated with enamelled flowers, is in the collection of Kenneth Snowman, London. Such rings are dated *c.* 1600, with the cameos from *c.* 1575.

émail en blanc (French). Literally, white enamel. ENAMELLING by the use of only white enamel; it was the usual style of ÉMAIL EN RONDE BOSSE. It was often applied over figures IN THE ROUND placed over a gold ground or polychrome enamelling or close to gemstones. It was a style characteristic of the 14th–16th centuries, and was often used on brooches.

émail en résille sur verre (French). Literally, enamel in network on glass. ENAMELLING executed by carving on a plaque of glass (usually dark blue or blue-green) or crystal, backed with FOIL, a design in slightly concave depressions and then lining the depressions with GOLD LEAF and filling them with powdered transparent coloured enamels so as to make a decorative design. The enamels were fused at a temperature lower than would result in melting the glass. The technique was used for a brief period by a few French enamellers in the first half of the 17th century. Some pendants were made with plaques so enamelled from designs made, *c.* 1619–24, by VALENTIN SEZENIUS, *See* PERTÁBGARH JEWELRY.

émail en ronde bosse (French). Literally, enamel on an object IN THE ROUND. Decoration with opaque ENAMEL (usually white) applied thickly on a raised or modelled metal surface to form a relief decoration, or applied over metal figures in the round. Several layers of enamel were applied, but when different colours were used, they were laid on evenly over the surface (sometimes roughened to help becoming affixed) so as not to overlap. After each layer or colour was applied, the piece had to be refired and, after fusing, smoothed and sometimes polished, sometimes requiring up to ten firings. This style is associated with Renaissance jewelry as, although it was used in France and Spain during the 14th and 15th centuries, it became the style generally used by jewellers in the 16th century. Also called 'encrusted enamel'. *See* ÉMAIL EN BLANC; DUNSTABLE SWAN JEWEL.

embossing. A technique of producing relief decoration by raising the surface of thin metal from the reverse to form the design. The technique is the same as in REPOUSSÉ work, but the term is sometimes strictly applied to work done by mechanical means, such as the use of metal or stone dies (called 'embossing dies') as distinguished from repoussé work that is done by hand by the use of punches and hammers. The process is usually applied to flat metal, but it is sometimes used to decorate hollow ware by means of a snarling iron that impresses the design from the interior.

emerald. A variety of BERYL, and one of the rarest and most valuable of the PRECIOUS STONES. It is green, ranging from pale to dark, the most valuable being very dark 'velvety green'; the colour is derived from the presence of traces of chromium. Flawless stones are extremely rare, and most specimens contain INCLUSIONS, called the JARDIN (garden) of the emerald. It is not affected by changes of light as is a SAPPHIRE. Other, inferior, stones that are similar in appearance are green CORUNDUM, green TOURMALINE, DEMANTOID, DIOPSIDE, CHRYSOLITE, and HIDDENITE.

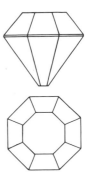

eight cut
side and top views

émail en résille sur verre. Pendant depicting 'The Adoration of the Shepherds' from a design dated 1623 by Valentin Sezenius. H. 5 cm. Victoria & Albert Museum, London.

Emeralds were known in Egypt from the 19th century BC and in the Red Sea region from the 1st century BC; they were used in abundance by the Indians in Colombia before the Spaniards arrived *c.* 1538. The finest, dark green, were found in the Muzo Mine in Colombia by the Spaniards *c.* 1587, and these, known as OLD MINE EMERALDS, were used as rounded pebbles called 'Chibcha stones', many of which were shipped to India and Persia; the next finest emeralds, of yellow-green colour, were from the El Chivor Mine (closed in 1625 but reopened in 1920). Other important sources have been India, the Ural Mountains of Russia, Rhodesia (now Zimbabwe) from 1955 (there called 'Sandawana emeralds' and being usually under one carat, but of good colour and free of inclusions), Zambia (from 1974), and Brazil (the stones having open veins that were filled with oil to improve the colour until the oil evaporated). In antiquity they were merely polished and drilled as beads or notched to be suspended (as still done in India and the Near East). In the West the stone is usually STEP CUT in rectangular shape (*see* EMERALD CUT); but some are cut EN CABOCHON (especially those that are CHATOYANT) or as a BRILLIANT. SYNTHETIC EMERALDS (*see* CHATHAM EMERALD; GILSON EMERALD) have been produced since 1930 (in quantity since 1946), as well as imitations in GLASS, which include FLAWS and inclusions but which are distinguishable by lack of dichroism. A deceptive practice to improve the appearance of an emerald of poor colour is painting its back and mounting it in a CLOSED SETTING for concealment. *See* DEVONSHIRE EMERALD; PATRICIA EMERALD; SOUDÉ EMERALD; CROWN JEWELS (IRAN); CROWN OF THE ANDES. *See* Benjamin Zucker, 'Connoisseurship in Emeralds', in *Connoisseur*, May 1980, p. 52.

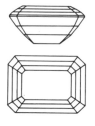

emerald cut
side and top views

emerald cut. The style of cutting a large transparent gemstone (usually an EMERALD or a DIAMOND) so that the TABLE and the contour of the stone are square or rectangular with chamfered corners and the sides are STEP CUT. It emphasizes, because of the large table, the colour of the stone rather than its brilliance, and results in less loss of weight than in a BRILLIANT CUT. This cut was developed in the late 19th century but seldom used until the 20th century. A recent modification is the ROYAL 144 CUT. *See* JONKER DIAMOND; VARGAS, PRESIDENT, DIAMOND.

emerald jade. The same as IMPERIAL JADE.

emeraldine. A misnomer of CHALCEDONY that has been stained green by DYEING with chromic oxide, so as to resemble the colour of an EMERALD.

Emerita. *See* SYMERALD.

en cabochon. Cut, as a gemstone, in the shape of a CABOCHON.

en plein enamelling. A style of ENAMELLING in which the enamel is applied in a smooth layer directly to the surface of the article rather than to panels (*plaquettes*) which are attached to it. When such enamelling is done is reserved areas, it is called *en plein sur fond réservé*. It was much used by CARL FABERGÉ.

en suite (French). Modelled and decorated in like style so as to form a set, e.g. a PARURE (or SUITE). *See* DRESS ORNAMENT; DRESS SET; DUO; ÉCHELLE; EQUIPAGE.

enamel. A pigment of a vitreous nature composed usually of powdered potash and silica, bound with oil, coloured with metallic oxides, and applied to PORCELAIN, GOLD, SILVER, COPPER, GLASS, etc., as a surface decoration by low-temperature firing. *See* ENAMEL COLOURS. Enamels are usually mixed with a flux to facilitate melting at a low temperature. They often sink deeply into the glaze of artificial porcelain, but are not absorbed into the feldspathic glazes of true porcelain or into the surface of gold, silver, copper or glass, and so remain on the surface of these, easily palpable to the finger-tips. The French term is *émail*, the Italian *smalto*, and the German *Schmelz*.

enamel colours. Colours applied in ENAMELLING that are fixed in a muffle furnace. Enamel colours are metallic oxides mixed with a frit of finely powdered glass. When used for painting, they are suspended in an oil medium for ease of application with a brush, the medium burning out during firing. The actual colours develop in the kiln. Enamel colours were originally opaque (owing to the inclusion of tin), but in the 17th century a transparent enamel was develop, and it is the variety most often used on enamelled jewelry.

enamelling. The technique of decorating various materials (e.g. gold, silver, copper, porcelain, glass, but as to jewelry usually only the first three) by the use of ENAMEL on the surface to paint scenes, figures or inscriptions (*see* PAINTED ENAMEL; EN PLEIN ENAMELLING; GRISAILLE) or in grooves or depressions in metal by filling in certain areas (*see* CHAMPLEVÉ; CLOISONNÉ; BASSE TAILLE; PLIQUE À JOUR; TAILLE D'ÉPARGNE; WIRE ENAMELLING; FILIGREE ENAMEL). The process of using ENAMEL COLOURS was known in Egypt from about 1600 BC and in the Mycenaean world from about 1400 BC; it was used to a limited extent in Greece (*see* DIPPED ENAMELLING) but extensively in Byzantium in the 6th century, in Venice from the 15th century, and elsewhere in Europe from the 16th century, especially at Limoges, which became a centre for decorating with PAINTED ENAMEL (*see* LIMOGES ENAMEL). It was used in Britain from the 9th century, and especially from *c.* 1750; *see* BATTERSEA ENAMELLED WARE; BILSTON ENAMELLED WARE. It has been used to decorate jewelry by all of the above-mentioned methods, employing a base of gold, silver or copper, and sometimes iron or bronze for use with opaque enamel; it has also been used on a glass or crystal base (*see* ÉMAIL EN RÉSILLE SUR VERRE) and on figures and relief work (*see* ÉMAIL EN RONDE BOSSE). Enamelling on metal by painting was originally unsuccessful but was solved by COUNTER-ENAMELLING. *See* ÉMAIL EN BLANC; SWISS ENAMELLING.

encrusted enamel. The same as ÉMAIL EN RONDE BOSSE.

engagement ring. A finger ring of no generally accepted form that is given by a man to his fiancée as a token of marriage engagement, in the manner of the earlier BETROTHAL RING, and indistinguishable in form or style. In recent years such rings have normally been set with a gemstone, usually a diamond (or any stone other than the ill-reputed OPAL), as a SOLITAIRE, of varying sizes, cuts, styles, and cost, but in the 19th century some were set with a PEARL. In the same century the custom arose in England of separate engagement ring and WEDDING RING, and in very recent years such rings have sometimes been made EN SUITE as a matching pair of similar style. *See* POSY RING.

English Dresden Diamond. A diamond found in 1857 in the Bagagem Mine in Brazil, weighing rough 119.50 old carats and cut into a pear-shaped BRILLIANT weighing 76.50 old carats. It is so pure that the KOH-I-NOOR DIAMOND appears slightly yellowish beside it. It was named after E.H. Dresden, a London merchant who bought it in Rio de Janeiro and had it cut by Coster of Amsterdam. In 1864 it was sold to an English merchant in Bombay, whose estate sold it to Mulhar Rao, Gaekwar of Baroda; it was acquired after 1934 by Cursetjee Fardoonji of Bombay. *See* DRESDEN DIAMONDS.

English square cut. A modification of the BRILLIANT CUT of a diamond that has an 8-sided TABLE to which abut 8 triangular FACETS alternating with 8 more triangular facets (the bases of which abut the GIRDLE), and that has on the PAVILION 8 similar triangular facets (the bases of which abut the girdle) and 4 large isosceles-trapezoid facets that meet at a point at the bottom (or 4 large 5-sided facets if they abut a CULET), totalling 28 facets (plus the table and culet). The CROWN is not as deep as the pavilion. The result is to take maximum advantage of the strong colour dispersion, but the fewer facets detract from BRILLIANCE. Also called the 'English brilliant cut'.

English star cut. A style of cutting a diamond that is somewhat similar to the ENGLISH SQUARE CUT except that on the PAVILION there are, extending from the GIRDLE to the CULET, 4 triangular facets alternating with 4 isosceles-trapezoid facets.

engraved gemstone. A gemstone decorated with a carved or engraved design, monogram, portrait or inscription, incised as an INTAGLIO or in relief as a CAMEO (*see* GLYPH). The stones most frequently so used were the AGATE and SARDONYX, which could be carved in a two-colour effect, but

English square cut
side and top views

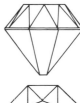

English star cut
side and top views

enkolpion. Gold pectoral of two joined discs with repoussé scene of the Annunciation (on reverse, Baptism of Christ). Byzantine, *c.* 6th century. W. 7.5 cm. Israel Department of Antiquities and Museums, Jerusalem.

enseigne. Gold with gemstones and enamelling. German, *c.* 1620. H. 8.5 cm. Schmuckmuseum, Pforzheim, Germany.

some diamonds bear engraved names, dates, and inscriptions (remarkable in view of their HARDNESS and the primitive tools available at the time), e.g. the SHAH DIAMOND, the AKBAR SHAH DIAMOND, the DARYA-I-NUR (IRAN) DIAMOND, and the JAHANGIR DIAMOND, and some RUBIES (e.g. the TIMUR RUBY) and EMERALDS were also so engraved. The work was done originally with a bow-drill, and later on a grinding wheel with the stone, attached to a dop-stick, held against it; a modern process uses a revolving burr. The early process was used from ancient times in Mesopotamia, mainly for designs in intaglio on a SEAL; later in Greece, in the Hellenistic period, gems were cut as a cameo to be worn ornamentally. The process was much used in Egypt for making SCARABS and in Minoan, Mycenaean, Greek, Etruscan, and Roman jewelry, especially for cameos and intaglios depicting persons and mythological characters. It was popular again in the Middle Ages when many of the cameos were thought to have amuletic powers. During the Renaissance engraved gemstones were made with original designs as well as copying the classical examples. Such engraved gemstones continued to be popular in the 17th and 18th centuries; among leading Continental engravers of the 18th century were the Italian JOHANN ANTON PICHLER, the French JACQUES QUAY, and the German Johann Lorenz Natter. Leading English engravers of gemstones were Edward Burch (1730-1814) and his pupil NATHANIEL MARCHANT (1739-1816), who depicted classical and contemporary subjects; others also produced accurate copies of ancient gems, but forgers, notably Thomas Jenkins in Rome, made cheap imitations. Important collections of engraved gemstones were assembled by Pope Paul II (1417-71) and at the courts of the Gonzaga, the Este, and the Medici (some made for Lorenzo de' Medici are inscribed with an abbreviation of his name, *Lau. R. Med.*) and also in England, e.g. by Thomas Howard, Earl of Arundel (1585-1646) and the 2nd Duke of Devonshire (*see* DEVONSHIRE COLLECTION). Imitations of cameos and intaglios were made in JASPER earthenware by Wedgwood and in paste by James Tassie (*see* TASSIE MEDALLION). Important engraved gemstones have been set in jewelry in recent years, e.g. the emeralds in the FARAH DIBA CROWN. Some of the gem-engravers of antiquity are identified by their MARK. Many engraved gemstones are too large to be worn as jewelry and were made as ornaments for a gem cabinet; for this reason such examples (e.g. the Gemma Augustea) are beyond the scope of this book. *See* John Boardman, *Engraved Gemstones* (1968).

engraving. The technique of decorating the surface of a hard material (e.g. metal or a gemstone) from the front by incised lines, characters, patterns, portraits, etc., cut into the surface. When the decoration on a gemstone is so made, it is an INTAGLIO; *see* ENGRAVED GEMSTONE. Engraving on gold was done from the third millennium BC, with crude tools of flint, bronze, copper and later iron; in Germany in the 15th century it was done with a dry-point needle. In modern times engraving is done by hand by means of a sharply-pointed steel tool (called a burin or graver) while the metal is held on an engraver's block. Engraving of monograms and inscriptions has been done by craftsmen skilled in calligraphy. *See* CHASING.

enkolpion (or **encolpium**) (Greek). A type of Byzantine circular PECTORAL, made with a central ornamental medallion depicting in REPOUSSÉ relief a Biblical scene or the portrait of an emperor, and having at the top two crosswise loops for suspending it at the breast from a necklace, neck-ring or TORC. They were usually made, in the 3rd-7th centuries, of sheet gold with repoussé relief, some being made of two such discs joined together with space between for a relic. One example, found in Palestine, is made of two such thin discs, one depicting the Annunciation and the other the Baptism of Christ. Such medallions were generally surrounded by a plain gold frame. The Christian examples, although forbidden by the Church, were worn as an AMULET. *See* BRACTEATE; EPIPHANY MEDALLION.

Enkomi Pendant. A gold PENDANT in the shape of a pomegranate, decorated overall with GRANULATED GOLD in a DIAPER pattern grouped in adjacent horizontal rows of inverted triangles and surmounted by a cylindrical suspensory loop. It is an example of MYCENAEAN JEWELRY of the 14th century BC, found at Enkomi, Cyprus, in 1896. *See* CYPRIOTE JEWELRY.

enriched surface. The surface of an article made of an ALLOY that is brightened by increasing the proportion of the more valuable metal in all or part of the surface, as in DEPLETION GILDING, DIFFERENTIAL PICKLING or DEPLETION SILVERING.

enseigne. A type of badge, worn on the hat or cap of a man of prominence, that evolved from the medieval PILGRIM BADGE. It was made in the 16th century, decorated with mythological or Biblical themes or with the portrait, monogram or device of the wearer or of his patron saint. Some were worn pinned on the underside of the rim of a turned-up hat, but most had loops at the edge or pierced holes so as to be sewn to the head-dress. From the mid-16th century they were worn also by women. Such pieces were made often of gold (but sometimes of bronze or copper) with enamelled decoration or an inlaid CAMEO, and occasionally were embellished with an encircling band of gemstones. They became less often used from the 1570s, and from the early 17th century the AIGRETTE became fashionable instead. *See* MORSE; NOUCH.

enstatite. A variety of gemstone that contains varying amounts of iron and that is transparent and often green, but as the iron increases the colour darkens (then called hypersthene). It is sometimes green-brown, called bronzite. The stones are usually faceted, but some specimens showing ASTERISM or CHATOYANCY are cut EN CABOCHON. It is dichroic and may resemble the green GARNET (DEMANTOID).

epaulet(te). A shoulder ornament worn on a military uniform, usually terminating in a fringe. Some worn in England have been made of gold, silver or plated ware. Examples worn in Russia, Portugal, and other Continental countries in the late 17th and early 18th centuries, with the insignia of military orders, were sometimes elaborately set with diamonds and other gemstones. A pair in the CROWN JEWELS (IRAN) is almost entirely covered with gemstones.

epaulet cut. A style of cutting a diamond (or other transparent gemstone) so that the TABLE is in the shape of an isosceles triangle bordered by 3 long trapezoidal FACETS and with 2 small triangular facets at the ends of the base.

epiasterism. The type of ASTERISM that is observed by reflected light, as from an ASTERIA (star stone), in contrast to DIASTERISM observed by transmitted light.

epidote. A group of minerals of similar chemical composition and related crystal structure, of which the best known as a gemstone is also called 'epidote'. It is usually of a unique colour similar to that of the pistachio nut, hence its alternative name 'pistacite', but specimens of brownish-green to brownish-black are known. Other varieties include allanite, clinozoisite, orthite, piemontite (sometimes called 'piedmontite'), TANZANITE, tawmawite, and zoisite.

Epiphany medallion. A type of ENKOLPION of which the decoration on one side of the central medallion is a depiction in relief of the Baptism of Christ. Such pieces were made in connection with a baptism at the Feast of Epiphany celebrated originally, and still in the Eastern Church, to commemorate the Baptism of Christ. One made of solid gold, and found in Cyprus, is said to have been issued at Constantinople by the Emperor at the time of the baptism of his son at Epiphany in AD 584 and given to a small number of courtiers and high officials. Numerous imitations were made of thin sheet gold with pressed relief, especially in southern Italy and among barbarian tribes; the Cyprus example is the only known surviving original.

episcopal ring. The same as a BISHOP'S RING.

Epsom Cameo. An irregularly-shaped CAMEO carved on a GARNET depicting in high relief the head of a bearded man wearing a Phrygian cap. The stone is set in a gold, late-7th-century, Anglo-Saxon PENDANT, but the date of the cameo (possibly antique) is uncertain. It was found at Epsom, Surrey, England.

Epiphany medallion. Gold medallion framed as enkolpion, depicting Baptism of Christ, with St John and two angels; on reverse (not shown), Virgin and Child between two angels. Probably Constantinople, 583–4. W. 6.5 cm. Dumbarton Oaks Collection (Harvard University), Washington, DC.

Epsom Cameo. Garnet cameo (possibly antique) carved to portray bearded man in Phrygian cap. Mount of gold with beaded wire edge. Anglo-Saxon, late 7th century. L. 3.85 cm. British Museum, London.

equal-armed fibula. Cast silver gilt with chip-carving. Anglo-Saxon, 5th century. L. 9.3 cm. Museum of Archaeology, Cambridge University.

erotic jewelry. Gold finger ring with emerald cameo bezel and phalluses on shoulders. Roman, *c.* 3rd century AD. From Guilhou Collection. Courtesy of Wartski, London.

esclavage. Gold and silver gilt with enamelling. Avranches, France, 19th century. Musée de Normandie, Caen, France.

Eskimo jewelry. Shaman's charm. Carved bone depicting 'Spirit Canoe' with 7 spirits. Alaska, 1825–75. L. 12.5 cm. Museum of the American Indian, Heye Foundation, New York.

equal-armed fibula. A type of FIBULA of ANGLO-SAXON JEWELRY of the 5th century, made in the form of the letter H resting on one side. Such pieces were cast of silver gilt, sometimes elaborately decorated with animal figures executed in CHIP-CARVING. It has been suggested that they may have been made by a Continental or an early British workshop.

equipage. A collection of small articles for personal use, such as a CHATELAINE with its suspended scissors, nail trimmer, tweezer, thimble, pencil, and the small container (ÉTUI) for such articles, or sometimes suspended articles for designing, e.g. a ruler, pair of compasses, and pencil. Such pieces became popular in the 18th century, some having the catch-plate of the chatelaine and the étui decorated EN SUITE with HARDSTONES.

erotic jewelry. Articles of jewelry with erotic decorative motifs, known from a wide area and over many centuries. A phallus has been used on amulets from ancient Egyptian and Roman times, and has been used to decorate brooches, finger rings, etc., throughout the ages. Examples of such motifs are carved on CAMEOS from the Hellenistic era and the Renaissance period. Many examples have been found in PRE-COLUMBIAN JEWELRY, especially in the MOCHICA JEWELRY and the CHIMÚ JEWELRY of Peru. Pornographic BUTTONS were made in the 18th century in France, and also in Japan and India. Modern pieces are known from Germany.

esclavage (French). Literally, slavery. A type of necklace composed of three chains or strings of beads or jewels in which the chains or strings hang approximately equidistant from each other. They were worn in Normandy as PEASANT JEWELRY in the mid-18th century.

Eskimo jewelry. Articles of jewelry made by the Eskimos, the native inhabitants of the arctic and subarctic region of North America, especially those from Alaska, Hudson's Bay, British Columbia, and Greenland. Although their artifacts were usually wooden masks and carved stone and jade tools, they made some jewelry, such as beads, BANGLES, and ear-rings, but particularly CHARMS (*see* SHAMAN'S CHARM) carved of WALRUS IVORY, moose or reindeer HORN, or BONE, to be worn as decoration on the robes of the shamans (medicine men). Some comparable work was done by the Lapps of northern Scandinavia. *See* FINGER MASK; TUPILAQ.

essence d'orient (pearl essence). A substance used to coat glass beads in the production of IMITATION PEARLS, to provide an iridescent effect so as to resemble a PEARL. It is made of silvery crystals (guanine) from the lining of the scales of certain fish (formerly bleak, but recently mainly herring). The crystals are pulverized, suspended in a solvent, and mixed with a lacquer, which is then applied, originally to the interior but later to the exterior, by spraying or dipping the glass beads (made with a string-hole). Up to ten coats are usually applied. It was originally made in France until *c.* 1940, but now it is made elsewhere, mainly in Canada near the Bay of Fundy and in Norway and South Africa.

Essex crystal. *See* REVERSE INTAGLIO CRYSTAL.

Essex Ring. An ELIZABETH I PORTRAIT RING with a gold, oval BEZEL set with a SARDONYX CAMEO of the head and shoulders of Elizabeth I, carved *c.* 1580 and set *c.* 1600. The back of the bezel is decorated with an enamelled floral scroll on a blue ground. The ring has been associated, but without confirmation, with a ring said to have been given by Elizabeth to the Earl of Essex with the stipulation that, if ever in desperate trouble, he should return it as a signal; he did so but his messenger, told to give it to Lady Scrope, handed it to her sister, the Countess of Nottingham, whose husband, an enemy of Essex, withheld it. She later confessed and the ring was said to have been given then to the widow of Essex, whose descendants sold it in 1911. Such a ring was purchased in 1927 and donated to Westminster Abbey, but it has been questioned whether it is the original ring.

essonite. The same as HESSONITE.

etching. The technique of decorating a metal surface by use of acids. The usual process is to cover the design on the surface with an acid-resisting substance and then to immerse the piece in acid that eats away (corrodes) the uncovered portions; but for decoration of fine lines, the entire piece is covered with the acid-resisting substance and the design is scratched through it with a sharp tool and then the piece is immersed in the acid. The covering is often a type of wax or varnish, and the usual acids for metalwork are nitric acid for silver and copper and aqua regia for gold and platinum. The process is sometimes used in modern times in lieu of ENGRAVING or CHASING. It is similar to the process of etching glassware and ceramic ware, except that there hydrofluoric acid is used. Sometimes tautologically called 'acid etching'.

eternity ring. A type of finger ring in the form of a circular band set with a continuous row of gemstones (usually diamonds) of the same size and cut. It is a type of modern WEDDING RING set with encircling gemstones. When the gemstones extend only on half of the SHANK, it is called a 'half-eternity ring'. The stones are secured in a CHANNEL SETTING or in adjacent single-stone COLLET SETTINGS. Modern examples are usually made of platinum, and sometimes depart from the traditional form by having two or three adjacent rows of stones, each row of different coloured gemstones, and sometimes having the two outer rows extend only halfway around the hoop. The history of the eternity ring extends back into antiquity, an example being known from Ur 4,000 years ago. In the Elizabethan period some examples were made in the form of an encircling snake swallowing its tail. It is sometimes called an 'alliance ring'.

Ethelswith Ring. A gold Anglo-Saxon finger ring having a circular BEZEL, in the centre of which, on a background of NIELLO, is a crude AGNUS DEI flanked by the letters A and D, and on each shoulder a small animal. The interior of the hoop is incised 'EADELSVID REGNA'. It has been identified with Queen Ethelswith of Mercia (853-89), the daughter of Ethelwulf, King of Wessex, 839-56, and sister of Alfred the Great (849-901). It was found in 1870 at Aberford, Yorkshire, by a farmer (who for six months tied it to his dog's collar before discovering that it was made of gold) and was bequeathed in 1897 by Sir A.W. Franks (who had acquired it from Canon Greenwell) to the British Museum. *See* ETHELWULF RING; ALHSTAN RING.

Ethelwulf Ring. A gold Anglo-Saxon finger ring with a BEZEL in the shape of a bishop's mitre with one peak, and having decoration depicting two facing peacocks reserved in gold on a background of NIELLO. On the hoop is an inscription 'ETHELVVLF R'. The ring is ascribed to the 9th century and is said probably to be associated with Ethelwulf, King of Wessex, 839-56, father of Alfred the Great and Queen Ethelswith of Mercia. It was found in 1780 between Salisbury and Laverstock, England, and was donated in 1829 by the Earl of Radnor to the British Museum. *See* ETHELSWITH RING; ALHSTAN RING.

Etruscan jewelry. Articles of jewelry (usually of gold) made with great skill and artistry in Etruria (now western Tuscany). The Etruscans were a non-Italic people whose culture, based on Greek culture, influenced the Romans from the 7th century BC until the 5th century BC, when they were invaded by the Gauls and again in the 4th and 3rd centuries BC until they were overcome by the Romans. The jewelry is of two periods: (1) the Early Etruscan Period, from the 7th century BC to the 5th, when the Etruscans excelled in developing their own characteristic styles and methods of workmanship, producing many pieces of technical perfection and great variety; and (2) the Late Etruscan Period, 4th-3rd centuries BC, when the work was of a coarser quality. During the Early Etruscan Period they developed the art of GRANULATED GOLD, using finely grained gold by a process only recently rediscovered, and making such articles as FIBULAE (some ornamented with animal figures IN THE ROUND), BRACELETS, EAR-RINGS (*see* BAULE EAR-RING), and NECKLACES. They also made articles in FILIGREE having openwork patterns without a backing, and often used coloured BEADS from Phoenicia, inlay and enamelling. In the Late Etruscan Period the decoration became meagre, mainly EMBOSSED work on convex surfaces rather than the earlier granulated and filigree work; the pieces included bracelets (some made as wide bands) and now finger rings, BULLAE, and burial WREATHS. The many finger rings were often made with a SCARAB or a long, oval BEZEL engraved or set with a

Essex Ring. Gold with onyx cameo of Elizabeth I. Westminster Abbey, London.

Ethelswith Ring. Gold finger ring; decoration reserved in niello. Anglo-Saxon, 9th century. W. 2.6 cm. British Museum, London.

Ethelwulf Ring. Gold finger ring; decoration reserved in niello. Anglo-Saxon, 9th century. W. 2.8 cm. British Museum, London.

Etruscan jewelry. Gold ear-ring with repoussé decoration and granulated gold. 4th/3rd centuries BC. H. 14.2 cm. British Museum, London.

étui. Enamelled case containing 9 implements. South Staffordshire, *c.* 1770. H. 11 cm. Courtesy of Halcyon Days, London.

gemstone. Most of the pieces known today have been found in Etruscan tombs and cemeteries. After *c.* 250 BC Etruscan jewelry continued to be made but was purely in Hellenistic style. In the 19th century the styles of ancient Etruscan jewelry were reproduced by FORTUNATO PIO CASTELLANI.

étui (French). A small ornamented case fitted with miniature implements for a woman's daily use, such as scissors, bodkins, needles, thimble, a tiny knife, pencil, ivory writing-tablet, etc. The cases were variously shaped, delicately decorated with enamels, and richly mounted with gilt hinges and collars. Porcelain examples were sometimes made in fantasy shapes, e.g. a maiden's leg with stocking, shoe, and garter, a lady's arm with sleeve, cuff, and ringed finger, a stick of asparagus or broccoli. They were also made in GOLD, SILVER, and PINCHBECK. Some were worn suspended from a CHATELAINE by loops of silken cord or chain attached to the cover. They were worn in the 17th-19th centuries. A heavier version was also used by a man, for a watch, watch key, keys, and seals. *See* EQUIPAGE.

eudialyte. A mineral that occurs in MASSIVE or crystal form, and is brownish-red to pink. The red crystal variety was once mistaken for GARNET until it was demonstrated in 1819 by the German chemist, Friedrich Stromeyer (1776-1835) that it dissolved in hydrochloric acid. It was discovered in south Greenland. *See* NAUJAITE.

Eugénie Blue Diamond. A heart-shaped, bright-blue, faceted diamond, weighing 31 carats, said to have once belonged to the Empress Eugénie, wife of Napoleon III. It was acquired by HARRY WINSTON, who sold it to Mrs Marjorie Merriweather Post, by whom it was donated to the Smithsonian Institution, Washington, DC. It is now mounted in a finger ring within a border of small white diamonds.

Eugénie Diamond. An oval BRILLIANT, weighing 51 carats, that was worn by Catherine the Great at her coronation in 1762 and was given by her, *c.* 1787, to her then favourite, Grigori Potemkin (hence it is sometimes called the 'Potemkin Diamond'). Later it was purchased from the grand-niece of Potemkin by Napoleon III as a wedding gift for his wife, Empress Eugénie (1826-1920), and was set in a diamond necklace. After the collapse of the Second Empire in 1870, the diamond was sold to Mulhar Rao, Gaekwar of Baroda. It was later reported as owned by Mrs N.J. Dady of Bombay, but its whereabouts since her death is unknown.

Eureka Diamond. Famed as the first diamond to have been found in South Africa. It was found along the Orange River in 1866 by Erasmus Jacobs, a young son of a Boer farmer, and was regarded as a pebble and given away. Before being identified as a diamond, it came into the possession of John O'Reilly, a travelling trader (hence it is still sometimes called the 'O'Reilly Diamond'), who sold it to the Governor of Cape Colony, Sir Philip Wodehouse. It was shown at the Paris Exposition of 1867. In 1946 it was bought at Christie's, London, by Peter Locan, a London collector, who had it cut from 21.50 carats rough to a 10.73-carat BRILLIANT. It was bought in 1966 by De Beers Consolidated Mines Ltd, and was presented by the company to the Parliament of South Africa at Cape Town.

Europa pendant. A type of PENDANT portraying Europa and the Bull. Some examples have the body of the bull made of a BAROQUE PEARL and its head and legs of enamelled gold. Other examples made of gold have the bull set with diamonds and rubies and Europa made in ÉMAIL EN RONDE BOSSE; they have been attributed to Italian make, 16th century. Another such pendant has the same motif carved in a chalcedony CAMEO set in a gold mount embellished with gemstones. Examples dating from the Renaissance are known from Spain and the Netherlands. *See* BAROQUE PEARL JEWEL.

European brilliant cut. A variation from the AMERICAN BRILLIANT CUT, involving changes in the size of the TABLE and depth of the CROWN. The European style was calculated in 1940 by Dr W. F. Eppler, and is recognized in Germany. In 1970 a new set of calculations of sizes and angles was developed in Scandinavia, known as 'Scan. D.N.'

eutectic welding. A process of joining small parts of a gold article, too small for SOLDERING, by which an ALLOY (having its components in such proportion that its melting point is the lowest possible with those components together, and lower than that of either of the components alone) is used as a welding agent. It is sometimes used by jewellers today when producing some types of gold jewelry. *See* COLLOID HARD-SOLDERING.

Evyan Aquamarine. An AQUAMARINE weighing 1,000 carats that was found in the Morambaya Mines, Minas Gerais, Brazil, and is greenish-blue, SCISSORS CUT (CROSS CUT). It was donated in 1963 by Evyan Perfumes, Inc. to the Smithsonian Institution, Washington, DC.

Excelsior Diamond. A famous bluish-white diamond found in 1893 at Jagersfontein, Orange Free State, South Africa. It was the largest known diamond until the CULLINAN DIAMOND was found in 1905. It weighed rough 995.20 carats, but was cut in 1903 by I. J. Asscher into 21 BRILLIANT CUT stones (10 of which weighed from 69.68 to 13.86 carats), totalling 373.79 carats, a loss in weight of 62.44%, due to the irregular shape of the stone. The cut stones were all sold separately, many through Tiffany & Co., but the present owners are unknown.

expandable bracelet. A type of BRACELET made of a series of identical segments that are pierced lengthwise with two holes so that strands of elastic can be threaded through and thus make the piece capable of fitting wrists or arms of different sizes.

eye agate. A variety of banded AGATE (or CHALCEDONY, ONYX or SARDONYX) having the bands of different colours in circular or oval shape, and hence suggesting an eye. Also called ALEPPO STONE.

eye bead. A type of BEAD of several varieties, all somewhat resembling an eye and decorated with contrasting spots. Such beads were generally made of glass and were almost always regarded as TALISMANS. The chief varieties are: (1) 'spot beads', each with a single spot of glass of one colour stuck on or pressed into the surface of the matrix; (2) 'stratified eye beads', each with a spot of coloured glass pressed into the surface, and another spot affixed on it, and so on; (3) 'ring eye beads', each with a ring or rings of glass of a different colour pressed into the surface; and (4) 'cane eye beads', each with a slice of a cane pressed into the surface. The first two types were made as early as 1300 BC, the third *c.* 9th century BC, and the fourth *c.* 6th century BC, and all continued to be made during Roman times. Such beads were also made in China in the 4th/3rd centuries BC, being the earliest form of Chinese manufactured glass.

Europa pendant. Baroque pearl and enamelled gold set with gemstones; figure in *émail en ronde bosse.* Italian, 16th century. W. 6.8 cm. National Gallery of Art (Widener Collection), Washington, DC.

F

Fabergé, (Peter) Carl (1846-1920). The Russian renowned for his artistic and imaginative creations in gold, enamelling, and gemstones, and best known for his jewelled eggs made from 1884 as Easter gifts from the Tsar to the Tsarina. He was born in St Petersburg, studied at several European centres, and then joined the jewelry firm that his father Gustav (1814-81) had started in 1842. Upon his father's retirement in 1870 he took over and soon, with his brother Agathon, enlarged the business. Later he was joined by his sons Eugène and Alexander. He achieved international recognition after the Paris Exposition of 1900, and thereafter made articles for the Russian Court, for Edward VII, and for other European royalty. Branches were opened in London and elsewhere, and the business grew to employ over 500 craftsmen. Fabergé himself, although he probably designed some of the work, was not a goldsmith or enameller, but excelled in supervising the creation of the pieces as to which he required the most meticulous craftsmanship and controlled the selection of the types of stones, enamelling, and settings. Each type of work was executed in a specialized workshop, and many of the pieces were signed with the marks of the individual workmasters, including, for the Easter eggs, Michael Perchin and later Henrik Wigström, and, for jewelry, Alfred Thielemann and later August Holmström. The articles were mainly OBJECTS OF VERTU, such as carved animals and jewelled flowers in vases, as well as useful objects, e.g. frames, boxes, clocks, etc., but he also produced a small amount of jewelry, mainly conventional pieces (e.g. tie pins, cuff-links) reputed for the precision of their settings; see EGG PENDANT. He specialized in the varied use of enamels, such as work in PLIQUE À JOUR enamel and *tour à guillocher* (see GUILLOCHÉ), articles of metal of different colours, and a great variety of gemstones (often ROSE-CUT diamonds and coloured stones cut EN CABOCHON). Many pieces were made in ART NOUVEAU style. The factory closed after the Revolution of 1918 and Fabergé escaped to Switzerland. *See* A. Kenneth Snowman, *The Art of Carl Fabergé* (1953) and *Carl Fabergé* (1979).

Fabulite. A trade-name for STRONTIUM TITANITE.

face. A plane, such as those that bound a CRYSTAL in its natural state, as distinguished from a man-made FACET.

facet. One of the small, ground, plane surfaces of a cut diamond (or other transparent gemstone). Such facets are of various shapes and sizes, and the many arrangements of the facets depend on the style of cutting the stone. *See* BEZEL; BREAK FACET; CROSS FACET; CULET; FACETING; GIRDLE FACET; KITE FACET; LOZENGE FACET; MAIN FACET; PAVILION FACET; QUOIN; SKEW FACET; SKILL FACET; STAR FACET; TABLE; TEMPLET.

faceted girdle. The GIRDLE of a diamond on which a band of small FACETS has been cut to increase the BRILLIANCE. It was introduced by Ernest G. H. Schenck. A girdle with 40 small facets has been developed by Louis H. Roselaar in the United States, and is found on a MULTI-FACET DIAMOND and on a ROYAL 144 CUT diamond.

faceting. The process of cutting a diamond (or other transparent gemstone) so as to have its surface completely covered with FACETS. The facets, if properly shaped and placed, result in greater BRILLIANCE by reducing the amount of refracted light that escapes; but some stones are cut to emphasize the colour rather than brilliance. There are a number of styles of faceting that are well established, some for many years, some recently developed. The earliest were the TABLE CUT and PYRAMID CUT. The ROSE CUT was introduced in the 15th century and was popular in the 16th/17th centuries until the invention of the BRILLIANT CUT. The rose cut has several modifications, e.g. the DUTCH ROSE CUT ('crowned rose'), the BRABANT ROSE CUT ('Antwerp cut'), the DOUBLE ROSE CUT, the CROSS ROSE CUT, the ROSE RECOUPÉE CUT, and the BRIOLETTE. The brilliant cut also has many modifications. Other recent styles of faceting are the BAGUETTE, CUT-CORNER TRIANGLE CUT, EMERALD CUT, EPAULET CUT, HEXAGON CUT, KEYSTONE CUT, KITE CUT, LOZENGE CUT, MIXED CUT, PENTAGON CUT, SQUARE CUT, and TRAPEZE CUT. The lapidary, when faceting a stone, must avoid over-heating from friction (doing so by means of a stream of water) as excess heat might lead to 'thermal expansion' of the stone, resulting in defective facets or a split stone. *See* STEP CUT.

facial ornament. An article of various types worn by a person on the face for practical or ornamental purposes, and often made of precious metal and embellished with gemstones. These include such vision aids as spectacles, lorgnette, and quizzing glass, as well as decorative pieces, including the FOREHEAD ORNAMENT and LABRET, and the many types of EAR ORNAMENT and NOSE ORNAMENT, including the Indian jewels set in the forehead, the cheek, and the side of the nose.

faience. Tin-glazed earthenware, especially that made in France, Germany, and Scandinavia. Owing to its easily chipped glaze, it is not suitable in general for jewelry, except BEADS. It is not the same as the ware incorrectly called EGYPTIAN FAIENCE. *See* PORCELAIN JEWELRY.

fake. A genuine article that has been altered or added to for the purpose of enhancing its market value, such as: (1) a finger ring that at a later date

Falize family. Gold necklace with enamel decoration in Japanese style. Alexis Falize. Ashmolean Museum, Oxford.

has been enamelled in black to make it appear to be a rare piece of
MEMORIAL JEWELRY or MOURNING JEWELRY; (2) a piece of jewelry to which
some additional gemstones have been added later; (3) a piece of jewelry to
which an inscription or maker's MARK has been added; (4) a gold or silver
article bearing a HALLMARK, where the mark has been altered or a new
one soldered on in order to indicate an earlier date; (5) a diamond that
has been subjected to IRRADIATION to change its colours; *see* TREATED
DIAMOND; (6) a ZIRCON made colourless by HEAT TREATMENT to simulate a
diamond. *See* FORGERY; COUNTERFEIT; REPRODUCTION. *See* Otto Kurz,
Fakes, 2nd ed. 1967.

falcon's-eye. The same as HAWK'S-EYE.

Falize family. Three generations of Parisian jewellers. Alexis Falize
(1811-98) started his own workshop in 1838 and acquired a reputation for
his gold jewelry with CLOISONNÉ enamelling and his adaptations of
antique jewelry. Upon retiring in 1876, he was succeeded by his son
Lucien Falize (1838-97) who became a partner of Alfred Bapst until 1879
(succeeding him as goldsmith to the French government) and then of the
latter's son, Germain Bapst, from 1880 to 1892. He was succeeded by his
son, André Falize (1872-1936), who, with his brothers Jean and Pierre
operated as Falize Frères, specializing in ART NOUVEAU jewelry. *See* BAPST
FAMILY.

false filigree. A style of decoration on metal that is an imitation of
FILIGREE work. It has been made mainly either: (1) by soldering
ornamental wire to a punch and then hammering it into a sheet of metal
from the back; or (2) by CASTING a piece from a model that was already
decorated with true filigree. A somewhat different technique was used for
decorating TUNJOS made as COLOMBIAN JEWELRY, where wax strands were
extruded as wire and affixed to the wax model before the metal piece was
cast.

false lapis. (1) A misnomer for JASPER stained blue by DYEING to imitate
LAPIS LAZULI. Also called 'German lapis' and 'Swiss lapis'. (2) A misnomer
for LAZULITE.

false topaz. A misnomer for CITRINE.

fan holder. A small receptacle for carrying a lady's fan, used in Europe
in the 16th/17th centuries. Some examples are in the form of a flower,
caduceus, etc., made of gold and decorated with enamelling or
gemstones, and having a small suspensory ring at the bottom of the stem.
Several examples were found in the CHEAPSIDE HOARD.

fancy-coloured pearl. A variety of pearl that is of an unusual natural
colour (other than the pink of the ROSÉE PEARL), e.g. faint tinges of blue,
green, yellow, bronze, grey, brown or black. Their value is usually less
than that of a rosée pearl of comparable size and quality. The colours,
derived from the water of the source, are dependent upon the translucency of the outer skin and the character of the interior layers of calcite,
aragonite or conchiolin, and also sometimes upon material in the
absorbed water; thus, white pearls are often initially greenish until they
become dry when the water has evaporated. *See* BLUE PEARL; STAINED
PEARL.

fancy diamond (or **stone**). A diamond of one of various pronounced
colours. *See* DIAMOND COLOURS.

Farah Diba Crown. The CROWN designed and made in 1967 by VAN
CLEEF & ARPELS, Paris, for Farah Diba, wife of Mohammed Reza Pahlavi,
Shah of Iran (died 1980), for her coronation. The crown is composed of
1,646 gemstones that were in the Royal Treasury of Iran, necessitating
their being set in Tehran in the gold and platinum mounting produced in
Paris to fit the particularly chosen stones. The principal stones are two
carved EMERALDS. *See* PAHLAVI CROWN.

Farah Diba Tiara. The TIARA made for Farah Diba upon her marriage
in 1959 to Mohammed Reza Pahlavi, Shah of Iran (died 1980). It is made
of platinum, set with 324 diamonds and has 7 upright ornaments, each set

fan holder. Gold with white enamel
and cabochon emeralds. English, 17th
century. L. 16 cm. British Museum,
London.

Farah Diba Crown. Gold and
platinum set with 1,646 gemstones.
1967. Courtesy of Van Cleef &
Arpels, Paris.

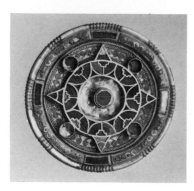

Faversham brooch. Silver gilt disc brooch with *cloisonné* inlay of garnets, niello, and gold filigree. Anglo-Saxon, 7th century. W. 5 cm. British Museum, London.

fede ring. Gold. Late 16th century. Ashmolean Museum, Oxford.

with a CABOCHON emerald, and has below the central emerald the pink NUR-UL-AIN DIAMOND. It was created by HARRY WINSTON.

fausse montre (French). Literally, false watch. An imitation watch that was carried on the right-hand side, in addition to the genuine watch that was carried on the left side, or carried on one end of a MACARONI. The former did not have a time-keeping movement, but included a small mirror, a pin-cushion, or a VINAIGRETTE. Although many were made inexpensively of gilt metal, some were almost as luxurious as the real watch, with a gold or silver case having an enamelled or jewelled back. Such pieces were carried by men and women in the late 18th century.

Faversham brooch. A type of circular DISC BROOCH of which about 50, from the early 7th century, have been found in Saxon graves near Faversham in Kent, England. They are silver-gilt examples of POLYCHROME JEWELRY with free-standing CLOISONS and gold FILIGREE on a separate plate, and sometimes have decoration in NIELLO. Some are set with GARNETS backed with FOIL or with green or blue glass.

feather. A type of microscopic internal incipient crack or fissure in a crystal that has been filled with gas, liquid or some subsequently introduced substance and that has a feathery appearance. Such flaws are found in some RUBIES and SAPPHIRES, varying in form depending on the origins of the stones, and in some genuine and synthetic EMERALDS.

feather agate. A variety of AGATE where the layers have been broken so as to resemble a black feathery form.

fede ring (from Italian, *fede,* trust). A type of finger ring, often worn as a BETROTHAL RING or an ENGAGEMENT RING, but sometimes merely as a token of affection, having as decoration an engraved pair of clasped right hands or two such hands moulded to form the BEZEL. They were usually made of silver (some of gold). On some examples from the 15th century the hands are at the back of the ring, and the bezel is ornamented, sometimes with a gemstone or a woman's head or a heart. Occasionally the fede ring was made in the form of a GIMMEL RING, with the hands on separate hoops and made to link together; these were sometimes separated so that each of an engaged couple could wear half until the marriage. Fede rings were used from Roman days, and were popular throughout Europe from the 12th until the 18th century. Some have an inscription (usually amatory, but sometimes religious or magical) around the hoops. The term 'fede' is said to have been introduced by 19th-century ring collectors from the Italian *mani in fede* (hands in trust). Links in the form of clasped hands were used in marriage chains of the 16th century.

fei-ts'ui. The Chinese term ('kingfisher plumage') applied to JADEITE. It was formerly used for a variety of green NEPHRITE, and recently has been applied to both varieties of JADE.

feldspar. A large group of minerals that is found in a wide area of the earth, but only a few of its members are suitable for gemstones. Feldspars are divided into several series: (1) orthoclase (embracing MOONSTONE and ADULARIA) and microcline (embracing AMAZONSTONE); (2) plagioclase (embracing SUNSTONE, AVENTURINE FELDSPAR, LABRADORITE, and PERISTERITE); and (3) celsian; each with several intermediate series. The group has also been called 'feldspath' but now is generally called 'feldspar'. The names of the varieties refer to the nature of the CLEAVAGE ('clase', derived from the Greek *klasis,* cleaving), with a prefix denoting the direction or nature of the cleavage.

Felicini Jewel. A pendant having a circular form with eight lobes decorated with red enamel and between each pair a pearl; the centre is set with a large AMETHYST with many FACETS and surrounded by enamelling. From the bottom is suspended a pear-shaped pearl. It was made by Francesco Raibolini, known as FRANCIA, being copied in an altar-piece painting for the Church of Sta Maria della Misericordia, Bologna.

ferronière (French). A type of FOREHEAD ORNAMENT in the form of a band worn around a woman's forehead and ornamented with a jewel in the centre. They were of Italian origin, worn in the 15th century in the form of a silken cord or velvet ribbon knotted at the back of the head. The style was revived in the early 19th century when the band was in the form of a fine gold chain or sometimes a string of beads, but was abandoned when hair styles made it unsuitable. The term is said to be derived from a portrait ascribed to Leonardo da Vinci and in the Louvre, portraying a lady wearing such a jewelled band; she was once thought to have been a blacksmith's wife (*ferronière*) greatly admired by Francis I, but now is generally considered to be Lucretia Crivelli, the mistress of Ludovico Moro, Duke of Milan. A later version of the *ferronière* had two additional pendants hanging at the temples.

fetter chain. A type of CHAIN of which the principal links are elongated. Usually there are, between each pair of long links, a group, of variable number, of short links, sometimes simple small ovals but often of the types found on a TRACE CHAIN, CURB CHAIN, etc.; where the number of short links in each group is three, the chain is called a 'fetter and three', and correspondingly for other numbers. There are many varieties of the basic fetter chain, e.g. the long links may be oval or rectangular and are sometimes twisted (called a 'snaffle chain') or 'fancy' (e.g. ornamented with crossbars or intertwined into knots).

Feuillâtre, Eugène (1870–1960). A French jeweller and designer who, after working with RENÉ LALIQUE, started his own workshop in 1899, specializing in the development of techniques for enamelling on silver and platinum and in making pieces with PLIQUE À JOUR enamelling. His work was mainly in the ART NOUVEAU style.

fibrolite. A mineral often of fibrous character from which some gemstones are derived. The stones are compact and usually of greyish shades of brown and green, but some transparent specimens are sapphire-blue. Some show CHATOYANCY. They resemble SAPPHIRE, CORDIERITE, and euclase. Pebbles of the massive fibrous variety are sometimes shaped by TUMBLING to form stones of baroque form. Also called SILLIMANITE.

fibula. A type of ancient garment-fastener brooch consisting usually of a straight pin (ACUS) that is coiled to form a spring and extended back to form a BOW and a CATCH-PLATE to secure the pin (the most common form of which resembles the modern safety-pin). The early form had no catch and was used by passing the pin twice through the fabric and then bending it upward behind the head to secure it. Mycenaean and later examples were made with the pin coiled at one end to form a spring for a more secure fastening. Later they were made of two pieces of metal with the pin hinged to a bar having around it wire coils attached on each side of the hinge (a double-twisted or bilateral spring); this type was the precursor of the safety-pin invented in the 19th century. Later the bow and the catch-plate were highly ornamented. Examples of the fibula have been made in gold, silver, and bronze. Some have been found at Etruscan sites in Italy, attributed to the 7th/5th centuries BC; it has been suggested that some of these were probably made locally, albeit some have also been found in the Illyrian region (now Jugoslavia). Many fibulae have been ascribed to Anglo-Saxon make, an example with triple pendants has been recorded of Byzantine make, and there are a number of varieties from Romano-British sources. A fibula is sometimes referred to as a 'safety-pin brooch'. The term 'fibula' has been sometimes loosely used to refer to any type of ancient brooch, and conversely the term 'brooch' has been sometimes used to refer to a fibula; but clarity would be better served if the two terms are respectively confined to the two basically different types

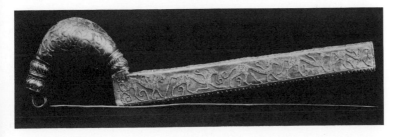

fibula. Gold with powder granulation. 7th century BC. Museo Archeologico, Florence.

figural brooch. Gold with *émail en ronde bosse* and gemstones. Netherlands, 1430–40. W. 5 cm. Schatzkammer, Kunsthistorisches Museum, Vienna.

figural ring. Germany, *c.* 1540. Kunstgewerbemuseum, Cologne.

of fasteners. *See* BIRD FIBULA; BOLT FIBULA; CERTOSA FIBULA; COMB FIBULA; CRUCIFORM FIBULA; HARP-SHAPED FIBULA; HORSE FIBULA; LEECH FIBULA; RADIATED FIBULA; SERPENTINE FIBULA; SMALL-LONG FIBULA; SPECULATE FIBULA; SQUARE-HEADED FIBULA; TIERFIBELN; VILLANOVAN FIBULA.

figural brooch. A type of brooch in the form of a RING BROOCH with the rim shaped like a floral stem with nodes, sometimes decorated with gemstones, and in the central space a variety of figures of persons or animals made of chased and enamelled gold. Such brooches were worn in the late 14th and early 15th century in England, France, Italy, Germany and Spain. A group of such brooches is in the Cathedral of Essen, Germany.

figural jewelry. Articles of jewelry, usually a pendant or a brooch, decorated with some story-telling theme portrayed by figures. The style was introduced in French jewelry under Francis I, 1515–47, and continued until the end of the reign of Henry II, 1547–59. Examples were designed by ÉTIENNE DELAUNE, inspired by the work of HANS HOLBEIN THE YOUNGER.

figural pendants. A type of PENDANT having as its decoration the figure or figures of persons, usually Biblical, mythological or allegorical, or of fantastic animals such as sea-horses, dragons, lizards, and birds. They were made of two types: (1) having the body IN THE ROUND, often in the form of a BAROQUE PEARL, with decoration of enamelling and gemstones (*see* BAROQUE PEARL); or (2) having the human figures placed against a background in ARCHITECTURAL STYLE. Such jewelry was especially made during the second half of the 16th century, often designed and made in Germany and Italy.

figural ring. A type of finger ring having its SHANK composed mainly of figures IN THE ROUND postured to form the loop. Designs for such rings were made by ALBRECHT DÜRER.

filigree. A type of decoration on metalware made by use of fine wire, plain, twisted or plaited. The wire was usually of gold or silver (sometimes of bronze in late Roman work), and was used to form a delicate and intricate design. It was executed in two styles: (1) the wire was affixed by SOLDERING to a metal base, this method having been used on BYZANTINE, CAROLINGIAN, ETRUSCAN, GREEK, OTTONIAN, and ROMAN JEWELRY, as well as on ANGLO-SAXON JEWELRY, and used later in the 13th century in Germany and Italy; and (2) the wire was used without a metal foundation, thus forming an openwork design. The latter method is found on European jewelry until the 15th century, and was revived in England in the Victorian era, being used especially for openwork portions of necklaces and brooches and also for finger rings having a gemstone encircled by such filigree or the shoulders decorated with it. Filigree was also used on some JEWISH MARRIAGE RINGS and on some Spanish and Portuguese PEASANT JEWELRY. In England it is found on some MOURNING JEWELRY, laid over locks of hair or made into a monogram. The openwork filigree is still popular in Portugal, the Ligurian coast of Italy, and Norway, especially on inexpensive jewelry for the tourist trade. For filigree work with the space filled in with enamel or slices of gemstones, *see* CLOISONNÉ ENAMEL and CLOISONNÉ INLAY. *See* FALSE FILIGREE.

filigree enamel. A type of decoration in the manner of CLOISONNÉ enamelling but having the CLOISONS made of twisted wire (rather than flat strips of metal) soldered to the base, and filled in with opaque enamel. After the powdered enamel in the spaces is fused and, upon cooling, has contracted, the wire shows above the surface. The style originated in Greece in the 5th century BC. Later, it flourished in or near Venice in the second half of the 14th century and spread throughout Europe, but mainly to Spain in some Hispano-Moresque work and to Hungary in the 15th/16th centuries. *See* WIRE ENAMELLING; HUNGARIAN ENAMEL; TRANSYLVANIAN ENAMEL.

fillet. A type of HEAD ORNAMENT in the form of a narrow band worn to encircle the hair. Fillets, worn by Greek, Etruscan, and Roman men and women, were often made of gold in the form of WREATHS of ivy, oak or myrtle leaves. In the medieval period, fillets were in the form of ribbons but later were bands of hinged pieces of gold. *See* BANDEAU; BANDELET(TE); CHAPLET.

findings. As to jewelry, small metal parts used as components in the making or repairing of various articles by jewellers, bought ready-made from refiners, e.g. BOLT RINGS, GALLERY STRIP, SETTINGS for stones, the ACUS and CATCH-PLATE for a brooch, links for a CUFF-LINK, etc. They are made by machine and mass-produced. When hand-made, they are sometimes called 'fittings'.

fineness. The proportion of pure GOLD or SILVER in jewelry, coins, etc., usually expressed in parts per thousand. English gold coins that are 11/12th pure gold are 0.9166 fine, and United States gold coins that are 9/10th pure gold are 0.900 fine. As to the fineness of gold and silver in jewelry, *see* GOLD ALLOY and SILVER ALLOY. *See* CARAT.

finger mask. A type of finger ring worn by Eskimo women, as a ceremonial article of jewelry, in the form of a ring, usually with two adjacent hoops (to be worn on adjacent fingers), to which is attached a large (width 8.5 cm) flat wooden disc bearing a carved human face. The discs are sometimes painted red and blue, with two teeth protruding from the open mouth, and are sometimes edged with downy feathers. The rings are usually worn in pairs, one on each hand. *See* DOUBLE-HOOP FINGER RING.

finger ring. A type of RING to be worn by a man or a woman on one of the fingers, or sometimes on the thumb. The ring consists of two parts: (a) the circular band, called the SHANK or HOOP, and (b) the raised part on the front, called the BEZEL, which is often broadened to support a COLLET for setting a gemstone, or which bears an engraved, stamped or enamelled motif or a SEAL (*see* SIGNET RING) or a SCARAB (*see* SCARAB RING). The part that includes the bezel and the set stone is sometimes called the CHATON. Such rings are of many forms, often depending on (1) the occasion for their use, e.g. CORONATION RING, BETROTHAL RING, ENGAGEMENT RING, WEDDING RING, GUARD RING, KEEPER RING, COCKTAIL RING, MOURNING RING, SERJEANT RING, ARCHER'S THUMB RING; or (2) the religious significance of the use, e.g. DEVOTIONAL RING, ECCLESIASTICAL RING, PAPAL RING, ICONOGRAPHIC RING, DECADE RING. Other such rings are of many shapes and styles, e.g. BROWNING RINGS, BUNCH RING, CHARM RING, CLUSTER RING, COILED RING, COIN RING, COMMEMORATIVE RING, CROSSOVER RING, DOUBLE-HOOP FINGER RING, ETERNITY RING, FEDE RING, FINGER MASK, FOB RING, GIARDINETTO RING, GIMMEL RING, GLOVE RING, GRASSHOPPER RING, GYPSY RING, HANDKERCHIEF RING, INVESTITURE RING, JET RING, KEY RING, LOCKET RING, LOVER'S-KNOT RING, MARQUISE RING, NUN'S RING, POISON RING, POLYHEDRON RING, PORTRAIT RING, POSY RING, PUZZLE RING, REGARD RING, SCIENTIFIC RING, SNAKE RING, SPLIT RING (or twin-bezel ring), STIRRUP RING, SWIVEL RING, THUMB RING, TRINITY RING, WATCH RING, WIDOW'S RING, WIRE RING. *See* O. M. Dalton, *Catalogue of Rings at the British Museum* (1912); Charles Oman, *British Rings (at Victoria and Albert Museum) 800–1914* (1974); John Boardman, Gerard Taylor, and Diana D. Scarisbrick, *The Ralph Harari Collection of Finger Rings* (1977).

—— *how worn.* Originally only one finger ring was worn by a person, but from Roman times, and later in the 17th century, men and women wore several rings on any finger as well as on the thumb (and not only on the bottom joint), and often several on the same finger, including sometimes a guard ring. From the 16th century finger rings were worn by women in various manners, e.g. sewn to a dress or tied on by a bow. From *c.* 1600 in England such rings, when worn on a finger, were sometimes attached to a long black thread or ribbon tied around the wrist, or were worn suspended from a ribbon around the neck or threaded on a cord around a hat. Men in Germany sometimes wore rings strung on a hat band. When having a portrait painted, especially in Tudor and Stuart times, men and women often wore all of their rings. A wedding ring was originally worn by the bride on the third finger of the left hand (the belief being that from there a vein, *vena amoris*, connected with the heart), but in the Middle Ages it was worn, for a then reversed belief, on the right hand. The wedding ring was placed on the left hand in England, but after the ceremony it was worn on any finger or on the thumb. The wearing of

filigree. Detail of gold bracelet with Heracles knot. 4th century BC. Museo Nazionale, Taranto, Italy.

finger mask. Wood, painted red and blue. Eskimo. W. 8.5 cm. Whatcom Museum, Bellingham, Washington.

finger ring. Gold with bezel set with engraved gemstone; shoulders decorated with filigree and granulated gold. Anglo-Saxon, 5th century. British Museum, London.

a wedding ring by a man, while frequent on the Continent and now also in the United States (and customary in the East), is less frequent in England. Persons wearing gloves sometimes wore a ring over the glove (*see* BISHOP'S RING) or slashed the glove to reveal it underneath.

fingernail shield. An article of gold jewelry worn to simulate exceptionally long fingernails, some being about 50 cm long, such as those worn continuously day and night by Tsz'i Hsi (1834–1908), Dowager Empress of China.

fingerprint. A type of INCLUSION in certain gemstones, e.g. SAPPHIRES from Sri Lanka (formerly Ceylon), in a net-like form, sometimes called 'butterfly wings'. It results from interior cracks that have 'healed' and show under magnification.

'Finglesham Man' Buckle. A gilt-bronze BUCKLE, the decoration of which is a cast figure in low relief of a man whose helmet bears horns terminating in beaks; he carries a spear in each hand and wears nothing except a belt. It has been suggested that the figure represents a version, possibly made in Kent, England, of traditional symbolic heathen religious art from northern Germany or Sweden from the 7th century. The buckle was found in 1964 in an Anglo-Saxon cemetery at Finglesham, near Deal in east Kent.

Finiguerra, Tommaso (Maso) (1426–64). A Florentine craftsman of the Renaissance period famed for his work in NIELLO.

Finnish jewelry. Articles of jewelry from *c*. AD 500–1100, known as Kalevala jewelry, and modern very accurate reproductions of it, as well as articles made of gold and silver by Finnish craftsmen from *c*. 1950, the style emphasizing simplicity and featuring the use of native gemstones rather than intricate design. *See* John Haycraft, *Finnish Jewellery* (1962).

fire. The brilliant display of flashes of prismatic hues in certain gemstones due to a high dispersive power and a high refractive index, emphasized by faceting. The fire in a correctly faceted diamond is greater than in any other natural colourless gemstone (next is ZIRCON), owing to the high dispersive power combined with its high refractive index; but it is surpassed by SYNTHETIC RUTILE and synthetic STRONTIUM TITANATE and also by such coloured stones as DEMANTOID (green GARNET), and SPHENE. Such stones as the emerald, ruby, and sapphire, although they may have BRILLIANCE, do not have fire.

fire-mark. A small crack that is visible near the edges of the FACETS of CORUNDUM (natural or synthetic) and that is the result of overheating while the stone was being cut or polished. Also sometimes called 'chatter-mark'.

fire opal. A variety of PRECIOUS OPAL that is transparent to translucent, and whose background is reddish-brown to orange-red, sometimes having patches of different colours in the same stone, but with very little or no prismatic colours. When viewed in certain directions, it sometimes shows IRIDESCENCE. Such stones are faceted as a BRILLIANT or cut EN CABOCHON. The main source is Zimapán, in the State of Hidalgo, Mexico, and the centre for cutting is at Querétaro, in the State of Querétaro, Mexico. Also called GIRASOL or 'gold opal'.

firestone. A treated QUARTZ that is an imitation of RAINBOW QUARTZ, produced by heating ROCK CRYSTAL to cause internal cracks and then suddenly cooling it in dyed water that enters the cracks and creates an iridescent effect.

firing. The process of altering a material by exposing it in a kiln to the requisite degree of heat. It is necessary in order to fuse ENAMELS and cause them to be affixed to a metal base; and in some cases (e.g. PAINTED ENAMEL) there must be several successive firings when different colours are used.

fish jewelry. Articles of jewelry made in the form of a fish. The fish has been used as a jewelry motif from ancient times, e.g. as the form of a gold

and green feldspar pendant made in Egypt, *c.* 1900 BC–1800 BC, and
worn as an AMULET (called a *nekhaw*) attached to the sidelock of children,
and as a jade pendant made in China as an amulet, 13th to 10th centuries
BC. Some articles of early Christian DEVOTIONAL JEWELRY were made in
the form of a fish or were inscribed or enamelled with the word ICHTHUS.
In SINÚ JEWELRY pendants were made in the form of a mythological flying
fish, with horizontal fins and a vertical tail. In modern times small
pendants are made, especially in China, in the form of a fish with
ARTICULATED parts and enamelled decoration. *See* PÁTZCUARO FISH
NECKLACE.

Fisherman's Ring. A gold SIGNET RING (*anulus piscatoris*) worn by the
Pope and used by him to authenticate papal documents. The BEZEL is
engraved with the Pope's name encircling a depiction of St Peter casting a
net from a boat. Such rings were first mentioned in 1265. A new ring is
made for the investiture of a new Pope, the old ring being destroyed and
the new one, after being first placed on his finger, is removed to have his
papal name, then chosen by him, engraved on it. One existing ring,
ascribed to the 18th century and set with a bloodstone INTAGLIO depicting St Peter and with a blank space for a name, has been said to be a
Fisherman's Ring that was never papally used; but it has been hinted that
it may have been made by a jeweller for private sale, and doubts based on
its form have been expressed as to its authenticity as a Fisherman's Ring.

Fishpool Hoard. A HOARD of articles of English and Continental mid-
15th-century jewelry buried at Fishpool, near Mansfield, Nottingham-
shire, England, and found in 1966. It included 1,237 gold coins which indicate that the burial was in 1464. Its relatively high value has suggested
that the owner was a rich merchant or a prominent person involved in the
Wars of the Roses. Many of the articles are decorated with black-letter inscriptions and flowers and foliage.

flame opal. A variety of PRECIOUS OPAL that shows flashes of red over the
entire surface of the stone. *See* FLASH OPAL.

fish jewelry. Gold pendant with
gemstones. Afghanistan, *c.* 100 BC–AD
100. National Museum of Pakistan,
Karachi.

Flaming Star Diamond. A pear-shaped diamond weighing 21.9 carats
that is remarkable in that under normal light it has a fine white colour but
under ultraviolet light it glows a very intense and brilliant orange. It was
found at the De Beers Mine, in South Africa, weighing 88 carats rough. It
was purchased and cut in 1967 by Baumgold Bros., Inc., New York City,
who reported in October 1979 that it had been sold to royalty.

flange. Any internal or external attachment to a piece as a support for
another part, e.g. a bearing inside a COLLET of a finger ring upon which a
gemstone is set.

flash opal. A variety of PRECIOUS OPAL that shows flashes of a single colour which tends to disappear when the stone is moved. *See* FLAME OPAL.

flaw. An internal fault or imperfection in a gemstone, as distinguished
from a BLEMISH, which is a marring of the surface. Flaws may be due to
the INCLUSION of a foreign material, to a small crack or cleavage, or to a
liquid-filled cavity. A flaw usually detracts from the value of a gemstone
(especially in a diamond), but less so in an EMERALD which almost invariably has some minute inclusion. In some stones a technical flaw does
not detract but adds to the character of the stone, e.g. the inclusions that
cause the ASTERISM in a RUBY or SAPPHIRE, the dendritic inclusions in a
MOSS AGATE, and the structure of an OPAL. A stone is said to be 'clean' or
'flawless' if no flaws are noticeable under a jeweller's lens that magnifies
ten times (or 'VVSI' if 'very very slightly imperfect'). Some flaws can be
concealed by the manner in which the stone is set.

flèches d'amour (French). Literally, love arrows. Thin hair-like sparkling crystals of RUTILE found as INCLUSIONS in some colourless transparent
quartz called RUTILATED QUARTZ.

flint glass. A variety of GLASS containing oxide of lead (now usually called LEAD GLASS) but inferior to CRYSTAL GLASS. It is sometimes used for
COSTUME JEWELRY, owing to its brilliance when faceted, but it is easily
scratched.

Flöckinger, Gerda. Necklace with pendant of oxydized silver, gold, coloured pearls, and gemstones, and chain of silver and pearls. 1978. Courtesy of Gerda Flöckinger, London.

Flora of Pistrucci, The. Gold finger ring with cornelian breccia depicting Flora. Benedetto Pistrucci, Italy, *c.* 1810. L. 2.3 cm. British Museum, London.

Flöckinger, Gerda (1927–). A London DESIGNER-MAKER of contemporary jewelry. Born in Innsbruck, Austria, she came to London in 1938, from 1945 studied and later conducted a course in art and jewelry, and in 1956 opened her own workshop. Her early work featured enamelling in abstract and pictorial forms, but from 1963 she developed a technique of fusing and texturing silver and gold to create flowing patterns, highlighted by one or more gemstones or pearls. Her work has been exhibited in England and abroad, with showings at Goldsmiths' Hall and in 1971 the first one-man show that the Victoria & Albert Museum had ever held for a living jeweller. All her work is personally designed and executed. *See* Brian Beaumont-Nesbitt, 'Gerda Flöckinger', in *Connoisseur*, September 1973, p.28; Graham Hughes, 'Gerda Flöckinger', in *Connoisseur*, February 1964, p. 111.

Flora of Pistrucci, The. A gold finger ring set with a cornelian BRECCIA depicting in high relief the profile head of Flora (the Roman goddess of flowers) wearing a floral wreath. When Richard Payne-Knight, a British collector, purchased the ring from an Italian dealer, Bonelli, he insisted that it was an antique CAMEO, despite the assertions of BENEDETTO PISTRUCCI that he had carved it. To support his assertion, Pistrucci carved several imitations. The ring was bequeathed in 1824 by Payne-Knight to the British Museum, where it is now regarded as modern, *c.* 1810.

floral brooch. A type of brooch the decoration of which is in the form of a bouquet of naturalistic flowers, usually set with gemstones of several colours and with green-enamelled leaves and gold stems; some also have a ribbon bow set with gemstones. They became popular during the ROCOCO period of the 18th century, and continued well into the 19th century, especially those pieces designed by OSCAR MASSIN. *See* SPRAY.

Florentine Diamond. A famous diamond, weighing 137.27 carats, cut as a DOUBLE ROSE, whose long history has been variously related. One story, now discredited, is that it was lost by Charles the Bold of Burgundy in the Battle of Grandson in 1476, was found by a soldier, sold successively until it came into the possession of Duke Ludovico Sforza of Milan, then of Pope Julius II, and later of the Medici. Its recorded history dates from its being listed in a 1621 inventory which described it as faceted on both sides and encircled by a gold, diamond-encrusted band, and stated that it was bought uncut by Ferdinand I de' Medici and was cut at the time of Cosimo II, *c.* 1609–21 (hence not the stone lost by Charles the Bold). It was seen in 1657 by Jean-Baptiste Tavernier in the possession of Ferdinand de' Medici, Duke of Tuscany, and was described by him as of yellow colour and faceted. It was again listed in an inventory made in 1740 of the personal jewels of Anna Maria de' Medici, the widow of Gian de' Medici (1671-1737), Duke of Tuscany and the last of the Medici line. She resisted the attempts to seize the Tuscany Crown Jewels made by Francis Stephen (1708-65), Duke of Lorraine (from 1729), when Tuscany was settled upon him in 1735 in exchange for Lorraine, and she bequeathed them to Tuscany for future Grand Duchesses. Francis Stephen married in 1736 Maria Theresa (daughter of Holy Roman Emperor Charles VI). When Anna Maria died in 1743 the Florentine and other personal Medici jewels, then found in her cabinet, were seized and taken to Vienna by Francis Stephen, as Duke of Tuscany. He wore the diamond in his crown upon his coronation in 1745 as Francis I, Holy Roman Emperor, and after his death in 1765 the Florentine and other Medici jewels passed, through the widow, Maria Theresa, to the Austrian branch of the Habsburgs and into the Austrian Treasury in Vienna. The diamond had been previously set in an elongated hat ornament. It was so displayed at the Hofburg in Vienna until 1919 when it was removed by Emperor Charles I in anticipation of his abdication, and was then either taken by his brother or an agent to Switzerland and sold, or taken to the United States (and possibly sold in 1955) or to South America. One view is that it has been cut into three pieces. It is sometimes called the 'Austrian Yellow Diamond' or the 'Tuscany Diamond'. *See* Lord Twining, *Crown Jewels of Europe* (1960), pp. 16–18; Kirsten Aschengreen-Piacenti, 'Jewels of the Electress Palatine', *Apollo*, September 1974, p. 231.

Florentine finish. A style of textured surface on a metal article made by ENGRAVING parallel lines closely in one direction and then cross-hatching at 90° with parallel lines engraved more lightly. *See* TEXTURED GOLD.

Florentine mosaic. A type of MOSAIC made in Florence, composed of tiny pieces of opaque varicoloured HARDSTONES, selected and arranged so that the colours and gradations of tones created and enhanced a pictorial effect, usually of flowers or scenes, and cemented on a background of white or black marble. Sometimes called 'intarsia' (although that term is mainly applied to inlaid woodwork) or *commesso di pietre dure* (*see* COMMESSO), referring to the hardstones used. It is used mainly in plaques and boxes, but sometimes in pieces of jewelry.

florid cruciform fibula. A type of FIBULA related to the CRUCIFORM FIBULA, but heavily and excessively decorated, with the wide cross arms and the foot dominating the short arched BOW. Examples in ANGLO-SAXON JEWELRY were made in the 7th century.

flower jewelry. An article of jewelry, usually a brooch or a pendant, whose decorative motif is a flower, enamelled or IN THE ROUND. Examples are known featuring many species of flowers. *See* Geoffrey Munn, 'A Garden of Earthly Delights', *Connoisseur*, July 1979, p. 96.

flush setting. A style of SETTING a flat-top stone in a finger ring so that the top of the setting edge is forced over the oblique FACETS of the stone and ground down so as to be level with the TABLE of the stone.

fly jewelry. (1) A type of PENDANT made in Egypt in the shape and with the markings of a house-fly, made of GOLD FOIL moulded over a composition core and having a suspension ring soldered to the head, or cast in solid gold with a pierced head for stringing onto a necklace. Such pendants are said to have been made originally as military awards but probably were later a decoration for any courtier, and examples are known to have been worn by women. Some were worn as an AMULET. They were made during the New Kingdom, *c.* 1552 BC-1070 BC, and were possibly connected with the worship of the Canaanite god Baal-Zebub, whose name was 'Lord of the Flies'. (2) A type of pendant or brooch in the form of a fly, made in England in the Victorian era; some were set with SEED PEARLS and small gemstones. (3) A type of finger ring having on the BEZEL a relief figure of a fly; examples were made of silver in the 17th century.

fob. (1) A small ornament suspended from a WATCH CHAIN, e.g. a FOB SEAL. The word 'fob' originally referred to a small pocket, particularly a small pocket in a man's trousers just below the waistband, in which a POCKET WATCH was carried; but when it became the custom to wear a watch on a chain, the word became associated with the chain (i.e. 'fob chain') and later it designated an ornament suspended from the chain. (2) A ribbon, mesh band or similar article attached to the 'bow' (ring) of a watch when it is carried in the watch pocket, hanging from the pocket and having some decorative ornament or fob seal attached to it.

Florentine mosaic. Gold brooch with polychrome hardstone mosaic. Italian, *c.* 1840. W. 3 cm. Courtesy of S. J. Phillips Ltd, London.

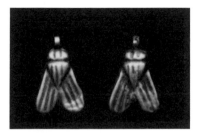

fly jewelry. Gold amulets. Tell el-Ajjul Treasure. 1900 BC-1200 BC. Israel Department of Antiquities and Museums, Jerusalem (photo by Israel Museum).

fob seals. Gold with hardstone seals. English, 18th century. Courtesy of Wartski, London.

fob ring. A type of finger ring that has a small loop or cylinder on the back of the hoop, opposite the BEZEL, for suspension on a CHATELAINE, FOB or WATCH CHAIN, sometimes along with a WATCH KEY, KEY-RING or SIGNET RING.

fob seal. A seal mounted on the base of a shank that is about 2.5 cm to 5 cm long and has a small ring for suspension from a CHATELAINE or WATCH CHAIN. The shanks were made of a variety of materials, including GOLD, SILVER, and HARDSTONES, as well as GLASS decorated with twists or in millefiori style. In some examples the seal was set so as to swivel in the arms of the shank. Some unusual Swiss specimens have a musical mechanism built into the shank. During the second half of the 18th century such pieces were made in England of gold very ornately decorated in a great variety of styles and designs.

foil. A thin sheet of metal (gold, silver, copper or an ALLOY made by various formulae depending on the colour desired to match the stone to be foiled), used in jewelry as a backing to certain mounted gemstones to enhance the colour or brilliance. Foil has been used from earliest civilizations. It is made by hammering sheet metal to the thinness of paper, and is applied by beating it to a metal object or by means of a fixative. In the 16th century it was sometimes used to back a diamond (cut as a POINT DIAMOND or a TABLE CUT diamond) so as to add to its brilliance, but usually a diamond is not foiled but occasionally tinted. Foil has also been used to back GARNETS in ANGLO-SAXON JEWELRY and in jewelry of the 17th to 19th centuries. Sometimes, to heighten the brilliance, the foil is pricked or cross-hatched. When beaten very thin, foil is known as LEAF, and is used as a decorative covering for cheaper metals; *see* GOLD LEAF; SILVER LEAF. Sometimes foil has been used deceptively to give to some inferior material the appearance of a gemstone. The French term is *paillon*. *See* MIRROR FOILING; DUTCH METAL.

foiling. The process of changing the apparent colour or appearance of certain gemstones by backing with FOIL. *See* MIRROR FOILING.

Fontenay, Eugène (1823–87). A prominent French jeweller who wrote an important history of jewelry and who is best known for his carvings of Chinese JADE mounted in ear-rings and other articles in Classical and neo-classical styles.

fool's gold. Iron PYRITES (PYRITE) which has some resemblance to gold, having a brassy-yellow colour and a brilliant METALLIC LUSTRE. The term has been incorrectly applied to MARCASITE.

forehead ornament. Gold and inlaid green and pink stones. Uzbekistan, *c.* 1750–70. Israel Museum, Jerusalem.

forehead ornament. An ornament, of various styles, worn on the forehead, usually suspended from a HEAD ORNAMENT and often being a gold pendant set with gemstones. Such ornaments were worn by women of certain primitive civilizations, e.g. of tribes in Uzbekistan, an ancient region of present-day USSR, *c.* 1750–70, and of tribes of pre-Columbian Indians in America, and by women in India. They have also been worn during the Renaissance and later, until modern times, by ladies in evening dress as a form of exotic jewelry. *See* FERRONIÈRE; FRONTLET.

forgery. An article made in order to be falsely represented and sold as a genuine ancient work, being dependent for its value mainly on the workmanship that it imitates. The making of such pieces is a development of relatively modern times when the demand for old jewelry, as with other antiques, has made their production profitable. Among the articles that have been forged are gold GREEK JEWELRY (especially INTAGLIO gems) and ETRUSCAN JEWELRY, medieval finger rings, enamelled Renaissance pendants, and PILGRIM BADGES (*see* BILLY AND CHARLEY). One insidious forgery practice is to reset a genuine old mount with modern stones or paste; another is to sell a forged PARURE in an old shagreen case or a new case made to fit it and 'aged'. *See* COUNTERFEIT; FAKE; REPRODUCTION; PONIATOWSKI COLLECTION; ROUCHOMOWSKY.

fortification agate. A variety of AGATE that shows, on a polished surface, angular concentric markings suggestive of a fortification. Sometimes called 'bastion agate'. The German term is *Festungsachat*. *See* RUIN AGATE.

fossil. A petrified organic substance (or the imprint of a fossilized plant or animal), the organic material having decomposed and been replaced over centuries by an inorganic mineral. Fossilized plants produce BOGWOOD and JET. Fossilized material is found in fossilized AGATE, JASPER, and OPAL. Several varieties of fossilized animal life have been incorporated into articles of jewelry, including opalized snails and mussels, AMMONITE (shell of snail-like molluscs), turrilite (shell of a spiral-turreted mollusc), and lumachella (shell of triton-like mollusc). *See* BELEMNITE; GLOSSOPETRA; ODONTOLITE; TRILOBITE.

fossil ivory. A variety of IVORY from the tusk of the mammoth or the walrus that has been buried long enough to have acquired a yellow, sepia, variegated or blackish colour, but is not actually fossilized. It is found mainly in the frozen ground of Siberia, and is brittle and often cracked, with a tendency to turn yellow. It differs little from ELEPHANT IVORY.

fossil turquoise. A misnomer for ODONTOLITE.

Founder's Jewel. A gold LETTER JEWEL in the form of a crowned letter M in Lombardic cursive script, being the monogram of the Virgin Mary. The two sides of the letter are set with alternate emerald and ruby CABOCHONS (two missing) and in the centre line a large ruby is set in an enamelled vase flanked by rubies from which rise three white-enamelled symbolic lilies. The spaces between the lines of the letter are in the form of architectural niches in which stand, facing each other, figures in ÉMAIL EN RONDE BOSSE, of the Virgin and the Angel of the Annunciation, the latter's wings being of translucent green enamel. The piece is said to have been possibly the central jewel on the mitre of William of Wykeham or a NOUCH. It is part of the 14th-century WILLIAM OF WYKEHAM JEWELS now at New College, Oxford. Reproductions were made by ALESSANDRO CASTELLANI. *See* E JEWEL.

Founder's Jewel. Gold jewel set with gemstones. English (?), 14th century. New College, Oxford.

'Founder's Ring'. The PONTIFICAL RING sometimes said, but without historical basis, to have belonged to Bishop William of Wykeham. It is of gold or silver-gilt, with an irregular-shaped BEZEL set with a pale SAPPHIRE in a scalloped COLLET. The cast hoop has shoulders decorated with an unidentified winged figure, below which are floral ornaments and a saltire cross. It is in the collection of WILLIAM OF WYKEHAM JEWELS at New College, Oxford.

Fouquet, Georges (1862–1957). A Parisian jeweller who in 1891 joined the jewelry business of his father, Alphonse Fouquet (1828–1911), at 35 Avenue de l'Opéra, and took over its direction when his father retired in 1895. After winning international awards, he, *c.* 1902, opened a new showroom at 6 Rue Royale designed by ALPHONSE MUCHA, who from 1895 to 1905 designed much of the jewelry executed by Fouquet, including some for Sarah Bernhardt. His other designers included Tourrette and Charles Desroziers. The jewelry was mainly in the ART NOUVEAU style, using enamelling and coloured gemstones, but was more symmetrical and less imaginative than that of RENÉ LALIQUE. He also made neo-classical pieces of heavily worked and chiselled gold. His son Jean joined the business in 1919, making some pieces in ART DECO STYLE. *See* CLEOPATRA BRACELET.

Fouquet, Georges. Gold and enamel brooch in Art Nouveau style. Design by Desrosiers. French, 1901. W. 12.8 cm. Victoria & Albert Museum, London.

four-colour gold. *See* GOLD À QUATRE COULEURS.

fracture. The texture of a freshly broken surface, e.g. that of certain gemstones that show no trace of CLEAVAGE. A fracture has distinct characteristics in certain stones, but it is not generally an aid in identifying an uncut stone. *See* CENTIPEDE.

Francia (1450?–1518). A goldsmith of Bologna, Italy, whose name was Francesco Raibolini, but who adopted the name of his tutor, Francia. Before he became a well-known painter he made gold, silver, and bronze medals, and was highly regarded for his work in NIELLO. He also made articles of jewelry, including some gold chains. *See* G. C. Williamson, *Francia* (1901). *See* FELICINI JEWEL.

Frankish jewelry. Articles of jewelry made in Gaul (present-day France and Germany) during the Frankish monarchy from *c.* 481 until the 10th century, including MEROVINGIAN JEWELRY and CAROLINGIAN JEWELRY.

Frankish jewelry. Belt buckle, French, 7th century. Found at Amiens, France. British Museum, London.

Froment-Meurice, François. Pendant, gold with enamelling. French, *c.* 1830. Victoria & Albert Museum, London.

frontlets. Pinchbeck with white and coloured paste. French and English, early 19th century. L. 15/17 cm. City Museums and Art Gallery, Birmingham, England.

Fuller Brooch. Silver disc brooch with niello. Anglo-Saxon, 9th century. W. 11.4 cm. British Museum. London.

fraternity jewelry. Various articles of jewelry (e.g. a finger ring, a small brooch) that are decorated with the emblem, monogram or initials of a fraternity (or sorority) and that are worn by its members. Such pieces include MASONIC JEWELRY and articles of the fraternities (or sororities) of colleges in the United States. They are usually made of gold and are frequently enamelled or set with diamonds or pearls.

French jet. Black GLASS imitative of JET. It has a hard bright glitter, unlike velvety jet, and is cold to the touch.

fresh-water pearl. A variety of pearl produced by several types of fresh-water molluscs, e.g.: (1) MUSSEL PEARL, produced by the PEARL MUSSEL; and (2) CLAM PEARL. Such pearls are usually inferior to the pearl of the PEARL OYSTER; they are of various colours. Fresh-water pearls are found in rivers of Scotland, Canada, the Mississippi River basin, and the Amazon basin. Those from the Mississippi region are usually of irregular shapes, hence called 'dogtooth', 'wing', and 'petal'. The largest known fresh-water pearl, owned by W. H. Moore, of Arkansas (USA), weighs 122½ grains; the largest from Scotland, found in 1967, weighs 44½ grains.

fringe necklace. *See* STRAP NECKLACE.

frog jewelry. An article of jewelry (usually a brooch or a pendant) made in the form of a frog (or toad) and set with coloured gemstones. Such pieces were worn as an AMULET, as the frog had various symbolic significances in different countries, being in Rome the emblem of marital happiness. Examples are known in COCLÉ JEWELRY as well as in PRE-COLUMBIAN JEWELRY from Panama and Costa Rica, the frog being sometimes depicted with bent legs and outspread, flat, stylized feet.

Froment-Meurice, Émile (1837-1913). A Parisian goldsmith and jeweller, the son of FRANÇOIS-DÉSIRÉ FROMENT-MEURICE, who succeeded to his father's business that had been carried on after his death by the widow. His work continued in the Romantic style until *c.* 1900 when he experimented in ART NOUVEAU styles. He made some pieces decorated in NIELLO.

Froment-Meurice, François-Désiré (1802-55). A Parisian goldsmith and jeweller who succeeded to the family business founded in 1774 by his father, François Froment; the son added the surname of Pierre Meurice, also a goldsmith, whom his widowed mother had married. His work was in the GOTHIC REVIVAL (Romantic) style, but also from 1839 in Renaissance style or ARCHITECTURAL STYLE, some of his designs featuring, against a background of Gothic architecture, enamelled figures of knights, angels, and saints, which appear to be cast IN THE ROUND. Some of his jewelry was enamelled by Lefournier. On his death, the business was inherited by his son, Émile.

frontlet. A FOREHEAD ORNAMENT in the form of a broad band worn in the 19th century on the upper part of a woman's forehead and over the hair. Such bands were decorated with pearls, gemstones or CAMEOS, or sometimes made of PINCHBECK and decorated with PASTE. The French term was *tour de tête.*

Fuller Brooch. A silver DISC BROOCH engraved and inlaid with NIELLO depicting in a central, dished panel human figures representing the Five Senses and having a border decorated with 16 roundels with various motifs. The attachment pin at the back is missing. It is Anglo-Saxon, 9th century, and the decoration is in the TREWHIDDLE STYLE. Its provenance is unknown. Although formerly considered a forgery, its authenticity has been established and it has been named after its part-donor, Captain A. W. F. Fuller.

funerary crown. A CROWN that was interred with a deceased crowned person. Such crowns were used from the 11th century in western Europe, but usually were not made of precious metal or set with gemstones. Sometimes they were accompanied by other royal REGALIA.

funerary jewelry. Articles of jewelry not intended to be worn by the living but with which the dead were buried, as in ancient Egypt (*see*

TUTANKHAMUN JEWELRY). In Egypt, during the VIth Dynasty (*c.* 2400 BC–*c.* 2250 BC) and the XVIIIth Dynasty (*c.* 1552 BC–*c.* 1296 BC), the SCARAB, which had significance as to resurrection and immortality, was often so interred, especially the HEART SCARAB. Some such articles were made of thin gold sheet to cover parts of the dead body, e.g. the eyes, mouth, ears, breast, navel, pudenda, some being in the form of the part to be covered; these were produced in many Eastern Mediterranean regions, such as Egypt, Cyprus, the region near the Black Sea, and the Palestinian–Phoenician coast. Related to these burial articles was the gold death MASK for covering the face. Many pieces of this type were made of gold PRE-COLUMBIAN JEWELRY. *See* MOUTHPIECE; FUNERARY CROWN.

—— , *Chinese.* In very ancient China, from the 4th/3rd millennia BC, various articles of JADE were interred with the dead, each having some ritualistic significance, e.g. the PI and the HUANG. The most imposing were the funeral suits such as those made of 2,690 pieces for Prince Liu Sheng and of 2,160 pieces for his wife, Princess Tou Wan, from the Western Han Dynasty (206 BC–AD 8), found in 1968 on their bodies in their tomb in the district of Hopei; the pieces of jade were sewn together with gold and silver thread.

fur clasp. Gold with *guilloché* design and set with cabochon gemstones. Courtesy of Wartski, London.

fur clasp. A device for fastening the two ends of a fur piece when being worn, in the form of two ornaments to be sewn on the ends, one having a short attached chain and the other a BOLT RING to be fastened to one of the links of the chain. Such pieces were often made of gold and decorated with gemstones.

fur jewelry. Originally a pelt of sable or marten, but later the head and claws were replaced by gold replicas, decorated with enamelling and with the eyes made of rubies or sapphires. Such pieces, popular in Italy, were also worn in Germany during the 15th and 16th centuries, initially for warmth but later for adornment. Some jewels in the form of the head of a sable were made of gold (sometimes of crystal), embellished with gemstones. Designs for such pieces were made by ERASMUS HORNICK, *c.* 1562. The Italian term is *zibellino*, and in Germany the pelts were sometimes called a *Flohpelz*.

fusiform bead. A type of BEAD that is shaped like a spindle or a cigar, tapering to each end.

G

gahnite. A variety of zinc SPINEL, crystals of which are dark-green to light-green; the latter colour is used in gemstones. A synthetic gahnite has a different refractive index and specific gravity. The mineral was named after J. G. Gahn (1745-1818), a Swiss chemist.

gahnospinel. A rare variety of SPINEL that is blue, being rich in zinc.

Gaillard, Lucien (b. 1861). A Parisian jeweller and enameller, succeeding in 1892 to the jewelry business started in 1840 by his grandfather, Amédée Gaillard, and carried on after 1860 by his father, Ernest Gaillard (b. 1836). His early work was as a silversmith, but from *c.* 1900 he became interested in ART NOUVEAU style under the influence of his friend, RENÉ LALIQUE. He worked in ivory and horn and decorated pieces with ENAMELLING (some in PLIQUE À JOUR enamel) and in Japanese techniques.

Gainsborough Ring. A gold finger ring having set in the BEZEL an oval piece of MOSS AGATE with markings suggesting trees in a landscape. It is so called because it was originally owned by the English painter, Thomas Gainsborough (1727-88); it was donated by a descendant to the Ashmolean Museum, Oxford.

Gaillard, Lucien. Gold pendant with diamonds and *plique à jour* enamel. Victoria & Albert Museum, London.

Gainsborough Ring. Moss agate suggestive of trees in landscape. Ashmolean Museum, Oxford.

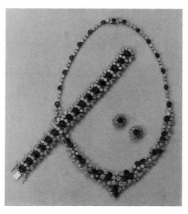

Garrard & Co. Ltd. Parure of diamonds and sapphires. Courtesy of Garrard & Co. Ltd., London.

galanterie (French). Various small trinkets given in the 18th century by gentlemen to ladies. They were intended to be carried in the pocket or a reticule, kept in a dressing-table or displayed in a cabinet. Included are étuis, snuff bottles, scent bottles, smelling bottles, patch boxes, cachou boxes, carnets de bal, needle-cases, etc. The German term is *Galanteriewaren.* A modern term in trade jargon for such pieces is 'smallwork'. Such decorative articles are usually classed as OBJECTS OF VERTU rather than as jewelry, and so do not fall within the scope of this book.

gallery. A strip of metal that is pierced with a continuing pattern, often framing vertical lozenge-shaped openings within an upper and lower band. Such strips are used by jewellers to make a CLAW SETTING for a finger ring after slicing the strip horizontally so that it becomes a series of points which hold the stone. The complete gallery is called 'closed' and the half-section is called 'open'.

garnet. A group of minerals that includes six main varieties of gemstones, closely related as to chemical composition, some varieties being so close as to be difficult to differentiate. The traditional colour is dark red, but the stones are found in many colours and shades, depending on the chemical composition. The principal varieties are: GROSSULAR (HESSONITE, rosolite); PYROPE (RHODOLITE); ALMANDINE; ANDRADITE (DEMANTOID, MELANITE, TOPAZOLITE); SPESSARTITE; and uvarovite. Formerly the stones were cut EN CABOCHON, but today they are faceted, either STEP CUT or MIXED CUT. Garnets were used by the Egyptians, Greeks, Romans, and Celts, often cut into thin slices and inlaid, as in CLOISONNÉ INLAY. When red garnets were mounted in ANGLO-SAXON JEWELRY or VICTORIAN JEWELRY, they were usually backed with gold or silver FOIL. Local misnomers applied to garnet are 'Cape ruby' and 'Bohemian ruby'. *See* SYNTHETIC 'GARNET'.

Garrard & Co. Ltd. A leading London firm of jewellers, goldsmiths, and silversmiths. Its founder was silversmith George Wickes who registered his mark in 1722; he transferred an interest in 1747 to Edward Wakelin, the firm later becoming Wakelin and Taylor, and under Edward Wakelin's son John took as a partner in 1792 Robert Garrard (1758-1818). The latter became the owner in 1802, and his sons Robert II, James, and Sebastian inherited the business. In 1830 the firm succeeded RUNDELL, BRIDGE & RUNDELL as Crown Goldsmiths, and in 1843 was appointed as Crown Jewellers, in which capacity it has since been responsible for the maintenance of the Regalia and the Crown Jewels and their preparation for the coronations. The descendants of Robert Garrard directed the firm until 1946, and in 1952 it was amalgamated with the Goldsmiths and Silversmiths Co. (founded in the 1880s by William Gibson and John Langman), and moved to its present address at 112 Regent St, London, maintaining the name Garrard and continuing to have the patronage of the Royal Family. It is now owned by Sears Holdings Ltd. Its craftsmen continue to make jewelry in all categories, and also sporting trophies and prestigious silverware for prominent persons and firms. *See* Christopher Lever, 'Garrard', in *Connoisseur,* June 1974, p. 94.

Gaskin, Arthur (1862-1928). An English silversmith and jeweller from Birmingham, who, with his wife Georgina (1868-1934), made from 1899 gold and silver jewelry. His early style featured curling tendrils of wire, with coloured gemstones as flowers, and this was used in some CYMRIC jewelry that they made for Liberty & Co., London. He designed some pieces with filigree wire executed *c.* 1912 in collaboration with W. T. Blackband.

gaud (or **gaudee**). A trinket, such as was attached at the end of a ROSARY. Some were in the form of a CROSS or crucifix; some were in the form of a CHARM decorated with a depiction or figure of a saint, such as were made in Germany in the 15th and 16th centuries. Another example is the NUT in the form of a spherical openwork case enclosing carved figures.

gedanite. A variety of AMBER. Its source is near Gdańsk (formerly Danzig), now in Poland, whose Latin name was Gedanum, hence the name.

gem. A gemstone, pearl or organic or non-organic substance that has intrinsic value based on its rarity, quality, size, durability, and beauty, but apart from any SETTING, and usually based on applied workmanship, as the quality of the cutting of a gemstone or the carving of a piece of HARDSTONE, CORAL, AMBER, IVORY or JET used as jewelry. The term 'gem' was originally applied to a gemstone decorated with carving or engraving, but since the last century it has been extended to any gemstone of quality, usually one that has been faceted, but exclusive of SYNTHETIC GEMSTONES and GLASS. *See* JEWEL.

Gem of the Jungle. A colossal SAPPHIRE found in 1929 in Burma, weighing 958 carats in the rough. The purchaser, Albert Ramsay, had it cut into 9 stones, the largest of which weighed 66.50 carats.

gem-set imitations. *See* COSTUME JEWELRY.

gemel ring. The same as GIMMEL RING, the term 'gimmel' being generally applied today by writers and jewellers (but not dictionaries) to a twin finger ring. The word 'gimmal' is, according to the *Oxford English Dictionary*, an 'altered form' of 'gemel' which is derived from the Latin *gemellus*, the diminutive of *geminus*, twin (just as the name of the zodiacal sign *Gemini* is derived from *geminus*). The spelling 'gimmal' (but not 'gimmel') is the spelling listed in the *Oxford English Dictionary*, in *Chambers's Dictionary* (1973), and in *Webster's Dictionary*, as the alternative to 'gemel'. Hence 'gemel' would appear to be historically and etymologically the correct term, but as 'gimmel' has the sanction of widespread usage, it must now be accepted to designate finger rings of this type (as it is for other appliances made of two joined rings, e.g. a horse bit).

gaud. Silver gilt. South German, 16th century. H. 6.8 cm. Schmuckmuseum, Pforzheim, Germany.

gemstone. Any mineral (natural or synthetic) that is composed of crystallized matter and the atoms of which are regularly arranged throughout the structure, thus including the approximately 100 principal mineral species used in jewelry, e.g. all PRECIOUS STONES, and also other stones formerly referred to as SEMI-PRECIOUS STONES, as well as the OPAL (which is non-crystalline), but excluding all types of glass and plastics. The quality of a gemstone that makes it desirable for use as jewelry (as distinguished from primarily utilitarian use) depends on varying degrees of BRILLIANCE, HARDNESS, colour dispersion, and refraction, on its being transparent, translucent or opaque, or colourless or of a wide range of colours, as well as being sometimes glyptic and usually susceptible of being given a polished surface, and also free of FLAWS. Some gemstones are identifiable superficially by colour, coolness, optic qualities, and sight, but most require some scientific examination, e.g. comparison of specific gravity, refractive index, hardness, dichroism, crystal system, absorption spectra, melting-point, etc. *See* G. F. Herbert Smith, *Gemstones* (1972); Robert Webster, *Gems* (3rd ed. 1975).
[*Plates VI and VII*]

—— *nomenclature.* The names used by jewellers and many persons for most gemstones are based on long usage, and in many instances differ from the correct names now used by mineralogists. This is now regarded as regrettable (and sometimes deceptive), especially when the old names, or even some names adopted later, include with some qualifying word or geographical name a mineralogical name that is incorrect for the particular stone (e.g. 'white sapphire', 'Cape emerald', 'Cornish diamond'). The preferable nomenclature in most cases is to use the correct mineralogical name of the stone preceded by the particular colour, rather than a geographical name preceding the name of a stone of a different species, e.g. 'green tourmaline' rather than 'Ceylon peridot'. Such misnomers should be discontinued, especially now that the Gemmological Association of Great Britain has promulgated a list of admissible names, and false names can lead to prosecution for illegal misdescription. Such terms as 'Oriental' or 'Brazilian' preceding a name often are intended merely to suggest a superior variety of the named stone, but are misnomers if the source of the stone is elsewhere or if the succeeding word is the name of a stone of a different species. Most names of gemstones end with the suffix '-ite', adopted in English from French, but sometimes '-ine' is used in England, e.g. 'almandine' for 'almandite'. The term 'synthetic' may properly be used as a qualifying term to designate a SYNTHETIC GEMSTONE, provided that the stone name used is that of a natural stone to which the synthetic one corresponds, not merely one of like colour. Likewise, the term 'reconstructed' should be restricted to stones built up from fragments, not formed from powder.

Geneva enamels. Articles, called 'Geneva ornaments', decorated with ENAMELLING made in Geneva, Switzerland, from the 17th century to the 19th when it was a leading centre for such work, with over 200 artists so engaged. The principal motifs were girls in regional peasant costumes and local landscapes. The work was sometimes highly skilled, but much was made merely for the tourist trade. The pieces were praised by John Ruskin in 1885. The principal maker was the firm of Bautte et Moynier, founded in the late 18th century by Jean-François Bautte (1772-1832), a watch-maker who turned to gold jewelry decorated with enamelling; such work continued until at least 1846.

Geneva ruby. A so-called RECONSTRUCTED STONE that simulates a natural RUBY. It was said to have been produced by fusing a number of small ruby crystals with an oxyhydrogen blowpipe. They were offered for sale in 1885 in Geneva as genuine rubies. They proved unsatisfactory, and later research has suggested that the material was purified alumina, in which case they were not 'reconstructed stones'.

geometric style. A decorative style for jewelry developed in the 1920-30s in which the form is in abstract geometric shapes, produced with great precision, and the articles generally are smooth and highly polished. Such jewelry was a development of the ART DECO style, and the designers who worked in this style included GEORGES FOUQUET, RAYMOND TEMPLIER, and Wiven Nilsson.

George. An insigne of the Order of the Garter, being a jewel with an enamelled figure of St George (patron saint of England) slaying the dragon. It is worn suspended from the collar of the Order. *See* LESSER GEORGE.

Georgian jewelry. Articles of jewelry from Georgia, a region in western Transcaucasia and since 1921 a republic of the USSR. The metalwork dates from very early pre-Christian times to the 18th century and was highly developed, with the processes of gold SOLDERING and FILIGREE being known from *c*. 1500 BC. Examples from the Akhalgori Treasure of the 6th century BC include elaborate gold head-dresses and ear-rings, as well as pieces set with gemstones cut EN CABOCHON. From the 3rd century AD work was done in CLOISONNÉ ENAMEL and CHAMPLEVÉ ENAMEL, especially in the 13th and 14th centuries. The greatest cultural period was under Queen Tamara in the 12th and 13th centuries, when the master jeweller was Beka, founder of the Opiza style. During the Persian-Turkish wars of the 16th century, the arts declined, but were revived in the 19th century, when work was done in NIELLO and with filigree decoration; cloisonné enamel was again used, with the cloisons fixed to a copper base by cold soldering. At all times the Georgians emphasized polychrome decoration by their lavish use of enamels and gemstones. *See* RUSSIAN JEWELRY.

Gérard, M. Double collar; neckband separable to form bracelet. Diamonds and Burma sapphires. Courtesy of M. Gérard, Paris and London.

Gérard, M. A leading French jeweller and since 1975 the largest French exporter of high-quality jewelry. The form was founded in 1968 by Louis Gérard (b. 1923), who, after some years with and becoming General Manager of VAN CLEEF & ARPELS, opened his own boutique in Paris. The firm specializes in important luxury jewelry that emphasizes the gemstones and design. Its Paris address is 8 Avenue Montaigne, and it has branches at Monte Carlo, Lausanne, Gstaad, London, Geneva, and Cannes.

geyserite. A variety of COMMON OPAL that is whitish or greyish. It is found near some geysers and hot springs.

giardinetto ring. Gold and silver, set with gemstones. 2nd half of 18th century. Schmuckmuseum, Pforzheim, Germany.

giardinetto ring. Literally, small-garden ring. A type of finger ring of which the BEZEL is made in an openwork floral design and set with small gemstones of various colours. The stones are usually (but not invariably) arranged to form a bouquet of flowers, or a basket or a vase holding flowers. Such rings were made in Italy in the late 17th and the 18th centuries, and also in England where they were popular from the end of the 17th century until the end of the 18th; those from the later period have open-back SETTINGS, better to display the stones. Many examples are still extant, as the stones did not justify resetting. Sometimes loosely called a 'flower-pot ring'.

Gika (Jiqa) of Nadir Shah. A noted AIGRETTE in the CROWN JEWELS (IRAN) in the form of a plume with a large, central, cabochon emerald and five emerald drops, the entire piece studded with diamonds. The piece, weighing 781 carats, was often worn by Reza Shah the Great, who founded in 1925 the Iranian Pahlavi dynasty. It is named after Nadir Shah who invaded India in 1739–40 and recovered many of the former Persian jewels.

gilding. The process of overlaying or covering any metal, wood, etc., with a thin layer of gold or gold alloy. The technique has been used since ancient times, and was practised by the pre-Columbian American Indians. The methods include: (1) oil gilding or water gilding, by attaching GOLD LEAF by means of an adhesive (called a 'mordant'); (2) mercury gilding, by applying an AMALGAM of gold and mercury with a brush, then heating the object to cause the mercury to vaporize and to leave a thin film of gold; (3) friction gilding, by rubbing the surface with ashes of linen rags soaked in a solution of gold chloride, then burnishing and polishing; and (4) electroplating, by depositing a layer of gold by an electric current, leaving a thin 'flash' of gold or a substantial covering, or leaving a more durable layer by 'hard gold plating'. After certain gilding processes, the effect was enhanced by 'tooling', i.e. by incising the gold surface to create a design or a textured surface. *See* DEPLETION GILDING; DIFFERENTIAL PICKLING; ROLLED GOLD.

Gilson emerald. A type of SYNTHETIC EMERALD developed by Pierre Gilson, of France, who also developed a type of synthetic opal. Such stones should be designated as 'synthetic emerald (opal) by Gilson'.

gilt bronze. BRONZE that has been covered with GILDING. It has been used extensively in France to make MOUNTS for some OBJECTS OF VERTU. *See* ORMOLU.

gimmel (or **gimmal**) **ring.** A type of finger ring that is composed of 2 (sometimes 3) separate hoops linked together, having the same SHANK split lengthwise so that the hoops can be fitted together unnoticeably as one hoop. The BEZEL is also split so that when joined it forms one ornament; it is sometimes decorated with clasped hands (*see* FEDE RING) or a heart-shaped ornament. Such rings were worn as an ENGAGEMENT RING or a WEDDING RING, appropriately engraved on the facing sides of the hoops. They were made of gold or silver, sometimes with NIELLO decoration or set with a gemstone. They were made in the mid-15th century. The hoops could be separated only by cutting one of them, but they were sometimes separated and worn in this way until rejoined by a goldsmith following the marriage. *See* GEMEL RING; PUZZLE RING.

girandole. A type of ear-ring composed of a bow-shaped ornament, or more usually a large circular gemstone (generally a diamond) at or near the top of the SETTING, and having suspended at the bottom three pear-shaped faceted diamonds (cut in PENDELOQUE form) or sometimes three pearls or PASTE gems. There were many variations, including one having suspended from a large diamond a silver oval hoop in the centre of which was suspended another diamond; another variant had the three pendent stones separated from the upper stone by openwork silver. The style (which was employed also for a brooch) was used in the 17th (*see* GILLES LÉGARÉ) and 18th centuries. The precursor of such girandoles was the CHANDELIER EAR-RING of ROMAN JEWELRY.

girasol. (1) The same as FIRE OPAL. The name is derived from the Latin words *girare* and *sol* (turn to the sun). (2) A designation applied to some gemstones that show flashes of FIRE, e.g. 'girasol sapphire' or 'girasol scapolite'. (3) A trade-name for a variety of IMITATION PEARL.

girdle. (1) The thin band that forms the widest circumference of a BRILLIANT and that separates the CROWN above it from the PAVILION below. The girdle is usually left in its bruted state and is matt; but to achieve more BRILLIANCE the girdle is sometimes ground (*see* BEARDED

gimmel ring. Silver gilt with gemstones and engraved interior inscription. German, late 16th century. Ashmolean Museum, Oxford.

GIRDLE; FACETED GIRDLE; POLISHED GIRDLE). (2) The edge of a gemstone to which the SETTING is attached. Sometimes called the 'setting edge'.

girdle book. A small devotional book, often bound within elaborately decorated gold covers, carried in the 15th/17th centuries by women of rank or wealth, worn suspended from a chain attached to a GIRDLE. Two pen-and-ink drawings for covers of such a book, with ARABESQUE designs to be enamelled on gold, were made, *c.* 1633-40, by HANS HOLBEIN THE YOUNGER, but possibly were never executed. Queen Elizabeth I had a number of such miniature girdle books, and several are recorded as owned by ladies of rank. An example at Rosenborg Castle, Copenhagen, made, perhaps, in 1613 by CORVINIANUS SAUR, for Princess Augusta of Denmark, has covers of sheet gold with CHAMPLEVÉ enamelling. Two gold covers, possibly for such a book, with enamelled decoration depicting Biblical scenes, are in the British Museum. *See* EDWARD VI PRAYER BOOK; BOOK COVER.

girdle facet. One of the FACETS that extend along the GIRDLE of a faceted gemstone, especially a BRILLIANT; those that extend upward toward the TABLE are now called the 'upper girdle facets' and those that extend downward toward the CULET are now called the 'lower girdle facets' (these terms replacing the former names 'skill facet' and 'cross facet' previously employed).

Gisela, Empress, Treasure of. A group of articles in OTTONIAN JEWELRY found in 1880 in a cellar in Mainz, Germany, and once believed to have been worn by Empress Gisela at her wedding in Rome at Easter 1027 to Conrad II, German King and Holy Roman Emperor, 1024-39, but more recently thought in part to have been made subsequently and deposited about a century later. The group included necklaces, brooches, and finger rings, decorated with gemstones, raised FILIGREE work, and CLOISONNÉ enamelling. Most of the pieces were sent to the Schlossmuseum, Berlin, where they survived World War II; the GISELA BROOCH and three other pieces are in the Mittelrheinisches Landesmuseum, Mainz.

Gisela Brooch. Pectoral brooch of gold, with enamelling and gemstones. Early 11th century. H. 10 cm. Mittelrheinisches Landesmuseum, Mainz.

Gisela Brooch. A large, gold, pectoral brooch (sometimes called a FIBULA) of OTTONIAN JEWELRY in the form of a circle enclosing, within an openwork border, an erect heraldic eagle with spread wings and outward-turned claws (a Western version of an Islamic motif) and whose head extends into the circular border. The eagle's wings, head, and tail are decorated with CLOISONNÉ enamelling of dark blue, turquoise blue, green, and white, but the enamel of the breast of the eagle is no longer there, so that all that can now be seen is the outline of the imbricated feathers made by the CLOISONS. Above the eagle's head, in a frame extending slightly above the border, are 3 sapphires. The openwork border is decorated with characteristic raised FILIGREE patterns in which are 8 floral motifs of cloisonné translucent green enamel. The brooch is said to have belonged to the Empress Gisela (*see* GISELA, EMPRESS, TREASURE OF) and to have been made in the Rhineland in the 11th century; it was found at Mainz in 1880.

Giuliano family. A family of jewellers from Naples whose members are well known for their work done in London, especially jewelry simulating antique and Renaissance styles. The best known is Carlo Giuliano (1831-95) who worked in Naples for ALESSANDRO CASTELLANI and was established by him in London as a branch of the Casa Castellani. He soon left Castellani and from 1867 worked for ROBERT PHILLIPS, Harry Emanuel, Hunt & Roskell, and HANCOCKS, prominent London jewellers. In 1875 he set up his own workshop as goldsmith, doing creative work in adapting designs of Renaissance style and developing new techniques. He is highly regarded for his work in GRANULATED GOLD and ENCRUSTED ENAMEL (ÉMAIL EN RONDE BOSSE), and for making pendants in Greek and Etruscan style inspired by Castellani. He was assisted from 1874 by his Italian chief designer and technician, Pasquale Novissimo (d. 1914), who had worked for Castellani in Italy. His workshop from 1861 to 1877 was at 11 Frith St, London, and in 1874 he set up a retail outlet at 115 Piccadilly. Competition was carried on from 1876 by his younger brother Federico and the latter's son, Ferdinando, working from 1883 until 1903 at premises in Howland St; no signed piece of their work in known but

Giuliano family. Fringe necklace of blue and white cylindrical beads with pendants of gold satyr heads and lapis lazuli alternating with pearls. Carlo Giuliano, *c.* 1870. Courtesy of Wartski, London.

some examples have been identified by the cases. The business of Carlo in Piccadilly was inherited by his sons, Carlo and Arthur, who moved in 1912 to 48 Knightsbridge, continuing there until 1914, but selling there less accomplished pieces. Their mark was C & A G; that of Carlo Giuliano was C G. *See* M. L. d'Otrange, 'The Exquisite Art of Carlo Giuliano', in *Apollo*, January 1954, p. 145; Geoffrey Munn, 'The Giuliano Family,' in *Connoisseur*, November 1975, p. 156.   [*Plate IV*]

glass. An AMORPHOUS, artificial, non-CRYSTALLINE substance, usually transparent but often translucent or opaque. It can be distinguished from most gemstones by its single refraction and consequent lack of dichroism and by comparison of the refractive indices. *See* Harold Newman, *Illustrated Dictionary of Glass* (1977). *See* FLINT GLASS; CRYSTAL GLASS; OBSIDIAN; BERYL GLASS; RHINESTONE; MOLDAVITE.

glass bead. A type of bead, made of glass, transparent, translucent or opaque, and smooth or faceted, including beads of coloured, colourless, MILLEFIORI, enamelled, gilded or iridescent glass, being solid or hollow, and of various shapes and sizes. The earliest material having the character of glass was used in Egypt, before *c.* 4000 BC, as a glaze to cover beads of stone or clay in imitation of coloured precious stones. Later this glaze was used in Egypt to make beads as the earliest objects made wholly of glass, *c.* 2500 BC. Glass beads are known from Mycenae from the 16th to the 13th centuries BC. The earliest decorative patterns on glass beads, from *c.* 1500 BC, were stripes and spots; later developments were EYE BEADS and beads with zigzags and chevrons. The early glass beads were normally of opaque glass, frequently blue, with decoration often in yellow. The Roman beads followed the Egyptian tradition. In Venice, in the 11th century and subsequently, glass beads were made for trade. Later they became popular in Bohemia and elsewhere, being made in many forms and styles and in various colours. Coloured glass beads may be either inferior varieties coloured only on the surface or made entirely of coloured glass. Today the principal sources of glass beads are Venice, Japan, and the Goblonz region of Czechoslovakia; some are of good quality and are used for COSTUME JEWELRY, but vast quantities serve merely as tourist souvenirs.

glass jewelry. Various ornaments for personal adornment that have been made of, or decorated with, GLASS, e.g. beads, bangles, finger rings, brooches, pendants, and necklaces. Glass has been so used for jewelry since earliest times in Egypt and the Roman Empire, and also in Venice probably before the 11th century. It has been used in modern jewelry by RENÉ LALIQUE and by Louis Comfort Tiffany (*see* TIFFANY & CO.) and recently by Steuben (*see* STEUBEN JEWELRY). Glass has also been used to imitate gemstones and in COMPOSITE STONES, as well as in PASTE JEWELRY. Much glass jewelry has been made in Czechoslovakia, France, Germany, and Austria. *See* CRYSTAL GLASS.

glass jewelry. Necklace of mould-pressed translucent blue glass rosettes with glassy 'faience' links. Mycenaean, 14/13th centuries BC. L. 28 cm. Toledo Museum of Art, Ohio.

Glenlyon Brooch (front and back). Silver ring brooch with transverse bar and two pins. W. 13.3 cm. Scottish, 15th century. British Museum, London.

glassie. A natural octahedral diamond with flat glass-like FACES. When the faces were polished, it was the earliest style of cut diamond, called a POINT-CUT DIAMOND.

Glenlyon Brooch. A silver RING BROOCH in the form of a flat ring that is set with pearls in tall cone-shaped turrets, alternating with pieces of CRYSTAL and AMETHYST. There is a bar placed across the ring, decorated with gemstones and on it rest the points of two short pins that are hinged to the inside edge of the ring. On the reverse of the ring, in black letters within 9 arches, are the names of the three Magi (Jaspar, Melchior, and Balthasar) and the word *consumatum [sic]*. The brooch, of Scottish origin, *c.* 1500, was formerly owned by the Campbells of Glenlyon and was sold at Christie's, London, 21 May 1897. *See* THREE KINGS.

Gloria. One of the beads on a ROSARY, being the one to follow each DECADE (group of ten beads) and on which the *Gloria Patri* is said; but in many cases it is omitted and the PATERNOSTER beads serve in its place.

gloss. The appearance of the surface of some minerals or gemstones that is a superficial LUSTRE, especially when smooth and polished.

glossopetra. A FOSSIL shark tooth. It was used as a CHARM, usually suspended from a chain or necklace worn around the neck of an infant.

glove ring. A type of finger ring that is worn over a gloved finger and hence larger than the usual finger ring. Some rings were thus worn during the Renaissance, but more often the finger of the glove was slit to accommodate and display a large ring. An ecclesiastical ring (*see* BISHOP'S RING) was sometimes worn over a glove.

glyph. A gemstone that is carved or engraved to depict a figure or figures, a monogram or inscription, being, if incised, an INTAGLIO or, if in relief, a CAMEO. Such pieces when incised are usually about 2.5 cm wide but those in relief are usually twice as wide and even up to 25 cm wide. *See* ENGRAVED GEMSTONE.

Gnostic seals. SEALS used by the believers in Gnosticism, a philosophical and religious movement that developed in the Roman era and was based on different elements of various religions, primarily the belief that salvation was dependent on knowledge (*gnosis*). It spread in the 2nd century AD to Gaul, Germany, and Britain, using emblems and iconography of the Egyptian religion and the Mithraic creed. The seals were carved as TALISMANS and as a means of mutual recognition, depicting such deities as Abraxas, Anubis, and Horus, along with planetary symbols and inscriptions. *See* ABRAXAS STONE.

Godstow Ring. A finger ring so called because found at Godstow Nunnery, near Oxford. It is a broad gold band, formerly enamelled, having the outside chased with three lozenges in which are engraved the Trinity, the Virgin and Child, and a male saint, and having on the interior an engraved amatory inscription suggesting that it was a LOVE RING despite the iconographic ornament. It has long been called 'Fair Rosamond's Ring'. It is English, early 15th century, and is in the British Museum.

Golconda diamond. Any diamond found at the Golconda mine in Hyderabad, India; the mine is no longer productive. Such cut stones were usually very shallow, probably owing to having been recut after the original thin cutting by Indian lapidaries.

gold. A metallic element that is very heavy, the most malleable and ductile of all metals, and unalterable by heat, moisture, and most corrosive agents. Pure gold is too soft for most practicable uses, but as an ALLOY with SILVER, COPPER or other metals it serves ordinary purposes as jewelry or coins. Gold is not susceptible to compression, so that when beaten it increases its surface area while losing thickness. It is basically yellow, but when alloyed it appears whitish, greenish, reddish or other hues (*see* GOLD ALLOY; GOLD À QUATRE COULEURS). The proportion of gold in an alloy is expressed in FINENESS and CARATS. Gold has a high melting-point (1063 °C., 1945 °F.). It is the most precious metal used as a medium

Godstow Ring. Gold finger ring with engraved iconography and chasing. English, early 15th century. British Museum, London.

of monetary exchange, but PLATINUM is more valuable as a metal. Gold is used in GILDING (*see* GILT BRONZE; GOLD LEAF; FOIL). Earliest gold objects were made of sheets of gold decorated in relief by being punched and hammered (*see* EMBOSSING; REPOUSSÉ) or by STAMPING, or in the case of objects IN THE ROUND by the LOST WAX (CIRE PERDUE) process or being beaten into two hemispherical moulds and then soldered together. It was also used decoratively as strips, rods, and wire. *See* PINCHBECK; TOUCHSTONE; SIMILOR; GRANULATED GOLD; SOLID-GOLD; GOLD FILLED; ROLLED GOLD; TEXTURED GOLD. For illustrations of many articles of gold jewelry, *see* C. H. V. Sutherland, *Gold* (1959).

gold à quatre couleurs. Gold of 4 (sometimes 3 or 5) different shades, used simultaneously in a piece of jewelry. The shades so used were usually GREEN GOLD, RED GOLD, WHITE GOLD, and BLUE GOLD. The technique involves inlaying and soldering each different colour in layers. It became fashionable after *c.* 1750, although it had been used previously. It is most attractive when the inlays are decorated with CHASING in relief so that the planes can be differentiated. The leading exponents were French, of whom one of high reputation was Jean Ducrollay. Early goldwork used the technique sparingly but later it was used for borders and for overall decoration on some snuff boxes.

gold alloy. An ALLOY of GOLD with various other metals, e.g. SILVER, PALLADIUM, COPPER, nickel, iron, etc., depending on the hardness and colour desired and the intended use, gold being too soft for practicable use alone. All alloys diminish malleability and increase resistance. The purity (FINENESS) of gold alloy is expressed in CARATS, 1 carat being 1/24th part by weight. The legal standards for gold alloy in Great Britain, in carats, are 22 (91.66%), 18 (75%), 14 (58.5%), and 9 (37.5%), and these are the only HALLMARKS employed, even though a slightly higher proportion of gold is used; most gold jewelry is of 14 or 18 carats, but 9 carats for some chains, etc., that require hardness. Different standards are used in other countries. *See* BLUE GOLD; GREEN GOLD; GREY GOLD; RED GOLD, WHITE GOLD, YELLOW GOLD; ELECTRUM; TUMBAGA.

gold filled. Covered with a layer of gold, of any specified FINENESS, by its being bonded to a base metal by electroplating. Such articles must, in the United States, have a layer of gold equal to at least 1/20th of the total weight of the metal in the piece, and the piece must be marked 'gold filled', with the phrase preceded by the appropriate carat fineness, e.g. '10-carat gold filled'.

gold leaf. LEAF of gold of extreme thinness, ranging from 1/200,000th to 1/250,000th of an inch (about 0.005 mm) in thickness. It is used for GILDING. *See* DUTCH METAL.

gold nugget. A lump of native gold in the form of a water-worn mass washed from the rock-bed and deposited in a river or stream, usually weighing from 20 grams to 50 kilograms. Small nuggets are sometimes mounted as decoration on some articles of jewelry, especially a BROOCH, occasionally with added decoration in the form of a shovel and a pick.

gold opal. The same as FIRE OPAL.

gold quartz. A variety of QUARTZ that is colourless (or white) but with INCLUSIONS of grains or fibres of gold.

golden beryl. A variety of HELIODOR (a type of BERYL) that is of a golden-yellow colour.

Golden Fleece. The emblem of the Order of the Golden Fleece (*Le Toison d'Or*), an Order of Chivalry founded in 1429 by Philip the Good, Duke of Burgundy (1396 1467), in honour of the Virgin and for the protection of the Church. It was maintained for persons of royalty and high nobility in Austria, England, France, Portugal, Russia, Spain, etc. The emblem is a suspended ram's fleece, usually of gold and often ornately set with gemstones. It has been used suspended from pendants of various styles, examples having been made in several European countries. The pendants are often in the form of 3 vertically connected gems, the lowest having on each side jewelled horizontal rays (representing sparks

Golden Fleece. Pendant of gold and silver gilt with diamonds and large stone (originally a blue diamond, replaced by glass). Munich, 1761. W. 6.8 cm. Schatzkammer, Residenz, Munich.

from the 2 pieces of flint, an emblem of the Dukes of Burgundy), and suspended from it the Golden Fleece. At least 11 such pendants are in the Green Vault, Dresden. One such pendant was presented to the Duke of Wellington and is at Apsley House, London.

gondola pendant. A type of SHIP PENDANT with a suspended ornament in the form of a Venetian gondola. Some examples depict a typical gondola, and show two lovers seated under a central canopy and a gondolier at the stern, a lute-player at the bow. Others show a stylized gondola, with similar bow and stern, and with two gondoliers and two lute-players. Ornamentation below the gondola is suggestive of waves. The pieces, of enamelled gold set with gemstones, were made in Venice and Germany, 16th/17th centuries. One of two known examples of the former type has been attributed to GIOVANNI BATTISTA SCOLARI. One of the latter type (at Waddesdon Manor, and said to have been given by Queen Anne, 1702-14, to Sir George Allardice and to have been acquired by Baron Edmond de Rothschild), also attributed to Scolari, has figures of a tall couple in Roman costume standing in the centre; these figures, it has been suggested, were possibly added at a later date. See Yvonne Hackenbroch, 'Jewels by Giovanni Battista Scolari', in *Connoisseur*, July 1965, p. 200.

gondola pendant. Gold with coloured enamel and gemstones. German or Italian. Late 16th/early 17th century. H. 8.5 cm. National Trust, Waddesdon Manor, Aylesbury, England.

gorget (American). (1) A circular artifact of BONE, stone or conch shell, having one or more pierced holes for suspension as a breast ornament and decorated usually with figures realistically carved in outline. Examples have been found in several southern states of the USA. (2) A crescent-shaped silver pendant; *see* INDIAN-TRADE SILVER JEWELRY.

gorget (European). A woman's metal collar in the form of a flat band, either PENANNULAR or circular and hinged at the back. An example of such a penannular collar, having at each terminal a circular cupped ornament and decorated with REPOUSSÉ ribbing, was made in Ireland during the Irish Bronze Age, 7th century BC; *see* SHANNONGROVE GORGET. A hinged circular collar decorated with PLATE INLAY, made *c*. 6th/5th centuries BC, is part of the PETROSSA TREASURE; *see* PETROSSA GORGET.

goshenite. A variety of BERYL that is colourless, or nearly so. Colourless beryl has been used to imitate other stones since the 1st century AD. It has been made to imitate emerald by the use of a backing of green FOIL or paint, and diamond by backing with silver or aluminium foil, and DOUBLETS have been made with a thin layer of SYNTHETIC EMERALD.

gorget (American). Shell with incised decoration. Tennessee. W. 10 cm. Museum of the American Indian, Heye Foundation, New York.

Goth jewelry. Articles of jewelry made in Europe during the Dark Ages, *c*. AD 410-870, by the invading Goths who overran the West and brought with them, to change the styles of classical jewelry, influences from the East. An important feature was the use of PLATE INLAY and CLOISONNÉ INLAY, with gold articles being inlaid with slices of GARNET or red glass, including BROOCHES and CROWNS so decorated. Outstanding among the work of the period are examples of ANGLO-SAXON JEWELRY. *See* BARBARIC JEWELRY.

Gothic jewelry. Articles of jewelry made in Continental Europe in the 14th/15th centuries, inspired by the designs of contemporary Gothic architecture. The pieces were more delicate than previously, and included ornaments of human figures in full relief and much openwork .design. Enamelling was used (including BASSE TAILLE, ÉMAIL EN RONDE BOSSE, and ÉMAIL EN BLANC). Gemstones when used were generally cut EN CABOCHON. Such jewelry was worn extravagantly, especially by members of the French and Burgundian Courts. Articles worn as jewelry included mainly brooches, finger rings, and jewelled belts with ornate BUCKLES. It must be distinguished from the GOTHIC REVIVAL JEWELRY. *See* SCHAFFHAUSEN ONYX.

Gothic Revival jewelry. Articles of jewelry made *c*. 1835-50 at the time of the Gothic Revival movement in England and France imitating the styles of the Middle Ages. It includes buckles, brooches, and bracelets decorated with figures IN THE ROUND of angels, saints, knights in armour, and pages and ladies in medieval costume, all against a background of ogival forms. It is said to have been introduced by its leading exponent, FRANÇOIS-DÉSIRÉ FROMENT-MEURICE. Sometimes called 'Romantic

Gothic', it is wholly unrelated to the GOTH JEWELRY of the Dark Ages or the GOTHIC JEWELRY of the 14th/15th centuries.

Gotlandic bracteate. A type of BRACTEATE that was made in Gotland, Sweden, and is seldom found elsewhere. Such pieces, made in the 8th century, are of sheet gold with concentric stamped decoration around a central roundel executed by stamping and with REPOUSSÉ work. The suspension loop at the top and a triangular decoration below it were enriched with FILIGREE and GRANULATED GOLD.

grain. (1) A unit of weight for pearls (sometimes formerly used for diamonds) equal to ¹/₄ of a CARAT. It is sometimes called a 'carat grain' or a 'pearl grain'. CULTURED PEARLS were formerly sold in Japan by the unit of weight called the momme, which equalled 75 grains. *See* POINT. (2) The line along which a diamond is divided by CLEAVAGE.

grain setting. A style of SETTING for securing a gemstone in a finger ring by making small shavings in the SHANK at intervals around the stone and bending them so that each forms a bead against the stone to hold it in place. Sometimes two such beads are made adjacent to each other and a third behind them to form a triangular ornament. Such a setting is used for expensive jewelry. It is sometimes called 'thread and grain setting'. *See* MILLEGRAIN SETTING.

granite jewelry. Articles of jewelry made of pieces of pink or grey granite rock cut into cylinders or prisms and capped with silver or gold, usually joined to form a bracelet. Such pieces were made in Scotland, mainly by Rettie & Sons, Aberdeen, during the Victorian era.

granulated gold. Gold used as decoration on the surface of jewelry by affixing the gold in minute grains to the metal base, sometimes massed in an area of the piece but sometimes placed in linear or outline decoration or used to make a design in reverse silhouette by covering the background of the design. The grains were made by pouring into water molten gold which then formed drop-like granules, or by placing gold cuttings in a crucible with charcoal and then heating and rotating so that the gold formed small spheres. The process of gold granulation was used from the 3rd millennium BC by the goldsmiths of the Eastern Mediterranean region (*see* TROJAN TREASURE; SUMERIAN JEWELRY; PHOENICIAN JEWELRY) and in Egypt, and was carried on and refined especially by the Etruscans (*see* ETRUSCAN JEWELRY). The gold granules were made separately and apparently soldered on, but by a technique whereby the SOLDERING was invisible. In the finest Etruscan examples, minute gold granules (sometimes only 0.25 mm to 0.14 mm in width) were sprinkled on the surface but in later examples larger grains were used. The style was also used by the Greeks. The style (although not the early technique) was adapted in Rome, *c*. 1826, by the goldsmith FORTUNATO PIO CASTELLANI who, with his two sons, developed a process of soldering gold grains on the surface of jewelry; the art was carried on by Carlo Giuliano (*see* GIULIANO FAMILY). The style was again used as decoration for Victorian jewelry. The Etruscan technique, long forgotten, was rediscovered and patented in 1933 by an Englishman, H. A. P. Littledale, and called COLLOID HARD-SOLDERING. A more recent technique was developed in Rome by F. Magi and V. Federici, involving making the gold granules by pouring molten gold from a height onto a stone slab, after which the granules were welded to the metal object by resin under red heat, the tars in the resin acquiring adhesive properties. It is sometimes referred to as 'granulation'. *See* SWEATING.

grasshopper ring. A type of finger ring having on the back of the BEZEL the green enamelled grasshopper badge of the financier Sir Thomas Gresham (1519?-79) and on the front of the bezel a crystal engraved with a shield bearing a coat of arms. They were probably gifts by Gresham to his friends and associates, *c*. 1557-75, each having his own shield of arms on the bezel. There are 7 known examples, of which one was sold at Christie's, London, on 19 December 1977, one on 9 May 1978, and another is in the Victoria & Albert Museum, London.

Great Mogul Diamond. A famous diamond that is said to have been found in the Kollur Mine near Golconda, southern India, in 1650 or earlier,

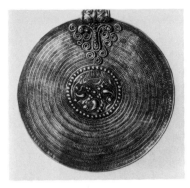

Gotlandic bracteate. Sheet gold pendant with concentric stamped decoration around central roundel, and with filigree and granulation. Probably Gotland, Sweden, 8th century. W. 5.6 cm. British Museum, London.

granulated gold. Gold pin with repoussé work. Etruscan, 7th century. W. 20 cm. Museo Poldi-Pezzoli, Milan.

and presented to Shah Jehan, the Great Mogul, Emperor of India. It was shown by his son, Shah Aurangzeb (1618–1705), to the French traveller and jewelry merchant Jean-Baptiste Tavernier (1605–89), who weighed, measured, and sketched it, showing it in conoidal shape with eight rows of facets and stated its weight as 280 carats. The stone had previously been inefficiently cut from rough 787½ carats by the Venetian cutter, Ortensio Borgio. In 1739 the stone was taken to Isfahan by Nadir Shah (1688–1747), the Persian ruler, after he invaded India and sacked Delhi. Although early writers have questioned its identity, it has been recently said to be the stone from which the KOH-I-NOOR DIAMOND was cut. Attempts to identify it with the DARYA-I-NUR DIAMOND have been discredited, as well as the opinion that it was the same stone as the ORLOV DIAMOND, both having been ROSE CUT and having a bluish tinge.

Great Southern Cross. A group of large pearls naturally joined together in the form of a cross. It has been suggested that originally there were only 8, and that the ninth has been attached to make the group symmetrical. It was found in 1886 in a PEARL OYSTER fished from the beds off the coast of Western Australia. Although 2 or even more pearls are sometimes found joined, it is rare to find a large group.

Great Table Diamond. A diamond that was seen by the French traveller Jean-Baptiste Tavernier at Golconda, India, in 1642, and was described by him as being a large, tabular, pale pink stone which weighed 242 French carats (the equivalent of 250 old carats). A sketch by Tavernier shows it to have been almost rectangular but with one chamfered corner. Its history is uncertain but it is believed to have been found in the Kollur Mine at Golconda and to have been taken to Persia by Nadir Shah after he looted Delhi in 1739. An examination in 1791 of the DARYA-I-NUR DIAMOND suggested that that stone was a part of the Great Table, and a 1966 study of it and of the NUR-UL-AIN DIAMOND has confirmed that they were both cut in the 19th century from the Great Table. *See* V. B. Meen, A. D. Tushingham and G. G. Waite, *Lapidary Journal*, April 1967, vol. 21, no. 8.

Greek jewelry. Articles of jewelry made, after the decline of the Minoan and Mycenaean cultures (*see* MINOAN JEWELRY; MYCENAEAN JEWELRY), on the Greek mainland and islands under foreign influence until about the 7th century BC and thereafter when native styles and techniques began to be developed and thrived, especially during the Classical period *c.* 475–323 BC (*see* CLASSICAL JEWELRY), and the Hellenistic period, *c.* 322–27 BC (*see* HELLENISTIC JEWELRY), until the absorption of Greek culture by the Roman Empire. Gold was used to a great extent, with decoration in GOLD GRANULATION and FILIGREE work, but few gemstones were used until the Hellenistic period. Among the articles principally made were finger rings, wreaths, diadems, necklaces, pectorals, ear-rings, and bracelets. Several Greek jewellers of the present day (e.g. Lalaounis and Zolotas) are making gold and silver jewelry as copies or modern adaptations of the ancient forms. *See* CYPRIOTE JEWELRY; RHODIAN JEWELRY.

Greek pin. A type of long PIN made in ancient Greece with various styles of heads, including geometrical patterns, helical ornaments, figures IN THE ROUND. Most examples starting from *c.* 1100 BC are of bronze; but such pins were also made of iron, silver or gold. The lengths vary greatly, from *c.* 12 cm to *c.* 40 cm, and extremely long ones are up to 82 cm. *See* Paul Jacobsthal, *Greek Pins* (1956).

green gold. An ALLOY of gold, made with varying percentages of silver (25%–40%), zinc or cadmium, and being 18- to 14-CARAT gold. It has a greenish colour. Three shades were generally made: *vert de pré* (meadow gold), *vert feuille* (leaf gold), and *vert d'eau* (water gold).

greened amethyst. An AMETHYST of natural purple colour that has been converted by HEAT TREATMENT to a green colour. *See* PRASIOLITE.

greenstone. (1) The same as NEPHRITE. (2) A misnomer for CHLORASTRO-LITE.

grelot. A small elongated BEAD suspended as a pendant from a necklace or collar.

Greek pin. Head of gold pin. Eastern Mediterranean, 3rd century BC. Full length 12.5 cm. Ashmolean Museum, Oxford.

Gresley Jewel. A gold PENDANT enamelled and set with table-cut gemstones and pearls. On the front is the cover of the locket, decorated with an oval onyx CAMEO of the bust of a Negress, the cover being surrounded by enamelled and jewelled bands flanked by gold figures of cupids with bows and arrows; at the top there is a jewelled pediment to which is attached the suspensory ring. Within the locket there is a painted portrait of Sir Thomas Gresley (1522–1610) and on the back of the cover a portrait of his wife, Catherine Walsingham (1559–85), both by NICHOLAS HILLIARD. It is a family tradition that the piece was a wedding gift from Elizabeth I and descended in the family until the late 19th century; thereafter it was in the collection of Lord Wharton and it is now in a private collection.

grey gold. An ALLOY of GOLD, made with 15%–20% iron.

Grima, Andrew (1921–   ). A London jeweller and designer of contemporary jewelry, appointed in 1970 as a Crown Jeweller. In 1946 he formed the H. J. Company Ltd, to manufacture traditional pieces, but soon progressed toward modern designs featuring pieces of OBJETS TROUVÉS in cast textured gold. He creates designs that combine originality with tradition, often emphasizing the display of unusual gemstones. He has designed WATCH-CASES for Omega of Switzerland. His main shop is in Jermyn St, London, with several branches world-wide.

grinding. The technique of cutting a diamond (or other transparent gemstone) so as to give it its final shape (*see* BRUTING) and the desired facets (*see* FACETING). It is done by making flat surfaces by means of the abrasive action of a rotating wheel (scaife) charged with diamond powder.

grisaille. A type of decoration in PAINTED ENAMEL in which the picture or design is in monochrome, usually shades of grey on a white ground. The process involves first applying to the entire surface of a metal base a coating of dark enamel (usually black) that is then fired, then covering it with transparent or translucent white enamel which is fired, after which the design is outlined and developed by successive painting in shades of grey, white, and black, in varying thicknesses so that the design appears as if in relief. Sometimes the monochrome is in shades of purple or brown. The leading exponents of the technique in the 16th century were NARDON PÉNICAUD and LÉONARD LIMOUSIN of Limoges, France; they further extended the technique by developing painted grisaille (tinted grisaille) in various shades and tints laid on over a greyish foundation. Grisaille enamel decoration in imitation of carved hardstone CAMEOS was executed *c.* 1790 by Jacques-Joseph de Gault.

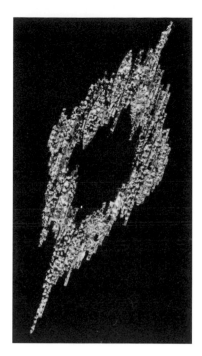

Grima, Andrew. Yellow-gold textured wire brooch-pendant with diamonds. 1960-68. H. 10 cm. Courtesy of Andrew Grima Ltd, London.

grossular(ite). A variety of GARNET (sometimes called 'grossular garnet') that is found in several colours and sub-varieties that merge into each other. Grossular when pure is colourless, but it usually exhibits some shade of red, pink, yellow, brown, or especially green (its name is derived from the Latin *grossularius,* the green gooseberry). The orange to orange-brown variety is HESSONITE ('essonite'), which when golden-yellow is called CINNAMON STONE. The pink variety, which sometimes includes small speckles of black magnetite, includes rosolite, landerite, and xalostocite. A pale green, MASSIVE variety, found in the Transvaal, South Africa, is sometimes given the misnomer 'Transvaal jade' or 'African jade'; but it can be distinguished from JADEITE or NEPHRITE. A reddish-brown variety has been given the misnomer 'hyacinth', and a reddish-orange variety the misnomer 'jacinth'; both those terms, now discarded, have been applied also to ZIRCON and SPINEL of those colours. Grossular is easily confused with SPESSARTINE. The interior of some stones shows oil streaks, sometimes called 'treacle'.

Grundy, Hull, Collection. A collection of more than 1,000 pieces of jewelry, mainly European jewelry from the period from *c.* 1700 to *c.* 1930, donated in 1978/80 to the British Museum by Prof. John Hull Grundy, and Mrs Anne Hull Grundy, of Hampstead, London. The collection is composed of many pieces of historical interest and artistic merit judiciously selected over many years by Mrs Hull Grundy, including many DOCUMENTARY SPECIMENS, as evidenced by their being accompanied by original cases bearing the name of the source. Mrs Hull Grundy also donated in 1975-6, to the Iveagh Bequest, Kenwood (London), a collection of 18th/19th-century jewelry, displayed at Kenwood, including examples of PASTE, BERLIN IRON JEWELRY, CUT STEEL, MOSAICS, CAMEOS, etc.. A great amount of other jewelry, totaling thousands of pieces, has

Guarrazar Treasure. Votive crown, gold with gemstones and pendent cross. Spanish, *c.* 621–80. Museo Arqueológico Nacional, Madrid.

guilloché. Gold buttons with enamelled engine-turned *guilloché* decoration and diamonds. Fabergé, *c.* 1900. Courtesy of Wartski, London.

been donated by the Hull Grundys to about 60 museums and institutions throughout the United Kingdom, especially to the Glasgow Art Gallery, the Ulster Museum, Belfast, and the Castle Museum, Norwich. *See* Hugh Tait and Charlotte Gere, *The Jeweller's Art: An Introduction to the Hull Grundy Gift to the British Museum,* London 1978.

Grundy's, Anne Hull, Gardens. A collection of about 200 varied small articles of jewelry, mainly with botanical, naturalistic or sentimental motifs, and dating from the period 1820–90, given by Prof. John Hull Grundy to his wife, Anne Hull Grundy, and donated by her, with the HULL GRUNDY COLLECTION, to the British Museum.

guard. A type of CHAIN, originally one from which a watch and various objects were suspended, but later any long chain, usually of gold. They were worn from the first quarter of the 19th century until the first quarter of the 20th century.

guard ring. A type of close-fitting finger ring that is put on after placing on the same finger a more valuable ring (or rings) so as to prevent the latter from slipping off. Such rings have no special form but are usually a simple hoop of gold or silver, often bearing an inscription. *See* KEEPER RING.

Guarrazar Treasure. A group of 11 jewelled gold VOTIVE CROWNS found in 1858 at La Fuente de Guarrazar, near Toledo, Spain, by peasants who broke them up and sold the pieces; some came into the possession of José Navarre, goldsmith to Queen Isabella, and he reconstructed 9 of them, smuggled them to France, and sold them in 1859 to the Government. They were displayed in the Cluny Museum, Paris, until 1942 when the Germans sent 6 to Madrid where they are now at the Museo Arquelógico Nacional, leaving at the Cluny 3 and a part of another. Two crowns were found later and were sent to the Armería del Palacio Real, Madrid, from which one was stolen in 1921. The crowns, dating from AD 621 to 680, are heavy and are made with various styles of decoration, including OPUS INTERRASILE, REPOUSSÉ work, and CHASING, and are set with varicoloured gemstones. All the crowns have attached suspensory chains, some ornamented, which has suggested that the crowns may not have been intended to be worn but were probably votive crowns. The two most famous have chains hanging from the rim and supporting cut-out letters forming the name of a Visigothic king, these being the CROWN OF KING SVINTHILA, 621–37 (stolen in 1921 from the Armería) and the CROWN OF KING RECESVINTHVS, 652–72. One crown has suspended chains from which a cross hangs down through its centre. *See* SONNICA, CROWN OF.

guilloché (French). A style of engraved decoration that, in jewelry and OBJECTS OF VERTU, is made on metal by means of an engine-turning lathe having an eccentric motion that can cut a variety of patterns, the most elaborate of which are done with a guide called a 'rosette', hence 'rose-engine-turned'. (It is different from the meaning of 'guilloche' as decoration on ceramic ware, and also on some Costa Rican jade jewelry, which is a border pattern in the form of 2 or 3 bands, twisted alternately over and under each other in a continuous series, in such a manner as to leave openings that are sometimes filled in with an ornamental motif; it was a speciality of Sèvres in the second half of the 18th century). The French term for the work is *guillochage.* When such engraving is covered with transparent enamel that reveals the pattern beneath, as found on some pieces by CARL FABERGÉ, it is called *tour à guillocher.*

gypsy ring. A type of finger ring having a wide gold band and a stone or stones set in a GYPSY SETTING.

gypsy setting. A style of SETTING for securing a gemstone in a finger ring, the stone being secured without a COLLET but only within a circular or oval recess in the body (SHANK) of the ring and held in place by a narrow turned-over flange so that the TABLE of the stone is level with the metal surface. This setting is suitable for soft stones that are thus protected. Sometimes claws are cut into the opening as a means of further securing the stone, and sometimes the shank is engraved to simulate rays extending from the stone. *See* BELCHER SETTING; CROWN SETTING; ROMAN SETTING.

H

hair jewelry. Articles of jewelry made of or embellished with human hair. Hair was used in several styles: (1) woven as a background for a gold-wire monogram set under a crystal or formed into a necklace, brooch, etc.; (2) plaited (braided) to form a bracelet or watch chain, or the rim around the BEZEL of a ring; (3) made into a floral or funereal design or a motif such as the Prince of Wales's feathers; and (4) a lock or plait of hair enclosed in the compartment of a brooch, hair locket or finger ring. Hair was used in the 17th century in MOURNING JEWELRY, but the fashion was revived in the 19th century for use also as a token of sentiment or affection for a living person, and amateurs made examples with their own hair. For methods of the use of hair in jewelry, *see* Alexanna Speight, *The Lock of Hair* (1871). *See* HAIR WORK; HORSEHAIR JEWELRY.

hair locket. A small LOCKET made especially to enclose a lock of hair and to be worn for sentimental reasons. Some were in the form of a small reticule, note-case, etc.

hair net. A type of HAIR ORNAMENT in the form of a skull-cap made of a flexible gold net having at the intersections a set gemstone and having at the top a REPOUSSÉ ornament, sometimes depicting the head of Medusa, all affixed to a metal headband set with gemstones and decorated with FILIGREE. Such pieces are found in HELLENISTIC JEWELRY.

hair ornament. Any of various types of ornaments worn in the hair by men and women of the Western and Eastern worlds. Such pieces are mainly the HAIR PIN, COMB, and SLIDE, but also the HAIR NET, HAIR RING, HAIR SPIRAL, etc., all made in various styles and degrees of ornateness, and often of a precious metal, CORAL, TORTOISE SHELL, JET, etc., with gemstones. In the Orient the hair pins are of the 1-pin and 2-pin types, and the combs are elaborate. *See* AIGRETTE.

—— , *Chinese.* A hollow ornament, made of JADE or gold, worn to fit over and hold in place a small bun of hair.

—— , *Hungarian.* An ornament attached to a short single pin, often set with gemstones in a floral pattern.

hair pin. A PIN with one or two blunt points for fastening or decorating the hair. There are two basic types: (1) One-point pins. Such pins have a single attenuated stem, straight or slightly irregularly bent, having a dull point at one end and a knob or other ornament at the top end. Some early Greek and Romano-British pins, and some from China, *c.* 13th/15th centuries, have elaborate heads, sometimes in the form of a human bust, flower, animal or figure. Those of the Etruscans and Romans were sometimes very long, ornately decorated with motifs of fruit. Anglo-Saxon examples often had a bird motif and were set with GARNETS. In the 18th and 19th centuries they were elaborately decorated, some with gemstones and some with ornaments that were made so as to vibrate. Somewhat different are those made in Japan and elsewhere in the Orient that are very long, without head ornament, and worn with the ends projecting for some distance from opposite sides of the hair. (2) Two-point pins. Such pins are U-shaped, sharply bent at the head so that the two shanks extend parallel and equally. They also were made in ancient times; some, from China, 3rd/8th centuries, and from Korea, 12th/14th centuries, have thin shanks, others have thick and bulging shanks, but later examples from both countries are delicately made and elaborately ornamented. Many such pins of both types have been made of gold or silver. Modern Western pins are of the two-point type and are generally prosaic, being usually made of cheap material and without ornamentation. *See* BODKIN.

hair jewelry. Pendant with hair inset. Swedish, 19th century. Nordiska Museum, Stockholm.

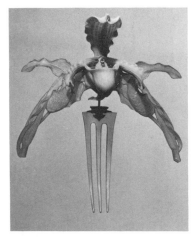

hair ornament. Ivory and horn. Signed by René Lalique. W. 16 cm. Gulbenkian Foundation, Lisbon.

hair pins. Left and right: silver; centre: bone. Romano-British, 1st/4th centuries AD. Full lengths 10.5, 19.4, 12.8 cm. British Museum, London.

hair pins. Bronze and carved bone. Roman, 1st/4th centuries AD. L. 5/15 cm. Museum of London.

hair rings. Gold 'ring money'. Ireland, 1200 BC–800 BC. W. 2 cm. Ashmolean Museum, Oxford.

hair ring. (1) A type of HAIR ORNAMENT, worn by a man or woman, in the form of a short, thick rod beaten into a corkscrew shape or into a spiral of several closely-spaced coils. Such pieces were articles of SUMERIAN JEWELRY, *c.* 2500 BC. (2) A type of hair ornament in the form of sheet gold made into a hollow PENANNULAR ring with slightly tapered ends. Such pieces, from the Irish Late Bronze Age, *c.* 1200 BC–800 BC, have been found in Ireland and Scotland; they are similar to the contemporary Egyptian hair rings, but have sometimes been called 'ring money' and said to have been used as a form of currency; *see* CURRENCY JEWELRY. (3) A type of finger ring worn as MOURNING JEWELRY and made in various styles with strands of human hair, the hair held (a) along the SHANK by flanges, (b) under a hinged lid, or (c) in a hollow tubular ring but visible through several apertures.

hair spiral. A type of HAIR ORNAMENT in a spiral shape with 4 or more turns, sometimes terminating with ornaments, such as a female head on one end and a rosette on the other. Such articles, made of gold, silver, or gold-plated bronze, are known from the Near East since the second millennium BC, in MINOAN JEWELRY and MYCENAEAN JEWELRY and in later periods of CYPRIOTE JEWELRY. Some examples from the 11th century BC have the wire bent double and then spiralled.

hair work. A type of HAIR JEWELRY made of hair of a deceased person and woven or plaited into strands that were given a gold mount so as to be used as a bracelet, necklace or watch-chain. Such pieces were worn as a form of Victorian MOURNING JEWELRY.

hairstone. A variety of QUARTZ that is thickly penetrated with hair-like crystals of RUTILE.

half-hoop bracelet. A type of BANGLE having decoration only on approximately one-quarter to one-third of the circumference, the decoration being usually a setting of gemstones. A finger ring similarly embellished is called a 'half-hoop ring'.

half pearls. Parts of pearls and SEED PEARLS that were popular in making designs of flowers and scrolls in jewelry in the 1890s, sometimes having coloured gemstones intermingled, or used in a setting as a frame for a miniature portrait.

hallmark. The mark(s) stamped on some articles of gold or silver in Great Britain and some Continental countries (but not officially in the United States) to attest the purity of the metal, in compliance with legally established standards, and other relevant data. Some such marks are required for jewelry except exempted articles, e.g. small pieces or delicate work that would be damaged. The hallmarks in Great Britain include the: (1) 'Maker's mark', stamped by the maker before the piece is submitted for assaying; (2) 'Assay Office mark', to indicate the office that does the assaying; (3) 'Standard mark', to attest the purity of the metal; and (4) 'Date letter', to show the date of assaying. Marks less often used include a 'Foreign goods mark' (to show date of importation), 'duty mark' (formerly used, to show payment of import duty), and 'Commemorative mark' (used seldom, during the period of some special event). A 'Design Registration mark' indicates the registration of a design (the date of registration, not the date of manufacture). Hallmarks were introduced in England in 1300 by Edward I, and the various marks gradually evolved. The standard hallmark in London is affixed at Goldsmiths' Hall (hence the term 'hallmark') of the Worshipful Company of Goldsmiths, organized as a guild before 1180, which maintains a record of all hallmarks. Booklets of hallmarks can be obtained from most jewellers. *See* C. J. Jackson, *English Goldsmiths and their Marks* (1921, 1964).

halo. (1) A type of head ornament in the form of a crescent-shaped band from which emanate a series of vertical pointed ornaments simulating rays of light, sometimes being alternately straight and wavy. Such pieces are popular forms of jewelry made in Spain and Mexico to adorn statues of the Virgin and of saints, and are attributes of sanctity. (2) A circular nimbus that surrounds a head. *See* AUREOLE.

hammer pearl. A type of BAROQUE PEARL that is shaped like the head of a hammer.

hammering. A process used in making gold jewelry by which the metal is beaten (alternately with annealing) to stretch and planish it in order to produce sheet metal, to make flat discs or plaques, and sometimes to alter the flat parts of some cast pieces. It was a process greatly used in making PRE-COLUMBIAN JEWELRY, the tools used being hard unhafted stones.

Hancocks. A London manufacturing and retailing jewelry firm founded in 1848 at 39 Bruton St by Charles Frederick Hancock (d. 1891), making silver plate and jewelry. In 1856 it made the DEVONSHIRE PARURE, and has been the sole maker of the Victoria Cross since it was first bestowed in 1857. In 1866 Hancock's eldest son, Charles (d. 1909), became a partner, as did his brother Mortimer (d. 1901) in 1869. In 1870 the firm's name was changed to Hancock & Co. and it is now known as Hancocks. In 1916 their successors moved the shop to Vigo St, and since 1970 it has been at 1 Burlington Gardens. *See* REVERSE INTAGLIO CRYSTAL.

hand amulet. A type of AMULET, worn as a pendant, in the form of a hand with the fingers in positions of varying significance. The hand, usually of IVORY, CRYSTAL, JET or WOOD, sometimes extends from a gold and jewelled suspensory mount made as part of a sleeve with a frilled cuff. Such amulets were worn in the 16th/18th centuries, mainly in Spain, as a deterrent against the 'evil eye'. When the hand is clenched with the thumb protruding between the index and third fingers (*mano in fica*), the amulet is called in Spain a HIGA, although that term has sometimes been extended to refer to such an amulet in the form of a woman's right hand (occasionally having jewelled finger rings on the index and third fingers) with the thumb and index finger forming a loop in a position regarded formerly as a gesture against the evil eye, but today as a gesture of accord. The gesture known as the *mano cornuta* (horned hand, denoting cuckoldry), with the index and little fingers extended upward, has also been used on amulets. *See* F. T. Elworthy, *The Evil Eye* (1895), p. 255.

hand ornament. An article of jewelry worn by a person on the hand for ornamental purposes, and often made of a precious metal and embellished with gemstones. The most frequently worn such ornament is the finger ring, of which there are a great many types and styles, including the ceremonial WEDDING RING and ENGAGEMENT RING, and also the SIGNET RING, and those worn as an AMULET such as the SCARAB RING. Another hand ornament is the glove, of which examples are known made of gold or embellished with gemstones. *See* CLEOPATRA BRACELET.

handkerchief ring. A type of finger ring that was worn on the little finger and to which was attached by a small chain a larger ring in which a lady's handkerchief was carried.

'Hanover' Jewels. Various pieces of jewelry (including a diamond crown) that had been owned by the British Royal Family and were awarded in 1858 to the then King of Hanover. (*See* HANOVER PEARLS.) The pieces were some that had been bought by George III for Queen Charlotte, and they were surrendered in 1858 and taken to Hanover.

'Hanover' Pearls. A famous pearl necklace that originally was composed of 6 very long ropes of pearls with 25 large drop pearls. Its extended history started when Pope Clement VII gave it to his niece, Catherine de' Medici, upon her marriage in 1533 to the second son of Francis I, the future Henry II of France. It passed in 1558 (when her son, Francis, Duke of Guise, became the first husband of Mary, Queen of Scots) to Mary, from whom it was purchased by Elizabeth I (it is shown in her portrait by Isaac Oliver). It was inherited in 1603 by James I who gave it to his daughter, Princess Elizabeth, upon her becoming Queen of Bohemia by marriage in 1658 to King Frederick V of Bohemia (it is shown in her portraits by van Miereveldt and by Daniel Mytens). The necklace then passed to their daughter, Electress Sophia of Celle, who in 1658 married the Elector of Hanover (from which marriage were derived the name and the later claim) who became in 1714 George I of England, the first Hanoverian king, and who brought the pearls back to England. Their son, George II, inherited the necklace, and it later passed to George III and then William IV. Upon his death in 1837 and the accession of his niece, Queen Victoria, the throne of Hanover passed by the Salic law (which banned succession in the female line) to her uncle, Ernest

halo. Gilded copper with enamel and gemstones. Spanish, *c.* 1630. W. 34 cm. Victoria & Albert Museum, London.

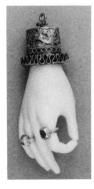

hand amulet. Ivory hand mounted in gold pendant with *cloisonné* enamel and gemstones. Spanish, 16th century. H. 6.7 cm. British Museum, London.

Augustus, Duke of Cumberland, the fifth and only living son of George III. He asserted against Queen Victoria the Hanoverian claim through the Electress Sophia. After litigation, and hearings before two commissions, as to whether the jewelry belonged to the Royal Family (and hence had passed to Hanover) or to the Crown, most of the jewelry (except the so-called 'HANOVER' JEWELS) was awarded in January 1858 to Queen Victoria on the grounds that they were Stuart heirlooms. The necklace has been said by Lord Twining to have been so awarded, and also said to have been worn by Queen Victoria and later by Queen Mary (as suggested by the portrait of her by Sir William Llewellyn), but there is no record of the necklace today among the royal jewels, and its present whereabouts is unknown. *See* Lord Twining, *A History of the Crown Jewels of Europe* (1960), pp. 165-6, 368-70.

Hanseatic jewelry. Articles of jewelry made in the 14th century in the German Hanseatic towns. (A mercantile league, called the Hanseatic League, was formed in 1358, centred on Lübeck and Hamburg; it continued until the 17th century.) The jewelry, much of it probably made in the wealthy town of Lübeck, often has decoration of relief animal motifs suggested by medieval heraldry, embellished by set gemstones. Examples have been found on the island of Gotland and in Ostergotland, Sweden.

Hanseatic jewelry. Gold brooch. Central sapphire, with rubies and emeralds. Possibly Lübeck, 14th century. W. 19 cm. Statens Historiska Museum, Stockholm.

hardness. The power of a gemstone, mineral, glass or other hard object to resist being abraded, i.e. the cohesion of the particles on the surface of such a body, as determined by its capacity to scratch another or to resist being scratched. Most gemstones, which possess hardness to a high degree, have an almost uniform degree of hardness; but such hardness may vary slightly in different directions or for the same species of stone from different localities. The hardness is measured by comparison with that of other selected minerals according to the MOHS' SCALE; it is indicated by the symbol 'H' followed by the numeral indicating its rating on the scale. Hardness can be tested by a jeweller by use of hardness plates or hardness points. *See* BRITTLE; TOUGHNESS.

hardstone. A vague term loosely applied to any opaque stone such as is usually used in making a MOSAIC, or to certain hard opaque gemstones that are carved as a CAMEO, e.g. ONYX, SARDONYX, AGATE, CORNELIAN, etc.

Harlech Torc. A gold TORC large enough to be worn around a waist, being 127 cm long and 35.5 cm in diameter. It is in the form of a circular cruciform flange, spirally twisted, with recurved solid terminals hooking into each other. It has been attributed to the second part of the Middle Bronze Age II, *c.* 1200 BC-1000 BC. It was found in 1692 near Harlech Castle, Merionethshire (now Gwynedd), Wales, owned by Sir Roger Mostyn; it remained in his family until sold by Lord Mostyn, at Christie's, London, on 12 July 1977. It is now in the National Museum of Wales, Cardiff. *See* WESTMINSTER TORC.

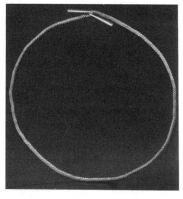

Harlech Torc. Gold girdle torc, spirally twisted with recurved terminals, Middle Bronze Age II, *c.* 1200 BC-1000 BC. L. 1.27 m. Courtesy of Christie's, London.

harlequin opal. A variety of PRECIOUS OPAL that has, on a reddish background, a mass of small points of different colours that appear to be shifting. When the points are very small pinpoint size, it is called PIN-POINT OPAL.

harlequin ring. A type of finger ring set with a band or cluster of dissimilar gemstones of different colours, with sometimes the initial letters of the names of the stones spelling a word (*see* ACROSTIC JEWELRY; REGARD RING). Such rings were often ornamented with FILIGREE work. They were popular in England in the Victorian era.

harp-shaped fibula. A type of FIBULA of safety-pin form, having a curved BOW extending into a straight bar, the terminals being connected by the pin, and so suggestive of a harp.

hat badge. *See* ENSEIGNE.

hat band. A decorative band encircling a hat which in the 16th century was decorated with gemstones.

hatpin. A long PIN for securing a lady's hat, used especially from Victorian times until *c.* 1940. Its head was decorated with ornaments of various materials and in many styles, including gemstones, JET, JADE, ornaments of glass (e.g. a coloured BEAD, a flower, a bird, etc.) or metal (e.g. gold or silver), etc. *See* LAPPET HATPIN. *See* Sonia Roberts, 'Hazardous Hatpins', in *Collectors Guide*, December 1979, p. 108.

haüyne (or **haüynite**). A rare mineral that is a component of LAPIS LAZULI. Sometimes it is found as an independent stone and, when sufficiently transparent, is used as a gemstone. It is bright-blue to greenish-blue and yellow. It was named after Abbé René Just Haüy (1743-1822), an eminent French mineralogist.

hawk jewel. A type of PECTORAL in the shape of a hawk, sometimes found in Egypt on the breast of a mummy. Fine examples were made of gold with the talons clutching a pair of signet rings.

hawk's-eye. A variety of CAT'S-EYE (QUARTZ) formed from infiltrated and silicified CROCIDOLITE and that has retained its original greenish-blue colour without being oxidized, in contrast to TIGER'S-EYE. Sometimes called 'falcon's-eye'. Former names that should be discarded are 'sapphire-quartz' and 'azure-quartz'.

head bead. A type of bead in the form of a human head IN THE ROUND. Phoenician examples were made of glass of several colours and with a suspension loop, suggesting that they may have been worn as a pendant on an EAR-RING as well as an element of a necklace. Examples are also known from Egypt, from the Ptolemaic period, *c*. 3rd/1st centuries BC.

head ornament. A head-dress of various types worn by men and women of the Western and Eastern worlds for ceremonial or ornamental purposes, usually made of a precious metal and embellished with gemstones. They include the CROWN, CORONET, CIRCLET, DIADEM, and TIARA, and also some rare gold antique WREATHS and HELMETS, as well as the less ornate FILLET, BANDEAU, BANDELET(TE), CHAPLET, and FERRONIÈRE, and types of HAIR ORNAMENT (including COMB, HAIR PIN, SLIDE). In the Orient they included a variety of styles, dating from articles of SUMERIAN JEWELRY, *c*. 2300 BC, to elaborate creations of gold or silver worn in China from the Sung Dynasty (960-1279) onwards and to pieces of TIBETAN JEWELRY; the Chinese examples were sometimes in the form of a domed cap enclosed within a crown and from which projected ornaments in the form of gold plumes and framework pieces with decoration of flowers, fruits, and butterflies. Several types are found in PRE-COLUMBIAN JEWELRY, including a type of DIADEM and a helmet.

heart. A popular shape for many types of jewelry, including the brooch, pendant, locket, charm, etc. Such pieces are made of gold, silver, and other metals, decorated with enamelling, gemstones or pearls. *See* HEART BROOCH.

heart brooch. A type of BROOCH in the shape of the outline of a heart, or sometimes two adjacent or interlocking hearts, and having a transverse or vertical pin. Such brooches, made of gold or silver, were constructed in the same manner as a RING BROOCH. They were popular in Europe during the 14th and 15th centuries, being given as love tokens, some having an amatory inscription on the front or the reverse. Some Scottish examples made from *c*. 1708 are surmounted by a crown, with occasionally a bird's head (*see* LUCKENBOOTH BROOCH).

heart scarab. A type of Egyptian SCARAB made to be buried as a TALISMAN with the dead, placed on the breast in lieu of the heart which was removed upon mummification. Such scarabs, often larger than the scarabs worn as an AMULET, were ritualistically carved of a variety of grey stone and mounted in gold, inscribed on the flat bottom with a quotation from the *Book of the Dead* (knowledge of which was believed to aid the journey of the soul), expressing a wish to the heart not to testify against the deceased at the moment of judgement before Osiris. On some such pieces, made in the Middle Kingdom (*c*. 2035 BC–*c*. 1668 BC), the beetle was carved with a human head. *See* TUTANKHAMUN JEWELRY.

heart-shaped diamond. A diamond that is faceted in the style of a BRILLIANT but the GIRDLE of which is heart-shaped. There are usually 36

hatpin. Blackamoor of black onyx with pearls and diamonds. Germany, 17th/18th centuries. Rijksmuseum, Amsterdam.

heart brooch. Silver with brass pin. Amatory inscription on reverse. Scottish, early 18th century. National Museum of Antiquities of Scotland, Edinburgh.

facets on the CROWN and 27 on the PAVILION, plus the TABLE and CULET. *See* BLUE HEART DIAMOND; EUGÉNIE BLUE DIAMOND.

heat. Most gemstones are good conductors of heat and so, when held in the hand or especially when touched to the tongue, they feel colder than imitations in glass.

heat treatment. (1) The process of changing or eliminating the colour of a natural gemstone or a synthetic gemstone by the application of controlled heat, due to a rearrangement of the atoms of the tinctorial agent. Examples are: (a) an AMETHYST which, when heated, becomes yellow (and resembles CITRINE) or green, and when more highly heated becomes colourless; (b) a yellow TOPAZ which changes to rose-pink; (c) a ZIRCON of reddish-brown colour which changes to blue or yellow or becomes colourless; (d) a dark QUARTZ (MORION) which becomes brown and then colourless; (e) an AQUAMARINE or BERYL of greenish-yellow colour which changes to blue. The changes are not in all cases permanent. (2) The process of changing the colour of a metal by heating. Examples are: (a) GOLD which changes to reddish when the presence of the copper in a low-carat ALLOY sometimes results in a varicoloured effect; (b) COPPER which changes as a layer of cuprous oxide forms, going through yellow, red, and violet to black; (c) STEEL which changes through yellow, bronze, light blue, and dark blue.

Hedeby Hoard. A HOARD of VIKING JEWELRY dredged in 1979 from the mud of the harbour of Hedeby, in Jutland. It includes an amber finger ring, a gold filigree ear-ring, gold and bronze pins, and carved bone combs and images. Especially significant are 40 bronze relief blanks over which metal was pressed in making gold and silver jewelry, such blanks having been found in a leather bag thought possibly to have been dropped *c.* 1000 by a jeweller engaged in mass production of jewelry. The articles are at the Schleswig-Holsteinisches Landesmuseum für Vor- und Frühgeschichte, in Schleswig, Germany.

hei-tiki (Maori). A grotesque form of flat pendant made of NEPHRITE, in the shape of a contorted human figure, sometimes having eyes made of paua shell. Such pieces have been worn by the Maoris of New Zealand.

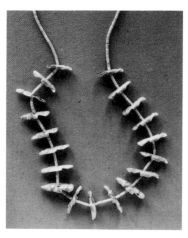

heishe. Necklace with fetish beads of carved stone birds. Santo Domingo Indian. Tom Bahti Indian Art Shop, Tucson, Arizona.

heishe (American Indian). A hand-drilled shell or stone BEAD made by the Santo Domingo Indians of south-western United States. Such beads are strung in strands, and many strands (up to 20) are combined to form a necklace, which is sometimes ornamented with suspended carved shell or stone fetishes in the form of animals, turtles or fish.

helical (or **volute**) **pattern.** A decorative pattern in the form of a HELIX or volute. It was used in volute form on three-dimensional pieces, as on some hollow beads of SUMERIAN JEWELRY made at Ur, *c.* 2300 BC. It is found more often as a helical curve on flat articles made of a continuous strand of coiled wire or as a REPOUSSÉ or incised pattern in such form. The helical pattern made of wire is found on some GREEK PINS and as terminals on some gold arm-rings, bracelets, brooches, and ear-rings made in Central Europe during the Central European Middle and Late Bronze Age, *c.* 13th/10th centuries BC. It is also found as a relief decoration incised or in repoussé work on pieces of jewelry from many regions in antiquity, such as jewelry from Ur *c.* 2300 BC and from Troy *c.* 2000 BC, and on MINOAN JEWELRY of the 17th century BC, on MYCENAEAN JEWELRY *c.* 1600/1400 BC, and on some gold bracelets made in Greece in the Classical period, 5th/4th century BC. In modern times the helical pattern made of coiled wire is characteristic of some jewelry made by ALEXANDER CALDER. *See* POSAMENTERIE STYLE.

heliodor. A variety of BERYL that is transparent and yellow. The preferable variety is golden-yellow, called 'golden beryl'; a specimen from Brazil weighing 2,054 carats, now at the Smithsonian Institution, Washington, DC, is the largest known cut golden beryl. Heliodor may contain a small amount of uranium, hence it is sometimes radioactive, but the yellow colour is due to traces of iron. The name is derived from the Greek words meaning 'sun-gilded'. Heliodor was discovered in 1910 in South-West Africa, but yellow beryl was used in ancient Egypt and India in AMULETS.

Hellenistic jewelry. Gold necklace. Greece, 3rd century BC. L. 33.6 cm. British Museum, London.

Helios brooch. A type of circular gold BROOCH having in the centre a head, in relief, of the Greek sun-god Helios, surrounded by a sunburst of triangular rays. A Hellenistic example, 3rd century BC, is in the Louvre, Paris. A similar piece was made by FORTUNATO PIO CASTELLANI, *c.* 1860, said probably to have been inspired by the Hellenistic piece while it was still in Italy in the Campana Collection (sold to the Louvre in 1861).

heliotrope. The same as BLOODSTONE. The name is derived from the Greek words meaning 'sun' and 'direction', and was first applied to a green CHALCEDONY which, when placed in water and facing toward the sun, appeared red. *See* PLASMA.

helix. A spiral curve moving around a focal point, as a watch spring. *See* HELICAL PATTERN.

Hellenic jewelry. *See* CLASSICAL JEWELRY.

Hellenistic jewelry. Articles of jewelry from Greece produced during the Hellenistic Age, from *c.* 323 BC (the death of Alexander the Great and the end of the Classical period) until *c.* 27 BC (the time of the Roman conquest of Greece) and some centuries thereafter when the Greek culture was absorbed in styles of Roman jewelry. Hellenistic culture was influenced by that of the various lands conquered by Alexander the Great, and jewelry styles in particular underwent changes. Owing to the greater availability of gold, jewelry became plentiful, and was characterized by three principal new features: (1) the use of new motifs, e.g. the HERACLES KNOT (reef knot), jars, birds, the crescent imported into Greece, and the indigenous figure of Eros; (2) the use of new techniques, e.g. DIPPED ENAMELLING and the lavish use of coloured gemstones and GLASS as inlays, all combined in the so-called 'polychrome style'; and (3) the introduction of new forms, e.g., ear-rings with suspended animal- and human-head ornaments (*see* ANIMAL-HEAD EAR-RING), diadems and bracelets with the Heracles knot and later with relief and filigree decoration, and finger rings with an oval BEZEL set with a gemstone or a CAMEO.

helmet. Gold helmet of Mes-Kalam-Dug, *c.* 2450 BC. Found at Ur. State Antiquities Organization, Baghdad.

helmet. A headpiece of armour made in a variety of styles. An example from Ur (*see* UR TREASURE), made of gold, is in the form of a close-fitting headpiece modelled as a wig bound by a diadem; it was made for Mes-Kalam-Dug, *c.* 2700 BC (the original is in the Iraq National Museum, Baghdad, but an ELECTROFORMED copy is in the British Museum, London). Helmets of TUMBAGA were made in the Quimbaya region of Colombia (*see* QUIMBAYA JEWELRY) by raising the form from a sheet of tumbaga, with decoration made in REPOUSSÉ work and CHASING, often with an ENRICHED SURFACE. *See* OORIJZER.

hem pearl. A type of pearl that is found near the mantle of the mollusc. It is usually dark, somewhat brownish, owing to a high proportion of CONCHIOLIN.

helmet. Tumbaga with repoussé decoration. Quimbaya style. W. 10 cm. Museum of Mankind, London (photo copyright Times Newspapers Ltd).

hematite. An iron ore that is found in many forms, e.g. (1) in MASSIVE form, and when showing a metallic LUSTRE called 'specularite'; (2) in botryoidal or nodular form, sometimes called 'kidney stone'; (3) in druses of crystals, especially in Cumberland (now Cumbria), England; and (4) as thin, transparent flakes which form a many-petalled rosette, called an 'Alpine rose' or 'iron rose'. It is blue-black, but when in fragments or powder it is blood-red (hence the name, from the Greek *haema*, blood), and when the stone is rubbed on an unpolished surface it leaves a red STREAK. It has been used in jewelry since Egyptian times, as a SEAL carved in INTAGLIO, as a CAMEO on a SIGNET RING (often depicting a warrior's head), as a CABOCHON set in a pendant or finger ring, and as beads strung in a bracelet or necklace (sometimes to imitate a black pearl). It is found as an INCLUSION in some AVENTURINE QUARTZ and SUNSTONE. Sometimes called 'iron glance', owing to its metallic lustre.

Heneage Jewel. *See* ARMADA JEWEL.

Heracles knot. A decorative motif, in the form of a reef knot, introduced in HELLENISTIC JEWELRY. It is found, inlaid with GARNETS, as the central ornament on some gold DIADEMS, flanked often with decoration in ENAMELLING and FILIGREE work. A similar reef knot is also found on some finger rings of ROMAN JEWELRY and of the 14th/15th centuries. The motif is said probably to have been imported from Egypt where it had for centuries been accorded amuletic significance. *See* LOVER'S-KNOT RING.

Heracles knot. Gold with filigree decoration. Grecian, 4th century BC. L. 3.5 cm. Schmuckmuseum, Pforzheim, Germany.

heraldic ring. A type of SIGNET RING worn in England from the 14th/15th centuries, bearing originally the crest or badge, later the coat of arms, of the owner. Some specimens from the Elizabethan era had the arms engraved on CRYSTAL in the BEZEL and the tinctures (colours) of the arms painted on the reverse, so that they would not be marred by use.

Heriot, George (1563-1624). The Crown Jeweller to James I. Born in Edinburgh, he was admitted there to the Goldsmiths Guild in 1588 and became jeweller and goldsmith to James VI of Scotland, having been previously appointed in 1597 as Court Jeweller to his consort, Anne of Denmark (1574-1619). Following the King to London when he became James I in 1603, Heriot made many jewels for Anne, most of them set with diamonds, but none is known to have survived. He also reset royal jewelry, including the THREE BROTHERS JEWEL.

Herkimer diamond. A local misnomer for ROCK CRYSTAL found in Herkimer County, New York.

Heron, Susanna (1949-   ). An English DESIGNER-MAKER, working in London, whose early interest was the production of ACRYLIC JEWELRY, often combining the coloured material with silver. Later she developed an original technique for making jewelry with RESIN of various colours, enclosed within a narrow, flat, silver (occasionally gold) frame, originally circular but later a broken circle integrated with the resin and silver pattern; the early motifs were boats and flowers, then silhouette bird forms, but recently she has tended toward abstract patterns, with flecks of colour in the resin. The resin is usually translucent so that the colour changes when viewed from different angles or worn over different fabrics.

hessonite. A sub-variety of GROSSULAR. It is transparent and brownish-yellow to yellow-orange in colour, and appears to best advantage under artificial light when it becomes fiery red. It contains many small inclusions, visible under a microscope, which give it a granular appearance visible to the naked eye; the interior also sometimes shows oily-looking streaks known as TREACLE. Hessonite is often confused with HYACINTH (reddish-brown ZIRCON) or SPINEL. Also called 'essonite' or 'cinnamon stone'.

hexagon cut. A style of cutting a diamond (or other transparent gemstone) so that the TABLE is 6-sided, in the form of a regular hexagon, and is bordered by 6 isosceles-trapezoidal facets.

hiddenite. A variety of SPODUMENE that is transparent, and emerald-green (owing to the presence of chromium). It has a high LUSTRE and strong pleochroism, so that the direction of cutting is important to feature the green colour. The green variety (sometimes miscalled 'lithia emerald' owing to the presence of lithium) resembles EMERALD. Hiddenite was discovered *c.* 1880 at Stony Point, North Carolina (USA), and was named after its discoverer, the mine superintendent, W.E. Hidden (1853-1918), of New York. The yellow and yellow-green varieties strongly resemble CHRYSOBERYL, but are lighter and softer.

higa (Spanish). A type of HAND AMULET in the form of a hand with the thumb protruding between the index and third fingers in a gesture of contempt and insult used since Roman times and ever since in all Latin countries, where it is associated with a fig, being called in France *figue,* in Italy *fica,* and in Spain *higa*. The term *higa* has sometimes been extended to refer to other such hand amulets in which the fingers are shown in different positions.

Hilliard, Nicholas (1547-1618). A famous English painter of miniature portraits who was painter, limner and engraver to Elizabeth I and from 1617 to James I, the first English-born artist to be so recognized at Court. Among his miniature portraits were those in the LYTE JEWEL, ARMADA JEWEL, NUTWELL COURT PENDANT, and 'HILLIARD' JEWEL. He and his brother John designed gold enamelled jewelry, especially lockets for his miniatures, but it has not been established that he executed any piece as a goldsmith. *See* Erna Auerbach, *Nicholas Hilliard* (1961); Roy Strong, *Nicholas Hilliard* (1975). *See* PHOENIX JEWEL.

'Hilliard' Jewel. A gold, enamelled locket pendant having on the front an oval onyx Italian CAMEO depicting the bust of a Negress, framed in a gold and blue enamel border encircling which is a white band set with rubies, and having on each side a gold figure IN THE ROUND of a Negro shooting an arrow. Above the cameo is a jewelled pediment and below are three suspended pearls. On the back there is a foliated design in translucent enamel. Behind the cameo is a locket; on one of the interior sides is an enamelled portrait of a man, on the other side is an enamelled portrait of a lady. The portraits, long unidentified, have recently been said to be of Sir Thomas Gresley (1522-1610) and his wife Catherine Walsingham (1559-85), painted by NICHOLAS HILLIARD, *c.* 1585-90. The jewel, possibly a wedding gift to the couple from Elizabeth I, is said probably to have been designed by him, but it has not been established that he executed it. The jewel was exhibited in 1862 at the South Kensington Museum (now the Victoria & Albert Museum), London, on loan from Lady Sophie des Voeux, and was sold at Christie's, London, in November 1957 by the American owner, Mrs B.C. Jago; it is now in a private collection. *See* Hugh Tait, 'Renaissance Jewellery', in *Connoisseur,* November 1963, p.152.

hinge pearl. A type of FRESH-WATER PEARL that is formed near the hinge of the fresh-water mussel. It is an elongated BAROQUE PEARL that has two pointed ends.

hippocamp(us) jewelry. Articles of jewelry of which the decorative motif is a hippocamp(us), a fabulous animal with the head and forequarters of a horse and the tail of a dolphin or fish. It is found on Renaissance pendants made in Spain, sometimes as a BAROQUE PEARL JEWEL, sometimes of gold decorated with enamelling and gemstones.

hippopotamus ivory. A variety of IVORY from the tusks (incisor and canine teeth) of the African hippopotamus. It is harder and whiter than ELEPHANT IVORY, and is covered with a layer of enamel that must be removed before carving.

historiated jewelry. Articles of jewelry, made in the 16th century, that depict scenes based on Biblical, mythological or allegorical subjects, with figures IN THE ROUND and enamelled; such pieces, made in England, France, and Italy, were usually an ENSEIGNE or a pendant. For an example, *see* SAMARIA, WOMAN OF, ENSEIGNE. *See* Hugh Tait, 'Historiated Tudor Jewellery', in *Antiquaries Journal* (1962), vol. XLII, part II, pp. 226-46.

hoard. A group of articles, sometimes including jewelry, buried or hidden deliberately for concealment and safe-keeping and found together

higa. Jet hand mounted in gold pendant with enamelling and gemstones. *c.* 1600. H. 8.5 cm. Courtesy of Christie's, London.

at a date much later than the period of production, and usually serving as
DOCUMENTARY SPECIMENS as distinguished from articles buried for other
purposes, such as funerary objects, and later excavated, known as a
TREASURE. *See* AJJUL HOARD; CHALCIS HOARD; CHEAPSIDE HOARD; FISHPOOL
HOARD; LARK HILL HOARD; THAME HOARD.

Holbein, Hans, the Younger (1497-1543). An outstanding artist,
especially a portrait painter and jewelry designer. He was born in
Augsburg, spent from 1514 to 1526 in Basle as a painter, becoming a
friend and illustrator of Erasmus, and then, after a short stay in Antwerp,
went to London where, through an introduction from Erasmus, he
became a close friend of Sir Thomas More (*see* SIR THOMAS MORE
PENDANT). After a brief return to Basle, he settled in London in 1530 and
continued as a portrait painter. In 1534 he entered the royal service and
designed jewelry that was executed in London and Basle. By 1536 he
became a Court painter to Henry VIII, making many portraits of him and
his wives. He also designed for craftsmen in several fields and, although
not a jeweller, made many designs for jewellers (including his friend JOHN
OF ANTWERP), especially some MONOGRAM PENDANTS. His designs for 179
articles, now remounted from the original *Holbein's London Sketch-
Book,* were bequeathed by Sir Hans Sloane in 1753 to the British
Museum. No known surviving jewel has been definitely attributed to a
Holbein design. *See* HOLBEIN GEORGE.

Holbein George An ENSEIGNE modelled in high relief with a figure of St
George and the Dragon, having in the background the figure of the
Princess Sabra (the daughter of the King, rescued by the hero). It is of
enamelled gold, finely chased, and surrounded by an open-wire
balustrade enamelled in green. Although named after HANS HOLBEIN THE
YOUNGER, there is no evidence that he was associated with it; it has been
said to date from the early 16th century and to be of South German
origin. It is traditionally believed to have been worn by Henry VIII and to
have been given by him to the Emperor Maximilian; it is now in the Royal
Collection at Windsor Castle. *See* GEORGE.

Holbein George. Gold enseigne with
enamelling. Probably South German,
early 16th century. At Windsor
Castle. Reproduced by gracious
permission of Her Majesty the Queen.

Holbeinesque. A style of certain jewelry made in England in the 1870s,
said to have been inspired by the Renaissance designs of HANS HOLBEIN
THE YOUNGER. It was used on oval pendants decorated with a large central
coloured gemstone surrounded by a wide border in a simple pattern of
multicoloured CHAMPLEVÉ enamel and with four or more spaced
diamonds and a drop pearl or diamond. The back has no signature but is
decorated with fine foliate engraving.

Hollar, Wenceslas (1607-77). A leading engraver who made prints for
jewelry, many based on the designs of ALBRECHT DÜRER. He was born in
Prague and emigrated in 1637 to England where, under the patronage of
the Earl of Arundel, he made a series of engravings for women's dress in
addition to his engravings of jewelry.

Holy Thorn Reliquary. *See* ST LOUIS RELIQUARY.

Honours of Scotland, The. The REGALIA of Scotland, the earliest
recorded being the crown, sceptre, and sword that Edward I of England,
after conquering Scotland in 1296, took back to London and that later
disappeared, possibly destroyed during the Commonwealth. After
Scotland regained independence in the 14th century, new Honours were
provided. After a turbulent history, they were used at the investiture of
Charles I in 1633. After a long period of discord relating to the Honours,
they were found in the Crown Room by Sir Walter Scott in 1818, and have
since then been on display at Edinburgh Castle. They include: (1) the
Crown, the oldest in Britain and remodelled under James V in 1540; (2)
the Sceptre, given to James IV by Pope Alexander VI in 1494; and (3) the
Sword of State, given to James IV by Pope Julius II in 1507.

hoop. The band of a finger ring that encircles the finger. Also called the
'shank'.

hoop ear-ring. (1) A type of ear-ring in the form of a curved wire or band
that extends somewhat like a hoop below the lobe and from which was

suspended some type of pendant. Some such ROMAN JEWELRY ear-rings were threaded with gemstones and glass beads. (2) A type of ear-ring that is a PENANNULAR hoop having at one end the figure of an animal or human head and then tapering to the other, thin, end that passes through the lobe (*see* ANIMAL-HEAD EAR-RING). Sometimes the decoration is not an animal head but the forepart of a horse; *see* PROTOME EAR-RING.

Hope Chrysoberyl. A flawless, faceted CHRYSOBERYL, yellowish-green, weighing 45 carats, and cut as a BRILLIANT. It was in the collection of Lord Henry Philip Hope. It was bought at Christie's, London, in 1866, by J. R. Gregory and sold by him in 1866 to the British Museum, and is now displayed at its Museum of Natural History. It is considered to be the largest known cut example of such a stone.

Hope Collection. An important collection of gemstones and pearls formed by the London banker Lord Henry Philip Hope (d. 1839), who was a descendant of an Amsterdam family of merchant bankers. The collection (which was inventoried for him by Bram Hertz in a catalogue published in August 1839, containing detailed descriptions and line drawings) included the HOPE DIAMOND, the HOPE CHRYSOBERYL, and the HOPE PEARL (but not the so-called HOPE SAPPHIRE), and also 41 uncut FANCY DIAMONDS and numerous other diamonds. The collection passed to his nephew, Henry Thomas Hope (1808-62), and the Hope Diamond was inherited by the latter's daughter, Henrietta Adéla, and then by her son, Lord Francis Hope (1866-1941) who, to secure the inheritance, had changed his name and whose wife, May Yohe Hope (1869-1938) twice wore it and later a copy of it. Lord Francis Hope (who in 1928 became the 8th Duke of Newcastle), after bankruptcy and family litigation, sold the Hope Diamond in 1901. The chrysoberyl had been sold at Christie's, London, in 1866, and 62 uncut diamond crystals were bought by James Tennant and were acquired in 1849 by the British Museum (Museum of Natural History).

Hope Diamond. A famous diamond, named after Lord Henry Philip Hope, that is of rare deep-blue colour, cushion-shaped (*see* CUSHION CUT) and of MIXED CUT, with 60 facets plus facets on the GIRDLE and weighing 45.52 carats. Its early history is uncertain, but it has been mentioned by writers since 1812, and is now considered to be a part of the BLUE DIAMOND OF THE CROWN. It appeared in the London market in 1830 and was sold then to Hope by Daniel Eliason, a London diamond merchant. It was inherited by Lord Francis Hope (*see* HOPE COLLECTION) and sold in 1901 by him to Simon Frankel, of New York, who resold it in 1908 to one Habib, of Paris (who may have bought it for, and later repurchased it from, Abdul Hamid II, Sultan of Turkey). It was bought in 1909 at the Habib auction in Paris by one Rosenau, who sold it to CARTIER. In 1912, it was sold by Cartier to Evalyn Walsh McLean, wife of Edward B. McLean, publisher of Washington, DC, who wore it (sometimes with the STAR OF THE EAST) until her death in 1947. In 1949 it was bought from her estate (with 73 other pieces of her jewelry) by HARRY WINSTON who in 1958 donated it (in Mrs McLean's original setting within a circle of 16 diamonds and suspended from a 48-diamond necklace) to the Smithsonian Institution, Washington, DC, where it has since been on display in its Hall of Gems, except when exhibited in 1962 at the Louvre, Paris, and in 1965 in South Africa. It has had a reputation of bringing tragedy to its owners. *See* Susanne Steinem Patch, *Blue Mystery: The Story of the Hope Diamond* (1975).

Hope Diamond. Brilliant cut diamond set as pendant in diamond necklace. Smithsonian Institution, Washington, DC.

Hope Pearl. The largest known pearl of modern times. It is nearly cylindrical, with a slight swelling at one end. It measures 5.1 cm in length, 11.4 cm in circumference at the thicker end, 8.3 cm at the thinner end, and weighs about 450 carats (1,800 pearl grains). It is white with a fine ORIENT except for about one-quarter that has a greenish-bronze tint. When owned by Lord Henry Philip Hope before 1839, it was mounted under an arched gold crown, enamelled and set with diamonds, rubies, emeralds, and sapphires. Apart from a suggestion that it may have been one of the French crown jewels, its later history is not recorded except for an offer of sale privately in 1974 for $200,000.

'Hope sapphire.' A misnomer for a SYNTHETIC GEMSTONE that, resulting from the early unsuccessful attempt to produce a SYNTHETIC SAPPHIRE by

Hornet Pendant. Gold pendant. Middle Minoan period, *c.* 17th century BC. H. 4.6 cm. Heraklion Museum, Crete.

horse fibula. Silver. Langobardic jewelry, 6th/7th centuries. L. 50 cm. Museo Civico, Ascoli Piceno, Italy.

Hu, Mary Lee. Neckpiece, silver and gold. 1976. H. 28 cm. Yale University Art Gallery, New Haven, Conn.

the VERNEUIL FURNACE, is a synthetic blue SPINEL. When the addition of cobalt as a colouring agent failed to produce the desired synthetic sapphire, magnesium oxide was added as a flux, and the resulting BOULE proved to have the HARDNESS, specific gravity, and absence of dichroism of a spinel. Stones so produced were cut and marketed as a 'Hope sapphire', perhaps to have them associated with the blue HOPE DIAMOND.

Hopi jewelry. Articles of jewelry made by the Hopi Indians of the southwestern United States, originally made from the late 1890s in the style of silver NAVAJO JEWELRY and ZUÑI JEWELRY, but since 1938 pieces have been executed by the process of OVERLAY as well as by the process locally known as SAND CASTING.

horn. The fibrous, pointed growth on the heads of some animals which, being tough, light, and easily worked, has for centuries been used in various forms for ornamental wear and utilitarian purposes. The horn principally used was ox-horn, ranging from white to dark brown, which has been made into buckles, brooches, etc. In China articles have been made of RHINOCEROS HORN. The use of horn was revived by RENÉ LALIQUE (who employed it for making decorative COMBS, HAIR ORNAMENTS, and elaborate TIARAS) and by LUCIEN GAILLARD.

Hornet Pendant. A gold pendant (hollow, with flat back) in the form of two confronting hornets having their curved bodies, seen in profile, forming a circle in the centre of which they hold a honeycomb decorated with GRANULATED GOLD. The bodies and wings have FILIGREE decoration. Above the heads is a bead enclosed within a CAGE. Three discs with granulated edges are suspended. It is an outstanding example of MINOAN JEWELRY, from the Middle Minoan period, *c.* 17th century BC. It was found at Mallia, Crete, hence is sometimes referred to as the 'Mallia Pendant'.

Hornick, Erasmus (fl. 1540-83). A Flemish goldsmith and designer of jewelry, born in Antwerp, who worked there in 1540-50, then emigrated as a Protestant refugee in the 1550s and settled in Augsburg in 1555; he worked in Nuremberg, 1559-66, and then returned to Augsburg where he became a citizen in 1578, working as an independent artist until 1582 when he left to go to Prague as Court Goldsmith to Rudolf II. While at Nuremberg he published in 1562 and 1565 two series of engraved designs for pendants, many depicting mythological, Biblical, or allegorical figures (the bodies in the form of BAROQUE PEARLS) or dragons and hippocampi, and having one or three suspended baroque pearls. He developed in his engravings of 1562 a new ARCHITECTURAL STYLE for pendants with a small niche in a columned background in which was placed a figure or a group, enamelled in white or colours, often with *putti* in the framework (*see* CHARITY PENDANT). He also made designs for gold TOOTHPICKS, FUR JEWELRY, handles for fans, and watch faces. His designs are in extreme Mannerist style and are said to have influenced some of the designs of HANS COLLAERT THE ELDER. He was a practising goldsmith but no jewel has been definitely attributed to him, although several have recently been said, on stylistic grounds, to be possibly from his designs or made by him. *See* Yvonne Hackenbroch, 'Erasmus Hornick as a Jeweller', in *Connoisseur,* September 1967, p. 54.

hornstone. A variety of QUARTZ, similar to flint but more brittle. It has been artificially coloured blue and used in the Victorian era as an imitation of LAPIS LAZULI, but is distinguishable by the absence of inclusions of PYRITES.

horse fibula. A type of FIBULA of LANGOBARDIC JEWELRY in the form of a horse (with the horse in various postures) made of silver with a pin and a catch-plate (usually missing) on the back. Five such pieces have been found in a tomb in the necropolis of Castel Trosino, near Ascoli Piceno, Italy. They have been attributed to the period of the Barbarian invasion of Italy in the 6th/7th centuries. The designs are said to be only ornamental, with no significance attached to the horse.

horsehair jewelry. Articles of jewelry made of natural or dyed horsehair, usually woven or twisted into patterns and set in gold or silver mounts in chains, brooches, etc. Such pieces were popular in the Victorian era. *See* HAIR JEWELRY.

horticultural style. A style, that developed in the 17th century, of decorating articles of jewelry with representations of naturalistic flowers (an outgrowth of the PEAPOD style). In Paris a hothouse was started by Jean Robin to furnish models for designers of jewelry and embroidery, and by 1634 this trend was magnified by the advent of tulipomania. Flower designs expressly for jewelry were published in 1602 by Jean Vovert, and many engravers adopted the style especially GILLES LÉGARÉ, JEAN VAUQUER, GIDÉON LÉGARÉ, François LeFebvre, Balthasar Lemersier (*c.* 1626), Paul Symony (*c.* 1621), J. P. Hauer (*c.* 1650), Heinrich Raab, Jacques Huon (*c.* 1660) and BALTHAZAR MONCORNET. The designs were executed in enamelling on the back of WATCH-CASES, MINIATURE CASES, and PENDANTS, and later on pierced and engraved silver in the late 17th century.

howlite. A white chalky mineral, sometimes veined with black. It is porous and so is sometimes dyed blue in imitation of TURQUOISE. It was named after Henry How, a Nova Scotian mineralogist.

Hu, Mary Lee (1943-   ). An American DESIGNER-MAKER now teaching at the Michigan State University. She has specialized since 1966 in working with wire and uses processes associated with fibres such as weaving, coiling, plaiting, etc., but in combination with traditional methods of metal joining.

huang (one of a pair). Green nephrite. Chinese. 5th/4th centuries BC. L. 31.8 cm. Indianapolis Museum of Art (Gift of Mr & Mrs Eli Libby).

huaca (Middle American Indian). Literally, a grave. Originally, a term applied by Middle American Indians to any article that was an object of worship (in Peru, spelled *huaco*), and used by the Spanish Conquistadors to refer to gold figures made by the Inca Indians to represent ancestors; but it has later been applied to any Indian artifact.

huang (Chinese). An element of a group of horizontal, arc-shaped pendants strung together, worn probably by being suspended from the neck by a cord attached through a hole at the centre and having holes at each side to support other ornaments. Such pieces were of ritual significance in China. Examples from the period of the Warring States, *c.* 481-205 BC, and made of NEPHRITE have at each end a carved dragon head, with an opening in the jaws for a suspensory cord.

hummingbird jewelry. Articles of jewelry having decoration (1) representing a hummingbird, with setting of diamonds and coloured gemstones, or (2) made of an actual dead bird, surrounded by a gold border set with gemstones and showing the broken or scuffed wings. Such articles were made in England in the Victorian era.

Hungarian enamel. A variation of FILIGREE ENAMEL in which the design is made on small plaques which are attached to the article to be decorated. The designs have mainly floral motifs. The work is found most often on church furnishings, but also on some Hungarian jewelry from the late 14th and 15th centuries.

Hungarian jewelry. Articles of jewelry made in Hungary, principally during the 14th to 17th centuries. Gold was plentiful, and the art of the goldsmith flourished, especially at the height of the Middle Ages; but royal decrees regulated its use, and much of the jewelry was made for export trade. Among the popular articles were gold and gilded silver bracelets, anklets, finger rings and ear-rings, as well as spangles and buttons to be sewn on garments, but mainly buckles and clasps for leather belts from which were suspended shield-shaped sabre tacheplates. In the 11th century Byzantine influence was conspicuous; later, Gothic styles prevailed with motifs drawn from chivalry. In the early 16th century the conquest by the Turks led to a decline in the making of jewelry until it was revived in Transylvania. During the Renaissance the goldsmiths again flourished, and BAROQUE styles were introduced. Pearls were lavishly used to embellish jewelry or were worn in ropes (with up to 2,000 large pearls or over 4,000 seed pearls on a single rope) made into necklaces or into wide bracelets (worn in pairs) or used in HAIR ORNAMENTS. Gold jewelry was extravagantly worn from the 17th century, often decorated profusely with gemstones, and ornate pieces were worn at weddings and social occasions. During the 18th/19th centuries articles of indigenous design were made. *See* Angéla Héjj-Détári, *Old Hungarian Jewelry* (1965). *See* RING BROOCH; 'PRETZEL' BRACELET; EAR-DROP; SNAKE BRACELET; NÁSFA; TREMBLANT.

Hungarian jewelry. Gold ear-rings, brooch, and bracelet; decoration of almandines and pearls. The clutched ring of blue enamel. Mid-19th century. Hungarian National Museum, Budapest.

hunt button. Jasper. Wedgwood (after
Stubbs), *c.* 1790. Wedgwood
Museum, Barlaston, England.

Hunterston Brooch. Penannular pin
brooch with filigree and amber.
Scottish, early 8th century. W. 12 cm.
National Museum of Antiquities of
Scotland, Edinburgh.

hunting belt. Gold plaques with
enamelled scenes. German, *c.* 1760.
Victoria & Albert Museum, London.

Hungarian opal. An OPAL of several varieties that was originally found
near Cervenica (now Czerwenitza), in Hungary; although the area is now
in Czechoslovakia, the name has persisted. The stones have a milky-white
ground with a varicoloured display of fire. The Hungarian mines were the
main source of opal before the stone was discovered in Australia in 1849,
and were probably the source of the opals known to the Romans. Many
such opals in the Hungarian National Museum lost their play of colour in
1956 due to heat from explosions during the Soviet invasion, but were
regenerated by restoring the water content.

Hungarian Opal, The. A pear-shaped OPAL, said to be the largest
known opal. It is from the Czerwenitza Mines, formerly in Hungary, and
was mounted in the first quarter of the 17th century in a gold pendant in
the form of three clasps that hold the stone. The opal weighs 17 oz and is
the size of a man's fist. The jewel is now in the Schatzkammer of the
Hofburg, Vienna.

Hunsdon Collection. A private collection of jewelry (sometimes referred
to as the 'Berkeley Heirlooms') that, by tradition, were presented *c.* 1579
by Elizabeth I to her cousin Henry Carey, Lord Hunsdon (d. 1596), who
bequeathed them to his son George, the second Lord Hunsdon, by whom
they were bequeathed to his wife in 1603 and thereafter to his daughter
Elizabeth, with the injunction to retain them in the family. The jewels,
upon the marriage of Elizabeth Carey to Lord Berkeley, came into the
possession of the Berkeley family and are preserved at Berkeley Castle.
The collection includes the DRAKE PENDANT and the STAR JEWEL (Drake
enseigne).

hunt button. A type of BUTTON used on a hunt jacket in England. Some
made by Josiah Wedgwood & Sons Ltd, *c.* 1790, depict horses from
studies by George Stubbs; they are of blue dip JASPER with white reliefs.
Similar jasper plaques were used on STOCK PINS.

Hunterston Brooch. A Scottish Celtic early 8th-century penannular PIN
BROOCH, made of silver part-gilt, and somewhat similar to the TARA
BROOCH, but without any enamelling, gemstones or attached chain. Its
ornament is a variety of interlaced work in fine gold FILIGREE and cells set
with AMBER. Its back is decorated with scratched runes, 10th/11th
century (the characters spelling the names of two former owners), and
with the Celtic TRUMPET PATTERN. It was found in 1826 on the estate of
Robert Hunter, of West Kilbride, Ayrshire (now Strathclyde), Scotland.
See LONDESBOROUGH BROOCH.

hunting belt. A type of livery belt worn by huntsmen in Germany. Some
ornate examples were made of a series of gold plaques decorated with
enamelled scenes depicting wild game.

hyacinth. A variety of ZIRCON or SPINEL that is of reddish-orange colour,
differing from JACINTH which is more reddish-brown. The term has been
used in the past in many confusing senses, sometimes referring to a blue
stone such as the SAPPHIRE, and sometimes to reddish-brown GROSSULAR.
It is still used as a prefix to the names of several stones that are reddish-
orange in colour, e.g. 'hyacinth quartz', a misnomer for reddish-brown
CITRINE, and 'hyacinth topaz', a misnomer for reddish-brown zircon,
while 'hyacinth sapphire' is sometimes applied to a sapphire that is
reddish-orange, and 'Oriental hyacinth' to reddish-brown CORUNDUM. It
has been recommended that the term be discarded. *See* HESSONITE;
BELLA, LA.

hyalite. A variety of OPAL that is transparent with sometimes a bluish
light reflected from the depth of the stone. When exhibiting a weak play
of colours, it is called WATER OPAL. It somewhat resembles a MOONSTONE.
The name is derived from the Greek word for 'glass'. Also called MÜLLER'S
GLASS.

Hyderabad, Nizam of, Collection. Reputed to be one of the world's
most magnificent collections of jewelry, owned by the Nizam of
Hyderabad (d. 1977) and partly (37 articles, including 22 emeralds
weighing 414.25 carats) offered for sale in September 1979 in order to pay
taxes. The sale was under the supervision of the Supreme Court of the
Indian province of Andhra Pradesh, which required a deposit of 210,000

million rupees (about £11,000,000) to qualify as a bidder or to inspect the jewels in the custody of the Mercantile Bank of Bombay. The sale, as well as two previous attempts to sell, failed owing to inadequate bids. Among the diamonds owned by the present Nizam (but not included in the proposed sale) were the NIZAM DIAMOND and also the Jacob Diamond (100 carats).

hydrophane. A variety of OPAL that is translucent and dehydrated, so that it becomes IRIDESCENT only upon immersion in water, owing to thin internal cracks that totally reflect light until the water enters the cracks and causes interference of light and consequent refractivity. The name is derived from the Greek words meaning 'appearing in water'.

I

ichthus. A representation of a fish, an ancient talisman symbolizing fertility, but later used as a Christian symbol, the word in Greek being regarded as a Christian acrostic. Some articles of DEVOTIONAL JEWELRY were shaped in such form or were decorated with the word in ENAMELLING. *See* FISH JEWELRY.

icon. A representation, made in mosaic, painting, or low relief (but never sculptured) of Christ, the Virgin Mary, or a saint, executed in Byzantine style. Icons were usually made as a wall ornament, but some were of small size and were worn as a pendant, especially in TRIPTYCH form.

iconographic ring. A type of finger ring having on the BEZEL (sometimes on the SHOULDER) a pictorial representation of the subject, the term having been applied by Victorian collectors of those rings which depict religious figures or motifs. The earliest known example has an engraving of the Virgin and Child (*c*. 1325), but by the mid-14th century most examples showed figures of patron saints (15 have been identified). Such rings (made only in England and Scotland, as DEVOTIONAL RINGS), were discontinued after the Reformation, but later examples bore such motifs as the Annunciation, the Trinity, the Instruments of the Passion, the Five Wounds of Christ, and the Five Joys. The rings were of gold, silver or, rarely, LATTEN. They were usually engraved (often filled in with NIELLO) but some were made by stamping or by the CIRE PERDUE process. Some examples bore religious inscriptions and some early ones are in the form of a DECADE RING.

ID (identity) bracelet. A type of BRACELET (modern) worn for identification of the wearer, originally by military, naval, and air force personnel and bearing the wearer's name and other basic data inscribed on a horizontal plate affixed midway between the links of the bracelet.

idocrase. A variety of gemstone that is found in several colours; it is usually olive-green or yellowish-brown but sometimes is blue or yellow. It was found first near Mt Vesuvius, hence its alternative name VESUVIANITE. A compact greenish variety that resembles JADE is called CALIFORNITE, a transparent yellowish-brown variety is called XANTHITE, and a sky-blue or greenish-blue variety is called CYPRINE. The stones that are transparent can be faceted; the MASSIVE stones are cut EN CABOCHON or as beads.

Idol's Eye Diamond. A diamond found at the Golconda Mine in India, *c*. 1600, so named as it is said to have been set in an idol's eye in an Indian temple. It is pear-shaped and of a fine blue-white colour, weighing 70.20 carats (rough weight unknown). It was seized in 1607 by the East India Company from the Persian Prince Rahab in payment of a debt, and did not reappear until 1906 when the Turkish Sultan Abdul Hamid II sold it

icon. Silver triptych pendant with enamelled icon. Russian, 17th century. Victoria & Albert Museum, London.

iconographic ring. Silver gilt depicting the Virgin and Child and, opposite, the Angel of the Annunciation. Found at Hume Castle, Berwickshire. Mid-15th century. National Museum of Antiquities of Scotland, Edinburgh.

in Paris to a Spanish nobleman who sold it in 1947 to HARRY WINSTON. It was resold in 1949 to Mrs May Bonfils Stanton, of Colorado, from whose estate it was bought at auction by the Chicago jeweller Harry Levinson, who exhibited it in 1967 at Johannesburg and was reported in 1978 to be still the owner, having offered it for sale at $1,000,000. It was owned in 1980 by Laurence Graff, the London diamond merchant.

Igmerald. A trade-mark for a type of SYNTHETIC EMERALD that was produced in 1934 by the I. G. Farbenindustrie (hence the name), at Bitterfeld, Germany, after experimenting since 1911. Production was terminated in 1942.

IHS pendant. A type of pendant (decorated with the letters I H S, a Christian sacred monogram (the insigne of the Jesuits) combining the initials of a Latin phrase, the words of which have been variously stated. The earliest known example is from *c.* 1480. Such pendants were popular in all countries of Western Europe in the 15th to 17th centuries, being shown in many portraits, e.g. Mary of Burgundy, Henry VIII, Queen Anne of Denmark, and Alethea Talbot, Countess of Arundel. *See* MONOGRAM PENDANT.

IHS pendant. Jesuit badge. Gold with polychrome enamel. Spanish, 17th century. Wallace Collection, London.

ikhoko (West African). A type of PENDANT made of IVORY in the form of a miniature replica of an anthropomorphic mask, usually triangular and about 5 cm long. The reverse is flat, but the front depicts in high relief a mask with characteristic facial features. Such pieces were made by skilled artisans of the Pende tribe of Benin in Nigeria, and were worn by men, attached to a string around the neck, for their alleged curative powers. *See* BENIN JEWELRY.

illusion setting. A style of SETTING a gemstone in a finger ring in which the stone is placed in a COLLET of reflective and brightly burnished metal, and then the metal edges are cut or shaped so that, when bent around the stone, they create the illusion of being a part of the stone. Such a setting is used mainly for a small diamond so as to enhance its apparent size. The style was invented by the French jeweller OSCAR MASSIN in the 1860s. The French term is *monture illusion.* Also called a 'deceptive setting' or a 'mirage setting'.

imitation gemstone. An artificial stone that is man-made to imitate, often by its colour, the appearance of a natural gemstone, but having wholly different physical characteristics (e.g. HARDNESS, specific gravity, colour dispersion, double refraction, dichroism) as well as different chemical composition, and hence also distinct from a SYNTHETIC GEMSTONE. Examples (called 'simulants') are usually made of various types of GLASS (e.g. PASTE or STRASS) or PLASTIC; such copies are moulded and hence are not required to be cut or faceted.

imitation (or **artificial**) **pearl.** An artificial man-made imitation (produced by several methods) of a natural pearl or of a CULTURED PEARL. Such imitations were first made in France before the 15th century in the form of a hollow glass bead dipped into acid to produce an iridescent surface and filled with wax to provide solidity and weight; they were used profusely as scattered trimmings on dresses and hats. In the 17th century an improved version was produced in France by first coating the interior of hollow glass beads with ESSENCE D'ORIENT to provide a nacreous appearance; they were called 'Roman Pearls'. In the 19th century a further improvement was developed in France by spraying the exterior of solid glass beads (having a string hole) with *essence d'Orient,* sometimes applying up to ten coats; they were called 'Venetian Pearls'. Such imitation pearls are identifiable by an unridged surface, by a smooth feeling when passed over the teeth, by showing a mark when pressed by a pin-point, or by being readily scratchable, as well as by X-ray and by testing for specific gravity (usually higher than 3.0). There are many trade-names for imitation pearls. *See* MALLORCAN PEARL.

Imperial Crown (Crown of the Holy Roman Empire). German, *c.* 962, with later additions. H. (front panel) 15.6 cm. Schatzkammer, Hofburg, Vienna.

Imperial Crown (Reichskrone). A CROWN of great historical and religious significance. It was formerly said to have been the Crown of Charles the Bold of Burgundy or a gift by Pope Benedict VIII to Henry II, Holy Roman Emperor from 1014; however, it is now considered to have been made at the workshops of the Monastery of Reichenau, on Lake

Constance in Germany, for the coronation in 962 of Otto the Great (although often called 'The Crown of Otto the Great', it has not been established that it was actually used at his consecration by Pope John XII in Rome as the first Emperor after the union of Germany and Italy). It has sometimes been referred to as the 'Crown of Charlemagne' (although he died in 814) because of historical continuity dating back to Charlemagne. It is said to have been worn by several Kings of Germany who were crowned at Aix-la-Chapelle (Aachen) or Frankfurt, but proof is lacking. The crown is of unique symbolical shape, composed of eight detachable gold arched panels, alternately set with varied gemstones and decorated with attached plaques depicting in CLOISONNÉ enamel scenes from the Old Testament; the front and rear panels are joined by a single gold arch bearing a Latin inscription made with pearls (the present arch being a substitute added by Conrad II, 1024–39) surmounted by a cross (a later replacement). All the parts are studded with gemstones, some of which are later additions. The original crown had *pendilia* that have not been preserved. The top stone in the brow plate, added in the 14th century, replaces the famous 'stone of wisdom' referred to by Walther von der Vogelweide (fl. 1198–1228) and last mentioned in 1350. The crown was kept after 1424 at Nuremberg but in 1796 it was moved, to avoid capture by Napoleon, and was taken to Vienna in 1800. It was returned to Nuremberg by Hitler in 1938, and after World War II it was hidden until returned in 1946 to Vienna where it is now in the Schatzkammer of the Hofburg. It is sometimes called 'The Nuremberg Crown' or 'The Vienna Crown'.

Imperial State Crown (British). With Second Star of Africa, Black Prince's Ruby, and St Edward's Sapphire. Crown copyright, HMSO.

Imperial (Victoria, Great White) Diamond. A large South African diamond that is said possibly to have been smuggled into London from Cape Town in 1884. Its characteristics have indicated that it was from the Jagersfontein mine. Its rough weight was 469 carats, but it was cut in Amsterdam into two stones, one, an oval BRILLIANT, weighed 184½ old carats, and the other, a circular brilliant, 20 old carats. The large one was sold to the Nizam of Hyderabad.

imperial jade. A variety of JADEITE (JADE) that is translucent and emerald-green. It is the most valuable type of jade. It is sometimes called 'emerald jade'.

Imperial State Crown. The British CROWN remade in 1838 for the coronation of Queen Victoria (used instead of ST EDWARD'S CROWN) and which each Sovereign has since worn when leaving Westminister Abbey after the coronation ceremony and on all later State occasions. It is part of the CROWN JEWELS. It consists of a pearl-bordered, gold circlet set with large gemstones within clusters of diamonds, the circlet being heightened by four diamond-encrusted CROSSES FORMÉE alternating with four diamond-encrusted fleurs-de-lis. Rising from the crosses are four arches set with diamonds and pearls, upon the intersection of which rests a diamond-encrusted MONDE upon which rises a diamond-encrusted cross formée set with ST EDWARD'S SAPPHIRE; from the top of the arches hang two pearls said to be from the so-called 'QUEEN ELIZABETH'S EAR-RINGS'. The front cross formée on the circlet is set with the BALAS RUBY (SPINEL) known as the BLACK PRINCE'S RUBY. In the circlet, below the balas ruby, is the diamond known as 'The Second Star of Africa' (Cullinan II); *see* CULLINAN DIAMOND. At the rear of the circlet is the STUART SAPPHIRE. The crown was reset for George VI in 1937.   *[Plate V]*

Inca jewelry. Articles of PRE-COLUMBIAN JEWELRY made by the Inca Indians of Peru (and also of neighbouring regions of Ecuador, Bolivia, and northern Chile) from *c.* 1200 until the Spanish conquest under Francisco Pizarro and the fall of Cuzco, the Inca capital, in 1533. When the Emperor (Inca) Atahualpa came in 1532 to Cajamarca to meet Pizarro he was imprisoned and a vast amount of gold artifacts (some 6,000 kg.) that had been assembled to ransom him was treacherously taken by Pizarro and much of it was melted and sent as ingots to Spain. Some gold jewelry was spared destruction owing to its having been buried with the dead and to the disapproval by the Church of plundering graves and tombs (this was, however, done extensively in later centuries). The Inca jewelry had been made exclusively for the gods and for the Emperor and his Court; the supply of the metal, as of most other resources, was under State control. The pieces included small gold anthropomorphic figures of

Inca jewelry. Hollow bimetallic figure; upper half gold, lower silver, with mussel-shell eyes. Peru, 1438–1532. H. 13.8 cm. Museum für Völkerkunde, Berlin.

Indian jewelry. Bazu band, gold with enamelling and gemstones; silk cord with pearls. 18th century. L. (ornament) 9.3 cm. British Museum, London.

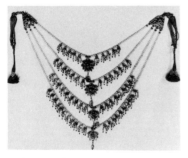

Indian jewelry. Necklace, gold with gemstones, pearls, and enamelling. Mughal, 18th century. Victoria & Albert Museum, London.

men and women, often only scantily clothed but wearing replicas of jewelry. *See* PERUVIAN JEWELRY.

inclusion. A foreign material (solid, gaseous or liquid), usually minute in size, that is enclosed within a natural mineral, but not in a SYNTHETIC GEMSTONE. An inclusion may result from: (1) a pre-existing material that was enveloped by a growing crystal, e.g. specks of iron; (2) a substance formed when the crystal was being formed, e.g. a gas bubble; or (3) a change after the crystal was formed, e.g. by heating which causes chemical alteration and recrystallization. Examples of solid inclusions may be: (1) a NEEDLE of RUTILE in ASTERIA; (2) specks (piqués) of carbon in some diamonds; (3) specks of mica in AVENTURINE QUARTZ; (4) insects, etc., embedded in AMBER. Examples of liquid or gaseous inclusions may be water or carbonic gas, with sometimes a bubble of gas in the liquid (a 'two-phase inclusion'), and sometimes also an included crystal (a 'three-phase inclusion'). *See* FEATHER; SILK; FINGERPRINT; DENDRITE; CENTIPEDE FLÈCHES D'AMOUR. *See* Eduard J. Gübelin, *The Internal World of Gemstones*, 2nd ed., Zurich 1979.

incrustation. A style of securing a gemstone in a finger ring by sinking the stone into a space cut in the metal hoop and securing it by pushing some of the metal inward over the GIRDLE of the stone. It is contrasted with a SETTING which secures the stone in a specially constructed separate mount.

India(n) cut. The type of cutting of a gemstone that is imperfect and without symmetry, as has been done sometimes in India, especially before the development of the modern techniques of DIAMOND CUTTING. Sometimes called 'Mughal (Mogul) cut'. *See* NATIVE CUT.

Indian jade. A misnomer for green AVENTURINE QUARTZ, containing fuchsite (a chromium mica); it is found in India. It is not found as a single crystal of quartz but as an aggregate called 'quartzite'.

Indian jewelry. Articles of jewelry made in India, known from recorded examples from as early as *c*. 2500 BC and from finds at Taxila from the 5th century showing Hellenistic and Parthian influence. The early indigenous pieces reflect Persian influence until the emergence of local styles, especially during the Mughal period (*see* MUGHAL JEWELRY). Jewelry was worn profusely by men and women, not only as ornament but as a status display of invested wealth or often for reasons of superstition. Articles were worn to adorn every part of the body, and many pieces were worn simultaneously. Gold articles were often made of thin sheet metal beaten over a core of lac or pitch, and are characterized by intricate designs displaying fine workmanship. Many pieces are decorated with GRANULATED GOLD, FILIGREE work, pearls, large coloured gemstones, and CHAMPLEVÉ enamelling The polychrome enamelling of Jaipur is renowned (*see* JAIPUR JEWELRY) but fine enamelling was also done at Delhi, Varanasi (in pink), Lucknow, and Hyderabad. The styles, which varied in the different regions, were generally massive, featuring numerous suspended ornaments and tassels. *See* T. H. Hendley, 'Indian Jewellery', in *Journal of Indian Art and Industry*, XII (1906); Jamila Brij Bhushan, *Indian Jewellery* (*c*. 1950). *See* PERTÁBGARH JEWELRY; NAVRATNA.

Indian (United States) jewelry. Articles of jewelry made by craftsmen of many tribes of American Indians that live on reservations in wide areas of the United States, including the Navajo, Hopi, Zuñi and Santo Domingo (New Mexico and Arizona), Sioux (North Dakota), Choctaw (Mississippi), Seneca (New York), and Iroquois (north-eastern United States and Canada). The articles, consisting of pendants, necklaces, bracelets (often of rigid penannular form), finger rings, and beads, as well as such indigenous pieces as the SQUASH-BLOSSOM NECKLACE, NAJA, BOLA, and CONCH BELT, have traditionally been made of silver decorated with REPOUSSÉ work and TURQUOISE; but modern styles include gold settings, inlays of coral, jet, mother-of-pearl, shell, and wood, and designs made by the OVERLAY and SAND CASTING techniques. New styles and techniques are continually being developed for the jewelry that has now a thriving market for expensive pieces as well as tourist items. *See* NAVAJO JEWELRY; HOPI JEWELRY; ZUÑI JEWELRY; WAMPUM.

Inquisition pendant (front and back). Gold set with emeralds; on reverse, the insigne of the Holy Office of the Inquisition. Spanish, late 17th century. L. 6.4 cm. British Museum, London.

Indian topaz. A local misnomer for saffron-yellow CORUNDUM (SAPPHIRE) found in India.

Indian-trade silver jewelry. Articles made of silver that were given during the 18th century by white traders to North American Indians in exchange for furs. The pieces included brooches (called 'shirt buckles' and sometimes bearing Masonic emblems), necklaces, head bands, buckles, crosses (with 2 or 3 cross arms), PENANNULAR wrist bands, and especially crescent-shaped gorgets; *see* GORGET (AMERICAN). *See* Charlotte Wilcoxen, 'Indian-trade silver of the New York colonial frontier', in *Antiques,* December 1979, p. 1356.

indicolite (or **indigolite**). A variety of TOURMALINE that is indigo-blue.

inlaid bead. A type of BEAD found among SUMERIAN JEWELRY that was made sometimes of a gemstone, e.g. LAPIS LAZULI, inlaid with a spiralling wire of gold, and often having a gold cap on each end, but more often made of gold inlaid with stones.

inlaying. The process of decorating by inserting shaped pieces of a material (not ENAMEL or NIELLO) into the surface or ground of an object so that the surfaces of both are level. Articles of jewelry have been inlaid by insetting into metal thin pieces of gemstones (*see* CLOISONNÉ INLAY) or of metal or other material. This is distinct from the various methods of decorating with ENAMELLING into the surface, e.g. CLOISONNE, CHAMPLEVÉ, PLIQUE À JOUR, and BASSE TAILLE, and also from niello. Other styles of inlaying in metal can be executed by several methods: (1) by inserting thin strips of gold, silver or other metal into narrow grooves in a metal surface, e.g. damascened ware; (2) by cutting a pattern into a sheet of metal which is then soldered to another metal sheet and filling in the spaces with thin pieces of a soft decorative material, e.g. IVORY or TORTOISE SHELL (*see* PIQUÉ) or with thin slices of gemstones cemented into place; (3) by making a recess in a piece of metal by chiselling or etching, and then filling it in with another hard material that is not enamel.

Inquisition pendant. A type of pendant bearing the insigne of Spain's Holy Office of the Inquisition. In 1603 Philip III decreed that ministers of the Holy Inquisition should exhibit the insigne on their clothing during religious functions and public acts. By 1680 certain officials at Madrid wore such pendants.

inro (Japanese). A small Japanese case (measuring about 10 x 5 x 2 cm) having several compartments, worn suspended by a cord from the sash

inro. Three-case, wood lacquer, with ojime and gold netsuke with silver disc. 19th century. Courtesy of Douglas J. K. Wright Ltd, London.

intaglio. Carved agate scaraboid. Greek, *c.* 530 BC. British Museum, London.

(*obi*) that fastened a kimono, along with other objects such as a NETSUKE. Such articles were used to carry seals, small shrines, and powdered medicine. They were usually made of IVORY, metal, or lacquered wood, often with inlaid decoration, but occasionally of tortoise shell, porcelain or other material. They were skilfully decorated with a great variety of motifs, and were used from the late 16th century, but mainly in the 17th/18th centuries, until the early 19th century. *See* Melvin and Betty Jahss, *Inro and other Miniature Forms of Japanese Lacquer Art* (1972).

inscription. Words inscribed on some articles of jewelry to record information about the circumstances in which the piece was made or used (e.g. MOURNING JEWELRY; COMMEMORATIVE JEWELRY) or to set forth some relevant motto (e.g. SERJEANT RING) or, more often, some sentimental expression (e.g. POSY RING; WEDDING RING). Some Saxon finger rings bear inscriptions stating the name of the owner. *See* MARK.

intaglio. A style of decoration (or an object so made) created by ENGRAVING or CARVING below the surface so that the apparent elevations of the design are hollowed out and an impression from the design yields an image in relief. The background is not cut away, but is left in the plane of the highest areas of the design. It is the opposite of a CAMEO. It is sometimes called 'hollow relief' or 'coelanaglyphic'. Greek goldsmiths did intaglio work on metal, but such decoration is more often found on gemstones (*see* ENGRAVED GEMSTONE), CORAL, and CRYSTAL (*see* CRYSTAL OF LOTHAIR), or on the the JASPER ware of Wedgwood or the TASSIE MEDALLIONS. Articles in intaglio were sometimes worn as an ornament alone, or mounted in a FINGER RING, BUTTON, BROOCH, PENDANT, etc., and especially a SEAL, and occasionally were surrounded by gemstones. *See* NICOLO; REVERSE INTAGLIO CRYSTAL.

intarsia, Florentine. Decoration made by inlaying, usually in wood (marquetry), but the term is sometimes loosely applied to FLORENTINE MOSAIC.

Investiture Coronet, Prince of Wales's. *See* WALES'S, PRINCE OF, INVESTITURE CORONET.

investiture ring. A type of finger ring that was used (1) when conferring an office (e.g. the BISHOP'S RING conferred upon his consecration or the FISHERMAN'S RING conferred on the Pope) or (2) as a symbolic device in connection with the transfer of land. The latter type was used from the 10th century and was common in the Middle Ages, when it was used by monarchs or the clergy to vest title in lands, sometimes – both in England and on the Continent – being attached to the charter of conveyance.

investment casting. The same as CENTRIFUGAL CASTING.

iolite (or **iolith**). A mineral from which is derived a gemstone of various shades of blue. It has a VITREOUS LUSTRE and exhibits strong DICHROISM; it shows deep blue when the stone is viewed along the length of the crystal, and should be cut accordingly. Transparent stones are usually faceted, and cloudy specimens are cut EN CABOCHON or engraved as a SIGNET RING; some are AVENTURESCENT, owing to flaky inclusions of HEMATITE, or show ASTERISM from silky inclusions. It resembles blue TOURMALINE and SAPPHIRE. Also called 'cordierite' and 'dichroite', as well as by the misnomers 'water sapphire' and 'lynx sapphire'. *See* PRASEOLITE.

Iranian Diamonds. A countless number of diamonds in the CROWN JEWELS (IRAN). They include a group of 23 diamonds studied in 1966 by Dr V. B. Meen and Dr A. D. Tushingham, of Toronto, 4 of which are probably Indian (3 being white and 1 peach-coloured) and 19 South African and yellow; the stones weigh from 152.16 to 38.18 carats, and are of various shapes. The yellow diamonds are included in the 48 so-called 'Iranian Yellows' bought in Europe in 1889 by Nasser-ed-din Shah, 5 of which weigh more than 114 carats each. The important diamonds in the Iranian Crown Jewels are the DARYA-I-NUR, the NUR-UL-AIN, and the TAJ-I-MAH.

iridescence. The phenomenon of the soft rainbow-like play of prismatic colours in certain gemstones sometimes caused by the interference of light reflected from (1) air-filled cracks which create layers of different refraction, e.g. as in RAINBOW QUARTZ (iris quartz), (2) INCLUSIONS of a thin layer or a film of LAMELLAR nature that has a different refractive index than the mass of the stone, or (3) the minute spheres within PRECIOUS OPAL. Iridescence is to be distinguished from (a) ordinary absorption colours by its shifting character, the colours changing with the angle of viewing or the variation of the angle of incidence of the illumination, and (b) OPALESCENCE. *See* SCHILLER; SHEEN.

iris (quartz). The same as RAINBOW QUARTZ.

iris agate. A variety of banded AGATE that has bands so close together that they diffract light, resulting in a rainbow effect. Also called 'rainbow agate'.

iris opal. The same as WATER OPAL.

Irish torc. A type of massive TORC made of gold in Ireland during the late Celtic period. The largest known is more than 1.50 m long and weighs more than 765 grams; it is said to have been worn over a shoulder and across the breast.

iron. A metallic element that has been used for making some jewelry in the form of cast iron and wrought iron. *See* IRON JEWELRY; BERLIN IRON JEWELRY.

Iron Crown, The. Six panels set with gemstones. 9th century. Cathedral Treasury, Monza, Italy.

Iron Crown, The. The CROWN in the form of a DIADEM that was used to consecrate Napoleon I, dating, according to legend, back to the 6th century, although now regarded as having been made in the first half of the 9th century. It was used for a number of kings consecrated in Italy, and was taken from Italy to Vienna when the Austrians left Lombardy in 1859; it was returned to Italy in 1866, and is now kept in the Cathedral at Monza, where it is carried in an annual solemn procession. The crown is a circlet made of six detachable rectangular gold panels, each decorated with green, blue, and white CLOISONNÉ enamel and set with gemstones, all the panels being connected by an interior narrow iron band traditionally said to have been made from a nail from the True Cross, given by St Helena, the mother of Constantine the Great. For its detailed history, *see* Lord Twining, *The History of the Crown Jewels of Europe* (1960), pp. 420–26.

iron jewelry. Articles of jewelry made of IRON, some from ancient times but in small quantity until the 18th century in Europe (*see* BERLIN IRON JEWELRY). A few examples are known of CELTIC JEWELRY and of ANGLO-SAXON JEWELRY, mainly BUCKLES.

iron pyrites. *See* PYRITE; MARCASITE.

irradiated diamond. *See* TREATED DIAMOND.

irradiation. The process of exposing certain gemstones to a radioactive substance with the effect of artificially inducing a change of colour. This has been done with some diamonds (*see* TREATED DIAMOND). The original colours are sometimes partly restored by heating.

Israelite jewelry. Articles of jewelry found in the Holy Land, in several HOARDS and finds, dating from *c.* 1000 BC until the conquest of Jerusalem by Nebuchadnezzar in 587 BC, before the styles were influenced by the Achaemenian, Phoenician, and Cypriote styles. The articles are of little artistic quality, consisting mainly of beads, simple ear-rings, and plaques, except for some unusual seals and amulets.

ivory. Arm-ring carved in Etruscan Orientalizing style. 1st half, 7th century BC. From Tivoli, Italy. Ashmolean Museum, Oxford.

ivory. A hard, creamy-white, opaque dentine that forms the tusks of elephants and some other mammals. (*See* ELEPHANT IVORY; HIPPOPOTAMUS IVORY; WALRUS IVORY; NARWHAL IVORY; FOSSIL IVORY). It is translucent when cut in thin sheets. It is initially white but ages with a yellow to brownish patina, and is marked with delicate horizontal graining. Different ivories show different colours under ultraviolet light. It has long been used for making jewelry in the form of finger rings, brooches, beads, BANGLES, NETSUKE, fans, etc., either smooth and polished or intricately carved, and also in inlay designs set in gold (*see* PIQUÉ work) and JET, and as the base for miniature paintings. Ivory can be readily carved and has been used from earliest times in China and Japan for highly carved ornaments, plaques, and jewelry. It has been used from antiquity, and in the West especially from the 13th century, particularly in the Victorian era. During the 19th century the centre for European ivory carving was Dieppe, France, until *c*.1870. Ivory carving was established in the late 19th century at Erbach, Germany, and the Erbach School, which still flourishes, is known for its ivory jewelry, especially the 'Erbach rose' that was copied from the 'Dieppe rose' (*see* ROSE). Ivory carving, using mainly walrus ivory and mammoth ivory, has been done in Russia since the 10th century, mainly making pieces with pierced designs; but the ware is principally objects of vertu rather than jewelry. The use of ivory was revived by RENÉ LALIQUE and WOLFERS for use in ART NOUVEAU jewelry. The largest pieces of carved ivory come from Benin (*see* BENIN JEWELRY) and Zaire; *see* IKHOKO. Ivory can be dyed, and it is coloured with bright colours in Tibet. Imitation ivory ware is made from the seed of a South American and an African palm; it is known as VEGETABLE IVORY. Ivory is imitated in celluloid, made of comparable weight and colour as well as with artificial graining, but it is distinguishable by being softer and more sectile. Real ivory will split or warp in extremes of temperature. The term 'ivory' without qualification refers to elephant ivory. *See* CHRYSELEPHANTINE. *See* G. C. Williamson, *The Book of Ivory* (1938).

Ixworth Cross. Pectoral cross. Gold with *cloisonné* enamel and garnets. Anglo-Saxon, 7th century. W. 3.75 cm. Ashmolean Museum, Oxford.

Ixworth Cross. A gold PECTORAL CROSS with 4 arms of equal length and having rounded extremities, all extending from a large central ornament of 3 concentric rings. The arms and the central ornament are decorated with rectangular and step-shaped cells formed by prominent CLOISONS and set with GARNETS backed with FOIL. At the top is a horizontal BUGLE BEAD for suspension; it may have been attached at the time of a later repair. It is Anglo-Saxon, 7th century, and was found in a grave at Stanton, Ixworth, near Bury St Edmunds in West Suffolk, England (hence sometimes called the 'Stanton Cross'). *See* WILTON CROSS; ST CUTHBERT'S CROSS.

J

jabot pin. A type of pin generally similar to a TIE PIN, worn on a jabot (a ruffle formerly worn by men on the front of a shirt or by women on the front of a dress).

jacinth. A variety of ZIRCON that is reddish-brown, similar to HYACINTH which is more reddish-orange. The term has been used in many confusing senses, such as for a reddish-brown GROSSULAR and SPINEL. It has been recommended that the term be discarded.

Jacobite jewelry. Articles of English COMMEMORATIVE JEWELRY worn by adherents of the royal house of Stuart to show loyalty to, or later in memory of, the exiled James II (1633-1701) after his abdication in 1698, and his descendants, James Edward Stuart, the 'Old Pretender', and his son Charles Edward Stuart (1720-88), 'Bonnie Prince Charlie' or the 'Young Pretender'. The themes depicted on the jewelry were, in the early period until 1745, the rose of England representing the Crown, and later, 1746-70, mottoes and disguised symbols. Some finger rings had on a lid on the BEZEL a portrait of the reigning monarch, William III (1650-1702), but inside a portrait of the Old Pretender. *See* STUART, CHARLES EDWARD, RING.

jade. A name that for many years was generally applied to two distinct minerals, JADEITE and NEPHRITE (until distinguished in 1863 by A. Damour), having different chemical compositions and other

V *Imperial State Crown*. The British Coronation crown, consisting of a pearl-bordered gold circlet set with gemstones and diamonds, and four arches set with diamonds and pearls, surmounted by a diamond-encrusted monde and cross formée. On the front, in the circlet, the 'Second Star of Africa' (Cullinan II diamond), and above it the Black Prince's Ruby. Remade 1838. Crown copyright, HMSO.

VI *gemstones*. 1 topaz 2 brazilianite 3 opal 4 scheelite 5 danburite 6 beryl (emerald) 7 fire opal 8 garnet (almandine) 9 cordierite (iolite) 10 topaz 11 corundum (purple sapphire) 12 beryl 13 labradorite 14 apatite 15 tourmaline 16 beryl (morganite) 17 topaz 18 quartz (citrine) 19 moonstone 20 spinel 21 garnet (pyrope) 22 fluorite 23 garnet (hessonite) 24 sinhalite 25 spinel 26 black opal 27 tourmaline 28 diopside 29 topaz 30 beryl 31 danburite 32 tourmaline 33 orthoclase. From the collections of the Geological Museum, London. (Photo courtesy of the Institute of Geological Sciences, London)

VII *gemstones*. 1 fluorite 2 zircon 3 tourmaline 4 tourmaline 5 garnet (hessonite) 6 garnet (demantoid) 7 phenakite 8 zircon 9 sphene 10 garnet (spessartine) 11 corundum (yellow sapphire) 12 olivine (peridot) 13 quartz (amethyst) 14 beryl (heliodor) 15 spodumene (kunzite) 16 beryl (aquamarine) 17 quartz (rock crystal) 18 chrysoberyl 19 zircon 20 zircon 21 sphalerite 22 tourmaline 23 apatite 24 amblygonite 25 spinel 26 scapolite 27 andalusite 28 zircon 29 fluorite 30 chrysoberyl 31 sillimanite (fibrolite) 32 tourmaline 33 zircon. From the collections of the Geological Museum, London. (Photo courtesy of the Institute of Geological Sciences, London)

VIII *Mughal jewelry*. Gold enamelled ear-rings, turban ornament, collar (reverse) and armlet, set with flat diamonds, emeralds, rubies, and natural pearls, and on reverse coloured Jaipur enamel. 19th century. Courtesy of Bonds, London.

characteristics (although 'jade' is still often used to refer to them in-discriminately). They resemble each other, both being hard, compact, and usually light-green with white markings ranging to emerald-green, but found in a wide range of colours. Both are too hard to be carved, and are shaped by abrasives rather than cutting tools; large pieces are divided by a taut cord or thin slate charged with an abrasive (as the 'string-cut' jade of Costa Rican Indians). Both varieties have long been used in the Far East, for weapons and tools, and also (in China from the Han Dynasty) for ornaments and (especially jadeite) for jewelry (e.g. beads, bracelets, finger rings, belt hooks, girdle ornaments, hair ornaments, and combs). Jade was regarded there as at least equal to, if not finer than, gemstones generally; the Chinese and Japanese words signify both the mineral jade and in general all precious stones. Jade was used extensively in Mexico and Costa Rica (see PRE-COLUMBIAN JADE JEWELRY), but its source has not been identified. Many other stones have the appearance of jade but vary in colour, LUSTRE, and HARDNESS, and can be readily distinguished, e.g. green SERPENTINE, green CHALCEDONY, BOWENITE, CALIFORNITE, ANTIGORITE, and PREHNITE, as well as so-called AMAZON JADE, AMERICAN JADE, CHINESE JADE, INDIAN JADE, SNOWFLAKE JADE, STYRIAN JADE, SWISS JADE, TRANSVAAL JADE, and WYOMING JADE. Jade has been imitated in both GLASS and PLASTIC, but the stone is easily distinguishable. It has also been dyed to improve its colour or to simulate antiquity, but the organic dye does not penetrate and the colour soon fades. The name 'jade' is derived from the Spanish *piedra de ijada* (loin stone), the name given to it by the Spanish Conquistadors in the 16th century based on the belief that it eased kidney pains; and later European physicians called it *lapis nephriticus* (kidney stone) for the same reason, whence the name for the variety nephrite. *See* CHLOROMELANITE; CHICKEN-BONE JADE; TOMB JADE; FUNERARY JEWELRY (CHINESE). *See* S. Howard Hansford, *Chinese Carved Jade* (1968).

Jacobite jewelry. Necklace with enamelled roses and portrait pendant of Charles Edward Stuart; also heart-shaped badge inscribed 'I live and dy in loyaltye'. 18th century. Inverness Museum, Inverness.

jade albite. A form of albite rock that contains chrome-rich JADEITE with spots and veins that are dark green to black.

jade amulet. An AMULET made of carved JADE such as those made in China from the Shang-Yin Dynasty (1766 BC-1122 BC) in two principal types: (1) Jade animals (e.g. buffalo, fish, cicada, bird, stag), the proto-types of which are found in Chinese bronze animal figures. Some were made IN THE ROUND, some flat, and sometimes with incised lines to limn the features. They usually had a pierced hole so as to be attached to a robe or suspended as a pendant. (2) Jade pendants, some of which were worn in combination with others as part of formal or ceremonial dress to provide a clinking sound, or were placed in the coffin of the dead to pro-mote the ascent to heaven. Such pieces often were suspended from carved arc-shaped pendants, and occasionally were decorated with spirals and scrolls, characteristic motifs of the Chou Dynasty (1122 BC-249 BC). *See* J. Ayers and J. Rawson, *Chinese Jade Throughout the Ages* (1975).

jade matrix. A mineral that is a mixture of NEPHRITE and albite. Sometimes called 'snowflake jade' or 'Wyoming jade'.

jadeite. The superior and much rarer of the two gemstones generally referred to as JADE. It was recognized as a separate species and so named only in 1863. It is harder than NEPHRITE, the other variety of jade, frac-tures more easily, and has a glossy appearance. It is varicoloured, often either white with streaks of emerald-green or green with streaks of lavender; but it is also occasionally found in intense hues of orange, yellow, brown, blue, violet, pink, and black. The most valuable variety is translucent and emerald-green, called IMPERIAL JADE or 'true jade'; the Chinese term is *fei-ts'ui* (kingfisher plumage). Jadeite is normally found in fine-grained and compact masses, suitable for making intricate objects of vertu and for beads or stones cut EN CABOCHON. Its surface, when polish-ed, has a slightly dimpled appearance. Jadeite was used by the Olmec and Maya Indians of Mexico from *c.* 1500 BC, but it was not known in China until imported from Burma *c.* AD 1780. Although it is sometimes called 'Chinese jade', it is not generally found in China, but is imported there to be carved. *See* SPINACH JADE; CHLOROMELANITE.

jadeite triplet. A COMPOSITE STONE made by cementing together three CABOCHONS of white JADEITE, the other two being cut as hollow cabochons and enclosing a double cabochon, all bonded with a green jelly-like cement. When set so that the join is not visible, the deception is difficult to detect.

Jaipur jewelry. Gold locket to hold perfume; enamelled gold. Jaipur, India, *c.* 1700. H. 5.7 cm. Cleveland Museum of Art, Ohio.

jager. The highest classification in the colour grading of diamonds, being applied to a rare white stone with a very faint bluish tinge, caused possibly by a slight bluish fluorescence. It was originally applied to such stones from the Jagerstontem Mine in South Africa. Only such diamonds are, strictly, classified as a BLUE-WHITE DIAMOND.

jaguar ornament. A type of ornament of PERUVIAN JEWELRY in the form of a crouching jaguar. Several examples of such ornaments, almost identical, are of hollow gold alloy, each made of 12 cut-out sections of hammered metal, soldered and welded together, with decoration in REPOUSSÉ work. Some of the examples contain a pebble, to form a rattle. The pieces all have small perforations, said to indicate that they were intended to be sewn to a garment or attached to a necklace. They were found in 1924 at Pampa Grande, in the Lambayeque region of northern Peru. The jaguar is frequently depicted also on articles of MEXICAN JEWELRY; *see* MONTE ALBÁN TREASURE.

Jahangir Diamond. A pear-shaped diamond of 83 carats engraved by Indian lapidaries in Persian characters with the names of the Mughal Emperors Shah Jahangir, 1605-27, and of his son Shah Jehan, 1627-58. It has a hole drilled near the top, and is said to have been suspended from the beak of the jewelled peacock on the Mughal's Peacock Throne. It was sold by the Maharajah of Burdwan in 1954 to Stavros S. Niarchos. In 1957 it was bought at Sotheby's, London, by C. Patel, an Indian businessman.

Jahangir Pendant. A pendant on the front of which is an agate CAMEO with a profile portrait of an unidentified lady, made in Italian COMMESSO technique, *c.* 1580-90, set within a gold frame. On the reverse is a gold plaque engraved in England, *c.* 1610-15, with a portrait of Jahangir, Mughal Emperor from 1605, encircled by an inscription that includes his earlier name, Salim. It has been suggested that the piece, now in a private collection, was sent by James I in 1616 with his first ambassador to India as a gift to Jahangir.

Jaipur jewelry. Articles of jewelry made in Jaipur (formerly called Jeypore), a state in north-west India founded in the 12th century and under Mughal supremacy in the 16th/17th centuries, and since 1929 joined into the state of Rajasthan (formerly called Rajputana). The articles are made of gold and include flexible collars, necklaces composed of many suspended pendants, brooches with a suspended pendant, and enamelled BANGLES. The gold pendants and brooches are usually decorated on the front with diamonds (generally unfaceted polished TABLE CUT stones in closed settings) and on the back are traditionally decorated with floral designs in CHAMPLEVÉ enamel, renowned for the high quality of the translucent red enamel, often with details in green, white, and blue. Similar enamelling was also done in Delhi and is often indistinguishable. *See* S. S. Jacob and T. H. Hendley, *Jeypore Enamels* (1886).

James I jewelry. Articles of COMMEMORATIVE JEWELRY decorated with a portrait of James I, 1603-25. A LOCKET enclosing such an enamelled portrait has on the inside of the cover a depiction of the Ark, slightly different from that on the ARMADA JEWEL, and with the altered motto 'stet salva per undas'. *See* ARK LOCKET.

James I jewelry. Locket with enamelled portrait and Ark. English, 17th century. Victoria & Albert Museum, London.

Jamnitzer, Wenzel (1508-85). A leading German goldsmith and jewelry designer who worked with his father Hans and his brother Albrecht (d. 1555). Born in Vienna, he moved before 1534 to Nuremberg and became a founder of the Mannerist style. He was skilled at modelling, embossing, engraving, and enamelling, and became best known for his figures cast from nature realistically depicting shells, insects, and reptiles (counterparts of the pottery made by Bernard Palissy in 1542-62). He was succeeded by his son Hans II (*c.* 1538-1603). Albrecht's son Bartel (*c.* 1548-96) became a master engraver of jewelry designs in 1575, and Christoph (1563-1618), the son of Hans II, became a master engraver in 1592. *See* J. Haywood, in *Connoisseur* (1957), pp. 148-54.

Japanese jewelry. Articles of jewelry of very limited types made in Japan. During the Great Tombs period of the 3rd/6th centuries AD the use of MAGATAMA beads was revived after they had been in disuse since the late Jomon period, c. 1000 BC. As articles of personal adornment have been traditionally seldom used in Japan (until recent decades) and as few gemstones are produced, there are few examples of pre-20th-century Japanese jewelry other than lacquered combs and pins worn as hair ornaments by young women, and some simple forms of ear-rings. Some 3rd/5th-century stone bracelets in the form of faceted discs, found in coffins, are thought to be copies of metal bracelets worn during lifetime. In recent years interest in jewelry has developed, but it is mainly reflected in mass-produced imitative pieces, although some original gold jewelry is emerging. *See* NETSUKE; INRO; OJIME.

jardin (French). Literally, garden. The group of three-phase, moss-like INCLUSIONS that are to be seen in almost every EMERALD and that constitute an acceptable, sometimes attractive, FLAW.

jargoon. A variety of ZIRCON that is pale yellow or pale grey to colourless, usually as a result of HEAT TREATMENT. It has been recommended that the name be discarded.

jarretière (French). Literally, garter. A type of metal bracelet having the appearance of a strap with a BUCKLE on one end and a MORDANT at the other, the buckle sometimes being in the form of a slide and occasionally having a pointed tongue.

jaseron chain. A type of CHAIN of fine gold links, worn as a necklace in the 19th century; from it were suspended several crosses and pendants.

jasper. (1) A MASSIVE variety of QUARTZ consisting of a mass of microscopic grains with many impurities that provide the various colours and render it opaque. The colours include, in addition to monochrome black and white, shades of brown, green, yellow, blue, and red. The colours may appear (similar to AGATE) in stripes (called 'ribbon jasper'), bands, or zones (called 'Egyptian jasper' or ORBICULAR JASPER). The blue variety is called 'porcelain jasper'. Jasper sometimes is found as patches in other stones, e.g. BLOODSTONE and JASPER AGATE. (2) A hard, fine-grained, unglazed, sometimes slightly translucent, stoneware introduced in 1764 by Josiah Wedgwood. The body or the surface is stained with metallic oxides in several colours, of which cobalt blue is most used; and decoration in relief is generally white, simulating a CAMEO. It has been used in jewelry for BUTTONS, BROOCHES, and MEDALLIONS.

jasper agate. A variety of AGATE with alternating bands of JASPER. Also called 'agate jasper'.

Jellinge style. A Viking style of decoration used in the 9th/10th centuries, named after an animal that is a decorative motif on a silver cup found at Jelling, Jutland. The animal has a sinuous body and a sort of pigtail. *See* VIKING JEWELRY.

Jensen. A prominent Danish firm of silversmiths founded in 1904 by Georg Jensen (1866-1935) in Copenhagen and having branches now in many large cities world-wide. Its present chief designer is his son Soren Georg (b. 1917). Although its reputation is based on its many years of designing and producing cutlery, tableware, ornaments, and jewelry of sterling silver, and recently of stainless steel and other metals, it also now designs and makes gold and silver jewelry in modern styles, usually with a smooth shiny surface, and often set with gemstones. Its jewelry designer has been Nanna Ditzel. Some of its work in the 1920s was in ART NOUVEAU style, but tempered by Scandinavian influences.

jet. A compact, velvet-black substance that is a variety of lignite or coal, being formed by pressure, heat and chemical action on ancient driftwood. It has a glossy brownish-black surface and a black interior. There are two varieties, hard jet and soft jet, of equal hardness but the latter, more recent, being more fragile and so less often used in jewelry; even hard jet is easily broken, and so jet articles, when skilfully carved, were expensive. Its principal source in ancient times (examples are known

jasper (2). Achilles and Hector. Green and white jasper. Wedgwood, *c.* 1785. W. 11.2 cm. Manchester City Art Gallery (photo courtesy of Wedgwood, London).

Jellinge style. Annular brooch, bronze with gold plates with filigree and gold granulation, and silver-plated with niello. Gotland, Sweden, 10th/11th centuries. 9.8 cm. Statens Historiska Museum, Stockholm.

Jensen. Silver brooch with gemstones, *c.* 1908. H. 5.5 cm. Courtesy of Jensen, Copenhagen and London.

jet. Parure with jet cameos. Museo Poldi-Pezzoli, Milan.

from the British Iron Age) and in Roman times and thereafter was the Liassic shales of the Yorkshire coast near Whitby, England, whence jet was mined and shipped to Rome during the Roman occupation. Whitby became the centre of the jet industry from *c*. 1808 to *c*.1875, after which jet was largely superseded by CHALCEDONY that was dyed black (sometimes called 'black onyx'), as well as by black TOURMALINE (SCHORL) and black ANDRADITE (MELANITE). Jet can be effectively carved, engraved, faceted, and highly polished, so was extensively used for MOURNING JEWELRY and BUTTONS, and consequently was popular in England after the death of Prince Albert (1861). It was made into ear-rings, finger rings, beads, pendants, brooches, and lockets. It can be distinguished from black gemstones and from GLASS and PLASTIC imitations by touching it with a heated needle (this releases an odour of burning coal). An inferior quality of jet has been produced in Galicia, northern Spain, and used there extensively for making AMULETS, especially for the 15th-century pilgrims to Santiago de Compostela. The present source of jet is still the Whitby region. *See* FRENCH JET; BOGWOOD; VAUXHALL GLASS; MELFORT NECKLACE.

jet ring. A type of finger ring made of JET, usually a simple hoop, but sometimes carved with clasped hands (as a FEDE RING) or engraved with a posy (*see* POSY RING). Such rings were apparently made for a jeweller's stock, not to order.

jewel. An article of JEWELRY that is of substantial value and intended to be worn on the person decoratively or usefully, being usually composed of a precious metal and/or a gemstone or gemstones, and made with art-istry or superior craftsmanship. The term would ordinarily exclude those articles of jewelry intended to be carried on the person but not to be worn, as well as such OBJECTS OF VERTU that, even though intended for some purpose closely identified with an individual's convenience or pleasure rather than primarily some utilitarian purpose, are not articles to be worn on some part of the body. *See* CROWN JEWELS. The term 'jewelled' normally means set with one or more gemstones.

Jewelled State Sword, The. The sword, with scabbard, that is part of the British CROWN JEWELS and that is the most important one of the five 'Swords of State'. The sword hilt and scabbard are of dull gold set with gemstones, those on the scabbard forming the national emblems of the rose thistle, and shamrock. The blade is of engraved Damascus steel. The sword, made for the coronation of George IV in 1820, is known as the 'Sword of Offering' and is used in the coronation ceremony.

jewelry (in Great Britain, usually **jewellery**). Any decorative article, including any JEWEL, that is made of metal, gemstones or certain organic materials, of high quality and with artistry or superior craftsmanship and intended to be worn or carried on the person for personal adornment or, in the broader sense of the term, used by a person for some purpose closely identified with his convenience or pleasure rather than only for a utilitarian purpose (*see* SMALL WORK). It includes ancient, primitive, and modern objects of such character. Only by a loosely used extension of the term does it include COSTUME JEWELRY or JUNK JEWELRY. The French distinguish BIJOUTERIE, JOAILLERIE, and ORFÈVRERIE.

Jewish marriage ring. A type of finger ring used at a Jewish wedding ceremony on the Continent, by being placed by the groom on the middle finger of the bride's right hand, and not intended to be worn thereafter but preserved by the family or the congregation. The early examples, made in Venice in the 16th century, have a wide band and mounted on the BEZEL a model of a building with a cupola or high roof, said to represent a synagogue or a symbol of the marital home. Later they were decorated with FILIGREE and GRANULATED GOLD, and some with enamelling but not gemstones. Some examples have a high-gabled roof and pierced windows, occasionally with a movable weathervane at the peak. Hidden within the bezel or inscribed inside the band are the Hebrew words *Mazal Tov* (Good Luck) or the Hebrew initials of these words. Some rings also depict on the hoop biblical scenes or symbols. The rings were usually made of gold, but later ones are of silver or gilded metal. Known examples are from Germany or Venice from the 16th and 17th centuries, but earlier ones are said to have existed. A few such rings were made as a LOCKET, with the building on the bezel hinged to cover a space for concealing some token. In England there is no record of such rings being used, but instead a plain hoop of gold (or other metal) without a gemstone but with a Hebrew inscription. *See* STEEPLE RING.

joaillerie. The French term for the type of jewelry that is composed mainly of gemstones, the pieces being referred to as *joyaux. See* BIJOUTERIE; ORFÈVRERIE.

John the Baptist Enseigne. A gold ENSEIGNE portraying the head of John the Baptist on a salver, enamelled in white on a red ground and encircled by a gold mount bearing an openwork Latin inscription. It is French, early 16th century.

joining. The process, by various methods, of assembling the shaped sections of multi-piece objects, including SOLDERING, COLLOID HARD-SOLDERING, DIFFUSION BONDING, pinning (by attaching with small pins), clinching (by overlapping, folding, and hammering down the edges), EUTECTIC WELDING, etc.

Jonker Diamond A famous diamond found in 1934 by a prospector, Jacobus Jonker, at his farm at Elandsfontein, near Pretoria, South Africa. It weighed rough 726 carats, measuring 63 by 38 mm. Jonker sold it at once to the Diamond Corporation in Johannesburg, which resold it to HARRY WINSTON after he had studied it for a month. He had it cleaved in 1936 by the famous cutter, Lazare Kaplan, of New York, and then cut into 12 stones, 11 being EMERALD CUT and 1 MARQUISE CUT, of which the largest, called the Jonker, weighed 142.90 carats, later recut to 125.65 carats. In 1949 the Jonker was sold to King Farouk of Egypt and is reported to have been sold by him in 1959 to Queen Ratna of Nepal, and later resold in Japan. The other 11 stones were sold privately, 4 of them reportedly to the Maharajah of Indore.

Joseph-in-the-Well Pendant A Tudor gold pendant with an oval scene depicting, in REPOUSSÉ work and enamelling, 'Joseph in the Well' surrounded by seven of his envious brothers; the figure-scene is enclosed within an inner and an outer frame of scrollwork, from which are suspended three pearls. The pendant hangs by two chains of gold links separated by enamelled beads and is suspended from a gold ornament set with a table-cut diamond above a pendent pearl. On the reverse is a design in translucent BASSE TAILLE enamel depicting a pecking bird under a baldachin. It is English, *c.* 1550-60, said to have been designed and possibly made by ÉTIENNE DELAUNE.

Josephine Tiara. A platinum TIARA set with 1,040 diamonds (weighing in all about 260 carats) given by Napoleon to his first wife, Josephine

Jewish marriage rings. Gold. Top, hinged-roof bezel and enamel; and canopy with pearls. 16th century. Ashmolean Museum, Oxford.

John the Baptist Enseigne. Gold with enamelling. French, early 16th century, Victoria & Albert Museum, London.

Joseph-in-the-Well Pendant (front and back). Gold pendant with repoussé scene, and (on reverse) *basse taille* enamelling. English, *c*. 1550-60. W. 6.3 cm. British Museum, London.

Josephine Tiara. Platinum and diamonds. French, *c*. 1802. Courtesy of Van Cleef & Arpels, Paris.

(1763-1814), and worn by her at her coronation in 1802. It was bequeathed by her to her daughter Hortense (by her first husband, de Beauharnais), from whom it passed to her son Napoleon III (1808-73) and was sold by his wife, the Empress Eugénie, before her flight from France in 1871. The tiara was bought from Lady Mond in 1948 by the French firm VAN CLEEF & ARPELS.

jour, à (French). (1) Pierced or openwork decoration, cut in metal so as to show light or to make a pattern which often forms the background of a design. *See* AJOURÉ WORK; OPUS INTERRASILE; PLIQUE À JOUR. (2) The same as OPEN SETTING.

Jourado diamond. A misnomer for a colourless SYNTHETIC SPINEL; the term was introduced when such stones were first produced and should be discarded.

jubilee cut. A style of cutting a large diamond, of which the main feature is the absence of a TABLE, in lieu of which there are on the CROWN 8 trapezium-shaped BEZEL FACETS rising to a central apex, and abutting these 8 smaller trapezium-shaped bezel facets, all making a symmetrical pattern that is surrounded by 16 STAR FACETS and then 16 CROSS FACETS, the sides of which form the GIRDLE. On the PAVILION there are 16 facets in addition to the usual 24, and no CULET. There is thus a total of 88 (sometimes only 80) facets. The cut was developed, as an American modification of the BRILLIANT CUT, in the early 20th century and named in honour of Queen Victoria's jubilee (1897); sometimes called the 'Twentieth-century cut'.

jubilee cut
side view

Jubilee (or **Reitz**) **Diamond.** A famous diamond found in 1895 in the Jagersfontein Mine in South Africa, weighing rough 650.80 carats. A flawless, cushion-shaped stone, BRILLIANT CUT, was cut from it, weighing 245.35 carats, and also a PENDELOQUE BRILLIANT weighing 13.34 carats.

The large stone was first named Reitz after F. W. Reitz, then President of the Orange Free State; but in 1897, after it had been cut, the name was changed to the Jubilee Diamond to commemorate the 60th (Diamond) anniversary of the coronation of Queen Victoria. The large stone was shown at the Paris Exposition of 1900, and, after several sales, it was acquired by Paul-Louis Weiller, a Parisian manufacturer, and loaned by him in 1961 to the Smithsonian Institution, Washington, DC, and in 1966 to the De Beers Diamond Pavilion in Johannesburg. It is said to be the most perfectly cut of all large diamonds.

Judgment of Paris Pendant. A gold PENDANT having a figure group depicting 'The Judgment of Paris' in ÉMAIL EN RONDE BOSSE, and set with rubies, emeralds, and other gemstones. It is of German make, *c.* 1570–1600, and is one of the jewels of the Green Vault, Dresden.

junk jewelry. A very recent extension of the term COSTUME JEWELRY that embraces articles made of a great variety of materials, including PLASTIC, GLASS, base metal, feathers, etc., and consisting of a wide assortment of articles of personal adornment, often of highly original and unusual patterns, but of an inferior quality, ephemeral styles, short life, and cheap production. Much of it is mass produced or made by amateur craftsmen. It is generally sold at various types of shops other than jewelry stores. Such articles are not considered to be within the scope of this book.

Judgment of Paris Pendant. Gold with gemstones and enamelling. German, *c.* 1570–1600. Staatliche Kunstsammlungen, Dresden.

K

Kames Brooch. A gold RING BROOCH with a transverse pin. The front is decorated in relief with six encircling dragons with glass eyes. The reverse has an encircling religious inscription and on the back of the pin is the word 'Atropa' (Atropos, one of the Fates). It is Scottish, 14th century, and was an heirloom of the Bannatynes of Kames, Bute, Scotland.

Kandy Cat's-Eye. The largest known CAT'S-EYE, weighing 313¼ old carats, mounted in a gold circle set with gemstones. It was taken from the King of Kandy, in Ceylon, when conquered by the British in 1815, and was presented to Queen Victoria in 1886.

Kandy spinel. A misnomer for a type of pale-red GARNET from Sri Lanka (formerly Ceylon).

kauri gum. A resinous product of the kauri-pine tree that grows in New Zealand and that is used as an imitation of AMBER. It is found in the form of yellowish or brownish lumps embedded deep in the ground where the trees have grown. It can be distinguished by its ready fusibility. Also called 'kauri resin' or 'copal resin'. *See* COPAL.

keeper ring. (1) The same as a GUARD RING. (2) A type of finger ring that is made with some device to prevent it slipping from the finger, such as with a close-fitting hoop attached at the back of the main ring, or sometimes two such hoops, one on each side of the main ring.

Kerch Treasure. A TREASURE of ancient GREEK JEWELRY and SCYTHIAN JEWELRY excavated by the Russian Government in 1831 at the Koul-Oba tumulus near Kerch (ancient Panticapaeum) in eastern Crimea, Russia, between the Black Sea and the Sea of Azov, near the site of the NYMPHAEUM TREASURE. It is now at the Hermitage Museum, Leningrad.

key-and-heart locket. A type of LOCKET given as a love token, made in the form of a heart to which is attached by a thin chain a replica of a key to unlock the heart. Some such lockets enclosed a lock of hair or a portrait.

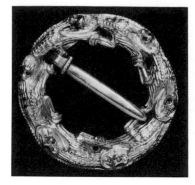

Kames Brooch (front and back). Gold ring brooch with encircling 6 relief dragons with glass eyes. On the reverse: religious inscription and, on pin, 'Atropa' (Atropos, one of the Fates). Scottish, 14th century. W. 4 cm. National Museum of Antiquities of Scotland, Edinburgh.

key finger ring. A type of finger ring to which is attached the ward of a key. Roman key finger rings were of two types: (1) the ward projecting vertically from the BEZEL; and (2) the ward projecting from the side of the SHANK, which when worn permitted the ward to be along the finger rather than dangerously projecting; most were made of BRONZE but some exist of precious metal. A Byzantine example of such a key finger ring has a flat tongue projecting from the side of the shank, to be used to lift a latch.

keystone cut. A style of cutting a diamond (or other transparent gemstone) so that the TABLE, in the conventional keystone pattern, is in the form of an isosceles trapezoid, each side being bordered by a FACET in the form of a trapezoid and sometimes having at each corner a small triangular facet. When there are two or more rows of such facets, the stone is STEP CUT.

Kiani Crown. Literally, Royal Crown. A CROWN made at Isfahan, Persia (Iran), during the reign of Fath Ali Shah (1797-1834) as a coronation crown. It is thickly set with 1,800 pearls, 300 emeralds, and 1,500 SPINELS. At the top are two jewelled AIGRETTES, below which is the Aurangzeb Spinel weighing 120 carats. The crown weighs 4.5 kg.

kidney stone. (1) The same as NEPHRITE, so called perhaps because some 'jade' stones were kidney-shaped. (2) The same as HEMATITE, so called perhaps for a similar reason.

king coral. A variety of CORAL that is black and grows in the form of thin tree-like stalks. The Italian name is *giojetto,* and in Malay it is called *akabar.* In Java it has been made for over 2,000 years into BANGLES to be worn as an AMULET against poisoning and as a cure for gout, and also as prayer-beads and necklaces. In the West Indies long straight stalks are used as walking-sticks.

king cut
side view

king vulture pendant. Cast gold. Costa Rica, Diquis culture, *c.* 800-1520. H. 14.9 cm. Museum für Völkerkunde, West Berlin.

king cut. A style of cutting a large diamond that is a modification of the BRILLIANT CUT. It has a 12-sided TABLE with 48 facets on the CROWN and 36 facets on the PAVILION, plus sometimes a CULET. The crown includes 12 small triangular facets abutting the table and 24 small triangular facets abutting the GIRDLE, between which are 12 LOZENGE-shaped facets of which two of their points touch the table and the girdle, respectively. The girdle is 24-sided, making it circular in appearance.

king topaz. A local misnomer for the yellow CORUNDUM (SAPPHIRE) found in Sri Lanka (formerly Ceylon).

king vulture pendant. A type of pendant of PRE-COLUMBIAN JEWELRY made of flat hammered and cast gold or TUMBAGA depicting a king vulture with outspread wings, broad tail feathers, bent claws, long beak, and a typical carunculated head. Such birds are known from Mexico south to Paraguay, and pendants depicting them are known from the Diquis culture of Costa Rica, *c.* 800-1520, and also in TAIRONA JEWELRY. Sometimes the piece is called a 'golden eagle pendant' from the name of such vultures said to have been applied by Columbus on his fourth voyage; the local name is *zopilote.* Such pendants are sometimes included in the broad classification of EAGLE PENDANT.

kingfisher-feather jewelry. Articles of jewelry whose overall decoration is made of the blue feathers of the kingfisher, usually mounted flat over a thin gold or silver plate, and sometimes further decorated by being set with a few beads of JADE or CORAL or a few small gemstones. The articles are mainly HAIR ORNAMENTS mounted on HAIR PINS, but also include brooches and pendants. Such pieces have been made in China since the 18th century. *See* FEI-TS'UI.

King's Orb, The. The larger of the two ORBS that form part of the British Crown Jewels, the smaller one being the Queen's Orb (made for Mary II as Queen Regnant, 1689); *see* ORBS, THE ROYAL.

King's School, Canterbury, Brooch. A DISC BROOCH found (in fragments) in 1957 by a gardener within the precincts of Canterbury Cathedral and donated by King's School to the British Museum on condition that it be so named. It consists of two silver dished sheets nailed together to clasp a number of gold plates (some now missing). The upper sheet is pierced by 8 circular holes, 4 square holes, and 8 comma-shaped holes, each set with a gold plate bearing filigree scroll patterns and NIELLO decoration; in the central hole there is a gold roundel with a gold rivet head. The space between the holes is decorated with niello zoomorphic and interlaced decoration. The entire face is ornamented with dome-shaped rivet heads. The border is a band of silver. The back of the rear plate was mounted with a fastening pin. It has been attributed to ANGLO-SAXON JEWELRY, 10th century. *See* David M. Wilson, in *Medieval Archaeology*, vol. IV (1960), p. 16.

King's School, Canterbury, Brooch. Silver disc brooch with inset gold plates and niello. Anglo-Saxon, 10th century. W. 14.1 cm. British Museum, London.

Kingston Brooch. A COMPOSITE BROOCH made of two gold circular plates bound together at the rim by a narrow band of beaded gold and secured by three clasps. The interior is filled with a clay-like substance, possibly cuttlefish bone. The front plate, slightly convex, is decorated with five concentric rings ornamented with gold CLOISONS making a multitude of tiny cells of various shapes, each filled with gold FILIGREE work or CLOISONNÉ INLAY set with GARNETS (some missing) or blue glass. There is a large central boss and four smaller ones spaced around it, all similarly decorated. The reverse has a bronze fastening pin with an elaborate catch-plate, in the form of an animal-head ornamented with filigree and a safety loop. The brooch was found in 1771 in a grave at Kingston Down, in Kent, and is of the early 7th century. It has been owned by the Merseyside County Museum since it was donated to it in 1867 (although on loan to the British Museum after World War II), having been given by Joseph Mayer, who had acquired it and other pieces of Anglo-Saxon jewelry from the owners of the collection of the finder, the Rev. Bryan Faussett, of Kent.

Kingston Brooch. Gold composite brooch set with garnets and blue glass. Anglo-Saxon, 7th century. W. 8 cm. Merseyside County Museum, Liverpool.

Kirkoswald Brooch. A silver trefoil Anglo-Saxon brooch with filigree scroll decoration and originally set, at each of the three points, with a GARNET (two now missing). It was found at Kirkoswald, Cumberland (now Cumbria), England. The brooch has been attributed to the 8th/9th century, based on the presence of coins found with it that date the deposit to *c.* 850-60.

kite cut. The same as LOZENGE CUT except that two adjacent sides of the TABLE are shorter than the other two sides.

kite facet. The modern name for the 8 LOZENGE-shaped FACETS on the CROWN of a BRILLIANT that extend to touch the GIRDLE and the TABLE, and also for the 8 elongated lozenge-shaped facets on the PAVILION that extend to touch the girdle and the CULET (or that meet at a point when there is no culet). An alternative modern name is MAIN FACET. Names formerly used for such facets were LOZENGE FACET, QUOIN, TEMPLET, and BEZEL.

knife wire. A type of jewelry WIRE made with a sharp edge that is always employed turned upwards to reflect a thin line of bright light so as to provide an almost invisible setting. Some brooches are made of a horizontal piece of such wire and have at the extremities small gemstones; and some brooches and GIRANDOLES have gemstones suspended by such wire from a supporting gemstone. Occasionally a necklace is made with links of such wire at the back to enhance the appearance of lightness.

Kirkoswald Brooch. Silver trefoil with filigree and set with garnets. 8th/9th centuries. L. 3.5 cm. British Museum, London.

Knight's Amulet (front and back). Silver medallion with enamelling. Upper Rhineland, *c*. 1340-50. Kunstgewerbemuseum, West Berlin.

kol't. Temple pendant; gold with *cloisonné* enamel. Russo-Byzantine, 11th/12th centuries. W. 6 cm. Metropolitan Museum of Art (gift of J. Pierpont Morgan), New York.

Knight's Amulet. A flat silver AMULET in the form of a MEDALLION, with a suspensory ring and having enamelled decoration on the front and the back. On the front is depicted the standing figure of the Virgin Mary surrounded by 4 angels holding a ribbon with a German inscription beseeching mercy for the knight. On the back is a figure of the risen Christ surrounded by symbols of 3 of the Evangelists, the fourth (Matthew) being represented by the kneeling knight in the foreground, all intertwined with a ribbon bearing a similar German inscription. It is said to have been made by an enameller of the Upper Rhineland, *c*. 1340-50.

Koh-i-Noor (Koh-i-Nur) Diamond. (Persian for 'Mountain of Light' Diamond). One of the world's most famous (although not the largest or finest) diamonds, weighing 186 carats until recut in 1852 to its present weight of 108.93 carats. According to Indian legend, its origin dates back some 5,000 years to ancient India and its early history, prior to recent research, was the subject of conflicting writings. Formerly it was generally accepted that it was the same diamond that had been in the possession of Sultan Baber (1480-1530), founder of the Mughal Empire in India (having been taken in 1304 from Al-in-Din, Rajah of Malwi, 1288-1321), and then known as 'Baber's Diamond', and that was inherited by his son, Humayun and later given, *c*. 1544, to Shah Jehan, Mughal Emperor of India, 1627-58. However, recent opinion distinguishes 'Baber's Diamond' (reported to have weighed 186 carats) from the Koh-i-Noor and contends that the latter (formerly called the 'Great Mogul Diamond' and weighing originally 787½ carats) was discovered *c*. 1655 in the Kollur Mine in Golconda, southern India, belonging to Mir Jumla, of Golconda, and that he presented it, *c*. 1655-7, to Shah Jehan, from whom it was inherited by his son, Aurangzeb, Emperor of Hindustan, 1658-1707. In 1655 a diamond (now thought to have been the GREAT MOGUL DIAMOND and identified with the Koh-i-Noor) was shown by Aurangzeb to Jean-Baptiste Tavernier, the French traveller and diamond merchant, who weighed, measured, and sketched it. In 1739, when Nadir Shah (1688-1747), the Persian ruler, invaded India and, after sacking Delhi, carried off the original Peacock Throne, he also took the diamond (allegedly having obtained it by trickery from the Mughal Emperor) to Isfahan, Iran, when it was given its Persian name, Koh-i-Nur. In 1747 it was inherited by Nadir's grandson, Shah Rukh Mirza, who in 1749 gave it, in gratitude for military support, to Ahmad Shah (1723-73), of the Dirrani tribe and ruler of Afghanistan; it was taken to Kabul and kept there until his brother and heir, Shah Shuja, surrendered it in 1813 to Ranjit Singh (1780-1839), 'Lion of the Punjab', the Sikh ruler of the Punjab, in return for military aid. It was taken by the latter to his capital, Lahore, and remained there until claimed from his son by the British when they annexed the Punjab after the Second Sikh War, 1848-9. It was then taken by the East India Company to England where in 1852, to celebrate the Company's 250th anniversary, it was presented to Queen Victoria. The diamond had at one time been cut by an Indian lapidary from its reputed 787½ carats to an oval stone in its natural domed shape, but with facets, weighing about 186 carats. In 1852 Prince Albert ordered the stone to be recut in London by the Amsterdam cutter Voorsanger, of the Coster firm, and it was reduced to 108.93 carats, so that it is now a shallow ROSE CUT stone, poorly proportioned and with little FIRE. It was worn by Queen Victoria in a brooch and a bracelet, and in 1858 it was reset for her in a circlet. It has never been worn by a British king, perhaps owing to the legend that it had often brought disaster to male owners; but it is more likely owing to the fact that when it was given to Queen Victoria it was as a personal gift, not as a CROWN JEWEL, and the belief grew that if it were ever worn by a male sovereign the British Empire would lose India, and hence Victoria bequeathed it not to Edward VII but as a royal heirloom to his wife, Queen Alexandra, in female entail for successive Queens Consort. It was later set in the coronation crowns made for Queen Alexandra in 1902 and for Queen Mary in 1911, and is now set (below the BLACK PRINCE'S RUBY) in the CROSS FORMÉE of the crown made for Queen Elizabeth (now the Queen Mother) and worn at her coronation in 1937. In recent years there has been some discussion, as a consequence of the independence of India, as to whether the diamond should be returned to India as a national heritage. *See* Stephen Howarth, *The Koh-i-Noor Diamond* (1980).

kol't (Russian). An article of Russo-Byzantine jewelry worn as part of a head-dress by aristocratic men and women during the 11th and 12th centuries. The *kol't* is a small, hollow, lunate ornament made of two convex discs joined by a thin metal strip around the edge and having a semi-circular opening at the top across which is a pivoted attachment hasp. *Kolti* were worn near the temples (hence sometimes called a 'temple pendant'), suspended from rings attached to a head-band, or from the hair or strings of beads; being hollow, they perhaps contained an aromatic oil. There are two types: (1) gold, decorated front and back with enamelling depicting the Tree of Life (an ancient Near East motif) between two stylized birds or depicting sometimes saints or sirens, and having around the edge an attached string of pearls or beads or an openwork border; and (2) silver, with a small disc soldered on the front with NIELLO decoration, often of geometric motifs. Examples are part of a TREASURE excavated at Kiev in 1906 and donated by J. Pierpont Morgan to the Metropolitan Museum of Art, New York, and to the British Museum. *See* Katherine Reynolds Brown, 'Russo-Byzantine Jewellery', *Apollo,* January 1980, p. 6.

Korea jade. A misnomer for BOWENITE, a green variety of SERPENTINE.

Korean jewelry. Articles of jewelry made in Korea, some being made in ancient times when the art of working gold, including the techniques of GRANULATED GOLD and FILIGREE work, had been learned from the Chinese. By the 5th/6th centuries, during the Silla Dynasty, indigenous styles had been developed; the production included gold crowns, necklaces, ear-rings, bracelets, and pendants, cut from sheet metal and decorated with openwork and inlaid with gemstones, as well as gold girdles having many suspended thin elongated pendants. In the 10th/11th centuries hair pins of the two-pin type were made of bronze and of silver. *See* R.-Y. L. D'Argence, 'Reflections on Korean Art', in *Apollo,* September 1979, p. 176, plates VII–X.

kornerupine. A variety of gemstone that is transparent to translucent, grey-greenish to brownish-green. It sometimes shows ASTERISM or CHATOYANCY and is strongly dichroic. It is cut EN CABOCHON or faceted. It is named after A. N. Kornerup, a Danish geologist, and was first found in Greenland in the late 19th century.

kulone (Russian). A type of PENDANT decorated with gemstones. A so-called pair, found perhaps in Odessa and made in the 4th/5th century, are of gold, decorated with GRANULATED GOLD and inlaid garnets; their use is uncertain, but it has been suggested that they might be a type of head-dress for an affluent woman.

kunzite. A variety of SPODUMENE that is transparent and lilac-blue, violet or pink, showing strong pleochroism when deeply tinted. Some Brazilian stones mined since the 1960s also show tan, but lose the tan and bluish colours when subjected to HEAT TREATMENT or exposed to strong light, retaining only the rose-violet. Owing to its pleochroism, the direction of cutting is important so as to feature the violet colour. The stones sometimes resemble pink TOPAZ but are lighter and softer. Kunzite was named after George F. Kunz (1856–1932), an eminent American gemmologist.

kulone (one of a pair). Gold decorated wth granulated gold and garnets. 4th/5th centuries. L. 7.3 cm. Römisch-Germanisches Museum, Cologne.

L

labradorescence. The phenomenon of the play of colour seen in a LABRADORITE resulting from reflection of light from the LAMELLAR plates within the stone. *See* ADULARESCENCE.

labradorite. A variety of plagioclase FELDSPAR which has a flashing display of varied colours suggestive of the Northern Lights. Although it

lady-in-waiting brooch. Gold with initials M A (in Cyrillic script) and Russian Imperial Crown, set with 262 diamonds, W. 4.5 cm. Hillwood, Washington, DC.

Lalique, René. Necklace plate. Head in chrysoprase set in gold with gold enamel. Signed by René Lalique. W. 19 cm. Gulbenkian Foundation, Lisbon.

has a dirty-grey colour before being cut, the cut stones, when placed in a certain position (but no other) before the viewer, change tremendously, acquiring a metallic LUSTRE and a beautiful SHEEN, due to the LAMELLAR composition and the property of ADULARESCENCE, which in this stone is called 'labradorescence'. The usual colour is blue, but a variety (called 'spectrolite') found in Karelia, Finland, shows the colours of the spectrum. The stones are usually cut with a flat surface, and have been carved as CAMEOS. The original source, *c.* 1770, was the island of St Paul, Labrador. *See* BLACK MOONSTONE.

labret. An ornament worn through a perforation near the lower lip, usually by peoples of low culture in widely scattered regions. Examples made of gold or TUMBAGA were popular ornaments of PRE-COLUMBIAN JEWELRY, especially in the Nariño and Tairona regions of Colombia. Some were of low (height *c.* 2.5 cm) cylindrical form with hammered decoration, some were cast in undecorated mushroom shape with the stem on a wide flattened base that rested against the teeth, with the head protruding below the lip, and a few were cast in very long (*c.* 5.5 cm) ornate form. In Mexico some gold examples of crescent shape indicated high rank, and some of the Aztec culture, made of OBSIDIAN, *c.* 800–1000, indicated low rank. Sometimes a gemstone was so worn. Also called a 'lip plug'.

lace pin. A type of brooch intended to fasten a fichu or flimsy lace scarf worn by a woman. In order to secure several folds of lace, the front of the brooch was usually curved and the pin on the back rather long.

LaCloche. A firm of manufacturing and retail jewellers established in Paris in 1897 by the LaCloche brothers, Fernand, Jules, Léopold, and Jacques, making luxurious enamelled jewelry in Oriental style, and later in the 1920s doing work in ART DECO style.

lady-in-waiting brooch. A type of brooch given by a Russian Tsarina to a lady-in-waiting and worn at the Imperial Court during the 19th and early 20th centuries. The usual such brooch was in the form of the openwork initial(s) of the donor(s), above which was the Russian Imperial Crown, all set with diamonds. One example with the initials M and A in Cyrillic script was owned by Mrs Illarian V. Mishtowt (lady-in-waiting to the Dowager Tsarina Maria Feodorovna and to Tsarina Alexandra Feodorovna) from whom the brooch was acquired in 1968 by Mrs Marjorie Merriweather Post, who donated it to Hillwood, Washington, DC.

Lahun Treasure. A TREASURE of Egyptian jewelry excavated in 1914 by Sir Flinders Petrie and his assistant, Guy Brunton, at the tomb of Sesostris II, 1897 BC–1878 BC, at Lahun. In the burial chamber of his daughter, Sit-Hathor-Yunet, was found an alcove containing her jewelry, including a wig-box, toilet case, and jewelry casket, the last containing many necklaces, armlets, bracelets, and pectoral ornaments. The wig-box contained a gold crown and a dressed wig ornamented with hollow gold tubes. Most of the treasure is now in the Metropolitan Museum of Art, New York. *See* SIT-HATHOR-YUNET CROWN.

Lalique, René (Jules) (1860–1945). The leading French designer and maker of jewelry and glassware in the ART NOUVEAU style, creating new techniques and highly original designs. He was born at Ay, on the Marne, was apprenticed at 16 to the Parisian silversmith and jeweller, Louis Aucoq, attended art schools in Paris and London, and upon returning to Paris made designs for Aucoq, CARTIER, BOUCHERON, and others. He managed, and in 1886 took over, the workshop of Jules d'Estape. After making, in 1891–4, several pieces of jewelry for Sarah Bernhardt, he exhibited his work at the 1894 Paris Salon, and was acclaimed for his Art Nouveau jewelry, especially after his success at the Paris Exhibition of 1900 which led to his vogue with royalty and the aristocracy. In 1895 he attracted the attention of Calouste Gulbenkian who became his patron and friend, and who commissioned many of his jewels, of which over 140 are now owned by the Gulbenkian Foundation Museum in Lisbon. In 1902 he designed and opened galleries in his home in the Cours la Reine in Paris, and in 1905 opened his shop in the Place Vendôme. His jewelry combined the use of gold with gemstones and enamelling in designs which often depicted the human female figure, nude or draped, and fantasized with butterfly or dragonfly wings. He made bracelets, necklaces, pendants, combs, and pectorals with themes emphasizing forms from nature, such as peacocks, snakes, insects, blossoming branches, orchids, etc. He often experimented with glass, using it in some articles of jewelry, and this led him to buy in 1910 a glassworks at Combes-la-Ville. Thereafter he devoted himself almost exclusively to making glass; and from 1914 ceased making jewelry, except possibly some mounted glass plaques.

Lamballe Necklace. A necklace composed of a gold chain on which are strung at intervals 11 round beads made of IVORY decorated with gold PIQUÉ work. It is traditionally said to have been a gift from Marie Antoinette to the Princesse de Lamballe (1749–92). It was later purchased by the 4th Marquess of Hertford.

Lambayeque style. The style of certain gold PRE-COLUMBIAN JEWELRY made in the Lambayeque Valley, in northern Peru, from the MOCHICA/CHIMÚ period. Characteristic of the style are representations of the human face with a sharply upturned outer corner of the eyes (known as a 'Lambayeque eye'); sometimes the eye-ball is made of a TURQUOISE bead, with a pierced hole to indicate the pupil. Such faces are sometimes found on a TUMI. Much of such jewelry was found at a ruined site of Batan Grande, Peru. *See* PERUVIAN JEWELRY.

lamellar. Composed of layers of thin plates or scales (laminae) of material, e.g. as in MOONSTONE and LABRADORITE, the result of which, when causing interference of light, is called LABRADORESCENCE or ADULARESCENCE. When the lamellar structure of labradorite causes polarization effects, the stone has a blue colour rather than its other colours.

landscape nephrite. A variety of NEPHRITE with green and other coloured markings suggesting natural scenery.

Langdale Rosary. A ROSARY (CHAPLET) of enamelled gold beads, composed of 5 DECADES and 6 PATERNOSTERS, and having a suspended gold enamelled GAUD. The beads are decorated with black NIELLO depicting saints. It belonged to the old Yorkshire Catholic family of Langdale; it has been suggested that it once belonged to Lord William Howard, third son of the 4th Duke of Norfolk. It is of English make, *c.* 1500. It was acquired in 1934 by the Victoria & Albert Museum under the bequest of Captain H. B. Murray.

Langobardic jewelry. Articles of jewelry made by the Langobardi (Lombards), a Germanic people who invaded northern Italy in AD 568, established a kingdom in the region that is now Lombardy, and at one time, especially in the 8th century, conquered much of the peninsula. The pieces included gold and silver BUCKLES, BASKET EAR-RINGS, FIBULAE, and PECTORAL CROSSES made in the 6th to 8th centuries. *See* HORSE FIBULA.

lapel watch. A type of small WATCH made to be worn on a lapel of a jacket or dress. Such watches are of two styles: (1) a watch suspended from a brooch; or (2) a watch with a fixed stud that is inserted in a lapel buttonhole. The former are usually decorated with gemstones.

lapis lazuli. A gemstone that is massive, typically of a deep-blue colour, but sometimes with mottlings of white. It is a complex mineral, composed of grains of several blue minerals, including HAÜYNE, LAZURITE, and SODALITE, in a MATRIX of calcite, and sometimes spangled with inclusions of brassy-coloured PYRITES. The varying proportions of the minerals determine the colour of the stone. As it is opaque, it is cut EN CABOCHON or flat, and never faceted; it has a poor LUSTRE and is dull except when it is given a polished surface. It has been used since ancient times (known then as 'sapphire'). In some ANGLO-SAXON JEWELRY the inlaid decoration, once thought to be lapis lazuli, is now considered to be blue GLASS. It has been made synthetically, and has been used to produce ultramarine, a colouring pigment now also made synthetically. The stone has been imitated by SWISS LAPIS (blue-dyed JASPER), by dyed AGATE, by sintered SYNTHETIC SPINEL, and also by PASTE, blue enamel, and ceramic ware, all of

Lamballe Necklace. Ivory beads with piqué work. French, 17th century. Wallace Collection, London.

Langdale Rosary. Chaplet of gold beads with niello decoration depicting saints. English, *c.* 1500. Victoria & Albert Museum, London.

Langobardic jewelry. Pectoral cross of thin gold sheet, 8th century. Museo Archeologico Nazionale, Cividale del Friuli, Italy.

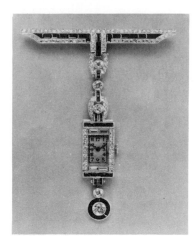

lapel watch. Art Deco style, set with diamonds and emeralds. Courtesy of Christie's, New York.

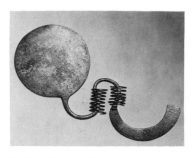

latchet. Bronze with spiral attachment. Irish, 6th/7th centuries. L. 17.5 cm. British Museum, London.

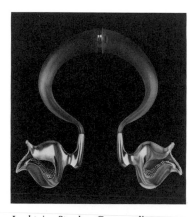

Lechtzin, Stanley. Cast acrylic neckpiece with electroformed silver gilt terminals and 100 pearls. 1978. W. 26 cm. Courtesy of Stanley Lechtzin, Philadelphia.

which are readily distinguishable. Some lapis has been stained to make it darker. *See* LAZULITE.

lappet hatpin. A type of HATPIN, worn on a maid's lace cap, that has a short stem and an ornament that is set at right-angles rather than as a finial.

Lark Hill Hoard. A HOARD of articles of English jewelry and coins found at Lark Hill, Worcester, in 1851, and dating mainly from the 12th century but including a finger ring from Viking times. It included rings and also coins of Henry I of England, 1100–35, and David I of Scotland, 1124–53.

lasque (or **lask** or **laske**). A thin flat diamond (as cut by Indian cutters) or an inferior stone bevelled for use as a glass in a watch case or over a miniature portrait. Also called a 'portrait stone'. *See* LAXY DIAMOND; PORTRAIT DIAMOND.

latchet. A type of metal fastener, possibly for a dress. An example in CELTIC JEWELRY, made of bronze, 6th/7th century AD, is of unique shape and has two spiral attachments that make its method of use uncertain; it was found in the River Shannon, in Athlone, Northern Ireland.

latten (or **laton**). An ALLOY having the appearance of BRASS, composed of varying base metals, that was used in the Middle Ages for some inexpensive types of finger rings (especially SIGNET RINGS) and for studs of some girdles. It was usually gilded.

Laub- und Bandelwerk. *See* STRAPWORK.

lava jewelry. Articles of jewelry, usually a mounted CAMEO or INTAGLIO, made of the lava from Mt Vesuvius and carved in Italy. The pieces are of a variety of colours, usually pale shades or greys and browns, and the surface is matt. It was a popular form of inexpensive jewelry of the 19th century.

lavalier (or **lavaliere** or **lavallière**). A type of CHAIN worn around a woman's neck and from which is suspended one or more gemstones. Its name is probably derived from Louise de La Vallière (1644–1710), mistress of Louis XIV. *See* NÉGLIGÉE.

Lavernite. An undesirable trade-name for a variety of SYNTHETIC PERICLASE.

laxy diamond. A trade term for a flat BRILLIANT DIAMOND; perhaps the name is derived from LASQUE.

lazo (Spanish). A type of brooch in the form of a bow-knot made of openwork gold and set with gemstones and sometimes a pendent stone. The reverse is engraved with a floral design. These pieces were popular in Spain in the 16th and 17th centuries.

lazulite. A mineral that is compact and opaque, with a VITREOUS LUSTRE; its colour is shades of blue, and, being dichroic, it shows dark blue in one direction, sky-blue in the other. It is used in ornamental ware but seldom as a gemstone. It somewhat resembles TURQUOISE but differs in that it does not contain copper. It is entirely different from LAPIS LAZULI, but is sometimes referred to as 'false lapis'. *See* LAZURITE.

lazurite. An opaque and azure-blue mineral that is a component of LAPIS LAZULI. Owing to the confusion of the name with LAZULITE and lapis lazuli, it has been suggested that the name be discontinued.

lead. A heavy metallic element, soft and malleable. It was used in the Middle Ages for some cheap jewelry, and especially PILGRIM BADGES. It is used in various ALLOYS; and also as lead oxide as a constituent of CRYSTAL GLASS such as is used to imitate gemstones.

lead glass. A type of GLASS containing a high percentage of lead oxide (today from 24% to 30%). Lead oxide, in a small percentage, had been used in ancient Mesopotamia and again, to enhance the brilliance of glass (especially in the manufacture of artificial gemstones), before the 11th century, but its importance stemmed from its first use, *c.* 1676, by George Ravenscroft in England, originally as a remedy against the crisselling of glass. Lead glass is soft, and has high colour dispersion that gives it strong brilliance, especially when in the 18th century and later it was decorated with FACETING. The process was independently discovered in 1781 in France by the St Louis Glass Factory. *See* CRYSTAL GLASS; FLINT GLASS; PASTE; STRASS.

leaf. A very thin sheet of metal (usually 0.005 mm thick), thinner than FOIL. It is made by hammering a metal sheet placed between plates of copper or sheets of parchment. It is used for GILDING. *See* GOLD LEAF; SILVER LEAF.

lechosos opal. A variety of FIRE OPAL that exhibits characteristic flashes of deep green.

Lechtzin, Stanley (1936-   ). An American DESIGNER-MAKER who from 1964 was among the earliest users of the technique of ELECTROFORMING, which he developed to make relatively large but lightweight articles. Recently he has sometimes combined such work with plastics and pearls, and often decorated it with forms derived from nature. He teaches at the Tyler School of Art, Temple University, Philadelphia, and also lectures on jewelry. His work is in many permanent collections and he has had a number of one-man exhibitions.

Leda and the Swan Jewel. An OVAL gold ENSEIGNE (a COMMESSO) decorated with an enamelled scene showing 'Leda and the Swan' attended by an amorino; the encircling frame is decorated with gold C-scrolls alternating with diamonds and rubies. The drapery is gold. The torso, head, and foot of Leda are fragments of an antique CAMEO of AGATE that was formerly said to be a cameo mentioned by BENVENUTO CELLINI as made by him in Rome, *c.* 1524, for Gabbriello Cesarino, but later views are that it is probably Milanese, *c.* 1550-75, or French, *c.* 1540. On the back are the enamelled arms of Francis I of France, 1515-47.

leech bead. A type of glass bead in the form of a hollow cylinder that is slightly curved to resemble a leech (or boat). Such beads (or a lengthwise section of such a bead, called a 'runner') were sometimes used to cover the bow of a FIBULA. Some examples were made of glass in Etruria in the 7th century BC, with marvered combed decoration that produces a feather pattern.

leech ear-ring. A type of ear-ring made of a sheet of metal folded and joined to form a hollow, leech-shaped piece, with a curved wire attached at the top to pass through the lobe. Such ear-rings were popular in Egypt in the XVIIIth Dynasty (*c.* 1552 BC-1296 BC), being worn by women, often in a pair on each lobe. Some examples of Greek jewelry of the CLASSICAL STYLE, 4th century BC, were made with much decoration in FILIGREE work and with suspended ornaments.

leech fibula. A type of FIBULA of which the BOW is in the form of a hemi-cylinder that is slightly curved to resemble a leech (or boat). Examples were made of gold during the 7th century BC. The term has also been applied to a fibula having an undecorated, asymmetrical, arched bow (hollow or solid) that is thicker at the top; these have also been called a 'boat fibula' or a 'kite fibula'.

Lefébure, François (fl. 1635-63). A jeweller who in 1635 published his *Livre des Fleurs et des Feuilles* with engraved designs that showed the transition to the use of naturalistic flowers which was developed in the BAROQUE period. His later designs of 1663 featured ear-rings.

Légaré, Gidéon (1615-76). A Parisian goldsmith, enameller, and designer of jewelry to whom Louis XIV in 1671 granted quarters in the Louvre. He created designs in the PEAPOD style, but from *c.* 1640 emphasized in his designs the flower motifs that became characteristic of the BAROQUE period, being later used extensively by GILLES LÉGARÉ, BALTHAZAR MONCORNET, and JEAN VAUQUER. *See* HORTICULTURAL STYLE.

Leda and the Swan Jewel. Enseigne with agate cameo and enamelling. *c.* 1550-75. Kunsthistorisches Museum, Vienna.

leech ear-ring. Gold with bow decorated with filigree and chains supporting 5 acorn ornaments. Classical style, 4th century BC, Museo Nazionale, Taranto.

Légaré, Gilles (b. c. 1610). A goldsmith and enameller of Chaumont-en-Bassigny, France, who worked in Paris and was jeweller to Louis XIV. He is best known for his treatise *Livre des Ouvrages d'Orfèvrerie,* the outstanding book of jewelry design published in the 17th century, which included designs for brooches, CLASPS, ear-rings, pendants, etc., in bow-shaped and floral forms (such as SÉVIGNÉ brooches and large GIRANDOLE ear-rings) set with diamonds that were TABLE CUT and ROSE CUT, as well as articles without stones, such as finger rings, SEALS, CHAINS, etc. He also designed enamelled pieces, and his masterpiece is considered to be a garland of enamelled flowers in openwork relief that surrounds a miniature painted by Jean Petitot. *See* Joan Evans, 'Gilles Légaré', in *Burlington Magazine*, April 1917, p. 140. *See* BOW-KNOT BROOCH; HORTICULTURAL STYLE.

legionnaire ring. A type of finger ring from the Roman era, made of BRONZE, on the flat BEZEL of which is engraved a Roman numeral. Some of the numbers are so high as to exceed the number of the Roman legions, so the present view is that they have no relationship to the legions, but are identification rings of soldiers.

Lemercier, Balthasar (fl. 1620–30). A Parisian goldsmith and designer of jewelry whose work was usually in the PEAPOD style. He made books of engravings with such designs.

Lemonnier. A French jeweller of the 19th century whose work (including jewels made for the Queen of Spain) was exhibited at the Great Exhibition of 1851 in Hyde Park, London, and attracted the attention of Napoleon III, so that the firm became Court Jewellers and remounted jewels for his marriage in 1853 to Eugénie de Montijo.

Lennox Jewel. The same as the DARNLEY JEWEL.

leontine. A type of CHAIN decorated with tassels and slides made of coloured gold, and later of silver, that was worn by ladies as a WATCH CHAIN. It was named after a celebrated actress.

Lesotho Diamonds. A group of diamonds found in the 1960s in Lesotho (formerly Basutoland) in southern Africa. A brownish stone, rough 601.25 carats, found in 1967, was, after several transfers, acquired by HARRY WINSTON who had it cut in 1969 into 18 stones (the largest 71.73 carats), all of which were sold privately. Others, white or brownish, have been cut and sold privately.

Lesser George, The. An insigne of the Order of the Garter, secondary to the GEORGE, but also being a jewel with an enamelled or carved figure of St George slaying the dragon, encircled by a buckled garter. It is worn suspended from a blue sash that extends from the left shoulder across the breast to the right hip where the insigne hangs. A number of examples exist. Three CAMEOS are in the Royal Collection at Windsor Castle, one with a miniature of the Raphael painting of St George and another from the early Stuart period said to have been given to Charles I on the scaffold by Archbishop Juxon. Another, at the Ashmolean Museum, Oxford, is of gold or gilded silver that originally belonged to Thomas Howard, Earl of Arundel, and was given to Elias Ashmole by Thomas Howard, Duke of Norfolk. Another, at the Victoria & Albert Museum, was owned by Thomas Wentworth, Earl of Strafford (d. 1641).

letter jewel. A type of jewel in the form of a capital letter. An important example is the FOUNDER'S JEWEL featuring the letter M. Another is a Saxony LOCKET in the form of the letter E; *see* E JEWEL. Another is in the form of a B, referring to Blanca, the mother of King Haakon of Denmark, who in 1372 redeemed it from pawn. A brooch shaped like the letter M and another like the letter B are listed in the inventory made in 1328 of the jewels of Queen Clementia, second wife of Louis X of France. An English example in the form of an A was recorded in 1857. Such letter jewels are known to have been made in the 14th century, but surviving examples are rare.

Leubingen Treasure. A TREASURE of articles of jewelry found on the skeleton of a girl buried in a tumulus (barrow) of the 16th century BC in

Lesser George, The. Pendant set with cameo; setting for missing diamonds. Said to have been given to Charles I. At Windsor Castle. Reproduced by gracious permission of Her Majesty the Queen.

Thuringia, in central Germany, that was excavated in the 19th century. The jewelry included a massive gold penannular bracelet with engraved decoration, gold pins, a recurved wire finger ring, and a spiral hair ornament. The articles are now in the Landesmuseum, Halle.

Leuhusen Chain. A heavy gold CHAIN of 97 rectangular links having the surfaces decorated with very fine FILIGREE. It was made in Sweden, *c.* 1530, and is said formerly to have been owned by Anna Leuhusen (d. 1550), who was Abbess of the Nunnery of the Order of Poor Clares in Stockholm.

Leuhusen chain. Detail of gold chain of 97 links. Sweden, *c.* 1530. Statens Historiska Museum, Stockholm.

Liberator Diamond. A diamond weighing rough 155 carats that was found in 1942 in Venezuela and was named in honour of Simón Bolívar (1783-1830), the liberator of the country. It was bought in 1943 by HARRY WINSTON who had it cut into 3 EMERALD CUT stones (weighing 39.80, 18.12, and 8.93 carats) and a MARQUISE stone (weighing 1.44 carats). Winston sold the largest, Liberator I, to May Bonfils Stanton, of Colorado, but in 1962 rebought it at auction. All four stones are last reported as owned privately.

ligament pearl. A type of natural pearl that is found near the ligament at the hinge that joins the two valves of the shell and that is opposite the opening of the shell. Such pearls are usually dark, somewhat brownish, owing to a large proportion of CONCHIOLIN.

Light of Peace. A diamond, said to have been found in 1970 in Sierra Leone, weighing 430 carats rough, which was cut into a large pear-shaped stone of 130.27 carats. It was exhibited by its owner, Zale Corporation, New York, which announced that it was not to be sold but to be permanently exhibited, with the proceeds to be donated to a cause for peace. *See* SIERRA LEONE DIAMONDS.

lily bead. A type of bead generally in a form suggestive of a lily, with two everted volutes. Examples in several variations are found from the Middle Minoan III Period, *c.* 1700 BC-1600 BC and the Late Minoan and Mycenaean Period, *c.* 1600 BC-1100 BC, including some with two adjacent lilies. *See* WAZ LILY BEAD.

Lim, Auguste (1830-95). A well-known French jeweller whose speciality was making CHAINS in a great variety of styles and at inexpensive prices, many to be exported to England. The chains were variously named, e.g. Écossais, Impératrice, Napolitain, etc.

Limavady Treasure. A TREASURE of gold objects discovered in 1896 at Broighter, near Limavady, in County Londonderry, Northern Ireland, near Lough Foyle. It includes a TORC made of twisted wire, two chains, and a hollow collar made of two plates soldered together and decorated in REPOUSSÉ style. They all have been attributed to the 1st century AD, based on the style of the decoration. The objects were purchased by the British Museum in 1897, but Ireland claimed them as treasure trove and, despite the Museum's contention that the pieces were not necessarily of Irish origin, the Chancery Court upheld the claim; the pieces were accordingly awarded to the Crown and presented to the National Museum of Ireland, Dublin.

lime dipper. A long, thin object of PRE-COLUMBIAN JEWELRY, being a type of narrow spatula or blunt pin, made of cast gold, with an ornate head, used to remove the powdered lime from a POPORA. They ranged from about 15 cm to 45 cm long and the heads were of a great variety of forms, e.g. a bird, warrior, bell, funnel, or masked anthropomorphic figure.

lime dipper (detail of head, without pin). Cast gold. Calima style. L. of figure, 2.5 cm.; of entire dipper, 25.8 cm. Museo del Oro, Bogotá.

Linea Viaja jewelry. Gold male figure holding rope. Costa Rica. H. 5.3 cm. New Orleans Museum of Art.

lime flask. *See* POPORA.

Limoges enamel. (1) A type of ENAMEL work on copper in the style of CHAMPLEVÉ enamel, found on much ware made at Limoges, France, in the late 12th and the 13th centuries, but infrequently used on jewelry. The metal in the cells was first covered with a dark enamel, and then the design was built up with translucent enamels (usually lapis-lazuli blue or sea-green) with the dark showing through as the background, and the unenamelled metal areas generally being gilded. (2) PAINTED ENAMEL that was executed at Limoges and elsewhere during the 15th century and that has continued to be produced there today. Leading exponents of such work were NARDON PÉNICAUD and LÉONARD LIMOUSIN. *See* GRISAILLE.

limonite. A dark-brown ironstone that is sometimes found as an inclusion in TURQUOISE or the brown-veined MATRIX in which turquoise is sometimes found. When cut together, the stone is called TURQUOISE MATRIX. The mineral with sandstone often forms a matrix for Queensland OPAL.

Limousin, Léonard (*c.* 1505–*c.* 1577). An enamellist of Limoges, France, who was the leading exponent of enamelling in GRISAILLE. He was a follower of NARDON PÉNICAUD. *See* LIMOGES ENAMEL.

Lincoln Sapphire. A SAPPHIRE, weighing rough 2,302 carats, that was carved by Norman Maness as a representation of the head of Abraham Lincoln. Three other large sapphires, weighing rough between 1,743 and 2,097 carats, and all also found in 1948 in Queensland, Australia, have been carved by Harry B. Derian as heads (each about 6.2 cm high) depicting US Presidents Washington, Jefferson, and Eisenhower, respectively. All four, together with the 733-carat Black Star of Queensland, were donated in 1957 by James and Harry Kazanjian, of Pasadena, Cal., to the Smithsonian Institution, Washington, DC.

line bracelet. A type of flexible bracelet with identical or graduated gemstones arranged in a single line without any embellishment. Usually there is only one variety of gemstone, but occasionally two are alternated, e.g. diamonds with emeralds or sapphires, and, rarely, a border, added on each side, is made of gemstones of the same or a different variety.

Linea Viaja jewelry. Articles of PRE-COLUMBIAN JEWELRY made by the Indians of the Linea Viaja (Old Line) region of Costa Rica along the Caribbean coast (so named after an early railway there). The articles, made of gold cast by the CIRE PERDUE process, included animal figures (e.g. a two-headed frog) and anthropomorphic figures with high topknots on their head. Many pieces are extremely small, owing to the scarcity of local gold. *See* PANAMANIAN JEWELRY.

link bracelet. A type of flexible bracelet composed of a series of links of various styles and sizes, ranging from simple small metal links such as are used for a CHAIN to large ornamental links decorated with enamelling or set with gemstones or made in complicated openwork patterns. Such ornamental link bracelets were a popular article of VICTORIAN JEWELRY, often several of different styles being worn on the same arm.

Linnean pearl. An early type of CULTURED PEARL proposed, *c.* 1760, by Carolus Linnaeus (Carl Gustav von Linne; 1708–78), the famous Swedish botanist, the method involving boring a small hole through the shell of a PEARL OYSTER and inserting a limestone pellet connected to a fine silver wire so that the nucleus could be moved to prevent its adhering to the interior of the shell while it was being covered with NACRE. Such pearls were never commercially produced.

Linobate. A trade-name for synthetic LITHIUM NIOBATE.

Lion Jewel. A LOCKET having in the centre of its front a large BAROQUE PEARL suggestive of a lion's head, and set with ruby eyes and surrounded by a gold mount in the form the mane and forepaws, decorated with rubies and diamonds. The reverse is an irregularly-shaped plaque with multicoloured enamelling of a bird amid arabesques and scrolls. The pendant is suspended by 3 enamelled and jewelled gold chains hanging

Lion Jewel. Gold pendant with baroque pearl and gemstones. South Germany, *c.* 1595. The National Trust (Anglesey Abbey, near Cambridge).

from an escutcheon bearing a relief lion's-head mask (the heraldic emblem of the Wittelsbach family of Bavaria-Palatinate); from it is suspended a large pear-shaped pearl. The piece has been attributed, based on the style of the enamelling on the reverse, to CORVINIANUS SAUR, and is said to have been made in south Germany, c. 1595. It has been suggested that the jewel was made for a woman, probably Elizabeth Renata (b. 1574), daughter of Charles II of Lorraine, who married in 1595 Duke Maximilian I, later Elector of Bavaria, or possibly for Louise Juliana, daughter of William I of Orange-Nassau ('The Lion of the Netherlands'), who in 1593 married the Elector Palatine Frederick IV. The jewel later appeared in England, possibly owned by John Farquhar who in 1823 bought treasures from William Beckford, known to have owned some Wittelsbach relics. In 1966 it was bequeathed by Lord Fairhaven, of Anglesey Abbey, near Cambridge, to the National Trust. *See* Charles R. Beard, 'The Lion Jewel', *Connoisseur*, January 1938, p. 72.

Loch Buy Brooch. Silver with cabochon crystal set on central reliquary box; 10 turret collets set with pearls. Scottish, 16th century. W. 12 cm. British Museum, London.

lip plug. The same as a LABRET.

lithia (or lithium) emerald. A misnomer for the emerald-green variety of HIDDENITE (green spodumene).

lithium niobate. A SYNTHETIC GEMSTONE having no counterpart in nature. It has properties similar to STRONTIUM TITANITE, but is distinguishable by several features. It is grown as a colourless stone but can be tinted in various colours from red to violet. It has been marketed under the trade-name of 'Linobate'. The preferable term is 'synthetic lithium niobate'.

Littledale, H. A. P. An Englishman who patented in 1933 a process for reproducing ancient GRANULATED GOLD by COLLOID HARD-SOLDERING. For examples of his work, *see* A. R. Emerson, *Hand-made Jewellery* (1953).

livery collar. A type of CHAIN with a pendent badge bearing the heraldic device and motto of a guild or of a royal family, a member of which had bestowed such a chain, as a mark of favour, on a relative or person of rank. Examples from the 14th to 16th centuries were worn in England and France. The badge sometimes showed the device or motto of the recipient. *See* SS COLLAR; ARCHER'S COLLAR.

lizard jewelry. Articles of jewelry of which the main decorative motif was the representation of a lizard. Such pieces were made in several types: (1) a bracelet, sometimes ARTICULATED, depicting fairly realistically a lizard, with curved body, often set with green gemstones and ruby eyes; (2) a pendant, in the form of a lizard with its body made of a BAROQUE PEARL and its head and tail of gold with enamelling and gemstones; and (3) a pendant made of cast TUMBAGA, in the form of a lizard, by the Colombian Indians (*see* QUIMBAYA JEWELRY). *See* CORTÉS EX VOTO JEWEL.

lizardite. A variety of SERPENTINE that is found, in shades of green and red-brown, on the Lizard promontory in Cornwall, England.

Loch Buy Brooch. A silver DISC BROOCH having a raised central RELIQUARY box on which is set a large CABOCHON crystal. On the outer band of the brooch are ten turret-like COLLETS, each set with a PEARL. It was made in Scotland in the 16th century, and bears an inscription on the reverse. It was in the possession of the MacLeans of Loch Buy in the Isle of Mull, then later in the collection of Ralph Bernal, an English collector, from whose dispersal sale it was acquired in 1855 by the British Museum.

locket. Gold with enamelled decoration and suspended baroque pearl. British Museum, London.

locket. A small case, usually with a hinged lid, for a memento, such as a photograph, miniature, lock of hair, etc., and usually worn suspended from a NECK CHAIN. Such pieces have been made of gold, silver or other metal, decorated with enamelling or engraving and often set with gemstones. The locket was a development of the hinged RELIQUARY pendants of the Middle Ages and the Renaissance. In the 16th century the Sovereign presented hinged pendants that enclosed a portrait of him- or herself (*see* ARMADA JEWEL; LYTE JEWEL), and other lockets of a more personal nature were made (*see* DARNLEY JEWEL). In succeeding centuries gold lockets, decorated with enamelling and gemstones, were worn as jewelry, but often enclosing miniature portraits and locks of hair, and later

Londesborough Brooch. Silver gilt, chip-carved and engraved, set with blue glass. Irish, 8th century. L. 24.2 cm. British Museum, London.

loop-terminal torc. Two twisted bars of gold alloy. South British Late Iron Age, 1st century BC. W. 21.2 cm. British Museum, London.

Lothair, Crystal of. Morse with copper-gilt frame (15th century) enclosing rock crystal plaque (9th century) engraved in intaglio with scenes of Susanna. British Museum, London.

photographs, many being in the 18th and 19th centuries (and especialy in the Victorian era) betrothal or sentimental gifts. Lockets are worn less often today, but antique examples are much sought. *See* KEY AND HEART LOCKET; MINIATURE CASE.

locket ring. A type of FINGER RING of which the BEZEL is a small LOCKET. On an example from *c.* 1576, now at Chequers, the hoop and the cover of the locket are set with gemstones and inside are portraits of Elizabeth I and Anne Boleyn(?).

Logan Sapphire. A blue SAPPHIRE weighing 423 carats that was found in Sri Lanka (formerly Ceylon). It is now mounted in a finger ring surrounded by 20 ROSE CUT diamonds, and is in the Smithsonian Institution, Washington, DC, donated by Mrs John A. Logan. It is said to be probably the largest known sapphire of such dark-blue colour.

Londesborough Brooch. A penannular PIN BROOCH of CELTIC JEWELRY similar to the TARA BROOCH, made of silver gilt with chip-carved (*see* CHIP-CARVING) and engraved decoration in zoomorphic and other patterns and set with blue glass bosses engraved with cell patterns. It is from Ireland, 8th century AD, and was acquired from the collection of Lord Londesborough by the British Museum. *See* HUNTERSTON BROOCH.

longchain. A type of CHAIN that is very long (usually more than 1 m) and that, worn by a woman, was tucked into the girdle or attached to her bodice to form two festoons over her bosom. Such chains were made with many styles of links. They were sometimes worn by a man around his neck and with an attached WATCH placed in a waistcoat pocket.

loop-in-loop chain. An ancient type of CHAIN, from *c.* 2500 BC, of which the links are initially of oval shape and are bent back against themselves so as to form a U-shape, after which each link is threaded through the looped end of the preceding link, resulting in a somewhat square section (hence sometimes called a 'square chain'). A more compact variation is the 'double loop-in-loop' where each added link is slipped through the loops of the two preceding links. The last link of each such chain is closed by SOLDERING. Some such chains are made broad by cross-linking two to eight basic chains; *see* CORD-CHAIN; STRAP CHAIN.

loop-terminal torc. A type of TORC of which the terminals are loops formed as an extension of the twisted wire rod that forms the PENANNULAR hoop, or are cast loops attached to simulate such extensions. Such torcs were made in the South British Late Iron Age, 1st century BC, and have been found near Ipswich, Suffolk, England.

lost-wax process. The same as the CIRE PERDUE process. It is sometimes referred to as 'lost wax casting'. *See* CENTRIFUGAL CASTING.

Lothair, Crystal of. A circular plaque of engraved ROCK CRYSTAL that was mounted, to be used as a MORSE, in a 15th-century copper-gilt circular frame set with four gemstones (now missing). The crystal is of lenticular shape and is engraved with eight miniature scenes, from the story of Susanna, from the Apocrypha. It is carved in INTAGLIO, but it is said that it was intended to be looked at from the other side through the crystal body, in which event the design appears to be in CAMEO. The piece has a long history: it is said to have been made for Lothair II, King of Lotharingia, 855–69, and belonged in the first half of the 10th century to the wife of Eilbert, Count of Flanders, who pawned it to the Canon of Rheims Cathedral; the latter denied it but the Count recovered it from him after burning the Cathedral, and in repentance gave it to Vasor Abbey at Florennes, near Dinant. After two later sales, it was bought by Ralph Bernal, an English collector, from whose dispersal sale it was acquired in 1855 by the British Museum. The crystal is of the 9th century.

Lotharingian jewelry. Articles of jewelry made in the Rhineland during the 13th century, influenced in style by the cathedral sculpture of northern France. It is exemplified by the work of NICOLAS OF VERDUN, the outstanding Lotharingian goldsmith of the early 13th century. (Lotharingia is the former name of Lorraine, and it originally included modern Alsace-Lorraine, the Low Countries, and part of north-west Germany.)

Louis Treize enamel. A style of ENAMELLING that featured the depiction of naturalistic flowers, painted on a monochrome ground, usually white but sometimes black or light blue, in the technique developed *c.* 1619 by JEAN TOUTIN. The name has been said to be misleading, as most pieces decorated in that style were painted in the second half of the 17th century, after the death of Louis XIII in 1643. The style was used to decorate WATCH-CASES and LOCKETS, and sometimes the reverse of plaques that formed a bracelet.

love ring. A type of finger ring worn to evidence a sentimental attachment, including the FEDE RING and the POSY RING. Before the use of the posy ring, some rings were so worn engraved with a simple inscription or merely an appropriate symbol.

lover's-knot ring. A type of finger ring, often worn as a BETROTHAL RING or an ENGAGEMENT RING, but sometimes merely as a token of affection, having the BEZEL made from twisted wire so as to form a complicated four-loop knot. Such rings were used from Roman times to the medieval period. *See* BOW-KNOT BROOCH.

lozenge. A decorative shape in the form of a diamond figure, having four equal and straight sides making two equal and opposite acute angles and two equal and opposite obtuse angles. The corners are sometimes rounded. *See* KITE CUT.

lozenge cut. A style of cutting a diamond (or other transparent gemstone) so that the TABLE is in the shape of a LOZENGE. When each of the four sides is bordered by a sloping trapezoidal FACET, or a descending row of such facets, the stone is 'lozenge step cut'.

lozenge facet. The former name for the 8 LOZENGE-shaped FACETS on the CROWN or the 8 on the PAVILION of a BRILLIANT. Former alternative names were QUOIN, TEMPLET, and BEZEL; but now all such lozenge-shaped facets are each called a KITE FACET or a MAIN FACET.

Luckenbooth brooch. A type of Scottish BROOCH that is heart-shaped (sometimes two hearts, side by side), occasionally surmounted by a crown, and sometimes set with a gemstone. They are of medieval Scottish origin, but continued to be popular in the 18th/19th centuries. Many bear on the reverse the word 'Love' or a posy (*see* POSY RING), hence they presumably were love tokens. They were so called because they were often sold in the Luckenbooths, which were street stalls near St Giles Kirk, on the High St in Edinburgh. Some examples, from the 19th century, include a cut-out M, and so they were sometimes called a 'Queen Mary Brooch'.

Lulls, Arnold (fl. 1600-20). A Dutch goldsmith and designer who came to England and in 1605 became jeweller to James I, 1603-25, and there designed AIGRETTES and other jewels for Anne of Denmark, the Queen Consort. Lulls's name appears often in the Court records. An album of his paintings, made in watercolours on parchment, and preserved at the Victoria & Albert Museum, shows 41 pieces, most contemporary but some dating from the second half of the 16th century, including pendants, necklaces, GEORGES, and aigrettes, many of them enamelled but mainly decorated with gemstones, often ROSE CUT or TABLE CUT. These paintings were thought until recently to be designs, but it is now recognized that the album constitutes a pictorial inventory. Another such pictorial inventory was made by HANS MIELICH.

lunate. Crescent-shaped, as the form of a CRESCENT BROOCH or of some ear-rings.

lunette. A style of cutting a diamond (or other transparent gemstone) in STEP CUT style but shaped in the form of a semi-circle.

lunula. A crescent-shaped ornament made of a thin plate of gold (or other metal). At the points of the crescent there are sometimes rounded rectangular terminals twisted at right-angles to the crescent; when these are overlapped to close the ornament (perhaps with a thong), the lunula becomes conical, with both the inner and outer edges forming circles that would enable the piece to rest on the neck as a collar or to be worn on the

Lotharingian jewelry. Silver buckle. *C.* 1230. L 8.5 cm. Statens Historiska Museum, Stockholm.

lover's-knot ring. Gold with twisted wire Heracles knot. Possibly English, 14th/15th centuries. Schmuckmuseum, Pforzheim, Germany.

Luckenbooth brooch. Silver. Scottish, *c.* 1850. L. 7 cm. National Museum of Antiquities of Scotland, Edinburgh.

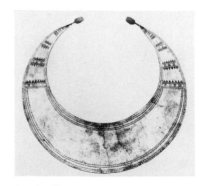

lunula. Sheet gold with engraved decoration. Irish, *c.* 1800 BC–1500 BC. Found near Ross, County Westmeath. W. 27.3 cm. National Museum of Ireland, Dublin.

 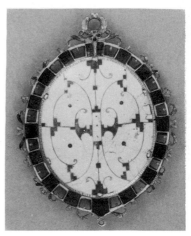

Lyte Jewel (front, back, and cover). Gold locket with jewelled monogram cover and enamelled back, enclosing portrait of James I within gold rim set with diamonds. English, 1610. H. 6.2 cm. British Museum, London.

head as a diadem. The original use is uncertain, and, although they are often referred to as a 'neck-ring', it has been suggested that such use could be dangerous to the wearer. The metal is usually decorated with CHASING in parallel vertical geometric patterns concentrated toward the terminals, but some also have rows of conical studs. More than 100 examples have been recorded in north-western Europe, the great majority in Ireland (some of which may have come from Brittany). They have never been found in graves but in isolated fields or HOARDS. Some have been attributed to the Irish Early Bronze Age, *c.* 1800 BC–1500 BC, and some are examples of CELTIC JEWELRY of the pagan period.

lustre. The appearance of the smooth surface of a mineral or some other substances due to the reflection which results from light striking the surface. It is a quality of opaque or translucent stones. There are several kinds of lustre: (1) metallic, the most brilliant, as shown by polished metals and many metallic minerals, e.g. crystalline HEMATITE; (2) adamantine, characteristic of diamonds; (3) vitreous, as shown by RUBY, SAPPHIRE, and GLASS; (4) resinous, as shown by AMBER and other RESINS, a greasy lustre and a waxy lustre being rather similar; (5) pearly, as seen on the surface of pearls and on the CLEAVAGE faces of some crystals; and (6) silky, as shown by CAT'S-EYE and other fibrous minerals. Lustre is seen on a smooth surface where no ridges are present to reflect the light in many directions. The degrees of lustre, indicating intensity, are 'splendent' (mirror-like), 'shining' (indistinct), 'glistening' (feeble), and 'dull' (almost none). Lustre should not be confused with SHEEN. *See* GLOSS.

lustreware jewelry. Articles of jewelry made of pottery covered with a metallic lustre. Examples are rare, but one known piece is a necklace composed of 14-sided lustreware beads.

lynx sapphire. A misnomer for a blue variety of IOLITE (CORDIERITE).

Lyte Jewel. An oval gold and enamelled LOCKET enclosing a miniature portrait of James I (possibly by NICHOLAS HILLIARD or Isaac Oliver) on the back of which is white enamel with decoration of delicate gold lines and ruby enamel. The locket (probably made by GEORGE HERIOT) has an oval gold rim, set with 16 square table-cut diamonds, and an openwork hinged lid with the monogram 'I R' (Latin, Iacobus Rex, for James VI of Scotland, later James I of England), the monogram being set with 8 square-cut diamonds and 4 rose-cut diamonds; the reverse of the lid is enamelled in red and blue. The locket was given by James I in 1610 to Thomas Lyte (1568–1638) of Somerset, as a reward for preparing an illuminated genealogical tree of the King. In 1747 a great-grandson of Lyte bequeathed the locket to his daughter whose descendants sold it to the Duke of Hamilton; the Hamilton Collection was sold in 1882 to Baron Ferdinand Rothschild who in 1898 included the locket in the Waddesdon Bequest to the British Museum. A portrait of Lyte dated 14 April 1611 shows him wearing the locket, which then had a trilobed drop instead of the present single pearl drop. *See* MONOGRAM PENDANT.

M

Mabe pearl. An early type of CULTURED PEARL produced *c.* 1896 by Kokichi Mikimoto, in the form of a BLISTER PEARL, by inserting an irritant in the mollusc and later by removing the nucleus and replacing it with a small bead cemented in and backed with MOTHER-OF-PEARL.

macaroni. A longer version of a CHATELAINE, made without a suspensory hook to be attached to the girdle but worn slung over a close-fitting belt or girdle with the two ends hanging down at equal lengths. On one end was an ornamented medallion with several (usually five) small hooks for suspending a WATCH (open-face, so as to be readily viewed), a SEAL, and other articles and decorative tassels, and on the other end more tassels or a hook for a FAUSSE MONTRE or a GIRDLE BOOK. Such pieces were made of enamelled gold links separated by enamelled plaques and often set with gemstones or pearls. They were fashionable from *c.* 1770 intermittently until the late 19th century, when some late examples were made of steel or JET.

macle (or maccle). (1) A triangular-shaped twinned natural crystal of a diamond, usually fairly flat but sometimes thick enough to be cut into a BRILLIANT, but with wide GIRDLE, TABLE, and CULET to compensate in weight for the thinness. (2) The same as CHIASTOLITE.

magatama. A type of bead made in Japan; it is characteristically comma-shaped and has a pierced hole near the top. They are known in Japan, made of stone or jade, from as early as the late Jomon period (*c.* 1000 BC), but disappeared until revived during the 3rd/6th centuries AD, perhaps, it has been said, because such beads were popular in Korea at that time. The form changed slightly during subsequent centuries. The later examples were made of stone but also some of GLASS. They were probably strung for necklaces or attached as dress ornaments, and possibly worn as talismans. Such beads were also made in Korea, in the early 6th century, sometimes of JADE, and were made into pendants capped with a gold ornament. Both Japan and Korea claim priority for the production of such beads which, it has been suggested, were of shamanistic origin.

magatama. Carved stone beads. Japan, 3rd/5th centuries. L. 1.5/2 cm. British Museum, London.

magical jewelry. Articles of jewelry which, during the Middle Ages and later, were regarded, by belief or superstition, as having magical or medicinal powers, and so were worn for other than ornamental or sentimental reasons. Early forms were the AMULET, BULLA or finger ring bearing an astrological, magical or religious inscription, word or symbol, or set with a SCARAB or a MAGICAL STONE (*see* ABRAXAS STONE). A later example was the RELIQUARY, as well as certain articles of DEVOTIONAL JEWELRY that sought the intercession of a saint. Some articles were supposed to have magical powers from extrinsic circumstances of their creation, e.g. the CRAMP RING or TOUCHPIECE. *See* CHARM; PHYLACTERY PENDANT; TALISMAN.

magical stone. A stone believed in the Middle Ages and even later to possess magical or healing powers (apart from the SETTING or any inscriptions on it; *see* MAGICAL JEWELRY). Such beliefs and traditions extend far back into antiquity, but sometimes had some recognizable basis in the nature of the stone, e.g. a transparent hard diamond to make the wearer invincible, a purple AMETHYST to prevent intoxication, a BLOODSTONE to stop bleeding, an EMERALD (impervious to light) to aid eyesight, etc. Some minerals and other substances were similarly regarded as magical, e.g. TOADSTONE, ADDER STONE, NARWHAL IVORY ('unicorn horn'), EAGLE STONE, SWALLOW STONE, BEZOAR STONE. Some such substances were administered in powdered form as medicine until the early 18th century. *See* Joan Evans, *Magical Stones of the Middle Ages and Renaissance* (1922). *See* BIRTHSTONE.

magna cut
side view

magna cut. A style of cutting a diamond that is a modification of the BRILLIANT CUT. It has a 10-sided TABLE, 60 FACETS on the CROWN, 40 facets on the PAVILION, and sometimes a CULET, totalling 102 facets. It is a 20th-century cut used for large stones to avoid waste but at the loss of some brilliance.

Maierhofer, Fritz (1941-). A DESIGNER-MAKER born in Vienna who emigrated to London and worked with ANDREW GRIMA. From 1970 he worked exclusively in acrylic (*see* ACRYLIC JEWELRY) but since 1973 has combined it with gold and alloys.

main facet. An alternative name for a KITE FACET. The 8 such facets on the CROWN of a BRILLIANT are each called an 'upper main facet' and the 8 on the PAVILION are each called a 'lower main facet'.

make. The quality of the cut of a diamond, depending on the correctness of the proportions (height of CROWN to PAVILION, and width of TABLE to CULET), the precision in placing and cutting the FACETS, and the measurement of the angles of the facets. Each facet is usually symmetrical, and the angle to the rest of the stone must not vary more than half a degree from the prescribed angle. A diamond cut to the ideal specifications is said to be of 'good make' or 'fine make', but of 'poor make' if it varies, sometimes dictated by the original shape of the rough stone and an intention to save weight at a loss of BRILLIANCE.

malachite. A mineral of which the compact green variety, with alternate irregular bands of light and dark green, is used mainly for table tops, vases, and veneers, but also in jewelry when cut EN CABOCHON or carved as flat brooches or pendants. It occurs often in botryoidal form which, in cut section, reveals a concentric pattern called 'malachite peacock eye'. Related AZURITE is sometimes called 'blue malachite' to distinguish it from green malachite. The name is derived from Greek *malache* (mallow), owing to its colour which resembles that of the mallow leaf.

Maltese cross. Silver and gold pendant, set with diamonds. 19th century. Courtesy of Wartski, London.

Mallorcan pearl. A variety of IMITATION PEARL made on the island of Mallorca (Majorca) in the Balearic Islands, Spain.

Maltese cross. A type of CROSS having four equal arms that widen as they extend from a central focal point and have the arm ends indented, resulting in its having 8 points. It was named after the white cross worn as an emblem on the black robes of the Knights Hospitallers, a military and religious order that grew from the Hospital of St John of Jerusalem, established in the 11th century to care for pilgrims to the Holy Land and that became powerful and wealthy, with headquarters in Malta, and that still survives in Catholic Europe. The cross was a popular motif in England in the mid-19th century, brooches and pendants being made in its shape and ornamented lavishly with diamonds, often in PAVÉ SETTING. Sometimes called the 'Cross of St John'. *See* CROSS FORMÉE.

mamillary fibula. A type of PENANNULAR brooch having the terminals of the penannular ring in the form of small knobs. It was an early type of CELTIC brooch of the penannular type.

mammoth ivory. *See* FOSSIL IVORY.

manchette (French). Literally, cuff. *See* CUFF BRACELET.

Mancini Pearls, The. Drop-shaped natural pearls set in leafage caps suspended from detachable diamond-set ear-rings. Courtesy of Christie's, New York.

Mancini Pearls, The. A pair of large, pear-shaped, natural pearls weighing over 400 grains, set in detachable drops in a pair of ear-rings, the drops being suspended from a floral ornament set with diamonds. The ear-rings were a wedding gift in 1625 to Queen Henrietta Maria of England (Consort of Charles I) from her parents, Henry IV of France and Marie de' Medici. She kept the ear-rings, despite the need to raise funds, until as an impoverished widow living in exile, she sold them to her nephew, Louis XIV, who gave them to Maria Mancini (1640-1715), niece

of Cardinal Mazarin. After Maria Mancini in 1661 married Prince
Colonna and moved to Italy, the ear-rings were kept in the Colonna
family, and later in the Rospigliosi family into which a Colonna princess
had married. They were acquired by an anonymous collector who sold
them at Christie's, Geneva, in October 1969, and they were sold again at
Christie's, New York, on 16 October 1979, for $230,000 (plus 10%). The
pearls have been depicted in many portraits by Van Dyck and others.
Most of the setting is modern.

Mandarin necklace. A type of Chinese NECKLACE that is very long,
having an attached pendant that is worn on the wearer's back and 2 or 3
short strands of beads hanging on the sides at the front.

manjū netsuke. A type of NETSUKE that is circular with a spindle in the
centre that was pierced for the suspensory cord. Examples are made of
IVORY or HORN carved to depict a wide variety of subjects, including
human figures, animals, scenery, etc.

mano cornuta (Italian). Literally, horned hand. *See* HAND AMULET.

mantle. The film of tissue, in the form of lobes or flaps, within a PEARL
OYSTER that surrounds the body and separates it from the shell. It is
composed of epithelium cells which secrete the material that forms the 3
layers of the shell, as well as the concentric layers of an oyster pearl. The
shell layers are: (1) the outer dark-brown layer that is composed of an
organic material, called conchiolin; (2) the prismatic middle layer
composed of calcite or crystalline calcium carbonate (carbonate of lime);
and (3) the smooth inner layer, called MOTHER-OF-PEARL, that is
composed of overlapping plates of crystalline calcium carbonate in the
form of aragonite, bound together by conchiolin, being the IRIDESCENT
material known as NACRE and which is also the material that forms the
layers of the oyster pearl.

manju netsuke. Carved ivory. 19th
century. W. 3.5/5 cm. Courtesy of
Sydney L. Moss Ltd, London.

mantle pearl. The same as a CYST PEARL.

Maori jade. A green variety of NEPHRITE (JADE) that is found in New
Zealand. It was used there for ornaments and weapons. Also called 'Maori
stone', 'axe-stone', and 'New Zealand greenstone'. It was also used in New
Zealand for carving TIKIS.

marcasite. Originally and strictly, common crystallized iron PYRITES, an
iron sulphide mineral; later the word became a misnomer for iron
disulphide (pyrite or white iron pyrites) that is of the same chemical
composition and resembles it but is of different structure and lower
specific gravity. True marcasite (which is almost white, resembling pale
bronze) was used in jewelry by the Greeks and the Incas, but the substitute
PYRITE was used extensively in Europe from the 18th century onwards,
especially in France. Marcasite and pyrite have been imitated with GLASS,
CUT STEEL, and PLASTIC, but are readily distinguishable from these,
although not from each other. Having been sometimes set in a MARQUISE
RING, it has occasionally been erroneously spelled 'marquisite'. Marcasite
is usually set in silver (sometimes pewter), and is generally ROSE CUT or
mounted in a PAVÉ SETTING to enhance its sparkle, due to surface
reflection rather than internal light. Some cheap examples are set in
rhodium-plated mounts made of a base metal, sometimes set with PASTE
and enamelled. It has been sometimes referred to incorrectly as FOOL'S
GOLD which is a term for pyrite. The term 'marcasite' is today often
loosely applied in the trade to cut steel or even any white metal cut with
facets.

Marchant, Nathaniel (1739-1816). A noted gem-engraver, born in
Sussex, England, who worked in Rome, 1772-88, and returned to
England to become official Gem Engraver to the Prince Regent. He
revived the art of engraving gemstones, carving classical subjects and
contemporary portraits, and published a catalogue showing his casts
which were all in INTAGLIO.

Mari diamond. A local misnomer for ROCK CRYSTAL found in India and
used for cheap necklaces.

Maria Theresa Bouquet. Bouquet of gemstones in crystal vase. Vienna, 1660. H. 49 cm. Naturhistorisches Museum, Vienna.

Marie Antoinette Ear-rings. 36-carat diamonds set in platinum. Smithsonian Institution, Washington, DC.

Marie Louise Tiara. Silver with diamonds and cabochon turquoises. French, *c.* 1811. Smithsonian Institution, Washington, DC.

Maria. A Parisian jeweller who published *c.* 1765 a series of ROCOCO designs, *Livre de Dessins de Joaillerie et Bijouterie*, for brooches, clasps, aigrettes, chatelaines, finger rings, buckles, seals, etc.

Maria Theresa Bouquet. A bouquet of 73 gemstones (diamonds, rubies, etc.) made into 61 flowers, on some of which are butterflies, beetles or other insects, all set in a rock crystal vase. It was made in Vienna in 1760 by Johann Michael Grosser, Court Jeweller, upon the order of Empress Maria Theresa (1717–80) for presentation by her to her husband, Francis I, in recognition of his important collection of gems. Although not an article of jewelry, but an OBJECT OF VERTU, it is included here as an outstanding example of the jeweller's art.

Marie Antoinette Ear-rings. A pair of ear-rings owned by Marie Antoinette until she was captured in Varennes in June 1791 after fleeing from Paris. Each includes a 36-carat diamond (their origin is unknown) now set with a platinum mount (replacing the original silver mount) and suspended from a triangular jewel. They are now in the Hall of Gems in the Museum of Natural History (Smithsonian Institution), Washington, DC, having been donated by Mrs Eleanor Close Barzin.

'Marie Antoinette Necklace'. A famous diamond NECKLACE (or RIVIÈRE), sometimes so called although never owned by Marie Antoinette (1755–93), Consort of Louis XVI. The necklace was made by the Paris jewellers Bassange and Böhmer for Louis XV, to give to his mistress, Mme du Barry, but it was not completed until after his death (1774) and it was then offered to and refused by Louis XVI and Marie Antoinette as too expensive (about £90,000). In 1784 a Court intriguer, Jeanne de St-Rémy (Comtesse de la Motte), induced Cardinal de Rohan to buy it for the Queen as a means of regaining her favour. He obtained it on credit from the jewellers and handed it to an accomplice of St-Rémy for delivery to the Queen, but the accomplice fled with it to England where he sold the diamonds. When the jewellers, who believed de Rohan was acting for the Queen, demanded payment from her, the plot was revealed. St-Rémy and her husband, la Motte, were imprisoned, de Rohan was exiled, and the Queen's unpopularity was intensified. The necklace has been described by Thomas Carlyle as of several graduated strings set with diamonds, 'a princely ornament', and an engraving of it shows a necklace of 3 festoons with 17 brilliants and 4 pendants, together with a double *rivière* with 4 diamond tassels. It is sometimes called the 'Collier de la Reine'.

Marie Louise Necklace. A NECKLACE (RIVIÈRE) given by Napoleon to his second wife, Marie Louise, on the occasion of the birth in 1811 of their son, later Napoleon II. The necklace, made by Étienne Nitot et fils, in 1811, included 172 diamonds (28 being large ROSE CUT stones, from which are suspended 19 pear-shaped diamonds), all weighing 275 carats and set in a silver mount. It was bequeathed by Marie Louise to her sister-in-law, Sophie, Archduchess of Austria (two large diamonds having been removed to make ear-rings). The necklace is now in the Smithsonian Institution, Washington, DC, as the gift of Mrs Marjorie Merriweather Post.

Marie Louise Tiara. A TIARA given by Napoleon to his second wife, Marie Louise, daughter of Emperor Francis II of the Holy Roman Empire (Francis I of Austria) and grandniece of Marie Antoinette, on the occasion of the birth in 1811 of their son, later Napoleon II. The tiara is of silver, set with 950 diamonds weighing 700 carats and originally also set with emeralds that have been replaced by 79 turquoises cut EN CABOCHON and weighing 540 carats. It was bequeathed by Marie Louise to the Archduke Leopold of Austria, and became the property of the Imperial Family of Austria. It was later acquired by Mrs Marjorie Merriweather Post who donated it to the Smithsonian Institution, Washington, DC.

mark. Generally, the identifying mark of the maker of an article of jewelry, comparable to the maker's mark on ceramic ware and the decorator's mark on some glassware. Among the names engraved on some Greek and Roman ENGRAVED GEMSTONES are Aulos, Dioskorides, Gnaios, Solon, Sostratos, and Tryphon. Some pieces of Anglo-Saxon jewelry, e.g. CANTERBURY COIN BROOCH, bear the maker's name. Modern jewelry often bears the mark of the individual DESIGNER-MAKER, or of the firm that had it made by its own craftsmen from the design of an employed designer. Often the most effective method of identifying the designer, especially of jewelry made in the 17th/19th centuries, is by reference to the many design books that have been left. Other marks seen on jewelry include a HALLMARK, patent mark, design registry mark, and trade-mark.

Marlborough Diamond. A diamond that belonged to the late Gladys Marie Spencer-Churchill, Dowager Duchess of Marlborough (d. 1977), wife of the 9th Duke of Marlborough, and that was sold at Christie's, London, on 5 July 1978, lot 85. When so sold it was a cushion-shaped diamond, weight 48.01 carats, cut with no table but having at the apex eight converging triangular facets and set in a brooch flanked by smaller diamonds; the sale price was £60,000. The diamond was acquired by Laurence Graff, the London diamond merchant, who had it recut in the form of a sun-burst (so-called 'radiant cut'), weighing then 45 carats. It was mounted in a diamond necklace (stolen on 11 September 1980).

marquise. A diamond that is cut in a modification of the BRILLIANT CUT, so that the GIRDLE is boat-shaped (elliptical and pointed at both ends), with a hexagonal TABLE, surrounded on the CROWN by 32 trapezium-shaped and triangular FACETS. The PAVILION has 24 facets (as on the pavilion of a PENDELOQUE CUT stone) and a CULET. It is sometimes called a 'navette'. *See* MARQUISE ROSE CUT.

marquise ring. A type of finger ring that has a vertical elliptical BEZEL pointed at both ends and is set with (1) a large gemstone (usually a diamond) or PASTE, sometimes with a surround of small diamonds, (2) a cluster of diamonds, seed pearls or small gemstones, or (3) a CAMEO or a JASPER medallion made by Wedgwood. Some examples used as MOURNING JEWELRY have enamelling on the bezel in purple or black or enclose under the bezel a miniature, usually of a woman weeping by a willow or urn. Such rings were introduced in the second half of the 18th century.

marquise rose cut. A style of cutting a diamond (or other transparent gemstone) in a modification of the ROSE CUT, so that the stone is elliptical and pointed at both ends, but having a flat base and no TABLE. It is cut generally similar to the PENDELOQUE ROSE CUT, with usually 4 or 6 horizontal rows of triangular FACETS (7 in each of the 2 middle rows and 3 or 5 in the terminal rows), totalling 24 or 30 facets.

marquise setting. A style of SETTING for a finger ring that is elliptical in shape but pointed at both ends.

marriage belt. A type of belt (given by a groom to his bride, but not necessarily as a part of the marriage ceremony) made of gold and thought to be of Greek rather than Syrian use; such belts are composed of linked discs, with two large central discs that serve as the fastener. Each large disc is ornamented with relief depiction of a figure of Christ, with a figure of a bride and a groom at His sides, and a Greek inscription. The smaller discs, sometimes 22 of them, bear relief depictions of Dionysiac figures of different types. The discs are pressed from moulds. An example found in Turkey is attributed to *c.* AD 600 and at least one similar example is recorded.

Martelé. The trade-mark used, *c.* 1900-10, on jewelry and silverware by Gorham & Co., prominent jewellers of Providence, Rhode Island.

Martinazzi, Bruno (1923-). A Turin sculptor and a leading DESIGNER-MAKER of contemporary jewelry. His early work emphasized

Marie Louise Necklace. Rivière of 172 diamonds. French, 1811. Smithsonian Institution, Washington, DC.

marquise
top view

marriage belt (detail). Gold with 2 large plaques depicting bridal couple with figure of Christ and 21 small plaques with busts of Dionysiac figures. Constantinople, 6th/7th centuries. L. 75.5 cm. Dumbarton Oaks Collection (Harvard University), Washington, DC.

textural effects, but more recently he has developed a technique of combining layers of gold of different colours to achieve a sculptural and contrasting effect, with sometimes the inclusion of diamonds in PAVÉ SETTING. Since *c.* 1965 he has often used as decorative motifs stylized human eyes and lips, but his recent work has featured other motifs, such as an apple. His pieces are signed, and replicas made by him are numbered.

Mary, Queen of Scots, Pendant. A gold pendant set with a crystal (?) engraved on the underside with the achievement (arms) of Mary, Queen of Scots (1542–87), set on a field of blue. The crystal is similar to that on the MARY, QUEEN OF SCOTS, SIGNET RING. The reverse of the pendant is decorated with CLOISONNÉ ENAMEL. The central medallion is encircled by a gold band set with gemstones.

Mary, Queen of Scots, Signet Ring. A gold SIGNET RING with an oval BEZEL containing a crystal engraved with the achievement of Mary, Queen of Scots (1542–87), set on foil painted with the proper tinctures on a blue field. On the underside of the bezel is the engraved cipher formed by the Greek letters Φ and M (for Francis II of France, her first husband, and Mary), so that the ring is presumed to have been made between 1548 (when she went to France) and 1558 (the marriage). The history of the ring is unknown after her death in 1587 until 1792 when the ring was owned by Queen Charlotte; it later was owned by the Duke of York who sold it at Christie's in 1827 to Richard Greene, from whom it was acquired by the British Museum in 1856. *See* DARNLEY RING.

Mary, Queen of Scots, Pendant (front view). Gold with arms carved in crystal and tinctured. French (?), mid-16th century. National Museum of Antiquities of Scotland, Edinburgh.

mask. A representation of a face in a naturalistic or stylistic manner, sometimes made in primitive countries of hollow metal depicting the human face with relief features and sometimes adorned with replicas of jewelry. Examples used as FUNERARY JEWELRY are known from all the early Mediterranean cultures, including the Egyptian, Phoenician, Mycenaean, and Etruscan, but not from the Classical period in Greece. The best known are the mask of Tutankhamun and the mask alleged traditionally to be the mask of Agamemnon. An example made in the Quimbaya region of Colombia, *c.* 500–1500, is of cast gold, the figure wearing a NOSE ORNAMENT and suspended gold plaques. Although the last was worn for personal adornment, masks in general are mainly of a ritualistic character, and are not within the scope of this book.

Masonic jewelry. Various articles of jewelry decorated with emblems or insignia of the Freemasons.

Massin, Oscar (b. 1829). A Parisian jeweler born in Liège whose designs emphasized the naturalistic floral patterns that had become popular in the 18th century and who invented the ILLUSION SETTING in the 1860s, using MOUNTS lighter in weight than the attached gemstones and so almost concealed.

massive. Composed of densely-packed crystals of microscopic size but of no regular form, e.g. LAPIS LAZULI. *See* AMORPHOUS.

Master of Animals, The. A pendant of MINOAN JEWELRY, 17th century BC, depicting in cut-out relief work a Nature-god holding in either hand the neck of a water-bird; suspended from the pendant are five discs. The piece is part of the AEGINA TREASURE.

Matara (or Matura) diamond. A local misnomer for a natural colourless or smoky ZIRCON found in the Matara (Maturai) district in southern Sri Lanka (formerly Ceylon).

Mary, Queen of Scots, Signet Ring. Gold with engraved achievement covered with crystal. French (?), *c.* 1548–58 (?). W. 2.25 cm. British Museum, London.

matrix. (1) The natural rock or material in which any crystal or gemstone is embedded. (2) A gemstone, e.g. a TURQUOISE or OPAL, cut with a part of its surrounding matrix. *See* OPAL MATRIX; TURQUOISE MATRIX. The matrix is sometimes not removed so as to provide added strength to the stone, although detracting from its value. (3) A mould or die, made of metal or stone, for casting or pressing an article so as to impart the decorative picture or design that had been made on the matrix, thus permitting repeated production of identical articles. *See* DIE STAMPING.

matrix (3). Bronze. Corcyra, Corfu, *c.* 600 BC. L. 12.3 cm. Ashmolean Museum, Oxford.

Mayan jewelry. Articles of PRE-COLUMBIAN JEWELRY made by the Maya Indians of southern Mexico and Yucatán, and the neighbouring regions of Belize (formerly British Honduras) and Guatemala, mainly during the so-called Old Empire, *c.* AD 317-987, and the New Empire (Classic period) from *c.* 987 until the Spanish conquest by Francisco de Montejo in 1527-46. Gold was not found locally, and metal-working techniques were consequently not well developed, so that most articles of metal jewelry that have been found in the region were imported from Costa Rica and Panama. The principal objects were large discs, possibly breastplates, worked with intricate REPOUSSÉ designs and made of thin gold backed by wood or of gilded copper. The local jewelry was made principally of JADE, and included pendants, NOSE ORNAMENTS, LABRETS, necklaces, bracelets, and ANKLETS. Much of the extant jewelry was recovered by Edward H. Thompson by dredging, 1904-7, a well, known as the Cenote of Sacrifice, at Chichén Itzá, Yucatán, Mexico, where offerings to the rain god had been thrown. *See* MEXICAN JEWELRY. *See* Samuel K. Lothrop, *Metals from the Cenote of Sacrifice* (1952).

Mazarin cut. The style of cutting a diamond similar to the CUSHION cut, with 16 facets above the GIRDLE and 16 below, plus a large square TABLE and a small square CULET. The style was long ascribed to Cardinal Jules Mazarin (1602-61), but in 1965 Herbert Tillander, of Helsinki, declared that it was invented *c.* 1620, before the period of Mazarin's prominence as a diamond collector, and that no stone so cut was among the MAZARIN DIAMONDS.

Mazarin Diamonds. A collection of 18 diamonds owned by Cardinal Jules Mazarin (1602-61), Chief Minister under Louis XIII and under the regency and early reign of Louis XIV. He bequeathed the collection to the French Crown, stipulating that they should be known as the 'Mazarin Diamonds'. An inventory of 1691 lists the stones with their weights and descriptions, but an inventory of 1791 stated different weights, suggesting that there may have been some recutting or substitutions (the SANCY DIAMOND was stated in 1691 at 53¾ old carats, in 1791 at 33¾ old carats). The diamonds were stolen with other gems from the French Garde Meuble in 1792; 5 were recovered and listed in an inventory of 1818. When the French Crown Jewels were auctioned in 1887, 15 were listed as Mazarin Diamonds, but only 5 were identifiable as being from the previous inventories. Among the Mazarin Diamonds were the Sancy and the MIRROR OF PORTUGAL.

medal medallion. A medal, usually of cast gold, mounted in the form of a MEDALLION, sometimes with enamelled and jewelled mounts, and sometimes hung with pearls. Such pieces were often worn suspended from a chain. They were the subject of gifts in Germany, in the 16th/17th centuries, as a mark of special favour from persons of royalty or nobility whose portrait was on the medal. The medals were frequently made in more than one copy, e.g. three replicas, dated 1612, are known (in the British Museum, the Victoria & Albert Museum, and the Morgan Collection) of one such medallion depicting Maximilian, Archduke of Austria (1558-1620); the medals are set in a circular frame of pierced enamelled scrolls with four shields of arms and suspended by an escutcheon with the arms of Austria. Such medallions are typically German but were adopted in Scandinavia. The German term is *Gnadenpfennig*. See COIN PENDANT.

medallion. A thin flat tablet, usually circular or oval, bearing a portrait, design or inscription. Such pieces were made of GOLD, PORCELAIN, GLASS, IVORY, CORAL, PASTE, etc., and some were decorated with miniature painting, ENAMELLING, ENGRAVING, or a CAMEO, INTAGLIO or carved gemstone. They were used principally for personal adornment, as on a brooch or a pendant, as distinguished from a 'plaque' used mainly for wall

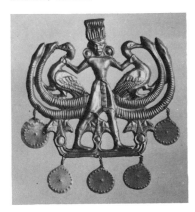

Master of Animals, The. Gold pendant, Minoan, 17th century BC. H. 6 cm. British Museum, London.

Mayan jewelry. Jade pendant carved to depict head of Mayan deity. W. 4 cm. Museum of Mankind, London.

medal medallion. Portrait of Maximilian, Archduke of Austria (1558-1620), German, dated 1612. H. 10 cm. British Museum, London.

medallion. Cameo bust. Venice, 15th century. Walters Art Gallery, Baltimore, Md.

Medici, Carlo de', Cross of (front and back). Gold cross, set with gemstones; reverse engraved and *champlevé* enamel strapwork. Florence (?), 1610-20. Bargello, Florence.

or furniture decoration. Many portrait medallions in relief were made by Josiah Wedgwood in JASPER or black basaltes, and were framed in metal. Such medallions were also made in glass paste by James Tassie (*see* TASSIE MEDALLION). *See* MEDAL MEDALLION.

Medici, Carlo de', Cross of. A gold pendant in the form of a CROSS with equal limbs, the front decorated with alternating large and small TABLE CUT diamonds closely set in square COLLETS, and the reverse smoothly curved and decorated with STRAPWORK silhouettes in translucent CHAMPLEVÉ enamelling. It was made for Carlo de' Medici (1595-1666), probably in Florence, *c.* 1610-20, and was formerly in the Church of S. Lorenzo, Florence.

Medusa. The depiction of the head of Medusa (called a 'Gorgoneion'), often found as a decorative motif carved on a CAMEO. Examples are set in some ear-rings of ROMAN JEWELRY and also in some later brooches (*see* MÖLSHEIM BROOCH). The Medusa head was also carved on some cameos set in Roman finger rings worn because of an amuletic belief; some such finger rings from the 2nd/3rd centuries have been found in Britain. Among other examples are cameos made in Italy in the 16th century.

meerschaum. A whitish to ivory-yellow, smooth, porous mineral composed of crystal fibres and AMORPHOUS material. It is soft and clay-like, and when dry it is light enough to float; when heated it hardens and becomes white. Since the 18th century it has been exported from Asia Minor to Germany where it is made into tobacco-pipe bowls and cigar and cigarette holders, being often ornamentally carved. After use it becomes stained from brown to mahogany colour. It is also carved for some articles of jewelry, e.g. the BEZEL of a finger ring, or an ornament on a brooch. The name is the German word derived from *Meer* (sea) and *Schaum* (foam). Also called SEPIOLITE.

mélange. In the classification of diamonds according to size, small stones of mixed qualities and sizes but larger than stones classified as MÉLÉE.

melanite. A sub-variety of ANDRADITE that is sparkling black. It can be distinguished from other black stones (e.g. CHALCEDONY and TOURMALINE) and black GLASS by its high specific gravity. It is a modern substitute for JET and has been used for MOURNING JEWELRY. Its name is derived from the Greek word *melas* (black).

mélée. (1) In the classification of diamonds according to size, a small stone weighing, if rough, between 0.2 and 1.4 carats (called a 'sawable') and, if cut and polished, between 0.2 and 0.5 carats. Smaller stones are sometimes classified as 'sand'. *See* MÉLANGE. (2) A group of small diamonds set close together but not as compact as in a PAVÉ SETTING.

Melfort Necklace. A necklace of JET from the North British Early Bronze Age, *c.* 1800 BC-1500 BC, found at Melfort, Argyll (now Strathclyde), Scotland, on a skeleton in a cist (stone-lined grave). The

necklace, made of two varieties of jet (one black and well polished, the other brownish and having a crazed surface) consists of: (1) one triangular TOGGLE bead; (2) two triangular TERMINAL BEADS, decorated in POINTILLÉ technique; (3) six trapeze-shaped SPACER beads, also with *pointillé* decoration; and (4) 51 FUSIFORM BEADS of various dimensions (longest, 2.8 cm). Examples of such necklaces, that imitate the form of the LUNULA, have been found in Scotland and also in northern and eastern England.

Melillo, Giacinto (1846-1915). A Neapolitan jeweller and goldsmith whose designs were in Classical style but adapted to his own interpretations. He also made some pieces by the CIRE PERDUE process. Some of his reproductions of ancient jewelry, inspired by the work of the Casa Castellani (*see* FORTUNATO PIO CASTELLANI), for which he worked, were sometimes sold by unscrupulous dealers as antique. His pieces are rarely signed (mark: 'G M') and are usually identifiable only by their fitted and labelled wooden cases. *See* Geoffrey Munn, 'Giacinto Melillo', in *Connoisseur*, September 1977, p. 20.

melon bead. A type of bead of ETRUSCAN JEWELRY that is hollow, globular, and ribbed. Such beads were made during the Early Etruscan Period. The process involved the making of two equal hemispherical pieces by beating gold sheet into a mould and then SOLDERING together the two sections.

memento mori (Latin). Literally, remember you must die. A motif used as decoration on various articles in the form of a reminder of mortality, e.g. as a coffin, a death's-head or a skeleton. Such pieces were not in remembrance of a departed person, but were an abstract warning of death, especially in the 16th and 17th centuries. They include finger rings, brooches, enseignes, pendants, watch cases, pomanders, etc. The articles were usually made of gold with black enamelled motifs or set with gemstones. *See* MOURNING JEWELRY; TOR ABBEY JEWEL.

memorial jewelry. The same as MOURNING JEWELRY.

menet bird. A bird used as a motif in EGYPTIAN JEWELRY, portrayed supporting on its back a globe symbolizing the sun. The bird, believed originally to be a swallow, was identified by Howard Carter as an Egyptian swift. It is said to have provided an image into which people could be metamorphized after death, but also possibly it symbolized a minor deity. An example in CORNELIAN is among the TUTANKHAMUN JEWELRY

menilite. A variety of COMMON OPAL that is found in brownish or dull grey concretions. It was named after Ménilmontant, near Paris, where it was found. Also called 'liver opal'.

merchant's-mark ring. A type of finger ring bearing on the BEZEL an arbitrary distinctive engraved device, as the mark of a merchant not entitled to a coat of arms, but recognizable by those with whom he dealt. Such rings, usually of silver or bronze, rarely gold, were used in Europe in the 14th to 16th centuries. *See* F. A. Girling, *English Merchants' Marks* (1962).

mercuric gilding. *See* GILDING.

mermaid pendant. A type of pendant in the form of a mermaid, the torso being a BAROQUE PEARL and the head, arms, and tail being enamelled gold set with gemstones, and having suspended pearls. One example, set with diamonds, a ruby and red stones, has been attributed to south Germany, *c.* 1580-85. *See* BAROQUE PEARL JEWEL.

Merovingian jewelry. Articles of jewelry made during the dynasty of the early Frankish kings from *c.* 481 to *c.* 751 (after which period, under Charlemagne, the custom of burying objects with the deceased was discontinued), found throughout Europe, but principally in Belgium and the Rhineland, hence the surmise that they were made there. Such jewelry is sometimes called 'Frankish jewelry' or 'Teutonic jewelry'. Characteristic are CLOISONNÉ INLAYS of coloured gemstones and animal

Medusa. Pendant with chalcedony cameo in enamelled gold frame set with gemstones. North Italian, probably Milanese, 16th century. W. 6.8 cm. National Gallery of Art (Widener Collection), Washington, DC.

meerschaum. High-relief ornament on gold brooch. Italian, *c.* 1840. H. 5.5 cm. Metropolitan Museum of Art, New York.

Melillo, Giacinto. Gold brooch with figures of child and birds among flowers. W. 3.75 cm. Courtesy of Wartski, London.

menet bird. Cornelian bird supporting the sun's disc; to be mounted by a swivel on a bracelet. Tomb of Tutankhamun. Photograph by Egyptian Expedition, Metropolitan Museum of Art, New York.

mermaid pendant. Baroque pearl and enamelled gold with gemstones. South German, *c*. 1580-85. W. 7.6 cm. Chain, Italian, *c*. 1570. National Gallery of Art (Widener Collection), Washington, DC.

Merovingian jewelry. Circular brooch of gold and silver, set with garnets and *pâte de verre*. 7th century. W. 4.3 cm. Römisch-Germanisches Museum, Cologne.

and bird motifs. The articles included the RADIATED FIBULA, BIRD FIBULA, and DISC BROOCH, also large polygonal ornaments suspended from earrings, finger rings, seal rings, and large bronze, copper, iron or silver inlaid buckles. *See* CAROLINGIAN JEWELRY.

metal-capped bead. A type of bead found in Egypt, from the XIIth Dynasty, *c*. 1991 BC–1784 BC, capped at each end with a silver or gold disc with a central hole over which a small tube is soldered; the tubes cover an inner cylinder of rolled metal stuck into the hole of the bead. Some metal-capped INLAID BEADS have been found among SUMERIAN JEWELRY.

metallic lustre. The type of LUSTRE shown by polished metal, the highest form of lustre, or by MARCASITE or OPAQUE gemstones (e.g. HEMATITE), appearing when the refractive index is more than 2.5. Sub-metallic lustre is somewhat less.

metamict stone. A stone whose crystal structure has been subjected to radioactivity, which resulted in the gradual disintegration of its crystals so that it has become AMORPHOUS. Examples are ekanite and green ZIRCON.

meteorite. A metallic or stony body that has fallen to earth from outer space as a fragment from a meteor. They usually show a pitted surface with a fused crust, due to the intense heat created by the rapid travel through the atmosphere. Pieces of meteorites have been worn for centuries as jewelry, usually as a TALISMAN. In recent years they have been incorporated in jewelry made by GILBERT ALBERT.

Mexican jade. JADEITE, found in Central America, which is more mottled and opaque than Oriental jade. It has been found in many shades of green, as well as ranging from grey to white. It was much used in PRE-COLUMBIAN JEWELRY by the early Indians. In modern usage the term 'Mexican jade' is often a misnomer for a green-dyed variety of calcite or ONYX.

Mexican jewelry. Articles of jewelry made: (1) from *c*. AD 700–900, during the pre-Columbian period and until the conquest by Hernando Cortés, *c*. 1520 (*see* OLMEC JEWELRY; MAYAN JEWELRY; AZTEC JEWELRY; MIXTEC JEWELRY; TOLTEC JEWELRY; TARASCAN JEWELRY; ZAPOTEC JEWELRY; YANHUITLÁN BROOCH); (2) later by European craftsmen in Renaissance style and by peasants in various indigenous styles (*see* YALALAG CROSS; PÁTZCUARO FISH NECKLACE), such peasant articles including mainly crosses, crucifixes, heart pendants, coin jewelry, gold HALOS, *milagros* (ex-voto replicas of parts of the body cured by prayer, as well as of animals, babies, broken hearts, all usually of gold, sometimes of silver), and combs (e.g. *peinetas* of carved TORTOISE SHELL and *cachirulos* of semi-circular tortoise shell with wide gold or jewelled bands along the top); and (3) from *c*. 1930 by designers and silversmiths who created the jewelry centre at Taxco, near Mexico City, developing new styles introduced by William Spratling and his numerous followers of recent years who produce a great variety of traditional and modern jewelry, mainly of silver and often decorated with turquoise, and much of it made for the tourist trade.

Mielich (or **Muelich**), **Hans** (1516–73). A German court artist working in Munich at the Court of Albrecht V of Wittelsbach, Duke of Bavaria, from 1550. Although not a designer of jewelry, he made in 1552–5 a series of painted illustrations for the inventory (*Kleinedienbuch*) of the jewelry in the collection of Anne of Austria, wife of Albrecht, and also of some jewelry belonging to Albrecht. The only article in the inventory known to have survived is a collar of the Order of St George. The articles often featured on the backs delicate Moresque patterns. Another such pictorial inventory was made by ARNOLD LULLS.

Mignot, Daniel (fl. 1590-1616). A French goldsmith who was a Huguenot refugee to Augsburg. He produced from 1596 to 1616 a series of engraved designs for pendants decorated in MORESQUE SILHOUETTE STYLE. His work represented a transition from the designers of the late 16th century, who emphasized the design of the goldwork, to those who introduced designs that featured engraved and enamelled STRAP-WORK and cartouches and also pieces set with gemstones. Some of his designs showed three sections of a jewel: a backplate pierced in a strapwork pattern, a plate to be jewelled and pinned on, and a plate for a separate rosette.

Milanese paste. A type of PASTE made in the 15th and 16th centuries by jewellers in Milan who specialized in pastework, imitating EMERALD and SAPPHIRE, as mentioned by BENVENUTO CELLINI in his writings.

military insignia. Articles worn by members of the military forces, such as badges, medals, etc., some being made of a precious metal and occasionally set with small gemstones of colours appropriate to the member's unit.

milk opal. A variety of COMMOM OPAL that is translucent and milky. When it includes DENDRITES it is called MOSS OPAL.

millefiori (Italian). Literally, a thousand flowers. A style of ornamented glass made from slices of canes of coloured glass embedded in clear glass, usually in flower-like designs. The style was known in Alexandria from the 3rd century BC and in Rome in the 1st century AD, but it was so called only after it was revived and modified at Venice in the 16th century. Such *millefiori* slices have been used to decorate some articles of jewelry, e.g. brooches and finger rings, especially at Venice.

millegrain decoration. A style of decoration made by passing a knurling tool over a metal strip, the wheel of the tool having indentations to form the pattern.

millegrain setting. A style of SETTING a gemstone in a finger ring by which the GIRDLE of the stone is secured in the COLLET by a series of minute adjacent beads (grains) of metal that are raised by passing a knurling tool (millgrain tool) around the top edge of the collet and that are bent over the girdle of the stone. This style was developed in the 19th century. *See* GRAIN SETTING.

Milton Brooch. A gold DISC BROOCH decorated with a pattern of CHIP-CARVING in which are four bosses around one large central boss, all made of some material originally white, probably ivory or shell. It is English, 7th century, and was found at the village of Milton, near the town of Abingdon (hence sometimes called the 'Abingdon Brooch'), in Oxfordshire, England.

miniature. A very small painting, usually a portrait, made on IVORY, metal, etc. Such pieces were worn as jewelry suspended from bracelets or necklaces, or to ornament the clasps on such objects or some brooches and finger rings. They were often used to decorate MOURNING JEWELRY. A chain at the Victoria & Albert Museum includes miniatures depicting girls wearing different Swiss regional costumes; *see* SWISS ENAMELLING.

miniature case. A type of case, similar to a LOCKET, used to enclose a MINIATURE, but without a ring for suspension from a chain.

miniature jewelry. Tiny articles in the form of normal pieces of jewelry (e.g. bracelets and brooches) made in extremely small size, to be placed on mannequin dolls to display fashions current in the 19th century. Such pieces are distinct from some jewelry specially made in small size for use by children.

Minoan jewelry. Articles of jewelry made in Crete during the Minoan civilization, named after the mythical King Minos. The examples in gold from the Early Minoan Period (*c*. 2500 BC-2000 BC), found mainly in eastern Crete near Mochlos, show Babylonian influences. In the Middle Minoan Period (*c*. 2000 BC-1600 BC), techniques of Western Asia were introduced. The Late Minoan Period was *c*. 1600 BC-1100 BC, but from *c*. 1450 BC the styles and techniques were influenced by the conquering Mycenaeans (*see* MYCENAEAN JEWELRY). Only a few articles of jewelry were found by Sir Arthur Evans (1851-1941) in his excavation from 1899 to 1930 at Knossos in Crete. Many examples of Minoan jewelry from the 17th century BC are said to have been found on the island of Aegina; *see* AEGINA TREASURE. The gold Minoan jewelry of the Middle Period has decoration of FILIGREE and GRANULATED GOLD, and some has inlaid

Mexican jewelry. Mid-section of cast gold ear ornament depicting coxcoxti bird. Mixtec culture, *c*. 1400-1520. H. 10 cm. Museum für Völkerkunde, West Berlin.

millegrain decoration. Gold pendant with millegrain decoration and set with diamonds. Fabergé, *c*. 1900. Courtesy of Wartski, London.

Milton Brooch. Gold disc brooch with chip-carving. English, 7th century. Ashmolean Museum, Oxford.

miniature case. Gold with enamelled decoration, enclosing early 17th-century miniature of Henry III of France. British Museum, London.

Minster Lovel Jewel. Gold mount with granulated gold and *cloisonné* enamel. Anglo-Saxon, 9th century. L. 3 cm. Ashmolean Museum, Oxford.

gemstones in CLOISONNÉ settings. The articles include pendants, bracelets, necklaces, hair pins, diadems, beads, finger rings, and (from *c.* 1700 BC) ear-rings. Some early pieces were made of thin gold foil beaten around other materials. During the Middle Period engraved gemstones were carved as seals. *See* HORNET PENDANT; CAGE.

Minster Lovel Jewel. A gold mount, probably for a stave or pointer (*aestel*) having a socket with a cross-rivet. Within a circular bent wire and granulated setting above the socket there is a roundel of CLOISONNÉ enamel on gold; its design on a dark-blue ground is a four-pointed green star with a white centre and with white cells at the tips of the points of the star, and between the points hoop-shaped cells of light-blue enamel. The reverse is plain. Its purpose has not been determined, but possibly it was the head of a pointer or even the foot of the pointer topped by the ALFRED JEWEL, with which it has some similarities. It is Anglo-Saxon, from the late 9th century. It was found *c.* 1860 at Minster Lovel, near Oxford, and was presented by Rev. John Wilson, President of Trinity College, Oxford, to the Ashmolean Museum, Oxford.

minuterie (French). A word used loosely with various meanings: (1) miscellaneous small articles such as were worn attached to a CHATELAINE; (2) articles of jewelry that are decorated by STAMPING; (3) as used by Italian writers, articles of jewelry worn on the person (*minuteria*) as distinguished from *grosseria*, applied to articles made of precious materials for household use or ornament.

mirror foiling. A technique of FOILING by which a colourless transparent stone was painted on the back with an amalgam (an ALLOY of mercury) in the manner of a mirror, so that the amalgam was in contact with the stone, unlike foiling with a metallic LEAF that was attached to the supporting metal. It has been used since *c.* 1840, especially to give a colour to PASTE and so that it could be set in an OPEN SETTING. *See* REFLECTOR.

Mirror of Great Britain. An ENSEIGNE in the form of a lozenge-shaped jewel, set with a gemstone at each corner (1 large TABLE CUT ruby, 1 table cut diamond, and 2 smaller diamonds, one of which was known as 'The letter H of Scotland' and 'The Great Harry') and having suspended the SANCY DIAMOND. The jewel was made to commemorate the union of England and Scotland in 1604, and is shown in a portrait of James I (1566–1625). It, together with the THREE BROTHERS JEWEL and another hat ornament known as 'The Feather', was pawned by James I and in 1642 was sold on the Continent by Henrietta Maria, the wife of Charles I. *See* Roy Strong, 'Three Royal Jewels', in *Burlington Magazine*, CVIII, July 1966, p. 350.

Mirror of Portugal. A diamond, weighing 25⅜ old carats, that was in the 16th century among the Crown Jewels of Portugal. When King Henry died in 1580 and his illegitimate nephew Don Antonio de Castro claimed the throne but was defeated by Philip II of Spain, he took the diamond and other jewels to England to raise funds. He pledged them to Elizabeth I for naval assistance, and she kept them. The large diamond remained in the English Crown Jewels under James I and later Charles I until his wife, Queen Henrietta Maria, took them in 1644 to France to raise funds on them. She pawned them (with the SANCY DIAMOND) to the Duke of Éperon, who sold them to Cardinal Mazarin (*see* MAZARIN DIAMONDS). It was among the jewels stolen in 1792 from the Garde Meuble and never recovered.

mirror pendant. A type of pendant having on the back a small mirror, such as were worn by ladies in the late 15th/early 16th centuries. In some cases the front was decorated with a Biblical subject.

mise en couleur (French). The same as DEPLETION GILDING.

Miseroni, Ottavio (fl. 1585–1624). A Milanese gem-cutter who was brought to Prague in 1588 by Rudolf II, King of Hungary and Bohemia, and became Court Lapidary. He, with his son Dionysio, carved a PORTRAIT CAMEO of Rudolf. Later he developed a version of the COMMESSO technique that was more like mosaic in relief. After the death of Rudolf in 1616, Ottavio did some work for Empress Anna, consort of Matthias, Rudolf's brother and successor, and had charge of the Kunstkammer; his son took charge of the workshop.

Mississippi pearl. A variety of FRESH-WATER PEARL found in the Mississippi Valley in the United States, including pearls from the PEARL MUSSEL and the NIGGERHEAD. Such pearls are generally of irregular shape and are of comparatively little value.

Mistress of the Beasts, The. A depiction of a Winged Artemis standing between two lions rampant, executed in relief (by stamping or moulding or by being made as separate figures soldered to the base), found on gold rectangular plaques made to be worn as a PECTORAL ornament. The figure of Artemis was a popular motif in RHODIAN JEWELRY of the 7th century BC, sometimes being accompanied by birds, occasionally without attributes; such figures are shown on some individual plaques found in tombs at Camirus, Rhodes.

mixed cut. The style of cutting a diamond (or other transparent gemstone) with two different cuts, e.g. the CROWN being BRILLIANT CUT and the PAVILION being STEP CUT or sometimes vice versa. The depth of the two parts is not fixed, so they can be cut deeper or shallower to enhance the colour. In some variations the TABLE is additionally cut with square facets in a chequerboard fashion.

Mixtec jewelry. Articles of PRE-COLUMBIAN JEWELRY made by the Mixtec Indians who settled in the Oaxaca region of southern Mexico, c. AD 1000, during the decline of the Zapotec culture. The Mixtecs were skilled craftsmen in gold and silver, making small pieces of jewelry cast with FALSE FILIGREE by the CIRE PERDUE process, some with ARTICULATED ornaments. They made jewelry of JADE, ONYX, TURQUOISE, ROCK CRYSTAL, and OBSIDIAN, and also carved SHELL and BONE. Their articles included pendants with cast gold anthropomorphic heads having articulated earrings and suspended CASCABELES, sectional EAR ORNAMENTS depicting heads of mythical birds, and brooches (a rare example is of stone inlaid with gold). Finger rings were made, some with false filigree, some with attached pendants, and some with cast heads of local gods. A large TREASURE of Mixtec jewelry has been found at Monte Albán, at Tehuantepec, Oaxaca. *See* MONTE ALBÁN TREASURE; YANHUITLÁN BROOCH; BACK ORNAMENT; TIGER'S-CLAW JEWELRY; MEXICAN JEWELRY.

Mizpah ring. A type of finger ring in the form of a wide gold band having on it the engraved or embossed word *Mizpah* (literally, 'watchtower', but in modern use a Hebraic parting salutation). It was worn as a TALISMAN, especially as a gift to departing soldiers, the name implying watchfulness by the donor, being derived from a parting salutation in Genesis xxxi, 49.

Mocha stone. A variety of AGATE that is sometimes regarded as the same as MOSS AGATE, but more commonly it is the variety with black or brown dendritic markings. The name is derived from the port of Mocha, on the Red Sea coast of Yemen.

Mochica jewelry. Articles of PRE-COLUMBIAN JEWELRY made by the Mochica (or Moche) Indians living in the north Peruvian coastal region,

Miseroni, Ottavio. Pendant with jasper cameo by Miseroni (?), Prague, c. 1600, in jewelled mount. German, 18th century. H. 25 cm. Schatzkammer, Residenz, Munich.

Mistress of the Beasts, The. Relief gold plaques from pectoral ornament, with granulation. Rhodian. 7th/5th centuries BC. H. 4.2 cm. British Museum, London.

Mixtec jewelry. Cast gold pendant depicting human figure wearing movable ear ornaments and mask suspended from lip-plug. *c.* 1000 1500. H. 8.5 cm. Museum of Mankind, London.

c. AD 300–600. Although their culture is known mainly from their architecture and pottery, they made jewelry of gold, silver, copper, bone, and shell. Most of the techniques of working metal were known to them by the 4th century AD, including simple and CIRE PERDUE casting, REPOUSSÉ work, enamelling, and alloying, as well as the making of mosaics with coloured stones. Large quantities of such jewelry, for adornment of the living and for burial with the dead, have been found, including bracelets, diadems, pendants, and ear-rings. Also found are a ceremonial cloak made of gold discs and gold gloves worn by deceased nobility and priests. *See* PERUVIAN JEWELRY.

mock-champlevé. A style of ENAMELLING on the surface of metal that imitates the appearance of CHAMPLEVÉ enamel in engraved cells. It is found on some ANGLO-SAXON JEWELRY in the SUTTON HOO TREASURE. *See* SHOULDER CLASP.

Mohs' scale. A scale for measuring the HARDNESS (resistance to abrasion or scratching) of a specimen of mineral or other hard substance, prepared in 1812 by the Austrian mineralogist Friedrich Mohs (1773–1839), being a series of ten specified minerals in the order of their relative hardness — the intervals between the listed minerals not being equal or proportionate — against which the specimen is rated. The minerals on the scale are: (1) talc; (2) gypsum; (3) calcite; (4) fluorspar; (5) apatite; (6) orthoclase (feldspar); (7) quartz; (8) topaz; (9) sapphire (corundum); (10) diamond. Intermediate measurements are indicated by fractions. All the important gemstones have a hardness of at least 5, but PEARL and CORAL are lower.

moldavite. A variety of tektite (natural glass) that has been found since 1787 near the Vltava River (in German, Moldau, hence the name) in Bohemia and Moravia (now Czechoslovakia). It is transparent and bottle-green to greenish-brown. It is occasionally used as a gemstone, being FACETED and polished. It is sometimes called 'bottle-stone' or 'water-chrysolite'.

mollusc cameo. *See* SHELL CAMEO.

mollusc shell. The calcareous SHELL of all the species generally called 'shellfish' other than crustaceans, and including the oyster, clam, mussel, sea-snail (including porcelain snail), conch, top shell, round-mouthed shell, NAUTILUS, and ABALONE. In addition to the pearls produced by some molluscs, all of these have shells which are used, owing to the nacreous lining, to make buttons, beads, and other inexpensive articles of jewelry, as well as set in slices in jewelry. Some such shells are used to make SHELL CAMEOS. *See* PEARL OYSTER; PEARL MUSSEL; ANTILLES PEARL; BURMESE SHELL; OPERCULUM; COWRIE SHELL.

Mölsheim Brooch. A brooch (sometimes called a FIBULA) made of ornamented gold mounted on a brass base. It is basically of square shape, but with hemispherical protrusions on each side in which are set pieces of green PASTE in circular COLLETS, alternating with like paste set in square collets at each corner, and each such piece of paste alternating with drop-shaped ALMANDINES. In the centre there is a raised collet holding a CAMEO of triple-banded AGATE carved with a portrait of MEDUSA. The gold ground is decorated with a FILIGREE pattern. The piece was made in the 7th/8th centuries, and found at Mölsheim, near Worms, Germany. It has been said to indicate the transition from MEROVINGIAN JEWELRY to CAROLINGIAN JEWELRY.

Moncornet, Balthazar (fl. *c.* 1670). A painter and engraver who worked in Rouen and Paris, and who published a book of jewelry designs in 1670. His designs show pendants, ear-rings, and brooches set with gemstones, accompanied by designs of garlands of natural flowers. *See* HORTICULTURAL STYLE.

monde. A globular ornament, similar to an ORB, usually of small size, that rests at the intersection of the two arches of a closed CROWN or at the top of a SCEPTRE, or on a sceptre below a cross or an emblem (such as a dove) that is superimposed on the monde. Sometimes the monde, instead of being gold, is formed by a globular gemstone, as the amethyst monde on the British Sovereign's Sceptre (*see* SCEPTRES, THE ROYAL).

Mölsheim Brooch. Gold with almandines and green paste, and central agate cameo of Medusa. 7th/8th centuries. W. 8 cm. Hessiches Landesmuseum, Darmstadt.

monkey. A decorative motif found on some NOSE ORNAMENTS of PRE-COLUMBIAN JEWELRY, sometimes as REPOUSSÉ work and sometimes in silhouette form along the edge of a flat angled strip extending almost horizontally on each side of the nose. The motif is found also on some EAR ORNAMENTS. Such pieces are found in NARIÑO JEWELRY.

Monkton Brooch. A COMPOSITE BROOCH of which the front is gold, decorated with an inner band and a border of CLOISONNÉ INLAY, connected by four points making a star-like design, between the points being four circles of cloisonné inlay, each of them enclosing a CABOCHON ornament (three missing); the back-plate was reused from another brooch and shows the markings of a CLOISONNÉ pattern. Some of the cloisons are of bronze rather than gold. It was found in 1971 during an excavation two miles from Sarre, in Kent, and its workmanship has been criticized as greatly inferior to that of the SARRE DISC BROOCH and the AMHERST BROOCH. It dates from the 6th/7th centuries, and was purchased by the Ashmolean Museum, Oxford, in 1972.

monogram pendant. A type of pendant made in the form of, or featuring in its design, an openwork monogram, sometimes enamelled or set with gemstones. Such pieces became important during the 16th and 17th centuries. Several are said to have been designed by HANS HOLBEIN THE YOUNGER for Henry VIII, incorporating his initial and sometimes that of one of his wives or daughters or of his sister. Some such pendants have been thought to have been made by HANS MIELICH. *See* AA PENDANT; LYTE JEWEL; IHS PENDANT; VENERA.

Monte Albán Treasure. A TREASURE of PRE-COLUMBIAN JEWELRY and other articles discovered in 1932 by Dr Alfonso Caso in Tomb 7 at Monte Albán (the sacred 'White Mountain' of the Zapotec Indians) near Oaxaca, in southern Mexico. The tomb was used first by the Zapotec Indians and later, after the 10th century and until shortly before the arrival of the Spanish Conquistadors, by the Mixtec Indians, to whom the articles have been ascribed. They are mostly of cast gold, some of silver or copper, with decoration of FALSE FILIGREE and REPOUSSÉ work, including PECTORAL ornaments, pendants, and necklaces with CASCABELES, as well as finger rings, ear-rings, and nose ornaments. Also found were beads and carved objects of gold, onyx, rock crystal, jade, turquoise, pearl, amber, jet, OBSIDIAN, and bone, and some wooden articles decorated with mosaic. Among the most important articles are the PECTORAL OF THE UNIVERSE and the gold pectoral (11 cm high), *c.* 1412–65, depicting 'The Lord of the Dead', the local deity, wearing a jaguar head-dress and a mask over the lower part of his face and having two suspended flat rectangles with calendrical notations. The treasure is now in the Regional Museum, Oaxaca, Mexico. *See* MEXICAN JEWELRY; MIXTEC JEWELRY.

Montezuma's head-dress. An Aztec head-dress now in Vienna that is often said to have been given to Hernando Cortés by Montezuma, the Aztec ruler, but in fact is one of hundreds of similar head-dresses that existed in Mexico at the time and of dozens that were brought to Europe. It is composed of a circular band of feathers (mainly green quetzal feathers, but some blue and red feathers), to which are affixed variously shaped small plaques sewn on in horizontal rows (the original plaques being of gold with silver content, but some replacement parts from 1878 being of gold-plated brass). Originally there was attached to the section above the forehead a small golden bird's head ornament which made the head-dress appear to be a bird perched on the wearer's head; but the ornament was stolen in the 18th century. The German term for such a piece is *Federkopfschmuck.*

Monte Albán Treasure. Cast gold finger rings. Mixtec culture. Oaxaca, Mexico, *c.* 1250–1500. Museum of the American Indian, Heye Foundation, New York.

moonstone. A variety of orthoclase FELDSPAR that is transparent or translucent. When cut EN CABOCHON, it has a SHEEN known as ADULARESCENCE, due to including alternate layers of albite which spread the light falling on the dome. The colour of the sheen is bluish on the finest stones, and whitish on more common stones having thicker layers. The stones are almost always cut as cabochons, and sometimes show CHATOYANCY in the form of a translucent band that merges into a transparent band of ADULARIA. Moonstone has been imitated in GLASS and also by SYNTHETIC SPINEL that has been heated. 'Black moonstone' is a misnomer for a dark variety of LABRADORITE, and 'pink moonstone' for pink scapolite. *See* BLUE MOONSTONE; CENTIPEDE.

Montezuma's head-dress. Coloured feathers with gold plaques. *c.* 1520. H. 1.15 m. Völkermuseum, Vienna.

mordant. A metal piece, sometimes jewelled, enclosing one end of a belt or girdle and opposite the end attached to the BUCKLE, the purpose being to enable the end to pass easily through the buckle. Also called a 'chape' or 'buckle tag'. Sometimes the buckle and the mordant were made so as to result in a unified design when attached.

More, Sir Thomas, Crucifix. A gold crucifix pendant, *c.* 1520-30, with three pendent pearls and on the detachable back-plate a Renaissance-style decoration in black NIELLO and a Greek inscription (translated) 'This is a relic of Thomas the Apostle'. It was mentioned by George Vertue (*Note Books*, Vol. II) as being owned in 1728 by Thomas More, Esq., a descendant of Sir Thomas More (St Thomas More, 1477/8?-1535), Lord Chancellor of Henry VIII. It (together with the SIR THOMAS MORE PENDANT) was presented in 1775 by Thomas More (1722-95), a Jesuit Father who called himself 'the last of the family of Sir Thomas More', to the Jesuit College at St Omers, France, and was taken by the College when it moved to Bruges (1762), to Liège (1773), and finally to Stonyhurst, Lancashire, England (1794).

More, Sir Thomas, Pendant. A pendant presented in 1775 by Thomas More, a Jesuit Father, to the Jesuit College at St Omers, France (*see* MORE, SIR THOMAS, CRUCIFIX). The pendant consists of two enamelled gold roundels in a gold frame, one depicting the mounted figure of St George slaying the dragon, with the figure of the Princess in the background, and the other the figure of Christ risen from the open sepulchre, together with the busts (cast in gold and attached by clips) of those who betrayed or denied him, and also some of the emblems of the Passion. Both sides of the frame have a narrow circular rim decorated with enamelled flowers and having around the edge a Latin inscription from Virgil's *Aeneid*. Enclosed is a badly faded miniature portrait that may be of Sir Thomas More. The origin of the pendant is unknown. It has been said that 'It does not appear to be of English manufacture' (Joan Evans, *A History of Jewellery*, 1953, p. 81) and also that it is 'no doubt' not from an English workshop, but is probably Italian, late 15th century (Hugh Tait, 'Historiated Tudor Jewellery', in *Antiquaries Journal*, XLII, 1962, p. 244); on the other hand, it has been suggested, based on stylistic grounds, that it (and the Sir Thomas More Crucifix) were designed by HANS HOLBEIN THE YOUNGER and executed in the third quarter of the 16th century, not in Italy, but in London by an Antwerp goldsmith, and that the original unknown donor may have been Erasmus or a relative of Sir Thomas More (Yvonne Hackenbroch, 'Two Relics of Sir Thomas More', in *Connoisseur*, January 1977, p. 43).

Moresque silhouette style. A style of decoration on jewelry, used in the late 16th and early 17th centuries, which was in the form of intricate filigree-like patterns, mingling the earlier Moresque style with scrollwork, executed in black enamel in the manner of silhouette decoration. Among its exponents were ÉTIENNE DELAUNE, HANS COLLAERT THE ELDER, and THÉODORE DE BRY, and later CORVINIANUS SAUR, DANIEL MIGNOT, VALENTIN SEZENIUS, and GUILLAUME DE LA QUEWELLERIE. The German term is *Schweifgrotteske*. A related style is found on some articles decorated in NIELLO. Such designs were used to decorate completely some pieces of jewelry, but more often were used as motifs to decorate borders and other details; they were used on the shoulders of finger rings and on watch cases.

Moresques. Decorative motifs similar to ARABESQUES, especially those derived from Moorish sources in Spain and Sicily, both of which were at one time under Saracen domination. The term is also sometimes applied to motifs based on Roman decorative motifs which are more usually termed GROTESQUES. *See* MORESQUE SILHOUETTE STYLE.

morganite. A variety of BERYL that is rose-pink, owing to the presence of lithium. It was named after John Pierpont Morgan (1837-1913).

morion. A variety of SMOKY QUARTZ that is dark smoky-brown or blackish.

moroxite. A variety of APATITE that is blue or bluish-green.

More, Sir Thomas, Crucifix (front and back). Gold crucifix with pendant pearls and niello back. *c.* 1520-30. H. 9.5 cm. Stonyhurst College, Lancashire, England.

morse. A type of CLASP primarily for fastening a cope in front, for use by the clergy and decorated with a representation of a religious subject. Such clasps are often very large, known examples being from 12.5 to 17.5 cm in diameter, and are of various materials and shapes, with decoration of ENAMELLING, CHAMPLEVÉ, BASSE TAILLE, gemstones, cameos, etc. Most examples were made to be fixed to one side of the cope and attached to the other side by a pin or hook, but others were meant to be only decorative, being hung by a ring or sewn on through a suspensory hole. The French term is *mors de chape*. *See* NOUCH.

mosaic (as applied to portable objects, including articles of jewelry, rather than to architectural mosaic embedded in cement in floors, walls, and ceilings of churches and rooms). An object decorated with many small adjacent pieces (*tesserae*) of inlaid varicoloured glass or stone arranged to form a picture or design. For articles of jewelry, the mosaic was usually made in the form of medallions set in brooches, pendants, necklaces, finger rings, ear-rings, parures, etc. Such work has been done principally in Italy, some being executed with skill and artistry in the 19th century, but many pieces being made in recent years as tourist souvenirs, with large *tesserae* of stone or glass that are roughly set, and sometimes with some painted portions. Pieces of good quality were mounted in gold frames, including some made by the Casa Castellani in Rome (*see* FORTUNATO PIO CASTELLANI). The fashion for mosaic jewelry in England was mainly in the period 1820–60. Mosaic work in jewelry was of two types: (1) Roman or Byzantine mosaic, with the *tesserae* made of glass, set into molten glass, and fused together; (2) FLORENTINE MOSAIC. (Venetian mosaic, made of slices of coloured glass canes, usually making a *millefiori* pattern, was seldom used for pieces of jewelry.) In both types the decorative motifs were often pictorial views of ancient ruins or famous buildings, and in the 1820s Egyptian motifs, but by the mid-19th century the usual subjects had become more sentimental, e.g. flowers and pet dogs. The Florentine mosaic was imitated in Derbyshire, England, in the late 18th to early 19 century, by using local black marble and feldspar.

mosquito agate. A variety of AGATEZ having the layers broken so as to resemble a multitude of tiny irregular-shaped black forms suggestive of mosquitoes.

mosquito agate. A variety of AGATE that has black, red, brown or green moss-like or dendritic markings (DENDRITES) due to the INCLUSIONS of various other minerals projecting from the outer skin into the main mass, sometimes producing a 'scenic agate'. Also called MOCHA STONE. The stone was sometimes simulated by enamelling on plaques set into snuff boxes. *See* TREE AGATE; GAINSBOROUGH RING.

moss opal. A variety of COMMON OPAL (MILK OPAL) that contains INCLUSIONS of DENDRITES which produce a moss-like pattern.

mother-of-pearl. The hard, smooth IRIDESCENT inner lining of the shell of certain molluscs (e.g. PEARL, OYSTER, abalone, nautilus, river mussel), consisting chiefly of plates of calcium carbonate (in the form of aragonite or calcite) secreted by the MANTLE in thin overlapping plates and cemented together with an organic substance, conchiolin, to form the iridescent substance known as NACRE. The iridescent effect is due to the interference of light reflected by the layers of nacre. The iridescence can be destroyed by exposure to sunlight, so that the shell is then said to be 'blind'. The principal producer is the large Australian pearl oyster (*Pinctada margaritifera*) rather than the pearl-producing variety (*Pinctada vulgaris*). It has been used in thin slices for decorative inlays, but also for some jewelry, e.g. carved pendants and buttons.

mount (or **mounting**). The metal framework in which gemstones are set to make various articles of jewelry.

mourning jewelry. Various articles of jewelry worn in memory of a deceased person during periods of mourning, the styles of which underwent changes from the impersonalized MEMENTO MORI jewelry of the Middle Ages and the 16th and early 17th centuries to the specifically commemorative pieces of the late 17th century and onwards. Throughout the period such jewelry preserving hair of the deceased was popular, and

More, Sir Thomas, Pendant. Gold enamelled roundels joined to enclose miniature portrait. 3rd quarter of 16th century (?). W. 6.6 cm. Stonyhurst College, Lancashire, England.

morse. Gold. French, 16th century. Victoria & Albert Museum, London.

mosaic. Finger ring with glass mosaic. Italian, 19th century. Schmuckmuseum, Pforzheim, Germany.

mouthpiece. Gold sheet with repoussé design (showing lips). Cypro-Mycenaean, *c.* 1400 BC–1300 BC. L. 10 cm. Ashmolean Museum, Oxford.

muff chain. Gold with hand-shaped clasp. English, 18th century. Courtesy of Wartski, London.

Mughal jewelry. Neck ornament. Gold with enamelling, gemstones, and pearls. Indian, 18th century. Victoria & Albert Museum, London.

in the 19th century jewelry was made of such hair (*see* HAIR JEWELRY). The jewelry was decorated with sentimental motifs from the Romantic period of the late 18th century onwards; frequent motifs were a Grecian maid bending over an urn, a weeping willow, or a broken column. The articles so worn included brooches and pendants, often ornamented with pearls or amethysts, but sometimes with diamonds or PASTE; but the principal articles of mourning jewelry were MOURNING RINGS. Such pieces were especially worn in the Victorian era after the death of Prince Albert in 1861, when they were generally made of JET (or cheaper black glass) in sombre styles. *See* GUSTAVUS ADOLPHUS PENDANT; CHARLES I JEWELRY.

mourning (or **memorial**) **ring.** A type of finger ring that was worn in memory of a deceased person. Originally in the Middle Ages rings of the deceased were given to and worn by relatives and friends, but when these proved insufficient in number or the values of owned rings varied too much, the custom developed from the 15th to the 17th centuries of providing in a will that a number of identical and relatively inexpensive rings (with the price sometimes stipulated) be made and donated to mourners. Many of such rings were of the MEMENTO MORI style, but in the 17th and 18th centuries special forms were developed. Some had the interior of the hoop engraved with the name and dates of the deceased and the exterior enamelled in black to depict a skeleton or a foliage pattern. Other examples had the dates of the birth and death of the deceased inscribed on the outside of the SHANK (the latter date did not necessarily indicate the date of the making of the ring, as sometimes such dates were added to rings formerly belonging to the deceased). The BEZEL of some mourning rings was set with a crystal over the initials of the deceased made in gold thread over a ground of silk or hair (*see* HAIR JEWELRY). After *c.* 1770 a lock of hair, a portrait or an enamelled mourning motif (an urn, weeping willow or broken column) was set under a crystal in the bezel. Some such rings were made in MARQUISE shape, decorated with SEED PEARLS, and were given by the male mourners to their wives to be generally worn. In the early 19th century some such rings were set with small gemstones, or black or violet enamelling was added to a gem-set ring owned by the deceased. In the late 19th century mourning rings ceased to be worn by the upper classes, but continued to be mass-produced, some set with JET or with a photograph in the bezel. *See* NELSON RING; ROYAL MOURNING RING; COMMEMORATIVE RING.

mouthpiece. An article of FUNERARY JEWELRY made of thin sheet gold in the form of an elliptical band with REPOUSSÉ decoration (sometimes with representation of the lips) to place over the mouth of a deceased person upon burial. Such pieces were made in many Eastern Mediteranean regions, such as the Cypro-Mycenaean examples, *c.* 1400 BC–1300 BC, and also of PRE-COLUMBIAN JEWELRY.

Mucha, Alphonse Marie (1860–1939). A native of Moravia, in present Czechoslovakia, who worked in Paris, Berlin, and Prague as a painter, graphic designer, and decorator. He was a leader of the ART NOUVEAU movement, and designed jewelry in that style for execution by GEORGES FOUQUET, whose shop in the Rue Royale, Paris, he created. His designs often featured girls with wildly flowing hair. From 1894 to 1900 he made posters for Sarah Bernhardt and published designs for Art Nouveau jewelry. His most famous piece is the CLEOPATRA BRACELET designed for Sarah Bernhardt in that role and executed by Fouquet.

Muelich, Hans. *See* HANS MIELICH.

muff chain. A very long CHAIN to be suspended around the neck and having fasteners at the terminals to be attached when the chain was passed through a lady's fur muff. Such chains were popular in England in the 18th century and later. Such a chain, set with diamonds, was a wedding gift to Lady Churchill.

Mughal (Mogul) jewelry. Articles of INDIAN JEWELRY made from the beginning of the Mughal Empire in 1526 until its gradual disintegration after Aurangzeb (1658–1707) and thereafter for some time during the period of British control. The characteristic features are the extravagant use of the abundant local gemstones and strings of seed pearls, the use of many pendent ornaments and tassels, and the decoration in polychrome enamel. The articles, often made of several components linked together, include: necklaces made of scores of strands of beads or pearls, with suspended pendants and tassels; FOREHEAD ORNAMENTS suspended from the hair; head ornaments with tinkling pendants; AIGRETTES to adorn turbans; EAR ORNAMENTS, sometimes worn by a band encircling the ear and so heavy that they had to be supported by attached ornate hair pins; NECK ORNAMENTS; large NOSE ORNAMENTS worn through the pierced septum or as studs on one side of the nostril; bracelets and ARMLETS; penannular BANGLES having animal and bird terminals; numerous FINGER RINGS and TOE RINGS, sometimes set with a mirror; ARCHER'S THUMB RINGS; ANKLETS connected by chains to foot ornaments; BUCKLES; and jewelled belts and sashes. The decoration featured CHAMPLEVÉ enamel (*see* JAIPUR JEWELRY), fine gold and silver FILIGREE work (the most noted being from Cuttack and Dacca), and the profuse use of diamonds (characteristically unfaceted polished TABLE CUT stones), emeralds, rubies, sapphires, and pearls, and sometimes turquoises. The lavish jewelry for members of the Court and the aristocracy was supplemented for the masses by pieces, worn with equal prodigality, made of gold and also of base metals set with glass.   [*Plate VIII*]

Muisca jewelry. Articles of PRE-COLUMBIAN JEWELRY made by the Chibcha-speaking Indians in the Muisca region of Colombia. One tribe, living on the high plateaux of central Colombia near present-day Bogotá and near the sacred Lake Guatavita, was ruled by the legendary 'El Dorado' (The Gilded Man), at whose installation as new ruler he and the chiefs, going to the centre of the lake on a raft, threw gold jewelry and emeralds into the lake as offerings to the gods. The region produced no gold but acquired it in abundance in exchange for its vast production of emeralds and salt. Among the articles made of gold and TUMBAGA were the characteristic TUNJOS, and also PECTORALS, NOSE ORNAMENTS, and openwork pendants, all produced by all the customary metal techniques. Another piece of such gold jewelry is a necklace composed of many identical small figures of birds and abstract forms, presumably made by the use of a local invention, the MATRIX, for mass production.

Müller's glass. The same as HYALITE. It is named after its discoverer.

multi-facet diamond. A diamond cut with a FACETED GIRDLE. Such a diamond that is BRILLIANT CUT has 40 facets on the girdle, and thus a total of 98 facets. It was developed by L.H. Roselaar, of the United States.

Murrle, Norbert (1948–). A DESIGNER-MAKER of jewelry, born in Pforzheim, who since 1970 has created pieces of highly original design, such as gold, steel, and ACRYLIC brooches with ivory motifs in the form of three-dimensional split cows depicted as half-entering, half-exiting a landscape. His work has been exhibited in many German cities, as well as London and Tokyo.

muscle pearl. A type of natural pearl that is found near the muscle that connects, and opens and closes, the two valves of the shell.

musical jewelry. Articles of jewelry that embody a small musical mechanism. An example is a gold enamelled pendant in the form of a harp, French, *c.* 1809, given by Eugène de Beauharnais (1781–1824) to his wife Auguste Amalie, Duchess of Leuchtenburg (d. 1851).

musk ball. A globular article used as a BOÎTE DE SENTEUR for containing musk (a substance obtained from the male musk deer that emits a strong odour) or more often some artificial product emitting a pleasant scent. *See* POMANDER.

mussel pearl. The variety of FRESH-WATER PEARL produced by the PEARL MUSSEL (genus *Unio*). Such pearls are white, pink, bluish or black, but inferior to those of the PEARL OYSTER, having a poor ORIENT. *See* NIGGERHEAD.

mutton-fat jade. A variety of NEPHRITE (JADE) that is pale, almost translucent, yellowish or greenish-grey, and has a greasy LUSTRE. It sometimes shows patches of pale or intense green, or more rarely streaks of carmine red. It is used more for ornaments than jewelry. The Chinese term is *yang-chih-yü*.

Mughal jewelry. Ear ornament. Gold with gemstones. Late 19th century. Victoria & Albert Museum, London.

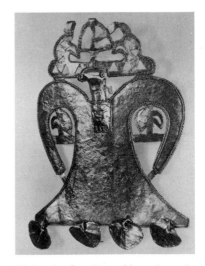

Muisca jewelry. Cast gold pendant of crested bird. H. 7.8 cm. Museo del Oro, Bogotá.

Mycenae Treasure. A TREASURE of gold jewelry and other Achaean objects discovered in 1876 in shaft graves at Mycenae, in the Peloponnese, Greece, by Dr Heinrich Schliemann (1822-90) and his wife Sophia. It included masks of beaten gold found in the so-called 'Tomb of Agamemnon' and diadems, necklaces, ear-rings, bracelets, beads, and pins, as well as vases, goblets, etc. The Treasure is now in the National Archaeological Museum, Athens.

Mycenaean glass bead. A type of glass bead made in the Mycenaean world between *c.* 1400 BC and *c.* 1100 BC in the form of a small thin plaque of which one end is ribbed and pierced for threading. Such beads are circular, rectangular or triangular, and of dark-blue or turquoise-green glass. They are decorated with Mycenaean motifs in relief, such as rosettes, ivy or spirals. They were generally used as beads strung on a necklace, or as decoration sewn on garments, but it has been suggested that they were also used occasionally to adorn DIADEMS. The plaques were sometimes covered with gold FOIL to simulate similar plaques made of sheet gold. *See Journal of Glass Studies* (Corning), X (1968), p. 1.

Mycenaean jewelry. Gold ear-rings. Mid-16th century BC. National Archaeological Museum, Athens.

Mycenaean jewelry. Articles of jewelry made by the Achaeans (or by Minoan craftsmen) in the Mycenaean world, *c.* 1600 BC-1100 BC. Many of the styles paralleled the Minoan styles (*see* MINOAN JEWELRY), with lavish use of the abundant supply of gold, often found in pieces decorated with GRANULATED GOLD, and with some of the earliest known examples of jewelry with ENAMELLING. Among the characteristic articles are: (1) MYCENAEAN RELIEF BEADS and MYCENAEAN GLASS BEADS; (2) gold SIGNET RINGS; and (3) SEALS carved from gemstones. *See* MYCENAE TREASURE; ENKOMI PENDANT.

Mycenaean relief bead. A type of gold bead found in Crete in burials dating from the 17th century BC and produced in great number by methods of mass production into the 13th century BC. The beads were made of sheet gold stamped to form a shallow relief decoration on the front; a flat piece was soldered on the back after filling the interior space. The designs depicted flowers, animals, fish, rosettes, etc., and were sometimes accented by GRANULATED GOLD. The beads were pierced with one or more suspensory holes.

mythological subjects. Subjects or figures derived from Greek or Roman mythology, sometimes used as a decorative motif on pendants or other articles of jewelry, e.g. Leda (*see* LEDA AND THE SWAN JEWEL), Climon and Pera (*see* THE ROMAN CHARITY), MEDUSA, THE JUDGMENT OF PARIS, Hercules, Aphrodite, Amphitrite, Orpheus, Europa, and many BAROQUE PEARL JEWELS depicting tritons, nereids, sirens, centaurs, hippocampi, dragons, etc.

N

Nabataean jewelry. Articles of jewelry made by the Nabataeans, Semites of the Kingdom of Transjordania (present-day Jordan), much of which has been found in a cemetery at Mampsis, dating from the early 1st to the mid-2nd century AD. It includes ear-rings of hoop and crescent shapes, some decorated with GRANULATED GOLD and REPOUSSÉ work and with suspended pendants, as well as examples of NOSE ORNAMENTS in the form of a ring.

nacre. The IRIDESCENT material that is a component of a pearl and of MOTHER-OF-PEARL. It is the secretion from the MANTLE of certain molluscs and consists of crystalline calcium carbonate (carbonate of lime) and conchiolin.

naif (or **naife, nyf, naive**). (1) The natural surface or 'skin' of an uncut and unpolished diamond. A small part (called a 'natural') of the naif is sometimes left on the GIRDLE of a cut stone to indicate that the maximum diameter of the stone has been retained. (2) A type of diamond that has a lustrous appearance in its natural and unpolished state.

naja (Navajo Indian). A horseshoe-shaped or crescent-shaped peńdant, made by the Navajo Indians of south-western United States, that is worn suspended from a SQUASH-BLOSSOM NECKLACE or attached to a silver-mounted bridle. The form varies, early examples being a single unornamented PENANNULAR hoop, but later ones having double, sometimes triple, arms. The arms are usually of triangular section, but some are flat or rounded, and many have decoration of filed or stamped designs. The terminals of the arms are decorated with rounded buttons, flat discs, tiny replicas of human hands, or other ornamental motifs. Usually there is dangling within the hoop a piece of turquoise or a pomegranate-shaped or other form of silver ornament. Such pendants, contrary to popular belief, are merely ornamental, and are not charms or amulets (nor fertility symbols, as sometimes stated today), although they were adapted from an amulet worn in the Middle East and North Africa, and later in Europe, to ward off the evil eye, and were copied by the Conquistadors who brought them to the New World where they were adapted by the Navajos, either directly or through other Indian tribes. *See* NAVAJO JEWELRY.

name brooch. An inexpensive article of sentimental jewelry of the late 19th century, being a silver brooch bearing a feminine given name, usually in relief, but sometimes cut-out. Such brooches, generally horizontal, are of many fancy shapes; a few are circular within a decorative frame.

Napoleonic conspiracy ring. A finger ring made for the conspirators who planned the escape of Napoleon from Elba in 1815. The ring has a hinged BEZEL forming a locket within which is a gold relief head of Napoleon and on the cover of which are enamelled three flowers within a wreath. It is said that only 6 such rings were made.

Nariño jewelry. Articles of PRE-COLUMBIAN JEWELRY made in the Nariño region in the southernmost Andes of Colombia, bordering Ecuador. The objects were made of gold or TUMBAGA, and some of pale gold (indicating an alloy with silver). The objects were usually of flat hammered metal with cut-out or REPOUSSÉ decoration and highly burnished, and often featured a MONKEY motif. The main articles were cut-out crescent-shaped EAR-ORNAMENTS (width 6 to 14 cm) and cut-out NOSE ORNAMENTS, both with monkey figures, and metal discs with a pierced hole, probably to be suspended as mobiles.

narwhal ivory. A variety of IVORY from the tusk (horn) of the Arctic male narwhal whale. It is coarse, and marbled grey and white. In modern times it is used mainly in Japan, often to make NETSUKES. *See* UNICORN HORN; DANNY JEWEL.

Naseby Jewel. A TROPHY JEWEL made as an ENSEIGNE of openwork gold with enamelling and set with rubies, depicting a knight armed with two swords and a shield (in which is set a large ruby) and surrounded by trophies of arms; at his feet crouches a lion, and a flag bears the St Andrew's Cross. It is said to have been lost by, or stolen from, Charles I at the Battle of Naseby on 14 June 1645 when his Royal Army was defeated by the army of Cromwell. It has been suggested that the jewel may have been made upon the order of the King of Denmark as a gift to James I, 1603-25. It is considered to be German, *c.* 1600-15. It was exhibited in 1755 and thereafter had several successive owners.

násfa (Hungarian). A type of pendant or brooch worn on the front of a bodice in Hungary in the 16th century, often in the form of a flower or floral design enamelled and set with gemstones or pearls.

Nassak Diamond. A famous colourless diamond that is said to have been once set by the Mahrattas, conquerors of India in the 17th/18th centuries, in the eye of a statue of Shiva in a Hindu cave temple near Nassak (now Nasik), north-west of Bombay. When in 1818 the British

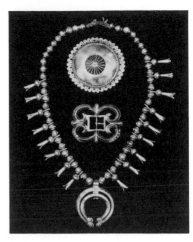

naja. Silver squash-blossom necklace (L. 35.5 cm) with suspended *naja.* Also brooch and buckle. Navajo jewelry. New Mexico. Museum of the American Indian, Heye Foundation, New York.

Nariño jewelry. Cast and hammered ear ornaments with monkey motifs. W. 6 cm. Museo del Oro, Bogotá.

Naseby Jewel. Trophy jewel, enamelled gold set with rubies. German, *c.* 1615. W. 9.3 cm. Sir John Soane's Museum, London.

nasfa. Gold pendant with baroque pearls. Hungarian, mid-16th century. H. 11.5 cm. Hungarian National Museum, Budapest.

subdued the region, the diamond (then triangular, cut in Indian fashion, weighing 90 old carats) was taken by the East India Company, then brought by Governor-General Warren Hastings to London, and sold to the London jewellers Rundell & Bridge (*see* RUNDELL, BRIDGE & RUNDELL) who had it recut, still in triangular shape, with 90 facets and weighing 80.59 carats. In 1831 it was purchased at auction by Emanuel Bros., London, and in 1837 purchased by the 1st Marquess of Westminster and mounted in the hilt of his sword. In the early 20th century it was bought by Georges Mauboussin, Parisian jeweller, who exhibited it in 1926 in the United States. Later it was bought by HARRY WINSTON who had it recut as a CUSHION CUT stone weighing 43.38 carats and sold it to Trabert & Hoeffer, New York jewellers. In 1944 it was bought by Mrs William B. Leeds, of New York, and in 1970 purchased at auction by Edward Hand, of Greenwich, Connecticut. Thereafter it was acquired by BULGARI, of Rome, who have resold it privately.

native cut. A gemstone that has been cut, faceted, and polished by the miners where the stone was found, consequently having a shape that is often not symmetrical and facets that are not uniform, the intention being to lose minimum weight and to enhance colour rather than brilliance. *See* INDIAN CUT.

naujaite. A rock that includes particles of EUDIALYTE, and so has a mottled reddish and greyish colour. It has been cut and polished for use in jewelry. The name is derived from Naujakasik, in Greenland, where it was found.

nautilus. A mollusc of which the pearly nautilus variety produces (1) the COQUE DE PERLE and (2) a nacreous shell. The shell resembles a snail shell, and when it is periodically enlarged by additional secretions, a new MOTHER-OF-PEARL partition (septum) behind it is also secreted, forming a number of chambers. The outer shell is used for carving oval convex ornaments and the inner septum for pieces of jewelry with engraved designs. The sources are the Indian Ocean and Pacific Ocean.

Navajo jewelry. Articles of jewelry made from *c.* 1850 by the Navajo Indians, a nomadic tribe that inhabited south-western United States, and since they were subdued in 1863-4 have lived on reservations in Arizona, New Mexico, and Utah. They learned metalwork from the Mexicans *c.* 1850, and by *c.* 1900 silver-making was well established. They have continued to make attractive silver jewelry, usually decorated with pieces of turquoise; however, much jewelry of the type is now being imitated, especially in Mexico, and sold in the United States as souvenir jewelry. Some Navajos now create new styles of better-quality jewelry, some made of multicoloured hardstones. *See* BOLA; CHANNEL WORK; CONCHA BELT; NAJA; SQUASH-BLOSSOM NECKLACE.

Navajo jewelry. Silver bracelet with turquoise inlays. New Mexico. W. 6.5 cm. Museum of the American Indian, Heye Foundation, New York.

navette. The same as a MARQUISE diamond.

navratna (Indian). A type of Indian jewel decorated with nine different varieties of gemstones, sometimes in the form of a necklace, pendant, bracelet or armlet. Such pieces were formerly regarded as AMULETS.

Nazca jewelry. Articles of PRE-COLUMBIAN JEWELRY made by the Indians living on the southern coast of Peru, *c.* AD 300-800. The best-known artifacts are their pottery decorated with elaborate polychrome painting of geometrical motifs and stylized birds, fish, animals, and anthropomorphic heads, but they also made metalwork decorated with such motifs, including jewelry made of cut and hammered thin sheets of gold with REPOUSSÉ work. The examples include bracelets, nose ornaments, mouth masks, and funerary masks. Some pendants were made of shell decorated in mosaic style with coloured shell and stones. Much of the extant jewelry was discovered in graves, *c.* 1901. *See* PERUVIAN JEWELRY.

Nazca jewelry. Cut-out sheet gold depicting deity with 19 radiating serpents. Peru. H. 19.7 cm. Museum of the American Indian, Heye Foundation, New York.

neck chain. A long CHAIN worn encircling the neck, sometimes wound in several loops, and extending down upon the breast, and occasionally having a suspended pendant. Although worn in ancient times and the Middle Ages, they were more popular during the Renaissance, when they were worn by men and women in the form of heavy chains of pure gold;

occasionally several were worn simultaneously. Some were worn by men as evidence of membership in orders or guilds, but most were worn decoratively, were massive and heavy, and were often royal gifts. Those worn by women in the 16th century were often embellished with gemstones. Some of exceptional length were raised and fastened in a loop high on the breast, so as to form two loops. Such chains are still popular today.

neck ornament. An ornament, of various forms, worn suspended from a chain or ring encircling a woman's neck. Examples made in India during the Mughal period sometimes were (1) a close-fitting wide band set with gemstones and having a dangling fringe of pendants and tassels, or (2) made of several components linked together, often with a crescent-shaped gold and jewelled pendant with dangling beaded ornaments and gemstones, all suspended from multiple pearl chains. *See* MUGHAL JEWELRY; JAIPUR JEWELRY.

neck ring. A rigid circular ornament worn around the neck, as distinguished from a flexible necklace or NECKLET. Ancient examples were made of bronze or gold in the North European and Iberian Late Bronze Ages, *c.* 8th/6th centuries BC. Such rings were popular in Scandinavia and northern Germany, being worn by high-ranking women. Some examples were made as a ring with an opening at the front that was joined by bent ornamented loops that hooked together, and some had a hinged section at the back for fastening. Some gold examples, made of a ribbon-like twisted gold band, have been found in Ireland; *see* RIBBON TORC. Pieces of similar shape and form, made of gold or silver, and sometimes set with gemstones, are worn today; for an example in PENANNULAR form with one ornamented terminal, *see* CHAUMET & CIE.

necklace. A flexible ornament worn around the neck, loosely rather than close-fitting (*see* CHOKER; DOG COLLAR) and not long (*see* NECK CHAIN). It can be in the form of a string of gemstones, beads, pearls, etc., or a band set with gemstones or pearls, or a chain embellished with gemstones, pearls or other objects. Often there is suspended from a necklace an ornamental PENDANT, CROSS or single gemstone or cluster of gemstones or pearls. *See* PEARL NECKLACE; NECKLET; SHEBU; BAYARDÈRE; RIBBON NECKLACE; MARIE ANTOINETTE NECKLACE; MARIE LOUISE NECKLACE.

necklace tiara. A type of circular necklace composed of a series of jewelled ornaments, each of which has a tiny hook that can be attached to a tiny ring on the adjacent ornament so that all the ornaments will be thus brought into a vertical position to form a TIARA. Sometimes it is in the form of a necklace that can be attached to a wire frame to convert it into a tiara.

necklet. Generally, any ornament worn around the neck, but usually a short, somewhat close-fitting type of necklace with unpretentious decoration, sometimes a simple wire band, often with only a single small gemstone.

needle. (1) A thin, needle-like crystal that is an INCLUSION in certain varieties of RUTILATED QUARTZ and of CORUNDUM, e.g. a RUBY from Sri Lanka, formerly Ceylon, or Burma. They intersect at different angles and produce a SHEEN or a type of SILK. Sometimes called a 'rutile needle'. (2) A long thin ornament worn as PEASANT JEWELRY in the Netherlands. They are worn in pairs (usually silver on weekdays, gold on Sundays), suspended from the lace cap at the temples, but in some provinces only one is worn, at the left side by a married woman, at the right side by a single woman. *See* OORIJZER.

nef pendant. *See* SHIP PENDANT.

négligée (French). A flexible chain of beads, pearls, links of a precious metal, or rope-like strands, about 50 to 75 cm long, that is hung or looped around a woman's neck, having no clasp and usually terminating with tassels on each end. *See* LAVALIER; SAUTOIR.

Nele, E. R. (1932-). A DESIGNER-MAKER of jewelry, born in Berlin, who studied in London and Berlin. She works in Frankfurt am Main and her work has been exhibited in Pforzheim and London. Among her best-known pieces

neck ornament. Gold with pearls, gemstones, and enamelling. Benares (Varanasi), India, 19th century. Victoria & Albert Museum, London.

neck ring. Gold, three bars with cups as decoration. Iberian Late Bronze Age, *c.* 7th century BC. W. 13.1 cm. British Museum, London.

necklace. Gold with diamonds and amethysts. English, mid-19th century. Victoria & Albert Museum, London.

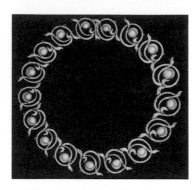

necklace tiara. Gold with pearls and diamonds. Russian, *c.* 1900. Courtesy of Wartski, London.

are brooches made of coral and hardstone that combine human faces or limbs with leaves or branches.

Nelson ring. A type of MOURNING RING made and distributed upon the death of Admiral Lord Nelson in 1805, having some appropriate decoration. One important example is a plain gold band having a black enamelled oval BEZEL decorated with a viscount's coronet above an N and a ducal crown above a B (for Brontë, the dukedom in Sicily that he accepted from King Ferdinand of Sicily), below which is inscribed 'Trafalgar'; the wide hoop is engraved outside with a Latin motto and inside with an obituary inscription.

Nepal Diamond. A white pear-shaped diamond, weighing 79.41 carats, whose early history is unknown, but which is said to have been found in the Golconda Mine in India, and to have been owned by successive generations of Nepalese rulers until acquired by HARRY WINSTON, who exhibited it in 1959 and sold it in 1961 to a private collector.

nephrite. The less valuable and more abundant of the two gemstones generally referred to as JADE. It is less hard than JADEITE, the other variety of jade. Its colour is subdued, and ranges from white to the more usual dark green (sometimes called 'greenstone') and shades of grey or brown to black. It is translucent with a greasy LUSTRE when polished, and is of great toughness and durability. It is used today for carved (i.e. ground) art objects and beads more than for jewelry. It is the variety of jade that has been used by the Chinese since Neolithic times and long before the importation of jadeite *c.* 1780, having been imported from Turkestan and the Baikal region of Siberia and later found in various regions of China and Taiwan (Formosa). A dark-green variety was discovered in the 19th century near Lake Baikal; other sources include New Zealand (*see* MAORI JADE; NEW ZEALAND GREENSTONE). *See* BOWENITE; LANDSCAPE NEPHRITE; MUTTON-FAT JADE.

netsuke (Japanese). An ornamental pendant fastened by a toggle at the end of a cord suspended from a girdle (obi) worn to close a Japanese man's dress (kimono). As the kimono had no pocket, there were also suspended from the cord such objects as a purse, tobacco pouch, pipe, snuff bottle, and INRO. The netsuke (measuring about 2.5 x 6.2 cm) is made of a wide variety of materials, usually lacquered wood, but also IVORY, TORTOISE SHELL, CORAL, enamelled metal, and sometimes HORN, SHELL, JADE, AMBER or porcelain, and often has inlaid decoration. They are made in an infinite variety of forms, usually figures to depict humans, animals, and birds, as well as religious subjects, feats of strength, the months, mythical animals, proverbs, etc., carved IN THE ROUND but sometimes in flattened form. They were originally utilitarian but later were worn as decorative ornamental objects. Each type and style has its individual name. They are usually signed by the maker (over 2,000 carvers' names are listed) using his professional name (sometimes with that of his tutor or sometimes only the latter as a mark of respect). They were worn by persons of all classes, but especially those of lower social rank, from the 15th century, and mainly in the 17th/18th centuries, until they went out of general use in the mid-19th century. They were usually made with two suspensory holes except those in the form of a figure where the limbs served to attach the cord; in older examples one such hole was larger, to conceal the knot of the cord. *See* Raymond Bushell, *The Netsuke Handbook of Ueda Reikichi* (1961), and *Netsuke, Familiar and Unfamiliar* (1975). *See* MANJŪ NETSUKE; OJIME.

New Jade. A misnomer for yellowish-green BOWENITE marketed from China under that name as an imitation of JADE.

netsuke. Carved ivory. Centre, figure of Gama Sennin, by Yoshinaga, Kyoto, 18th century. Courtesy of Sydney L. Moss Ltd, London.

New Zealand greenstone. The variety of dark-green NEPHRITE (JADE) found in New Zealand. The same as axe-stone and MAORI JADE. A dark-green BOWENITE (SERPENTINE) is also found there.

Niarchos Diamond. A diamond found in the Premier Mine in South Africa in 1964, weighing in the rough 426.50 carats, and originally called the 'Ice Queen' and the 'Pretoria'. It was bought from De Beers Consolidated Mines Ltd, as part of a purchase of 50,000 stones, by HARRY WINSTON in 1956, who had it cut by his chief cutter, Bernard de Haan, working on the project for a year, into a pear-shaped, ice-blue PENDELOQUE stone having 58 main facets with 86 more around the girdle, and weighing 128.25 carats. It was sold in 1957 to Stavros Niarchos, the last known owner. From the rough stone were also cut a 40-carat EMERALD CUT stone and a 30-carat MARQUISE; both are now privately owned.

Nicolas of Verdun. The most outstanding Lotharingian goldsmith of the late 12th/early 13th century. Although best known for his large altar-pieces, he also made some jewelry that displayed his realism in modelling human figures. A CLASP attributed to him is of gilt bronze, decorated with figures in sculptural style depicting a king and queen, each with an attendant. He also did work decorated with CHAMPLEVÉ enamel. See LOTHARINGIAN JEWELRY.

Nicolas of Verdun. Clasp of gilt bronze. Lotharingian, early 13th century. W. 7.5 cm. Metropolitan Museum of Art, New York.

nic(c)olo. (1) A variety of ONYX (AGATE) that has a thin layer of faint bluish-white over a thick layer of black. (2) A CAMEO or INTAGLIO that is carved in such a stone, with the design cut in the upper translucent bluish-white layer; the black shows through the translucent carving to provide a bluish tinge. Such pieces were made in the Early Christian Era, *c.* AD 400 and in the Roman period.

niello. An inlay used in decorating in black on silver (infrequently on gold) that is somewhat related to CHAMPLEVÉ work except that the effect is metallic rather than vitreous. The process involved engraving (or, for large areas, using other indenting processes) the design into a metal plate, then filling the indented portions with a powdered black matt ALLOY made of metallic sulphides (sulphur with silver, copper, and lead) according to various formulae, together with a flux, after which the piece was heated until the alloy melted (at 1200° C.) and became fused in the grooves and depressions of the design; the piece, when cooled, was scraped and polished until the niello was removed except in the then contrasting design. Niello decoration is found on Bronze Age non-jewelry articles (usually of gold) and was reintroduced in ROMAN JEWELRY in the 4th century AD, and was also used in Egyptian and early Byzantine jewelry, as well as ANGLO-SAXON JEWELRY (*see* ETHELWULF RING; FULLER BROOCH); however, the method for executing such work was different, in that the inlay was of silver sulphide alone, and it was not melted but merely heated until plastic, then inlayed and burnished. In the 11th century the niello formulae were developed, and it was used on GOTHIC JEWELRY and on some pieces made during the Renaissance (*see* MORESQUE SILHOUETTE STYLE). Niello has been used also in India and Islamic countries, and also in Russia (*see* TULA WORK). An imitative process was used in the Balkans by inlaying lead alone, and also by Dutch engravers during the late 16th and mid-17th centuries by applying niello as a background. Its use was revived in the 19th century by KARL WAGNER; and it was used in France by ÉMILE FROMENT-MEURICE and in London by S.H. and D. Gass. In recent years it has been simulated by painting on the surface with a niello preparation as a background or a design. Some niello work is being done today in the Far East. The German term is *Schwarzornamente*. *See* TOMMASO FINIGUERRA.

niello. Gold buckle and buttons for belt. Hungarian, 2nd half of 13th century. W. (buckle) 4.4 cm. Hungarian National Museum, Budapest.

niggerhead. (1) A local name for a variety of TOURMALINE that is found in Elba and that is pink, yellowish or green, sometimes parti-coloured, and black at the top of the crystal. (2) A species of PEARL MUSSEL found in the rivers of the Mississippi Valley of the United States, the shell of which has a diameter of up to 10 cm; the shells are used to make MOTHER-OF-PEARL buttons. Such mussels are sometimes incorrectly called 'niggerhead clams'.

Nizam Diamond. A diamond said to have been found at the Golconda Mine in southern India about 1835, the weight in the rough being

originally estimated at 340 old carats but later, after it had been broken up in the Indian Mutiny of 1857, estimated at 440 old carats. It was cut in irregular INDIAN CUT to retain maximum weight, and then weighed 277 old carats. It is said to have been owned continuously by the Nizams of Hyderabad, the 7th Nizam having said in 1934 that he had seen what may have been this stone on his father's desk, used as a paperweight. *See* HYDERABAD, NIZAM OF, COLLECTION.

Noah Cameo. An oval CAMEO carved of ONYX, depicting a scene showing Noah and his family, with animals and birds, leaving the Ark. It is mounted in a gold frame with floral motifs on the reverse, characteristic of French metalwork of the 14th/15th centuries. On the doors of the Ark are the incised words 'LAVR MED' (the mark of Lorenzo de' Medici). The origin of the cameo, attributed to various sources in antiquity and later periods, is still undetermined, but one now favoured opinion is that it cannot be antique and that it is from the Court workshop, *c.* 1204–50, of Frederick II Hohenstaufen (1194–1250); it has been listed in the inventories of Piero de' Medici (1465) and of Lorenzo de' Medici (1492), and was purchased in Paris in the 18th century by the 4th Earl of Carlisle, with whose collection it was acquired by the British Museum.

noble opal. Several varieties of OPAL that present a characteristic play of brilliant or delicate tints, as distinguished from the COMMON OPAL. The noble opal (also called 'precious opal') includes the BLACK OPAL, FIRE OPAL (GIRASOL), HARLEQUIN OPAL, and WATER OPAL.

noble serpentine. A variety of SERPENTINE that is hard and TRANSLUCENT, and of a rich green colour.

non-nucleated pearl. A type of CULTURED PEARL grown by the insertion of a piece of the MANTLE of a Japanese fresh-water mussel. Such pearls are generally whitish and are in the form of a BOUTON PEARL.

Norman cross. An article of Norman silver PEASANT JEWELRY in the form of a cross. The type used near St Lô and Caen has 5 high bosses, one on each limb of the cross and one at the centre, all set with a foiled ALENÇON DIAMOND cut as a BRILLIANT, 4 being round and the one on the lower limb (which is usually hinged) being pear-shaped (PENDELOQUE). Around the bosses are sprays of silver set with small crystals in ROSE form. The crosses of the other regions of Normandy vary in style.

Northumberland Brooch. A pendant BROOCH in two sections, the upper part being a circular EMERALD decorated with Mughal carving of stylized tulips (a motif dating from 1620), and the lower droplet being a smaller PENDELOQUE emerald. Both emeralds are within frames of gold and silver, set with diamonds, thought to have been made in 1820 by the King's jewellers. The brooch was sold by the Duke of Northumberland at Sotheby's, London, on 20 April 1978 for £250,000. It is thought to be the brooch listed among the family jewels in the 1863 inventory of the 3rd Duke of Northumberland.

nose ornament. An ornament worn on the nose by both men and women, mainly in India and in America in the pre-Columbian period. The examples of MUGHAL JEWELRY were either (1) jewelled studs worn on one side of the nostril, or (2) large, ornate gold pieces, with pendants and dangling chains, worn suspended through the septum. Those of PRE-COLUMBIAN JEWELRY were made of gold or TUMBAGA, including: (1) a ring suspended through the septum; (2) a pin in the form of a straight bar worn horizontally through the septum (but sometimes made of JADE as articles of MAYAN JEWELRY; (3) a thick, solid or tubular, PENANNULAR ring, sometimes with a lower projecting ornament; (4) a long, angled strip extending almost horizontally on either side of the nose, with various ornamental motifs (sometimes a monkey figure) attached; (5) an openwork semi-circular disc with small arms at the top for attaching to the septum; or (6) an elaborate ornament of hammered sheet metal of considerable size, made in an openwork pattern, sometimes with dangling discs, cylinders or pendants or in the form of a cut-out anthropomorphic face with the features in REPOUSSÉ work.

nose stud. An ornament, usually a gemstone, worn inserted on one side of the nose by men and women in India, Pakistan, and countries of the

Middle East. It is usually on the left side, but on the right in southern India. An example made of bone has been found from the Meroitic era in Nubia. The word used for a nose stud varies in different regions; it is sometimes called a *chemki*.

nouch. An archaic term for an OUCH, being derived from combining the words 'an ouch' into 'a nouch'. The term has been sometimes spelt 'nowche'.

Nubian jewelry. Articles of jewelry made and worn by the people of Nubia, a country that in antiquity extended south of Egypt below the site of the Aswan Dam to present-day Khartoum in the Sudan, and that had a rich culture as early as *c.* 3300 BC; often conquered by the Egyptians, the country was revived *c.* 2000 BC under the Kerma kings, but vanquished again *c.* 1550 BC until becoming the kingdom of Kush from *c.* 850 BC until *c.* AD 350. Treasures from the Kushites were excavated in pyramids by Giuseppe Ferlini in the 19th century, including intricately designed gold finger rings and ARMLETS, and pendants of EGYPTIAN FAIENCE, some of which were exhibited in the USA in 1978-79. Additional Nubian jewelry was found *c.* 1964 by Keith Seele in Egyptian tombs threatened by the construction of the Aswan Dam.

nugget. *See* GOLD NUGGET.

Nunkircher jasper. A misnomer for a variety of flint that is dyed blue and marketed in Germany and Switzerland as LAPIS LAZULI.

nun's ring. A type of finger ring received by a nun upon making her profession as a bride of Christ. The only known identifiable surviving example, *c.* 1300, is a gold, ridged hoop inscribed in Latin 'With this ring of chastity I am espoused to Jesus Christ'; but there probably are many more that remain unrecognized because of lack of an explicit inscription. They were worn by nuns throughout Europe. *See* ABBOT'S RING.

Nuremberg egg. The nickname for a type of WATCH made at Nuremberg in the 16th century that was somewhat spherical rather than strictly egg-shaped. The nickname derives from a mis-translation of the medieval German term *Uhrlein*, meaning 'little clock', which is said to have been confused with *Eyerlein (Eierlein)*, meaning 'little egg'. Authentic examples from Nuremberg are rare, but there are some in such form from England and Holland from the 1600s, and many imitations were made in the 19th century in Switzerland and Italy with long oval and slightly pointed cases. Such watches were often worn suspended from a chain around the neck.

Nur-ul-Ain (Nur-ol-Eyn) Diamond (Persian for Light of the Eye Diamond). The world's largest rose-pink diamond of BRILLIANT CUT, weighing 60 carats. It is set in the FARAH DIBA TIARA. It has been established that it and the DARYA-I-NUR (IRAN) were cut from the same stone that Jean-Baptiste Tavernier called the GREAT TABLE DIAMOND.

nut. A type of GAUD attached as an ornament to a ROSARY. Such pieces were in the form of a spherical case (sometimes made of BOXWOOD) with a hinged opening and having on the interior of each hemisphere a number of minute carved figures of saints or Biblical figures or scenes. Some (*c.* 1500) were made of HARDSTONE with interior carved and enamelled figures. Sometimes all of the beads on a rosary were nuts. Occasionally called a 'prayer-nut'. The French terms are *noix* or *grain de chapelet*, and the German term for those of wood is *Betnüsse*. *See* DEVONSHIRE ROSARY.

Nutwell Court Pendant. A diamond-shaped pendant in the centre of which is an oval Renaissance CAMEO of Oriental SARDONYX carved with two portraits, one in the light-coloured lower layer depicting a classical head almost concealed by another in the dark upper layer depicting a Negro. The cameo is within an ornamented enamelled border (blue, red, yellow, and green) set with diamonds and rubies. On the reverse is a miniature portrait of Elizabeth I by NICHOLAS HILLIARD dated 1575. Suspended from the pendant is a grape-like cluster of pearls from which hangs a pear-shaped pearl. It was presented to Sir Francis Drake by Elizabeth I in 1579. In a portrait of Drake by Federigo Zucchero, an

nose ornament. Sheet gold with three repoussé animal motifs. Pre-Columbian, Early Calima style. H. 17.3 cm. Museo del Oro, Bogotá.

nut. Gaud of carved boxwood. Flemish, early 16th century. W. 4 cm. Wallace Collection, London.

Nymphaeum Treasure. Gold necklace with hollow acorn and lotus pendants suspended from band of rosettes. Scythian, late 5th century BC. L. 31 cm. Ashmolean Museum, Oxford.

Italian painter, he is shown wearing the pendant suspended from a gold and red cord.

Nymphaeum Treasure. A TREASURE of SCYTHIAN JEWELRY and also objects of silver, bronze, and pottery, buried in six graves in a necropolis at Nymphaeum, near Kerch, in the Crimea, Russia, in the late 5th century and found in tumuli excavated in 1868 by the explorer Franz Biller; it was donated in 1880 to Oxford University by Sir William Siemens, the German engineer. The jewelry includes bracelets, finger rings, necklaces, ear-rings, and many dress ornaments, some in the form of hares. An exquisite necklace consists of 22 rosettes with acorns suspended from them alternately with stylized lotuses, all made of sheet gold edged with beaded gold wire, and possibly once enamelled. The jewelry has been since 1885 in the Ashmolean Museum, Oxford. *See* Michael Vickers, *Scythian Treasures in Oxford* (1979).

object of vertu. A small object of artistic quality and of value, made of a precious metal and often embellished with gemstones, such as a snuff box, ÉTUI, etc. They are not articles of jewelry in the strict meaning of that term (not being worn on the person, although sometimes they are made for personal use and carried as personal accessories); hence they are not within the scope of this book, nor are any objects of vertu that are made to be ornaments on a table. All such objects of artistry, rarity, and luxury, usually of the 17th to 19th centuries, are sometimes called an 'object of virtu', but since the word 'vertu' was applied by Horace Walpole, the term accepted by collectors is 'object of vertu'. The French term is *objet de vitrine* or the more general term *bibelot*. *See* Howard Ricketts, *Objects of Vertu* (1971).

objets trouvés (French). Literally, found objects. Objects sometimes worn as articles of personal adornment in the form in which they are found in nature, e.g. teeth, bones, shells, pebbles, feathers, beans, and fish vertebrae, without setting or ornamentation except a hole drilled for suspension. Such objects have been worn in the manner of jewelry from the palaeolithic period and presumably in all regions of the world, and are still worn by remote tribes. Some such objects have in modern times been set in mounts, especially as COSTUME JEWELRY, or are worn today strung as a necklace or a bracelet, and to that extent may be embraced within the term 'jewelry'. When such an object is altered by an artist, it is called an *'objet trouvé assisté'*. *See* DENTALIUM SHELL; MOLLUSC SHELL; SEED JEWELRY.

Obry, Hubert (1808-53). A Parisian carver of metal jewelry who specialized in making SEALS and SIGNET RINGS with motifs relating to the chase, which was his lifelong hobby.

obsidian. A solidified volcanic lava that is a form of natural GLASS which, owing to rapid cooling, did not have time to crystallize. It is usually so dark as to appear to be black and opaque, but some varieties have colour and are somewhat transparent. The splinters are transparent or translucent and have a VITREOUS LUSTRE. Some varieties are marekanite, rainbow obsidian, snowflake obsidian, and perlite; see APACHE TEAR. Obsidian, which breaks with a sharp cutting edge, was used by primitive people, and also by the Aztec and Maya Indians of Mexico, for arrow-heads, knives, and weapons, and also for some jewelry, e.g. LABRETS; it was also used for beads. Brown obsidian is carved in Italy and elsewhere for jewelry and cheap souvenirs. Sometimes bottle-green water-worn glass from the seashore in Cornwall, England, is sold as obsidian. A local misnomer for obsidian is 'Icelandic agate'. The name 'obsidian' was derived, according to Pliny, from 'Obsidius' (an erroneous form of 'Obsius'), who discovered it in Ethiopia.

obus. A 5-sided gemstone cut in the shape of a rectangle having its two long sides drawn to one point. The word means 'howitzer shell', which the shape suggests.

Occidental. Western, although not necessarily, as applied to a gemstone, from the Western hemisphere, but a loose term that often is prefixed (as a misnomer) to the names of stones that resemble other stones or sometimes to a stone of inferior quality. See ORIENTAL.

Occidental topaz. A misnomer for yellow QUARTZ (CITRINE).

octahedrite. The same as ANATASE. It is so called from its frequent shape as an 8-faced bipyramid.

octahedron. Generally, a solid bounded by 8 faces; but as applied to a crystal (e.g. a diamond) it refers to a regular octahedron, i.e. a solid (bipyramid) bounded by 8 equilateral triangles (being 2 equilateral pyramids with their square bases together). Diamonds before the 16th century were left in this natural shape and thus lacked BRILLIANCE. Thereafter, but before the ROSE CUT, some such diamonds were sawn in half (each called a DIAMOND POINT) and so worn. See POINT-CUT DIAMOND; GLASSIE.

odontolite. A FOSSIL bone or tooth of the mastodon or other extinct animal, made blue by impregnation of vivianite (iron phosphate) which has coloured the original organic material. It resembles TURQUOISE. The name is derived from the Greek *odon* (tooth). Also called 'bone turquoise' or 'fossil turquoise'.

Oeuf de Naple. A BALAS RUBY (red SPINEL) that was given by Pope Clement VII to his niece, Catherine de' Medici, upon her marriage in 1533 to the second son of Francis I, the future Henry II of France (1519-59). It was named after the city of Naples which was coveted by Francis. Henry II gave it to his mistress, Diane de Poitiers (1499-1566), to be worn by her, and after his death she returned it to the Crown. It was later pawned by Charles IX with the CÔTE DE BRETAGNE. Later Louis XV sent it to Jacquemin, the Court Jeweller, to be reset, and it was then mounted in the circle of a Star of the Order of Saint-Esprit, cut in the form of a dove and surrounded by pieces cut from the 'Roman A Diamond', resulting in great loss of value to both stones, as shown on an inventory of 1791. See SAINT-ESPRIT CROSS.

oil pearl. The same as ANTILLES PEARL.

ojime (Japanese). A sliding bead on the cords between an INRO and a NETSUKE that serves as a TOGGLE to tighten or loosen the cords.

Old Mine cut. The style of cutting a diamond that is an early version of the BRILLIANT CUT. It was introduced in Brazil soon after diamonds were discovered there, and was originally known as the 'triple cut'. The GIRDLE is cushion-shaped, and there was 32 FACETS on the CROWN plus an octagonal TABLE, and 24 facets on the PAVILION plus the CULET. The 'Brazilian cut' has a similar crown but 8 additional small facets surrounding the culet.

Old Mine cut
side view

Old Mine emerald. An emerald mined in Colombia before the 17th century from the Chivor Mine (the location of which the Conquistadors, *c.* 1538, tortured the Indians to reveal) and especially from the Muzo Mine (which the Spaniards discovered in 1587). The stones were in the form of rounded pebbles (called 'Chibcha stones' after the name of the Indian tribe), those from Muzo dark velvety bluish-green and those from Chivor yellowish-green. After being cut EN CABOCHON and usually drilled for necklaces, the stones were exported in quantity to India and Persia. They are still regarded as the highest-quality emeralds. Although both mines, abandoned in 1675, have been reopened, the Muzo in 1895 and the Chivor in the 1920s, the recent stones, found at greater depth, are inferior in size and colour.

olivine. A mineral of varying specific gravity and intensity of colour. The colour ranges from yellowish-green to dark leek-green; the yellowish-green has been misleadingly called CHRYSOLITE, and it has been recommended that that term be discontinued. It has a vitreous to oily LUSTRE. The name has been incorrectly applied to ANDRADITE (DEMANTOID) found in the Urals. The original source was the Egyptian island of Zebirget (St John) in the Red Sea. *See* SINHALITE.

Olmec jewelry. Articles of PRE-COLUMBIAN JEWELRY made by the Olmec Indians in the lowlands of Vera Cruz and Tabasco on the Gulf Coast of Mexico, *c.* 1000 BC–100 BC, particularly objects of JADEITE, NEPHRITE, SERPENTINE, and other HARDSTONES, often carved with great skill. *See* MEXICAN JEWELRY. *See* I. Bernal, *The Olmec World* (1969); A. Digby, 'Olmec Jades', in *Burlington Magazine*, May 1953.

Olmec jewelry. Carved jade pendant depicting human head, bordered by unidentified glyphs. 1000 BC – 100 BC, H. 10.5 cm. Museum of Mankind, London.

onyx. A variety of CHALCEDONY that is very porous and is composed of parallel straight layers of different shades of black and white, making it suitable for cutting as a CAMEO. Almost all onyx is artificially coloured (*see* DYEING), not only to enhance the colours but to emphasize the zonal structure; examples have been coloured deeper black, and also blue, green, and red. *See* BLACK ONYX; JET; NIC(C)OLO; SARDONYX.

oorijzer (Dutch). Literally, ear iron. Originally a type of iron head-dress worn as PEASANT JEWELRY by the women of Friesland, in northern Netherlands, but later adapted as a gold helmet fitting tightly over the head and worn under a lace cap. It has a cleft opening extending from the brow to the crown, derived from the 17th-century iron type, and is made with rosettes at the side that hide pins which secure it at the temples to the lace cap.

opal. A gemstone that is usually characterized by a flashing mixture of prismatic colours of delicate hues when light falls upon the surface. It does not have a CRYSTALLINE form but is an AMORPHOUS, gelatinous, hydrous silica containing a variable percentage (up to 20%) of water, with traces of impurities that are oxides of various metals. There are two principal varieties of opal: (1) PRECIOUS OPAL (or 'noble opal') that is IRIDESCENT, and (2) COMMON OPAL that has a white, milky appearance; there are many sub-varieties. The name 'opal' is derived from the Sanskrit word *upala* (gem). When precious opal is heated, the play of colours vanishes owing to the expulsion of the water; some opals (e.g. HYDROPHANE) show a play of colours only when dipped into water, or, more so, into oil, and lose the colour after evaporation. A 'treated opal', developed in the 1960s, is given a dark background by soaking it in a sugar solution and then carbonizing it with sulphuric acid, or by burying it in cinders and covering it with fired oil; such treatment is difficult to detect. The opal is usually cut EN CABOCHON, but sometimes (especially the fire opal) is faceted, carved or engraved. The opal sometimes loses water and may crack. The main source of the opal was Hungary (*see* HUNGARIAN OPAL) until the stone was discovered in 1849 in Australia and later Mexico and elsewhere as to several varieties; the present greatest source is Australia. There has long been a superstition (perhaps of

Teutonic origin) that wearing an opal is unlucky, sometimes attributed to the ill-fortune brought to the owner of one in the novel *Anne of Geierstein* by Sir Walter Scott; it did not deter Queen Victoria from wearing them or giving them as gifts, and it has diminished since the discovery of fine opals in Australia. Among famous opals are the DEVONSHIRE OPAL; THE HUNGARIAN OPAL; PRINCE HARLEQUIN OPAL. *See* AMBER OPAL; BLACK OPAL; FIRE OPAL; HUNGARIAN OPAL; LECHOSOS OPAL; OPAL DOUBLET; OPAL MATRIX; PROSPECTOR'S BROOCH; SLOCUM STONE; STAR OPAL.

opal agate. A variety of AGATE having alternate bands of OPAL. Sometimes called 'agate opal'.

opal doublet. A type of DOUBLET, made as a COMPOSITE STONE to imitate PRECIOUS OPAL, in which a thin film of good opal is mounted on poor quality opal, black ONYX or black PASTE, or a thin layer of opal is backed with OPAL MATRIX, OBSIDIAN or opalized wood. Sometimes a TRIPLET (called a 'triplex opal') is made by covering such a doublet with a dome of ROCK CRYSTAL cut EN CABOCHON, to afford protection, although reducing the lustre and iridescence. Such composite stones should be distinguished from those natural stones that are a layer of true opal over its MATRIX (*see* OPAL MATRIX). An inferior opal doublet is sometimes made by cementing a layer of QUARTZ or GLASS cut en cabochon over a thin layer of MOTHER-OF-PEARL.

opal matrix. A variety of PRECIOUS OPAL that is embedded in and cut with part of the surrounding MATRIX. Some stones have tiny iridescent multicoloured specks due to ironstone INCLUSIONS too numerous to be isolated, so that the whole mass is cut and polished. Some specimens have a film of BLACK OPAL over a layer of matrix. *See* OPAL DOUBLET.

opalescence. The phenomenon of a shimmering display of milky-white light, sometimes with a bluish tinge, in some gemstones that is caused by the interference of light due to the inclusion of small particles of matter within the stone, e.g. in CHALCEDONY and in some COMMON OPAL and MOONSTONE. The term has sometimes been applied to the play of colours shown in a PRECIOUS OPAL (which is caused by diffraction of white light from the closely packed and orderly arranged minute spheres that constitute the structure of the stone), but strictly that phenomenon is known as IRIDESCENCE; however, the terms are sometimes loosely used synonymously. *See* SCHILLER; SHEEN.

opaline. (1) A variety of CHALCEDONY that is of an opalescent yellow colour. (2) A translucent type of glass, produced in several pastel colours.

opalite. (1) A variety of BANDED OPAL with cinnabar-red bands. Also called 'myrickite'.

opaque. Not transmitting light at all; as applied to a gemstone, a stone through which light cannot be transmitted when sliced to a thickness of 0.04 mm. An example of an opaque gemstone is the TURQUOISE. *See* TRANSPARENT; TRANSLUCENT.

open setting. The style of SETTING a gemstone (usually a transparent faceted stone) in a finger ring or other article of jewelry so that the FACETS of the PAVILION are exposed to light, as opposed to a CLOSED SETTING. There are several variations of such settings that were introduced in the late 18th century and following years, usually having the stone supported by a circle of prongs projected upward from the SHANK or by an encircling open-bottom COLLET or by a BOX SETTING from which the bottom has been cut away. Also called an '*à jour* setting'.

openwork. A style of decoration of metal articles that shows openings in the material for the passage of light, by (1) thin wire not completely attached to the metal base of the article, or thin wire in a pattern entirely independent of any metal base (e.g. FILIGREE) or (2) piercing the metal that is the base of an article so as to make a pattern (e.g. OPUS INTERRASILE). *See* AJOURÉ WORK.

operculum. The horny or shell-like plate at the rear of the shell of the sea-snail that closes, as a 'door', to cover the aperture when the snail has retracted into the shell and that rests on the snail's back when it is moving. The opercula are slightly domed and range from 1 to 2.5 cm in diameter; they are greenish at the top, shading down to white and yellow at one edge and to reddish-brown at the other. The flat underside is covered with a brownish skin of conchiolin. They are used in the Far East, where the snails are found, as jewelry, being set in ear-rings, bracelets, necklaces, and brooches. Such pieces are sometimes referred to as 'shell-' or 'Chinese-' or 'Pacific-cat's-eye', owing to the shape and colouring, but unlike CAT'S-EYE stones they are not CHATOYANT. Some small specimens, called an 'eyestone', are used for inserting under the lid of a human eye to work out a foreign substance.

Oppenheimer Diamond. A large, pale yellow, uncut, octahedron diamond, weighing rough 253.70 carats, that was found in 1964 at the Dutoitspan Mine at Kimberley, South Africa (hence formerly called the 'Dutoitspan Diamond'). It was acquired by HARRY WINSTON and presented by him in 1964 to the Smithsonian Institution, Washington, DC, in memory of Sir Ernest Oppenheimer, formerly Chairman of De Beers Consolidated Mines Ltd. *See* DUTOITSPAN DIAMOND.

opus interrasile (Latin). A style of OPENWORK decoration of metal that was used in ETRUSCAN JEWELRY and later in ROMAN JEWELRY and in BYZANTINE JEWELRY, made by piercing the metal (usually gold) with a chisel or other tool to form an openwork pattern. It is found on bracelets, finger rings, ear-rings, and necklaces, and on borders of medallions. The work is of varied patterns and often made as the background of the design, sometimes so minutely pierced as to appear like gold lace. The style was superseded by an *ajouré* scroll style (*see* AJOURÉ WORK), and there is an intermediate style, Byzantine, 6th century, made by means of a large number of short tubes soldered side by side. The French term is *travail ajouré*.

Orange Pearls, The. Three ropes of graduated pearls and two pearl ear-rings that were made up, *c.* 1703, from pearls that had been inherited by King Frederick I of Prussia from his mother, Louisa Henrietta of Orange, who had married in 1646 Frederick William, the Great Elector. The pearls were included among the Crown Jewels of Kaiser William II in 1913, but their ownership now is unknown.

opus interrasile. Gold mount with openwork decoration depicting mounted horsewoman. Asia Minor, 4th century. W. 5.1 cm. British Museum, London.

orb. A spherical ornament that has, since its use by Roman and Byzantine rulers, been regarded as a symbol of sovereignty. Orbs were originally surmounted by a figure of Victory, but from Christian times by a jewelled cross; examples were used generally in Europe after the Middle Ages, especially by the Germanic rulers from the 5th century. They have been used as such symbols in most of the countries of Europe, varying somewhat in style and decoration, but usually encircled horizontally by a band (called the 'equator') set with gemstones and joined by another upright semi-circular band (called the 'meridian') arching over the top and surmounted by a cross. The orbs in the Russian REGALIA in the 17th century were almost completely covered with enamelled plaques and gemstones. There are two orbs in the British royal regalia; *see* ORBS, THE ROYAL. *See* MONDE.

orbicular jasper. A variety of JASPER that has a high percentage of INCLUSIONS of impurities, mainly clay and iron oxide of contrasting colour, in an orbicular effect, i.e. in spherical or orb-like shapes in successive concentric zones, creating an effect of spots on a background of a different colour.

Orbs, The Royal. The two ORBS that are included among the British CROWN JEWELS and that symbolize kingly power and justice, as well as dominion of the Christian religion over the world. An orb was used in England first in 1053, and first at a coronation by Henry VI in 1191. (1) The King's (Sovereign's) Orb, a globe of gold encircled by a band (equator) edged with pearls and set with rubies, emeralds, and sapphires, joined by a band (meridian) arching across the top and surmounted by a large amethyst above which is a jewelled CROSS FORMÉE. It was made for Charles II in 1661, but was reset several times until its use by Queen Victoria. It is considered perhaps the most sacred article in the Coronation REGALIA. It is placed in the left hand of the Sovereign during a part of the Coronation ceremony. (2) The Queen's Orb, a similar but smaller and lighter orb, made for Queen Mary II when she became Queen Regnant in 1689 with William III.

order. The BADGE or insigne worn by a member of any of various types of orders, such as the orders of royalty, nobility, chivalry or merit, e.g. Order of the Garter, Order of the Thistle, Order of the Bath. The badges were usually ornately enamelled and set with gemstones. Sometimes articles of jewelry were made in the general style of an order and worn as an ornamental piece. Such orders exist in a great number of countries. These badges, as well as the badges of guilds and other bodies, are in general beyond the scope of this book. *See* GOLDEN FLEECE; SS COLLAR; TRESS, ORDER OF THE.

orfèvrerie. The French term for the type of jewelry that consists mainly of gold or silver, the product of the goldsmith, as distinguished from JOAILLERIE and BIJOUTERIE.

orient. The IRIDESCENT lustre of the surface of a pearl and also of the nacreous lining (MOTHER-OF-PEARL) of the shell of a mollusc. It is a characteristic SHEEN that is more pronounced on pearls of highest quality. It is caused by the combined effect of (1) the interference of light from the succession of thin translucent laminae that compose the surface of the pearl, and (2) the diffraction of light that is reflected from the closely packed lines where such laminae meet the surface. Pearls having a fine orient are sometimes said to be 'ripe', those of poor quality being called 'unripe'.

Oriental. Eastern, although not necessarily, as applied to a gemstone, from the East, but a loose term that is often prefixed (as a misnomer) to the names of stones that resemble other stones (e.g. 'Oriental topaz' for 'yellow corundum') or sometimes to a stone of superior quality. The continued use of the word in such context today is probably a misrepresentation in law.

Oriental almandine. A misnomer formerly used for a violet variety of CORUNDUM (SAPPHIRE).

Oriental amethyst. A misnomer for a purple variety of CORUNDUM (SAPPHIRE), somewhat resembling an AMETHYST.

Oriental aquamarine. A misnomer for a light blue-green variety of CORUNDUM (SAPPHIRE), somewhat resembling an AQUAMARINE.

Oriental chrysolite. A misnomer for yellowish-green CORUNDUM (SAPPHIRE) and yellowish-green CHRYSOBERYL.

Oriental emerald. A misnomer for a rare deep-green variety of CORUNDUM (SAPPHIRE) that somewhat resembles an EMERALD.

Oriental pearl. A pearl from a PEARL OYSTER of the Persian Gulf and, by extension, from such oysters of the Red Sea and the Gulf of Manaar between Sri Lanka (formerly Ceylon) and India. It is the highest quality pearl. Such pearls were brought to Europe in medieval times and in the Elizabethan era, often being regarded then as more valuable than a diamond.

Oriental topaz. A misnomer for a yellowish variety of CORUNDUM that is properly a SAPPHIRE.

orle. A WREATH or CHAPLET encircling or surmounting the helmet of a 15th-century knight. Such pieces were made originally of two bands of ribbon twisted together, but later they were ornaments decorated with gemstones.

Orlov (Orloff) Diamond. A famous diamond that is white, slightly bluish-green, with its weight now recorded as 189.60 carats; it is of irregular hemispherical shape, still in its original Indian ROSE CUT form. Its early history is uncertain. One legend, no longer believed, is that it is a part of the GREAT MOGUL DIAMOND; another is that it was originally in the eye of the Hindu god Sri-Ranga in a temple at Srirangam, Madras, in India, and was stolen by a French deserter and resold several times. It is generaly agreed that it was purchased in Amsterdam in 1775 from an Armenian merchant by Prince Gregori Gregorievich Orlov (1734–83), whose name is engraved on it, and was presented by him to his patron, Catherine the Great of Russia. The diamond was set in the top of the Russian Imperial Sceptre that she had made and that is now in the Diamond Treasury in the Kremlin at Moscow.

ormolu (from French *or moulu*). Literally, ground gold. An ALLOY of COPPER, zinc, and tin, having the colour throughout of GOLD. It is similar in appearance to gilded brass and GILT BRONZE. Today the term is loosely applied in England and the United States to brass or bronze gilded by the process of fire gilding or mercury gilding, or even to copper so gilded as a cheap imitation. Ormolu has been used in England as a mount for objects of porcelain or glass, and only to a limited extent in jewelry. *See* Nicholas Goodison, *Ormolu* (1974).

orthoclase. A mineral of the FELDSPAR group. The term used alone usually refers to one variety that is sometimes used as a gemstone which is transparent or yellow. It is sometimes BRILLIANT CUT or EMERALD CUT, and resembles yellow BERYL. *See* MOONSTONE; ADULARIA.

Osman, Louis (1914–). An English DESIGNER-MAKER whose best-known work is the PRINCE OF WALES'S INVESTITURE CORONET made by ELECTROFORMING for the Investiture in 1969. He also made a replica of the Magna Carta that was presented as the gift of Great Britain to the United States upon its Bicentennial celebration in 1976.

Otto the Great, Crown of. *See* IMPERIAL CROWN.

Ottonian jewelry. Articles of jewelry made during and shortly after the reign of Otto I of Germany, 936–73, Holy Roman Emperor, 962–73, following the period of CAROLINGIAN JEWELRY. It shows the influence of contemporary Byzantine art. Among the examples are several brooches (sometimes called FIBULAE) with decoration depicting an eagle (*see* GISELA BROOCH) or decorated with gemstones in cruciform pattern, with raised FILIGREE work. With the introduction of Christian burials, interment with jewelry was discontinued, so surviving specimens are rare, being from abbeys, cathedrals, and royal treasuries. *See* GISELA, EMPRESS, TREASURE OF; IMPERIAL CROWN.

ouch. A type of brooch worn sewn to a garment instead of being attached by a pin. Sometimes called a NOUCH; but the term 'ouch' is found in the Bible, Exodus xxviii, 11, 13, 25, referring to a gold jewel enclosing an engraved onyx and worn on each shoulder of an *ephod* (a priest's garment), having attached to it a gold chain to support a breastplate. The term has sometimes been spelt 'ouche' or 'owche'. *See* DOWGATE HILL BROOCH.

overlay. The technique of decorating silverware by use of two sheets of silver and sweating them together (i.e. heating until they adhere). The process used by the Indians of south-western United States involves cutting a design into one sheet and sweating it to the other uncut flat sheet, then blackening the exposed areas of the bottom sheet to emphasize the design and to create the effect of a piece carved from a single solid sheet.

overlay. Cut-out upper plaque and complete piece. Hopi Indian. Tom Bahti Indian Art Shop, Tucson, Arizona.

owl's-eye agate. A variety of AGATE where there are two adjacent sets of concentric black circles surrounding a black pupil-like dot, and with the outer bands having feathery edges, the overall appearance being suggestive of the eye of an owl.

oxidation (or **oxidization**). The result of combining an element or metal with oxygen, producing an oxide that presents an 'antique' finish. It is not related, as often incorrectly stated, to the process by which SILVER acquires a TARNISH, that being due to contact with sulphurous fumes in the air. The process can be effected artificially by immersion of the metal in heated potassium sulphide solution. When silver is alloyed with copper, the latter is oxidized by the heating, so that the alloy must be immersed in PICKLE to remove the copper oxide. *See* SOLDERING; PATINA.

IX *Pre-Columbian jewelry.* Left, gold ornament representing a bird with projecting beak. Sinú River, Colombia. L. 15.8 cm. Centre top, gold bell with jaguar heads around edge. A clapper in the hollow belly of the centre figure completes the bell. Chiriquí, Panama. 7.6 x 7.6 cm. Centre bottom, gold human figure. Chiriquí, Panama. Right, gold figure pendant representing a deity. Morales, Colombia. L. 13.3 cm. Museum of the American Indian, Heye Foundation, New York.

X *Renaissance jewelry.* Top, pendant. Diana, with stag and hound. Enamelled gold set with a diamond, emeralds, rubies and pearls. Italian, 16th century. Left, pendant in the form of a lizard. Enamelled gold set with a Baroque pearl and emerald and hung with a pearl. Italian or Spanish, 16th century. Right, pendant in the form of a ship. Enamelled gold, the hull of crystal. Italian, 16th century. Bottom, pendant. Enamelled gold, surrounding an onyx cameo head of Hercules. The sapphire drop and emeralds set in silver gilt are modern additions. German, late 16th century. Victoria & Albert Museum, London.

Oxus Armlet. A gold ARMLET (of a pair) in PENANNULAR form, almost solid at the incurved back of the hoop but tubular towards the terminals that are in the shape of winged monsters (the Persian development of the griffin) with horns, high ears, body, and forelegs of a lion, and the wings, head, and hindlegs of an eagle. Parts are decorated with chased (*see* CHASING) decoration and attached wires (CLOISONS) from which the original inlays are now missing. The pair are of Persian origin, 5th/4th century BC, and are part of the OXUS TREASURE. One such armlet is at the British Museum, another at the Victoria & Albert Museum, London.

Oxus Armlet. Gold penannular armlet, Oxus Treasure. Persian, 5th/4th centuries BC. Victoria & Albert Museum, London.

Oxus Treasure. A TREASURE of many varied gold and silver articles, including jewelry, from the 5th/4th centuries BC that was found *c.* 1877 near the Oxus River (now the Amu Darya) in Bactria (in present-day Russian Turkestan adjoining Afghanistan). Its history is uncertain, but it has been said that it was sold by local bandits to Moslem merchants who carried it to India where they resold it to Captain F. C. Burton, an English official there. Most of it is now in the British Museum. Much of the jewelry has been attributed to Persian origin or to Persian influence, but it has been surmised, on stylistic grounds, that some of the pieces came from other sources, possibly from the areas of central Asia inhabited by the Scythians and the Sarmatians. The jewelry includes several gold ARMLETS and finger rings. *See* O. M. Dalton, *The Treasure of the Oxus* (3rd ed. 1964). *See* OXUS ARMLET; ZIWIYE TREASURE; SCYTHIAN JEWELRY; SARMATIAN JEWELRY.

oyster-shell pendant. A type of hollow pendant made of thin gold or ELECTRUM sheet in the form of the shell of a variety of oyster (*Avicula*). Some from the XIIth Dynasty in ancient Egypt (*c.* 1991 BC–1784 BC) were inscribed with the praenomen of the King; uninscribed examples were worn as an AMULET in the Middle Kingdom, *c.* 2035 BC–1668 BC. It has been surmised that natural inscribed oyster-shells were used as a military decoration, and perhaps metal ones also.

P

padpara(d)scha(h). A term, now regarded as unnecessary, applied to a variety of CORUNDUM (SAPPHIRE) from Sri Lanka (formerly Ceylon) that is pinkish-orange, and also to a SYNTHETIC CORUNDUM of similar colour, due to the nickel oxide used as a colouring agent. The word is derived from the Sinhalese word *padmaragaya* (lotus-colour).

Pahlavi Crown. The CROWN made in 1925 for the coronation of Reza Shah Pahlavi (1877–1944), designed by the jeweller Serajeddin and made of selected gemstones in the Iranian Crown Jewels. It has, above a circlet, 4 arches and 4 step-shaped panels projecting slightly outward, each panel decorated with a large diamond-set sunburst, the front sunburst including a 60-carat diamond. The crown is set with 3,380 diamonds, 369 matched pearls, and 5 emeralds that weigh 199 carats. It is surmounted by a jewelled and feather ornament. It was worn by Mohammed Reza Shah Pahlavi at his coronation on 26 October 1967.

painted enamel. Pendant with scene 'Solomon turning to idolatry'. Limoges, 16th century. Walters Art Gallery, Baltimore, Md.

paillon (French). (1) A small piece of FOIL. (2) A spangle of gold, silver or coloured enamelled material, cut into geometric or various other shapes, rolled very thin, and fired between two layers of translucent enamel. Such pieces were set as decoration on some small boxes and ÉTUIS, and were a speciality of Jean Coteau. A very small piece, called a *paillette*, was sometimes sewn as decoration on fabrics. (3) A tiny piece of gold foil, used in quantity, mixed with the enamel on or in the ground of some PAINTED ENAMEL jewelry to provide a flashing effect. (4) A small pellet of SOLDER that is placed between two metal parts to be joined by SOLDERING.

painted enamel. Enamel decoration on a flat surface with the enamel applied by painting with a brush, as in GRISAILLE, without any CLOISONS or depressions in the metal base to separate the colours, such as in CLOISONNÉ or CHAMPLEVÉ enamelling. Several layers of enamel are applied, using different colours to make the design, each layer being fused and polished (first on a carborundum wheel and then by a felt buff charged with pumice) before the next layer is applied; the later layers must each have a lower melting-point than the preceding layers to avoid mingling. This method was developed in the 15th century but was not successful until the introduction of COUNTER-ENAMELLING. It has become known as LIMOGES ENAMEL owing to its having been used extensively at Limoges, although not exclusively there. A modern version sometimes uses a stencil to outline the design. *See* EN PLEIN ENAMELLING.

painted grisaille. *See* GRISAILLE.

palladium. A rare metallic element of the PLATINUM group. It is similar to platinum, being silver-white, malleable, ductile, and in ordinary conditions non-tarnishable, but it is much lighter in weight. It is used in jewelry alone or as PALLADIUM ALLOY, as a less expensive substitute for platinum. It was discovered in 1803 by William Hyde Wollaston and named by him after Pallas, a newly discovered asteroid. Palladium is often used today, because of its being lighter and cheaper than platinum, to make wedding rings and jewelry that can be worn without 'drag' on dresses of silk or lightweight materials.

palladium alloy. An ALLOY of PALLADIUM and GOLD or SILVER, and sometimes, to provide hardness, with ruthenium, for making certain objects of jewelry. There are no legal standards for its quality.

Paltscho flowers. Brooch of rose bouquet; blossoms of yellow Mexican onyx, leaves of nephrite, with gold stems and diamonds. Courtesy of Ernst Paltscho, Vienna.

Paltscho flowers. Articles of jewelry (mainly brooches) in the form of various flowers, singly or in small bouquets, made of carved ROCK CRYSTAL and coloured HARDSTONES. The petals and leaves simulate natural colours, the stems are of gold, and most pieces are embellished with diamonds. Examples range from large orchids to a spray of lilies-of-the-valley. Some flowers, especially a rose, are made of carved coral. The designer is Ernst Paltscho (b. 1899) of Vienna, who owns and carries on the business of his father (d. 1929) which was started by the latter's father. In recent years imitations have been made by others in Vienna.

pampilles, en (French). A style of decoration of jewelry in the form of a cascade of several gemstones (or ornaments of PASTE), descending in diminishing size, and terminating with a thin, tapering, pointed 'icicle-shaped' ornament. It is found on brooches and ear-rings of the 19th century, and also on some pieces of CUT STEEL JEWELRY. *See* AIGUILLETTE.

panagia. A type of MEDALLION depicting the Virgin Mary, worn by bishops. The name is derived from the Greek word meaning 'All Holy', the epithet of the Virgin Mary. Some examples were mounted in Russia as a central ornament in a pendant, surrounded by decorative arrangements of large and small gemstones.

Panamanian jewelry. Articles of PRE-COLUMBIAN JEWELRY made, *c.* AD 500-1500, in regions of Panama, i.e. Coclé (*see* COCLÉ JEWELRY), Veraguas, and parts of Chiriquí adjoining Costa Rica. A few articles were made of hammered thin gold plates with REPOUSSÉ work and inlaid decoration, but most were made by the CIRE PERDUE process. They included bracelets, belts, head-bands, breast ornaments, finger rings, nose rings, ear ornaments, and distinctive twin-figure pendants. Many such pieces were decorated with a wide variety of zoomorphic motifs with suspended rectangular plaques hanging in front of the figure, and also deity figures with a human body but a head in the form of a bird, fish, shellfish, frog, alligator, deer, monkey, etc., some being double-headed figures. Some male figures were made naked except for replicas of articles of jewelry worn by the figure. The styles and workmanship were often very similar to those of the neighbouring Quimbaya region of Colombia (*see* QUIMBAYA JEWELRY). *See* VENADO BEACH TREASURE.

pampilles, en. Silver brooch with paste aiguillettes. English, *c.* 1840. Victoria & Albert Museum, London.

papal ring. A type of finger ring that is made of a gilded base metal and is massive in form, having a wide, heavy hoop and a high, square BEZEL, being characteristically too large to be worn on any finger, even securely on a thumb; it is often set with an inferior-quality foiled stone or PASTE. Such rings bear on the bezel the arms of a Pope or Cardinal (and sometimes also the arms of a contemporary temporal ruler) as well as such papal symbols as the triple crown and crossed keys, and sometimes on the hoop the symbols of the four Evangelists. They have been found in great number, some duplicated in form, all indicating that they were not intended for use by church dignitaries, much less the Pope. Their purpose is uncertain, but it has been surmised that they were worn or carried as a credential by a papal emissary to the indicated ruler or given by the Pope to pilgrims as souvenirs. Although some are from the 11th and 12th centuries, most are from the 15th and 16th centuries. *See* ECCLESIASTICAL RING; FISHERMAN'S RING.

paragon. (1) A term used in 16th-century Europe to describe a diamond weighing at least 12 carats, but today a flawless stone weighing at least 100 carats. (2) A type of pearl that is exceptionally large; some such pearls come from very large oysters, up to 30 cm wide, that are found in the South Pacific and off the coast of Australia.

parcel-gilt. Partial gilt, as on some silver jewelry, to form a design (by providing a contrast between the design and the background) or appearing on only part of the piece. Sometimes called 'party-gilt'.

Parian jewelry. Articles of jewelry of which the principal decoration is an object made of Parian porcelain (an unglazed biscuit porcelain that superficially resembles white marble). The porcelain parts are usually in the form of white flowers and bouquets. The ware was introduced in England by Copeland's at Stoke-on-Trent in 1846, and later unmarked examples were made by other English and American potters. Wedgwood introduced an improved Parian in 1860. The name was inspired by the Parian marble from the Greek island of Paros. The porcelain objects are set in a gold mount as a brooch. *See* CERAMIC JEWELRY.

Paris work. A Renaissance designation for jewelry that was hollow, with pierced work and filigree – not necessarily jewelry made in Paris. *See* SPANISH WORK.

parrot jewelry. An article of jewelry (usually a pendant) of which the decorative motif is a parrot. *See* BIRD JEWELRY.

Parthian jewelry. Articles of jewelry made in limited quantity in Parthia, a country of south-west Asia near the Caspian Sea in the region of modern Khurasan, Iran. The Parthian empire was at its height from the 1st century BC until the 1st century AD. The jewelry included buckles, ear-rings, and pendants made of gold with decoration of embossed work (*see* EMBOSSING), GRANULATED GOLD, and FILIGREE work, sometimes set with GARNETS.

parti-coloration. The effect of two or more distinct colours present in the crystals of different parts of the same gemstone, so that when the stone is cut the different colours are visible in separate parts. Such effect is found in some TOURMALINE and CORUNDUM.

parting. The quality of some gemstones (e.g. CORUNDUM) that makes it possible for them to split only along certain definite planes (e.g. some twinning planes) of the crystal, contrary to CLEAVAGE which leads to splitting anywhere parallel to the cleavage plane.

parure. A set of jewelled ornaments decorated EN SUITE or made of the same variety of gemstone, and intended to be worn at the same time, such as a necklace, bracelets, brooch, and ear-rings (and sometimes an AIGRETTE or SÉVIGNÉ). The modern term is sometimes a 'suite'. Less than a full set is called a 'demi-parure'. Such assemblages of jewelry became fashionable in the second half of the 16th century and were revived in the 19th century; they were made with diamonds for formal wear and other gemstones for daytime wear. Some were made of BERLIN IRON JEWELRY. *See* BRIDAL PARURE; DEVONSHIRE PARURE.

Pasfield Jewel. A pendant in the form of a pistol, with a whistle set in the mouth; within the barrel is a swivelled three-piece set of toilet

panagia. Pendant with painted medallion depicting the Virgin Mary. Russian, 19th century. Courtesy of Wartski, London.

Panamanian jewelry. Gold pendant. Coclé, *c.* AD 300–500. Museo del Hombre, Panama.

papal ring. Gilt bronze with crystal (or glass). Mid-15th century. W. (internal) 2.6 cm. City Museums and Art Gallery, Birmingham, England.

Parian jewelry. Brooches of Parian porcelain. English, *c.* 1850. L. (lower right) 4.5 cm. Courtesy of Geoffrey Godden, Worthing, England.

parrot jewelry. Gold pendant with enamelling, rubies, and pearls. H. 6.6 cm. National Trust, Waddesdon Manor, Aylesbury, England.

parure. Necklace, bracelets, brooch, and ear-rings of Berlin iron jewelry. Hallmark of Geiss, Berlin; *c.* 1820. Nordiska Museum, Stockholm.

implements (a TOOTHPICK, an EAR-PICK, and a nail cleaner). The piece is of gold, set with emeralds. It is English, late 16th century.

paste jewelry. Articles of jewelry that are decorated with PASTE, often said to simulate jewelry set with diamonds or other gemstones, but having its own characteristics. It became very popular in England and France, and somewhat in Spain, during the 18th century, owing to the demand of the middle classes for inexpensive jewelry, to new techniques for cutting stones to increase brilliance, and even to the prevalence of highwaymen who made the carrying of paste jewelry a lesser risk. So many persons were engaged in France in making paste jewelry after the invention of STRASS that there was a corporation, *c.* 1767, of *joailliers-faussetiers.* The articles, including brooches, bracelets, necklaces, and especially finger rings, were made of silver or occasionally of PEWTER, and are often found with a RUB-OVER SETTING or PAVÉ SETTING. Many examples have survived, as the low value of the stones and setting did not warrant the labour of remodelling, as was done with jewelry of gold and gemstones, and also such remodelling presented great technical difficulties. Paste jewelry can be fairly readily distinguished from other jewelry by several means: (1) the paste itself is warmer than gemstones and more easily scratched; (2) the paste stones are cut to fit the setting rather than in the conventional shapes of gemstones; (3) the settings are different, those for paste being generally closed and foiled settings, especially for pieces made before the 19th century: (4) genuine 18th-century pieces are lighter than later specimens, and the silver settings are usually without assay mark (*see* ASSAYING) because of the thinness; and (5) inspection for BLACK SPOT. *See* M. D. S. Lewis, *Ancient Paste Jewellery* (1970).

paste. GLASS of several types, but usually of great BRILLIANCE, that is cut and set in PASTE JEWELRY. The paste used by Italian jewellers of the 15th to 17th centuries (*see* MILANESE PASTE) and also in England for ANGLO-SAXON JEWELRY, was basically ordinary glass that was highly refractive and simulated the brilliance of diamonds. After George Ravenscroft developed, *c.* 1675, lead (flint) glass in England, it was used extensively there and elsewhere for paste jewelry. In France, such jewelry was made, from the mid-18th century, of STRASS. Paste is usually colourless, but some is tinted, although more often given a coloured effect by being backed with FOIL; the foil adds brilliance, but often becomes discoloured (especially when air or dampness enters the setting), resulting in a PATINA sometimes deemed desirable. Some stones are sometimes erroneously referred to as paste, e.g. RHINESTONE, BRISTOL DIAMOND, ROCK CRYSTAL. The term 'paste' (possibly derived from the Italian *pasta*), as used in England, dates from the translation by Christopher Merret of the book *L'Arte Vetraria* (1662) by Antonio Neri. Good-quality paste is extensively made today in France, Austria, and Czechoslovakia.

pâte de verre (French). Literally, glass paste. A material produced by grinding glass to a powder, adding a fluxing medium so that it could be readily melted, and then colouring it (or using powdered coloured glass). Objects were made of it in a mould and the material was fused by firing. The varied colouring was obtained by the positioning of different powdered ingredients in the mould. The process was used in ancient Greece to simulate gemstones set in finger rings and was revived in France in the 19th century, especially, as to jewelry, for articles made in ART NOUVEAU style.

paternoster. One of the large beads on a ROSARY, placed preceding each DECADE (group of ten AVE beads) and on which the Lord's Prayer is said. Such beads were made of various materials and in various forms. The makers (known as 'paternosterers') in France were grouped as specialists who made beads of (1) BONE or HORN, (2) CORAL or MOTHER-OF-PEARL, and (3) AMBER or JET. In London the makers were concentrated near the jewellers in Cheapside, in streets called 'Paternoster Row' and 'Ave Maria Lane'. By 1514 the term 'paternoster' was applied to any large gold bead, even one in an ordinary necklace. *See* DECADE RING.

patina. A thin, greenish film or discoloration that forms, after long exposure to the atmosphere, on bronze and copper, sometimes on jewelry of such metals, adding a prized artistic effect. The natural patina is a carbonate of copper that forms to protect the metal from further

OXIDATION. By extension of the term, it has been applied to a reddish patina-effect on ancient GOLD jewelry and to the so-called patina on SILVER that is a surface blur resulting from numerous shallow scratches. An artificial patina can be produced with acids.

Patricia Emerald. An uncut EMERALD found in 1920 in the Chivor mine, near Bogotá, Colombia, weighing 632 carats and measuring 6.5 by 2.5 cm. It was donated anonymously to the American Museum of Natural History, New York City

Pátzcuaro fish necklace. A type of necklace of Mexican PEASANT JEWELRY made in the lakeside villages (now tourist centres) near Lake Pátzcuaro, in Michoacán, west of Mexico City. It is composed of cast silver replicas of the local fish, stylized or resembling the local specimens, suspended between beads of imitation CORAL. Comparable ear-rings, made at Tlatlauqui, in Puebla, are of cast silver or gold, with pendent fish. *See* FISH JEWELRY; MEXICAN JEWELRY.

pavé setting. Literally, paving-stone setting. A style of SETTING in which many small gemstones (usually CALIBRÉ or faceted diamonds, sometimes TURQUOISE and half-drilled pearls) are set very close together in a mass so as to cover the entire piece and to conceal the metal. The stones (often backed with FOIL) are secured in holes drilled through the metal base and held in place by burrs pressed down over the edges of the stones. It is a style used for brooches, pendants, etc. that seek to emphasize the massed effect rather than any individual stone. On some dome-shaped jewels, the stones must be of graduated sizes, diminishing in concentric circles from the central stone, to permit accurate close spacing. *See* CARVED SETTING.

pavilion. The part of a BRILLIANT below the GIRDLE. It is sometimes called the 'base'. *See* BRILLIANT CUT.

pavilion facet. One of the 8 elongated LOZENGE-shaped FACETS on the PAVILION of a BRILLIANT, all extending down from the GIRDLE to the CULET. The 4 pavilion facets, alternating with 4 similar adjacent facets (formerly called QUOINS) are all now considered together as a group of 8 pavilion facets, the only differences being their orientation to the stone and the direction and sequence in which they are ground.

Peace Ruby. A RUBY found in Burma weighing 43 carats uncut and so named because it had been found on Armistice Day, 1919. Also called 'Chhatrapati Manick' (literally, 'Ruler's Jewel').

peacock ore. An iridescent variety of BORNITE.

peapod. A French decorative motif, of the 17th century, in the form of an elongated curved leaf-shape or a diminishing row of dots like peas in a peapod. It was used as enamelled decoration on some lockets, pendants, and watch-cases, and also as the shape of some elaborate AIGRETTES and frames for some miniatures. Occasionally it was used as the shape of a metal strip set with gemstones. The French term is *cosse de pois*, the German is *Schotenornamentik*. Among the leading exponents of the style were GIDÉON LÉGARÉ, JEAN VAUQUER, NATHANIEL MARCHANT, and JEAN TOUTIN.

pear-shaped. Pyriform, as applied to diamonds and pearls in this shape. Such a diamond is sometimes called 'drop-shaped'; if the narrow end is pointed, it is a PENDELOQUE. In the case of a pearl, it is sometimes called 'drop-shaped' or a 'drop pearl'.

pearl. A dense, lustrous concretion, formed within the shell of certain molluscs, that is used as a gemstone and classified with PRECIOUS STONES. The finest pearls (called ORIENTAL PEARL) are produced by the PEARL OYSTER. The pearl is composed of conchiolin and calcium carbonate (in the form of minuscule prisms of calcite or aragonite) that is secreted by the MANTLE of the mollusc and is deposited as NACRE in very many thin concentric layers to surround some foreign particle (usually thought to be a grain of sand, but now believed possibly a cellular tissue that causes a resistance) that has entered the shell by nature (making a 'true pearl' or a 'wild pearl') or has been inserted by man (making a CULTURED PEARL); but *see* IMITATION PEARL. The pearl is either attached to the interior of

Pasfield Jewel. Pendant in form of pistol with whistle and manicure set. Gold set with emeralds. English, late 16th century. L. 8 cm. Victoria & Albert Museum, London.

pavé setting. Brooch with *pavé* set diamonds and central pearl. Courtesy of Boucheron Ltd, London.

the shell (BLISTER PEARL) or formed within the body of the mollusc (MANTLE PEARL). The sizes vary (from SEED PEARL to PARAGON PEARL) as well as the form, from the finest, which are spherical, to the oval or egg-shaped or those that are irregularly-shaped (*see* BAROQUE PEARL; BOUTON PEARL; DROP PEARL; HINGE PEARL; HAMMER PEARL; POIRE). The colours also vary, usually depending on the water where produced, from pink (*see* ROSÉE PEARL) to various faint tints (*see* FANCY-COLOURED PEARLS) and blackish (*see* BLACK PEARL) but some are artificially coloured (*see* STAINING). The finest specimens have a satin lustre (*see* ORIENT; WATER). Pearls are used as beads in a PEARL NECKLACE, suspended from brooches, ear-rings, and pendants, and set in finger rings, pins, brooches, etc. Probably the largest known round pearl is *La Reine Perle*, weighing 111 grains.

—— *varieties.* In addition to those of the pearl oyster, pearls are produced by other molluscs and are generally designated by the name of the mollusc, e.g. ABALONE PEARL, CLAM PEARL, CONCH PEARL, MUSSEL PEARL. *See* COQUE DE PERLE; FRESH-WATER PEARL; MOLLUSC SHELL.

—— *drilling.* Pearls are usually pierced through the centre for stringing or part-way for setting in ear-rings, pendants, STUDS, etc. Most drilling of ORIENTAL PEARLS is done in Bombay by means of a bow-drill. Pearls to be strung are drilled from each side to make a straight hole; those to be set are partially drilled and are cemented to a metal peg. Some inferior pearls are CHINESE DRILLED.

—— *pricing.* The monetary value of a natural pearl is calculated by using the base system (once-the-weight method). Seed pearls are priced by the CARAT or ounce, and cultured pearls formerly by the momme.

—— *identification.* For several methods of distinguishing a natural pearl from a cultured pearl, *see* CULTURED PEARL.

—— *measurement.* The weight of a natural pearl is measured in GRAINS, of a cultured pearl formerly by the momme. The size of a circular pearl is measured in millimetres.

—— *care of pearls.* Pearls become damaged (1) by acid (as from the skin or some hair-lotions or cosmetics), owing to the effect on the aragonite in the pearl, resulting in the pearl (especially a cultured pearl) becoming barrel-shaped, with only two nacreous caps at the ends; (2) by grease (as from the skin or certain cosmetics), the grease entering the drill-hole by capillary attraction from the string; and (3) by dryness, from dry atmosphere or protracted storage, reducing the water content and causing surface cracking. Frequent wearing is advisable, also frequent restringing by a jeweller (using a nylon string and tying a knot between individual pearls to prevent loss if the string should break) and occasional cleaning by an expert.

—— *famous pearls.* Among the most famous are: THE HANOVER PEARLS; HOPE PEARL; MANCINI PEARLS; THE ORANGE PEARLS; PEREGRINA, LA.

pearl essence. *See* ESSENCE D'ORIENT.

pearl mussel. Any fresh-water mussel that produces a FRESH-WATER PEARL or, more often, MOTHER-OF-PEARL, and especially the genus *Unio* that is found in the Mississippi Valley of the United States (as well as the niggerhead mussel and the warty-back mussel) and the rivers of Scotland, north Wales, and Ireland, and parts of Germany, Austria, and Norway. Pearls are sometimes produced, but they are inferior to those of the PEARL OYSTER. The mother-of-pearl is used in great quantities to make buttons. *See* NIGGERHEAD.

pearl necklace. A necklace composed exclusively of pearls (except for the CLASP which is usually set with one or more gemstones). A necklace of good quality has pearls that are matched as to colour and ORIENT, and are well graduated from the largest one at the centre. Some necklaces consist of two or more strands of varying lengths. In a necklace the pearls should be strung with a knot between the pearls, to avoid loss in case of breakage. Some lengths are adjustable by a small attachment that forms a loop at the rear. Sometimes called a SAUTOIR or 'rope of pearls' when long. *See* BAYARDÈRE.

pearl oyster. A marine bivalve mollusc that resembles the true oyster but differs by having a byssus (a projecting tuft of filament by which the oyster attaches itself to rocks). Pearls are formed in various parts of the oyster, e.g. (1) CYST PEARL or MANTLE PEARL, (2) HEM PEARL, (3) MUSSEL PEARL, and (4) LIGAMENT PEARL.

peasant jewelry. Various articles of jewelry worn by peasants of most countries and usually made by local craftsmen in native tradition, uninfluenced by current artistic fashions until the 19th-century industrial revolution led to standardization. The major articles of various countries are: (1) *France*: A pendent cross, made in various regional styles, and worn suspended by a ribbon drawn by a jewelled slide (*coulant*) in the form of a bow-knot, heart or rosette; they were made of gold for married women and silver for girls, and were usually ornamented with foiled STRASS and sometimes gemstones. Other popular ornaments were the SAINT-ESPRIT CROSS, CROIX DE SAINT LÔ, CROIX A LA JEANNETTE, ESCLAVAGE, and NORMAN CROSS. (2) *Italy*: A large amount of peasant jewelry is worn, made in many forms, especially ear-rings and hair ornaments. Much of it echoes the styles of previous centuries. (3) *Belgium*: Long pendent crosses and ear-rings, as well as a pendent silver heart-shaped (*Sacré-Coeur*) pendant. Much of the decoration is in ROSE CUT diamonds. (4) *Netherlands*: Peasant jewelry has been, and still is, worn in abundance, especially gold, silver, and gilded ornaments worn with lace caps, some being spiral pieces worn on each side of the head with suspended pendants or pearl clusters and some merely beaten gold skull-caps (*see* OORIJZER; NEEDLES). Gold and silver buttons are worn, especially by men and boys. (5) *Germany*: Ornaments made of silver filigree, AMBER beads, and hollow silver beads. (6) *Scandinavia*: Silver ornaments with seldom any gemstones. Some buckles, crosses, and heart-shaped brooches are ornamented with suspended small concave metal discs. *See* BRIDAL CROWN; PENDANT; SØLJE; SWEDISH PEASANT PENDANT CROSS; SWEDISH PEASANT HEART BROOCH. (7) *Spain*: Articles decorated with filigree enamel and painted enamel, and the frequent RELIQUARY. (8) *Portugal*: Articles of gold filigree and long ear-rings and neck chains, many embellished with crystal; *see* RELOJ. (9) *Mexico*: Articles that vary in style in different regions, but usually adapted from the time of the Spanish conquest. Featured are large silver crosses, crescent-shaped ear-rings with filigree decoration, and (in the lake region near Pátzcuaro) necklaces made of silver fish, as well as gold coins set undamaged in finger rings and pendants (*see* MEXICAN JEWELRY).

pebble jewelry. Articles of jewelry made in Scotland since the mid-19th century, set with small pieces of AGATE and granite found in Scotland and cut in various shapes. The pieces of varicoloured stone are set in mosaic patterns in brooches with silver mounts, but some are of gold. Such jewelry achieved great popularity, and consequently was later made in Birmingham (some pieces with stones not from Scotland), and exported to the Continent.

pectoral. (1) A decorative ornament worn on the breast. In the Middle Ages such ornaments were usually sewn on a garment, although sometimes fixed by a pin as a brooch. Some were worn suspended by a cord or a string of beads, sometimes counter-balanced by a small tablet hanging on the back. They were worn by ecclesiastics, but also by laymen. Examples from Egypt (often made with a SCARAB) were suspended by a chain or ribbon, but they were also funerary ornaments (*see* HAWK JEWEL) placed on mummies; these were of various materials (rarely gold, usually gilded bronze, glazed earthenware or alabaster) and were sometimes decorated with gemstones or inlaid glass. (*See* PECTORAL CROSS.) Pectorals of beaten gold sheet or cast gold were made of PRE-COLUMBIAN JEWELRY. (2) A decorative breastplate such as worn by a Jewish High Priest. *See* DARIEN PECTORAL; ENKOLPION.

pectoral cross. A cross worn on the breast, usually by bishops and abbots, and sometimes by canons and laymen. *See* BERESFORD HOPE CROSS; AVERBODE, PECTORAL CROSS OF ABBOT OF.

pectoral disc. A type of PECTORAL in the form of a disc ranging in width from about 12 to 28 cm and with one or two suspension holes near the top. Examples in PRE-COLUMBIAN JEWELRY were made of gold or TUMBAGA, with hammered REPOUSSÉ decoration, sometimes depicting stylistic anthropomorphic figures or faces, sometimes birdlike or lizard figures. They were made in the Quimbaya style (*see* QUIMBAYA JEWELRY).

pectoral disc. Hammered tumbaga with repoussé figure and birds. Quimbaya style. W. 26.8 cm. Museum of Mankind, London (photo copyright, Times Newspapers Ltd).

pelican jewelry. Gold brooch in form of pelican in-her-piety. Gold set with ruby. North-west European (found in River Meuse), 15th century. L. 3.8 cm. British Museum, London.

penannular pin brooch. Uppland, Sweden, 10th century. L. 20.4 cm. Statens Historiska Museum, Stockholm.

Pectoral of the Universe, The. A long (21 cm) narrow PECTORAL of MIXTEC JEWELRY from the MONTE ALBÁN TREASURE that is composed of seven sections linked vertically, all made of cast gold. The top ornament is a panel from which is suspended a sun disc, below which are two openwork rectangular plaques supporting a row of four stylized faces, and then two rows of CASCABELES. It is in the Regional Museum, Oaxaca, Mexico.

Pedro, Dom, Emerald. The largest EMERALD from the famous Muzo mine in Colombia, now known as the DEVONSHIRE EMERALD.

peg setting. (1) A style of SETTING a flat-bottom stone (e.g. a ROSE-CUT diamond or a half-pearl) in a finger ring or EAR-STUD by which a peg is affixed to the metal base and cemented into a hole in the base of the stone. (2) A style of setting a massed group of gemstones by soldering wire pegs to the metal base in an arrangement so that the stones will fit closely among the pegs, with the top of the pegs being barely visible. In some cases the outer edge of the piece is cut away to form claws that are bent over the edges of the stones along the rim; this type is called 'peg-and-cut-away setting'.

pelican jewelry. Articles of jewelry of which the decorative motif is a pelican depicted in-her-piety, i.e. over her nest with wings extended and vulning (wounding) her breast, from which fall drops of blood. It was formerly erroneously believed that pelicans fed their young with their own blood. The fabled practice of the bird became symbolic of Christ and of charity. The motif was used on Renaissance pendants, brooches, and ENSEIGNES, usually decorated with a symbolic ruby and sometimes with pearls. A 15th-century example, made in north-west Europe, is said to have been found in the River Meuse in the 19th century, and examples are known from Spain from the 16th century (*see* SARAGOSSA, LADY OF THE PILLAR OF, JEWELS).

pelta. Strictly, a small shield worn, as depicted in art, by Amazons, and hence a type of ear-ring of HELLENISTIC JEWELRY in the form of a crescent-shaped shield from which is suspended a cone-shaped ornament.

penannular. Almost annular, e.g. a cleft ring that is not completely circular but has a small space between its two ends. Penannular ear-rings were among the articles in the TUTANKHAMUN JEWELRY, and such brooches were frequent in CELTIC JEWELRY and ANGLO-SAXON JEWELRY. *See* ANIMAL-HEAD BRACELET; ANIMAL-HEAD EAR-RING; GORGET.

penannular ear-ring. A type of EAR-RING that is in PENANNULAR form. Some examples are of curved rods or tubes of slightly tapering form, with an animal-head or other ornament on the larger terminal, e.g. Etruscan ear-rings, 600 BC–250 BC; some such pieces have ornamentation along the thick SHANK, and occasionally a suspensory ring for a pendant. Examples of HELLENISTIC JEWELRY have a shank that tapers to a thin end and a point for piercing the ear-lobe, and at the other end is an ornament in the form of an animal- or female-head; *see* ANIMAL-HEAD EAR-RING.

penannular finger ring. A type of finger ring that is in PENANNULAR form. Some such rings are merely cut across to make an opening, but usually the two ends terminate in knobs or broaden into discoidal ends.

penannular pin brooch. A type of brooch in the form of a PENANNULAR circle to which is attached a long pin whose length is at least double the diameter of the circle. The head of the pin is looped around the circle so that the pin can slide along the circle. When the pin is pushed through a fabric twice, the circle is rotated so that one terminal is pushed under the exposed end of the pin and the pressure of the fabric holds the pin in place. The terminals of the circle and the head of the pin were decorated over periods of time with increasing elaborateness, as well as the ornament on the circle which was sometimes so enlarged that it occupied a large portion of the inside of the circle. The space between the terminals was later closed by a bar and finally was completely closed, so that the brooch resembled a RING BROOCH. Such brooches were originated by the Celts in the Iron Age in Britain, and were developed by them during the Christian period (*see* CELTIC JEWELRY). Similar brooches were also later made in ANGLO-SAXON JEWELRY. *See* TARA BROOCH; HUNTERSTON BROOCH; LONDESBOROUGH BROOCH; MAMILLARY FIBULA.

pendant. An article suspended from a NECK CHAIN or NECKLACE (some Renaissance pieces were fastened to the sleeve), either as an auxiliary decoration or as an object worn for its own sake. Examples of the latter type include an AMULET, LOCKET, MINIATURE, PECTORAL CROSS or RELIQUARY, but also an ornamental piece of jewelry, usually made of gold or silver, enamelled or set with gemstones or consisting primarily of a large gemstone alone or a cluster of pearls or small stones. Most pendants are worn as ornaments but often they are an article of DEVOTIONAL JEWELRY, MOURNING JEWELRY, or MAGICAL JEWELRY, not primarily decorative, evidenced by being worn sometimes under a bodice. Pendants vary greatly in style and size, from the simple primitive examples to the symbolic ones of the Middle Ages and the elaborate jewelled ones of the Renaissance and modern times.

pendant frame. A small frame for a GLYPH or enamelled plaque, to be worn as a pendant. Such pieces were made in the 16th century, sometimes with enamelled decoration and set with coloured gemstones.

pendant watch. A type of woman's WATCH worn suspended in the manner of a PENDANT and usually decorated with enamelling and gemstones. Examples having a gold case, with or without a hinged lid, were made in France from *c.* 1600; such watches are still being made today.

pendeloque. A diamond or other gemstone that is somewhat pear-shaped (pyriform), but having the narrow end pointed. It is sometimes pierced near the apex so that it can be suspended as a pendant from a brooch or a necklace. *See* PENDELOQUE CUT; PENDELOQUE ROSE CUT.

pendeloque cut. A style of cutting a diamond (or other transparent gemstone) in a modification of the BRILLIANT CUT, so that the GIRDLE is somewhat pear-shaped (rounded at the bottom end and pointed at the top) with an irregular 8-sided TABLE. It has on the CROWN 8 large trapezium-shaped FACETS and 24 triangular facets, and on the PAVILION 8 large trapezium-shaped facets arranged as a central 8-pointed star and 16 surrounding triangular facets, thus a total of 56 facets plus the table and sometimes a CULET. It is sometimes pierced along its length (to be used in an ear-ring) or across its top (to be used as a pendant).

pendeloque rose cut. A style of cutting a diamond (or other transparent gemstone) in a modification of the ROSE CUT, so that the stone is somewhat pear-shaped (rounded at the bottom end and pointed at the top) but having a flat base and no TABLE. There are usually 24 triangular FACETS, cut in 4 horizontal rows, with 5 facets in the top and bottom rows and 7 facets in the 2 middle rows. Sometimes the stone is cut as a DOUBLE ROSE, in the form of two such cut stones placed base to base; it is then intended to be worn as a pendant.

Pénicaud, Nardon (or **Léonard**) (1470?-1542/3). A leading enamellist of Limoges, France, in the 16th century. He is highly regarded for his technique of using coloured ENAMELS on a ground of white enamel on a copper base and, after firing the piece, adding touches of opaque white and opaque red enamels as highlights, sometimes supplementing this with gold and with PAILLONS. He also was a leading exponent of work in GRISAILLE. Similar work was also done by members of his family, Jean I, Jean II, and Jean III Pénicaud, all of Limoges. An outstanding follower was LÉONARD LIMOUSIN.

Penicuik Jewels. A group of articles of jewelry (especially a LOCKET, pendant, and necklace) that are relics of Mary, Queen of Scots. Their recorded history dates from 1587 when Mary, on the day of her execution at Fotheringay Castle, gave them to her lady-in-waiting, Gillis Mowbray, whose grand-daughter, Mary Gray, inherited them and when she married John Clerk thus brought them into his family. He in 1646 bought the estate of Penicuik, Scotland, where the Clerk descendants still reside. The jewels were kept there by the Clerks of Penicuik until March 1923 when Sir George Clerk, the 9th Baronet, sent them to London to be sold. As reports had indicated that they might be bought away from Britain, a group, including members of the Royal Family, subscribed funds to retain them for Scotland. The relics were bought at auction through

pendant frame. Gold with enamelling and red stones. Flemish, 16th century. W. 5 cm. City Museums and Art Gallery, Birmingham, England.

pendant watch. Gold spherical watch set with diamonds, suspended from a brooch. *c.* 1910. Courtesy of Sotheby's, London.

pendeloque cut
side view

Penicuik Locket. Gold, enamelled and decorated with pearls; watercolour portraits, under crystal, of James I (James VI) and Mary, Queen of Scots. Scottish (?), *c.* 1576-9. W. (open) 6 cm. National Museum of Antiquities of Scotland, Edinburgh.

Penicuik Necklace. Gold filigree beads. Also, pendant for Penicuik Locket. Scottish, *c.* 1576-9. National Museum of Antiquities of Scotland, Edinburgh.

Spink & Sons, and have since been kept at the National Museum of Antiquities of Scotland, Edinburgh. *See* Walter Seton, *The Penicuik Jewels of Mary, Queen of Scots* (1923). *See* PENICUIK LOCKET; PENICUIK NECKLACE.

Penicuik Locket. A gold LOCKET that is one of the PENICUIK JEWELS. It is oval, having on both sections a wide band of floral openwork in the centre of each of which is a tiny miniature watercolour portrait under crystal: on the front, of James VI of Scotland (James I of England) as a young boy, on the reverse, of his mother, Mary, Queen of Scots. The front section has a border of openwork set with pearls. It is said to be possibly Scottish, *c.* 1576-9. Another jewel in the Penicuik group is a pendant of tall oval shape set with pearls, below which is suspended a gold ornament from which is a pendent pearl; this piece, once thought to be an ear-ring, is now considered to be a pendant to be attached to a loop on the locket.

Penicuik Necklace. A necklace that is one of the PENICUIK JEWELS. It is composed of 14 large oval gold beads of FILIGREE work, alternating with 13 smaller similar beads, and having a suspended oval bead from which hangs a pearl. It is possibly Scottish, *c.* 1576-9.

penis sheath. An article of PRE-COLUMBIAN JEWELRY worn by the Indians. Examples are known in 2 forms: (1) a wide-mouth, funnel-shaped cover, sometimes with a suspensory loop attached at the rim, and (2) a narrow elongated tapering cover. Such articles were made of gold in the Tairona and Sinú regions of Colombia, and examples have been reported in COCLÉ JEWELRY from Panama.

Penruddock Jewel. A Renaissance pendant believed to have been presented in 1544 by Catherine Parr, sixth wife of Henry VIII, to Sir George Penruddock of Compton Chamberlayne (Wiltshire). It is triangular, set in the centre with a large CABOCHON triangular SAPPHIRE surrounded by gold openwork enamelled and set with diamonds and rubies. The pendant is shown in a portrait of the donee by Lucas de Heere.

pentagon cut. A style of cutting a diamond (or other transparent gemstone) so that the TABLE is 5-sided, bordered by 5 facets, each in the form of an isosceles trapezoid.

'Percy' Signet Ring. A gold SIGNET RING with a circular BEZEL engraved with a lion passant and the inscription 'now:ys: thus'. It has been ascribed to the Percy family on the basis that it was found *c.* 1789 at Towton, near Tadcaster, Yorkshire, and that Henry Percy, the 6th Earl of Northumberland, fought and was killed at the battle of Towton on 29 March 1561, although there is no definite evidence that the family at that date used the lion passant as its badge. The ring has been attributed to the 15th century.

Peregrina, La. A famous pearl, said to have weighed originally 58.50 carats (234 grains) and to have been found off Panama before 1554 by a Spaniard who presented it in 1560 to Philip II of Spain, who gave it to Mary Tudor in 1554 upon their marriage. Upon her death it was returned to Spain and later worn by the Queens of Philip II, Philip III, Philip IV, and Charles II, and in 1679-90 was worn by Charles II; in 1706 the wife of Philip V tried to sell it. Maria Luisa of Parma, wife of Charles IV, had it remounted, *c.* 1790, with an oval gold ball set with diamonds, encircled by a band with the inscription 'Soy La Peregrina'. It was taken by Joseph Bonaparte when he conquered Spain in 1808, but remained in Spain until he abdicated in 1813 and took it to France. It was given to Hortense de Beauharnais when she married Joseph's brother, Louis Bonaparte, and in 1837 it passed to Louis Bonaparte, from whom it was bought by the then Marquess of Abercorn for his wife, who (as the pearl was then set unpierced) lost but recovered it three times. It later passed to the present Duke of Abercorn, of Omagh, Northern Ireland. Having then been pierced, it weighed 203.84 grains. The pearl (suspended in a platinum foliate mount set with diamonds) was sold at auction at Parke-Bernet Galleries, New York, on 23 January 1969 for $37,000 to Elizabeth Taylor Burton (now Mrs John Warner), who still owns it.

La Peregrina is to be distinguished from: (1) a pearl of similar size and shape found in 1691 and presented to Charles II of Spain and named after

him; it (sometimes called 'La Compañera de la Peregrina') and La
Peregrina were set in ear-rings worn by successive Queens of Spain until it
was destroyed in a fire in 1734 in Madrid; and (2) an ovoid pearl of 28
carats, called 'La Peligrina' that was given by Philip IV to his daughter,
Maria Theresa, when in 1660 she married Louis XIV of France, and that
was later bought in Moscow by Princess Youssoupoff. At the time of the
sale of La Peregrina in New York in 1969, its identification was
challenged by Spain's ex-Queen Victoria Eugenia, who claimed
ownership of a pear-shaped drilled pearl that she contended was La
Peregrina, but that pearl has been said to have weighed only 223.8 grains.
See AUSTRIAS, JEWEL OF THE.

perfume jewelry. Articles of jewelry made with a small receptacle for
some substance, e.g. musk, ambergris or perfume, that emitted a
pleasant scent. Some ear-rings, necklaces, and bracelets were made of
beads for containing perfume, and the POMANDER was made especially for
such purpose. Such articles were popular in the Middle Ages and the
Renaissance. Two sets of such jewelry were owned by Mary, Queen of
Scots. The French term is *accoutrements de senteurs*. *See* BULLA.

periamma. A circular breast ornament kept in place by crossed straps.
Certain Hellenistic medallions (*see* HELLENISTIC JEWELRY) are set in a
circular frame with double loops in four places, and it has been suggested
that these may have been such ornaments. Some circular examples are
decorated with FILIGREE, inlay, and enamel.

periclase. A mineral that is translucent and has a brilliant LUSTRE. It
ranges from colourless to shades of yellow and green. The crystals are
small round granules and some have been polished as gemstones. A
SYNTHETIC PERICLASE has been produced and cut for use in jewelry; its
trade-name is 'Lavernite'.

peridot. A GEM variety of OLIVINE that is golden-green, but also shades
ranging from dark leek-green to yellowish-green. It has been confused
with green CORUNDUM, EMERALD, and CHRYSOBERYL. The stones are
usually faceted, but some are polished by Tumbling or mounted in their
natural rough form. Some examples are CHATOYANT. A stone of brownish
colour, formerly called 'brown peridot', has since 1952 been recognized as
a different mineral, SINHALITE. In Sri Lanka (formerly Ceylon) water-
worn fragments of bottle-glass have been sometimes deceptively sold as
peridot. The name 'peridot' is generally pronounced like the French form
péridot; an alternative spelling 'peridote' is incorrect. The original source
in antiquity was the Egyptian island of St John's (now Zabargad) in the
Red Sea. *See* CHRYSOLITE.

peristerite. A variety of FELDSPAR that resembles MOONSTONE and shows
mixed flashes of green, blue, and brownish-pink, resembling the colours
of a pigeon (Greek *peristera*), hence the name. Sometimes called 'pigeon
stone'.

perlite. A variety of OBSIDIAN that is porous and greyish, and has
concentric curved cracks. *See* APACHE TEAR.

Pertábgarh jewelry. Articles of jewelry made in the small town of
Pertábgarh, in Rajputana, northern India, during the 19th century and
decorated with plaques made by a local technique that produced an
appearance resembling ÉMAIL EN RÉSILLE SUR VERRE. A patterned
openwork plaque was cut from a thin sheet of gold and decorated with
engraving, then it was placed, engraving down, on a sheet of transparent
mica and the openwork spaces were filled in with powdered glass (usually
green) that was then fused, so that the piece then had the appearance,
from the front, of a design carved in glass mounted on gold set in a clear
glass ground. Similar plaques (but sometimes with blue glass) were made
in the nearby town of Rútlám. Such ware has been sometimes erroneously
called 'quasi-enamel'. *See* INDIAN JEWELRY.

Peruvian jewelry. Articles of PRE-COLUMBIAN JEWELRY made by the
Indians of Peru from as early as the Chavín culture (*c.* 900 BC–500 BC)
until the conquest by the Spanish Conquistadors under Francisco Pizarro
in 1532. The earliest examples are CHAVÍN JEWELRY (*c.* 900 BC –750 BC),

'Percy' Signet Ring. Gold finger ring
with lion passant badge on bezel.
English, 15th century. W. 3 cm.
British Museum, London.

Pertábgarh jewelry. Brooch with
plaques of engraved gold and green
glass under mica. 19th century. W.
9.8 cm. Victoria & Albert Museum,
London.

then NAZCA JEWELRY and MOCHICA JEWELRY from *c*. AD 300–600, and CHIMÚ JEWELRY and INCA JEWELRY from *c*. AD 1000. Some pieces from the Vicús Valley in the north are closely related to the jewelry from neighbouring Ecuador and Colombia. The pieces are usually made from thin sheet gold, hammered and decorated with REPOUSSÉ work and linear, stylized CHASING, but some were made by the CIRE PERDUE process. Occasional pieces are made of combined gold and silver or with DEPLETION GILDING, and some have inlays of shell or turquoise. More than 2,000 examples are in the Miguel Mujica Gallo Collection at the Museo Oro de Peru, in Lima.

Peruzzi, Vincenz(i)o. A Venetian lapidary who is often said to have invented, *c*. 1700, the BRILLIANT CUT style for cutting a diamond, which thereafter superseded the ROSE CUT. However, it has been declared by Herbert Tillander, of Helsinki, that although a Peruzzi family came from Florence, there is no record of any member named Vincenz(i)o.

Peruzzi cut. A style of cutting a diamond, named after VINCENZ(I)O PERUZZI. It is CUSHION CUT with an octagonal TABLE surrounded on the CROWN by 32 FACETS, and with 24 facets on the PAVILION plus the CULET.

Peruzzi cut
side and top views

petoskey stone. A fossil limestone that is greyish-green and is found as pebbles along Lake Michigan (USA). It has been used for making some articles of jewelry, e.g. small CHARMS. It was named after an American Indian chief.

Petrossa Brooch. A large brooch of gold sheet, shaped into the form of the front of a hawk with closed wings. The head and neck are pierced in OPUS INTERRASILE style with heart-shaped openings to represent feathers, and the body was originally decorated with PLATE INLAY of CARBUNCLES and green glass (most pieces now missing). It is hollow and at the back there is an attachment for a missing pin. Suspended at the bottom on gold chains are 4 (2 now missing) QUARTZ ornaments. The piece, of Byzantine-Gothic origin, 4th or 5th century, is part of the PETROSSA TREASURE, which includes 2 other bird-shaped flat brooches, depicting eagles, one with a long neck and beak, and the other smaller and in stylized form, both decorated with garnets and suspended ornaments.

Petrossa Gorget. A GORGET of crescent shape, made of a gold plate (with a hinged section near the back, so as to be fitted on the neck), with an overlaid gold plate that is pierced with an openwork design and decorated with PLATE INLAY of slices of GARNET, vitreous green PASTE, and LAPIS LAZULI. It is said to be Byzantine–Gothic, made by Gothic tribes of Dacia, in Romania, in the 5th/6th centuries AD. It is part of the PETROSSA TREASURE in the Museum of Antiquities at Bucharest; an electrotype (*see* ELECTROTYPING) reproduction is in the Victoria & Albert Museum, London.

Petrossa Treasure. A TREASURE of gold vessels, jewelry, and other articles, some from the 4th/5th centuries AD, discovered in 1837 by quarrymen near the village of Petrossa (Pietroasa), about 40 miles from Bucharest, Romania. Some pieces were destroyed by vandalism, but some that had been badly damaged were recovered and restored, and were lent, *c*. 1868, to the South Kensington (now Victoria & Albert) Museum, London, and are now in the Museum of Antiquities, Bucharest. They were removed to escape the German invasion in World War II and were captured by the Russians, but were returned in 1956 to Bucharest. They include gold brooches decorated with PLATE INLAY of CARBUNCLES and glass, some of the earliest examples of such jewelry in Europe. *See* R. H. Soden Smith, *The Treasure of Petrossa* (1869); Alexandru Odobescu, *Le Trésor de Pétrossa* (French translation, 1976). *See* PETROSSA BROOCH; PETROSSA GORGET.

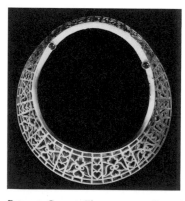

Petrossa Gorget. Electrotype replica of reconstructed damaged original, without plate inlay, *c*. 1869. W. 16 cm. Victoria & Albert Museum, London.

pewter. An ALLOY of varying constituents, of which the principal one is tin. It is silver-white and can be shaped by hammering, casting or spinning on a mould. It has been used mainly for domestic tableware, but also formerly for some mediocre articles of jewelry, including some SHOE BUCKLES and a few pieces of ANGLO-SAXON JEWELRY such as brooches. It has also been used for some inexpensive modern jewelry (*see* Miriam Browne, *Pewter Jewellery*, 1979).

phenakite (or **phenacite**). A variety of gemstone that is transparent, usually colourless or nearly so, but sometimes brownish, yellow or pink. It resembles QUARTZ (hence the name from the Greek *phenax*, deceiver); it is harder but almost totally lacks FIRE, hence is not often used in jewelry. *See* SHAH DIAMOND.

Phillips, Robert. A London jeweller who entered his mark (RP in skeleton form) at Goldsmiths' Hall on 3 June 1851 and a second one (RP on a shield) on 26 October 1853. He had a retail shop at 31 Cockspur St, and by 1869 he was reputed for his antique-style jewelry and also for articles of CORAL that he imported from southern Italy. He assisted CARLO GIULIANO to become established in Soho and was almost certainly his retail outlet before 1874 when Giuliano opened his own shop at 115 Piccadilly. Phillips probably visited ALESSANDRO CASTELLANI while the latter was exiled in Naples in the late 1850s. CARLO DORIA may have worked for him in the early 1860s, and many articles that bear a mark which until recently has been ascribed to Doria have been found in leather boxes that bear Phillips's name and address; it has been suggested that the mark may have been that of Phillips. By 1885 ownership of the shop had passed to Alfred Phillips, 23 Cockspur St, who entered a mark 'A P' on 24 April 1885; the shop ceased *c.* 1927.

Phoenician jewelry. Articles of jewelry produced by the Phoenicians from the period *c.* 1250 BC (but mainly from *c.* 900 BC to 325 BC) when, as renowned navigators, traders, and colonists, they dominated commerce in the Mediterranean, In addition to bringing home jewelry from Egypt and Assyria, they made native jewelry, much in styles adapted from Egypt and Assyria. Gold articles were made by SOLDERING, and they are said to have introduced, or refined, the process of GRANULATED GOLD. Phoenician jewelry from the 7th to 6th centuries BC has been found in Tharros, in Sardinia, and also near Cáceres, Spain (*see* ALISEDA TREASURE). Some articles of glass, e.g. pendants and amulets, found in eastern Mediterranean regions, have been considered probably Phoenician.

Phoenix Jewel. A gold pendant in the form of a circular wreath enclosing a relief profile bust of Queen Elizabeth I cut out in silhouette, and having on the reverse, in relief, a device of a phoenix in flames under a royal monogram, crown, and heavenly rays; the wreath has, on front and reverse, enamelled red and white Tudor roses with green leaves. Much uncertainty surrounds the piece: it has been said that the bust was modelled upon or cut from a medal of 1574, known as the 'Phoenix Badge', but this has not been definitively established; nor has the claim that the bust is by NICHOLAS HILLIARD been proved. The piece has been tentatively attributed by the British Museum to English production, *c.* 1570-80; it was acquired with the collection of Sir Hans Sloane in 1753.

phoenix jewelry. Articles of jewelry of which the decorative motif is a phoenix rising from flames. In Egyptian religion the phoenix was the embodiment of Ra, the sun-god, and was worshipped as a symbol of resurrection. The Chinese version of the phoenix (*huang* for the male,

Phoenician jewelry. Gold bracelet with repoussé design and granulated gold. Tharros, Sardinia, 7th/6th centuries BC. L. 12.8 cm. Museo Archeologico Nazionale, Cagliari, Sardinia.

Phoenix Jewel (front and back). Gold pendant with relief bust of Queen Elizabeth I within floral wreath. English (?), *c.* 1570-80. W. 4.6 cm. British Museum, London.

phoenix jewelry. Pendant with gold phoenix rising from enamelled flames. Gold set with gemstones. South German, *c.* 1610. Wernher Collection, Luton Hoo, Luton, England.

pi. Nephrite, greenish-yellow. Honan, China. 5th/3rd centuries BC. W. 16.5 cm. William Rockhill Nelson Gallery (Nelson Fund), Kansas City, Mo.

pilgrim badge. Silver badge of shrine at Hal, Belgium. 14th/15th centuries. W. 3.8 cm. British Museum, London.

fêng for the female) is found on porcelain articles and also on some Chinese jewelry, e.g. pieces from the Sung Dynasty (960-1279) made entirely of gold, unlike the usual inlaid ware. The phoenix was also an emblem of resurrection in Christian art; examples are found in jewelry from Germany and elsewhere from the 17th century. *See* PHOENIX JEWEL.

photographic jewelry. Articles of jewelry of which the principal decoration was a photograph, usually framed in a brooch or pendant made of gold or other metal. In the mid-19th century lockets enclosing a photograph of a deceased person were popular, but later they were worn with an enclosed photograph of the living.

phylactery pendant. A type of pendant which was worn as a phylactery, enclosing a parchment or paper on which was written a prayer or Scriptural passage. Such articles were common in the Jewish and Islamic religions, and examples made of crystal are known from Spain, *c.* 1600.

pi (Chinese). A flat disc, made of JADE or BRONZE, having a central hole, circular or square, so that several could be strung and worn, either alone or in combination with a HUANG, as part of Chinese ceremonial dress. The discs were often decorated with various carved and openwork patterns, sometimes extending over areas protruding outside the circular rim. The *pi* is known from at least the Eastern Chou Dynasty (5th/3rd centuries BC), and had symbolic significance.

Pichler, Johann Anton (called **Antonio;** 1697-1779). A noted gem-engraver, born in northern Italy, who finally settled in Rome in 1743. He engraved imitations of antique gems but also carved CAMEOS and INTAGLIOS of his own design. His 3 sons successfully followed his career, Giovanni (1734-91), Giuseppe (1770-1819), and Luigi (1773-1854), especially Luigi who took over his workshop in 1791 and Giovanni whose gems were often bought as antiques. The latter's son, Gian Giacomo (1778-1829), became a gem-engraver in Milan. Pichler instituted the custom that cameos should be signed by the artist to prevent fraudulent sales as antiques.

pickle. A bath of nitric acid or sulphuric acid, or a mixture of both, diluted with water. It is used by jewellers to remove from metal any oxides and flux remaining after SOLDERING and also for cleaning jewelry. *See* DIFFERENTIAL PICKLING.

picotite. A variety of SPINEL that is brown to black, containing CHROMIUM. It is named after Picot de la Peyrouse, the French botanist who described it. Also called 'chrome spinel' or 'chromite'. The crystals have been cut EN CABOCHON with a silvery shine.

pierre d'Alençon. The French term for cut ROCK CRYSTAL. Also called *caillou du Rhin. See* RHINESTONE.

pietra dura (Italian). Literally, hard stone. The term (although a singular form) refers to the various hardstones (e.g. CHALCEDONY, AGATE, JASPER, LAPIS LAZULI) used in flat slices in the type of MOSAIC produced in Florence during the Renaissance and continuing until today, and is sometimes applied to an example of the work. It is used sometimes in small articles of jewelry, e.g. brooches, pendants, and finger rings. Occasionally the stones are cut and shaped in the form of various fruits and then assembled into a varicoloured group; such work was done in Florence and also in Russia. *See* FLORENTINE MOSAIC.

pigeon's-blood ruby. The most valuable variety of RUBY, of which the colour is deep-red tinged with purple. Such rubies come from Mogok in Upper Burma, hence sometimes called a BURMA RUBY. Flawless specimens are rare, and are the next most valuable of the PRECIOUS STONES after the EMERALD. A specimen weighing 20 carats in the rough and 7.50 carats after cutting was found in 1933. A SYNTHETIC RUBY of this colour has been produced.

piggy-back diamond. A type of DOUBLET made with a flat diamond having a large CULET cemented above the TABLE of a smaller diamond so as to appear as one large natural stone.

pilgrim badges. Pewter or lead. 14th/15th centuries. Museum of London.

Pigot(t) Diamond. A diamond of Indian origin, said to have weighed 49 old carats and to have been given by an Indian Maharajah to Lord George Pigot, Governor of Madras, some time before his resignation in 1763 and his recall to England for having accepted gifts for protection. He brought it to England and his brothers either bought or inherited it. After several changes in ownership, it was acquired by Rundell and Bridge, the London jewellers, who sold it in 1818 to Ali Pasha, ruler of Albania under the Turkish Sultan. In 1822 Ali was recalled to Turkey, but was mortally wounded in resisting, and on his deathbed he ordered the stone to be destroyed (and his wife killed); one version is that it was crushed, but its true fate is unknown.

pilgrim badge. A small badge (usually made of lead or pewter, but sometimes of gold or silver for the nobility) or 'Pilgrim's Sign' given or sold to pilgrims visiting English and Continental shrines of saints or martyrs. They were issued by the attendants at the shrine, and bore the device or effigy of the local patron saint or martyr. Some were in the form of an *ampulla* for holy water. Such badges were pierced or attached to a pin so that they could be fastened to a pilgrim's hat or apparel to evidence his visit, and were worn thereafter as a charm. They were made by the pilgrimage churches and monasteries in the 13th to 15th centuries and issued in great quantities. Some were made and issued at Canterbury (one in the form of the shrine) and are mentioned in *The Canterbury Tales*. In 1466 the monastery at Einsiedeln, near Zurich, is said to have issued 130,000 for 2 pfennigs each. Many were issued to pilgrims to Santiago de Compostela, Spain, in the shape of the scallop-shell identified with St James. They were the precursor of the ENSEIGNE. Forgeries were sold in London in the 19th century; *see* BILLY AND CHARLEY.

pin. (1) A thin, straight (usually cylindrical), pointed and headed object, usually of metal, that is used to fasten garments or various articles, or sometimes worn ornamentally. Pins have been made of gold, silver, brass, iron, or other materials. Often the head has been decorated with enamelling, engraving or gemstones. *See* HAIR PIN; HATPIN; TIE PIN; STOCK PIN; PIN SUITE; GREEK PIN. (2) A similar pointed fastener at the back of a brooch or FIBULA and by which the piece is attached to a garment by being pierced twice through the fabric and secured by a catch-plate. *See* DISC BROOCH; PIN BROOCH; RING BROOCH; TARA BROOCH. (3) A pointed fastener (called an ACUS) that is formed by a complete and a 180-degree turn, producing a spring at one end and having at the other end a catch-plate and a guard to cover the point. *See* SAFETY PIN; COLLAR PIN.

pin brooch. A type of brooch in the form of a long pin (about 60 cm long) with a square-section attenuated shank. It is attached to a flat

pin. Gold. Mycenaean, 2nd half of 16th century BC. National Archaeological Museum, Athens.

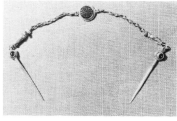

pin brooch (detail). Silver with gilt filigree and granular decoration; similar to Clonmacnois Pin. L. 24 cm. National Museum of Ireland, Dublin.

pin suite. Two gold pins set with garnets, linked to gold chain with glass ornament. Found at Roundway Down, Wiltshire, England. Anglo-Saxon. L. of pin, 10 cm. Devizes Museum, Devizes, England.

ornament, usually decorated with FILIGREE, NIELLO, and white enamel, so that the pin can be swivelled to secure it. Such brooches were made in Ireland in the Christian period of the Celtic era. An example is the CLONMACNOIS PIN whose whereabouts today is unknown; a similar pin brooch, with different decoration, is in the National Museum of Ireland. *See* TARA BROOCH; THISTLE BROOCH.

pin-fire opal. *See* HARLEQUIN OPAL.

pin suite. A group of two (occasionally three) similar, headed PINS linked together by a chain (sometimes a small bar) attached to the heads of the pins. Some were made of gold, set with GARNETS, to be worn as ornaments in the hair; but the paired suites were worn as cloak or tunic fasteners. *See* WITHAM PINS.

Pinchbeck, Christopher (1670-1732). A London watch-maker who invented, *c.* 1720, PINCHBECK, an ALLOY to imitate gold and that was named after him. He was a prominent maker of watches and clocks, as well as musical automata. He lived and worked in Clerkenwell until he opened a shop in Fleet St in 1721. He was succeeded in 1732 by his second son, Edward (1713-66). His eldest son, Christopher (1711-83), left his father's shop in 1738 and later became clock-maker to George III.

pinchbeck. An ALLOY of COPPER and zinc (about 83 to 17) that was invented, *c.* 1720, by CHRISTOPHER PINCHBECK. It resembled, but was much lighter than, gold and was used in making inexpensive jewelry, including WATCH-CASES, CHATELAINES, BUCKLES, CLASPS, snuff boxes, étuis, etc. It retained for a while a bright and unoxidized appearance. Sometimes it was covered with a wash of gold, but when some of the gilding wore off the difference in colour was barely visible. It was used in France, known there as 'pinsbeck' and 'pinsebeck'. It has been superseded by GILDING METAL and ROLLED GOLD, and also by 9-carat gold since its authorization in England in 1854. *See* SIMILOR.

pink moonstone. A misnomer for opalescent pink SCAPOLITE.

pinpoint opal. A variety of PRECIOUS OPAL that displays a mass of minute colour specks. *See* HARLEQUIN OPAL.

piqué (French). A style of decoration of small luxury articles (e.g. snuff boxes) of TORTOISE SHELL (sometimes IVORY) made with inlaid minute points (called PIQUÉ POINT) or strips (called PIQUÉ POSÉ) of gold or silver (sometimes also MOTHER-OF-PEARL). The process was introduced by Laurentini, a Neapolitan jeweller, in the mid-17th century, but credit for developing it into a minor art is usually accorded to Charles Boulle (1642-1732). After its use in France, the art was brought to England by Huguenot refugees, *c.* 1685, as well as to Holland and Germany, hence it is usually impossible to identify the origin of a piece. After the 1760s it was used in Birmingham, England, originally by skilled craftsmen; but handwork was superseded there in the 1870s by mass-production methods producing such decorated articles, popular in the Victorian era, as brooches, buttons, ear-rings, etc. *See* LAMBALLE NECKLACE; PIQUÉ D'OR.

piqué diamond. A diamond so classified for its lack of clarity (or purity) as a result of its having very small INCLUSIONS (piqués) of carbonaceous material, usually visible to the naked eye. There are grades of piqué diamonds according to the extent of the inclusions. Often referred to as 'PK'. *See* CLARITY GRADING.

piqué d'or (French). A type of PIQUÉ work in which tiny gold figures and ornaments were applied to the surface of TORTOISE SHELL to compose a pattern.

piqué point (French). The type of PIQUÉ work that was done with inlaid minute points of gold or silver. It was sometimes combined with PIQUÉ POSÉ, but the finest work is that done exclusively in '*petits et gros points*' with gold nails of various sizes, and dated to the late period of the reign of Louis XIV, *c.* 1700-15. Although the work is usually on dark TORTOISE SHELL, it was sometimes done in gold on blond tortoise shell, especially during the end of the reign of Louis XIV and the *Régence*, 1715-23.

XI *sphinx pendant*. Necklace with pendant representing a sphinx. North Italian, 16th century. National Gallery of Art (Widener Collection), Washington, DC.

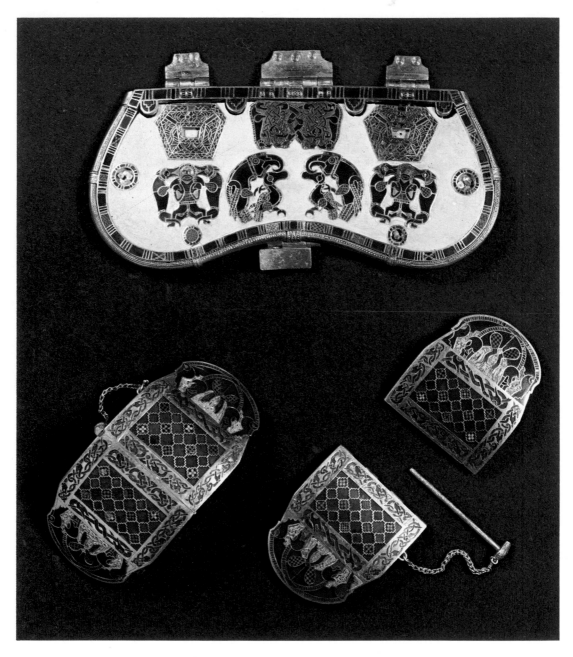

XII *Sutton Hoo Treasure*. Above, lid of a purse set with garnets and coloured glass, with plaques showing the 'Daniel in the Lions' Den' motif. Below, two clasps. 7th century. British Museum, London.

piqué posé (French). The type of PIQUÉ work that was done with inlaid tiny strips of gold or silver so as to compose a scene with figures. It was sometimes combined with PIQUÉ POINT into a pictorial scene, especially popular until the late 18th century.

pistacite. The same as EPIDOTE. It is so called from its unique greenish colour, resembling that of the pistachio nut.

Pistrucci, Benedetto (1784-1855). An outstanding Italian engraver of gemstones, including some so-called 'antiques' that he engraved, while living in Italy, for an Italian dealer Bonelli. He claimed in 1815 to have carved the FLORA OF PISTRUCCI. Pistrucci emigrated in 1814 to London and became Chief Engraver at the Mint (1817-49) where he carved the dies for the George and Dragon on the new coinage. He designed the 1819 medal commemorating the Battle of Waterloo and several royal commemorative medals. He was patronized by Elisa Bacciochi, sister of Napoleon I, and sponsored by Sir Joseph Banks. His work was always signed, but to circumvent dishonest dealers who eradicated the mark he later used a secret hidden mark. Many of his CAMEOS were sold as antiques. His work was carried on by his daughters, Elena (1822-86) and Maria Elisa (1824-81), after their youthful return to Italy, where they carved gems and SHELL CAMEOS.

Pitt Diamond. The same as the REGENT DIAMOND.

plaque brooch. A type of brooch in the general form of a plaque, usually rectangular (sometimes with curved corners) with the area within the border almost entirely filled in and with little or no decoration extending outside the border. Such brooches are usually heavily encrusted with gemstones, often in PAVÉ SETTING.

plasma. A variety of QUARTZ that is cryptocrystalline, opaque (or slightly translucent) and of various shades of green, due to INCLUSIONS of green earth. It is sometimes flecked with spots of white or yellow; when the spots are red, the stone is BLOODSTONE (HELIOTROPE). It is sometimes carved.

plaque brooch. Buckle style with diamonds in *pavé* setting. Courtesy of Sotheby's, London.

plastic. A synthetic substance that, being susceptible of being moulded by heat and pressure, is used for many modern purposes, including making articles of COSTUME JEWELRY and JUNK JEWELRY. Plastics can be manufactured in many varieties and in infinite colours and can be given a metallic appearance, and also can be treated by electroplating. The material is light in weight, soft, and sectile. It can be made to resemble any type of gemstone, and also certain natural substances, e.g. AMBER, CORAL, IVORY, JET, and TORTOISE SHELL, but they are readily distinguishable by the resinous LUSTRE, internal bubbles, low degree of HARDNESS, rounded edges, etc., of plastic. Plastics are made of varying components, the most common varieties being celluloid and nylon. Vinyl plastics and acrylic plastics are sometimes used in jewelry to imitate gemstones and also as the nucleus for an IMITATION PEARL. *See* ACRYLIC JEWELRY.

plate inlay. A type of decoration related to, and possibly preceding, CLOISONNÉ INLAY, produced not by the attachment to the metal base of thin CLOISONS of metal, but by piercing a design in a metal (usually gold) plate, backed by a second metal plate, and filling in the design in the upper plate with thin slices of coloured gemstones (usually GARNET) or coloured glass, often backed with FOIL and secured by mastic. It is found in GOTHIC JEWELRY (*see* PETROSSA GORGET).

platinum. A valuable, rare, metallic element that is very heavy, silvery-white, non-corroding, malleable, ductile, and of high tensile strength. As its price exceeds that of gold, it is used in jewelry only for fine articles, but in the form of PLATINUM ALLOY. It is fusible with great difficulty (its melting-point is 1773.5° C., 3190° F.), hence requiring great heat for annealing or SOLDERING. It is regarded by some as a desirable SETTING for diamonds, as it does not readily TARNISH and the colours are harmonious. Platinum was known by the Indians in Colombia and Ecuador before the 15th century, and was used there, for some articles of PRE-COLUMBIAN JEWELRY, as almost pure platinum or mixed with gold (not as an ALLOY but by SINTERING it into a hammered composite mass); *see* TUMACO

plique à jour. Gold pendant with peacock wings in *plique à jour* enamel and opal drop. Lucien Gautrait, Paris, 1900. H. 6.5 cm. Schmuckmuseum, Pforzheim, Germany.

JEWELRY. Not until the mid-19th century was platinum used in Europe, when methods were found to make it fusible. Its principal user in jewelry today is Japan. *See* PLATINUM ALLOY; PALLADIUM.

platinum alloy. An ALLOY of PLATINUM with various other metals, e.g. PALLADIUM, COPPER, rhodium, iridium, osmium, etc. Platinum to be used in jewelry must be made workable by being alloyed. Since 1 January 1975 platinum has required a legal HALLMARK in Great Britain. The usual proportion of platinum in alloy used for jewelry is 95%.

pleonaste. The same as CEYLONITE.

plique à jour (French). A technique of decoration in ENAMELLING by which the design is outlined in metal and filled in with variously coloured transparent enamels but with no backing behind the enamel, so that the effect is similar to that of a stained-glass window. One process involved mixing a FLUX into the enamel so that it would have sufficient consistency not to run, but more often an openwork metal mount was attached to a sheet of copper foil, the enamel was filled in and allowed to harden, and the copper was dissolved by dipping the piece in acid, leaving only the mount and the enamel. The work in jewelry was usually executed in a gold setting, but the technique has also been used with pierced porcelain. The method was discovered in the 15th century and used by BENVENUTO CELLINI and others during the Renaissance, and was reintroduced in France *c.* 1900. The German term is *Fensteremail* (window enamel). *See* CLOISONNÉ; CHAMPLEVÉ; À JOUR.

pocket watch. A type of man's WATCH, to be carried in a pocket of the waistcoat (usually worn attached to a WATCH CHAIN) or in a special small watch-pocket below the waistband of the trousers (usually so worn with a watch FOB attached). For some of the many styles of cases for such watches, *see* WATCH-CASE.

Pohl Diamond. A DIAMOND weighing 287 carats rough that was found in 1934 at the Elandsfontein diggings in South Africa by Jacob Jonker (finder of the JONKER DIAMOND). It was sold to HARRY WINSTON who had it cut by Lazare Kaplan, of New York, into one emerald-cut stone of 38.10 carats (sold to an opera singer in the 1930s and called the Pohl diamond) and 14 other stones. The large stone was sold at Christie's, London, in October 1976 to a private collector.

poinçon (de contrôle). The French term for the mark on silver similar to the English HALLMARK.

point. A unit of weight for a DIAMOND, being one-hundredth of a metric CARAT. It is used for weights that are decimal fractions of a carat, and all figures after the second decimal point are, in the diamond and jewelry trade, generally discarded. *See* GRAIN.

point-cut diamond. A diamond in the form of an octahedron, being the natural form of the stone, and merely polished; sometimes called a GLASSIE. It was the earliest style used, from *c.* 1475, and was seldom used after the early 16th century when it was largely superseded by the PYRAMID CUT and then TABLE CUT diamond.

pointillé. A technique of decorating metal with small points or dots, made with a sharp pointed instrument. It is found on some Bronze Age JET jewelry (*see* MELFORT NECKLACE) and some English pieces of the early 15th century (*see* CLARE RELIQUARY).

poire (French). Literally, pear. A natural pearl having a pear-like shape.

poison ring. A type of FINGER RING having a hinged BEZEL that conceals a compartment said to have held poison. Although no such use has been factually established, there are historical (e.g. Hannibal's death) and literary references to such rings. It has been surmised that the compartment may usually have contained perfume or a relic.

poissarde (French). Literally, fishwife. A type of EAR-RING with an elongated pendant. Such pieces were popular in France during the period of the Directory, *c*. 1795-9, when the fashion was for dresses in Greek style worn without much jewelry.

Polar Star Diamond. A diamond weighing 40.28 carats, believed to be from the Golconda Mine in India. It is cut as a square, about 2.5 cm wide, with facets to form a symmetrical eight-point star; the faceting is in the style done in Antwerp in the 16th/17th centuries. The diamond's history dates from its ownership by Joseph Bonaparte, brother of Napoleon, when the former is presumed to have acquired it while he was King of Naples, 1806-8. It was taken by him to Switzerland and sold in the 1820s to Princess Tatiana Youssoupoff, a wealthy Tsarist collector, and was sold by the Youssoupoff family in the 1920s through CARTIER, in Paris, to Sir Henry Deterding, who purchased it for his wife, Lydia. It was sold, as part of her estate, on 21 November 1980 at Christie's, Geneva, for 8,640,000 Swiss francs (almost £2,000,000), to Bazeen Saliah, a dealer of Sri Lanka, presumably acting for a client in Bombay. The diamond is noted for its brilliance and has been mounted in a ring by BOUCHERON.

polished girdle. The GIRDLE of a diamond that has been polished to give it a smooth curved surface. The process was developed by Monnickendam, of Portslade, Sussex, England, and requires the use of special machinery. It is sometimes called a 'cylindrical girdle'.

polishing. (1) Metals. The process, used by jewellers, of making metal smooth and glossy, after the piece has been fashioned and rubbed with any of various abrasives to give it its preliminary finishing. The polishing is done first by machine, using a polishing lathe fitted with various polishing brushes charged with emery powder and oil or with tripoli, and then by lathe or hand, using a polishing mop charged with tripoli, or rouge, after which the piece is completed by buffing with a buff stick. Small areas are polished by burnishing. Polishing the interior of a FINGER RING is done with either a felt cone attached to the spindle on the lathe or a ring-stick. (2) Gemstones. The polishing of gemstones is done on a rotating wheel (scaife) charged with various powders, including tripoli, putty powder, diatomite, rottenstone, and pumice. It is sometimes followed by an acid bath. A diamond requires no special polishing, as the stone, having no Beilby layer, is polished in the same operation as the FACETING.

polychrome jewelry. ANGLO-SAXON JEWELRY that is multicoloured by reason of being inlaid with garnets, blue and green glass, NIELLO, and white shell-like material. It is of two varieties: (1) so-called 'luxurious', with flat-cut foiled garnets and glass set in gold or silver cells built on a base of gold or silver, in the manner of CLOISONNÉ INLAY, forming patterns of zoomorphic motifs, with panels of FILIGREE wire ornament between the cells and along the border (*see* KINGSTON BROOCH); and (2) so-called 'humble', with the base and plate of silver or bronze cast in one piece, having a serrated edge in imitation of filigree, and cells of simple patterns set with garnets and niello rings. Such decoration is usually seen on DISC BROOCHES found in the counties of Kent and Suffolk, being an English style derived from, but an improvement on, Continental prototypes. After comparison with the SUTTON HOO TREASURE, it has been established that such pieces were made between AD 550/600 and 700, rather than earlier as formerly believed. The Sutton Hoo brooches of East Anglia have larger garnets and the cloison cells are of more complicated shapes than such Kentish brooches. A much earlier use of the polychrome style is found in HELLENISTIC JEWELRY and ROMAN JEWELRY.

polyhedron ear-ring. A type of EAR-RING in the form of a plain thin PENANNULAR hoop decorated with a polyhedron ornament. Some examples have a thin raised border on each face, and the enclosed space is decorated with varicoloured enamelling or set with GEMSTONES.

pomander. Originally, a mixture of highly scented spices and perfumes, made into a ball and carried in medieval times to counteract offensive odours, and also supposedly to protect against infection; later the term was applied to the receptacle, often shaped like an apple or a pear, that

polyhedron ear-ring. Gold with almandine stones. Gothic, *c.* AD 500. W. 2.8 cm. Schmuckmuseum, Pforzheim, Germany.

pomander. Gold, enamelled, and jewelled, with panels on 6 compartments bearing in *émail en résille sur verre* the names of the enclosed essences. French, *c.* 1600. Sold from Melvin Gutman Collection. Courtesy of Sotheby's, New York.

Pomodoro, Arnaldo. Pendant, white and yellow gold. 1968. H. 17.5 cm. Schmuckmuseum, Pforzheim, Germany.

Popayán jewelry. Eagle pectoral of cast tumbaga, H. 9.4 cm. Museum of Mankind, London (photo copyright, Times Newspapers Ltd.)

was worn like a PENDANT during the 14th–17th centuries. The receptacle was usually a perforated metal globular case, opening midway, to contain the ball, but some examples were made with four to sixteen hinged compartments that opened out like the segments of an orange, each containing a different scent whose name, or an identifying numeral, was inscribed on the separate lids (some without any pierced walls were primarily for storage of scents rather than being a true pomander). The segmented type often had an enclosed VINAIGRETTE as the core of the fruit. Examples in the form of a human skull were worn as a MEMENTO MORI. Articles made similarly were sometimes also devotional jewelry, with inscribed names of saints and with a religious figure in the centre. Women wore pomanders suspended from a GIRDLE or a CHATELAINE, and men by suspending them from a chain around the neck. Pomanders were made of gold or other metal, decorated with enamelling and sometimes gemstones, and in France some were made of CRYSTAL or ONYX. A rare specimen made in Spain, *c.* 1600, is in the form of a ball of gum benzoin (an aromatic resin) with gold mounts and studded with cabochon emeralds. They were sometimes called a 'scent ball' or a 'musk ball'. The German name is *Bisamapfel. See* W. Turner, 'Pomanders', in *Connoisseur*, March 1912, p. 151; Edward Wenham, 'Pomanders', in *Connoisseur*, April 1934, p. 228. *See* BOÎTE DE SENTEUR; SACHET.

Pomodoro, Arnaldo (1926–   ). An Italian sculptor who, with his younger brother Giò, a painter and sculptor, has contributed to contemporary design and greatly influenced later work. They made pieces in gold, often decorated with gemstones and especially CRYSTAL. Some pieces were made by CUTTLEFISH CASTING. During the 1950s they worked together, exhibiting extensively as 'Fratelli Pomodoro'. Arnaldo in the 1950s often created articles with roughened textures, while Giò leaned toward use of colour and gemstones. Their brother-in-law, Gian Carlo Montebello, employs many craftsmen to execute their designs and markets the pieces under the name 'Gem'.

Poniatowski Collection. A collection, consisting predominantly of forged ENGRAVED GEMSTONES, owned by Prince Josef Anton Poniatowski (1762–1813), who had inherited a collection of authentic gemstones from his uncle, Stanislas Augustus (1732–98), the last King of Poland and a famous collector of gems. The Prince was exiled to Italy and soon after his death the owner of the pension where he lived in Rome showed his collection of INTAGLIOS to an agent of Christie's of London; Christie's bought the collection, catalogued about 3,000 pieces, and sold them in 1839. Shortly thereafter several contemporary Roman gem-engravers claimed that they had carved them and that one of them named Odelli had been assigned to provide them with forged signatures of real and imaginary Graeco-Roman engravers of antiquity.

pontifical ring. A type of finger ring worn by a bishop on the fourth finger of his right hand, when celebrating the Mass. Such rings were large (being worn over a glove; *see* GLOVE RING) and were ornately decorated with several GEMSTONES. The earliest extant ring of this type dates from *c.* 1255; another early example is the FOUNDER'S RING. A bishop might have several such rings. The only persons entitled to such rings, other than a bishop, were those with offices at the Papal court.

ponytails. A type of INCLUSION in certain gemstones, consisting of fibres of asbestos (byssolite) that form a plume of thin curved lines. It is characteristic of the DEMANTOID. Sometimes called 'horse's tails'.

Popayán eagle. A type of PECTORAL, made of TUMBAGA in the POPAYÁ region of Colombia, that is in the form of an eagle with spread wings and tail, having helical ear ornaments, sometimes an anthropomorphic head, and sometimes attached human legs and phallus. *See* EAGLE PENDANT.

Popayán jewelry. Articles of PRE-COLUMBIAN JEWELRY made by the Indians of the Popayán region in the High Andes of southern Colombia, which are closely related to those of the nearby regions of San Augustin and Tierradentro. The articles included gold and copper discs, but most notably the POPAYÁN EAGLES.

popinjay. An ornament in the form of a popinjay (a bright-coloured parrot) that was made IN THE ROUND, usually wearing a crown, and worn suspended from a NECK CHAIN or as a pendant. A number of such pieces are of silver, made in Holland in the late 16th century; they were worn as a badge, suspended from an ARCHER'S PENDANT, by members of the Archers' Guild.

popora (Colombian Indian). A small, gold bottle ('lime flask') generally in the form of an anthropomorphic male or female figure, usually seated, and used, mainly in the Quimbaya region of Colombia (*see* QUIMBAYA JEWELRY), to contain powdered lime (made from shells) for mixing with coca leaves which the Indians carried in bags and chewed as a religious practice, keeping a wad in the cheek throughout the day. The flasks had a cover with a hole through which a thin spatula (LIME DIPPER) was kept for using the lime. The flasks were worn slung around the neck, as shown on gold figures wearing replicas of them. The figures were in many forms, including warriors with bow and arrows, nobles wearing a pendant, necklace, and sceptre, and women sometimes holding a baby; the figures were nude except for replicas of jewelry. Some of the figures carry small SNUFF TRAYS to hold the *yopo* (narcotic snuff) that they sniffed. The figures are usually made of sheet gold or TUMBAGA, with REPOUSSÉ decoration or of cast gold or tumbaga (but sometimes of a gourd or calabash), and usually they have an attached loop for a suspensory cord or necklace. Some flasks are in the form of a globular container. *See* PRE-COLUMBIAN JEWELRY.

porcelain jewelry. Various articles of jewelry made of porcelain or decorated with porcelain, including FINGER RINGS, MEDALLIONS, BROOCHES, PENDANTS, BUCKLES, CLASPS, BUTTONS, EAR-RINGS, and POSY-HOLDERS. Some pieces having flat plaques of porcelain are usually decorated with enamelled floral designs, sentimental motifs, or miniature portraits. Some factories made flowers IN THE ROUND which were mounted as brooches; examples were made of Belleek porcelain and of Parian porcelain (*see* PARIAN JEWELRY). Porcelain jewelry has been made also by the Worcester (Chamberlain's) factory, by the makers of Crown Staffordshire, by Lenox China, Inc., in the United States, and by some German factories. Medallions of bone china made by Josiah Wedgwood II (*see* WEDGWOOD JEWELRY) and other English porcelain factories were also mounted in jewelry. *See* BRELOQUE.

portrait bracelet. A type of bracelet that is decorated with a portrait, usually enamelled on a plaque and sometimes framed with SEED PEARLS or HALF PEARLS.

portrait cameo. A CAMEO of HARDSTONE carved with a portrait. Many examples were made during the late 15th and the 16th centuries in Italy and France. Some were mounted in a pendant ENSEIGNE or finger ring. A series of royal portrait cameos, representing every great sovereign of the age, can be seen at the Vienna Cabinet and the Paris Cabinet des Médailles. *See* ELIZABETH I CAMEO.

portrait diamond. A thin diamond with two large, flat, parallel surfaces so that a viewer can see through it to recognize an object under it, without distortion by refraction. The largest known is the 'Russian Table Portrait Diamond', 25 carats, 4 by 3 cm, now in the Kremlin, Moscow; it is thought to be a cleavage from a larger stone. Sometimes such a diamond is found in nature (called a 'flat') and is cut and bevelled for use as a glass over a miniature portrait or for a watch-case (called a 'portrait stone' or a LASQUE).

portrait jewelry. Various articles, principally brooches, pendants, bracelets, and finger rings, decorated with a portrait, usually executed by carving as a CAMEO or by enamelling as a MEDALLION on porcelain, bone china or COPPER, or painting on vellum set under a crystal. Rings made in the Roman period often bore portraits, as did enamelled pendants made in the 16th/17th centuries and enamelled rings, bracelet clasps, etc., made in the 18th century. *See* CHARLES V JEWELRY.

portrait medallion. A MEDALLION decorated with a portrait, usually an enamelled miniature but often in the form of a CAMEO, sometimes

popinjay. Silver pendant. Dutch, late 16th century. Victoria & Albert Museum, London.

popora (lime container). Cast tumbaga. Seated woman. Quimbaya style. H. 14.5 cm. Museum of Mankind, London (photo copyright, Times Newspapers Ltd).

porcelain jewelry. Pendants (one enamelled). Lenox China, Inc., Lawrenceville, New Jersey.

portrait bracelet. Gold rigid bracelet with portrait of future Edward VII; set with diamonds, emeralds, and amethysts and having relief facsimile signature on the back. English, *c.* 1880. W. (portrait) 3.2 cm. Courtesy of S. J. Phillips Ltd, London.

portrait cameo. Henry VIII and his son, by Richard Astyll. By gracious permission of Her Majesty the Queen.

mounted in a frame with gemstones. A notable example is a gold medallion bearing a low-relief profile portrait carved in CHALCEDONY, depicting a nobleman (traditionally thought to be Philip the Good, Duke of Burgundy, but now considered probably to be Robert de Masmines, wearing his collar as a Knight of the Golden Fleece); the hat (red) and costume (green) are in gold REPOUSSÉ covered with translucent enamel. During the 16th century silver portrait medallions were cast from medals. Enamelled portrait medallions were a popular form of personal adornment, worn suspended on a chain or a ribbon by ladies and gentlemen, during the late years of Elizabeth I and the reign of James I, and were also used as presentation pieces.

portrait ring. A type of finger ring that bears a portrait carved on a gemstone as a CAMEO, enamelled or moulded on the BEZEL, or painted on vellum and covered with a crystal on the bezel. Some Roman rings bore a portrait of a friend of the owner, and some Saxon rings a portrait of the owner. Rings have borne depictions of a number of English Sovereigns (*see* ROYAL PORTRAIT RING; ELIZABETH I PORTRAIT RING). Few such rings were made for private individuals, most preferring a portrait enamelled on a pendant, but from the 18th century some such cameos were made, probably carved in Italy and mounted in England, with a few bearing the name of the subject. Portraits are also on the rings mounted with TASSIE MEDALLIONS and with cameos made by Wedgwood (*see* WEDGWOOD JEWELRY).

Portuguese Diamond. A diamond said to be the largest known cut diamond found in Brazil. Its early history is unknown, but as all important diamonds found in Brazil during the Portuguese regime, especially during the reign of Regent John VI (1799–1824), became the property of the Portuguese Crown, it has been presumed that this stone was among several so owned. It was previously a 170-carat CUSHION CUT diamond (possibly originally cut from a much larger historic rough stone), but was recut in the late 1800s into a 150-carat oval shape, and in the 1920s cut again into the present EMERALD CUT stone of 127.02 carats. It was acquired from HARRY WINSTON in 1963 by the Smithsonian Institution, Washington, DC.

posamenterie style. A style of ancient jewelry characterized by designs formed by a length of gold wire tightly twisted into flat helical patterns. Sometimes the outer terminal of the wire of one such pattern was continued to form the bow and pin of a brooch or to form another such pattern which, connected by a looped section of the wire, made a pendant. Examples have been found on the banks of the Danube in Hungary, dating from the Central European Late Bronze Age, *c.* 11th/9th century BC. The modern term is derived from the German *Posament* (lace-work).

Post, Marjorie Merriweather, Handbag. An evening handbag made for Mrs Marjorie Merriweather Post and donated by her daughter, Mrs Augustus Riggs IV, to the Smithsonian Institution, Washington, DC. It is a silk octagonal bag attached to a platinum frame and covered completely with hand-sewn SEED PEARLS at about 100 to the square inch. The frame is decorated with leaflets made of carved alternating rubies, sapphires, and emeralds, with interspersed small diamonds. Suspended from the frame is a monogram 'M P D' (her initials at the time) set with diamonds.

posy holder. A small cornucopia-shaped container for holding a posy (a nosegay), sometimes intended to be worn attached to a dress. Examples are known made of porcelain in Berlin and elsewhere. Some made of silver are from Madras, India, 19th century; these usually have an attached clip to fasten to a garment and also a chain with a ring for a finger. A gold enamelled example may be from France, *c.* 1560.

posy ring. A type of finger ring that is engraved with a posy (a brief naive sentimental expression, the word being contracted from 'poesy' or 'poetry'; before the 15th century, called a 'reson'). The amatory inscription (often rhymed) was usually (and especially after the 16th century) hidden on the inside of the hoop, but sometimes was on the exterior, sometimes on both sides. The language of the inscriptions was usually Norman French, and the dating of the rings is generally determined by the script. Such inscriptions are also found on some SIGNET RINGS. The rings were usually, from the 17th century, an ENGAGEMENT RING or a WEDDING RING, but some of the inscriptions are ambiguous as to the use. Rings inscribed with a version of a posy were worn in Classical times, but their use ceased during the Dark Ages until they were revived with the rise of chivalry in the age of feudalism. They were principally worn in England from the 14th century (a few are French) until they were mass produced and went out of fashion in the 18th century. The engraving of sentimental inscriptions on the inside of a WEDDING RING has been somewhat revived in modern times. *See* Joan Evans, *English Posies and Posy Rings* (1931), reproducing about 3,000 posies.

potences, à (French). A style of setting a pearl with small gold projections on two sides.

Pouget, Jean (d. 1769). A Parisian jeweller, usually known as 'Pouget fils', who in 1762 wrote one of the most famous French 18th-century books about jewelry designs, which included lists of jewellers and stones, and discussed the effect of the introduction of the rococo style and the emphasis on coloured gemstones. *See Bulletin of the Metropolitan Museum of Art*, May 1921, p. 134.

prase. (1) A variety of QUARTZ that is cryptocrystalline, translucent, and leek-green, the colour being due to the presence of internal actinolite fibres. The name is derived from the Greek *prason* (leek). It has sometimes been called 'mother-of-emerald' because it was supposed to be the mother-rock of EMERALD. (2) A variety of CHALCEDONY that is microcrystalline and also dull leek-green. Sometimes now called 'green agate', especially when it is a grey AGATE that has been dyed green.

praseolite. A variety of IOLITE that is leek-green. *See* PRASIOLITE.

prasiolite. A variety of AMETHYST from Montezuma, Brazil, that has been changed by HEAT TREATMENT to a leek-green colour. The name is deprecated, owing to confusion with PRASEOLITE which was earlier so named. A variety of amethyst from Arizona has been similarly changed by heat.

prasopal. A variety of COMMON OPAL that is leek-green. The name is derived from the Greek *prason* (leek).

precious opal. One of the two principal varieties of OPAL (as contrasted with COMMON OPAL) which exhibits IRIDESCENCE due to a play of spectral colours when light falls upon its surface. It includes a regular structure of minute, closely set internal spheres of similar size but there may be variations of the sphere sizes between different stones which regulate the wave lengths of the reflected light, causing varicoloured interference of light. When heated, it loses water, turns dull, and loses iridescence. Most examples are somewhat transparent with backgrounds that are milky or varicoloured. The colour play shows in different patterns which establish various varieties, including principally the BLACK OPAL, FIRE OPAL, WHITE OPAL, and WATER OPAL, and also FLAME OPAL, FLASH OPAL, HARLEQUIN OPAL, PINPOINT OPAL, and HYALITE. The class is sometimes called 'noble opal'.

precious stone. A term that in past years has been applied to a gemstone of a small group limited to the diamond, emerald, ruby, and sapphire, with which the pearl, although not a stone, is usually included. The basic monetary value of such stones depends upon rarity, size, and intrinsic quality, although it is also affected by the quality of the workmanship, such as FACETING, but apart from considerations of SETTING. *See* SEMI-PRECIOUS STONE. The term 'precious' is sometimes used to indicate a variety of a stone, e.g. PRECIOUS OPAL. It is also sometimes loosely prefixed to the name of a gemstone to distinguish it from another variety of stone that resembles it, e.g., 'precious topaz' which is CITRINE; such usage involves a misnomer and should be discontinued.

pre-Columbian jade jewelry. Articles of PRE-COLUMBIAN JEWELRY made usually of JADEITE, but sometimes of SERPENTINE or green CHALCEDONY, in Middle America, principally in Costa Rica and Mexico, the pieces

portrait medallion. Carved chalcedony on gold with gold and coloured enamel on repoussé relief. Portrait of Philip the Good, Duke of Burgundy, or Robert de Masmines. Burgundy, *c.* 1440. Schatzkammer, Residenz, Munich.

portrait medallion. Enamel on gold. Portrait of Eleanore, wife of Leopold I. German, *c.* 1720 (portrait), *c.* 1650 (frame). H. 7.1 cm. Schmuckmuseum, Pforzheim, Germany.

portrait ring. Tassie medallion depicting George III. English, *c.* 1780. Ashmolean Museum, Oxford.

Portuguese Diamond. Emerald-cut diamond from Brazil. Smithsonian Institution, Washington, DC.

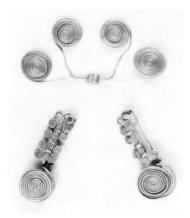

posamenterie style. Brooches of gold wire with helical terminals. Central European Late Bronze Age, *c.* 11th/9th centuries BC. British Museum, London.

Post, Marjorie Merriweather, Handbag. Silk with seed pearls and jewelled frame. Smithsonian Institution, Washington, DC (photo by Van Pelt, Los Angeles).

being in the form of beads and pendants. The pendants usually depict birds (*see* BEAK BIRD), animals or anthropomorphic figures (*see* AXE GOD) sometimes holding a pair of staffs, and are pierced horizontally so as to be strung facing frontally. *See* Elizabeth K. Easly, *Pre-Columbian Jade from Costa Rica* (1968).

pre-Columbian jewelry. Articles of jewelry, generally made of gold or TUMBAGA, but sometimes of JADEITE (*see* PRE-COLUMBIAN JADE JEWELRY), in many indigenous forms and styles, by the American Indians before the coming of Columbus (1492) and during the period thereafter until the conquest in the 16th century by the Spanish Conquistadors (hence sometimes called 'pre-Hispanic jewelry') in certain countries of Middle America (Mexico, Guatemala, Honduras, Costa Rica, and Panama) and South America (Colombia, Ecuador, Peru, and Chile). The gold pieces were usually made of flat sheet metal, hammered and decorated with REPOUSSÉ and FALSE FILIGREE work or cast by the CIRE PERDUE process, and with a total absence of enamelling on any known examples and occasional use of TURQUOISE or a few other gemstones. Such articles included mainly PECTORALS, MASKS, DIADEMS, LABRETS, NOSE ORNAMENTS, EAR ORNAMENTS, and NECKLACES, and certain objects indigenous to some regions. Most of the jewelry, pillaged by the Spaniards, was destroyed by them or in Spain for the gold content, and what survives today is mainly from robbed graves and tombs or from recent excavations. As there were trading posts throughout the region, some articles have been found far from the place of fabrication, at sites 4,000 miles apart, and from periods of time ranging through 1,500 years, thus creating unsolved problems of attribution. The dating of pieces is uncertain, and tentatively estimated dates vary in each region. *See* CHILEAN JEWELRY; COLOMBIAN JEWELRY; COSTA RICAN JEWELRY; ECUADORIAN JEWELRY; MEXICAN JEWELRY; PANAMANIAN JEWELRY; PERUVIAN JEWELRY. *See* André Emmerich, *Sweat of the Sun and Tears of the Moon* (1965). [*Plate IX*]

prehnite. A variety of gemstone that is opaque, sometimes translucent, with a green variety that may resemble NEPHRITE (JADE) and sometimes brown or yellowish. Some brown specimens cut EN CABOCHON show a CAT'S-EYE effect, and some transparent stones have been faceted. The stone was named after Colonel van Prehn who in 1774 brought it from the Cape of Good Hope. Stones from South Africa have been called by the misnomer 'Cape emerald'.

premier. A gemstone that is somewhat cloudy and has a bluish tinge that, in some lights, seemed to change to yellowish or brownish, but which has been determined to be caused by fluorescence. It was formerly referred to as a stone of 'false colour'. Such stones have been found in the Premier Mine, in South Africa.

Premier Rose Diamond. A diamond found in April 1978 at the Premier Mine (site of the discovery of the CULLINAN DIAMOND), near Pretoria, South Africa, weighing rough 353.90 carats. It was sold in May 1978 for $5,170,000 by De Beers Consolidated Mines Ltd, to a syndicate (the Mouw Diamond Cutting Works, of Johannesburg, and Goldberg-Weiss, Inc., New York) which had it sawn into 2 rough stones, weighing, respectively, about 270 and 80 carats. From the larger piece was cut a pear-shaped stone of 137.02 carats (named the Premier Rose or Big Rose, after Mrs Rose Mouw, who planned the cutting and marked it for sawing). The smaller piece was cut into 2 stones, a pear-shaped diamond (named the Little Rose) of 31.48 carats, and a circular BRILLIANT (named the Baby Rose) of 2.11 carats. The Big Rose, a blue-white stone cut with 189 facets (56 main facets and 133 facets on the GIRDLE) has been certified as flawless and of top-quality colour and purity. The full ownership of the 3 stones was acquired for a reported $12,000,000 by Goldberg-Weiss, Inc., which offered the Big Rose for sale in May 1979.

pressing. The same as STAMPING, except that it is done by a mechanical process rather than by hand

'pretzel' bracelet. A type of BRACELET of which the main decoration is a repoussé motif in the form of a pretzel, sometimes ornamented with a floral motif of gemstones. Such pieces were made in Hungary in the 19th century.

Priam, Treasure of. *See* TROJAN TREASURE.

priest's ring. A type of finger ring to be worn by a priest. The wearing of a ring by a priest was not customary, but there are existing examples of rings inscribed with the name and title of a priest. Such a ring was not permitted to be worn while celebrating the Mass (*see* PONTIFICAL RING).

Prince Harlequin Opal. A BLACK OPAL weighing 181.20 carats. It is in the Natural History Museum, New York City.

princess cut. The discontinued name for the PROFILE CUT.

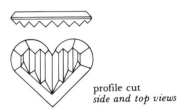

profile cut
side and top views

profile cut. A style of cutting a diamond (and some other transparent gemstones) that provides a large surface area with good total internal reflection while permitting economical use of the material. After a crystal has been sawn into thin parallel plates (about 1.5 mm thick), each plate is cut into any desired shape, then the top is polished and the bottom cut with a series of narrow, parallel V-shaped grooves (if all are parallel, the appearance is a series of BAGUETTE CUT stones, but it criss-crossed they appear as small STEP CUT stones; a border is then added of variously-shaped facets. The process was invented in 1961 by Arpad Nagy, a London cutter, and was originally called the 'princess cut'.

prophylactic jewelry. Articles of jewelry that from antiquity to the Renaissance and later have been considered by the wearers to contribute to the prevention or healing of disease, either by reason of an inherent magical quality of the gemstone or organic substance used (*see* MAGICAL STONES) or the power of certain magical words inscribed on them (*see* MAGICAL JEWELRY). Some such pieces were made with an open back to afford the magical quality closer access to the wearer's skin. Treatises have been written since 1592 on the powers of such jewelry. *See* AMULET; CHARM; TALISMAN; ANODYNE NECKLACE; PHYLACTERY PENDANT.

prospector's brooch. A type of brooch introduced in Australia at the time of the discovery there of OPALS, the brooch being in the form of a map of Australia with the states shown in opals of different colours within a gold frame.

protome ear-ring. A type of HOOP EAR-RING of which one terminal is in the form of a protome (a human bust or the forepart of an animal). Gold examples, in the form of the forepart of a horse, are known from the Doric colony at Messembria (now Nesebǔr) in Bulgaria, from the 3rd century BC. A Hellenistic gold example from the same period has been found in Cyprus.

provenance (or **provenience**). The source of an object; strictly, for clarity, with respect to a gemstone, pearl or other natural substance, the place of origin, and with respect to a jewel, the find-site, and in either case, the prior ownership as distinguished from the place of production of a fabricated article.

pseudophite. A mineral that resembles SERPENTINE and also JADE. It is normally green, massive, and of low HARDNESS. It is polished for use as ornaments, but also for COSTUME JEWELRY. The name is derived from the Greek *pseudo* (false) and *ophis* (snake).

Pugin, A(ugustus) W(elby) N(orthmore) (1812-52). An English architect and designer of French descent who was in England from *c.* 1837 where he made designs in many fields, especially for metalware. He

posy-holder. Silver with filigree decoration, and attached clip and ring. Madras, India, 19th century. Victoria & Albert Museum, London.

'pretzel' bracelet. Gold spun wire band with repoussé motif and gemstones. Hungarian, mid-19th century. W. 7 cm. Hungarian National Museum, Budapest.

protome ear-ring. Gold hoop ear-ring. Hellenistic; Cyprus, 3rd century BC. W. 1.75 cm. City Museums and Art Gallery, Birmingham, England.

Pugin, A.W.N. Gold brooch with gemstones; made by Pugin for Jane Knill. English, *c.* 1848. Victoria & Albert Museum, London.

purse mount. Gold with enamelling. Anglo-Saxon, 7th century (Sutton Hoo Treasure). British Museum, London.

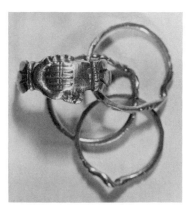

puzzle ring. Four hoops (one with fede ornament). Silver. Ashmolean Museum, Oxford.

also made designs for jewelry in Gothic style, most of which was executed by John Hardman & Co., Birmingham, of which firm he was a co-founder in 1838. He designed a well-known set of jewelry in 1846-7, which he made for his fiancée, Helen Lunsden, and altered (after the engagement was broken) for his third wife, Jane Knill; it was shown at the Great Exhibition of 1851. His jewelry featured work in CLOISONNÉ, CHAMPLEVÉ, and ENCRUSTED ENAMEL, with floral motifs in natural colours. In 1848 he produced a book of designs for jewelry depicting floral patterns.

purse mount. A decorative mount attached to a purse and suspended by hinges. An example in ANGLO-SAXON JEWELRY from the SUTTON HOO TREASURE is decorated with several plaques mounted in relief on a base (now missing) that originally was probably bone, wood or ivory, and now is a substitute material; the plaques are of gold, decorated with GARNETS and MILLEFIORI glass. It is attributed to East Anglia, 7th century.

puzzle ring. A type of finger ring that is composed of three or up to seven interlocking hoops which form a single hoop when assembled, but when disassembled are very difficult to restore to the original form. Usually there are small bulges along the hoops that further complicate fitting the sections together. In the 17th century some were made as a SIGNET RING with a seal in the BEZEL, and some were used as a LOVE RING, like a GIMMEL RING. They were popular, and still are in Turkey. Some were set with gemstones, but those made today are usually inexpensive novelties.

pyramid cut. An early style of cutting a diamond, being in the form of a square pyramid, cut by splitting a natural OCTAHEDRON-shaped diamond. It is said to have been first used by LUDWIG VAN BERGHEM, and was superseded by the TABLE CUT. *See* THREE BROTHERS JEWEL.

pyrite. A variety of PYRITES (iron sulphide), sometimes called 'IRON PYRITES'. It is pale brassy-yellow and has a brilliant metallic LUSTRE. It is of the same chemical composition as MARCASITE and resembles it, but is of a different structure and lower specific gravity. It is a very common mineral and was used extensively in Europe, especially in France, during the 18th and 19th centuries as a substitute for diamonds and marcasite. The 18th-century pieces of jewelry were well made, with PAVÉ SETTING for the stones, which were faceted and polished so that they reflected light from their surface; but in the 19th century pyrite was used for inexpensive jewelry, being cemented in the SETTING instead of having a RUB-OVER SETTING. It was set in silver or some WHITE METAL rather than more expensive and less harmonious gold. Small stones have for centuries been ROSE CUT and set in cheap jewelry. It was used in BUCKLES, FINGER RINGS, BUTTONS, COMBS, etc., and sometimes was set in narrow rows to form BOW-KNOT BROOCHES or in the frames of CAMEOS in LOCKETS. The centre for cutting pyrite (so-called 'marcasite') is in the Jura region of France, where the pieces are generally cut as low six-sided pyramids. Pyrite is found in particles dotting LAPIS LAZULI. It is sometimes called 'fool's gold'.

pyrites. Any of a number of metallic sulphides, of which the most common is iron pyrites (PYRITE, or 'fool's gold'). Other varieties are copper pyrites (chalcopyrite) and tin pyrites (stannite).

pyrope. The most popular variety of GARNET. It is transparent and fiery ruby-red, but sometimes it is tinged with brown or black and hence approaches ALMANDINE. It can be distinguished from the RUBY by its single refraction, the absence of dichroism, and lower refractive index. Some stones of less value are yellowish; these have been found mainly in Bohemia, near Trebnitz, and were ROSE CUT and set (sometimes backed with FOIL) in Victorian jewelry. The terms 'Bohemian ruby', 'Cape ruby', 'Arizona ruby', and 'rock ruby' sometimes applied to it are misnomers. It is sometimes called 'precious garnet'. The name is derived from the Greek words *pyr* (fire) and *ops* (eye or face). *See* RHODOLITE.

pyroxene. A group of minerals that have similar characteristics and when in crystal form include spodumene, HIDDENITE, KUNZITE, ENSTATITE, JADEITE, and DIOPSIDE.

Q

Qajar jewelry. Articles of jewelry made in Persia (now Iran) during the Qajar Dynasty (1794–1925), founded by Agha Mohammed Khan Qajar, who was succeeded by his nephew, Fath Ali Shah (1797–1834), a great collector of jewels, and descendants until the Pahlavi Dynasty took over in 1925. Apart from important jewelry made (e.g. the KIANI CROWN) or designed for the Court, the indigenous Qajar jewelry included gold articles decorated with coloured enamelling.

quartz. A mineral that is a form of silica which commonly occurs as crystals. When free from impurities it is colourless and limpid (ROCK CRYSTAL) but it is also found in many colours. There are three basic varieties: (1) CRYSTALLINE, including AMETHYST, CITRINE, ROSE QUARTZ, CAIRNGORM, MORION, SMOKY QUARTZ, MILKY QUARTZ, and CAT'S-EYE quartz; (2) cryptocrystalline, including CHALCEDONY (in several varieties), PLASMA (BLOODSTONE), and flint; and (3) MASSIVE including quartzite, AVENTURINE QUARTZ, and JASPER. Some quartz displays a CHATOYANT effect when properly cut EN CABOCHON, resulting in a variety of cat's-eye stones. Quartz has a VITREOUS LUSTRE and is piezoelectric, making it useful for broadcast emission and accurate timepieces. *See* RAINBOW QUARTZ; FIRESTONE; PRASIOLITE; SAGENITIC QUARTZ; SANG-DE-BOEUF; GOLD QUARTZ; RUBASSE.

quartz cat's-eye. *See* CAT'S-EYE.

quatre couleurs. *See* GOLD À QUATRE COULEURS.

Quay, Jacques (1711–93). The most highly reputed French gem-engraver of the 18th century.

'Queen Elizabeth's Ear-rings'. A legendary pair of ear-rings having each a pendent pear-shaped pearl, alleged to have been found after the death of Queen Victoria among her possessions in a packet labelled 'Queen Elizabeth's Ear-rings'. It has been related that Edward VII ordered the pearls to be suspended from the intersection of the arches of the IMPERIAL STATE CROWN in place of two pearls that had been placed there for the coronation of George IV in 1820, themselves in lieu of two poorly-shaped pearls previously on the Crown. Two pear-shaped pearls are now so suspended on the Crown but it has not been established that they were the pearls from the ear-rings and it has been said that in any event the ear-rings probably belonged, not to Elizabeth I, but to Queen Elizabeth of Bohemia (daughter of James I) whose pearls had been inherited by Queen Victoria.

Queen Mary brooch. *See* LUCKENBOOTH BROOCH.

Quewellerie, Guillaume de la (fl. 1611–35). A designer of jewelry from Amsterdam who published sets of engraved designs featuring the MORESQUE SILHOUETTE STYLE.

Quimbaya jewelry. Articles of PRE-COLUMBIAN JEWELRY made, strictly speaking, by the Quimbaya Indian tribe but, in customary usage, articles in the so-called Quimbaya style recovered from looted graves and tombs throughout the Middle Cauca Valley of the Andes in the middle of Colombia, made *c.* 400–1000, such as typified by the QUIMBAYA TREASURE. The articles include pendants and masks with humanoid faces, pectorals of cut-out humanoid figures (sometimes with suspended discs), POPORAS

Qajar jewelry. Gold brooch with enamelled portrait. Mid-19th century. L. 6.3 cm. Courtesy of Christie's, London.

Quimbaya jewelry. Cast gold mask. Face with ear and nose ornaments. Quimbaya style. H. 11.5 cm. Museum of Mankind, London (photo copyright, Times Newspapers Ltd).

Quimbaya Treasure. Cast tumbaga lime container (*popora*); seated man, nude except for jewelry. Filandia, Colombia. H. 12.5 cm. Museo de América, Madrid.

(lime flasks) and LIME-DIPPERS, EFFIGY FLASKS, HELMETS, finger-grips for spear-throwers, NOSE ORNAMENTS, EAR ORNAMENTS, and PECTORAL DISCS. The articles were made of gold or TUMBAGA, cut out from sheet metal and having REPOUSSÉ decoration or cast by the CIRE PERDUE process.

Quimbaya Treasure. A TREASURE of 121 items of QUIMBAYA JEWELRY and other articles, dating from perhaps 400–1000, found in 1891 in two graves at Le Soledad, Filandia, in the Quimbaya region of Colombia. It was presented in 1892 by Colombia to the Queen of Spain and is now kept in the Museo de América, Madrid; pieces from the Treasure were first seen outside Spain at the El Dorado Exhibition in London in 1978. A characteristic form of decoration on POPORAS (lime flasks) is the depiction of men and women, modelled IN THE ROUND, nude except for replicas of jewelry, which sometimes includes a suspended *popora*; the small feet of the figures extend outward to lend stability to the flasks.

quoin. The former name for 4 of the LOZENGE-shaped FACETS on the CROWN or on the PAVILION of a BRILLIANT, all having their apex touching the GIRDLE. Those on the crown extend up to touch the TABLE, and those on the PAVILION extend down to touch the CULET. The 4 quoins (formerly also called 'lozenges') on the crown, alternating with 4 similar adjacent TEMPLETS (BEZELS), were all usually considered together as a group of 8 templets, and likewise the 4 larger quoins on the pavilion, alternating with 4 similar adjacent PAVILION FACETS, were all usually considered together as a group of 8 pavilion facets, the only differences being their orientation to the stone and the direction and sequence in which they were ground. All such lozenge-shaped facets are now each called a KITE FACET or MAIN FACET.

quoit brooch. A type of RING BROOCH that is silver-gilt and has within the wide ring band an inner PENANNULAR ring with rope-like decoration (hence the name) along which slides the head of the hinged pin. The pin slides freely along the inner ring, the point passing through a notch opposite and being secured against one of two studs. The origin of such brooches has not been ascertained, but it has been suggested that they were made either by Jutish craftsmen with Scandinavian traditions working near Canterbury, England, in the late 5th or early 6th century or by craftsmen in northern Gaul or southern Scandinavia working in the Roman tradition. *See* SARRE QUOIT BROOCH.

R

radiated fibula. A type of FIBULA having an arched central portion and a semi-circular headplate from which radiate several (5 to 11) protuberances. The entire surface is usually divided into several zones, often decorated with CLOISONNÉ enamelling or FILIGREE ornamentation. Such pieces date from the 6th/7th centuries, and have been found at various places in Europe, including a few in Kent (England).

rainbow agate. The same as IRIS AGATE.

rainbow quartz. A variety of ROCK CRYSTAL (QUARTZ) that shows IRIDESCENCE as a result of interference of light due to natural tiny internal cracks that are filled with air and interfere with light waves. Also called 'iris' or 'iris quartz'. An artificially created imitation is called FIRESTONE.

Ramshaw, Wendy (1939–   ). An English DESIGNER-MAKER of jewelry known for her original designs for finger rings made to be worn on one finger in groups of five in changing order to vary the patterns on different occasions. The rings are of lathe-turned silver with upright spikes having different coloured gemstones set on the apexes.

radiated fibula (front and back). Silver gilt with garnets and niello decoration. From tomb of an Alemannic prince at Wittislingen, Germany. 7th century. L. 16 cm. Prähistorische Staatssammlung, Munich.

Raspoli Sapphire. A fine SAPPHIRE of 132 carats, known from the time of Louis XIV and now in the Musée National d'Histoire Naturelle, Paris.

rebus ring. A type of SIGNET RING having engraved on the BEZEL a rebus representing the name of the owner. Such rings, made of gold, silver or gilded brass, were popular in the Middle Ages. On some examples an object depicted might have several interpretations, making the correct name difficult to determine. Other articles of jewelry, e.g. a TIE PIN, were also sometimes made with a rebus.

Recesvinthus, Crown of King. The gold VOTIVE CROWN of King Recesvinthus, 653–72, the last Visigothic king in Spain. The crown is in the form of a gold circular band set with three rows of gemstones and pearls, and decorated in OPUS INTERRASILE style and with REPOUSSÉ work and CHASING. From it hang jewelled chains, each bearing a cut-out gold sheet letter forming the words 'Recesvinthvs Rex Offeret'. The crown is suspended by four chains composed of triangular plaques that hang from a jewelled ornament. The suspensory chains have suggested that the crown was not intended to be worn but probably to be a votive crown. The crown is part of the GUARRAZAR TREASURE and is now kept in Madrid. *See* SUINTHILA, CROWN OF KING.

Ramshaw, Wendy. Five finger rings, to be worn together; silver with amethysts and cornelians. 1971. Courtesy of Wendy Ramshaw, London.

reconstructed stone. A type of gemstone made by fusing together small crystals or fragments of crystals so as to make one large stone, sometimes enhancing the colour with a metallic oxide. The process was once said to have been used to imitate the RUBY (*see* GENEVA RUBY). The principle is used to combine pieces of AMBER into a large piece (*see* AMBROID). In some cases the crystals are bonded together by means of resin or a synthetic plastic, e.g. the so-called 'bonded turquoise'. Such reconstructed stones are now superseded by SYNTHETIC GEMSTONES. Some mis-called 'reconstructed turquoises' have been found, after X-ray examination, to be FAKES, made of chemical materials bonded together.

Red Cross Diamond. A large canary-yellow diamond found in the De Beers Company mine, Griqualand, South Africa, and given in April 1918 by the Diamond Syndicate of London to an art sale held in London to aid the British Red Cross Society and the Order of St John of Jerusalem. It originally weighed 375 old carats but after being cut as a square-shaped BRILLIANT it weighed 205 old carats. It was sold in 1918 at auction for £10,000. A curious feature is that inclusions visible through the TABLE are arranged to form a MALTESE CROSS. It was sold in Geneva, by Christie's, in November 1973, and was last reported as privately owned in Switzerland.

Recesvinthus, Crown of King. Gold with gemstones and pearls. Spain, *c.* 653, from Guarrazar Treasure. Museo Arqueológico Nacional, Madrid.

reliquary cross. Byzantine gold and *cloisonné* pectoral cross opening in half. Enamelled figure on front shows Virgin Mary between two busts. 10th century. H. 6.1 cm. British Museum, London.

red gold. An ALLOY of GOLD with COPPER (or copper and silver), usually about 1 part of copper to 3 parts of 24-carat gold.

reflector. A reflecting material that was formerly used as a mirror to increase the brilliance of a diamond (especially a pure colourless stone) by catching the light entering the stone and reflecting it back. It was placed below the stone in the bottom of the BEZEL in which the stone was set. This method was used in the 16th century. *See* MIRROR FOILING.

regalia. The emblems and symbols of regal authority. The British Regalia includes the CROWN, SCEPTRE, ORB, sword, spurs, finger rings, anointing vessel, etc., all being referred to together as 'Crown Jewels'. They include the Coronation Ornaments and the State Regalia for use on other State occasions, but not the personal jewels of the Sovereign privately owned and used on other than State occasions. *See* CROWN JEWELS (BRITISH). For the Scottish regalia, *see* HONOURS OF SCOTLAND, THE. *See* Lord Twining, *History of Crown Jewels of Europe* (1960) and *European Regalia* (1967).

regard ring. A type of finger ring set with a row of small gemstones of different varieties and of which the initial letters spell 'regard', such rings having been given as tokens of friendship or sentiment *c.* 1840. They were a type of ACROSTIC JEWELRY. The stones usually used in sequence were the RUBY, EMERALD, GARNET, AMETHYST, RUBY, DIAMOND. Such rings were generally a single hoop but in some unusual examples the stones were set individually in separate hoops that were joined, so that the stones formed a vertical row.

Regent (Pitt) Diamond. A diamond that is CUSHION CUT as a BRILLIANT, weighing 140.50 carats (originally 410 carats rough). It has a long history, having been found in the Parteal Mine in India in 1701 and, after several alleged thefts, was purchased in 1702 by Thomas Pitt (father of William Pitt), Governor of Fort St George, Madras, who sent it in 1710 to England where he had it cut (and then called the 'Pitt Diamond'). Fearing its theft, he sold it in 1717 to the Duc d'Orléans, Regent of France (whereupon its name was changed to the 'Regent Diamond'). It was worn by Louis XV in a SHOULDER KNOT in 1721 and again in his crown at his coronation in 1722, and then unset and worn by his Queen, Marie Leszczynska. Later it was worn by Marie Antoinette. It was stolen in 1792 from the Garde Meuble with other royal REGALIA but was returned by the thieves. In 1797 it was pawned to raise funds for the Directory, but Napoleon I redeemed it in 1802 and had it set in the hilt of the sword that he carried at his coronation in 1804. After his exile to Elba, the diamond was taken by Marie Louise, his second wife, to Blois, but it was returned to the French Government by her father, Francis I of Austria. Charles X wore it at his coronation in 1825, and after 1852 Napoleon III had it set in a diadem made for Empress Eugénie. At the auction of the French Crown Jewels in 1887 it was reserved, and thereafter (except when hidden at Chambord during World War II) has been displayed at the Galerie d'Apollon, in the Louvre, Paris.

Reimer, Hans (fl. 1555-75). A goldsmith and jeweller from Schwerin, Germany, who opened a workshop in Munich in 1855 and made jewelry for Duke Albrecht V of Bavaria and his wife Anna. The pieces included pendants, lockets, and ceremonial chains, some made from designs by HANS MIELICH. Most of his surviving pieces are in the Schatzkammer of the Residenz, Munich.

reliquary. A small casket, pendant, PECTORAL CROSS, or other receptacle for keeping or displaying a religious relic. Some, especially those made to contain an important relic, were often very highly decorated and ornamented with gemstones, but less pretentious types were made of silver or silver-gilt to contain relics of less importance. *See* BERESFORD HOPE CROSS; CHARLEMAGNE RELIQUARY; ST LOUIS RELIQUARY; CLARE RELIQUARY; DEVIZES PENDANT; ST JOHN, RELIQUARY OF THE TOOTH OF; DOVE.

reliquary cross. A type of RELIQUARY in the form of a CROSS. Byzantine examples from the 10th century, said to have been found at Istanbul, are of gold, decorated with CLOISONNÉ enamel. Such pieces were also made in

Spain in the 17th century, sometimes of hollow gold set with many gemstones amid enamelled decoration. Some examples have several compartments for a number of relics.

reliquary pendant. A type of RELIQUARY in the form of a pendant. Examples are known in many forms and styles. One handsome piece, *c.* 1400, is a pendant in the form of a TRIPTYCH with a suspended pearl, the two doors being slices of ROCK CRYSTAL that open to reveal an enamelled miniature depicting Christ between two angels holding the Crown of Thorns over his head and the space below the miniature being a compartment for a relic. Another is a circular LOCKET with 8 pin-set pearls projecting from the rim; on the front is the figure of an angel in ÉMAIL EN RONDE BOSSE, on the reverse is an engraved portrait of John the Baptist, and inside the locket the space is divided into compartments for relics; the piece is possibly French, early 15th century, and was sold from the Von Hirsch Collection by Sotheby's, London, on 22 June 1978 for £20,000. *See* WIRE ENAMELLING.

reloj (Portuguese). An article of Portuguese PEASANT JEWELRY in the form of an ear-ring or a pendant that has in the centre a decoration in the form of a rosette (that somewhat resembles the dial of a clock, hence the name) but that has the overall appearance of an ornate heart and bow-knot, such as was popular in the 18th century.

Renaissance jewelry. Articles of jewelry made during the period of the Renaissance from the 15th century until the early 17th. The style was developed in Italy, under the patronage of the Medici in Florence, the Sforza family in Milan, and the Renaissance Popes in Rome, and spread to France, the Low Countries, Spain, and the Courts at Prague and Augsburg, with relatively little impact in England. The most renowned of the early designers of jewelry were BENVENUTO CELLINI and HANS HOLBEIN THE YOUNGER, but a host of later designers (e.g. ERASMUS HORNICK, ÉTIENNE DELAUNE, DANIEL MIGNOT, HANS COLLAERT THE ELDER) published books of their designs which influenced goldsmiths and jewellers throughout Europe. The articles that were most popular were the ENSEIGNE (hat badge), the pendant (especially the BAROQUE PEARL JEWELS), and finger rings. Engraved gemstones and PORTRAIT CAMEOS were often used, and the decoration was frequently in ARCHITECTURAL STYLE or COMMESSO style or with ÉMAIL EN RONDE BOSSE. Among notable jewels of the period that are now in England are the CANNING TRITON JEWEL, DARNLEY JEWEL, BARBOR JEWEL, PHOENIX JEWEL, and LYTE JEWEL. It is difficult to establish the origin of many pieces, and some have been attributed by some writers to the country of the maker, by others to the country of his patron, and by still others on the basis of opinions as to style. *See* M. L. d'Otrange-Mastai, 'A Collection of Renaissance Jewels', in *Connoisseur*, March 1957, p. 126; Yvonne Hackenbroch, *Renaissance Jewellery* (1979); Anna Somers-Cocks, *An Introduction to Courtly Jewelry* (1980); Victoria & Albert Museum exhibition catalogue, *Princely Magnificence*, London, October 1980. [Plate X]

repoussé. A long established and universally used technique (often called EMBOSSING) of producing relief decoration on a metal plate by punching and hammering thin metal from the reverse in order to raise the design on the front. The metal plate is sometimes turned over so that some embossing can be done on the front to enhance the desired relief design. The work is done by means of hand punches and hammers, or sometimes by mechanical means by the use of metal or stone dies (called 'embossing dies'). The metal to be decorated is laid on a bed of a yielding material (e.g. wood, lead, leather sand-filled bag, or usually pitch) after the design has been scratched on with a tracer, and then the design is punched and hammered in, with periodic annealing to prevent the metal from becoming BRITTLE. On some examples the relief design is refined by CHASING on the front (sometimes called 'repoussé chasing') or ENGRAVING, or sometimes embellished by additional metal soldered to the front. Sometimes, in imitation of true repoussé work, the decorative design is not beaten from the reverse but pieces of metal are cut out separately, embossed, and affixed to the front. The process must be distinguished from STAMPING. *See* DOT-REPOUSSÉ.

reproduction. An article that is a close copy of a genuine article but made without any intent to deceive. It might be a copy of a genuine

reliquary pendant (front and back). Enamel front, engraved back. French (?), 15th century. W. 3.2 cm. Courtesy of Sotheby's, London.

repoussé. Pendant depicting three birds. Anglo-Saxon, 7th century. W. 3.8 cm. British Museum, London.

article that has been made at a prior date and recognized as a work of art, such as the copies of Etruscan articles with GRANULATED GOLD decoration made by FORTUNATO PIO CASTELLANI and his son Alessandro in the mid-19th century, and later by Carlo Giuliano (*see* GIULIANO FAMILY) and GIACINTO MELILLO. Reproductions of some important articles of jewelry have been made by the ELECTROFORMING process. Multiple reproductions of modern jewelry (e.g. pieces created by outstanding designers, with or without gemstones, and also COSTUME JEWELRY marketed by leading couturiers) are made with the same design and materials by the original maker and sold legitimately, with no intent to deceive. *See* FORGERY; COUNTERFEIT; FAKE.

resilla (from the French *résille*, network). A network of beads, usually pearls, coral or jet, worn as a lady's hair covering and kept in place by a jewelled ornament suitable for the purpose, e.g. a comb or clasp, or worn as a breast ornament.

resin. A solid organic substance exuded from pine- or fir-trees; it is amorphous, translucent, and yellowish to brown. It was used for some articles of EGYPTIAN JEWELRY, especially beads but sometimes a complete object, e.g. a HEART SCARAB in the TUTANKHAMUN JEWELRY; it has been stated that such Egyptian substance was probably a product of coniferous trees brought to Egypt from the region of Lebanon.

resin opal. A variety of COMMON OPAL that has a resinous appearance. Also called 'pitch opal'.

retinalite. A variety of SERPENTINE that is of a honey-yellow to greenish colour and has a waxy or resinous lustre. The name is derived from the Greek *rhetine* (resin).

reverse intaglio crystal. A CRYSTAL cut in the form of a CABOCHON, shallow or domed, that is carved in INTAGLIO on its flat back with a motif that is realistically painted in minute detail and is surrounded by a transparent ground. The deeper the carving, the more pronounced the three-dimensional *trompe l'oeil* effect, which is sometimes enhanced by a backing of a thin layer of MOTHER-OF-PEARL. The carved motif, for pieces mounted in a circular gold band as a tie pin, cuff links, button, or studs for men, was usually a racing horse, game bird or dog, and for pieces in a brooch or a locket for women, a floral design or a monogram; some examples depict an insect or a coaching scene. Sometimes two crystals are mounted back-to-back to form a spherical pendant, preferably with the motifs not identical but complementarily depicting the front and back views of the same subject, e.g. the head of a dog. Some examples consist of two or even three superimposed hollow cabochons, each carved with a different motif, thus increasing the effect of perspective. The technique was originated by Émile Marius Pradier, of Belgium (?), *c.* 1860 (he made the only known signed example). In England it was developed by Thomas Cook in the early 1860s and carried on by his pupil Thomas Bean and the latter's son Edmund and grandson Edgar (d. 1954). After the popularity of the pieces in the late Victorian era, the high quality deteriorated by the 1920s, when examples were also being made in France and the United States (some modern pieces depicting motor cars and aeroplanes). The crystals have long been identified with the HANCOCKS firm. The crystals have sometimes been referred to by the misnomers 'Essex Crystal' or 'Wessex Crystal', owing to the erroneous assumption that they were decorated *c.* 1860 by the enamel portrait painter William Essex (d. 1869). Imitations have been made of carved and painted glass, and even of a glass cabochon above a printed paper design. *See* Malcolm Carr, 'English Carved and Painted Crystals', in *The Antique Collector,* December 1974, p. 19.

Revolution ring. A COMMEMORATIVE RING distributed by King Gustavus III of Sweden in 1772 to royal sympathizers to commemorate the overthrow of the Russophile government. It has a diamond-encircled BEZEL which is surmounted by a crown, and on which is the diamond-set royal monogram 'G' above which is the enamelled date '21 Aug. 1772'.

rhinestone. (1) A variety of ROCK CRYSTAL that is used as an inexpensive imitation of diamond. (2) A misnomer for a colourless, iridescent GLASS that is so used. In the United States and Canada this misnomer has been sometimes applied to a colourless PASTE of high lustre, and in England sometimes also to a coloured paste. The French term for true rhinestone is *caillou du Rhin. See* STRASS.

rhinoceros horn. A variety of native HORN used in China from at least the 4th century to make various decorative personal ornaments, such as belt plaques and pendants.

Rhodian jewelry. Articles of jewelry from the Greek island of Rhodes, much of which was excavated in the cemetery of Camirus, Rhodes, in the 1860s. It was produced mainly in the 7th century BC. Examples include gold relief rectangular plaques strung together as PECTORAL ornaments depicting winged goddesses, sphinxes, griffins, etc., and ornamented with GRANULATED GOLD (*see* MISTRESS OF THE BEASTS, THE); the figures on such plaques were made separately and cut out, then soldered on the plate to provide a clearer outline. Related to such jewelry are some gold rosettes made on the island of Melos in the 7th century BC, used on DIADEMS.

rhodochrosite. A mineral that is usually MASSIVE and characteristically rose-pink, sometimes with light and dark wavy bands. After its discovery in a mine in Argentina said to have been worked by the Incas, it was first used in modern times mainly for ornaments and as thin plates to cover cigarette boxes, but it has since been used in jewelry as stones cut EN CABOCHON. A paler variety is found in Colorado (USA). The name is derived from the Greek *rhodon* (rose) and *chrosis* (colouring). It is sold under the trade-names of 'Inca rose' and 'Rosinca'.

rhodolite. A variety of GARNET that is intermediate between PYROPE and ALMANDINE, nearer to the former. It is mauve-red to rose-purple, and has high LUSTRE. Its name is derived from the Greek *rhodon* (rose) and *lithos* (stone).

rhodonite. A mineral containing manganese, the colour of which is several shades of pink, hence its name, derived from the Greek *rhodon* (rose). It is sometimes marred by veins or patches of black. It is used occasionally in jewelry when opaque and cut EN CABOCHON or as beads, but only rarely as a faceted translucent gemstone.

ribbon jasper. A variety of JASPER in which the mixed colours run in stripes, in contrast to EGYPTIAN JASPER.

ribbon necklace. A type of necklace in the form of a band of ribbon, usually of velvet, from which were suspended one or more jewelled pendants, often a large one in the centre flanked by two smaller ones. Such necklaces were popular in the early 18th century.

ribbon style. Belt buckle. Gold decorated in ribbon style in niello. Anglo-Saxon, 1st half of 7th century. L. 13 cm. British Museum, London.

ribbon style. A style of decoration suggestive of swirling ribbons, found on some ANGLO-SAXON JEWELRY of the late period, reflecting the introduction of Christianity into England which gradually influenced the prior pagan style. It is sometimes in the form of narrow lines (*see* WITHAM PIN), but more often is composed of wider broken and swirling lines decorated with stylistic forms of animals and snakes. An example of the latter type is on the 7th-century BELT BUCKLE in the SUTTON HOO TREASURE. The origin is unknown, but it has been suggested that it is derived from Scandinavia or Italy.

ribbon torc. A type of TORC made of a single ribbon or narrow strip of metal continuously twisted and having the ends fastened by a simple bent clasp. This type was made of gold in Ireland during the Irish Bronze Age; examples have been found in Ireland and Scotland. They may have been worn over a sleeve because of the rather sharp edges.

ring. A small circular band, generally referring to one worn on the finger (*see* FINGER RING), but also including other types of rings worn for personal adornment (*see* TOE RING; EAR-RING; NOSE ORNAMENT; ARMLET; BANGLE) or used functionally (*see* SIGNET RING; KEY FINGER RING; SCARF RING). Rings have been worn since the 3rd millennium BC (*see* WIRE RING) and were extensively worn by the Egyptians, Greeks, and Romans, and have been continuously worn ever since in all civilizations. They have been made of GOLD, SILVER, PLATINUM, and other metals, as well as CORAL, JET, TORTOISE SHELL, JADE, AMBER, etc. and decorated with gemstones, CAMEOS, MEDALLIONS, etc., as well as engraving and enamelling.

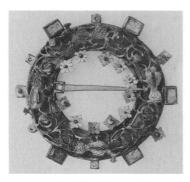

ring brooch. Gilded silver with cast peacock decoration. Gemstones and pearls missing. Hungarian, 18th century. W. 13.3 cm. Hungarian National Museum, Budapest.

ring brooch. A type of BROOCH in the form of a complete ring to which is usually hinged a horizontal pin slightly longer than the diameter of the brooch. The point of the pin rests on the ring opposite the hinge, and the brooch is worn by pulling the fabric up inside the ring, passing the pin through it twice and then drawing the fabric down so that it holds the pin in place. In some examples two short pins extend from the ring to a centre transverse crossbar. Such brooches were used frequently in medieval times, and examples have been found in HOARDS of buried ANGLO-SAXON JEWELRY and also among English jewelry of the 13th/14th centuries. Most specimens are plain but some are decorated with inscriptions or gemstones set around the ring. *See* QUOIT BROOCH; GLENLYON BROOCH; SHAWL PIN.

ring clip. A device placed inside the SHANK of a loose-fitting finger ring to make it fit securely. It is a narrow strip made of a hard, springy metal, silver or a gold alloy. There are two types: (1) the strip is soldered at one end to the inside of the shank, the balance being an unattached spring curve; (2) the strip has lugs at each end which are pressed over the edge of the shank.

ring dial. A type of finger ring, used for determining time, that is in the form of a flat band having around the outside a channel in which slides a narrow hoop in which is a pin-hole. On the band are the initials of the twelve months. When the ring is suspended by a small fixed loop on the band and the hoop is moved so as to bring the hole to the initial of the month during which the observation is being made and held toward the sun, the sun's rays pass through the pin-hole; the rays then fall on the figure, marked on the inner side of the band, from 4 am to 8 pm, to indicate the hour. Such dials were used in Germany in the 16th century, but ceased to be used when the watch was introduced. *See* SHEPHERD'S DIAL.

ring money. *See* HAIR RING; CURRENCY JEWELRY.

Ringerike style. Disc brooch. Silver gilt, cast. Gotland, Sweden, 11th century. W. 5.9 cm. Statens Historiska Museum, Stockholm.

ring-terminal torc. A type of TORC of which the terminals of the PENANNULAR hoop are massive, hollow, ring-shaped ornaments, usually decorated in relief, sometimes with CHASING and hatching. The rings are soldered to the ends of the hoop, which is often composed of strands of metal twisted as a rope-like tube, each strand being made of eight wires twisted together. Examples from the South British Late Iron Age, 1st century BC, have been found at Snettisham, Norfolk, England. *See* SNETTISHAM TORC.

Ringerike style. A Viking style of decoration used in the 10th/11th centuries, named after a group of sandstone slabs found in Ringerike, Norway, in which some examples of the style have been carved. It has also been used on some objects found in Britain. It is characterized by interlaced animal motifs, e.g. as on the SUTTON BROOCH. *See* VIKING JEWELRY.

river. A colour grading term formerly used for a diamond of pure white colour, occasionally with a prismatic blue radiance. 'Extra river' is the highest grade. The name was applied to the stones found in the river diggings of South Africa. *See* DIAMOND COLOURS.

riveting. The process of joining two pieces of metal with a rivet (a headed pin) by passing the shank through a hole in each piece and then beating down the plain end so as to make a second head as a fastener. The process has been used in jewelry, instead of SOLDERING, when it was not practicable to apply heat or when one part was to be left flexible for swivelling; it was also used to secure the studs to articles of CUT STEEL JEWELRY. It was the exclusive method used in making CELTIC JEWELRY. The rivets are of the same metal as the piece, and gold and silver rivets are today produced by refiners.

rivière (**French**). A type of NECK CHAIN or necklace that is strung with graduated gemstones of the same variety, usually individually set and without other ornamentation. Expensive examples were made with diamonds mounted in silver or platinum (as more harmonious than gold), but others were set with amethysts or other lesser gemstones, especially in the Victorian era. Sometimes two such chains, one longer than the other, were worn together, called a 'double *rivière*'. Some especially luxurious examples have a similar gemstone suspended from each stone of the necklace. *See* MARIE LOUISE NECKLACE.

rock crystal. Natural QUARTZ that is CRYSTALLINE, usually colourless (or nearly so), and transparent (or nearly so). Objects of rock crystal were carved in medieval Egypt, Iraq, and Persia, and were highly prized during the Renaissance. In modern times it is less often faceted, as lead glass (*see* CRYSTAL GLASS) is more readily available, but some pieces are carved as a CAMEO or INTAGLIO or as a SEAL. Rock crystal is also used for beads, bracelets, ear-rings, etc., faceted or merely polished. It is distinguishable from glass by its greater HARDNESS, coldness, and double refraction. It is sometimes used to simulate colourless gemstones (e.g. stones called 'diamond' with various geographical prefixes), but is distinguishable by its lack of FIRE. It is generally referred to merely as 'crystal', although that term is also now used for glass made with lead oxide and having a high brilliance like rock crystal. The German term is *Bergcristal*, the French is *cristal de roche*. *See* REVERSE INTAGLIO CRYSTAL.

rock ruby. A misnomer for the red PYROPE variety of GARNET.

rock turquoise. TURQUOISE speckled with a large amount of its MATRIX.

rococo. A style of decoration that followed, *c.* 1730, the BAROQUE style in France (where it was also called *rocaille*), the principal features of which are asymmetry of ornament and a repertoire consisting to a considerable extent of rockwork, shells, flowers, foliage, and scrollwork. It was developed in France under Louis XV, 1715-74, and spread to Italy, Germany, and Austria and to a lesser extent to England. Rococo was followed, after the mid-18th century, by the neo-classical style, generally termed in England 'Adam style'. As applied to jewelry, rococo was evidenced by the departure from the symmetrical arrangement of gem-stones (such as the frequent three pendent pearls) and the introduction, in patterns, of feathers, ribbons, and foliage. Leading exponents of the style among jewelry designers were Girolami Venturi (*c.* 1739), Thomas Flach (*c.* 1736), Albini (*c.* 1744), and Christian Taute (*c.* 1750). In the second quarter of the 19th century, there was a period of 'revived rococo' style.

rolled gold. A product resulting from fusing over a base metal a thin layer of GOLD, and then rolling it into sheets of varying thicknesses, depending on the intended use. From about 1817 it was made by fusing gold to a sheet of base metal and, if gold was desired on both sides, stamping on the sheet two identical patterns that were cut out and fused together with the gold sides outside; but a later development, which is less frequently used (but is suitable for some jewelry which is to show gold on both sides, e.g. some bracelets), is to fuse a sheet of gold on both sides of the base metal. In either method, the product can be made with different colours of gold. To make rolled-gold wire, a base metal core is enclosed within a rolled-gold tube and drawn to the desired diameter. As the thickness of the gold can vary, the quality is expressed in microns if the layer of gold is uniform, otherwise in millièmes.

Roman Charity, The. A decorative motif inspired by the legend of Climon who was imprisoned without food or water and was fed by his daughter Pera at her breast during fleeting daily visits, thus saving his life. The motif was used in an engraved design by HANS COLLAERT THE ELDER, dated 1581, and in three known jewels of the 16th century with figures in ÉMAIL EN RONDE BOSSE ornamented with cut gemstones: (1) a pendant in the Rijksmuseum, Amsterdam; (2) a pendant in a collection at the British Museum (*see* GRUNDY, HULL, COLLECTION), formerly in the Alfred de Rothschild, Loria, and Desmoni Collections; and (3) a pendant formerly in the Gutman Collection shown at the Baltimore Museum of Art in 1962-8. *See* CHARITY PENDANT.

Roman Charity, The. Émail en ronde bosse with gemstones and pearls. South Germany, late 16th century. H. 12 cm. Rijksmuseum, Amsterdam.

Roman gold. Gold having a matt finish, produced by electroplating an object with gold after it has been given a matt or frosted surface.

Roman jewelry. Articles of jewelry made throughout the Roman Empire after the Hellenistic Age, from *c.* 27 BC, when Roman styles absorbed Greek culture, until the founding of Constantinople in AD 330 and the gradual encroachment of Byzantine styles. During the early years of Rome, before *c.* 27 BC, the wearing of finger rings and other articles of gold, as well as the burial of gold articles, was legally restricted. Thereafter, during the period of the Empire, customs relaxed and jewelry was lavishly worn. With the expansion of the Empire, in the period AD 200–400, Roman techniques and styles were developed, including the making of articles decorated as OPUS INTERRASILE, the introduction of NIELLO, and the extensive use of coloured gemstones (especially emeralds) and glass (*see* POLYCHROME JEWELRY) with almost no settings and little use of GRANULATED GOLD or FILIGREE. Among the favoured articles then worn in abundance were ear-rings (including the BALL EAR-RING, CHANDELIER EAR-RING, BAR EAR-RING, and HOOP EAR-RING), NECKLACES (some with pendent coins), NECK CHAINS (some with pendants), BRACELETS, FINGER RINGS (especially the ENGAGEMENT RING, SIGNET RING, and COIN RING, and rings set with gemstones in the BEZEL or around the hoop — such rings often being worn several at a time by both men and women), and FIBULAE (especially the crossbow fibula). The centres of production were Rome, where foreign craftsmen settled, Alexandria, and Antioch.

Roman Pearl. *See* IMITATION PEARL.

Roman setting. A style of SETTING a stone in a finger ring that is a variation of the RUB-OVER SETTING, in that when the stone is set in the COLLET a groove is cut around the exterior of the collet and the resulting raised part of the rim is pressed (rubbed) over the stone to secure it. It is used to secure a SEAL in a SIGNET RING, and is a modern version of a setting so used by the Romans in the form of a GYPSY SETTING encircled by a ridge.

Romano, Giulio (Giulio Pippi; *c.* 1499–1546). An Italian painter and architect who was called in 1524 to the Gorgonza Court at Mantua where he also designed jewelry. An album preserves 71 designs by him or attributed to his studio. *See* F. Hartt, *Giulio Romano* (1958).

Romano-British jewelry. Articles of jewelry made or used in Britain after the Roman conquest, AD 43, under Emperor Claudius, in Roman and native styles, or in a combination of the two. The articles included necklaces, brooches, and some hair pins with ornamental IN THE ROUND heads in the form of busts of women wearing a high coiffure.

rondelle. A thin, circular piece of metal or gemstone that is pierced to be strung between beads on a necklace. Sometimes a thin, flat slice of a diamond is so cut and has the edge faceted, resulting in a many-sided shape.

rope chain. A type of TRACE CHAIN of which two or more links are attached to the adjacent link. Also called a 'double-trace chain'.

rosary. A string of beads used in counting prayers, each bead being named after the prayer it represents. The modern rosary is divided into 15 groups of beads, with each DECADE (group of 10 small beads, of which each is known as an AVE) being preceded by a PATERNOSTER bead and usually followed by a GLORIA bead (sometimes a single bead serving as the Paternoster and the Gloria). Strictly, a rosary originally consisted of 3 CHAPLETS each composed of 15 decades and 15 paternosters; since the Middle Ages the number of beads has varied. Attached to a rosary is usually a crucifix, a cross or an ornamental trinket (called a GAUD), and sometimes a finger ring. The larger beads were often made of gold or silver (sometimes engraved or enamelled) or of carved IVORY or BOXWOOD, or hollow with interior figures decorated in ÉMAIL EN RONDE BOSSE, and the smaller beads have been made of many materials, including HARDSTONES, CORAL, JET, JADE, AMBER, GLASS, wood, etc. A rosary was sometimes worn by a woman as a necklace or bracelet, and by a man tucked into his belt. The rosary was first used by the Eastern Christian Church and was brought to Western Christendom by the Crusaders; it is used also by the Moslems, Buddhists, and Hindus. *See* DECADE RING; LANGDALE ROSARY: DEVONSHIRE ROSARY.

rose. (1) A brooch made in the form of a full-bloom rose attached to its stem. Such pieces have been made of gold with small gemstones set on or bordering the petals and also set along the stem. (2) A brooch composed of carved pieces of CORAL and various HARDSTONES, set to form the petals and the stem (*see* PALTSCHO FLOWERS). (3) A mineral of which the natural form is in the shape of a rose, e.g. the 'Alpine rose' formed by HEMATITE and the 'Desert rose' formed by a variety of gypsum. (4) A ROSE DIAMOND. (5) An ornament of IVORY cut in the form of a rose, first made at Dieppe, France, and later at Erbach, Germany.

rose cut. A style of cutting a diamond (or other transparent gemstone) in one of several prescribed symmetrical forms, with the FACETS being of various shapes and relative sizes, but characteristically having a flat base and usually two horizontal rows of facets rising to a point. The standard rose (sometimes called the DUTCH ROSE CUT) has 24 triangular facets (6 STAR FACETS meeting at a point at the top and 18 CROSS FACETS). The rose cut style is said to have been developed by Dutch lapidaries in the mid-17th century, but may have been used earlier in India in a crude version (*see* MAZARIN CUT). It lost popularity when the BRILLIANT was invented in the early 18th century, but its popularity was revived in the early 20th century. It is used today mainly when too much of the stone would be lost if it were cut as a brilliant. When the stone is cut so that it is in the form of two rose-cut stones placed base to base, it is called a DOUBLE ROSE CUT. There are several other varieties of the rose cut, e.g. (1) the BRABANT ROSE CUT (Antwerp rose), (2) the ROSE RECOUPÉE CUT, and (3) the CROSS ROSE CUT, as well as the varieties of the brilliant having a flat base, i.e. the MARQUISE ROSE CUT and the PENDELOQUE ROSE CUT. Other simpler varieties are the 'six-facet rose' (with 6 triangular facets rising to an apex) and the 'three-facet rose' (with 3 such facets), each with a thin GIRDLE, and the corresponding 'mode rose' and 'chiffre' without a girdle. Sometimes the rose cut has been used for stones set in jewelry when the designer (e.g. FABERGÉ) wished the other ornamentation to dominate. Famous rose-cut diamonds include the GREAT MOGUL and the ORLOV.

rose diamond. (1) A diamond having its FACETS cut in ROSE CUT style. (2) A diamond of such small size that it can be cut only by a small amount or not at all.

rose quartz. A variety of QUARTZ that is CRYSTALLINE and rose-red to pale pink. Usually it is cloudy or streaked, owing to INCLUSIONS of small RUTILE needles; this MASSIVE type is often carved as an ornament or as a NETSUKE, but some pieces used in jewelry are shaped by TUMBLING or cut as beads or EN CABOCHON to show DIASTERISM. When a dome-topped piece is backed with black or strongly coloured enamel, the needles cause a star to appear. Some specimens, discovered in Brazil in 1960, occur as transparent crystals, and are sometimes faceted. The colour occasionally fades in strong sunlight.

rose recoupée cut. A style of cutting a diamond (or other transparent gemstone) in the basic ROSE CUT style but having a 12-sided base and 36 FACETS cut in two horizontal rows. There are 12 triangular facets in the upper row (called the CROWN), forming a low 12-sided pyramid, and 24 facets in the lower row in the form of isosceles triangles, 12 of which have their bases abutting the upper facets and their points touching the GIRDLE, and 12 alternating ones having their bases forming the girdle. A stone so cut is higher than one with a DUTCH ROSE CUT.

rose recoupée cut
side view

rose topaz. A type of yellow TOPAZ that is made pink by applied HEAT TREATMENT. It is to be distinguished from a rare natural pink topaz.

rosée pearl. A type of pearl of the highest quality that is of a delicate pink colour. It must also have a fine ORIENT and be perfectly spherical.

rosette. (1) A type of jewel in the form of a stylized rose, with a central gemstone surrounded by a circle of other stones. (2) A group of closely-set, shaped diamonds arranged in circular form like the petals of an open rose. Such rosettes were made in India by placing together about 6 small diamonds that, in order for each to have the correct shape, had to be cut with a loss of about 50% of the weight, a difficult and costly process that required highly skilled artisans; an example is in the collection of the Green Vault in Dresden. The style was used in southern Germany in finger rings and pendants to increase the effect of light before the introduction of the ROSE CUT.

Rosser Reeves Star Ruby. A STAR RUBY weighing 138.70 carats that has excellent colour and remarkable ASTERISM due to refraction of light caused by 3 sets of needle-like INCLUSIONS arranged at 60° angles to each other, resulting in a 6-pointed star. It is in the Smithsonian Institution, Washington, DC.

Rouchomowsky, Israel (fl. *c.* 1870-1906). A Russian jeweller and goldsmith from Odessa, who was notorious for having skilfully made gold jewelry as FORGERIES, especially in the style of ETRUSCAN JEWELRY and in other ancient styles, perhaps influenced by pieces found in the region of Odessa. His best-known piece is the TIARA OF SAITAPHERNES that was bought as genuine by the Louvre in 1896. He went to Paris for investigation by the Louvre, and then settled there, exhibiting there in 1904-6 and continuing to make gold articles in antique styles.

rough. The description given to a diamond (or other gemstone) as found and before being cut.

roumanite. A variety of AMBER that is found in Romania. It is darker in colour than the amber known as SUCCINITE, and sometimes is bluish, greenish or blackish in addition to the usual yellow, red, and brown varieties. It is highly fluorescent.

round, in the. Having the full form, as of a figure, projecting on all sides and not attached to any background, as distinguished from relief. *See* ÉMAIL EN RONDE BOSSE.

royal cut. A style of cutting a diamond that is a modification of the BRILLIANT CUT. It has a hexagonal TABLE surrounded by 32 triangular and isosceles-trapezium FACETS on the CROWN, with 72 facets on the PAVILION plus sometimes the CULET, and in addition has 48 facets along the GIRDLE (*see* FACETED GIRDLE) making a total of 154 facets. The 'royal 144' with fewer facets is for smaller stones.

royal 144 cut. A modern style of cutting a diamond that is a modification of the BRILLIANT CUT, intended to afford increased brilliance. In addition to the usual 56 FACETS as on a full cut brilliant, there are 40 small facets on the GIRDLE, and 48 small facets on the PAVILION near the GIRDLE, making a total of 144 facets, plus the TABLE and the CULET.

royal 144 cut
side view

royal mourning ring. A type of MOURNING RING originally made and worn in England in memory of a deceased Sovereign and later of a member of the Royal Family. Such rings were first made for Mary II (d. 1694) and then her husband William III (d. 1702). Inexpensive mourning rings were made for George I (d. 1727) and George II (d. 1760), and thereafter for most of the members of the Royal Family who died in the 18th and early 19th centuries, until the last was made by Queen Victoria following the death of Prince Albert (1861).

royal portrait ring. A PORTRAIT RING decorated with a portrait of a British Sovereign. In addition to several of Elizabeth I (*see* ELIZABETH I PORTRAIT RING), such rings were made with portraits of Charles I, Charles II, William III, Mary II, George III, and George IV. *See* CHARLES I RING.

Royal Rings, The. The gold finger rings that are a part of the British CROWN JEWELS and that have been used as a CORONATION RING or in connection with a coronation ceremony. They include: (1) the 'Sovereign's Ring' or Coronation Ring made for William IV (1830) and used at the coronation of every subsequent Sovereign except Queen Victoria (*see* below); in the centre is a large SAPPHIRE encircled by diamonds on which are set five RUBIES in the form of the cross of St

George. (2) the 'Queen Consort's Ring', made in 1830 for Queen Adelaide, wife of William IV; it is set with a ruby encircled by diamonds and has a band of small rubies encircling the hoop. (3) Queen Victoria's Ring, similar to the 'Sovereign's Ring' but smaller, and having engraved inside the hoop 'Queen Victoria's Coronation Ring 1838'.

royal signet ring. A type of SIGNET RING bearing the monogram or insigne of a member of royalty. An example is a gold hoop enamelled in relief with a rose and a thistle, together with the monogram 'H M' and having a BEZEL set with a diamond cut in INTAGLIO with a bearing and the monogram 'H M', the initials being those of Henrietta Maria, wife of Charles I; the engraving was made in 1628-9, at the order of Charles I, by Francis Walwyn, and the ring was acquired from the executors of William, Duke of Brunswick, and presented in 1887 to Queen Victoria. Another is Charles I's own signet ring.

rub-over setting. A style of SETTING a gemstone in a finger ring as in the COLLET SETTING but then bending (rubbing) the upper edge of the metal over the GIRDLE of the stone to secure it. A variation is the CRAMP SETTING.

rubasse. A variety of QUARTZ that is coloured red by iron oxide. Misnomers that have been applied to it are 'Ancona ruby' and 'Mont Blanc ruby'. It has been imitated by a crackled quartz dyed red and called 'rubace'.

rubellite. A variety of TOURMALINE that is red, ranging from pale rose-red to deep ruby-red. It is sometimes called by the misnomer 'Siberian ruby'.

rubicelle. A variety of SPINEL that is orange-red with a pronounced yellow or orange-yellow tinge. It is in no way except colour related to RUBY, and so the name should be discarded in favour of 'orange spinel'.

ruby. A PRECIOUS STONE that is a red variety of a transparent CORUNDUM. The colour ranges from pink to deep red; the PIGEON'S-BLOOD RUBY is deep red tinged with purple. Flawless specimens showing the most desirable colours are rare; the varieties of shades are due to the presence of a small quantity of oxide of chromium. Some rubies show ASTERISM; see STAR RUBY. Rubies may be cut as BRILLIANTS, but more often are MIXED CUT; sometimes they are cut and strung as beads. They are occasionally termed 'true ruby', 'red corundum' or 'Oriental ruby'. The principal sources are the Mogok district of Upper Burma for deep-red rubies, Sri Lanka (formerly Ceylon) for light red, and Thailand (formerly Siam) for dark brownish-red. The best rubies are more costly than diamonds of the same size, and are exceeded in value only by the emerald. Rubies contain some tiny irregular inclusions; SYNTHETIC RUBIES have bubbles that are perfectly rounded instead of being natural crystal shapes, and can be further identified by having striae in straight rather than curved lines. Among the famous true rubies are ANNE OF BRITTANY'S RUBY; DE LONG STAR RUBY; EDWARDES RUBY; PEACE RUBY; ROSSER REEVES STAR RUBY. Some well-known so-called rubies (known as a BALAS RUBY or RUBY SPINEL) are in fact red SPINEL. See Benjamin Zucker, 'Connoisseurship in Rubies', in *Connoisseur*, December 1979, p. 236.

ruby spinel. A misnomer for a variety of SPINEL whose colour is very close to the ruby-red of a RUBY. It also resembles in colour the GARNET. It is sometimes called a BALAS RUBY.

ruin agate. A variety of AGATE that is usually brownish and shows, on a polished surface, haphazard markings suggestive of a ruined area. *See* FORTIFICATION AGATE.

Rundell, Bridge & Rundell. A prominent and successful London firm of jewellers and goldsmiths, founded by Philip Rundell (1747-1827) who had come from Bath to London in 1769, worked for and became a partner of Thead & Pickett (founded in 1758), and in 1777 formed the firm of Pickett & Rundell. By 1800 Pickett's nephew, P. W. Rundell, became a partner. In 1804 J. W. Bridge, of Dorset, joined the firm. It became Crown Goldsmiths and Crown Jewellers to George III, and acquired an international reputation and clientele. Paul Storr, although

Royal Rings, The. Worn by: (1) William IV and later sovereigns; (2) Queen Adelaide; (3) Queen Victoria. The Jewel House, Tower of London, Crown copyright, HMSO.

Royal signet ring. Ring of Charles I, gold and steel, with lion and unicorn on shoulders; made by (?) Thomas Simon (c. 1623-55). By gracious permission of Her Majesty the Queen.

not employed by the firm, had a workshop with it *c.* 1811–19, and A. W. N. PUGIN worked for the firm *c.* 1827. The firm ceased in 1842 and was succeeded as Crown Jewellers and Goldsmiths by GARRARD & CO.

Russian jewelry. Articles of jewelry made in Russia from the time of the adoption of the Orthodox Christian Church, *c.* AD 1000, and which, although influenced by Byzantine art, had its own characteristics. Metalwork, which had been known for many centuries, included from the 10th century FILIGREE work, and in the 11th and 12th centuries EMBOSSING and CHASING, as well as decoration in CLOISONNÉ ENAMEL, GRANULATED GOLD, and NIELLO. The jewelry for secular use included finger rings, ear-rings, bracelets, necklaces, belt buckles, and filigree buttons. Some articles had pagan motifs, but also showed Norse and Oriental influence. Kiev in the 11th/14th centuries became the centre for high-quality *cloisonné* enamelware, made as plaques for necklaces and pendants, often with religious motifs. The centre for making fine jewelry shifted to Novgorod, and then in the 15th century to Moscow, where the repertory was increased to include jewelled covers for secular books and gold and silver covers for icons; enamelled ware was extensively made, with polychrome enamel dropped on REPOUSSÉ work or with small silver plaques affixed on top of the enamel. By the 18th century gemstones were popular embellishments to jewelry, several varieties being sometimes used on a single piece. Under Catherine the Great (1729-96), lavish jewelry in Western style was made for the Court. During the 19th century lacquer snuff boxes were made, especially by such artists as Pyotr Lukutin and his St Petersburg rivals. The culmination of Russian jewelry was reached in the work of CARL FABERGÉ. *See* GEORGIAN JEWELRY; TULA WORK; KOL'T; KULONE; CATHERINE I DEMI-PARURE; LADY-IN-WAITING BROOCH.

rutilated quartz. A variety of ROCK CRYSTAL (QUARTZ) having fine INCLUSIONS of RUTILE crystals (*see* FLÈCHES D'AMOUR). Such stones are usually cut EN CABOCHON. Also called 'Venus's-hair stone'. *See* SAGENITIC QUARTZ.

rutile. A mineral that is reddish-brown to red, sometimes yellowish, and has a brilliant lustre. It is sometimes found as needle-like INCLUSIONS in some gemstones, e.g. SAGENITIC QUARTZ and sagenite. Some transparent specimens are used in jewelry, occasionally being faceted or, when opaque, cut EN CABOCHON. A SYNTHETIC RUTILE was developed in 1948.

S

St Cuthbert's Cross. Gold with *cloisonné* inlay of garnets. Anglo-Saxon, 6th/7th centuries. W. 6 cm. Durham Cathedral, England.

sablé d'or (French). Literally, sanded with gold. A type of TEXTURED GOLD produced by lightly hammering a gold surface with a fine matting tool so as to impart a coarse sandy finish. It is used usually to emphasize the ground for a relief design, e.g. a border so made around a GUILLOCHÉ panel. It is sometimes called 'granulation' but has no relationship to the GRANULATED GOLD of antiquity.

sachet. A small container for perfume, made to be worn as a pendant but not in the spherical form of the usual POMANDER. An example of complex design was in the Melvin Gutman Collection, Baltimore, Maryland.

safety chain. A short, thin chain used to prevent loss of a bracelet or necklace by being attached to each terminal as security in case the clasp should come open. Such chains, made of gold links, are usually attached to pieces of high value. Occasionally a brooch has a safety chain attached, joined to a small safety pin.

safety pin. A type of metal fastener in the form of a PIN that originally was bent 180° so that the point was held in a CATCH-PLATE, but later was bent, first in a complete turn and then 180°, which resulted in a small spring that, by tension, more securely held the point in the catch-plate. Such pieces were the precursor of the FIBULA and of the modern safety pin. Modern examples have a guard over the catch-plate which protects the user from being pricked. The safety pin has four parts: (1) the ACUS (the pin); (2) the spring (or a springless joint); (3) the BOW (the part that joins the spring with the catch); and (4) the catch-plate. Some modern examples are made of gold, to be used as a COLLAR PIN or, in a large size, to fasten a Scottish kilt. *See* SAFETY-PIN FIBULA.

safety-pin fibula. A type of FIBULA made in the general form of a modern SAFETY PIN, with an ACUS, an arched BOW, and a CATCH-PLATE. Such fibulae were made in many variations, from Scythian examples (*see* SCYTHIAN JEWELRY) and Etruscan examples (*see* CERTOSA FIBULA) to some made in England during the Celtic Iron Age and the Roman era.

sagenitic quartz. A variety of QUARTZ that contains acicular or needle-like INCLUSIONS of other material, e.g. RUTILE (sometimes called 'rutilated quartz') or TOURMALINE (sometimes called 'tourmalinated quartz'), which produce attractive patterns but do not create CHATOYANCY. It is usually cut EN CABOCHON rather than faceted (*see* FACETING) as the inclusions are the main attraction.

St Cuthbert's Cross. A gold CROSS with the four arms of equal length and having rounded extremities, and with a closed conical gold cell riveted at the junction of the arms; the cell is set with a sliced GARNET resting on an exposed insert of shell. The closed cell is hollow to provide space for a small relic. The arms of the cross are decorated with CLOISONS inlaid with sliced garnets (without FOIL) and within a serrated and beaded border. The suspensory loop may be a later addition. The cross was found upon the opening in 1827 of the coffin of St Cuthbert (d. 687) in Durham Cathedral, along with other relics. It is said to have been made *c.* 640-70 by Northumbrian jewellers. It was broken and repaired both before and after its burial. A reproduction, with red enamel in place of the garnets, bears a mark that until recently has been associated with CARLO DORIA; it is in a box marked with the name and address of ROBERT PHILLIPS and is owned by HANCOCKS, the London jewellers.

St Edward's Crown. The British CROWN that is reputed by tradition to have had its origin in the crown of Edward the Confessor, 1042-66, and possibly Alfred the Great, 871-901, but without any actual connection, as the Royal Regalia was destroyed by Cromwell, although it has been surmised that the circlet itself may have survived. Its name and tradition survive in the crown made by Sir Robert Vyner for the coronation of Charles II in 1662 (originally set with paste and imitation pearls) and used (although reset for Queen Victoria) at every subsequent coronation, although not always for the actual crowning until George V in 1911 and always subsequently. It is in the form of a gold circlet bordered with silver pearls and set with twelve large gemstones outlined with diamond clusters, the circlet being heightened by four gold CROSSES FORMÉE alternating with four gold fleurs-de-lis, all set with gemstones; rising from the crosses are four jewelled arches, at the intersection of which rests a gold MONDE upon which rises a gold and jewelled cross formée from which are suspended two silver drop-shaped pearls. The whole weighs nearly 4 lb (1.8 kg.), is ornamented with about 440 gemstones, and is lined with the 'Cap of State' (a purple velvet cap, the bottom of which is edged with white miniver fur). The crown is sometimes referred to as the 'Crown of England'.

St Edward's Sapphire. A SAPPHIRE that is ROSE CUT and is now set in the diamond-encrusted CROSS FORMÉE surmounting the MONDE on the IMPERIAL STATE CROWN of the British CROWN JEWELS. It is reputed to have been set in a finger ring worn by Edward the Confessor, King of England, 1042-66, when he was buried, and removed in 1269 by the Abbot of Westminster as a holy relic and given by him to the King or to Westminster Abbey. It is the oldest stone in the Crown Jewels.

Saint-Esprit cross (French). Literally, the Holy Ghost cross. An article of French PEASANT JEWELRY, made in Flanders and other regions, being a gold or silver pendant in the form of the Holy Dove, sometimes holding in

St Edward's Crown. Sometimes called 'The Crown of England'. Crown copyright, HMSO.

Saint-Esprit cross. Silver and strass. Alençon, France, 18th century. W. 4.5 cm. Musée de Normandie, Caen.

St Hubert Pendant. Gold with bloodstone hunting horn and figures in *émail en ronde bosse*. German, 19th century (?). Photo courtesy of National Gallery of Art, Washington, DC, and Sotheby-Parke-Bernet, Inc., New York.

its beak an olive branch, a sprig of forget-me-nots or a bunch of grapes. The piece was usually set with crystal or coloured PASTE, and was worn suspended from an ornament in the form of a bow-knot with a rosette-shaped slide on the ribbon. Some pendants of expensive jewelry in the form of a dove, set with gemstones and having a suspended pearl, are sometimes referred to by the same name. *See* DOVE; OEUF DE NAPLE.

St George and the Dragon. A popular motif for decorating jewelry since the 16th century, depicting St George mounted on a horse slaying the dragon with his spear. It is found on some gold pendants and brooches decorated with enamelling and gemstones. *See* GEORGE; HOLBEIN GEORGE.

St Hilary Jewel. A jewel in the form of an oval CAMEO of SARDONYX carved with a profile bust of Emperor Augustus, 27 BC–AD 14, framed in a silver gilt mount (13th century) set with six large alternating EMERALDS and RUBIES between which are trefoils of small PEARLS. It was originally a PECTORAL on a silver RELIQUARY bust of St Hilary formerly in the Treasury of the Abbey of St Denis, Paris, and has since 1791 been in the Bibliothèque Nationale, Paris.

St Hubert Pendant. A gold pendant in the form of a horizontal hunting horn made of BLOODSTONE (HELIOTROPE) with coloured enamelling and gemstones, having at one end a figure in ÉMAIL EN RONDE BOSSE of St Hubert kneeling in prayer before a cross, suspended at the top between the antlers of a stag, and having at the other end a figure of a hound. The pendant was said in 1967 to be a badge of the Order of St Hubert of Jülich and Berg (which was founded in 1476, inspired by the victory in 1444 of Gerhard V, Duke of Jülich and Berg, and flourished until 1609) and to be German, *c.* 1540–50; but in the catalogue of the 17 October 1969 sale of the Milton Gutman Collection by Sotheby-Parke-Bernet, New York, it was considered to date from the 19th century.

St John, Reliquary of the Tooth of. A RELIQUARY in the form of a purse made of gold and set with very many gemstones. It is in the style of CAROLINGIAN JEWELRY and was made in the 8th century.

St Louis Reliquary (Reliquary of the Holy Thorn). A RELIQUARY in the form of two CABOCHON amethysts set in a hinged gold frame enclosing an interior case with two covers and a central leaf. On the inside of the covers and on one side of the leaf there are six scenes in translucent enamel depicting events associated with the life of Christ; on the reverse of the leaf is a manuscript illumination of the Nativity and the Annunciation to the Shepherds, and the inscription 'De Spina : Sancte : Corone'. Behind the leaf there is mounted in a crystal the Holy Thorn said to have been taken from the Crown of Thorns that was purchased by St Louis (Louis IX of France, 1226–70) from Baldwin II, Emperor of Byzantium from 1237 to 1261. The setting is said to be French from the second quarter of the 14th century. The piece was in the Paris collection of Baron Pinchon, and was donated in 1902 by George Salting to the British Museum.

St Martin's ring. A type of finger ring made in the 15th/18th centuries of brass or copper and produced or imported by goldsmiths at the 'Liberty of St Martin-le-Grand' (a sanctuary in London near Goldsmiths' Hall), who were excluded from the Goldsmiths' Hall as a result of restrictions imposed by its Wardens.

St Stephen, Crown of. The CROWN that is not merely a part of the REGALIA of Hungary but is a sacred symbol of its nationhood. Its history is subject to much uncertainty and disagreement. It consists of two main parts that have different origins and dates, but are believed to have been assembled in 1108–16. The lower part has generally been said (based on various factors) to have been sent, *c.* 1074–7, by the Byzantine Emperor Michael VII Dukas to the Hungarian King Géza I (but there are differing opinions as to the circumstances in which it reached Hungary); it is a forehead band, above the front half of which are 8 alternating *cloisonné* enamelled blue and green triangular and semi-circular plates (perhaps from a book cover), decorated with Byzantine enamelled miniatures portraying saints, alternating with large gemstones. The band, made of gold alloyed with silver, has along its edges a row of pearls. The upper part of the crown is generally said to have been a coronation gift in 1100

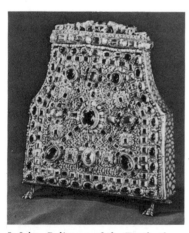

St John, Reliquary of the Tooth of. Gold set with green and blue gemstones. 8th century. Cathedral Treasury, Monza, Italy.

to Stephen I, first King of Hungary, from Pope Sylvester II; it consists of 4 curved plates joined to form 2 arches that are decorated with enamelled plaques (added later) and with gemstones, and surmounted at the intersection by a cross that is slanting (generally thought to have been accidentally bent between 1613 and 1793, but possibly so made). Suspended from each side of the crown are gold chains from which hang trefoil ornaments set with rubies; these chains, called *cataseistae*, were emblems of supreme power in Byzantium, worn only by the Emperor. The crown is lined with cloth of gold. The history of the crown, much debated, involves many changes of custody. At the end of World War II it, with other Hungarian regalia, was placed by Regent Horthy with the United States military to preserve them from the approaching Russians; it was kept in the United States until returned to Hungary on 6 January 1978, and it is now displayed in the Hungarian National Museum, Budapest. A reproduction has long been in the Vatican Museum, and another reproduction is now being made in Budapest. *See* Patrick J. Kelleher, *The Holy Crown of Hungary* (1951); Lord Twining, *European Regalia* (1967), p. 98.

St Louis Reliquary. Interior decorated with enamel scenes. French, 14th century. H. 3.8 cm. British Museum, London.

Saitaphernes, Tiara of. A gold so-called tiara in conoidal form heavily ornamented with an encircling frieze. It was made by ISRAEL ROUCHOMOWSKY and bought as an antique by the Louvre in 1896, but claimed by many to be a forgery when it first came on the market in 1895, as it was later confirmed to be. A miniature gold reproduction made by Rouchomowsky, *c.* 1904, is in the British Museum, London.

Samaria, Woman of, Enseigne. A Tudor hat-badge of REPOUSSÉ work and coloured enamelling with a scene depicting Christ talking to the Woman of Samaria at Jacob's Well (St John iv, 4–42), having on the well a black-enamelled inscription. The central figure-scene, the convex frame, and the four projecting loops are attached by BUTTERFLY CLIPS to a circular gold base-plate. It was made in England, *c.* 1540. Another smaller enseigne (diameter 3.7 cm) with an almost identical scene, but less skilfully executed, was made in England *c.* 1530–35, perhaps by the same workshop; it is reported to have been in the collection of Lord Wharton.

St Stephen, Crown of. Hungarian National Museum, Budapest. Photo courtesy of National Gallery of Art, Washington, DC.

Samarian Spinel, The. The largest known red gem SPINEL, weighing 500 carats. It is in the CROWN JEWELS (IRAN).

Sancy, The Little (Beau Sancy). A pear-shaped diamond weighing 34.5 carats that was once in the collection of Nicolas Harlay, Sieur de Sancy (*see* SANCY DIAMOND). When his collection was disposed of by his family after his death in 1627, the diamond was bought by Frederick Henry of Orange (1583–1647), who bequeathed it to his great-grandson, Frederick William I of Prussia, who placed it among the Crown Jewels of the Hohenzollerns; upon his death it was removed from his crown and was worn by Queen Elizabeth Christine (wife of Frederick the Great) and was inherited by successive Prussian rulers. It appeared in an inventory of 1913 as a pendant on a necklace among the Crown Jewels of Kaiser William II.

Sancy Diamond. A famous Indian diamond (sometimes called the 'Grand Sancy') that is pear-shaped and ROSE CUT (with a 5-sided TABLE), weighing 55.23 carats, regarding whose history there have been several versions. (The legend that it was once owned by Charles the Bold of Burgundy has been definitely disproved.) It was first recorded *c.* 1593 as being owned by Nicolas Harlay, Sieur de Sancy (1546–1629) who bought it while in Constantinople *c.* 1570 and took it to France. He lent it to Henry III of France (who wore it in his cap) and later to Henry IV (who pawned it) and in 1599 offered it for sale. Later Sancy's brother, Christopher, Comte de Beaumont, the French Ambassador to England, sold it before 21 March 1604 to James I who wore it in his hat. In 1625 it was inherited by James's son, Charles I, whose wife, Queen Henrietta Maria, took it and other jewels (including the MIRROR OF GREAT BRITAIN and the MIRROR OF PORTUGAL) to France and pawned them in 1647 to the Duke of Épernon. (The Sancy was sketched in 1625–47 by Thomas Cletscher, Court Jeweller.) After non-payment of the loan, the diamonds were acquired *c.* 1654 by Cardinal Mazarin who bequeathed them (*see* MAZARIN DIAMONDS) in 1661 to Louis XIV. (A different story, perhaps

Samaria, Woman of, Enseigne. Hat-badge, gold and enamelled with repoussé scene. English, *c.* 1540. W. 5.7 cm. British Museum, London.

relating to a different stone, is that Henrietta Maria, after the execution of Charles I in 1649, gave the Sancy to Somerset, Earl of Worcester, for safe-keeping, and he returned it in 1660 to Charles II, from whom it passed to James II who, after he fled to France following the Battle of the Boyne, 1690, sold it to Louis XIV.) After its acquisition by Louis XIV, a copy was set in the coronation crown of Louis XV, but the Sancy was worn in 1725–37 by Queen Marie Leszczynska, wife of Louis XV, and later by Marie Antoinette and by Louis XVI. (Although generally said to have been stolen in 1792 from the French Garde Meuble, the stone inventoried there in 1791 was stated, possibly erroneously, to weigh only 33¾ old carats, whereas the Sancy had been inventoried in 1691 as weighing 53¾ old carats.) Later it was pawned by the French Directory to the Marquis of Iranda in Madrid and never redeemed; it was acquired by Prince Manuel de Godoy (1767–1851), favourite of Spanish Queen Maria Luisa, from whom it passed to the Spanish Bourbons. In 1828 a diamond, now considered to be the Sancy, appeared in Paris, was offered unsuccessfully to Charles X, and was sold by a French merchant to Prince Nicholas Demidoff (d. 1829); his son Paul (not Anatol, as sometimes stated) took it to Russia and in 1865 his heirs sold it (then called the 'Demidoff') in London to a Bombay merchant, Sir Jamsetjee Jeejeebhoy. In 1867 it was exhibited in Paris by Germain Bapst. In 1906 a diamond now considered to be the Sancy (having the same shape and weight as the original) was bought by Lord William Waldorf Astor as a wedding gift for his daughter-in-law, Nancy Langhorne (Lady Astor), and was exhibited in 1962 at the Louvre, Paris. It was inherited in 1964 by her son, the 3rd Viscount Astor, and later by the present 4th Viscount Astor. In 1976 it was acquired by the Louvre and is now exhibited at its Galerie d'Apollon. (Another diamond, once said to have been the Sancy, was owned by the Maharajah of Patiala, but it has been found to weigh 60 old carats and to have different measurements, so it is considered now to be a different stone.) As to another diamond, sometimes confused with the Sancy, see SANCY, THE LITTLE. See *Journal of Gemmology*, XV, No. 5 (1977), p. 240 (E.A. Jobbins) and XVI, No. 4 (1978), p. 221 (Herbert Tillander); Pierre Verlet, 'Le "Sancy" Rentre au Louvre', in *Gazette des Beaux Arts*, Paris, November 1978, p. 165.

Sancy Diamond. Pear-shaped diamond. Photo courtesy of Institute of Geological Sciences, London.

sand blasting. A technique of obtaining a matt finish on a gold article by directing onto it a jet of sand by compressed air or steam. It was used in the 19th century to emphasize, by contrast, the brilliance of polished areas. It is the same process that has been used to decorate glassware.

sand casting. (1) A process of CASTING molten metal in sand which was used from the 14th century for making certain articles of jewelry. It involved using two adjacent iron boxes which were filled with tightly packed, wet sand so as to enclose a model, and after the boxes were separated and the model removed, the mould of sand was filled with molten metal to make the desired article. This method has been superseded by CENTRIFUGAL CASTING. (2) A technique, used by the Indians of south-western United States, locally called 'sand casting' but executed with a mould made of soft volcanic pumice or tufa. A design is carved into a flat slab, smoked to allow free passage of the molten silver, and covered with another flat smoked slab, after which molten silver is poured in the resulting mould. The casting, triangular in section, is then filed and polished, and sometimes additionally decorated by hammering.

sandwich stone. A jeweller's jargon term for a DOUBLET or TRIPLET.

sang-de-boeuf (French). Literally, ox-blood. A variety of QUARTZ that is dark reddish-brown.

sapphire. A precious stone that is a variety of transparent CORUNDUM of any colour other than red (which is a RUBY). The usual and preferable colour ('Kashmir blue') ranges from pale cornflower-blue to deep velvety blue; but less valuable varieties of corundum of other colours are included as sapphires, e.g. white, yellow, green, pink, purple, brown, and black. Any sapphire that is not blue is sometimes called a 'fancy sapphire'. The cause of the variety of colours is uncertain, but the blue colour is probably due to traces of oxide of iron and titanium. Some sapphires change colour in daylight from that in artificial light. Due to the Asiatic origin of the stones, the yellow variety is sometimes called 'Oriental topaz', the dark

green 'Oriental emerald', and the purple 'Oriental amethyst'; but these
are misnomers that should be discarded. Sapphires are usually cut as a
BRILLIANT or MIXED CUT, but sometimes they are cut and strung as beads.
Sapphires show strong dichroism, often ASTERISM (as in the case of the
STAR SAPPHIRE when properly cut EN CABOCHON), and occasionally
FEATHERS; they are extremely hard and have a vitreous LUSTRE. Zones of
different colours, or concentrations of one colour, are sometimes present
in stone, as a result of which, and also owing to the dichroism, the quality
of cut stones depends greatly on skilful cutting; faceting is done mainly in
Sri Lanka (formerly Ceylon). The finest stones came from India
(Kashmir) since 1862 and have a rich blue colour that does not 'bleed'
(i.e. change in different lights); the next finest blue sapphires (paler
varieties) came from Burma and some are still being found in Sri Lanka.
The colour of sapphires is sometimes altered by HEAT TREATMENT (which
dulls the colour) or irradiation (the effect of which fades). A SYNTHETIC
SAPPHIRE was developed in 1910. Among the most famous or largest
sapphires are the BISMARCK SAPPHIRE, LINCOLN SAPPHIRE, LOGAN
SAPPHIRE, RASPOLI SAPPHIRE, ST EDWARD'S SAPPHIRE, STUART SAPPHIRE,
and GEM OF THE JUNGLE, and among those that show asterism are the STAR
OF ASIA and STAR OF INDIA. *See* WINDOWS; PADPARA(D)SCHA(H). *See*
Benjamin Zucker, 'Connoisseurship in Sapphires', in *Connoisseur*, March
1980, p. 204.

*Saragossa, Lady of the Pillar of,
Jewels.* Gold pendant, in the form of
a pelican, with ruby and pearls.
Spanish, 16th century. Victoria &
Albert Museum, London.

Saragossa, Lady of the Pillar of, Jewels. A collection of jewelry owned
by the Cathedral of Nuestra Señora del Pilar, at Saragossa, Spain, and
sold on 30 May 1870 at auction in 523 lots by Don José Ignacio Miro, a
leading Madrid dealer in antiques, most of the pieces being from the
second half of the 16th century and the early 17th century. The sale was
to obtain funds for the completion of the building of the Cathedral begun
in 1681; some of the pieces were acquired by the Victoria & Albert
Museum, London, and some have been reacquired by the Cathedral. The
Cathedral was built to house the marble pillar on which legend says the
Virgin stood when she appeared before St James the Greater, AD 40, when
on his way to Compostela. Among the jewels are several gold pendants
with figures of the Virgin, sometimes flanked by angels, as well as jewelled
pendent crosses, crystal IHS PENDANTS, a PELICAN JEWEL, a PARROT JEWEL,
a pendant decorated in ÉGLOMISÉ style and a crystal PHYLACTERY
PENDANT; these pieces were made mostly in Spain and were probably
donated to the shrine. Many Spanish pendants made as inexpensive
PILGRIM BADGES depict the Lady of the Pillar. *See* Charles Oman, in
Apollo, June 1967, p. 402.

sard. A variety of CHALCEDONY that is light to dark brown, sometimes
orange-red, similar to but darker than CORNELIAN (sometimes called a
variety of cornelian). It is often used in a SEAL or a CAMEO. *See* SARDONYX.

sardonyx. A variety of ONYX that is marked by evenly spaced bands of
SARD (reddish-brown coloured) contrasting with the white colour of the
adjacent bands and hence often used to make a CAMEO with the raised
design and the background in different colours. *See* SCHAFFHAUSEN ONYX;
ESSEX RING.

Sark stone. Originally a variety of AMETHYST found on Sark, one of the
Channel Islands off England, but no longer found there. The name is now
applied to amethysts imported there from Brazil or to an amethyst-
coloured PASTE.

Sarmatian jewelry. Articles of jewelry attributed to the Sarmatians, a
nomadic people who emigrated from Asia in the 5th century BC, inhabited in
the 4th century BC the region near the lower Don River to the east of the
region of the Scythians, and conquered the latter in the 3rd/2nd centuries BC;
after warring for two centuries against the Romans, they were conquered by
the invading Goths. Their jewelry shows the influence of the Greeks with
whom they traded and of SCYTHIAN JEWELRY, but made extensive use of
polychrome decoration, with inset gemstones and coloured glass, paste
inlays, and CHAMPLEVÉ enamel and CLOISONNÉ enamel, and with animal
motifs in REPOUSSÉ work. A motif often featured was a large-beaked bird.
Some pieces in the OXUS TREASURE have been said to be from this source. A
large find known as the Novocherkassk Treasure was made in the early 20th
century.

Sarre Quoit Brooch. Silver gilt with zoomorphic decoration and three birds in the round. Anglo-Saxon (?), mid-5th century. W. 7.8 cm. British Museum, London.

Sassanian jewelry. Silver swivel ring with intaglio seal, 3rd/9th centuries. Courtesy of Wartski, London.

saucer brooch. Cast bronze. Found at Horton Kirby, Kent. Anglo-Saxon, 5th century. W. 4.8 cm. Maidstone Museum, Kent.

Sarre Disc Brooch. A gold DISC BROOCH having decoration in four concentric circles, each with cells of various shapes made of CLOISONNÉ enamel, separated by designs in gold wire. In the centre is a small boss decorated with gold in relief. The central boss and 4 four-lobed ornaments in the centre circle were decorated with garnets, now missing. It is Anglo-Saxon, c. AD 600, and was found at Sarre, Kent, England.

Sarre Quoit Brooch. A silver gilt QUOIT BROOCH, the band of which is decorated with two concentric zones beaten into the metal from the front, depicting stylized zoomorphic motifs within a beaded rim. Riveted to the hinge of the pin and also to the plate of the brooch are three dove-like birds cast IN THE ROUND. The brooch, of the 5th century, was found in a grave in an Anglo-Saxon cemetery at Sarre, Kent, England, but its origin is uncertain.

Sassanian jewelry. Articles of jewelry made by the Sassanians during the reign of the Sassanidae, the last dynasty of native rulers of ancient Persia, AD 224–642, and in the two succeeding centuries of Islamic rule during which the style survived; their territory extended over present-day Iraq and the neighbouring regions. The most important work of the period was in metalware, with decoration of embossed and engraved figures and with some partial gilding and inlaid NIELLO, but some examples of jewelry included gold articles in pairs with pierced designs of monsters or birds.

satin spar. A variety of English calcite or gypsum that is white and has a satin LUSTRE. It is sometimes cut EN CABOCHON or used to make BEADS.

saucer brooch. A type of brooch of ANGLO-SAXON JEWELRY, of the 5th/7th centuries, that is circular and concave, having a flat central disc with a deep flared rim. Such brooches have been found in several sizes and of two types: (1) cast solid in one piece of bronze, decorated with a design that was sharpened with a chasing tool and then silvered or gilded, the design having the appearance of CHIP-CARVING; and (2) made in two parts, one being a thin bronze cast plate, gilded or silvered, applied by cementing to a heavier disc of beaten bronze. The designs are usually stars, spirals, or geometric or zoomorphic motifs, with sometimes a human face much distorted. Sometimes a central bead of AMBER, GARNET, GLASS or enamel is cemented on, and occasionally also wing-shaped pieces of garnet. Such brooches, worn on the shoulder and sometimes made in pairs, have been found in Saxon cemeteries. They are sometimes called a 'cupelliform brooch'.

Saulini, Tommaso (1793–1864) and **Luigi** (1819–83). Outstanding Roman carvers of CAMEOS in hardstone and shell. Tommaso, having studied in Rome under the Danish sculptor Albert Bertel Thorvaldsen (1770–1844), established a workshop in Rome in 1836, moving in 1857 to 96 Via del Babuino where he and his son Luigi worked until their deaths. Some of their cameos were made from sketches of works by Thorvaldsen and also by the English sculptor Joseph Gott (1786–1860), and some were inspired by the sculpture of Antonio Canova (1775–1822); but they also created much original work. The cameos depicted Classical subjects from existing drawings or from their own original designs (many cameos being made expressly for the British Royal Family), but the Saulinis also carved portraits of contemporaries. Several of the cameos were mounted in gold frames designed by Sir John Gibson (1790–1866), the English neo-classical sculptor who was a friend of Tommaso living in the Via del Babuino in the 1840s, and from whose drawings they made a number of cameos; some of the frames were executed by ALESSANDRO CASTELLANI. See Malcolm Stuart Carr, 'Tommaso and Luigi Saulini', in *Connoisseur*, November 1975, p. 171.

Saur, Corvinianus (1555/60?–1635). A Bavarian goldsmith and jewelry designer who is best known for his designs for enamelled decoration in adaptations, in multicoloured patterns, of the MORESQUE SILHOUETTE STYLE. He was born at Mauerkirch, in Bavaria, went as a child with his mother to Augsburg, and trained there as a goldsmith with his stepfather. In 1591-7 he engraved and published a series of arabesque designs, as a result of which he came under the patronage of the nobility. In 1600 he was invited to Denmark by King Christian IV, in 1613 became Court Goldsmith, and continued to work there until his death. See LION JEWEL.

sautoir (French). A woman's long NECK CHAIN, worn loosely from the shoulders and usually extending down to below the waist. Some have a jewelled pendant or a tassel suspended at the bottom. Although usually worn from both shoulders, it was often worn draped over only one shoulder, then said to be worn *en sautoir sur l'épaule*. It was popular in the 19th century.

sawing. The technique developed in the early 20th century for dividing a rough diamond before BRUTING and FACETING, instead of the former method of splitting according to the CLEAVAGE of the stone. The process of sawing in general divides the octahedral stone against its grain and along its 'sawing grain', preferably near its greatest width, resulting in two unequal stones each suitable for making a BRILLIANT. The result is to require less bruting and to reduce the loss of weight. It involves fastening the stone in steel catches on a sawing machine and keeping it against the sharp edge of an extremely thin disc of phosphorized bronze that turns vertically, charged with a mixture of olive oil and diamond-powder. The duration of the operation may vary from a few hours to a few days, depending on the size and characteristics of the stone.

Saxon Diamonds, The. A large collection of diamonds started by Augustus the Strong of Saxony (1670–1733) at the end of the 17th century and added to by his successors. It included the DRESDEN DIAMONDS and many others, said to weigh in 1938 a total of more than 7,000 old carats and to include many heavier than 10 carats. They were kept among the Crown Jewels of Saxony in the Green Vault, Dresden.

Saxony chrysolite. A misnomer for a variety of greenish-yellow TOPAZ found in eastern Vogtland, in Saxony, Germany.

Saxony diamond. A misnomer for colourless TOPAZ.

scapolite. A mineral occurring in MASSIVE form or as crystals that are sometimes used as gemstones. They are colourless or in pastel shades of pink, yellow or violet, and some massive stones are CHATOYANT when cut EN CABOCHON (called 'scapolite cat's-eye'). Some resemble BERYL or QUARTZ. Also called 'wernerite'; related varieties are meionite and marialite. The misnomer 'pink moonstone' has been applied to the pink chatoyant variety.

scarab (or **scarabaeus**). A conventionalized representation of a dung beetle, made in Egypt of carved stone, STEATITE or gemstone, or of EGYPTIAN FAIENCE, usually with an amuletic inscription cut in the flat underside and the depiction of the beetle incised on the rounded upper side (the beetle being the symbol of Khepera, the god of the morning sun, and regarded by the ancient Egyptians as a symbol of resurrection and immortality). The style of the carving varied, from a bare outline to well-defined markings and sometimes partly in relief, and occasionally with the beetle having a human head. Such pieces were generally worn in pendants and TALISMANS, as well as being set in the BEZEL of a finger ring or of a bracelet, and also were buried with the dead (*see* FUNERARY JEWELRY). They were copied by the Etruscans, Phoenicians, and Greeks. *See* SCARAB RING; HEART SCARAB; BEETLE JEWELRY; SCARABOID.

sautoir. Diamond chain, links, and detachable tassel (brooch). Signed Cartier. Courtesy of Christie's, New York.

scarab. Gold bracelet with gold openwork scarab encrusted with lapis lazuli; border and shoulders set with gemstones. W. 5.4 cm. Tomb of Tutankhamun. Photograph by Egyptian Expedition, Metropolitan Museum of Art, New York.

scaraboid. Chalcedony intaglio. Late 5th century BC. Museum of Fine Arts, Boston, Mass.

scarab ring. A type of finger ring made in ancient Egypt, and in Phoenicia, Greece, and Etruria, with an ornament in the form of a SCARAB. Such rings were made in several forms: (1) The ring was a stirrup-shaped hoop with flattened pierced ends and a scarab was attached by a wire run through it so that the scarab could revolve when worn on a finger, with the underside (engraved with the name or device of the owner) turned up when to be used as a SEAL and the beetle side up when worn as an ornament. (2) A non-swivelling type, with the outside of the ring of the same stirrup shape and set with a scarab, but the inside circular to fit the finger; some such rings were made of two hoops united at the top and having cut on the long oblong BEZEL the name and titles, in hieroglyphs, of the owner. (3) A circular type, similar to a modern SIGNET RING, with an engraved scarab.

scaraboid. A Greek modification, made in the late 6th and 5th centuries BC, of an Egyptian SCARAB, with the stone being engraved only on the flat, oval base and the back being rounded but with no engraved imitation of a beetle.

scarf pin. The same as a TIE PIN.

scarf ring. An ornament, usually circular, through which are drawn the two ends of a woman's or man's scarf, the wearer then sliding it up to near the neck. Sometimes there are two adjacent rings ornamentally joined. Formerly called a 'belcher ring'.

sceptre. A staff or baton borne by a sovereign as a ceremonial emblem of authority. Sceptres were used in Cyprus as early as the 12th century BC, made of gold and surmounted by a sphere, sometimes decorated with figures of hawks and with enamelling. They became an article of royal REGALIA in Greece, Rome, and elsewhere, continuing to be used in the Middle Ages and thereafter until today; see SCEPTRES, THE ROYAL. Some sceptres are topped by a MONDE surmounted by a cross, some by a dove, and some by the 'Hand of Justice' (an upright hand with two extended fingers), e.g. the French sceptres of Henry II and of Napoleon I.

Sceptres, The Royal. The two SCEPTRES that are included among the British CROWN JEWELS. (1) The Sovereign's Sceptre with the Cross is held in the Sovereign's right hand during the coronation. It is surmounted by a diamond-encrusted MONDE above which is a diamond-encrusted CROSS FORMÉE set with a large emerald; the monde is formed by a superb round amethyst (set with gemstones) and below it is the great diamond known as 'The Great Star of Africa' (Cullinan I; see CULLINAN DIAMOND). The sceptre is 92 cm long, weighs 1.24 kg., and is set with over 300 gemstones. (2) The Sovereign's Sceptre with the Dove is held in the Sovereign's left hand during the coronation and signifies equity and mercy. It is a slender rod of gold, surmounted by a jewelled monde and a cross, upon the arms of which stands a white enamelled dove. It is 109 cm long and is set with 199 diamonds, 58 rubies, 10 emeralds, and 4 sapphires.

Schaffhausen Onyx. A medieval JEWEL, probably a brooch, consisting of a Roman CAMEO framed in an elaborate gold setting. The oval cameo, carved in SARDONYX (and encircled by bands of blue and brown OPAL) depicts a standing figure of Pax Augusta (the symbol of peace and prosperity in ancient Rome), holding a caduceus and a cornucopia. The deep setting includes high COLLETS set with SAPPHIRES, TURQUOISES, GARNETS, and PEARLS. On the border of the jewel are a number of tiny gold figures IN THE ROUND of standing lions in REPOUSSÉ work with cast heads looking outward, and stylized relief figures of eagles. The back of the piece is a silver gilt disc engraved with a figure of a knightly falconer, surrounded by an inscription referring to Count Ludwig II of Froborg (1210–59); it has been suggested that the piece was a gift from Frederick II to the Count, whose family seat was near Basle and whose coat of arms is suggested by the colours of the stones and the animal motifs. The piece has been attributed to Germany, mid-13th century.

Sceptres, The Royal. Detail of Sovereign's Sceptre with the Great Star of Africa. Crown copyright, HMSO.

scheelite. A mineral that is colourless or yellowish to brownish, but the orange variety is the only one used as a gemstone. A synthetic scheelite has been produced in several colours. The natural stone was named after K. W. Scheele (1742–86), a Swiss chemist.

Scherr, Mary Ann (1931–   ). An American DESIGNER–MAKER of jewelry who has lectured and exhibited internationally. She has experimented with stainless steel and aluminium. Her speciality is jewelry having medical or scientific functional purposes, such as bracelets that contain crystals to detect air pollution or that monitor the wearer's heartbeat.

schiller. A variously coloured IRIDESCENCE due to the reflection of light from minute INCLUSIONS or cavities in parallel positions within a gemstone or to the passage of light from one thin layer (lamella) of crystal to another. It is a characteristic of MOONSTONE and ENSTATITE. It is sometimes caused by alteration of the stone by HEAT TREATMENT. The term is derived from the German *Schiller* (play of different colours). *See* ADULARESCENCE; AVENTURESCENCE.

Schlumberger, Jean (1907–   ). A designer of luxury jewelry. Born in Alsace, his first venture in jewelry was mounting porcelain flowers on clips. After designing costume jewelry for *couturière* Elsa Schiaparelli, he was sponsored by her and patronized by wealthy socialites. In 1946 he opened his own salon in New York City for high-fashion clothes and jewelry, and in 1956 became associated with TIFFANY & CO., being made the director of a special designing department. He has revived old methods of enamelling and has created new styles for jewelry set with expensive gemstones, designing jewels of exotic form and very high cost.

Schmuck (German). Literally, jewelry, but usually applied in Germany and Austria to inexpensive ornaments of COSTUME JEWELRY ornately decorated with cheap gemstones, PASTE or coloured glass.

schorl (or **shorl**). A common opaque variety of TOURMALINE that is black in colour and never used as a gemstone except for some MOURNING JEWELRY. The name is derived from the German word *Schörl*, which was formerly applied to a variety of stones prefixed by the particular colour of the stone. It is a modern substitute for JET.

scientific ring. A type of finger ring, of several varieties, having some device of a scientific nature, e.g. a ring with several hoops opening to form an armillary sphere (*see* ASTRONOMICAL RING). Such rings were also made to measure time, e.g. the RING DIAL, SHEPHERD'S DIAL, COMPASS RING, and SUNDIAL RING, and at a later date the WATCH RING.

scissors cut. The same as CROSS CUT.

Scolari, Giovanni Battista (fl. 1567-83). A goldsmith from Trento, Italy, who worked in Munich from *c.* 1567. He is said to have made a GONDOLA PENDANT and some related SHIP PENDANTS, as well as the SLEIGH-RIDE PENDANT. One pendant with similar characteristics but with a devotional subject has been attributed to him, as well as a pendant portraying a female lute-player seated on a white doe. His jewelry reflects Italian influence modified to northern taste. *See* Yvonne Hackenbroch, 'Jewels by Giovanni Battista Scolari', in *Connoisseur*, July 1965, p. 200.

Scotch pebble. A variety of QUARTZ (often AGATE) found in parts of Scotland which, when cut and polished, is used in some jewelry, especially articles of Highland dress. It is usually precisely cut so as to be inlaid in a close arrangement. It has been a speciality of Edinburgh.

Scottish jewelry. Articles of jewelry made in Scotland, mainly (1) brooches made in various shapes and styles for over 2000 years, and (2) the 19th-century articles, made in response to the romantic interest in Scotland stimulated by the writings of Sir Walter Scott and the visit of George IV, such as PEBBLE JEWELRY, articles made of CAIRNGORM, grouse feet mounted in silver, the skean dhu (a type of dirk), and accessories for full Highland dress. Much Scottish jewelry is decorated with FRESH-WATER PEARLS from the Tay and Spey Rivers, especially that made in the Victorian era. *See* KAMES BROOCH; LOCH BUY BROOCH; HUNTERSTON BROOCH; DISRUPTION BROOCH; BALLOCHYLE BROOCH; LUCKENBOOTH BROOCH; PENICUIK JEWELS; GRANITE JEWELRY.

Scottish topaz. A local misnomer for (1) CAIRNGORM that is smoky yellow or brownish, and (2) the yellow QUARTZ known as CITRINE.

Schaffhausen Onyx (front, back, and side views). Cameo in gold frame with repoussé and cast decoration, set with gemstones. Germany, mid-13th century. W. 12.5 cm. Museum zu Allerheiligen, Schaffhausen, Switzerland.

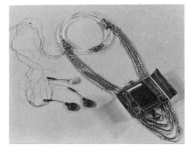

Scherr, Mary Ann. Silver portable electrocardiograph necklace. 1970. W. (pendant) 10 cm. Courtesy of Mary Ann Scherr.

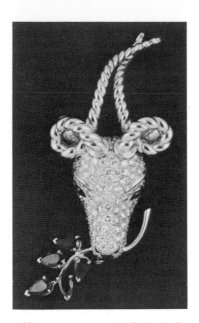

Schlumberger, Jean. Gazelle-head clip of *pavé* diamonds in platinum with gold horns and rubies. Tiffany & Co., New York.

Scythian jewelry. Gold safety-pin fibula with griffin facing a hippocampus. Perhaps Greek (Crimea), late 5th century. L. 20 cm. City Museums and Art Gallery, Birmingham, England.

Scythian jewelry. Articles of jewelry used by the Scythians, a nomadic people who inhabited the north shore of the Black Sea, in present-day Crimea, from the 6th century BC until they were overthrown by the Sarmatians in the 3rd century BC. A characteristic of the jewelry was the extensive use of bold motifs of animals distorted to subordinate them to the shape of the object and the artistic effect. Some pieces were decorated with geometric or floral motifs, in all cases covering almost the entire surface. Such jewelry was produced by Greek goldsmiths who in the 6th century BC settled in the region, and much was discovered upon the opening in 1831 of a tumulus at Kul-Oba, near Kerch, by the Russian government, and is now in the Hermitage Museum, Leningrad. *See* NYMPHAEUM TREASURE; ZIWIYE TREASURE; SARMATIAN JEWELRY. *See* 'From the Land of the Scythians', in *Bulletin of the Metropolitan Museum of Art*, XXXII/5 (1973-4).

seal. A device bearing a monogram or design in INTAGLIO for imparting an impression in relief on a soft tenacious substance, e.g. clay or wax. Seals have been made from ancient times, of clay and later of various substances, e.g. GOLD, CORNELIAN, and other gemstones, CORAL, GLASS, etc. The earliest forms were flat (called a 'stamp seal'), then on the outside of a cylinder (*see* CYLINDER SEAL), and later they were mounted on SIGNET RINGS and also on a SHANK, usually about 3 to 5 cm in height, made of gold, silver, enamelled ware, or steel, as well as of porcelain (such as those made at Chelsea in the form of figures, cupids, birds, animals, etc.). From the 16th century seals were worn suspended from a NECK CHAIN, girdle or CHATELAINE, and from the 17th century men wore seals dangling from a WATCH CHAIN (*see* FOB SEAL). The former term for a seal was a 'sphragis'.

seal ring. The same as a SIGNET RING.

seed jewelry. Articles of jewelry made of various plant seeds and fruit stones. Peach stones have been intricately carved in China and used as beads for necklaces.

seed pearl. A very small round pearl, natural or cultured (sometimes of irregular shape), that weighs less than one-quarter of a GRAIN. They are used in clusters or tassels suspended from ear-rings, set in the borders of frames or mounts, sewn ornamentally on dresses, or set as ornamentation of some brooches or other articles of jewelry. When set in jewelry the metal framework is covered with a thin sheet of MOTHER-OF-PEARL and the seed pearls are sewn on with horsehair, cat-gut, or silk thread; the designs are usually openwork, executed in pavé style (*see* PAVÉ SETTING), with sometimes large pearls intermingled in the design.

semi-precious stone. A term that has fallen into disuse among gemmologists and jewellers and has been discouraged vigorously by European jewellers' associations and the Gemmological Association of Great Britain on the grounds that it is (1) too vague (embracing a great variety of stones, some of which are used mainly for ornamental purposes rather than jewelry), and (2) misleading (as not taking into consideration various factors affecting the comparative values of stones, such as the quality of a smaller superior stone in relation to a poor-quality large stone). The term had always excluded SYNTHETIC GEMSTONES, GLASS, PASTE, and PLASTICS, as well as organic substances, e.g. CORAL, AMBER, JET, IVORY, TORTOISE SHELL. It is sometimes still used to refer to all gemstones other than PRECIOUS STONES, but is preferably to be avoided.

senaille. A small chip of a diamond that is cut in an irregular shape and with a flat base, usually somewhat in the form of a circular ROSE CUT. Such chips are used in inexpensive jewelry.

sepiolite. A mineral usually known as MEERSCHAUM. Its name is derived from the Greek *sepia* (cuttle-fish), the flat internal bone of which is similarly light and porous.

sepulchral jewelry. The same as FUNERARY JEWELRY.

sequin. A very small shiny metal disc or spangle, of various colours, used by being sewn on a handbag, dress, etc. as ornamentation, either overall or in a decorative pattern. The name is derived from the Italian *zecchino* (a Venetian gold coin from the late 13th century).

serekh bead. A type of bead in the form of a *serekh*, which is a rectangular frame at the bottom of which is a design of recessed panelling such as is found in Egypt on façades of early brick tombs and on false doors, and on top of which is perched the falcon of Horus; within the frame usually appears the Horus name of the king or a dotted design. Such beads were made of IVORY, GOLD, TURQUOISE, or EGYPTIAN FAIENCE, and were used in bracelets. Examples dating from the Ist Dynasty, *c*. 3000 BC, have been found in Egypt.

serjeant ring. Gold ring, inscribed 'Secundis dubiisq rectus'. English, 1770. Victoria & Albert Museum, London.

serjeant ring. A type of finger ring presented by an English barrister, upon being called to be a Serjeant-at-Law (a judicial post held before becoming a judge, abolished in 1875), to the Sovereign, judges, numerous officials, and also friends. Such rings were flat, gold bands, usually with moulded rims and encircling stripes between which was engraved a Latin motto, usually of legal significance. Each donor gave a large number of rings and as a number of serjeants were called simultaneously, the quantity of such rings was vast; but today they are rare, as most were melted for the gold. They varied in weight according to the rank of the donee, but all were fairly costly. The custom prevailed from the late 15th century until 1875. For a list of mottoes, *see* Charles Oman, *British Rings* (1974).

serpent bracelet. *See* SNAKE BRACELET.

Serpent Pectoral. A large PECTORAL made in the form of a serpent with a head at each end, and decorated with blue turquoise mosaic. As the heads of the serpent are decorated on the front and the back, thus visible from the sides, it has been suggested that the piece was possibly worn as a helmet ornament. The known example was used by the Aztecs of Mexico, and is believed to be part of the treasure given by Montezuma to Hernando Cortés *c*. 1520 and sent by the latter to Emperor Charles V of Spain.

Serpent Pectoral. Wood matrix with mosaic (mainly turquoise) decoration. Mexico, Aztec period. W. 43.5 cm. Museum of Mankind, London.

serpent ring. *See* SNAKE RING.

serpentine. A type of rock that, owing to its origin from the decomposition of various constituent minerals, varies considerably in appearance and characteristics. The most valuable varieties are of shades of green, resembling and sometimes sold as the NEPHRITE variety of JADE; and some bear misnomers, e.g. KOREAN JADE and NEW JADE. Often it is mottled with reddish-brown, hence its name. It is fairly soft, so that it has been used for carving CAMEOS and INTAGLIOS. A harder variety is BOWENITE, which is more used in jewelry than are the other varieties, e.g. WILLIAMSITE, ANTIGORITE, RETINALITE. Massive rocks of serpentine include several varieties of marble, and fibrous serpentine (chrysotile) is a source of asbestos. *See* STYRIAN JADE.

serpentine fibula. A type of FIBULA made in a variety of shapes but basically having a straight BOW extended to form a curved terminal ornament. Such pieces, of ETRUSCAN JEWELRY, were usually decorated with GRANULATED GOLD, but one exceptional example (18.6 cm long) has along the length of the bow a double column of animal figures IN THE ROUND.

serpentine jade. A misnomer for BOWENITE, one of the harder varieties of SERPENTINE.

serpent's stone. *See* ADDER STONE; DRACONITES.

Sesostris III Pectoral. An Egyptian gold PECTORAL, rectangular in shape, depicting apes with heads of hawks trampling vanquished monkeys, with overhead a vulture with outstretched wings and holding the SHEN symbol, all decorated in red and blue enamelling. The symmetrical design, around a central motif, symbolizes the victory of Sesostris (reigned *c*. 1878 BC–1842 BC) over his enemies. The piece was found at Dashur, and is from the XIIth Dynasty, *c*. 2035 BC–1991 BC. *See* EGYPTIAN JEWELRY.

serpentine fibula. Gold with granulation and figures of animals. Etruscan, 7th century BC. L. 18.6 cm. British Museum, London.

setting. (1) The mount in which a gemstone is set in a finger ring, pendant, brooch, etc. (2) The method in which a stone (or stones) is secured in a finger ring, either by a CLOSED SETTING or an OPEN SETTING, in contrast to the method of INCRUSTATION. There are many styles of settings and incrustations: AMERICAN SETTING; BELCHER SETTING; BOX SETTING; CARVED SETTING; CLAW SETTING; CHANNEL SETTING; CLUSTER SETTING; COLLET SETTING; CORONET SETTING; CRAMP SETTING, CROWN SETTING; CUT-DOWN SETTING; FLUSH SETTING; GRAIN SETTING; GYPSY SETTING; ILLUSION SETTING; MARQUISE SETTING; MILLEGRAIN SETTING; PAVÉ SETTING; PEG SETTING; ROMAN SETTING; RUB-OVER SETTING; SQUARE SETTING; THREAD SETTING; TIFFANY SETTING.

sévigné (French). A type of brooch in the form of a bow-knot, made of gold or silver in an openwork pattern and set with many small diamonds, sometimes having a suspended diamond or pearls. It was worn as a bodice ornament from the mid-17th century until the late 18th century. In early examples the bow-knot was simple, formal and flat, but later it became more naturalistic and three-dimensional, with unequal loops and dangling ends. It was named after the Marquise de Sévigné (1626–96), a member of the Court of Louis XIV who is famed for her letters to her daughter. *See* BOW-KNOT BROOCH.

Sezenius, Valentin (fl. 1619–24). A designer of jewelry who made engravings featuring designs in the MORESQUE SILHOUETTE STYLE. He also made designs that were executed in ÉMAIL EN RÉSILLE SUR VERRE.

Shah Akbar Diamond. *See* AKBAR SHAH DIAMOND.

Shah Diamond. A diamond probably found in the Golconda mines in India in the second half of the 16th century, and said to have weighed originally 95 carats but cut to 88.70 carats. It is of yellowish tint and of narrow oblong shape, with one faceted and three cleavage surfaces. On it are engraved the names of three rulers who have owned it, with the dates in Persian script of the Hegira era, being transliterated as follows: The Mughal Emperors Nizam Shah II, 1000 (AD 1591) and Jehan Shah, 1051 (1641) and the Persian ruler Kadjar Fatkh Ali Shah, 1242 (1824). After being taken by Nadir Shah after the capture of Delhi in 1739, it was kept with the Persian Crown Jewels until presented in 1829 to Tsar Nicholas I by the son of Shah Abbas Mirza on his visit to St Petersburg, as condolence for the assassination of the Russian ambassador to Tehran. It is now in the Diamond Treasury at Moscow. It has an encircling groove to hold a thin cord so that it could be suspended as a pendant. In view of the great difficulty in engraving a diamond, it has been suggested that the stone may be a PHENAKITE. *See* ENGRAVED GEMSTONES.

Shah of Persia Diamond. A yellow CUSHION-CUT Indian diamond, weighing 99.52 carats, that is said to have been part of the loot taken by Nadir Shah from Delhi in 1739 and brought to Persia. Near the end of World War I it was presented by the Persian government to General V. D. Starosselky, in appreciation of his services as Russian adviser to the Persian army, and he brought it to the United States. It was later owned by Carl D. Lindstrom, a Los Angeles jeweller, and passed in 1957 to HARRY WINSTON who sold it in 1965 to an undisclosed private buyer.

Shakespearean gemstones. Gemstones (and some organic stones) mentioned in the plays and poems of Shakespeare, of which 15 varieties have been noted. *See* George F. Kunz, *Shakespeare and Precious Stones* (1916).

shaman's charm. A type of CHARM that was worn or used by an Eskimo shaman (medicine man) in ceremonies as a fetish and that represented the spirit which he was calling to capture the soul of his intended victim. Such pieces were carved of WALRUS IVORY or moose or reindeer HORN, with decoration of haliotis (abalone) shell and rubbed-in colouring; they were of horizontal shape, about 12 to 20 cm wide. They were in the form of fantastic creatures representing the spirits of good or evil; one example depicted the 'Soul-catcher' in the form of Sisiutl, the mythical double-headed water monster who swallowed souls, and another was in the form of a 'Spirit canoe' depicting a combined sea-lion and octopus carrying a number of spirits. They were made by male Eskimos and used mainly in

shaman's charms. Carved bone charms. British Columbia, Eskimo, *c.* 1850. L. 19.7 cm. Museum of the American Indian, Heye Foundation, New York.

Alaska and British Columbia during the mid-19th century. Some comparable charms were made by the Lapps of northern Scandinavia.

shank. The part of a piece of jewelry or other object that connects the operative or decorative part with the part by which it is held, moved, or worn, e.g. the handle of a SEAL or the band (also called 'hoop') of a finger ring or the loop or pierced attachment on the back of a type of BUTTON by which it is sewn to a garment.

Shannongrove Gorget. An Irish GORGET made of thin gold and of PENANNULAR shape. It was made to be worn around the neck and resting on the shoulders, so it is slightly curved to conform to the body. It is decorated with concentric REPOUSSÉ ribbing and has at each end a circular cupped terminal, also with concentric ribbing. Near the rims are circles of gold granules. It was found near Shannongrove, County Limerick, Ireland. It was made in the Irish Bronze Age, 7th century BC. It was an heirloom of the Earls of Charleville and was given to the Victoria & Albert Museum in 1948 by Col. C. K. Howard Bury.

shawl brooch. A type of silver brooch in the form of the TARA BROOCH, but with a shorter pin that is only slightly longer than the diameter of the ring. Examples were made by Waterhouse in Dublin in the style of the Tara Brooch after its discovery in 1850, but comparable pieces with different decoration were made by West, jewellers of Dublin, after the design registered by them in 1849 based on a Celtic brooch found in County Cavan, Ireland.

shawl pin. A type of elongated straight pin, having an ornamented head, that has been used from ancient to modern times by Indian women of Chile and other South American countries as a fastener for their traditional shawls.

Shannongrove Gorget. Gold gorget with repoussé ribbing. Irish, 7th century BC. W. 29 cm. Victoria & Albert Museum, London.

shebu (or **shebyu**). The Egyptian term for a type of honorific necklace or collar composed of disc-shaped beads on two to four strings held closely together by an ornament at each end. The example in the TUTANKHAMUN JEWELRY has three strings, the inner string being composed of gold discs, but the two outer strings having groups of eight discs separated by two beads of blue EGYPTIAN FAIENCE; the two middle beads of each group are reddish in colour, resulting from applying to the surface a thin film of either iron oxide or iron pyrites and soda. Each string of that example is capped by an imitation of a lotus flower inlaid with such faience and CORNELIAN, and the terminals consist of CLOISONNÉ *uraei* with blue faience beads surmounted by solar discs. Such necklaces were worn by the kings, from Tuthmosis IV (*c.* 1419 BC-1386 BC) to the end of the XXth Dynasty, *c.* 1070 BC, but from the beginning of the XVIIIth Dynasty, *c.* 1552 BC, they were also used as rewards for valour or distinguished service, and in the Amarna period, *c.* 1356 BC-1339 BC, were given to women as well as men; sometimes more than one was awarded at a time.

shebu. Necklace with 3 strings of gold beads and intervening blue Egyptian faience and reddish beads; *uraei* terminals of *cloisonné* work. Tomb of Tutankhamun. Photograph by Egyptian Expedition, Metropolitan Museum of Art, New York.

sheen. The optical effect seen in some gemstones caused by reflection of light from linear or LAMELLAR features within the stone. The blue sheen of a MOONSTONE arises from the interference of light at the minutely thin laminae of different refractive index. Sheen must be distinguished from LUSTRE. *See* GLOSS; ADULARESCENCE.

sheet metal. A flat piece of metal, usually between 3 mm and 6 mm in thickness, made by setting an ingot on an anvil and hammering it; when the hammering causes it to become BRITTLE, the metal must be processed by annealing and quenching. Sheet metal is used to make articles of jewelry decorated with REPOUSSÉ work and related processes. Metal that is thicker is usually designated as 'plate metal'.

shell. (1) The outer hard covering of certain molluscs, turtles, etc., which is used for various purposes, including making or decorating certain objects of jewelry. The shell of molluscs is generally referred to, when applied to objects of jewelry (e.g. brooches and finger rings), as 'shell', but that of turtles as TORTOISE SHELL. Shell is sometimes carved as a CAMEO (*see* SHELL CAMEO). (2) The shell of the PEARL OYSTER and other molluscs, the lining of which is NACRE (from which articles of MOTHER-OF-PEARL are made). *See* MOLLUSC SHELL.

shell cameo. A type of CAMEO that is cut in SHELL rather than in a HARDSTONE. Such cameos have been made from many (at least ten) varieties of mollusc shell, especially those having, under the dark mottled outer layer that is usually removed and discarded, two colours, i.e., (1) a white layer into which the design is cut in relief, and (2) a lower layer (ranging from brown and violet to pink) which serves as the contrasting ground. Shells of several kinds of mollusc have been used: (1) *Cassis* mollusc, a genus that includes the 'Helmet conch', the 'Cameo conch', and the 'Queen conch', the shells of all of which provide a brownish ground; and (2) *Strombus* mollusc, a genus that includes the 'Giant conch' and the 'Fountain conch', the shells of both of which provide a pink ground. Shell cameos are cut by hand tools, not carved as is a gemstone cameo. The subjects depicted include Classical motifs, ruins, portraits of mythological characters and, later, portraits of contemporary personages. Some cameos were set in gold mounts, sometimes surrounded with gemstones or SEED PEARLS, or the inferior ones in ROLLED GOLD, in PINCHBECK or in gilded metal. They were worn as a brooch, ear-ring, finger ring, pendants on a necklace, etc. Such shell cameos were made in France and Italy from *c.* 1500, and became popular as jewelry in England and elsewhere in the early 19th century; in England they lost favour to the MEDALLIONS of Wedgwood and Tassie, but were revived in the mid-19th century and continued in wide usage into the 20th century, especially in Italy, where the centres of production were around Naples and in Sicily. In the late 19th century the standard of craftsmanship deteriorated, and in recent years imitations have been moulded in PLASTIC and mounted in cheap settings.

shell cat's-eye. (1) A variety of MOTHER-OF-PEARL that is brown, black or coloured and is carved to produce a moving streak of light, similar to the effect of CAT'S-EYE, hence CHATOYANT. (2) An OPERCULUM, so called because of its shape and colouring, but not chatoyant.

shen (Egyptian). A symbol of life and infinity in the form of a circle, held in each talon of the falcon or vulture that is found on many articles of EGYPTIAN JEWELRY, e.g. the SESOSTRIS III PECTORAL, and the ear-rings, falcon pectoral, and the vulture collar among the TUTANKHAMUN JEWELRY. The symbol is a red glass disc, surrounded by a blue glass circle, to the bottom of which is attached a horizontal bar with spiralling gold wire and blue glass terminals.

shepherd's dial. A type of ring, worn suspended from a finger ring, that is a diminutive and simplified form of a RING DIAL and was used in the same manner to determine time. It was in the form of a hoop that is the dial, on the interior of which are the hour numerals from 4 am to 8 pm, and on the exterior are the initials of the twelve months. A pin-hole in the ring permits the sun's rays to pass through to show the time on the dial. Sometimes there are three holes, for us at different seasons according to the angle of the sun. Such dials were used in England in the 16th/17th centuries.

Shibarghan Treasure. A TREASURE of gold articles, including some jewelry, found in 1977 by Soviet and Afghan archaeologists on skeletons in 6 graves in a mound near the town of Shibarghan, in northern Afghanistan. The region, known in antiquity as Bactria, had been under Indian, Mongolian, Parthian, nomadic, and Roman cultures until conquered in 331 BC by Alexander the Great. The articles have been attributed to 100 BC–AD 100, when the history of the region is shrouded in mystery, and they are said to have been made by local artisans using the techniques of the Scytho-Sarmatian nomads but incorporating decorative figures from Greek mythology with Chinese, Indian, and Parthian motifs in a steppe art form. Included are gold bracelets, necklaces, and pendants, some with turquoise decoration.

ship pendant. A type of pendant of which the decorative motif is a suspended enamelled and often jewelled gold model of a ship, with sometimes figures in ÉMAIL EN RONDE BOSSE, such as oarsmen, lute-players, or voyagers. The ship has been represented in various types, e.g. (1) a caravel (see CARAVEL PENDANT), galleon or caique, with one, two or three masts and rigging, (2) a stylized boat with a crescent-shaped hull or flat-decked, with a forecastle and poop, and (3) a Venetian gondola (see

ship pendant. Gold with crystal and enamel. French, *c.* 1600. Victoria & Albert Museum, London.

GONDOLA PENDANT). Some have an entirely fanciful form (*see* DANNY JEWEL), and some have the hull formed by a BAROQUE PEARL. Some such vessels have, as added decoration, a circular ornament midway on the hull. The pendants were made mainly in Venice, Spain, and Germany, but also in France and England, during the late-16th and 17th centuries when there was great interest in maritime matters. Ship pendants continued to be made at various centres in the Aegean and the Adriatic into the 18th century; *see* ADRIATIC JEWELRY. The motif is also found on some ear-rings (*see* CARAVEL EAR-RING). Some such pendants have been attributed to GIOVANNI BATTISTA SCOLARI, but most are by unidentified goldsmiths. Some have been referred to as a 'nef pendant' by analogy to some table ornaments or ewers made in the form of a ship and designated a 'nef'.

shoe buckle. A BUCKLE (always in a pair) attached to a man's or woman's shoe, of two types: (1) the ordinary form of buckle through which a pierced strap passes and is secured by a pointed tongue; and (2) the buckle that is attached by prongs or sewing to the top of the vamp of the shoe, not as a fastener but only as a decoration. The shape of the latter type is usually oval or rectangular, and examples have been decorated in a multitude of styles, with ornaments often of MARCASITE, cut steel, JET, PASTE, or, for luxury shoes in former days or the present, gemstones. The 18th-century shoe buckles ceased to be used as fasteners when shoe-strings were introduced. Modern shoe buckles are sometimes used decoratively at the side of the vamp. The Lady Maufe Collection of about 1,300 18th-century shoe buckles is at Kenwood House, London.

shoe buckles. Gold set with diamonds. English, 17th century. Courtesy of Wartski, London.

shoulder. The wide part of the SHANK of a finger ring that adjoins the BEZEL or central ornament. It was often decorated in the Renaissance period by a figure on each side, e.g. caryatids with their hands supporting the bezel.

shoulder clasps. Hinged CLASPS (in pairs) presumably designed to clasp a thick leather or fabric garment at the shoulders. A pair, in ANGLO-SAXON JEWELRY, early 7th century, found in the SUTTON HOO TREASURE, are of gold, each consisting of two curved halves fastened by a gold pin attached by a chain. The decoration consists of CLOISONNÉ INLAY set with GARNETS and MILLEFIORI glass in panelled designs bordered by zoomorphic interlacing MOCK-CHAMPLEVÉ patterns. On the reverse are staples for sewing it to a garment.

shoulder clasps. Gold with *cloisonné* inlay of garnets and glass, and mock-*champlevé* borders. Sutton Hoo Treasure. Anglo-Saxon, early 7th century. L. 12.7 cm. British Museum, London.

shoulder knot. A shoulder ornament worn by a woman and made in various styles, sometimes as a jewelled bow-knot or as a bow-knot from which was suspended a jewelled ornament. Examples are among the jewels in the Green Vault, including the one in which is set the 'Dresden Green Diamond' (*see* DRESDEN DIAMONDS).

showstone. A spherical piece of hardstone, e.g. AGATE, mounted as a pendant within a thin metal frame. Such pieces are said to have been used as TALISMANS and to have been found in Merovingian and Dark Ages graves.

Siam aquamarine. A local misnomer for a bluish-green ZIRCON whose colour is due to being subjected to HEAT TREATMENT at Bangkok, in Thailand (formerly Siam).

Siam zircon. A misnomer for ZIRCON, applied owing to the fact that many zircons are subjected to HEAT TREATMENT at Bangkok, in Thailand (formerly Siam), although the stones are brought there from Sri Lanka (formerly Ceylon), Kampuchea (Cambodia), Vietnam, and Burma.

Siberian chrysolite. A misnomer for the ANDRADITE or DEMANTOID varieties of GARNET.

Siberian ruby. A misnomer for RUBELLITE, a red variety of TOURMALINE; it is unnecessary and should be discarded.

siberite. A variety of TOURMALINE from Siberia that is reddish-violet.

Sierre Leone diamonds. Diamonds from Sierra Leone, in western Africa, where diamonds have been found since 1930, including: (1) the

STAR OF SIERRA LEONE; (2) the STAR OF INDEPENDENCE; (3) the LIGHT OF PEACE; (4) a stone found in 1945 in the Woyie River alluvial diggings, weighing rough 770 carats, the largest alluvial diamond ever discovered, which was cut by Briefel & Lemer, London, into 30 stones, the largest weighing 31.35 carats (called the 'Woyie River Diamond' or the 'Victory Diamond'); and (5) two, also found in the Woyie River, which were cut in 1959 by Lazare Kaplan & Sons, New York, into one of 75 carats rough (cut into a pear-shaped stone of 32.12 carats and sold to BULGARI, and a BRILLIANT of 3.95 carats) and one weighing rough 115 carats (cut into 2 pear-shaped stones of 27.14 carats total weight and 1 marquise of 15.78 carats), all sold to De Young, Boston, and resold privately.

signet ring. Gold, depicting fertility rite. Mycenaean, 15th century BC. National Archaeological Museum, Athens.

signet ring. A type of finger ring made with a signet or SEAL and used from earliest times for the utilitarian purpose of authenticating a document by impressing the seal, or later for ornamental wear. In Egypt such rings were in the form of the SCARAB RING or a ring with a gemstone cut in INTAGLIO. In Greece the signet ring was usually a gold hoop (sometimes hollow and filled with mastic) with a flat BEZEL engraved with a seal or set with an engraved gemstone. Roman signet rings were large and ornate, often with the seal engraved on a gemstone. Anglo-Saxon rings were more severe, roughly engraved. But medieval signet rings were very ornately decorated, some having engraved devices, e.g. animals, coats of arms, distinctive marks (*see* HERALDIC RING; MERCHANT'S-MARK RING; REBUS RING) and were often used by a messenger as a credential. In the 18th century the need for seals was less but signet rings were used as ornamental pieces, especially those with an engraved gemstone, as well as many with CAMEO or intaglio seals by Wedgwood and Tassie. From the 19th century signet rings were mainly simple gold bands having an intaglio initial or monogram on the flat bezel, or having a raised ornamental initial or monogram, and many were mass produced. *See* ROYAL SIGNET RING.

Sigsig Treasure. A TREASURE of gold objects of PRE-COLUMBIAN JEWELRY found in 1889 in a tomb in the province of Azuay, in southern Ecuador. Included are a crown with upright gold plumes and also several bracelets, dress ornaments, and seals. Most of the articles were acquired in 1906 for the Museum of the American Indian, New York. *See* Marshall H. Saville, *The Gold Treasure of Sigsig* (1924).

Sigsig Treasure. Gold crown with gold plumes. Chavín culture, Peru, *c.* 1000-1500. H. 35 cm. Museum of the American Indian, Heye Foundation, New York.

silhouette. The representation of a subject by outline filled in with a uniform colour, usually black, and most often used to make a profile portrait. Silhouettes were made by cut-out paper patterns or by painting on porcelain, ivory or glass, and were used to decorate some articles of jewelry, e.g. brooches, pendants, finger rings, snuff boxes, patch boxes, etc., during the late 18th and early 19th centuries. The silhouette was introduced in 1759 by Étienne de Silhouette (French Minister of Finance under Louis XV), its eponymous promoter, as an inexpensive form of household decoration as wall pictures so as to encourage economy. Although the French were especially skilled silhouettists, the style did not win favour in France, and silhouette jewelry became more popular in Germany and England, where it was used for MOURNING JEWELRY. The style ceased to be fashionable when the daguerreotype was introduced. Perhaps the greatest exponent of the art was Augustin Édouart (1789-1861), who cut out freehand in black paper over 200,000 portraits. The silhouette was known in England as a 'shade' or a 'profile'. *See* MORESQUE SILHOUETTE STYLE.

silk. Inclusions of minute (but larger than microscopic) crystals (NEEDLES) or interior lines that run parallel or criss-cross, visible when viewed in a plane at right angles to it, resulting in a sheen that resembles that of woven silk fabric. It is especially seen in some varieties of CORUNDUM, but (unless forming a perfect star) is considered a flaw in a RUBY (being found in some from Burma, but not those from Thailand) or a TURQUOISE.

sillimanite. The same as FIBROLITE. It was named after Benjamin Silliman (1779-1864), an American physicist.

silver. A metallic element that is medium heavy, ductile, and malleable. It is usually used in an ALLOY with COPPER to increase its hardness; *see*

SILVER ALLOY; STERLING SILVER. It has a melting-point of 961° C. (1762° F.) It takes a high degree of polish, but tarnishes by contact with sulphurous fumes in the air; *see* TARNISH. For use in jewelry it can be beaten, chiselled, rolled, and cast. Silver was not used in ancient times as much as GOLD for jewelry, being mainly made into tableware and Church plate, but in the mid-19th century silver jewelry became popular in England for a short period until superseded by PLATINUM. It was later used for ART NOUVEAU jewelry and more recently for medium-priced COSTUME JEWELRY, often hand-made and sometimes set with inexpensive gemstones. Silver is sometimes treated or plated to make it more durable or less susceptible to tarnish. *See* HALLMARK.

silver alloy. An ALLOY of SILVER with COPPER to produce a metal hard enough to be workable. In Great Britain, the legal standard (STERLING SILVER) is 92.5% silver (FINENESS of 0.925), but for Britannia silver (no longer made) it was 95.84%. The standard in the United States is 92.1%.

silver leaf. LEAF of SILVER that is extremely thin. It has been used for backing certain gemstones (e.g. GARNET) but is too thin and fragile to be satisfactorily applied to a base metal.

simetite. A variety of AMBER found along the banks of the River Simeto in Sicily. It is reddish-brown, and darker than the amber known as SUCCINITE. It is used today by Sicilian craftsmen to make a wide range of articles for local sale. Some varieties are bluish or blood-red.

similor. An ALLOY of copper and zinc, resembling gold in colour. It was invented in France by Renty, of Lille, *c.* 1729, and later improved by Leblanc, of Paris. It was an imitation of PINCHBECK, and was sometimes called 'goldshine'. The name is derived from Latin, *similis* (similar), and French, *or* (gold).

single cut. The same as the EIGHT CUT. A later version, called the 'rounded single cut', has similar shape and facets, but an almost circular GIRDLE.

sinhalite. A variety of gemstone that is transparent, and ranges in colour from yellowish-brown to greenish-brown. Owing to its colour, resulting from the presence of iron, and to certain physical properties, it was formerly considered to be a rare brownish variety of PERIDOT (and called 'brown peridot'); but in 1952 it was conclusively shown to be a new mineral species, and as the first specimens came from Ceylon (the Sanskrit name of which is Sinhala), the stone was named 'sinhalite'.

sintering. The process of causing a powdered or granular material to become a solid coherent mass by heating without completely melting it. Some PRE-COLUMBIAN JEWELRY was made of an ALLOY of GOLD and PLATINUM produced by heating grains of platinum and gold dust and then hammering them to form a mass; the Indians of Ecuador had learned that they could not produce heat sufficient to work the local platinum and developed the process of sintering. The secret was lost until it was rediscovered in the 19th century. The process is now used to produce a SYNTHETIC SPINEL in imitation of MOONSTONE or LAPIS LAZULI. The process is also called 'incipient fusion'.

Sintra Collar. A rigid gold collar in the form of three adjacent swelling bands, having at the back a curved, rectangular link with terminal projections that serve as a hinge and a hook. The central band is decorated with two lotus-like cups at each end. The size indicates that it was for a woman or child. It is from the Iberian Late Bronze Age, *c.* 7th century BC, and was found near Sintra, Portugal. *See* C. F. C. Hawkes, 'The Sintra Collar', in *British Museum Quarterly* 35 (1971).

Sinú jewelry. Articles of PRE-COLUMBIAN JEWELRY made in the Sinú region of northern Colombia, near Panama. Among the many articles made of gold and TUMBAGA are: (a) semi-circular EAR ORNAMENTS in lacy openwork patterns made by the CIRE PERDUE process, requiring great skill owing to the thread-like channels through which the molten gold had to flow before cooling; (b) wide, semi-circular breastplates of hammered metal with REPOUSSÉ breasts and decoration; (c) wide NOSE ORNAMENTS of

Sinú jewelry. Cast gold pendant; figure with head-dress and suspended discs. H. 11.6 cm. Museo del Oro, Bogotá.

Sit-Hathor-Yunet Pectoral. Gold with *cloisonné* inlay of gemstones. From Lahun Treasure. Egyptian, *c.* 1840 BC. W. 8.2 cm. Metropolitan Museum of Art, New York.

Sleaford Pin. Bronze pin with gilded stylized animal head. Anglo-Saxon, late 6th century. L. 15.25 cm. British Museum, London.

sleeve fastener. Gold, grooved with plain terminals. Irish Late Bronze Age, 8th/7th centuries BC. W. 2.3 cm. British Museum, London.

flat, slanting strips of metal; (d) pendants in the form of naturalistic or stylized anthropomorphic figures made of cast gold with repoussé work and FALSE FILIGREE decoration; (e) necklaces with gold beads; and (f) 'staff heads' (of unknown use) with animalistic tops. *See* DARIEN PECTORAL; FISH JEWELRY.

siren pendant. A type of pendant in the form of a siren, the torso being a BAROQUE PEARL and the other parts of the figure being enamelled gold set with gemstones, and usually having suspended pearls. An outstanding example is the CANNING SIREN JEWEL. *See* BAROQUE PEARL JEWEL.

Sit-Hathor-Yunet Crown. The CROWN of Sit-Hathor-Yunet, daughter of Sesostris II, *c.* 1897 BC–1878 BC, found as a part of the LAHUN TREASURE. It is a gold circlet with ornaments of inlaid LAPIS LAZULI and green EGYPTIAN FAIENCE, and having at the front a URAEUS. The crown was worn over a wig of many long curls, each extending through a series of short gold tubes (HAIR RINGS).

Sit-Hathor-Yunet Pectoral. An unframed, openwork, gold PECTORAL, suspended from a chain, that belonged to an Egyptian princess, Sit-Hathor-Yunet, daughter of Sesostris II, *c.* 1897 BC–1878 BC, and found in his pyramid in 1914 by Sir Flinders Petrie. The gold openwork design is entirely covered with 372 pieces of CLOISONNÉ INLAY of LAPIS LAZULI, CORNELIAN, TURQUOISE, and GLASS. It depicts the god Heh holding two palm branches between two large falcons, each standing on a SHEN symbol and holding an ANKH symbol; above the branches is the cartouche of Sesostris II, held by two *uraei* (*see* URAEUS). The symbolism is that the sun-god Ra, represented by the falcons, shall grant long life to Sesostris. The piece has been attributed to the Middle Kingdom, *c.* 1840 BC.

skew facet. A former alternative name for a CROSS FACET that is above the GIRDLE of a BRILLIANT.

skill facet. A former name for one of a number of relatively small triangular FACETS on the CROWN or on the PAVILION of a BRILLIANT, all abutting the GIRDLE. The eight skill facets on the crown, alternating with eight similar adjacent CROSS FACETS, and the eight skill facets on the pavilion, alternating with eight similar adjacent cross facets, are now all usually considered together as a group of 32 cross facets, as they are all of identical shape and the only differences are their orientation to the stone and the direction and sequence in which they are ground.

skin. (1) The natural surface of an uncut and unpolished diamond. *See* NAIF. (2) The exterior layer of the nacreous matter of which a pearl is composed. On a pearl of quality, it should be flawless.

slave bracelet. A type of bracelet composed of several narrow rings or sometimes a broad heavy ring, usually worn on the upper arm.

Sleaford Pin. A bronze PIN of ANGLO-SAXON JEWELRY, 6th century, having a gilded and silver-plated head in the form of a stylized animal head. Such a decorated terminal, usually found on a brooch, is not often seen on a dress pin of the period. The pin was found in a grave at Sleaford, Lincolnshire, England, and was donated in 1883 by Sir A. W. Franks to the British Museum.

sleeper. A small wire-like gold hoop worn as an ear-ring to keep open the piercing in the lobe of the ear.

sleeve button. A type of fastener that was used in the 17th/18th centuries to fasten the wrist bands of a sleeve; it was the precursor of the modern CUFF-LINK.

sleeve fastener. A type of PENANNULAR ring in the form of a swelling hoop that is wider in the middle and sometimes ribbed, and has at each end a large disc terminal. It has been said that, in view of the acute angle of the discs, such articles were for use in the manner of a modern CUFF-LINK, but that has been doubted in that some of the discs are too large for that purpose. It has also been suggested that they were intended for use as a special-purpose currency; *see* CURRENCY JEWELRY. Some similar larger articles, with flat, conical or trumpet-mouth terminals, have been designated as a DRESS FASTENER. Both types have been found in Ireland, and the smaller ones also in western Scotland; both have been attributed to the Irish Late Bronze Age, 8th/7th centuries BC. *See* WRIST CLASP.

Sleigh-ride Pendant. A figure group made of enamelled gold and depicting a horse-drawn sleigh carrying a seated girl and a standing driver. The subject is derived from a woodcut made by JOST AMMAN and has been attributed, on stylistic grounds, to GIOVANNI BATTISTA SCOLARI. The piece, decorated with coloured enamelling and gemstones, was originally the ornament of a pendant; it is now in the Rijksmuseum, Amsterdam.

slide. (1) A type of sliding fastener through which a belt or ribbon can be passed and secured (without a tongue, such as in a BUCKLE), usually in the form of an open frame with a vertical centre bar. (2) A type of clasp for holding in place a woman's hair, having a centre bar and a catch or some sort of spring fastener. Such articles are usually made of a base metal or PLASTICS, but some are made of GOLD, SILVER, TORTOISE SHELL, CORAL, JET, AMBER, etc. The term used in the United States is a 'barrette'.

slitting. The process of dividing a rough gemstone, other than a diamond (*see* SAWING), into two or more smaller stones suitable for FACETING, being guided by the crystalline structure of the rough stone. It has been done for centuries, and is still so done, by use of a small, very thin, revolving disc, made of bronze or soft iron, charged with diamond dust together with olive oil or paraffin as a lubricant. The stone is usually held by hand against the edge of the slitting disc, but in modern times mechanical holders have been introduced. After a stone has been so split, BRUTING is not needed before faceting.

Slocum stone. An artificial stone made of varicoloured pieces of glass fused together in CABOCHON form to simulate an OPAL. It was invented by John L. Slocum.

small-long fibula. A type of FIBULA that is a short variety of the CRUCIFORM FIBULA, being only about 6 cm in length, rather than the 8 to 18 cm length of the latter. It is less elaborate, and is of Anglo-Saxon origin in the 6th century. Such fibulae were very common, but of varied shapes. They were worn often in conjunction with a cruciform fibula, sometimes as a pair on the shoulders at each end of a necklace.

smallwork. *See* MINUTERIE; GALANTERIE.

smaragdite. A bright green mineral that resembles and is related to NEPHRITE. The name is derived from the Greek *smaragdos* (emerald).

Smaryll. The trade-name for an IMITATION GEMSTONE that is a variety of COMPOSITE STONE (DOUBLET) of which the CROWN and the PAVILION are made of layers of BERYL or of EMERALD of pale colour or poor quality, with an intervening layer, to provide the depth of colour, of emerald-green PLASTIC cement. It is a modification of the SOUDÉ EMERALD.

smoky (or **smoke**) **quartz.** A variety of QUARTZ that is transparent and blackish-brown to greyish-brown or a smoky shade of yellow. The deeply tinted blackish stones are called MORION and those brownish to yellow have been called CAIRNGORM but that name is now discouraged. It was formerly called 'smoky crystal'. It is sometimes shaped by TUMBLING, but some specimens are faceted (*see* FACETING). A variety that will turn yellow when heated has been found near Córdoba, Spain.

smoky topaz. A variety of TOPAZ that has a smoky appearance; but the name is often erroneously applied to SMOKY QUARTZ.

snake bracelet. A type of bracelet made in the form of a snake or serpent, being of two styles: (1) a solid band or a band of articulated parts (*see* ARTICULATED BRACELET) representing a snake, some examples being enamelled and set with gemstones, especially to represent the eyes; examples were made in England in the 19th century, often completely covered with small stones of turquoise cut EN CABOCHON and inlaid in

Sleigh-ride Pendant. Pendant ornament; gold with enamelling and gemstones. Scolari(?), *c.* 1567/83. Rijksmuseum, Amsterdam.

small-long fibula. Anglo-Saxon. L. 6.4 cm. Museum of Archaeology, Cambridge University.

snake bracelet. Gold decorated with blue enamel and gemstones. Austria (?), 19th century. W. 7 cm. Hungarian National Museum, Budapest.

PAVÉ SETTING; and (2) a long coil of a flattened narrow gold band extending in 3 or more loops, having incised scales and terminating at one end with the head of the reptile and at the other end with its coiled tail; examples of this type were made in Greece from the 3rd century BC, and also in the Roman Empire (some with a head at each end of the coil). Such bracelets have been worn as an ornament or as a TALISMAN, and are still being made in Greece today. Sometimes called a 'serpent bracelet'.

snake ring. A type of finger ring made in the form of a coiled snake, spiralling upward from the tail in three coils around the finger and terminating with the head at the top. Examples in gold, with the body having appropriate snakeskin markings, were made in HELLENISTIC JEWELRY. Later examples, usually with the snake tightly coiled and sometimes having a gemstone set in each eye, were worn during the Renaissance and later, especially in the Victorian era (sometimes as a MOURNING RING). Sometimes called a 'serpent ring'.

Snettisham Torc. A TORC, of the RING-TERMINAL TORC type, made in rope-like manner, with eight twisted strands of ELECTRUM, each strand being composed of eight thin twisted wires, and the ring terminals being large hollow knobs decorated in abstract relief. It is from the 1st century BC and was found at Snettisham, Norfolk, England, in 1950. Another torc, found at Snettisham in 1950, and also at the British Museum, is made of two bars twisted together in rope-like fashion and ending in coiled terminals.

Snettisham Torc. Ring-terminal torc of electrum. South British Late Bronze Age, 1st century BC. D. 19.5 cm. British Museum, London.

snowflake jade. *See* JADE MATRIX; WYOMING JADE.

snuff spoon. An implement used in taking snuff from a SNUFF TRAY, being in the form of a small spatula. Some were carved of BONE in Chile *c.* 1250–1500, for use by the local Indians. *See* CHILEAN JEWELRY.

snuff tray. A small, shallow tray of cast gold or TUMBAGA, with vertical sides and a long handle, that was used by the Colombian Indians to hold *yopo* (a narcotic snuff prepared from toasted seeds). The snuff was inhaled through Y-shaped hollow tube (length 16 cm) made of bird bones, terminating in two nostril-pieces. Sometimes a pottery snuffing pipe was used, having a small bowl with extended snuffing tube. Similar trays were made of carved wood by the Indians in Chile and elsewhere in South America, *c.* 1250–1500. Replicas of the trays are often seen on the figures forming a POPORA.

soapstone. The common name for STEATITE.

sodalite. A mineral that is a component of LAPIS LAZULI, but is also sometimes used alone as a gemstone. It is transparent to translucent, of vitreous to greasy LUSTRE, and of various colours but mainly blue, and sometimes with specks of PYRITES. Purplish varieties tend to lose colour when warmed or exposed to sunlight. The MASSIVE form is sometimes polished by TUMBLING or is cut EN CABOCHON or as beads.

solder. The metal that is used in molten form to join pieces of metal. Various solders are produced commercially for different types of SOLDERING, having different melting points for 'hard soldering' and 'soft soldering'. The solder for gold and silver must have the same proportions of the precious metal as the pieces to be joined, and such solders are now made by refiners with the prescribed proportions. Solders that melt readily are 'soft solders'; those that fuse only at red heat are 'hard solders'.

soldering. The process of joining pieces of metal by the insertion of SOLDER (molten metal) having a melting point lower than that of the metals to be joined. It is used in making and repairing jewelry. If the solder has a melting point only slightly below that of the metal pieces, it penetrates the metal and makes a firm join (called 'hard soldering' or sometimes 'brazing'); if its melting point is much lower it makes a weaker join (called 'soft soldering') that is seldom practicable for jewelry. The pieces to be joined must have clean surfaces and be coated with a flux to dissolve the oxide film that would impede the join, and after fusing the piece must be dipped in PICKLE to remove the flux. Soldering was used in Mesopotamia from the 3rd millennium BC and in the Minoan civilization from the 2nd millennium BC; the ancient process involved binding the pieces together with a metal wire and applying heat which would cause the base metal of the wire to oxidize, and so it required that the surface of the wire be coated with a flux (e.g. wine lees or natron) to prevent oxidation. *See* COLLOID HARD-SOLDERING.

solid gold. Made entirely of gold or a gold alloy (of any specified FINENESS), not of a base metal mechanically coated with gold, e.g. GOLD FILLED or ROLLED GOLD.

Solis, Virgil (1514–62). A designer of jewelry and silverware in Nuremberg who is especially known for designing a group of pendants in characteristic Renaissance style, with decoration featuring arabesques, animal and human figures, and scrollwork, and also for CROSSES set with gemstones. He also made designs for the backs of pendants, to be executed in CHAMPLEVÉ enamel in Moresque patterns, and for the links of the chains and necklaces for the pendants. A book of his designs for goldsmiths' work was published in England after his death. No article made by him has been identified.

solitaire. (1) A single gemstone (usually a diamond) or sometimes a symmetrical pearl set alone as the sole ornament for a piece of jewelry, usually a finger ring, but sometimes a pendant. The diamond solitaire became popular from *c.* 1880 when high-quality stones became more available, and is still favoured, especially for an ENGAGEMENT RING. (2) A finger ring set with such a stone.

sølje (Norwegian). A type of silver brooch worn in Norway as PEASANT JEWELRY. It is saucer-shaped and often very large (up to 10 cm wide), with an open centre in which is worn a decorated pin. The brooch is ornately decorated with FILIGREE and pendent ornaments. It is usually worn by a bride wearing a BRIDAL CROWN.

Sonnica, Crown of. A VOTIVE CROWN in the form of a band made of two gold semi-circles hinged and bolted together to form a circlet, each studded with three rows of gemstones and from the rim of which hang several gemstones. The crown is suspended by chains, with another chain hanging through the centre and having attached a pendent cross bearing a long inscription including the name Sonnica, probably a Visigothic queen in Spain. The crown is part of the GUARRAZAR TREASURE, being one of the three Guarrazar crowns kept at the Cluny Museum, Paris.

soudé emerald (or **émeraude soudée**). Literally, soldered emerald. A COMPOSITE STONE (TRIPLET) that is made in imitation of a natural EMERALD. It was originally composed of two layers of colourless QUARTZ enclosing a layer of green gelatin, so that it appeared emerald-colour when viewed from above the top; but the gelatin was unstable and turned yellow, so this method was discontinued. The next type was composed of two layers of green quartz enclosing a slice of sintered glass, and later the two layers were made of colourless SYNTHETIC SPINEL (this being described as *soudé sur spinelle*). Finally, the layers were made of slices of pale emerald or BERYL, and these have been marketed under the trade-name of 'Smaryll'. All such imitations are detectable if immersed in water or certain other liquids, when the layers become visible if viewed from the side.

South German jewelry. Articles of jewelry made during the 15th and 16th centuries at Augsburg and Nuremberg, and to a lesser extent at Munich. Although much jewelry has been loosely attributed to South Germany, some can be definitely so ascribed by reference to the engravings by such designers as ALBRECHT DÜRER and HANS HOLBEIN THE YOUNGER or by being the work of known goldsmiths (but no article has been identified with VIRGIL SOLIS). Much of the design was influenced by the Italian jewelry of the Renaissance period.

spacer. (1) A type of bead (or a bar or plaque pierced at intervals) that is threaded on a necklace or NECK CHAIN made of multiple strands so as to ensure that the strands will remain separated and correctly spaced in relation to each other. Among the earliest known examples are some found in a girdle from Egypt, *c.* 4000 BC. Others were made of TAIRONA

sølje. Silver brooch with filigree and pendant ornaments. Norwegian, early 19th century. W. 6.8 cm. Kunstindustrimuseet, Oslo.

spacer. Cast tumbaga bead for 12-strand necklace, with bird motif. Tairona style. H. 6.3 cm. Museo del Oro, Bogotá.

Spanish jewelry. Gold ear-ring with pearls and topaz. Spanish, *c.* 1800. H. 6.3 cm. Schmuckmuseum, Pforzheim, Germany.

Spanish jewelry. Gold pendant with enamelled figure of the Virgin and set with pearls. Spanish, 17th century. Courtesy of Wartski, London.

JEWELRY. Such beads have been made of various materials and in many shapes. (2) An ornament strung on a necklace to separate various large decorative objects. *See* MELFORT NECKLACE.

Spanish jewelry. Articles of jewelry made in Spain, especially during the 16th and 17th centuries, by the many native and immigrant goldsmiths and jewellers there. Owing to the wealth of the country, the jewelry was of a sumptuous nature. Characteristic articles were: (1) the LAZO; (2) the long pendent ear-ring decorated with ENAMELLING and set with pearls and gemstones; (3) the RELIQUARY, often decorated with a small panel of VERRE ÉGLOMISÉ, with enamelling and gemstones; (4) the badge (e.g. VENERA) worn by members of religious orders, some being of openwork gilded brass (sometimes of gold) and decorated with opaque enamelling in white, black, and blue; some badges of this type were square, rectangular, triangular or oval, and were made in two sections, a central area with an enamelled religious design and a surrounding frame with a rayed rim, and having a miniature on the reverse under a crystal. Much Spanish jewelry was set with EMERALDS imported from Peru (often stones with FEATHERS) and usually was decorated on the reverse with engraved designs. Green PASTE was sometimes used in imitation of emeralds. Related to the typical Spanish articles but different in style was the Hispano-Moresque jewelry, being more ornate and usually decorated with FILIGREE ENAMEL. *See* Priscilla E. Muller, *Jewels in Spain, 1500-1800* (1972). *See* PEASANT JEWELRY; INQUISITION PENDANT; HAND AMULET; HIGA; SARAGOSSA, LADY OF THE PILLAR OF, JEWELS.

Spanish topaz. A local misnomer for yellow to orange-brown QUARTZ found in Spain.

Spanish work. A Renaissance designation for jewelry of heavy enamelled gold with a scrolling pattern, as made at Prague. *See* PARIS WORK.

spark. A tiny gemstone that is sometimes used in a jewel setting among large precious stones to create a sparkling effect.

spectacle bead. A type of bead decorated with a single strand of wire coiled to form a spiral, or sometimes two connected spirals. The earliest examples were in the form of a tube with the wire drawn from the ends to form two spirals; it originated in Anatolia, *c.* 2400 BC. Sometimes a metal cylinder bead was decorated with several such spectacle forms encircling it. Later Mycenaean examples have the wire bound around the tube or soldered to the sides of the tube. *See* SPECTACLE FIBULA.

spectacle fibula. A type of FIBULA (somewhat resembling spectacles) that is made of a single strand of wire coiled to form two connected spiral discs. One end of the wire is at the centre of one disc and is bent to form a hooked catch; the other end of the wire is extended horizontally from the centre of the other disc to form the pin (ACUS) which meets the catch. Examples are known from the Hallstatt Bronze Age, *c.* 1200 BC-600 BC and from Greece, 8th century BC.

spessartite (or **spessartine**). A variety of GARNET. It is red, from hyacinth-red to brownish-red. The stones show under a microscope an internal wavy veil resulting from INCLUSIONS of tiny drops of fluid. It was named after the Spessart region of Bavaria, Germany, where it was first found.

sphalerite. A mineral that is the ore of zinc but from which some crystals are sometimes cut for use as gemstones. The stones are usually brownish-yellow to greenish when transparent, deepening to black as they become opaque. It is also known as 'blende' and 'zinc blende'. The name is derived from the Greek *sphaleros* (deceitful) because the stone is often mistaken for galena (lead sulphide) but contains no lead.

sphene. A gemstone that is brilliant and sparkles like a diamond, with a high degree of FIRE. The transparent stones are yellow and green; dark stones are made lighter by heat. The name is derived from the Greek *sphen* (wedge), which is the shape of the natural crystals. It is alternatively called 'titanite'.

sphinx bead. A type of bead used as a SPACER in Egypt, examples being known from the XIIth Dynasty (*c.* 1991 BC–1784 BC) and the XVIIth Dynasty (*c.* 1660 BC–1552 BC). Such beads, in the form of a recumbent sphinx on a pedestal, were made of thin gold foil. Each was made of two moulded parts joined together. The sphinx wore a chin beard and a head-dress with a URAEUS. A pierced hole provided for the passage of a suspensory thread.

sphinx pendant. A type of pendant of which the principal ornament is a representation of the sphinx (with head and bust of a woman, wings, and lion's body).   [*Plate XI*]

spinach jade. A variety of NEPHRITE that is dark olive-green, sometimes with black flakes (formerly believed to be graphite, but now said to be chromite).

spinel. A gemstone that is found in a wide range of colours and shades (colourless spinel being rare), of which the most valuable spinel is that which resembles in colour the red RUBY (*see* BALAS RUBY). In general the stones should preferably be designated as 'spinel' preceded by the particular colour, and not by the often-used misnomers such as 'ruby-spinel', 'balas ruby', 'balas spinel', 'almandine spinel' or 'rubicelle'; but some varieties have unambiguous and accepted names, such as CHLOROSPINEL (green), CEYLONITE or PLEONASTE (dark green or brown to black), PICOTITE (brownish-black), and GAHNOSPINEL (blue). The various spinels can be distinguished from other stones that they resemble in colour by their single refraction and lack of dichroism, but to distinguish the GARNET (ALMANDINE) depends on different refractive index and specific gravity. Spinels are usually faceted in the BRILLIANT CUT, STEP CUT or MIXED CUT. A SYNTHETIC SPINEL has been produced, examples being of blue and other colours. The largest known spinel is a polished pebble weighing 500 carats in the CROWN JEWELS (IRAN). For some well-known red spinels that have been called 'balas ruby', *see* BLACK PRINCE'S RUBY; TIMUR RUBY; CÔTE DE BRETAGNE; OEUF DE NAPLE. *See* SAMARIAN SPINEL.

spiral armlet. A type of ARMLET (or BRACELET) made in the form of a long coil of a flattened, narrow, gold band extending along the arm in three to six or more loops. Some gold examples of Greek, Roman, and Etruscan jewelry, 4th/3rd century BC, terminate at each end with a serpent's head. Some Chinese examples from the Sung Dynasty (960–1279) and later into the Yüan Dynasty (1260–1368) were in the form of such spirals extending in six or more loops, having the end loops fastened to the neighbouring loop with wire. *See* SNAKE BRACELET.

split ring. A type of finger ring that has its hoop split in front at the shoulders to provide for two BEZELS, each set with a gemstone, thus appearing to be two rings. Such rings are known from the 14th century. Also called a 'twin-bezel ring'.

spodumene. A mineral of which the transparent variety may be colourless or of several hues, often yellowish-green. It includes HIDDENITE and KUNZITE.

sporting jewelry. Articles of jewelry made in the form of, or decorated with a representation of, some object of sporting equipment, e.g. a tennis racquet, golf club, golf ball, fishing rod, riding crop, etc. Such pieces of novelty jewelry became popular in England in the late 19th century when women entered such fields of sport and wore related jewelry. Sporting equipment is a popular motif on modern CHARMS.

spray brooch. A type of brooch in the form of a naturalistic or stylized spray, being several small floral branches with leaves and flowers, sometimes having the leaves and flowers covered with small diamonds in PAVÉ SETTING and sometimes with small coloured gemstones interspersed as flower petals. Some examples were made in the form of a TREMBLANT. *See* FLORAL BROOCH; LEUCHTENBERG BROOCH.

spread diamond. A diamond that is cut with the width of the TABLE larger than 60% of the width of the GIRDLE (instead of the usual 50%) and with a low CROWN, resulting in less BRILLIANCE.

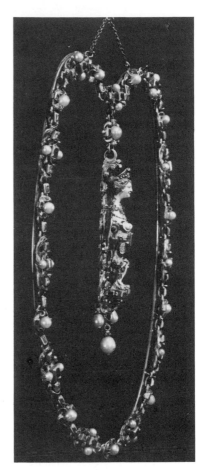

sphinx pendant (with necklace); side view. Enamelled gold, set with gemstones. North Italian, probably Florentine, *c.* 1570. W. (pendant) 5.2 cm. National Gallery of Art (Widener Collection), Washington, DC.

spiral armlets. Flattened gold bands. Chinese, Yüan Dynasty, 13th/14th centuries. L. 19 cm. British Museum, London.

spray brooch. Gold with brilliant- and rose-cut diamonds in *pavé* setting. French, *c.* 1850. Courtesy of Wartski, London.

square. A band of jewels that outlines a square neckline on a woman's gown, as used in the Renaissance period.

square cut. A style of cutting a diamond (or other transparent gemstone) so that the TABLE is square, bordered by four long narrow FACETS that are STEP CUT in the shape of equal isosceles trapezoids. When there are several rows of steps and the corners are chamfered, it is called EMERALD CUT.

square-headed fibula. A type of FIBULA related to the CRUCIFORM FIBULA, being of a somewhat cruciform shape but having a square head. Such examples of ANGLO-SAXON JEWELRY were made of silver or bronze, heavily decorated with CHIP-CARVING, NIELLO, and silver discs attached to the three foot terminals, with sometimes set garnets. They were made in Kent in the 6th/7th centuries, and it has been suggested that prototypes were originally brought there from the Rhineland in the 5th century. Fibulae of closely related form are known from Norway, 5th century.

square setting. A style of SETTING a small gemstone (or several) in a finger ring by securing it (or them) with tiny grains or round metal chips worked up from the surrounding metal. A variation, to make a stone appear larger, was to make sloping cuts in the square toward the stone from the framing edges, which sometimes were impressed with MILLEGRAIN DECORATION by use of a knurling tool.

squash-blossom necklace. A type of necklace that is a popular article of NAVAJO JEWELRY, having a fringe of small silver pendants in the form of squash blossoms, and often an attached centre pendant (usually a NAJA). Some related examples have the pendants in the form of crosses or coins. The style was adapted from a costume decoration of the colonial Mexicans in the early 1800s, and is now being made, although it is not a traditional American Indian design, over widespread areas of southwestern United States, with some versions embellished with turquoises. A similar type of necklace, with the pendants slightly less elongated, is known as a 'pomegranate necklace.'

SS collar. The insigne of a heraldic order in the form of a CHAIN or LIVERY COLLAR, made of silver gilt ornaments shaped like the letter S repeatedly joined by pairs of links to form a long chain, with usually a pendant in the form of a BADGE of a family, order, etc. The order was established by John of Gaunt (1340-99) for his Lancastrian retainers, and one such chain was presented by him to his son, Henry IV (1367-1413), and another by him to his nephew, Richard II (1367-1400). Such chains were also owned by Henry V and were revived by Henry VII, and it is known that Elizabeth I gave as presents a number of SS collars. They are still worn by England's Lord Chief Justice, the Chief Heralds, and the Lord Mayor of London (given in 1546 to the City of London by Sir John Alleyn, having been received by him from Henry VII or Henry VIII, and consisting of 28 gold letters S alternating with 14 enamelled roses and having a suspended pendant made of an onyx cameo carved in 1565 with the coat of arms of the City and surrounded by 254 diamonds). The significance of the letter S has not been established, but one theory is that it was originally a rebus for a swan (the Latin word for which, *cygnus*, was adapted *c.* 1307 to *signus*) and was used as a consequence of a vow of chivalry made to a swan, first by Edward III in 1306. Sometimes called an 'Esses collar'. *See* C.K. Jenkins, 'Collars of SS: A Quest', in *Apollo*, March 1949, p. 60.

square-headed fibula. Silver with chip-carving. Anglo-Saxon, 6th/7th centuries. Found in Norfolk, England. British Museum, London.

stained pearl. A pearl that has had its colour artificially changed by staining, usually in an effort to imitate a ROSEÉ PEARL. Some dark pearls are stained to simulate a black pearl by being soaked in a solution of silver nitrate or exposing them to ultraviolet rays or sunlight, then buffing them to give a lustrous effect.

staining. The process of changing the colour of certain gemstones by soaking the stone in an aniline dye or precipitating various chemicals within cracks or a porous structure. The colours are often permanent, but some organic dyes fade in time. The terms 'staining' and 'dyeing' are often used interchangeably.

stamping. The process of making a complete relief pattern on metal by forcing, by a blow of a hammer, a punch with the desired pattern in relief

XIII *Tutankhamun jewelry*. Gold pendants inlaid with gemstones and decorated with *cloisonné* enamel. Top, scarab within falcon wings. W. 10.5 cm. Below, falcon supporting red disc of rising sun and holding two *shen* signs attached to *ankh* signs. W. 12.6 cm. Museum of Antiquities, Cairo.

XIV *Vasters, Reinhold.* Gold and enamelled pendants in Renaissance style, with gemstones and pearls, and gold suspension chains. From the Spitzer Collection, sold in Paris, 1893, and Collection of Lord Astor of Hever, sold 27 November 1979. Courtesy of Christie's, London.

(cameo or male) into a metal sheet placed over a corresponding depressed (intaglio or female) mould, or vice versa. This process, unlike the REPOUSSÉ (EMBOSSING) process, permits the making of a number of identical objects, and was an early method of mass production. The process was used in ancient Greece for metal jewelry, and also in making Renaissance articles in the 16th century; it was highly developed in the 19th century to make mass-produced jewelry. It is now done by DIE STAMPING or on a mechanical press by machine stamping.

Stanton Cross. *See* IXWORTH CROSS.

star amethyst. A variety of Mexican AMETHYST that shows a star, not due to reflected light as in ASTERISM, but to thin fibres of HEMATITE upon the terminal faces. When the points of the crystal have been cut off and the crystal is turned over, the star appears, owing to the exclusion of light.

star brooch. A type of brooch made in the form of a star, with from five to twelve points, sometimes the points being of different shapes and lengths, and usually set with gemstones.

star facet. (1) A triangular FACET, 6 of which form the CROWN of a ROSE CUT diamond; from the base of these facets 18 smaller triangular facets, called CROSS FACETS (the 18 being together called the DENTELLE), extend down to touch the GIRDLE. (2) A triangular facet, 8 of which occur in the CROWN of a BRILLIANT and encircle the TABLE; along their two shorter sides are the larger facets formerly called TEMPLETS (BEZELS) and QUOINS (LOZENGES), but now called KITE FACETS. Star facets of slightly different shapes and sizes are on some stones of other cuts.

Star Jewel. An ENSEIGNE, circular in form, with 24 projecting rays (12 long alternating with 12 short) decorated with a red and black enamel ground set with RUBIES and OPALS. The centre is an engraved ruby, within a border of interspersed diamonds and opals. It was a gift from Queen Elizabeth I to Sir Francis Drake, and has been inherited by Sir George Meyrick, of Hinton Admiral, Dorset, the present owner. Sometimes called the 'Drake Enseigne'.

Star of Africa. Two diamonds cut from the CULLINAN DIAMOND and now among the British CROWN JEWELS, the Great Star of Africa (Cullinan I) being set in one of the Royal Sceptres (*see* SCEPTRES, THE ROYAL) and the Lesser Star of Africa (Cullinan II) in the IMPERIAL STATE CROWN.

Star of Arkansas. A diamond found in 1956 in the kimberlite pipe, 'The Crater of Diamonds', near Murfreesboro, Arkansas, USA. It is a colourless, flawless stone that weighed in the rough 15.33 carats; its finder, Mrs Arthur L. Parker, of Taos, New Mexico, had it cut by Schenk & Van Haelen, New York City, into a long MARQUISE of 8.27 carats. In 1968 it was acquired by N. Pfeiffer, a Tucson, Arizona, jeweller, who sold it to a private collector.

Star of Asia. A SAPPHIRE of clear deep-blue colour that weighs 330 carats and has a strong sharply-defined 6-ray star. One of the finest sapphires in the world, it is in the Smithsonian Institution, Washington, DC.

Star of Egypt. A Brazilian diamond said to have been found in the mid-19th century and to have belonged to and been sold *c.* 1880 by the Khedive of Egypt, but not known in Europe prior to its appearance in the London market in 1939, when it was an oval stone weighing about 250 old carats. It was recut into an EMERALD CUT brilliant weighing 106.75 metric carats. Its subsequent whereabouts is unknown.

Star of Independence. A diamond found in 1976 in Sierra Leone, weighing rough 204.10 carats and 75.52 after being cut in PENDELOQUE shape. It was acquired from De Beers Consolidated Mines Ltd by HARRY WINSTON and, before being exhibited by him at the Smithsonian Institution, Washington, DC, in November 1976, was sold privately. It was reacquired and, after being displayed at his Geneva shop, was again sold privately. It was named after the United States Bicentennial then being celebrated. It is one of the largest diamonds cut in the 20th century, and is of rare transparency and perfect quality.

SS collar. Silver gilt. English, 16th century. Victoria & Albert Museum, London.

Star of Independence. Uncut and cut in pendeloque shape, weighing 204.10 and 75.52 carats, respectively. Courtesy of Harry Winston Inc., New York.

Star of India. A SAPPHIRE weighing 563.35 carats, found in Sri Lanka (formerly Ceylon) about three centuries ago. It is noted for its size, clarity of its star, and near-freedom from flaws. It was donated by J. P. Morgan in 1901 to The American Museum of Natural History, New York City, from which it was stolen but has been recovered.

Star of Peace. A diamond recently reported (but without confirmation) to have been found, c. 1976, in central Africa and to be the largest known flawless diamond, weighing rough over 500 carats and 170.49 carats after being cut, and to have been sold in March 1981.

Star of Sierre Leone. A white diamond found in 1972 in Sierre Leone, weighing rough 968.90 carats and being the third largest gem diamond ever discovered. After examination had resulted in doubt if a large stone could be cut from it, it was bought by HARRY WINSTON who had it cut by Lazare Kaplan and Sons, New York, into 11 stones, including 1 of EMERALD CUT weighing 143.20 carats and 5 others of over 20 carats each, and later the largest was recut into 7 stones, of which 1 was emerald cut weighing 32.52 carats. See SIERRA LEONE DIAMONDS.

Star of South Africa (Dudley Diamond). A diamond found in 1869 by a native shepherd in the Vaal River diggings on the Orange River in South Africa, weighing rough 83.50 carats. It was the second diamond discovered there (after the EUREKA) and the one that started the diamond rush. It was bought by Schalk van Niekerk (who had seen the Eureka before it was confirmed as a diamond) and he sold it to the Lilienfeld brothers who, after bitter litigation about ownership, resold it to Louis Hond, an Amsterdam diamond-cutter. Hond cut it into an oval three-sided BRILLIANT of 47.75 carats and sold it to the Countess of Dudley, who had it mounted with smaller stones as a HAIR ORNAMENT. It was resold at Christie's, Geneva, on 2 May 1974 and its present ownership is unknown.

Star of the East. A diamond of pear-shape, weighing 94.80 carats. Its history before 1900 is unknown, but it is believed to be of Indian origin and is first recorded as having been among the jewels of Sultan Abdul Hamid II of Turkey in the early 1900s. At the time of the revolt in 1908 of the Young Turks, it and several other large gemstones appeared in Paris for sale by persons then believed to be agents of the Sultan. In 1908 it was sold by CARTIER to Evalyn Walsh McLean (who later bought the HOPE DIAMOND) and in 1949 was bought from her estate by HARRY WINSTON who resold it privately. One report is that it was taken into exile by King Farouk and that it was sold to a Middle Eastern princess in 1977.

Star of the South. A diamond discovered in 1853 at the Bagagem Mines in Minas Gerais, Brazil, the largest known Brazilian diamond. It originally weighed 261.88 carats until it was cut as a perfect BRILLIANT at Amsterdam, reducing the weight to 128.80 carats. It was bought by a Paris syndicate and shown at the London Exhibition of 1862. It was resold, c. 1867, to Mulhar Rao, Gaekwar of Baroda, India, and was reported by his son in 1934 to be in a necklace still owned by the family. It has later been rumoured to be owned by Rustomjee Jamsetjee, of Bombay.

star opal. A variety of OPAL which exhibits a star pattern due to ASTERISM.

star ruby. A variety of RUBY that has a silky structure and when cut EN CABOCHON shows a 6-rayed (rarely, 12-rayed) star in reflected light, due to the phenomenon known as ASTERISM. Such stones are natural or a SYNTHETIC GEMSTONE. Among important star rubies are the DE LONG STAR RUBY and the ROSSER REEVES STAR RUBY. See STAR SAPPHIRE.

star sapphire. A variety of SAPPHIRE that has a silky structure and when cut EN CABOCHON shows a 6-rayed (sometimes 12-rayed) star in reflected light, due to the phenomenon known as ASTERISM. The stone must be precisely cut, aligned with the vertical axis, as otherwise the result will be an off-centre, crooked or dim star, or even the absence of a star. Such star stones are natural or a SYNTHETIC GEMSTONE. The largest known star sapphire, grey-blue and weighing 12.6 kg (about 63,000 carats), was found in 1966 at Mogok in Burma. See STAR RUBY; TRIPLET.

star setting. A type of SETTING for a gemstone in which the stone is placed at the centre of an engraved star and secured by a small grain of metal at the base of each point.

star stone. The same as an ASTERIA.

Starilian. A trade-name for STRONTIUM TITANITE.

starlite. A fanciful name given to the blue variety of ZIRCON. The colour is produced in dark-brown stones by heating them with fluxes. They are so called from a supposed resemblance to starlight, being named by George F. Kunz (1856–1932), an American gem expert.

statuette pendant. A type of pendant in the form of a small statuette, such as were popular in Germany in the Middle Ages for use as an AMULET or as the symbol of a guild. Examples depict such favourite patron saints as St George, St Michael, St Christopher, St Sebastian, and St Martin. Most were mass produced in silver but some were of good quality.

staurolite. A mineral in which the prismatic crystals are often twinned as interpenetrant twins in the form of a cross; hence it has been used in its natural form as an AMULET. It is translucent to opaque, and the colour is brown, from reddish-brown to almost black. Some non-cruciform transparent crystals have occasionally been faceted. Imitations of such crosses have been offered to tourists. The stone is sometimes called 'lapis-crucifer' and in the United States 'cross stone' or 'fairy stone'. The name is derived from the Greek *stauros* (cross).

steatite. A MASSIVE variety of talc, of a greyish, brownish or greenish colour, and having a greasy LUSTRE, hence its common name 'soapstone'. Owing to its softness it is easily carved, and it has been glazed and used for small ornaments and articles of jewelry since ancient times in Mesopotamia and Egypt, and by primitive people such as Eskimos. Some pieces are carved in imitation of JADE, but are readily distinguishable by being easily scratched. Steatite is used in making moulds for casting some articles of gold and for making moulds from wax models for use in making articles by the CIRE PERDUE process.

steeple ring. A type of finger ring having on the BEZEL a representation of a tall Gothic building with a cross on its steeple. Such a ring, made in Germany, is comparable to a type of JEWISH MARRIAGE RING.

step brilliant cut. A style of cutting a diamond (or other transparent gemstone) that is a modification of the BRILLIANT CUT, having an extra shallow row of 12 triangular FACETS in the CROWN adjacent to the TABLE and also an extra row of 8 triangular facets in the lower part of the PAVILION and extending down to a CULET or point. Having 78 facets (20 more than in a brilliant cut), it has more BRILLIANCE.

step cut. A style of cutting a large diamond (or other transparent gemstone) so that, below the TABLE, there are a number of sloping, parallel rows of four-sided (isosceles-trapezoidal) FACETS that increase in size as they approach the GIRDLE and then decrease as they descend to the CULET, and thus give the impression of steps. The number of rows above the girdle is smaller than the number below, but the number of rows can vary, depending on the size of the stone. The shape of the table (and thus of the stone) is usually square, rectangular, hexagonal or octagonal, but some stones are cut with the table as oval, semi-circular (LUNETTE), LOZENGE-shaped, trapezoidal, drop-shaped, etc.; on some the corners are chamfered. The cut emphasizes the stone's colour at some loss of BRILLIANCE, and so is used mainly for coloured stones. Also called 'trap cut'. *See* PORTUGUESE DIAMOND, THE; SQUARE CUT; EMERALD CUT; CROSS CUT; BAGUETTE.

sterling silver. An ALLOY of SILVER that, when used for jewelry in Great Britain, usually has a FINENESS of 0.925 parts silver and 0.075 parts copper. In the USA it is 0.921 parts silver. *See* SILVER ALLOY; HALLMARK.

Steuben jewelry. Articles of GLASS JEWELRY made in recent years by Steuben Glass, Inc., a subsidiary since 1918 of Corning Glass Works, of

Steuben jewelry. Solid crystal heart pendant surmounted by prism with engraved birds. Design by Eric Hilton. L. 5.5 cm. Courtesy of Steuben Glass, New York.

stomacher. Silver gilt with diamonds and pearls. German, *c.* 1710-20. Schatzkammer, Residenz, Munich.

clear or coloured CRYSTAL GLASS. Such articles include pendants (some in the form of a strawberry or acorns), bracelets, finger rings, pins, cuff-links, etc. Among the pieces that combine crystal glass with 18-carat gold some are decorated with small internal air bubbles or air-twists, but the most important examples are solid crystal moulded in designs created by Eric Hilton and decorated by copper-wheel engraving, the designs emphasizing the changing light when viewed from different angles.

stick pin. The same as a TIE PIN.

stirrup ring. A type of finger ring of which the hoop is elongated so that the hoop and its extensions on the two sides of the BEZEL suggest the shape of a stirrup. Such rings were made in the Middle Ages; an example has been found in England from the mid-12th century, and others were made in England from *c.* 1200.

stock pin. A decorative PIN similar to a TIE PIN, but usually worn on a stock (a close-fitting wide band worn around the neck).

stomacher. A large ornamental piece of jewelry, triangular in shape, worn by a woman on a bodice and extending from the *décolletage* or below to the waistline. Such pieces were usually of floral or ribbon design, set with many small gemstones and sometimes with several pendants. Some were made sectionally so that they could be separated into two or three parts, to be worn individually. They were used in the 18th century and later, especially during the Edwardian period. Sometimes called a *devant le corsage* or a 'corsage brooch'.

stoning. The process of smoothing the ENAMEL used in making work with CLOISONNÉ, CHAMPLEVÉ, PLIQUE À JOUR or BASSE TAILLE decoration, done by means of rubbing with a stone (after initial smoothing by filing) until a uniformly even surface has been achieved. Sometimes a piece with transparent enamel must be refired to provide a glazed surface, and finally the piece is buffed.

strap chain. A type of broad CHAIN made by interlocking side-by-side several lengths of LOOP-IN-LOOP CHAINS. Such chains were popular in HELLENISTIC, ETRUSCAN, and ROMAN JEWELRY.

strap necklace. A type of necklace in the form of a circular, flexible band of gold mesh from which may be suspended, directly or from short chains, a great number and variety of closely-spaced gold ornaments made as flowers, acorns, scarabs, heads of river-gods, sirens, amphorae, and framed gemstones, giving the appearance of a fringe. Such necklaces were made from the 7th century BC to the 3rd century AD in RHODIAN, ETRUSCAN, HELLENISTIC and ROMAN JEWELRY, and again later by FORTUNATO PIO CASTELLANI. Also called a 'fringe necklace'.

strapwork. A decorative pattern in the form of crossing and interlaced straight or curved bands resembling straps. It was used on enamelled jewelry in the 16th century, and also as black-enamelled flat metal bands folded, crossed or interlaced in arabesque patterns on some Renaissance jewelry. In the later BAROQUE period it was more voluted and often accompanied by leafy ornaments (then called *Laub- und Bandelwerk*, German for 'leaf and strapwork'), owing something to the designs of Jean Bérain *père* in France; in such form it is found mainly on porcelain, but it was also used on some jewelry, especially some from south Germany.

strass. A brilliant PASTE made of lead glass and used to simulate various transparent gemstones. It is a borosilicate of potassium and lead, with small quantities of alumina and arsenic. When uncoloured it was used to simulate diamonds, being transparent and very refractive, although much softer; the addition of metallic oxides and salts produces coloured strass to imitate most known gemstones. It is named after Georges-Frédéric Strass (1701-73) who was born at Wolfsheim, near Strasbourg, where he learned to make jewelry and artificial gems; he moved to Paris in 1724, and there invented, from 1730 to 1734, new techniques for making imitation precious stones (imitation diamonds having been known in Paris in the 17th century). He ceded the making of such ware in 1752 to

strap necklace. Gold necklace with beads of river-gods, sirens, flowers, and scarabs. Etruscan, 6th century BC. L. 27.6 cm. British Museum, London.

Georges-Michel Bapst (1718–70), husband of his niece (*see* BAPST FAMILY). Such artificial gems are now made mainly in Czechoslovakia, Austria, and France. Many writers and standard dictionaries have attributed the invention to a Joseph Stras(s)(er) of Vienna, but no record of such a person is known, and the legend about him has been discredited. *See* Hans Haug, 'Les Pierres de Strass', in *Cahiers de la Céramique* (Paris), no. 23 (1961), p. 175. *See* RHINESTONE; PASTE JEWELRY.

streak. (1) The colour of the fine powder of certain minerals obtained by scratching or pulverizing it or preferably making a mark with the mineral by rubbing it against a hard white surface, e.g. a piece of unglazed porcelain or tile (called the 'streak plate'). The colour of the streak is often different from that of the mineral as a stone. It serves to identify certain stones, especially one with metallic LUSTRE. (2) The mark left on a TOUCHSTONE, e.g. HEMATITE, when it is rubbed by certain metals to be tested for their purity or to identify the metals in an ALLOY.

Strickland Brooch. A silver DISC BROOCH with a convex surface decorated in an openwork design with inlaid gold and NIELLO. The centre decoration is cruciform with animal-mask terminals, surrounded by a quatrefoil field with more animal masks. It has five domed rivets, and the animal eyes were originally of blue glass. The reverse has fittings for a missing pin. It is Anglo-Saxon, 9th century, and the decoration is in the TREWHIDDLE STYLE. Its find-spot is unknown, but it is said to have been probably part of a collection of Sir William Strickland (1753-1834) of Yorkshire. Its authenticity was once doubted but has been now established. It was purchased in 1949 by the British Museum after an export licence had been refused.

Strickland Brooch. Silver disc brooch with inlaid gold and niello, and 5 domed rivets. Anglo-Saxon, 9th century. W. 11 cm. British Museum, London.

striped agate. A variety of AGATE that has bands of alternating colours extending in straight, almost parallel, lines.

strontium titanate. A SYNTHETIC GEMSTONE that has no counterpart in nature. It was synthesized in 1953 by the flame fusion process of the VERNEUIL FURNACE. It is black until heated in a stream of oxygen (similar to SYNTHETIC RUTILE), when it becomes colourless and simulates the diamond, although it can be distinguished by being much heavier, by its having four times as much FIRE, and by several tests. Being of lower hardness it is less desirable for a finger ring than for a brooch or ear-ring, and the facet edges are not sharp. Some examples have been made into a DOUBLET with a CROWN of SYNTHETIC SPINEL or SYNTHETIC SAPPHIRE which can be given sharp-edged facets. The colourless stone was marketed first as 'Starilian', and later as 'Fabulite' and 'Diagem'. The preferred name for the stone is 'synthetic strontium titanate'.

Stuart, Charles Edward, Ring. Gold enamelled finger ring with gold medallic portrait (under crystal) of Prince Charles Edward Stuart. National Museum of Antiquities of Scotland, Edinburgh.

Stuart (or **Stewart**), **Charles Edward, ring.** A finger ring of English COMMEMORATIVE JEWELRY decorated with the portrait of Charles Edward Stuart (1720–88), the grandson of James II and known as Bonnie Prince Charlie (or the 'Young Pretender'). He led the Jacobite movement to restore his father (the 'Old Pretender'), until defeated in the Battle of Culloden (1746). His portrait, from an engraving by Sir Robert Strange, is found under a crystal, or under the hinged lid, on the BEZEL of some finger rings of JACOBITE JEWELRY.

sun disc. Found at Ballyshannon, County Donegal, Ireland. Early 2nd millennium BC. W. 5.1 cm. Ashmolean Museum, Oxford.

Stuart Sapphire. A fine SAPPHIRE that is now set in the British IMPERIAL STATE CROWN. It measures 3.8 by 2.5 cm, and weighs 104 carats. Its early history is obscure, but it has been said that it was perhaps worn in the mitre of George Neville, Archbishop of York, and later confiscated by Edward IV and set in his State Crown. It was sold during the Commonwealth and later set in the State Crown of Charles II. It was taken by James II when he fled to France in 1688 and bequeathed to his son, Prince James Francis Edward, the 'Old Pretender', and from him it descended to the Prince's younger son, Henry Benedict, Cardinal of York, last of the Stuarts. The Cardinal wore it in his mitre and sold it shortly before his death in 1807 to a Venetian merchant, Arenberg, who resold it to an Italian who bought it for George, Prince of Wales, later George IV. He gave it to Princess Charlotte, upon whose death it was returned to George IV as a Crown Jewel. At the coronation of Queen Victoria it was set in the new Imperial State Crown below the BLACK PRINCE'S RUBY, where it was displaced *c.* 1908 for the coronation of George V (1910) by the Second Star of Africa (*see* CULLINAN DIAMOND) and moved to its present position at the centre of the back.

stud. A type of fastener that is used not by being permanently attached to a garment as a button but by being inserted through two button holes or eyelets of a shirt, blouse, etc. Such studs are made in two forms: (1) with a fixed bar from a circular back-piece to the ornamented head; and (2) with a back-piece joined to the head by a hinged bar that slides through the holes and is then turned into a horizontal position in order to secure it. Such pieces are made of gold, silver, crystal, jet, etc., and are in many decorative forms, with luxury examples (especially for men's dress shirts) ornamented with gemstones or pearls. *See* CUFF-LINK; DRESS SET.

style cathédrale (French). A decorative style that featured ogival forms enclosing figures, IN THE ROUND, of saints, angels, and knights, together with attributes of chivalry. It was used to decorate some pieces of jewelry in France during the 19th century, e.g. some of the pieces designed by FRANÇOIS G. FROMENT-MEURICE.

Styrian jade. A local misnomer for PSEUDOPHITE.

succinite. A variety of AMBER that is found washed up along certain shores, especially of the Baltic Sea near Kaliningrad, and also on the coasts of eastern England and the Netherlands. It is usually yellow in colour, but in some instances is red, blue or green.

Suinthila, Crown of King. A gold CROWN of King Suinthila, 621–31, a Visigothic king in Spain. The crown (stolen in 1921 from the Armería de Madrid and probably destroyed) was in the form of a circular, hinged, gold band set with three rows of varicoloured gemstones and having suspended from it green stones from which were originally hung chains each bearing a letter forming the words 'Svinthilanus Rex Offerret' and also a long chain with a gold cross. The crown was suspended by five gold chains which has suggested that the crown was intended not to be worn but probably to be a VOTIVE CROWN. The crown was part of the GUARRAZAR TREASURE. *See* RECESVINTHUS, CROWN OF KING.

suite. The same as a PARURE.

Sumerian jewelry. Articles of jewelry made by the Sumerian people in southern Mesopotamia from the late 4th millennium BC until the 20th century BC. Among the surviving examples are articles found in royal graves, in mass interments, for a royal person and a retinue of female attendants who were buried side by side in their Court dress; *see* UR TREASURE. The main articles were made of gold, silver, CORNELIAN, and LAPIS LAZULI, and different colours were alternated, as in CAMEOS. Among the various articles that were made are pieces that have been assembled in the form of a head-dress, consisting of HAIR ORNAMENTS and gold hair ribbons; other surviving articles of Court jewelry include gold pendants, ear-rings, HAIR RINGS, CHOKERS, NECKLACES, DRESS FASTENERS, and inlaid BEADS. The decoration includes FILIGREE, REPOUSSÉ work and inlay work, and some GRANULATED GOLD. Some articles of male jewelry included gold finger rings, ear-rings, bracelets, pectorals, necklaces, roundels of CLOISONNÉ INLAY, and chains with bead ornaments worn as part of a head-dress.

sun disc. A circular object (probably a button cover) made of thin metal sheet decorated with various motifs in REPOUSSÉ work. Such pieces, made of gold or copper, are known from the early Copper Age of the late 4th and early 3rd millennia BC in eastern Europe, and spread westward to reach Denmark in the 3rd millennium BC, and later Brittany, Ireland, and Portugal. *See* PECTORAL DISC.

sunburst. A jewelled brooch representing the sun surrounded by up to 32 projecting rays. It usually has a central cluster of large gemstones, the rays being set with smaller stones. The rays are sometimes straight, sometimes wavy, and in some brooches are of different shapes and lengths. Sometimes referred to as the 'sun-in-splendour'. Such pieces made in semi-circular form have been called a 'rising-sun brooch'. *See* HELIOS BROOCH.

sundial ring. A type of finger ring that conceals in the BEZEL a miniature sundial. An example is known from the 16th century.

sunstone. The same as AVENTURINE FELDSPAR.

sureté pin. A type of TIE PIN having, as a protection against being lost, a safety device that slips up over the pointed end of the pin and is screwed on or is secured by an interior spring.

surface enrichment. The same as DEPLETION GILDING.

Sussex arm-ring (or **loop**). A type of bracelet or ARMLET made of BRONZE and wrought from a bar into a convoluted circular shape, having a rounded or diamond-shaped cross section. Such pieces have been found only in Sussex, England, normally in pairs. They have been attributed to the British Middle Bronze Age, 12th century BC.

Sutton Brooch. A gold DISC BROOCH decorated in RINGERIKE STYLE with motifs of animals and snakes. On the reverse is a long inscription, partly in Roman characters and partly in cryptic runes, that is a rhyming Anglo-Saxon Christian curse and perhaps the name of the owner with a prayer for protection. It is Anglo-Saxon, 10th/11th century. It was found in 1694 at Sutton, Isle of Ely, near Cambridge, England, in a lead casket with a hoard of silver coins from the time of William the Conqueror, 1066-87; it vanished from 1705 until 1951 when it was purchased from a Dublin dealer by the British Museum.

Sutton Hoo Treasure. A TREASURE including gold ANGLO-SAXON JEWELRY found in 1939 in a large rowing boat pulled from the sea and buried under a mound near Sutton Hoo, in Suffolk, England. The boat was a funeral monument or cenotaph to a Saxon king of the 7th century AD, probably Raedwald (d. *c.* 625) of East Anglia, and on it was built a wooden mausoleum that contained a vast treasure, including fine jewelry, weapons and armour, a sceptre, gold coins, drinking horns, a lyre, etc., as well as many silver household articles. It has been surmised that the boat may have come from eastern Sweden in the mid-6th century with a group who founded a dynasty of East Anglians. The owner of the land, Mrs E. M. Pretty, was awarded the treasure and donated it to the British Museum. Much of the jewelry is gold, decorated with inlaid GARNETS in MOCK-CHAMPLEVÉ style; these include a SHOULDER CLASP, BELT BUCKLE, PURSE MOUNT, and the mounts for a SWORD HARNESS. *See* POLYCHROME JEWELRY; RIBBON STYLE. *See* R. L. S. Mitford, *The Sutton Hoo Ship-Burial* (vol. 1, 1972; vol. 2, 1978). [Plate XII]

swallow stone. A variety of seashore pebble formerly said to have been fed by swallows to their young to give sight. It was worn as an AMULET.

Swan Jewel. *See* DUNSTABLE SWAN JEWEL.

Swedish peasant heart brooch. A type of brooch worn as PEASANT JEWELRY in Sweden in the late 18th and mid-19th centuries, especially in the southern province of Småland. The brooches were of silver gilt, in the form of a heart, from the sides of which were suspended a number (often 9 to 15) of circular concave pendants, and having at the top a crown-like ornament set with coloured glass stones. Such pieces were pinned at the centre of a fichu or neckerchief worn as a part of a woman's festival dress in Småland.

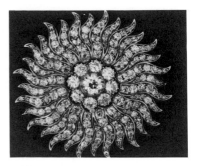

sunburst. Brooch of gold and silver, set with diamonds. English, 18th century. Courtesy of Wartski, London.

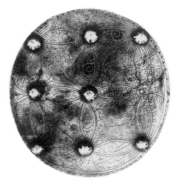

Sutton Brooch. Gold disc brooch with zoomorphic motifs. Anglo-Saxon, 10th/11th centuries. W. 5.9 cm. British Museum, London.

Swedish peasant heart brooch. Silver gilt with red glass stones. Hallmark of Adam Tillström, Wäxjö, Sweden, *c.* 1820-40. H. 12.4 cm. Nordiska Museum, Stockholm.

Swedish peasant pendant cross. Silver, parcel-gilt, with red glass. Hallmark of P. Wigren, Ystad, 1842. Nordiska Museum, Stockholm.

Swiss cut
side view

Swiss enamelling. Gold parure with polychrome enamelled plaques depicting girls in cantonal costumes (names inscribed on reverse). Swiss, *c.* 1830. L. 19 cm. Courtesy of S. J. Phillips Ltd, London.

Swedish peasant pendant cross. A type of pendant worn as PEASANT JEWELRY in Sweden in the late 18th and mid-19th centuries, especially in the southern province of Skåne. Such pendants were of silver gilt, in the form of a CROSS from which were suspended a number (usually 7 to 13) of circular concave pendants, and having usually superimposed on the cross a small crucified figure of Christ; they were usually set with coloured glass stones. Such pendants (the Swedish term for which is *Striglakor*) were frequently made in the city of Ystad, and were worn suspended from a NECK CHAIN as part of a woman's festival attire.

Swiss cut. A modification of the BRILLIANT CUT that is used for small stones. It has a CROWN similar to that of the ENGLISH STAR CUT but a PAVILION with 8 PAVILION FACETS and 8 STAR FACETS, i.e. 16 facets in the crown and 16 in the pavilion.

Swiss enamelling. A technique of decorating by ENAMELLING with a neutral colour over a gold panel to form a base (*fond*) and firing the piece, then painting a picture in colour on the matt enamel surface and refiring, and finally applying a transparent glaze. Examples are found on 19th-century plaques decorated with pictures of native girls wearing typical cantonal peasant attire.

Swiss jade. A local misnomer for a variety of green AGATE or for JASPER that is dyed green.

Swiss lapis. A misnomer for JASPER stained blue by DYEING to imitate LAPIS LAZULI. Also called 'German lapis' and 'false lapis'.

swivel catch. A type of metal fastener affixed to the end of a heavy CHAIN, such as an ALBERT CHAIN, for the purpose of attaching a WATCH or other article. It has an oval loop of which a section can be pushed inward so that the watch-ring can be inserted and then springs back into place as a fastener. The catch is made so as to swivel and allow free movement of the chain.

swivel ring. A type of finger ring having a PENANNULAR hoop between the ends of which is set a SEAL, gemstone or GLASS ornament that can swivel, perhaps with the intention that the carved decoration could be worn against the skin to prevent its being chipped.

sword harness. A suite of metal mounts, buckle, and clasp to be attached to a harness or belt for wearing a sword. Examples are rare; a superb set was found in the SUTTON HOO TREASURE, consisting of seven gold pieces, each decorated with CLOISONNÉ cells set with GARNETS cut in complex shapes. Continental examples are known. *See* BELT FITTINGS.

Symerald. The trade-name for a type of SYNTHETIC EMERALD that is a COMPOSITE STONE consisting of a seed of colourless or pale faceted BERYL covered with a thin coating of synthetic emerald that has been deposited by the hydrothermal process. It was first produced in 1960 by J. Lechleitner of Innsbruck, Austria. The name first used was 'Emerita'.

Symony, Paul (fl. 1621). A designer of jewelry from Strasbourg who was among the early designers of the PEAPOD style of decoration, leaving twenty-four such engraved designs.

synthetic gemstone. An artificial, man-made stone used in the same manner as a natural gemstone, having the same appearance, chemical composition, and physical characteristics, including crystalline structure, specific gravity, refractive index, colour dispersion, and HARDNESS. Such stones can be made colourless, or, by the use of metallic oxides, in many colours, and thus can be made to resemble many natural stones, including the diamond, SPINEL, EMERALD, and CORUNDUM (RUBY and SAPPHIRE). Although experiments in making synthetic rubies were successfully concluded in 1877 by the French chemists Edmond Frémy and Charles Feil, who produced SYNTHETIC CORUNDUM, it was not until the invention of the VERNEUIL FURNACE in 1904, and its production of the BOULE, that commercial production became feasible. Today many synthetic gemstones are mass produced. Some man-made stones have no counterparts in nature and so are not strictly synthetic stones but rather

are oddities (e.g. STRONTIUM TITANATE; LITHIUM NIOBATE; YTTRIUM-
ALUMINIUM-GARNET; CUBIC ZIRCONIA); however, they are generally
considered as synthetic gemstones except when presented to imitate a
natural gemstone, in which case they are considered a simulant. Synthetic
gemstones are usually sold by size in millimetres, rather than by weight.
Testing to distinguish a natural stone from a synthetic stone is usually
done by microscopic examination, as the minute internal INCLUSIONS
often vary between the natural stone and its synthetic counterpart. A
synthetic stone should be designated preferably, not by a coined trade-
name, but by the name of the stone that it simulates, preceded by the
word 'synthetic'. It must be distinguished from an IMITATION GEMSTONE.
See PERICLASE; PHENAKITE.

   synthetic alexandrite. A misnomer for a synthetic gemstone that is
either (1) a SYNTHETIC CORUNDUM (SAPPHIRE) coloured bluish-green by
oxide of vanadium, or (2) a SYNTHETIC SPINEL, both of which resemble
ALEXANDRITE. Such stones were once miscalled 'scientific alexandrite'
owing to their having the property of changing colour in the manner of
alexandrite. The synthetic corundum has been sold under the trade-name
of 'Syntholite'. An experimental synthetic CHRYSOBERYL has been
produced as a true synthetic alexandrite.

   synthetic beryl. A synthetic gemstone resembling the BERYL that is
coloured green by use of vanadium oxide.

   synthetic corundum. A synthetic gemstone that has been made with
many colouring agents, producing stones in many hues and shades. A
colourless variety, produced with pure alumina free from potash,
corresponds to white SAPPHIRE and has been called 'Walderite'. Another
variety simulates the ALEXANDRITE (*see* SYNTHETIC ALEXANDRITE); a
green variety has been called 'Amaryl'; and a yellow variety simulates
TOPAZ. The earliest synthetic corundum was the SYNTHETIC RUBY, next
the SYNTHETIC SAPPHIRE. Synthetic corundum stones can be produced as
ASTERIAS (STAR STONES), to simulate both STAR RUBY and STAR SAPPHIRE
by the addition of titanium oxide which, at high temperature, is
precipitated as NEEDLES of RUTILE. Such stones can be distinguished from
natural stones by use of a microscope which will reveal internal curved
striae, and also the presence of tiny spherical gas bubbles (although such
bubbles may be minimized by modern processes); more exact tests require
use of ultraviolet light and x-rays. Synthetic ruby and synthetic sapphire
are now produced by other methods, and detection is more complicated.

   synthetic diamond. A synthetic gemstone that resembles the natural
diamond, produced at very high temperature and under great pressure.
The earliest experiments were made before 1880 by a Glasgow chemist,
J.B. Hannay, who produced some small stones of doubtful authenticity.
Experiments by F.F.H. Moissan in the 1890s and by others later proved
inconclusive. In 1955 a successful process was developed using techniques
devised by Dr Percy W. Bridgman (1882-1961) for the General Electric
Co. in the United States, producing by high temperature and enormous
pressure some very small stones (1.2 mm in length). As a result, this firm
and others in Sweden and elsewhere now produce quantities of small
synthetic diamonds for industrial use, but they are not large enough for
gemstones and are more costly than natural stones. By 1970 General
Electric Co. had produced gem-quality synthetic diamonds that were
colourless or that showed yellow or blue, but they show technical
deviations from the natural stones and under a microscope have a 'dusty'
internal look. Some man-made stones are sold as simulants of diamonds
but are not synthetic diamonds, e.g. CUBIC ZIRCONIA; YTTRIUM-
ALUMINIUM-GARNET, and STRONTIUM TITANATE.

   synthetic doublet. A COMPOSITE STONE consisting of a piece of red
SYNTHETIC SPINEL or SYNTHETIC CORUNDUM cemented alongside a piece of
blue synthetic corundum, forming a pseudo-parti-coloured stone (*see*
PARTI-COLORATION).

   synthetic emerald. A synthetic gemstone resembling the natural
EMERALD, produced by several processes. Early experiments by P.C.
Hautefeuille and A. Perrey, *c.* 1890, produced stones too small to be cut
as gemstones, and later attempts by use of the VERNEUIL FURNACE failed
because the substance fused as GLASS rather than in a crystalline form.
The first success came in 1928 by use of the hydrothermal process by E.
Nacken, of Frankfurt. Then in 1934 a synthetic emerald of commercial
size, called IGMERALD, was produced in Germany by the I.G.
Farbenindustrie, using the flux fusion process, followed in 1935 by C.F.
Chatham in San Francisco, in 1963 by W. Zerfass in Germany and by

swivel ring. Gold. From Treasure of
the Cenotaph. Tell el-Ajjul, Israel,
2200-1550 BC. Department of
Antiquities & Museums, Jerusalem.

sword harness. Buckles and strap-
mounts. *Cloisonné* enamel. Sutton
Hoo Treasure. Anglo-Saxon, early 7th
century AD. British Museum, London.

Pierre Gilson in France, and in 1965 by the Linde Co. of California. (*See* SYMERALD.) These and other synthetic types later produced can be distinguished from natural stones by their being lighter and having lower refractive index and specific gravity, as well as by the use of a colour filter; but more effective tests are by microscopic examination which reveals in the synthetic stones the character of the FEATHERS (two-phase INCLUSIONS, rather than the three-phase inclusions of a true emerald) and by tests for fluorescence which is strong in the synthetic stones.

synthetic fluorspar. A synthetic gemstone that resembles natural fluorspar and is artificially coloured. As is the case with the natural stone, it is too soft to be serviceable for jewelry.

synthetic 'garnet'. A misnomer for a synthetic stone that has no counterpart in nature but is a compound synthesized by the Czochralski process (a variation of the flux fusion process); it is not a silicate as is a natural GARNET, but has a similar structure. One colourless variety has been called YAG (for YTTRIUM-ALUMINIUM-GARNET) or 'Diamonair'; it simulates the diamond. Other varieties are made in many colours. They have single refraction but can be distinguished from a natural garnet by several tests. *See* CARTIER DIAMOND.

synthetic opal. *See* GILSON EMERALD.

synthetic periclase. A synthetic gemstone that resembles the natural PERICLASE. It is almost colourless and has been produced by the flame fusion process with the VERNEUIL FURNACE. A trade-name for one variety is 'Lavernite'.

synthetic ruby. A synthetic gemstone resembling the natural RUBY. The first synthetic rubies were attempted by Marc Gaudin in 1837, and by 1877 thin platy crystals of ruby were produced by the French chemists Edmond Frémy and Charles Feil; later Frémy and Auguste Verneuil succeeded in producing rubies large enough to be ROSE CUT, but too small for general use as jewelry. A so-called RECONSTRUCTED STONE having the appearance of a ruby was produced *c.* 1885 (*see* GENEVA RUBY). Successful results from the VERNEUIL FURNACE process, using as a colouring agent oxide of chromium, were published in 1904, and today synthetic rubies (including the synthetic PIGEON'S-BLOOD RUBY) are commercially produced by modifications of that method, and also by the advanced hydrothermal process and flux fusion process. Synthetic rubies can be distinguished by the often 'too perfect' colour, by curved rather than straight striae, and by the typical internal bubbles, and sometimes by ultraviolet and X-ray tests.

synthetic rutile. A synthetic gemstone of the same composition as natural RUTILE but of different appearance. It has been produced since 1948 by a modification of the flame fusion process of the VERNEUIL FURNACE. The resulting BOULES are opaque black, but when reheated in a stream of oxygen they change to various colours. The variety most in demand commercially is pale yellow to colourless, resembling a diamond but distinguishable by its colour, greater FIRE, much higher colour dispersion, lower HARDNESS, and having strong double refraction. It has been sold under many trade-names, e.g. 'Titania', 'Titangem', 'Diamothyst', 'Titanstone', etc., or the misnomer 'Rainbow diamond'. It has been largely superseded by synthetic STRONTIUM TITANATE which is whiter.

synthetic sapphire. A synthetic gemstone resembling a natural SAPPHIRE, first produced by the VERNEUIL FURNACE process in 1910. Early experiments had used cobalt oxide, but the colour concentrated in patches, so magnesium oxide was added as a flux; this resulted in a stone that was a SYNTHETIC SPINEL rather than a synthetic sapphire (*see* HOPE SAPPHIRE). Later magnetic oxide of iron and titanic acid were added, and a clear transparent blue synthetic sapphire was produced. The synthetic STAR SAPPHIRE was produced by adding more titanium oxide which precipitated to form NEEDLES of RUTILE. A colourless variety (misleadingly called WALDERITE) has been produced by use of pure alumina, and various coloured varieties by use of different metallic oxides, e.g. with nickel oxide a pinkish-orange stone (*see* PADPARA[D]SCHA[H]) and with vanadium oxide a greenish stone resembling ALEXANDRITE. The synthetic varieties can be distinguished by their showing, when viewed through a miscroscope, curved colour bands as opposed to straight bands, and sometimes minute gas bubbles.

synthetic spinel. A synthetic gemstone that resembles the natural SPINEL. It was first produced accidentally in experiments to produce a SYNTHETIC SAPPHIRE by the VERNEUIL FURNACE process and using cobalt oxide and also magnesium oxide as a flux. It can be made now to imitate gemstones of several other species, e.g. RUBY, SAPPHIRE, DIAMOND, ZIRCON, TOURMALINE, AQUAMARINE, ALEXANDRITE, etc. The synthetic stones can generally be distinguished by lack of curved growth lines (striae), by colour banding, and by crystal INCLUSIONS, and also by occasional internal globular gas bubbles, as well as by slightly different colour, refractive index, and specific gravity. Other varieties of synthetic spinel include an imitation of LAPIS LAZULI (produced by SINTERING powdered colourless synthetic spinel and cobalt oxide) and of MOONSTONE (produced by applying HEAT TREATMENT to a colourless synthetic spinel). There is a synthetic blue spinel that can be distinguished from natural blue spinel by use of a colour filter, and a synthetic red spinel that resembles RUBY but is distinguished by its fluorescence.

synthetic turquoise. A misnomer for an IMITATION GEMSTONE made of blue GLASS to simulate TURQUOISE. An actual synthetic turquoise has now been produced. *See* VIENNESE TURQUOISE.

Syntholite. A trade-name for a type of SYNTHETIC CORUNDUM that is an imitation of ALEXANDRITE. *See* SYNTHETIC ALEXANDRITE.

szkofia (Polish). A type of ornament worn pinned to the left side of a man's head-dress in Poland, but of Hungarian origin. Such pieces, made of gold or silver gilt, were decorated with gemstones and pearls, with ÉMAIL EN RONDE BOSSE on the vertical pin, and filigree work on the wing. An example without enamelling was in the head-dress of Stefan Bathori, King of Poland, 1575–86, and is now in the Czartoryski Collection, National Museum, Cracow, Poland.

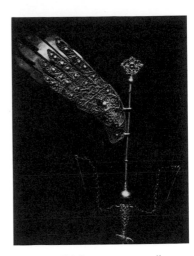

szkofia. Polish hat ornament, silver gilt with turquoises, almandines, and pearls, and filigree decoration. 2nd half of 16th century. L. (wing) 20.5 cm. National Museum, Cracow.

T

tabernacle style. The same as ARCHITECTURAL STYLE.

table. The large flat surface or central FACET at the top of the CROWN of a diamond (or other transparent gemstone), the sides of which surface are cut at angles depending on whether the table is square, octagonal, oblong, etc. If larger than normal, it is called an 'open table'.

table cut. The style of cutting a diamond (or other transparent gemstone) by removing the natural points of an octahedral crystal (*see* OCTAHEDRON), leaving a flat square or rectangular TABLE at the top and a similar but very much smaller parallel flat surface (CULET) at the bottom, with four abutting isosceles-trapezoid-shaped FACETS sloping upward and four downward from the GIRDLE (if the sloping facets are given chamfered corners, the number of sloping facets is increased from 8 to 16). This cut was introduced in the early 15th century and continued until the introduction of the ROSE CUT in the mid-17th century. A later modification has, extending downward from the girdle, 4 triangular facets that meet at a point at the bottom instead of a culet. Such table-cut stones are described as 'thin cut' or 'thick cut', depending upon the depth of the stone.

table cut

table down. The position in which a diamond (or other transparent gemstone) is placed, resting upon its TABLE, so as to be best examined for colour grading.

taille d'épargne (French). Literally, saving cut. A variation from CHAMPLEVÉ decoration in which engraved lines in the metal base are filled in with opaque enamel, without any variation in the depth of the lines, such as in BASSE TAILLE enamelling. It was often used in inexpensive MOURNING JEWELRY in the 18th century, and also to decorate some BANGLES, CHATELAINES, and WATCH-CASES. *See* NIELLO; JEAN BOURGUET.

Tairona jewelry. Pendant of cast tumbaga depicting a human figure wearing diadem, ear-rings, nose ornament, and lip-plug. H. 6.4 cm. Museo del Oro, Bogotá.

taille en seize (French). Literally, cut in sixteens. A style of CUTTING of a diamond with 16 facets. It was introduced in the mid-17th century in France as an improvement of an earlier cut.

Tairona jewelry. Articles of PRE COLUMBIAN JEWELRY made in the Tairona region of northern Colombia along the Caribbean coast by the Indian tribes who lived in towns of the lowlands and, when subdued by the Conquistadors, moved into the high valleys of the Sierra Nevada. Their descendants, the Kogi and the Ika, the only tribes remaining today from the early Indians, no longer make jewelry. The Tairona jewelry, made of gold or TUMBAGA, usually cast by the CIRE PERDUE process but sometimes flat and hammered, includes pendants in the form of (a) a mythological creature combining anthropomorphic, eagle, and bat characteristics, (b) an anthropomorphic figure wearing detailed miniature replicas of all types of local jewelry, and (c) a bird with a large beak. Other articles are non-representational pendants of anchor shape, LABRETS, EAR ORNAMENTS, NOSE ORNAMENTS, necklaces (some with CORNELIAN or stone beads), SPACER beads, and spiral spectacle-shaped ornaments. Two gold pendants have been found in Venezuela just east of the Tairona region; they have been ascribed to Tairona jewelry, as no other gold jewelry from Venezuela is known.

Taj-i-Mah Diamond (Persian for 'Crown of the Moon' Diamond). A diamond said to be from the Golconda Mine in southern India, weighing 115.06 carats; it is a flawless white diamond cut as an irregular oval. It has been considered to be a sister stone to the DARYA-I-NUR DIAMOND, taken with it by Nadir Shah after his sack of Delhi in 1739, and set in two arm-bands seen worn by Lutf Ali Khan Zand, a Persian ruler, in 1791 and seen again in the arm-bands in 1827. It is today among the CROWN JEWELS (IRAN) at Tehran.

talisman. A broad term for an object that is supposed to ward off evil or bring good fortune, including an AMULET and a CHARM, but especially such an object with some astrological or magical symbol. At one time the term was restricted to objects engraved with signs having an astrological significance, as distinguished from amulets bearing occult inscriptions; the Church in the early Christian era permitted generally the latter but condemned the former, although in time amulets and talismans were assimilated. During the Middle Ages objects of such natures, as well as certain gemstones, were all regarded as talismans. *See* ABRAXAS STONE; HIGA.

tallow-top. A gemstone cut in the general form of a CABOCHON but with a shallow dome.

tanzanite. A variety of EPIDOTE that is transparent and typically deep bluish-violet, but also sometimes of other hues. The paler stones are subjected to HEAT TREATMENT to produce the blue colour desired for gemstones. Transparent stones are faceted, cloudy ones are cut EN CABOCHON. A specimen called 'Midnight Blue', weighing 122.7 carats, is at the Natural History Museum, Washington, DC. The stones somewhat resemble SAPPHIRE but are lighter and softer. Tanzanite was discovered in 1967 in Tanzania (the state formed in 1964 by the merging of Tanganyika and Zanzibar) through the aid of Henry B. Platt, of TIFFANY & CO., and was so named by him; in 1968 it was introduced by Tiffany to the jewelry world.

Tara Brooch. Gilt bronze with enamelling, niello, and gemstones. Celtic, 8th century. National Museum of Ireland, Dublin.

Tara Brooch. A PENANNULAR PIN BROOCH made of white bronze, thickly gilded, that has a continuous ring partly filled with an ornament which, as well as the expanded head of the pin, is divided into a number of panels decorated with enamelled work, NIELLO, and inlaid gemstones. The metal is hammered, chased, and engraved. The enamels are CLOISONNÉ and were made separately and mounted. Attached to the brooch at one side is a finely plaited tapering chain (a similar one for the other side has been lost). The reverse of the brooch is engraved with the Celtic TRUMPET PATTERN. The brooch is Celtic, dating from the early 8th century. It was found in 1850 on the shore near Bettystown, County Louth, Eire, and was named 'Tara' after the hill of that name. The brooch has been copied by jewellers in Birmingham. *See* HUNTERSTON BROOCH; LONDESBOROUGH BROOCH; SHAWL BROOCH.

Tarascan jewelry. Articles of PRE-COLUMBIAN JEWELRY made from the 10th century in the Tarascan region of the province of Michoacán in west-central Mexico. Owing to the scarcity of local gold, much of the work is of copper thinly covered with TUMBAGA and gilded by the process of DEPLETION GILDING (*mise en couleur*). The local articles include effigy bells in the form of animals, covered entirely with snail-like spirals of cast wire.

tarnish. The altered lustre or surface colour of a mineral, due either to a slight alteration, as by a chemical process from contact with sulphurous fumes that tarnishes SILVER, or to a thin external deposit, e.g. dust. Tarnish of silver is not due, as often stated, to OXIDATION (or oxidization). It can be removed by a liquid that releases the sulphur, and can be protected against by plating the silver with rhodium.

tassie. A glass paste replica of an engraved gemstone made in the style of a TASSIE MEDALLION by any of many later English firms.

Tassie medallion. A moulded MEDALLION made of PASTE in London by James Tassie (1735-99) of Glasgow, or his nephew William (1777-1860), or by their successor from 1840, James Wilson. The medallions, in CAMEO or INTAGLIO form, were used in various articles of jewelry, being mounted and set in brooches, necklaces, bracelets, finger rings, buttons, etc., and the intaglios were used as SEALS. Tassie first made in Dublin reproductions of ancient ENGRAVED GEMSTONES, and later, *c.* 1766, he moved to London where he made, in a glass paste that he had developed, *c.* 1763, reproductions of gems and portrait medallions designed by contemporary artists, as well as some modelled in wax by himself. The paste was a finely powdered potash-lead glass, opaque white and coloured, which was softened by heating and pressed into plaster of Paris moulds. He also made some relief plaques. The medallions range from 2 to 11 cm in height; the reliefs are larger. The London subjects are royalty and famous persons, usually contemporaries. Some pieces bear an impressed mark 'T' or 'Tassie F'; those by William are marked 'W Tassie F'. A catalogue by R. E. Raspe published in 1791 lists over 15,000 subjects. Tassie made a set of his paste reproductions of ancient and modern gems for Catherine the Great. He also made, from 1769 to 1780, models for Josiah Wedgwood to use for casting JASPER ware medallions. *See* John M. Gray, *James and William Tassie*, 1894.

Tau cross. A type of cross that is shaped like a letter T but with its stem widening toward the bottom. It is the emblem of St Anthony and examples were worn as an AMULET in medieval times to ward off ergotism, a disease also known as St Anthony's fire. Such crosses were popular in England, Spain, and Denmark during the 16th/17th centuries. *See* ANKH.

Tavernier Diamonds. A group of diamonds brought back to France by Jean-Baptiste Tavernier (1605-89), the French traveller, diamond merchant, and memoir-writer, from his six voyages to India, where he saw many diamonds owned by the Great Mogul, Jehan Shah, and his son Aurangzeb. He described the diamonds, and sketched some, in his two books which have been translated into English (1889). Four diamonds were given names, of which one, the 'Tavernier Blue', was recut as the BLUE DIAMOND OF THE CROWN and is believed to be the stone from which later the HOPE DIAMOND was cut. The 'Tavernier A' was sold to Louis XIV and was among the stones stolen from the Garde Meuble in 1792. Tavernier also travelled elsewhere, including a trip to Italy in 1657 when he visited the Medici in Florence.

templet. The former name for four lozenge-shaped FACETS on the CROWN of a BRILLIANT. The four templets and the four similar QUOINS (LOZENGES) that alternate with them were usually considered together as eight templets. A former alternative name was BEZEL, but now all such lozenge-shaped facets are each called a KITE FACET or a MAIN FACET.

Templier, Raymond (1891-1968). A Parisian DESIGNER-MAKER descended from a Parisian family of jewellers, his grandfather being Charles Templier who founded the firm in 1849 and was later joined by his son Paul, Raymond's father. The firm became known as Paul and Raymond Templier. Their work has been widely exhibited.

Tau cross. Locket decorated in enamels with the Holy Family, and with a dove (symbolizing the Holy Ghost) suspended below. Spanish, late 17th century. Wernher Collection, Luton Hoo, Luton, England.

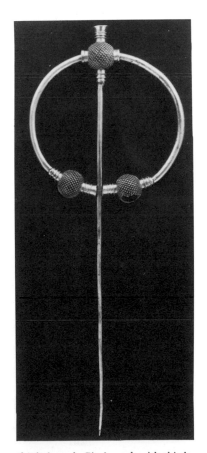

thistle brooch. Pin brooch with thistle ornaments. L. 60 cm. British Museum, London.

Thomas, David. Bracelet, yellow gold, with hinged sections and diamonds, 1975. Courtesy of David Thomas, London.

'Thor's hammer' pendants. Silver; Ostergotland, Sweden; 11th century. H. 4.3 cm. Statens Historiska Museum, Stockholm.

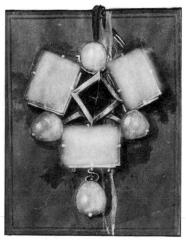

Three Brothers Jewel. As depicted in a miniature painting in the Historisches Museum, Basle.

terminal bead. A type of bead that is placed at the ends of a multiple NECKLACE or NECK CHAIN, pierced in one direction for threading with the other beads and sometimes also pierced at right angles to receive the tie-strings.

ternary alloy. A three-fold ALLOY composed, for example, of platinum/gold/silver or palladium/gold/silver; these can be used in SOLDERING. One such alloy of gold/silver/copper, with only about 15% gold, was sometimes used in PERUVIAN JEWELRY to permit a gold surface by use of DEPLETION GILDING, first removing the copper by heating and hammering, then removing the silver by applying a salt preparation that produced a black scale which was removed with another chemical solution.

Teutonic jewelry. The same as FRANKISH JEWELRY.

textured gold. A gold surface that has been subjected to some process to produce a textured, non-smooth effect as a modern style of decoration. The effect can be produced by making overall marking by ENGRAVING or with an electric drill or by heating the surface to the point where the surface gold becomes molten and runs to create the desired effect of texturing. *See* BRUSHED GOLD; FLORENTINE FINISH; BLOOMED GOLD; SABLÉ D'OR.

Thame Hoard. Articles of jewelry (mainly finger rings) and coins (English silver groats, from the reign of Edward III, 1327-77, to that of Henry VI, 1422-61), found on 21 April 1940 on the bank of the River Thames, at Thame, Oxfordshire. The rings are datable by the dates of the coins.

Thetford Treasure. *See* Addenda, p. 335.

thickness (of diamonds). The distance between the TABLE and the CULET of a BRILLIANT. Ordinarily one-third is occupied by the CROWN and two-thirds by the PAVILION.

thistle brooch. A type of PIN BROOCH having ornaments in the form of a thistle. Such brooches are composed of a long pin at the top of which is a PENANNULAR ornament to which the pin is affixed so that it can swivel in order to be attached to a garment and secured in the opening on the lower side of the ornament. The ornament has two small knobs on the terminals of the opening, to secure the pin. Such pins are of Viking style, and have been found in Cumberland, England, and in Scotland.

Thomas, David (1938–). An English DESIGNER-MAKER of 18-carat gold jewelry who has had his own workshop in London since 1961. He has designed some pieces for De Beers and had an exhibition at Goldsmiths' Hall, London, in 1974. He personally designs pieces expressly to order for clients and also creates designs and jewelry for the trade. His finger rings and bracelets, usually set with diamonds, originally featured a large number of thin metal rods and dots soldered together to create sunburst and other abstract forms, but his recent work emphasizes solidity and sinuous curves coupled with the use of contrasting massed, parallel, thin strips of gold.

thomsonite. A variety of gemstone that is somewhat transparent with circular bands, similar to AGATE, on a reddish, creamy-white or grey-green background. When heated it swells, giving off water and melting, and it is electrified by friction. It is sometimes CHATOYANT and cut EN CABOCHON, but some unpolished blue-green stones are sold as souvenirs along Lake Superior (USA). Owing to the banding it is sometimes called 'eyestone'. A related stone is CHLORASTROLITE.

'Thor's hammer' pendant. A type of pendant in the form of Thor's hammer, the magical weapon of the Norse god Thor, presumably symbolizing physical strength and having large staring eyes, one of Thor's attributes. It was worn as an AMULET in Scandinavia during the Viking period. Examples were made in Sweden in the 11th century. *See* VIKING JEWELRY.

Thracian jewelry. *See* BULGARIAN JEWELRY.

thread setting. A style of SETTING a gemstone in a finger ring by which a thin thread of metal is raised with a knurling tool and pressed over the stone to hold it in the COLLET.

Three Brothers Jewel. A pendant in the form of three rectangles (each set with a BALAS RUBY (SPINEL), known as 'The Three Brothers') in triangular arrangement, separated by three large pearls, in the centre of which was a deep diamond, PYRAMID CUT, and having a large pearl suspended from the lowest rectangle. It dates from 1400/10 and is recorded in an inventory of 1419. In 1467 it was inherited from his father by Charles the Bold (1433–77), last Duke of Burgundy, who carried it (together with the WHITE ROSE JEWEL) as a TALISMAN. It was taken from his tent by a soldier after his defeat by the Swiss at the battle of Grandson, 1476, and came into the possession of the Magistrates of Berne. They sold it in 1504 to Jacob Fugger of Augsburg, whose son negotiated its sale to Henry VIII, which sale, after his death in 1547, was completed in 1551 by his successor, Edward VI (but another version is that Edward VI bought it in Antwerp in 1551). Edward VI delivered it to the Treasury for safe-keeping and in 1554 it was given to his sister, Mary I, when she married Philip II of Spain. It was worn by Elizabeth I, mounted on a CARCANET, as shown in the Segar portrait made in 1585. It was described in the 1605 inventory of articles declared by James I as Crown Jewels and also in a 1623 list of jewels removed from the Tower of London by James I and delivered to GEORGE HERIOT, Crown Jeweller, for resetting, and again in a letter, referring to it as 'newlie sette', sent by James I to his son (the future Charles I) telling him to wear it as an ENSEIGNE on his (unsuccessful) visit in 1623 to Spain to woo the Infanta. It was pawned by Charles I in the Netherlands in 1626 and redeemed in 1639. In 1642 it and other jewels were taken to the Netherlands by Henrietta Maria, wife of Charles I, and pawned and later sold through a bank in Rotterdam. It was last seen in 1650. The diamond in the jewel was cut by LUDWIG VAN BERGHEM and is said to have been the first diamond cut in pyramid form. The jewel is shown in several drawings and engravings, as well as in a watercolour on vellum, made c. 1550, now in Basle. See Roy Strong, 'Three Royal Jewels', in *Burlington Magazine*, CVIII, July 1966, p. 350.

Three Kings (Magi), The. A decorative or amuletic motif on some articles of medieval jewelry in the form of the names of the so-called Three Kings of the East, the gift-bearing magi, whose bodies are said to have been brought by the Empress Helena (mother of Constantine the Great) to Constantinople and thence transferred to Milan and then to Cologne. There is a Shrine of the Three Kings in Cologne Cathedral and also in the Church of S. Eustorgio in Milan, and pilgrims to these shrines were given TALISMANS thought to be charms against epilepsy. The names (Gaspar, Melchior, and Balthasar) are inscribed on the COVENTRY RING, the GLENLYON BROOCH, and a number of DEVOTIONAL RINGS.

thumbpiece. A small projecting knob to be pressed by the thumb to operate a catch, as on some bracelets.

thumb ring. (1) A decorative ring worn as a finger ring on the thumb. (2) A broad ring originally designed to be worn by an Oriental archer to protect his thumb when drawing a bow-string, but later worn generally. They were made of BONE, JADE, IVORY, and also of glass in China during the K'ang Hsi period (1662–1772). See ARCHER'S THUMB RING.

tiara. A type of HEAD ORNAMENT worn by ladies, usually royalty or members of the nobility, on state or formal occasions. Tiaras vary greatly in form and degree of ornamentation but usually are a curved (less than a semi-circular) vertical band with a central peak, all encrusted with diamonds or other gemstones. In the Victorian era in England some necklaces were made so that the central part could be detached and worn as a tiara; in Russia and England a type of necklace could in its entirety be worn as a tiara (see NECKLACE TIARA). The term originally was applied to the head-dress worn by the ancient Persians; it is now also applied to the triple crown of the Pope. See CORONET; DIADEM; TIARA RUSSE.

tiara russe (French). A type of TIARA, derived from the Russian *kokoshnik,* in the form of a narrow band from which extend a series of closely-spaced, pointed, jewelled ornaments, sometimes of alternating

thumb ring. Gilt metal. Italian, late 15th century. Victoria & Albert Museum, London.

tiara. Diamond tiara of the Queen of Sweden, c. 1850. Royal Treasury, Stockholm.

Tibetan jewelry. Gilded copper crown, 19th century. Victoria & Albert Museum, London.

lengths. When worn as a tiara, the ornaments projected upward, but the piece can also be worn as a NECKLACE, unmounted from its frame and with the ornaments downward. An example is owned by the British Royal Family, having been worn by Queen Alexandra and by Queen Mary who bequeathed it to Queen Elizabeth II. Another, made by Bapst for the Empress Eugénie, was among the French Crown Jewels sold in 1887.

Tibetan jewelry. Articles of jewelry made in Tibet under the Lamaist culture which required a religious significance to be given to all the arts. This led to emphasis of the traditional styles, so that individual makers are not known and attributions to places and periods are difficult. Decoration was profuse, covering all available space on an object. The styles were influenced by those of neighbouring Kashmir, Nepal, China, and India, but they were submerged in the indigenous styles. Metalwork was made and decorated by all the metal processes, especially REPOUSSÉ work, damascening, ENGRAVING, and false GRANULATED GOLD; pieces were made of gold, silver, and gilded copper. Gemstones were used profusely, especially TURQUOISE that was from local and imported sources, EMERALD, ROCK CRYSTAL, CORAL, LAPIS LAZULI, and in the 19th century, coloured glass. Jewelry was universally worn, by men and women of all classes, and included finger rings (decorated with amuletic devices), hair clips and medallions, ear-rings, crowns, rigid penannular collars, and waist ornaments, as well as amuletic shrine boxes (*gahu*) that were worn as a pendant on a necklace and that contained prayers, images, and seeds.

tie clip. A detachable clip (modern) to secure, by tension, a necktie to a shirt by being slipped over the tie and the edge of the shirt. They have been made of gold or other metal, and are often monogrammed or otherwise inscribed. *See* TIE TACK.

tie pin. A decorative PIN worn inserted vertically into a necktie or scarf. The ornamental top has been made with a great variety of ornamentation, including gemstones, pearls, CORAL, etc., as well as a representation of many objects, animals, and other motifs. The pin was made in the 18th century with a zigzag grooving to prevent slipping, but those made in the 19th century usually have merely a few twists in the pin about two-thirds of the length up. Some such pins were made in pairs joined by a chain and worn together. Occasionally they are provided with a safety device, to prevent loss; *see* SURETÉ PIN. The same as a 'cravat pin', 'stick pin' or 'scarf pin'. *See* JABOT PIN; STOCK PIN.

tie tack. A detachable ornament (modern), often set with a gemstone, to secure a necktie to a shirt by being affixed to a very short pin that pierces the tie and shirt horizontally and is secured at the back by a spring clip.

Tierfibeln (German). Literally, animal fibula. A type of FIBULA having the BOW made in the form of an animal (e.g. a dog) IN THE ROUND. Such fibulae were made of bronze from the Central European Iron Age, 5th century BC.

Tiffany & Co. The leading American jewelry firm, founded in New York City in 1837 by Charles Lewis Tiffany (1812-1902) with John B. Young, the firm then selling miscellaneous inexpensive wares, but soon thereafter expanding to offer jewelry, diamonds, and watches. In 1841 J. L. Ellis became a partner, and Tiffany and Young travelled in Europe, buying large and important collections of jewelry. In 1853 Tiffany acquired the entire firm, thence known as Tiffany & Co. In 1850 it introduced the English Sterling Silver standard which later was legalized for American Sterling silverware. In 1868 it merged with Edward C. Moore & Co., silversmiths; Moore, who had been a Tiffany designer since 1851, influenced the introduction of Japanese styles. In 1886 Tiffany introduced the TIFFANY SETTING for diamond SOLITAIRE finger rings. His son, Louis Comfort Tiffany (1844-1933), an early exponent of the ART NOUVEAU style, introduced *c.* 1892 his Favrile iridescent glassware, and *c.* 1900 joined the firm. In 1940 the firm, having acquired an international reputation for jewelry, gemstones, and silverware, moved to its present luxurious premises at 5th Ave. and 57th St. Walter Hoving, who in 1955 assumed control from the Tiffany and Moore families, has retired. Henry B. Platt (the great-great-grandson of Charles Tiffany), now Chairman of the Board, was responsible for the discovery and naming of TANZANITE in

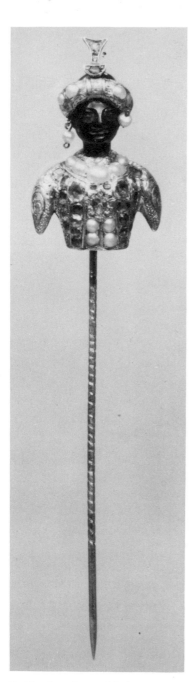

tie pin. Carved agate blackamoor with diamonds and pearls. 18th century. Courtesy of Wartski, London.

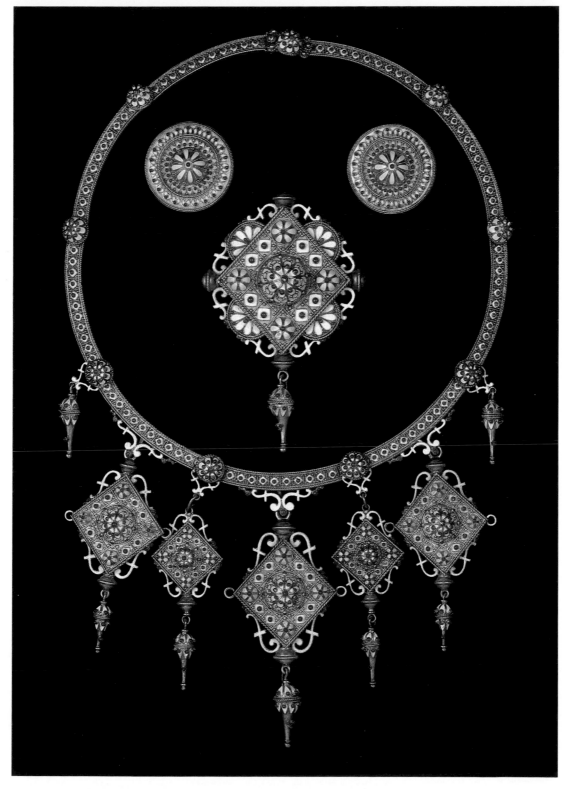

XV *Victorian jewelry*. Gold and enamelled suite: necklace, brooch, buttons. Probably English, *c*. 1860.
Courtesy of S.J. Phillips Ltd, London.

XVI *Winston, Harry.* Parure consisting of platinum necklace, bracelet, and ear-rings, with 88 pear-shaped emeralds and 295 marquise and 72 brilliant diamonds. Courtesy of Harry Winston, Inc., New York.

1968. Branches of the firm are in several American cities, as well as in Paris (since 1850) and London (since 1868). *See* TIFFANY DIAMOND; TIFFANY JEWELRY.

Tiffany Diamond. A canary-yellow diamond (largest known of such colour) weighing 128.51 carats and cut from a rough diamond weighing 287.42 carats that is believed to have been found in 1878 in the Kimberley Mine in South Africa. It is CUSHION CUT, cut in Paris with 90 facets, having 40 facets on the CROWN, 48 on the PAVILION, a TABLE, and a CULET, the 32 facets more than the standard BRILLIANT giving it extraordinary BRILLIANCE and FIRE. It was immediately purchased and is still owned by TIFFANY & CO., New York City, which has had it displayed at several exhibitions and continuously at its shop in New York City (valued in 1978 at $7,000,000). It was first worn in 1957 at the Tiffany Ball at Newport, Rhode Island, by Mrs Sheldon Whitehouse, set in a necklace of white diamonds. It is now mounted in a clip of platinum with touches of gold, designed by JEAN SCHLUMBERGER.

Tiffany jewelry. Articles of jewelry made by TIFFANY & CO., including that made after 1848 under the founder Charles L. Tiffany and later under his son Louis Comfort Tiffany (1844-1933) and his several successor companies. The latter after 1892 made jewelry of Favrile glass and the various other types of glass developed by him; after he took over direction of the jewelry workshops in 1902, jewelry became a major part of the firm's business. In 1956 JEAN SCHLUMBERGER was engaged as Special Designer of jewelry, being given his own studio. The present Design Editor is John Loring, and the leading staff designers are Elsa Peretti (b. 1940), creator of 'Diamonds by the Yard' (gold chains interspersed with diamonds) and of jewels of ebony and ivory; Angela Cummings (b. 1944), featuring diamonds set in exotic varieties of wood; and, since 1979, Paloma Picasso (b. 1949).

Tiffany setting. A style of SETTING a SOLITAIRE in a finger ring, the stone being secured by prongs cut into a small tubular holder that is set into the SHANK of the ring so as to extend somewhat above the circumference, with the bent prongs extending slightly over the GIRDLE of the stone. This setting is usually used for a diamond or other transparent stone. It was introduced by Charles L. Tiffany in 1886. *See* TIFFANY & CO.

tiger's-claw jewelry. Articles of jewelry made of the curved tapering claws of a tiger, with gold tips and mounts and occasionally with gemstones. They were sometimes mounted in India and China, and were also mounted in England in the Victorian era, *c.* 1860-80, e.g. by JOHN BROGDEN. They have been mounted as pendants and as drops on ear-rings or necklaces. A necklace with about forty pendent tiger's claws was made in PRE-COLUMBIAN JEWELRY by the Mixtec Indians near Oaxaca, Mexico. Comparable jewelry was also made with vulture claws.

tiger's-eye. A variety of CAT'S-EYE (QUARTZ) that has originated from CROCIDOLITE (a fibrous variety of asbestos) which has partially changed its original greenish-blue colour, by oxidation of the iron pigment, into golden yellow before replacement by quartz. It has a silky LUSTRE and, when suitably cut EN CABOCHON, has a high degree of CHATOYANCY. Its source is near West Griquatown, north of the Orange River in South Africa. *See* HAWK'S-EYE.

tiki (Maori). A PENDANT of MAORI JADE carved by the Maoris in New Zealand in the form of a symbolic figure representing an ancestor, sometimes having eyes made of MOTHER-OF-PEARL. In Polynesian mythology Tiki was the first man, or the god said to have created the first man, hence regarded as an ancestor.

Timur Ruby. An unfaceted red SPINEL, once said to be the largest known red spinel, weighing 352.50 carats (but a red spinel in the Imperial Russian Crown is recorded as weighing 414.30 carats). Known in the East for 600 years as Khiraj-i-Alam ('Tribute of the World'), it was acquired by Timur (Tamerlane) upon the fall of Delhi in 1398, and after being owned successively by Timur's descendants, and then the Safavid rulers of Persia and the Mughal Emperors, it came into the possession of the East India Company in 1849 upon the annexation of the Punjab and was

Tiffany & Co. Ribbon necklace of platinum and gold with brilliant diamonds in *pavé* setting and star bezels. Design by Jean Schlumberger, 1977. Courtesy of Tiffany & Co., New York.

Tiffany diamond. Canary-yellow, cushion cut diamond, 128.50 carats, set in platinum and gold clip with diamonds. W. 6.25 cm. Design by Jean Schlumberger. Courtesy of Tiffany & Co., New York.

tiger's-claw jewelry. Necklace with tiger's claws and gold filigree ornaments. Chinese, *c.* 1860. Victoria & Albert Museum, London.

donated by it to Queen Victoria. It was shown in the Great Exhibition of 1851, but not identified until 1912 when it was recognized by the engraved inscriptions on it (which still include the names of several of its former owners, the inscribed names of other former owners having been removed). The stone is now mounted in a diamond necklace with other Indian red spinels and is kept in the Indian Room at Buckingham Palace, London. For a detailed history and the names and dates of the many owners, *see* G. F. Herbert Smith, *Gemstones* (1972), p. 239.

tinted gold. Articles of gold coloured by GILDING the surface to provide a different hue. It was done mainly in the 19th century to conceal repairs when a matching gold was not available or when necessary to conceal oxidation resulting from SOLDERING an article decorated with ENGRAVING or engine-turning where damage to the design might result from use of a bath of sulphuric acid.

tinting. The process of improving the colour of certain gemstones by painting the FACETS of the PAVILION. It is also used to improve the BRILLIANCE of some yellowish diamonds by painting the facets of the pavilion with violet dye which neutralizes the yellow and gives a water-white appearance. Stones so tinted are usually given a CLOSED SETTING so as to conceal the tint. The process has been used for centuries, especially in the 16th century before the introduction of the BRILLIANT CUT. Tinting is also used on some specimens of HYALITE (WATER OPAL) from Mexico.

Titania. A trade-name for SYNTHETIC RUTILE that was marketed in 1948. It has a very high degree of colour dispersion and resultant FIRE.

titanite. An alternative name for SPHENE.

titanium. A metallic element, discovered in 1789, that has been used mainly in industry because of its lightness, strength, and high melting point, but has in recent years been used in some jewelry, owing to the attractive range of colours that it acquires by being heated. The colours, depending on the degree of applied heat, include blue, pink, and brown, and they can be produced on limited areas or in designs. The disadvantages to its use include its hardness, limited ductility and malleability, difficulty to cut, and inability to be soldered, thus making it suitable mainly for articles made of components that can be fitted together.

toadstone. (1) A bufonite (derived from the Latin *bufo*, toad), i.e. a fossil consisting of the petrified tooth or palatal bone of a fish (a type of ray or shark), which was supposed in the Middle Ages to be found in the head or body of a toad and to indicate poison by perspiring and changing colour, and hence said to be an antidote to poison. Referred to by Shakespeare, *As You Like It*, II, i, and by Ben Jonson, *Volpone*, II, 5. Such stones were set in the BEZEL of some finger rings as an AMULET. Also called 'crapaud stone'. (2) A name given to certain lavas, e.g. in Derbyshire, England.

toe ring. A decorative type of ring worn on a woman's toe. Such pieces were worn as jewelry, set with gemstones, especially in France during the Empire period. Examples were also made of gold in ASHANTI JEWELRY; some pieces were decorated with zoomorphic subjects made IN THE ROUND by the CIRE PERDUE process.

toe stall. A sheath to cover a toe, such as the gold examples found on the Royal Mummy in the Tutankhamun tomb. A separate sheath covered each toe, with the details of the toenails and the first joints indicated by engraving.

toggle. (1) A type of straight pin used to fasten a garment. *See* DRESS PIN. (2) A pierced cross-piece or bead strung on a chain or necklace to tighten it and prevent it from slipping. *See* MELFORT NECKLACE; OJIME; BOLA.

Tolima jewelry. Articles of PRE-COLUMBIAN JEWELRY made in the Tolima region of Colombia, south-west of Bogotá, inhabited by the Panche and Pijao tribes. Most typical are the large (height, *c.* 10 to 22 cm) PECTORALS of gold or TUMBAGA, made by the Pijaos, in the form of stylized 'silhouette' anthropomorphic figures of cast and hammered flat

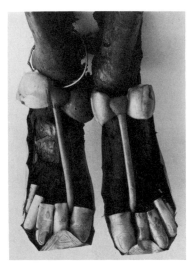

toe stalls. Gold with engraved details. Tomb of Tutankhamun. Photograph by Egyptian Expedition, Metropolitan Museum of Art, New York.

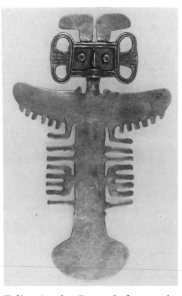

Tolima jewelry. Pectoral of cast and hammered gold. H. 17.7 cm. Museo del Oro, Bogotá.

sheet metal with angular arms and legs, sometimes a flat prolongation of
the spine as a sort of crescent-shaped tail, and sometimes FALSE FILIGREE
facial features. Some such pectorals were decorated with many
symmetrical openwork slits. Other articles were pendants of similar
silhouette form (sometimes strung on a necklace) in the form of fantastic
animals.

Toltec jewelry. Articles of PRE-COLUMBIAN JEWELRY made by the Toltec
Indians of central Mexico, from the 10th century until the conquest by
the Mayan Indians, *c.* 1116, when their capital, Tollán (present Tula,
Hidalgo), was destroyed. The Toltecs are credited with the discovery of
gold and silver in Mexico and the introduction of the use of metal. Their
workmanship included all of the processes of metalwork, especially
EMBOSSING designs on hammered sheet gold.

tomb jade. JADE that has been buried in a tomb and has acquired, from
proximity to bronze objects, an outer brownish or reddish skin. Such
effect is sometimes created by heating. *See* CHICKEN-BONE JADE.

tombac(k). An ALLOY consisting of copper and zinc (being various forms
of brass) used for making and GILDING cheap jewelry. When made as
FOIL, it is called DUTCH METAL or 'Dutch gold'.

tooth pendant. A type of pendant the main ornament of which is the
tooth of an animal, usually set in a metal collar with a suspensory ring.
Such pendants usually were worn as a AMULET, and have been found
mainly among peoples of ancient or primitive cultures. Examples are
known from the 7th century AD, found in Anglo-Saxon graves.

toothpick. A thin, pointed, instrument for removing particles of food
lodged between the teeth. Examples made of gold or silver were popular
in England during the Renaissance; some were enamelled or decorated
with gemstones, and were worn suspended from a NECK CHAIN. In Italy,
where toothpicks are still widely used, very ornate examples have been
made since the 15th century, sometimes having the head in the form of a
mermaid or other figure. A German example, 16th century, is in the
shape of a sickle. Some toothpicks have been made with an EAR-PICK at
the end opposite the point, and some have a toothpick and an ear-pick
joined by a swivel (*see* PASFIELD JEWEL). Modern examples made of gold
have the point retractable into a decorative case.

top and drop ear-ring. A type of ear-ring that has an upper ornament
suspended just below the lobe of the ear and then another ornament
(sometimes detachable, to be worn separately) attached as a drop. Such
ear-rings were popular in the 18th and 19th centuries.

topaz. A gemstone that is generally yellow, ranging from canary-yellow
to orange-yellow, but sometimes is colourless or of a wide range of other
hues, including pale blue, pale green, pink, golden-brown, and sherry-
brown. It is very hard but has strong CLEAVAGE and breaks easily; it has
double refraction, low dichroism and colour dispersion, and a vitreous
LUSTRE, and is pyroelectric. The topaz is often cut as a PENDELOQUE, but
sometimes mounted as MIXED CUT and some stones (especially when
colourless) are BRILLIANT CUT. The topaz is resembled by some other
gemstones, e.g. (1) the colourless variety, by DIAMOND, ROCK CRYSTAL,
and white CORUNDUM, (2) the yellow variety, by yellow SAPPHIRE
(sometimes miscalled 'Oriental topaz') and yellow QUARTZ (which, when
heated, is CITRINE, and sometimes called 'false topaz', 'Brazilian topaz' or
'Spanish topaz'), (3) the greenish-blue variety, by AQUAMARINE, and (4)
the pink variety, by TOURMALINE (especially pink RUBELLITE). Some
yellow topazes change colour by HEAT TREATMENT, e.g. the ROSE TOPAZ;
but quick heating can remove all colour. There is no commercial
synthetic topaz, but the term is sometimes applied to a coloured
SYNTHETIC CORUNDUM. Among the local misnomers that have been
applied to topaz is 'Brazilian ruby'. The name 'topaz' was for centuries
applied to a stone which was found on the Arabian Gulf island of
Topazos. *See* AQUAMARINE TOPAZ; BRAZILIAN TOPAZ; BRAGANZA STONE.

topazolite. A sub-variety of ANDRADITE (GARNET) that is yellow to
greenish-yellow and resembles in colour the yellow TOPAZ. It has been
recommended that the name be discarded in favour of 'yellow andradite'.

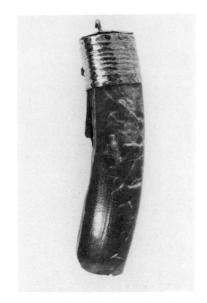

tooth pendant. Animal tooth set in
gold collar. Anglo-Saxon, 7th
century. L. 3.8 cm. British Museum,
London.

toothpick. Gold, set with diamonds
and rubies. Italian, 19th century.
Victoria & Albert Museum, London.

Tor Abbey Jewel. A pendant in the form of a MEMENTO MORI, being shaped as a coffin and made of gold with black CHAMPLEVÉ enamelled decoration. The coffin, when the lid is removed, reveals an ARTICULATED, white-enamelled skeleton. On the sides of the coffin is a devotional inscription. It was made in England, c. 1540–50, and was found at the site of Tor Abbey, Devonshire, England. A similar pendant, of inferior quality, is from Germany, 1st half of 17th century. See ADOLPHUS, GUSTAVUS, PENDANT.

Tor Abbey Jewel. Gold *memento mori* pendant, with enamelled decoration. English, *c.* 1560. Victoria & Albert Museum, London.

torc (or **torque**). A type of metal neck ring or ARMLET or, rarely, a girdle (*see* WESTMINSTER TORC; HARLECH TORC) in the shape of a PENANNULAR hoop, the terminals being in the form of ornaments of many forms and styles. Such pieces are generally associated with CELTIC JEWELRY, but an armlet (in the British Museum) of bent silver wire from Egypt, *c.* 1800 BC–1500 BC, has suggested possible early Asiatic sources. Examples are known from the La Tène culture, *c.* 5th/1st centuries BC, found mainly in eastern France; these are of solid cast bronze, almost undecorated except the hollow buffer or discoidal terminals (*see* BUFFER-TERMINAL TORC). Some have decoration in the WALDALGESHEIM STYLE, and some of the 2nd/1st centuries BC have terminals of a double-hour-glass style (*see* DOUBLE-HOUR-GLASS TORC). Among the examples found in Britain, at Ipswich, Suffolk, and Snettisham, Norfolk, from the British Later Bronze Age, 1st century BC, are some of gold alloy, made either as two circular bars twisted together or in rope-like style of twisted strands, and having ring or loop terminals, sometimes ornamented in relief or with engraving (*see* RING-TERMINAL TORC; LOOP-TERMINAL TORC). Examples found in Ireland from the Bronze Age are made from twisted rods or twisted flat metal strips (*see* RIBBON TORC). The torc, long regarded as the principal ornament of Celtic jewelry, has been mentioned by some writers as worn by Celtic warriors, but those that have been found in graves in England are around the necks of women and girls. It has been suggested that, in view of the precise weight of some examples (either alone or with some accompanying article as a makeweight), they may never have been made to be worn but were used as CURRENCY JEWELRY. See IRISH TORC; SNETTISHAM TORC; TWO-PIECE TORC.

toreutics. The process and art of decorating metalware, including gold and silver jewelry, by hammering, embossing, chasing, and other methods of doing relief work.

tortoise brooch. Viking bronze brooch, 10th century. L. 11.5 cm. Statens Historiska Museum, Stockholm.

tortoise brooch. A type of brooch that is oval and convex, in the form of the carapace of a tortoise, with characteristic markings. Such brooches were made of bronze, sometimes gilded, during the 9th/10th centuries. They are examples of VIKING JEWELRY, and have been discovered on female remains in burials in Sweden, Scotland, and France, worn as pairs on the bodies of the deceased.

tortoise shell. An organic material (not a shell) that is obtained, not from a tortoise, but from the overlapping horny top plates (called 'blades') covering the carapace (upper shell) of certain marine turtles, preferably the hawksbill turtle found off the West Indies and Brazil and the loggerhead turtle found near the Celebes. Such plates are translucent and of a dark-brownish colour marbled with yellow. A yellow (blond) variety is less often preferred; see YELLOW-BELLY. Tortoise shell can be moulded by heating (but excessive heat darkens the colour) and also thickened or enlarged by joining heated pieces under pressure. It has been used for inlaying (e.g. PIQUÉ and coulé decoration) and for making, since Roman days, various personal articles (e.g. COMBS) and pieces of jewelry (e.g. brooches, bracelets, ear-rings, bangles), including pieces carved as a CAMEO. Imitation tortoise shell is made from PLASTIC and stained HORN, but is identifiable by the smell from burnt samples or by microscopic examination which reveals in imitations an absence of small, spherical, reddish particles.

touchpiece. A coin formerly given by a British Sovereign (as late as Queen Anne, 1702–14) to a sick person whom he touched to heal him of scrofula (the 'King's evil') and sometimes suspended personally by the Sovereign around the recipient's neck. It was regarded as an AMULET, the magic power of which was supposed to be derived from the power of the King's touch to cure the ailment, hence its name.

touchstone. Generally, a black siliceous stone (usually basanite) related to flint that is used to test the purity of gold and silver by the streak left on the stone when rubbed by the metal. In recent years some other material is sometimes used for the purpose, the requirements being that it is black, harder than the metal to be tested, and finely grained, e.g. unglazed black basaltes made by Wedgwood.

toughness. The quality of a hard substance to resist being fractured by a blow or by being snapped. The toughness of a stone does not correspond to its HARDNESS. The converse of toughness is being BRITTLE.

tour à guillocher (French). *See* GUILLOCHÉ.

tourmaline. A gemstone that has a complicated and very varied chemical composition which, rather than internal impurities, accounts for its being found in a wide range of colours. The most common colour is black (SCHORL), but the transparent colourless variety (ACHROITE) is highly valued. The coloured varieties include blue, red, pink, green, brown, and yellow (with sometimes pink and green in the same crystal; *see* WATERMELON TOURMALINE), and are known as INDICOLITE, RUBELLITE, DRAVITE, and SIBERITE. Tourmaline shows strong dichroism, the effect being dependent on the manner of cutting, which is often MIXED CUT. Some specimens of all colours have fibrous INCLUSIONS and, when suitably cut, show CHATOYANCY (tourmaline CAT'S-EYE). The varieties can be readily distinguished from other stones of similar colours, e.g. yellow ZIRCON and green PERIDOT. Local misnomers that have been applied to tourmaline include 'Brazilian emerald', 'Brazilian peridot', 'Brazilian chrysolite', 'Brazilian sapphire', 'Ceylon chrysolite', and 'Ceylon peridot'. *See* NIGGERHEAD; CHROME TOURMALINE.

Toutin, Henri. Front of gold locket enamelled by Toutin, 1636. H. 4.4 cm. British Museum, London.

Toutin, Henri (1614–after 1683). The son of JEAN TOUTIN, who produced, at his workshops in Paris and Blois, enamelled gold plaques for WATCH-CASES and LOCKETS. One example, signed and dated 1636, consists of a gold locket bearing on the front and back covers and on the inside of one cover enamelled scenes, and on the inside of the other cover his signature and date. Another signed and dated example bears a miniature portrait of Charles I. These two are his earliest known dated and signed pieces. Another signed locket is datable *c.* 1640. He also made designs for finger rings.

Toutin, Jean (1578–1644). A renowned goldsmith and enameller of Châteaudun, France, who published in 1618–19 six plates with designs for WATCH-CASES and LOCKETS, to be enamelled in white reserved on black grounds, the patterns being scroll and leaf motifs and arabesques, and some in PEAPOD style. A new technique of PAINTED ENAMEL, attributed to Toutin, involved covering a gold or copper surface with an opaque monochrome (white, black or blue) background, over which was painted a design in opaque colours, fused at a lower temperature than the ground; the designs often depicted naturalistic flowers. No authenticated work by Jean Toutin is known to exist. He founded a school at Blois attended by his sons and by Jean Petitot. *See* HENRI TOUTIN; LOUIS TREIZE ENAMEL.

Towneley Brooch. Gold, with filigree decoration, enamelling, and pearls; probably 11th century. W. 5.6 cm. British Museum, London.

Towneley Brooch. A circular, gold brooch decorated with FILIGREE, having a central raised enamelled medallion within a circular gold band and with a border of 16 small roundels, alternate ones decorated with blue and green CLOISONNÉ enamel. The central medallion is decorated with a moline cross in blue on a green ground, with 4 small garnets at the centre. The gold band and the unenamelled roundels are each set with a small pearl. The brooch has been considered probably German (possibly Byzantine, French or Italian) and the enamelling probably Italian of the 11th century. It was acquired by the British Museum with the Towneley Collection in 1814 and is said to have been found in Scotland.

trace chain. A type of CHAIN that is composed of simple oval links of equal length which are linked alternately horizontally and vertically so that the chain can lie flat. There are a number of varieties, e.g. ALMA CHAIN, BARLEYCORN CHAIN, BELCHER CHAIN, DIAMOND TRACE CHAIN. Sometimes links of the trace-chain type are combined with the elongated links of a FETTER CHAIN.

tremblant. Hair ornament of gold with inset gemstones, 17th century. H. 8.7 cm. Hungarian National Museum, Budapest.

transichromatic. Having the property of changing colour temporarily, as when a diamond, after being in darkness, is brought into daylight and changes colour, but soon reverts to the original colour.

translucent. Permitting the passage of light but in a diffused manner so that objects behind cannot be distinctly seen. An example of a translucent gemstone is the MOONSTONE. *See* TRANSPARENT, OPAQUE.

transparent. Having the quality of transmitting light without diffusion, so that objects (even writing) behind can be distinctly seen. If semi-transparent, the object can be seen but blurred and indistinct. Most gemstones are transparent except when marred by FLAWS. Minerals that are TRANSLUCENT generally become transparent if cut sufficiently thin. *See* OPAQUE.

Transvaal jade. A local misnomer for a variety of massive green GROSSULAR which resembles JADE but from which it can be readily distinguished.

Transylvanian enamel. A technique of decoration in ENAMELLING that is a modification of CLOISONNÉ enamel. The design of floral motifs is made on the gold backplate of a piece by means of applied fine wire, and the enclosed design is filled in with enamels of appropriate colour. The range of colours used in the 16th century included blue, green, manganese, white, and yellow; later in the 17th century the enamels were painted over in various colours. The resulting appearance is of a design done by appliqué.

trap brilliant. A BRILLIANT that is STEP CUT.

trap cut. The same as STEP CUT.

trapeze cut. A style of cutting a diamond (or other transparent gemstone) so that the TABLE is in the shape of an isosceles trapezoid (a truncated isosceles triangle, with its longer parallel side being at the top), bordered by 4 narrow sloping FACETS, the 2 along the parallel sides being long isosceles trapezoids and the other 2 being of short trapezoid shape.

trapiche emerald. An unusual variety of EMERALD crystal found in 1964 in Colombia, South America, being a central hexagonal prismatic crystal from which radiate six dark spokes interspersed with white albite feldspar. The name is derived from a Spanish word meaning 'mill'. The clear emerald sections that form the spokes are cut as gemstones.

treacle. An oily-appearing streak visible within certain gemstones, especially HESSONITE.

treasure. A group of objects, sometimes including jewelry, buried for a purpose other than mere concealment (e.g. funerary objects) and later found in a tomb or cenotaph or in an excavated grave in a cemetery or tumulus (barrow), as distinguished from a HOARD, and usually serving as DOCUMENTARY SPECIMENS. Among important treasures that included jewelry are: AEGINA TREASURE; ALISEDA TREASURE; CARTHAGE TREASURE; CHILDERIC TREASURE; GUARRAZAR TREASURE; KERCH TREASURE; LAHUN TREASURE; LEUBINGEN TREASURE; LIMAVADY TREASURE; MONTE ALBÁN TREASURE; MYCENAE TREASURE; NYMPHAEUM TREASURE; OXUS TREASURE; PETROSSA TREASURE; QUIMBAYA TREASURE; SHIBARGHAN TREASURE; SIGSIG TREASURE; SUTTON HOO TREASURE; TROJAN TREASURE; UR TREASURE; VERGINA TREASURE; VIX TREASURE; X-GROUP TREASURE; ZIWIYE TREASURE; CENOTAPH, TREASURE OF THE. *See* NUBIAN JEWELRY; TUTANKHAMUN JEWELRY.

treated diamond. A diamond that has been treated by one of several modern scientific processes (e.g. exposure to radium bromide or bombardment with atomic particles, electrons or neutrons) which results in changing the colour to green or in some cases to blue or pink (on the surface or throughout, temporarily or permanently) and sometimes further changing to yellow or brown by applying heat. Some such processes leave the stones radioactive for varying periods of time. The early experiments of exposure to radiation were performed in 1904 by Sir

William Crookes, and some stones so treated by him are still radioactive, with the induced green colour unchanged. Few diamonds have been so treated, and they can be distinguished by various laboratory tests. Such diamonds are variously termed 'irradiated' (or 'radium-treated'), 'cyclotroned', 'electroned', 'neutron-treated', or 'pile treated'.

tree agate. A variety of AGATE similar to a MOSS AGATE but with the inclusions in a tree-like formation. *See* DENDRITE.

tremblant (French). A brooch, pendant, AIGRETTE or HAIR ORNAMENT decorated with a flower or other motif that has at the top stiff projecting wires (embellished with gemstones) that tremble when the piece is subjected to any movement. Sometimes the projections are finely coiled silver springs, such as were used in the 18th century, but some examples were made with tubular stems enclosing a strip of steel spring.

Tress, Order of the. An ORDER of knighthood founded in 1377 by Duke Albrecht III of Austria (1365-95) to honour the donor who had given him a tress of her hair to take on one of the Crusades. Its insigne was a collar in the form of a braided (plaited) tress. In the back of the curl there is a compartment for a relic or a token.

tresson. A head-dress in the form of a bandeau of network, usually embellished with gemstones.

Trewhiddle style. A style of decoration on ANGLO-SAXON JEWELRY of NIELLO on silver, so called after the HOARD of silver and coins (dating the deposit to *c.* 875) found in 1774 at Trewhiddle, near St Austell, Cornwall, England. The style, featuring animal motifs, dominated the decoration of Anglo-Saxon metalwork of the 9th and early 10th centuries. The use of silver, instead of the gold used in the 6th/7th centuries, is said to have been influenced by the quantities of Arab silver coins imported by the Vikings after exhaustion of the supply of Byzantine gold. *See* FULLER BROOCH; STRICKLAND BROOCH.

tribal jewelry. Articles worn by tribal peoples mainly in connection with tradition or ritual, not primarily as adornment or for reasons of artistry or value. Such articles include many OBJETS TROUVÉS. Unless they are made of or mounted in a precious metal or set with a gemstone, they are generally considered beyond the scope of this book. This applies to masks and to most ethnological objects of personal adornment, but not to such articles of precious metal and skilful workmanship as the pieces made as ASHANTI JEWELRY or BENIN JEWELRY, nor the sophisticated articles of PRE-COLUMBIAN JEWELRY or the skilfully made jewelry of some Indian tribes of the United States; *see* INDIAN (UNITED STATES) JEWELRY.

trilliant. A style of cutting a diamond in a rounded triangular shape, with 25 facets on the CROWN and 19 facets on the PAVILION, plus a POLISHED GIRDLE. It was developed by the firm of I. J. Asscher, of Amsterdam.

trilobite. A FOSSIL marine creature that lived in early geological periods and that has been mounted as decoration on some pieces of jewelry. Its flat, oval body, divided into three lobes crossed by many narrow furrows, was often 2 to 5 cm long.

Trinity Jewel. A gold MEDALLION (sometimes called a MORSE, but with no evidence of ever having had a clasp) with a scene in white ÉMAIL EN RONDE BOSSE depicting the Trinity encircled by the Crown of Thorns within which are four small angels. The piece is attributed to *c.* 1400, but the six-lobed frame may have been added in the 16th century. It has been reputed (without substantiation) to have been worn by Rodrigo Borgia (Pope Alexander VI, 1492-1503).

trinity ring. A type of finger ring in the form of three intertwined continuous strands carved out of one solid hoop of IVORY. The only known examples are three made by Stephen Zick, of Nuremberg, in the late 17th century.

triplet. A type of IMITATION GEMSTONE that is a COMPOSITE STONE made of three layers, two layers being of stone with an intervening layer at the

Tress, Order of the. Silver gilt collar, with (on the back at lower extremity) space for a relic. W. 19 cm. Steiermärkisches Landesmuseum, Johanneum (on loan from the Counts of Stubenberg), Graz, Austria.

Trinity Jewel. Gold and *émail en ronde bosse.* Burgundian, *c.* 1400 (frame possibly 16th century). W. 12.7 cm. National Gallery of Art (Widener Collection), Washington, DC.

triptych. Central onyx cameo, Italian, 13th century; side panels gold with translucent enamel. French, late 15th century. W. (closed) 5.7 cm. Cleveland Museum of Art (purchase from J.H. Wade Fund), Ohio.

triskelion brooch. Gold disc brooch with *cloisonné* triskelion motif and filigree decoration. Anglo-Saxon, 6th century. W. 4 cm. British Museum, London.

GIRDLE being coloured cement or gelatin that provides or enhances the colour. Some such stones have the outer layers of slices of the identical gemstone, e.g. EMERALD of pale colour, or BERYL (*see* SMARYLL), or ROCK CRYSTAL (*see* SOUDÉ EMERALD) or OPAL. In some cases the lower layer is an inferior stone or GLASS. A STAR SAPPHIRE triplet is sometimes made by having a star-stone of ROSE QUARTZ cut EN CABOCHON cemented over a layer of blue glass backed by a mirror (the mirror being needed because the star in rose quartz is seen only by reflected light). All such triplets are sometimes loosely referred to as a DOUBLET. *See* TRIPLEX OPAL; JADEITE TRIPLET.

triplex opal. A variety of TRIPLET made of two layers of OPAL, one of precious opal cemented over one of opal matrix, and having cemented over the top a dome of colourless QUARTZ, glass or plastic.

triptych. A picture or a carving made in three compartments that are hinged together side by side, some folding over each other completely, but more often with a central panel and two flanking panels half its size that fold over the central panel. Some, in contrast to large altar-pieces, were made small enough to be worn as a pendant. They were often decorated with enamelling depicting Biblical scenes or characters, and occasionally served as a RELIQUARY PENDANT. *See* DIPTYCH; ICON.

triskelion (or **triskele**). A decorative motif found on some pieces of jewelry that is composed of three branches, usually curved, that radiate and whirl from the centre, such as three human legs with bent knees (a symbol used in Sicily and the Isle of Man). *See* TRISKELION BROOCH.

Triskelion Brooch. A gold DISC BROOCH decorated with FILIGREE wire that frames a central Celtic TRISKELION motif consisting of three whirling arms in the form of birds' heads, at the centre of which is a boss set with a GARNET. The eyes of the animals are set with small gemstones cut EN CABOCHON. The brooch is Anglo-Saxon, 6th century, and was found at Faversham, in Kent, England.

triton pendant. A type of PENDANT in the form of a triton, the torso being a BAROQUE PEARL and the head, arms, and tail being enamelled gold set with gemstones, and having suspended pearls. One example, set with diamonds, rubies, and red stones, has been attributed probably to Spanish origin, *c.* 1590-1600, by an artist trained in south Germany. Another, formerly owned by Viscountess Lee of Fareham and sold at Christie's, London, is thought to have been designed and executed by BERNARDO BUONTALENTI; it is in the form of a bearded and helmeted triton, the breastplate being a baroque pearl and the other parts decorated with enamelling and graduated rubies. *See* BAROQUE PEARL JEWEL; CANNING TRITON JEWEL.

troida. A style of cutting a diamond that is a modern variation of the BRILLIANT CUT, but having 48 facets and being mainly used for MACLES. It was developed by Édouard Sirakiar, of Belgium.

Trojan Treasure. A TREASURE of jewelry excavated in 1873 by Dr Heinrich Schliemann (1822-90), at a Bronze Age site at Hissarlik, in present-day Asiatic Turkey (the ancient Troad), believed to have been the site of Troy. The Treasure has now been attributed to Troy II, *c.* 2500 BC-2200 BC, 1,000 years before Priam may be presumed to have lived. The so-called 'Treasure of Priam', as it was believed to be by Schliemann, includes finger rings, bracelets, PECTORALS, ear-rings, many beads, and especially two DIADEMS of intricate workmanship (one composed of 90 chains, some 38 cm long); most of the articles are made of gold, some being decorated with GRANULATED GOLD, and some made as openwork flowers decorated with LAPIS LAZULI and ROCK CRYSTAL. The treasure, over 8,000 pieces, was smuggled by Schliemann out of Turkey to Athens and later donated by him to the Berlin Museum for Early History, from where it is said to have been removed in World War II and never since found.

trophy jewel. A type of JEWEL that is decorated with various martial trophies. The trophy was originally the arms of a defeated enemy hung by the Greeks in an oak-tree to commemorate the victory; it became a decorative motif depicting martial trophies, including helmets, shields, swords, axes, drums, etc. An example is the badge of Duke Maximilian I of Bavaria (1573–1651) in the form of an enamelled breastplate with a flag and many projecting weapons; it is decorated with 245 faceted TABLE CUT diamonds and 6 large pear-shaped pearls, weighing together 410 grams. The reverse bears the Ducal emblem, an inscription, and the date MDCIII. The surviving bill states that it was made by the Augsburg goldsmith Georg Beuerl (Peyerl), and a painting of the Duchess Elizabeth shows it worn on her left sleeve. *See* NASEBY JEWEL.

trumpet pattern. A style of decoration found on some CELTIC JEWELRY of the La Tène culture of the pagan period and later of the Christian period. It is a spiral pattern in REPOUSSÉ work and is found on the back of the TARA BROOCH and the HUNTERSTON BROOCH, as well as some pieces in the LIMAVADY TREASURE.

tula work. A term used erroneously in the antique trade to designate certain articles (mainly snuff boxes) made at a number of Russian centres in the early 19th century with decoration with an ALLOY similar to NIELLO, and having as decorative motifs figures, flowers, geometrical forms, and sometimes maps. The term 'tula' strictly applies to an alloy of silver, copper, and lead that was made at Tula, in Russia, south of Moscow, and that was used in such work. *See* RUSSIAN JEWELRY.

Tumaco jewelry. Articles of PRE-COLUMBIAN JEWELRY made in the Tumaco region along the Pacific and extending across the border of present-day Colombia and Ecuador. The objects were made of gold and TUMBAGA, but also here of PLATINUM which was found in the local rivers. Some objects were made of almost pure platinum (e.g. nose ornaments); but usually the metal was mixed with gold dust and hammered (*see* SINTERING) into a composite mass, showing a change of colour to whitish or greenish-yellow, and when so used with gold it resulted in objects of contrasting colours.

tumbaga. An ALLOY of gold and copper (about four parts to one, with some accidental silver naturally in the gold) made and used by the Indians of the Andes, Central America, and Mexico for many articles of PRE-COLUMBIAN JEWELRY. It had a lower melting point and a greater hardness than either of the metals alone. It had a dull colour but was brightened, usually in limited areas to make a design, by use of heat and a mineral paste or a preparation of plant juices which removed the copper from the surface (*see* DEPLETION GILDING; DIFFERENTIAL PICKLING), and was sometimes further brightened by burnishing. Local terms for the metal were 'guanín gold', 'caricoli', and 'karakoli'.

tumbling. The process of shaping and POLISHING rough stones of inferior quality by mutual attrition, by spinning them in a revolving barrel together with water and first an abrasive and then polishing powder. The process was used from ancient times until the 1600s when FACETING was introduced; but in recent years tumbling has again come into use.

tumi (Peruvian Indian). A gold ritual knife made by the Inca Indians of Mexico, but the term is often applied also to the Chimú knife-like object made in the Lambayeque region of Peru. The latter was probably used for ceremonial rather than utilitarian or ornamental purposes, and is related to CHIMÚ JEWELRY in its method of production and style of decoration. The Chimú *tumi* is a flat knife-like object with a long handle vertical to a crescent-shaped blade (similar in shape to bronze knives made in Peru). Some are undecorated, but some examples are ornately decorated, with anthropomorphic figures incised on the handle and sometimes having at the top of the handle an elaborate decoration of a human or zoomorphic head cast in gold, with insets of turquoise and shell, and with dangling bird-like pendants said to be intended to reflect sunlight when swaying. On some pieces the handle is made of sections of gold and silver (*see* CASTING ON) in a chequerboard pattern. Gold pendants in similar form were made in COLOMBIAN JEWELRY.

tunjo (Colombian Indian). A small anthropomorphic votive figure (usually triangular) made by the Indians of the Muisca region of Colombia, always cast of gold or TUMBAGA, with the details of the features

triton pendant. Baroque pearl and enamelled gold, set with gemstones. Probably Spanish, *c.* 1590–1600. W. 7.6 cm. National Gallery of Art (Widener Collection), Washington, DC.

trophy jewel. Hat brooch, enamelled and set with gemstones by Georg Buerl, Augsburg, 1603. Schatzkammer, Residenz, Munich.

and apparel outlined in FALSE FILIGREE made by the wax threads on the models. The figures depict an individual in some routine occupation, but a few examples show groups in a genre scene. Such pieces were used as an offering to the gods, to propitiate or thank them, by being thrown into the sacred Lake Guatavita or buried in a funerary pot. Pilgrims to the lake used them in such large quantity that they were made in the Muisca region by a mass production method, using a stone MATRIX with the design carved on it for stamping many wax models for casting. The pieces were usually dull and roughly finished, perhaps because the subject matter was more important than the workmanship, but also because Muisca goldsmiths did not coat their wax models with charcoal and water to provide a smooth casting. The most remarkable piece is a gold representation, made of MUISCA JEWELRY, of a ceremonial raft used by each 'El Dorado' upon his installation, showing him and other figures (*see* COLOMBIAN JEWELRY).

tunjo. Cast tumbaga votive figurine holding lime flask and lime dipper. Muisca style, H. 7.9 cm. Museo del Oro, Bogotá.

tupilaq. A figure representing a weird mythical creature believed by Greenlanders to be sent to destroy enemies. Such figures were carved out of the curved pointed and conical teeth of the sperm whale, and worn or carried as an AMULET. *See* ESKIMO JEWELRY.

turban ornament. A decorative jewel worn affixed to the front of a turban by men in the Levant and in India, and generally by Moslems. Such pieces are often in the form of a gold feather, ornately decorated with gemstones, but examples exist in many shapes and styles. *See* GIKA OF NADIR SHAH.

turquoise. A gemstone that is bluish, greenish-blue or greyish-green, but the best quality is uniformly intensely sky-blue; some less valuable specimens are speckled with LIMONITE or with dark markings from the surrounding MATRIX (called 'rock turquoise'). Turquoise is usually opaque, hence often cut EN CABOCHON, but occasionally faceted; some flat pieces are engraved in Eastern countries with gilt characters. During the 19th century brooches and pendants were often set in pavé style (*see* PAVÉ SETTING) with small cabochon turquoises; and turquoises are often used as inlay to decorate silver jewelry in Mexico, Tibet, and Iran (*see* BEDOUIN JEWELRY), and some made by American Indians. Turquoise has a waxy LUSTRE and takes a high polish. It is porous and sometimes discolours, especially from grease; hence it is often protected with a plastic film. It shows double refraction. Some deeply coloured stones become pale when exposed to sunlight and lose value; the colour can be temporarily restored (and sometimes is, to promote sales) by burying the stone in damp earth or by immersion in ammonia. Pale turquoise is sometimes stained dark blue, but this can be detected by a drop of ammonia (turning it greenish) or by a surface scratch. Sometimes good-quality turquoise that retains its colour is called 'old rock turquoise', and an inferior grade 'new rock turquoise'. Turquoise was formerly called 'Turkish stone' (not actually from Turkey, but Persian stones shipped from there), hence the present name from the French *pierre turquoise*. The main sources for centuries have been the Sinai Peninsula and the Nishapur region of Iran (Persia). Some other stones resemble turquoise, e.g. ODONTOLITE, LAZULITE, HAÜYNE, SODALITE, VARISCITE, and WARDITE; and CHALCEDONY and HOWLITE are sometimes dyed blue to imitate it, as are glass and IVORY. A RECONSTRUCTED STONE is made by bonding small pieces of true turquoise. A plastic imitation of low density is now being made. *See* VIENNESE TURQUOISE; SYNTHETIC TURQUOISE; CHALCHUITE.

turquoise matrix. The brown-veined stone in which TURQUOISE is found and with which the turquoise is sometimes cut as a gemstone. *See* LIMONITE.

turritella agate. A variety of AGATE that has INCLUSIONS of masses of small shells of turritella (a snail-like mollusc having an elongated spiralling shell). It is found in Wyoming (USA). It is sometimes polished by TUMBLING and made into articles of jewelry.

turban ornament. Mughal, 17th/18th centuries. Victoria & Albert Museum, London.

turtle-back pearl. (1) A type of BLISTER PEARL that has a rather high dome or a surface that is uneven, resembling the carapace (upper shell) of a turtle. (2) A pearl from the variety of clam known as a turtle-back clam.

Tutankhamun jewelry. Objects photographed by Egyptian Expedition, The Metropolitan Museum of Art, New York:

cobra amulet. Thin sheet gold embossed and chased. H. 11.5 cm.

heart scarab (reverse). Black resin scarab mounted on gold plate; polychrome glass with figure of heron mounted on back. W. 3.45 cm.

Tuscany Diamond. The same as the FLORENTINE DIAMOND, also called the 'Austrian Yellow Diamond'.

Tutankhamun jewelry. Articles of jewelry found in the tomb of Tutankhamun, King of Egypt, *c.* 1339 BC-1329 BC, when discovered and excavated in 1922 by the 5th Earl of Carnarvon (1866-1923) and Howard Carter (1873-1939). The king's mummy, in a triple gold coffin in the burial chamber, was adorned with a MASK, DIADEM, breastplate, necklaces, finger rings, TOE STALLS, and ear-rings, all of gold, in addition to which there were many funerary objects never worn but interred for the after-life and for amuletic purposes. Many of the pieces have engraved or openwork decoration and are inlaid with EGYPTIAN FAIENCE or with varicoloured glass in imitation of turquoise, jasper, and lapis lazuli. The decoration includes representations of religious significance, such as deities or the vulture, falcon, heron or cobra, as well as the UDJAT EYE, SHEN, ANKH, SCARAB, MENET BIRD, and URAEUS. Almost all of the treasure was claimed by and is owned by the Egyptian Museum, Cairo. *See* SHEBU; DEITY AMULET; RESIN.   [*Plate XIII*]
—— *cobra amulet.* An AMULET representing a cobra in repose, made of sheet gold that is embossed and chased. At the back is a hole for a suspensory string. Its amuletic significance is unknown.
—— *diadem.* A gold DIADEM in the form of a circlet, to the front of which is fastened a detachable ornament having the gold head of a vulture and the body of a curved cobra, the cobra being inlaid with LAPIS LAZULI, EGYPTIAN FAIENCE, CORNELIAN, and glass. The ornament symbolizes the unification of

diadem. Gold with vulture's head and *uraeus* at front and suspended streamers. W. 17.5 cm.

vulture collar. Flexible gold wings of 250 sections inlaid with polychrome glass; talons grasping inlaid *shen* symbols. Attached counterweight worn on back. W. 48 cm.

Tutankhamun jewelry

ear-studs. Gold with hybrid birds (glass duck heads and inlaid falcon wings) and suspended gold and blue beads. W. 5.2 cm.

falcon pectoral. Gold with coloured stone inlays; talons grasping *shen* symbols. W. 12.6 cm.

tweezer. Hammered sheet gold. Valle del Cauca, Colombia. H. 4.1 cm. Museo del Oro, Bogotá.

Lower and Upper Egypt, *c.* 3100 BC. At the back of the band are a gold bow-knot ending in streamers and gold appendages ending with a cobra head.

—— *ear-studs.* An elaborate pair of EAR-STUDS from the shank of each of which is suspended a figure of a hybrid bird with gold CLOISONNÉ body, having the wings of a falcon and the head of a duck. The wings curve upward to form a circle and the talons hold the SHEN symbol of eternity. The heads are composed of translucent blue glass, and the wings and body are inlaid with QUARTZ, CALCITE, EGYPTIAN FAIENCE, and multicoloured glass. Extensions downward from the tails are composed of strands of gold and blue inlay. The studs each consist of two buttons attached to short tubes that fit one into the other. The front button is of glass covering a portrait of the King, made of particles of fused glass.

—— *falcon pectoral.* A PECTORAL in the form of a falcon that was the symbolic representation of the sun-god Ra. It is made of inlays of LAPIS LAZULI, TURQUOISE, CORNELIAN, and light-blue glass, with an eye that is probably OBSIDIAN. On the underside the details are chased in gold. The bird holds in each talon the SHEN symbol.

—— *heart scarab.* The HEART SCARAB found suspended by a strap and placed over the navel of Tutankhamun. It is made of black RESIN, has on the back an inlaid figure of a heron (in Egyptian, *benu*, a deified bird), and an atypical inscription seeking the restoration of his life.

—— *vulture collar.* A flexible gold collar representing the vulture-goddess Nekhbet, with extended wings divided into 250 small cells set with varicoloured glass in imitation of TURQUOISE, JASPER, and LAPIS LAZULI. The beak and the eye are set with OBSIDIAN, and the talons grasp the SHEN symbol. A floral-shaped ornament hung as a counterpoise down the back of the mummy. The vulture was worn on the King's chest, being 48 cm wide.

tweezer. A depilatory tweezer of which examples are found in PRE-COLUMBIAN JEWELRY, some in CALIMA JEWELRY from Colombia and some in PERUVIAN JEWELRY. Such articles are sometimes in the form of a simple unadorned bent-over strip of metal (about 4 to 9.5 cm long), with the terminals extended in a crescent shape; but some ornate examples have the front arm in the form of an anthropomorphic figure wearing a diadem, earrings, and nose ornament.

twentieth-century cut. The same as the JUBILEE CUT.

twin-bezel ring. The same as a SPLIT RING.

twisted rope ring. A type of finger ring made of gold in the form of a band of twisted rope, sometimes two or more such bands making a wide HOOP. On some examples the bands are not parallel and adjacent but are spread apart to form loops above and below the central band, and occasionally a band is wound diagonally around a plain hoop. Some similar rings are made with twisted strands of gold wire.

two-piece torc. A type of TORC that is in the form of a complete hoop rather than the usual PENANNULAR ring, having a detachable segment that is about one-sixth to one-eighth of the total circumference and that is attached to the larger portion by mortise-and-tenon joints. Such torcs, made of bronze, and sometimes decorated in WALDALGESHEIM STYLE, have been found only in Champagne, France, and were worn there by high-ranking women; they are of the Early La Tène culture, *c.* 4th century BC.

U

Udjat (or **Wedjet**) **eye.** An Egyptian symbolic motif in the form of a human eye and eyebrow, usually the right eye (representing the sun), sometimes the left (representing the moon). The eye usually symbolizes the eye lost by Horus and then restored and given to his father, Osiris, to restore him to life (the word *udjat* meaning 'sound' or 'healthy'), but in some pieces it symbolizes the eye of the sun-god Ra. The Udjat eye was the Egyptian AMULET next most popular after the SCARAB. One example among the TUTANKHAMUN JEWELRY, an eye of Ra, is exceptionally made entirely of blue EGYPTIAN FAIENCE, instead of the more usual inlaid gold or ELECTRUM.

Uncle Sam Diamond. A colourless diamond, weighing 40.23 carats rough, that was found in 1924 in Murfreesboro, Arkansas, and is the largest diamond found in North America. It was cut in the same year by Schenck & Van Haele, New York, into an EMERALD CUT weighing 12.42 carats. It was acquired in 1971 by Sidney De Young, a Boston diamond dealer, and is now owned by B. Beryl Peiken, New York City.

unicorn horn. The tusk of the Arctic male narwhal whale, being long, pointed, and having a twisted appearance, resembling the horn of the fabled unicorn. Hence it was considered in the Middle Ages and the Renaissance to be a 'unicorn horn', and it, or objects made from it, had alleged magical powers or great mystical significance. The most renowned example is the *Ainkhürn*, the complete tusk (length, 2.43 m) that has been treasured since 1564 as an inalienable heirloom of the Habsburgs and is now in the Schatzkammer in Vienna. *See* NARWHAL IVORY.

union pin. A type of pin, worn in the Victorian era, made in two sections, one the pointed pin and the other an ornament with a socket into which the point is secured.

unit-constructed jewelry. A modern type of inexpensive jewelry that is made by joining several items of prefabricated parts to develop a pattern, rather than using parts made expressly for the predetermined pattern. Many small identical units are used in the same piece, usually to make a symmetrical design. The units are generally pieces made by refiners, such as rings, lengths of wire or tube, and sheets of metal (called 'grids') with perforations to develop a design. The units are joined by wire or by SOLDERING or RIVETING.

Ur Treasure. A TREASURE of SUMERIAN JEWELRY and other objects found at the site of the ancient Sumerian city of Ur in southern Mesopotamia (now Muqqayit, in southern Iraq). It was identified as the Biblical 'Ur of the Chaldees' in 1854 by J. E. Taylor, the British Consul at Basra, and excavations between 1922 and 1924 led by Sir C. Leonard Woolley revealed the Royal Tombs, including that of Queen Pu-abi from *c.* 2500 BC. The tombs contained many varieties of jewelry, made of gold and set with gemstones, on the body of the Queen and her royal retinue buried in ceremonial costume. The jewelry included many objects decorated with naturalistic representations of animals, stylized flowers with up to 13 petals, and geometric motifs, including objects with FILIGREE and GRANULATED GOLD. *See* Sir C. Leonard Woolley, *Ur Excavations*.

uraeus. The representation of the sacred cobra affixed to the front of the head-dress of Egyptian rulers just above the forehead; it was a symbol of sovereignty. It is found on some SPHINX BEADS from Egypt, XIIth Dynasty

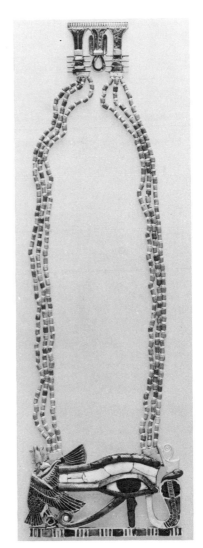

udjat eye. Gold inlaid with glass and gemstones, suspended from necklace with gold inlaid counterweight. W. 9.5 cm. Tomb of Tutankhamun. Photograph by Egyptian Expedition, Metropolitan Museum of Art, New York.

(*c.* 2035 BC–1991 BC) to XVth Dynasty, but some composed of four gold wire loops curving across the top of the head were characteristic of the reign of Sesostris I, *c.* 1800 BC–1788 BC. The *uraeus* occurs on several pieces among the TUTANKHAMUN JEWELRY. *See* EGYPTIAN JEWELRY.

Ural(ian) emerald. A local misnomer for the emerald-green DEMANTOID (ANDRADITE variety of GARNET). Other misnomers for the same stone are 'Ural(ian) olivine' and 'Ural(ian) chrysolite'.

Urartian belt. A type of wide belt from Urartu (the Assyrian name for a region in Turkey and Armenia), the Biblical Ararat, a kingdom which flourished in the 9th century BC and until it was destroyed in the 6th century BC. Many such belts are known. They were made from a bronze INGOT, rolled and cut, and decorated in REPOUSSÉ style by tooling from the front and reverse with animal motifs and some human figures. The belts were backed with a leather strip and have a fastening clasp. They were worn encircling a woollen robe or shirt or sometimes as part of armour. They are of various sizes and in width range from 5 cm to 16 cm. *See Boston [Mass.] Museum Bulletin*, vol. 75, 1977, p. 27.

Urartian belt. Bronze belt with repoussé decoration, 7th century BC. W. 10.2 cm; L. 97 cm. Museum of Fine Arts (Egyptian Curators Fund), Boston, Mass.

utahlite. A variety of gemstone that is the same as VARISCITE and is found in Utah (USA). It resembles TURQUOISE. It was initially named 'utahite' but as that is the name of another mineral, it has been recommended that it be discarded for this stone.

V

Vallum diamond. A local misnomer for QUARTZ that is found in the Tanjore district of Madras, India.

Van Cleef & Arpels. A leading French jewelry firm, founded in 1906 by Julien, Louis, and Charles Arpels and their brother-in-law Alfred van Cleef, all descendants of jewellers and diamond dealers. Its main shop is at 22 Place Vendôme, Paris, and it has branches in London, New York City, and fashionable resorts, catering for a clientele seeking jewelry of original design and high quality. In 1930 it created the first *minaudière*, the name being trade-marked by it. The management, which now includes the three sons of Julien Arpels, Claude, Jacques, and Pierre, has opened boutiques for less expensive articles and for watches. *See* FARAH DIBA CROWN.

Vargas, President, Diamond. A diamond discovered in Minas Gerais, Brazil, in 1938, weighing rough 26.60 carats, being the sixth largest known diamond. It is of the purest WATER except for yellowish tinges on two edges. It was named after Dr Getulio Dornelles Vargas, President of Brazil. It was bought in 1939 by HARRY WINSTON and cut in 1941 into 23 stones of which 8 of the largest, ranging from 17 to 48.26 carats each, were EMERALD CUT. The largest, retaining the name, was reported in 1961 to be owned by Mrs Robert W. Windfohr, of Fort Worth, Texas.

variscite. A variety of gemstone that usually is opaque, and is apple-green to bluish-green. It sometimes has brown veins, and sometimes WARDITE 'eyes'. It has a VITREOUS LUSTRE and takes a good polish; it is sometimes cut EN CABOCHON to be set in jewelry. It resembles CHRYSOPRASE and TURQUOISE. Its original source was Variscia (Vogtland), Germany (hence its name). *See* UTAHLITE.

Vasters, Reinhold (fl. 1853–90). A German goldsmith who worked as a restorer at the Aachen Cathedral Treasury and who had his own workshop. He is known to have made for his workshop drawings of a large number of pieces of Renaissance-style art objects (a collection of 1,079 such drawings has been given to the Victoria & Albert Museum), some of which depicted pendants (including one similar to the CHARITY PENDANT). He is said to have made a number of jewelled objects similar to his drawings with the intent that he or his purchasers would sell them as Renaissance articles. Pieces similar to the drawings are in a number of museums and collections and have been considered as of Renaissance workmanship until revealed in 1979 as made or restored by Vasters. A gold and jewelled agate bowl sold at Christie's, New York, on 28 March 1979 for £30,000 is the first piece sold with an attribution to him; and pendants and other pieces of jewelry from the Viscount Astor Collection were sold, attributed probably to him, at Christie's, London, on 27 November 1979. *See* Charles Truman, 'Reinhold Vasters', in *Connoisseur*, March 1979, p. 154.   *[Plate XIV]*

Vauquer, Jean (fl. 1670-1700). A French jewelry designer, engraver, and enameller who was a pupil of Morlière at Orléans and who worked at Blois between 1670 and 1700. He published in 1680 a book of jewelry designs that featured flowers and ornamental foliage, including the PEAPOD style, and was outstanding as an enameller and noted for his naturalistic flowers.

Vauxhall glass. A type of black GLASS that was used to imitate JET. Pieces made of it were usually mounted in japanned black metal frames.

Venado Beach Treasure. Articles of PRE-COLUMBIAN JEWELRY and other objects discovered accidentally in the late 1940s in a cemetery of an ancient Indian settlement near the Canal Zone of Panama as a result of excavations by United States soldiers from nearby Fort Kobbe, and excavated in 1951 by the Peabody Museum of Harvard University. The articles include superb gold breastplates, bracelets, pendants, and beads, and especially some cast three-dimensional effigy figures entirely of lacy openwork filigree made by means of very thin wax threads laid over a core removed before casting. The find has been attributed to COCLÉ JEWELRY of the 10th century AD. *See* PANAMANIAN JEWELRY.

venera (Spanish). A type of jewel worn in Spain, including the badges of the Spanish religious confraternities worn by members throughout the 17th century, such as the Order of Santiago de Compostela. One jewelled example is in the form of a gold openwork monogram 'M R', for the Virgin Mary, crowned above the monogram and set with gemstones.

venera. Gold openwork monogram pendant, set with table-cut emeralds forming the monogram of the Virgin Mary, with crown above and rosette below. Spanish, late 17th century. H. 9.3 cm. British Museum, London.

Venetian pearl. *See* IMITATION PEARL.

Venus Marina. A BAROQUE PEARL JEWEL depicting Venus Marina (after the marble statue 'Fortuna' by Giambologna) in ÉMAIL EN RONDE BOSSE standing on a dolphin whose body is a BAROQUE PEARL, with decoration in enamelling and gemstones. Its maker or even its country of origin has not been established, but a Flemish master at Vienna or Prague has been suggested as possible. *See* Yvonne Hackenbroch, 'Jewellery in the Style of Giambologna', in *Connoisseur*, September 1978, p. 34.

Venus's-hair stone. The same as RUTILATED QUARTZ.

Vergina Treasure. A TREASURE discovered in 1977-8 at the village of Vergina, near Salonika (ancient Thessalonika), in Macedonia, northern Greece, by Professor Manolis Andronikos, of the University of Salonika. The treasure, dating from *c.* 350 BC, was found under a tumulus in tombs which are believed by the finder to be those, *c.* 336 BC, of Philip of Macedon, father of Alexander the Great, and perhaps of his second wife, Cleopatra. Among the many gold articles found are a magnificent DIADEM of delicate flowers (on one of which is a golden fly), a circular regal head-band, two oak-leaf WREATHS, a woman's PECTORAL, and a man's breastplate, as well as many silver, bronze, and gilded vases, weapons, etc. The treasure now belongs to the Museum of Salonika, and in 1980 was exhibited in the United States.

vermeil. (1) Gilded silver, i.e. sterling silver covered with a layer of gold by plating or by other process. (2) A vermilion, or orange-red, colour exhibited by some gemstones, e.g. some GARNETS. (3) An orange-red garnet.

Vever. Pendant, gold with enamelling and gemstones. Maison Vever, Paris, 1901. H. 9.5 cm. Schmuckmuseum, Pforzheim, Germany.

Verneuil furnace. A type of blowpipe (*chalumeau*) invented by the French chemist Auguste Victor Louis Verneuil (1856–1913), with which he first made SYNTHETIC RUBIES. His results were published in 1904. The apparatus is used today (sometimes in banks of several hundred units) to make synthetic varieties of CORUNDUM and other SYNTHETIC GEMSTONES; but other processes have been developed that are used less frequently, e.g. hydrothermal, flux fusion, and Czochralski processes. The Verneuil process is sometimes referred to as 'flame fusion'.

verre églomisé (French). A style of decorating glass on the back by applying GOLD LEAF (occasionally SILVER LEAF, or both) and then engraving it with a fine needle point, but without firing the piece. As the work would readily rub off and was not durable, it was applied on the reverse of the surface to be viewed and then protected by a layer of varnish or metal foil or another sheet of glass. Sometimes there is supplemental background decoration in black or colour where the foil has been removed. The term is derived from the name of the 18th-century French writer, artist, and art dealer Jean-Baptiste Glomy (d. 1786) who used the process extensively, although it had been developed in ancient times and used on articles by the Egyptians and Romans (called *fondi d'oro*) and in Bohemia (called *Zwischengoldglas*). It is found mainly on glassware, but glass plaques so decorated are found on some gold snuff boxes and also on some jewelry made in Spain in the 16th and 17th centuries (e.g. some RELIQUARIES) and in Italy.

verroterie cloisonnée (French). The same as CLOISONNÉ INLAY.

vesuvianite. The same as IDOCRASE. It was first found near Mt Vesuvius, hence the name.

Vever, Maison. A leading Parisian jewelry firm founded in 1821 at Metz by Paul Vever who was joined by his eldest son Ernest in 1848. Ernest moved to Paris after France lost Alsace-Lorraine in 1871, and acquired the jewelry business, founded in 1850, of Marrett et Baugrand, formerly owned by Paul Marrett (d. 1853) and Gustave Baugrand (d. 1870). Ernest's sons, Paul II (1851–1915) and Henri (1854–1942), inherited the business in 1874; their work was mainly in ART NOUVEAU style, of which Henri was the foremost exponent after RENÉ LALIQUE. The firm won many awards at international exhibitions, and Henri wrote the leading history of French 19th-century goldwork and jewelry. The firm produced many busts carved in gemstones, embellished with elaborate enamelled and jewelled ornamentation. In 1904 the business was moved to its present location at 14 rue de la Paix, and in 1915 the management was taken over by the sons of Paul II, André and Pierre. Some of the firm's finest pieces were designed by Eugène Grasset (1841–1917).

vibrating jewelry. *See* TREMBLANT.

Victoria, Queen, Commesso. A COMMESSO style CAMEO brooch depicting the young Queen Victoria in robes of state and wearing the royal circlet made for George IV in 1820. The head and shoulders are cut from 'bull's-mouth' SHELL, and the robes are of gold, enamelled in black and white to simulate ermine; the ribbon and tassel are of chased gold, the Collar of the Garter is of gold set with gemstones, and the circlet is of silver. On the back is scratched 'Paul Lebas/Graveur/1851/Paris'; it has been presumed that the piece was made in France, for the Great Exhibition of 1851, by an artist working for F. Dafrique.

Victoria–Transvaal Diamond. A champagne-coloured diamond weighing 67.89 carats. When found in the Premier Mine, Transvaal, South Africa, in 1950, it weighed rough 240 carats. It was cut in 1950, by Baumgold Brothers of New York City, as a pear-shaped stone with 116 facets. It is set in a yellow-gold necklace, containing 108 other diamonds together weighing 44.67 carats, donated in 1977 by Leonard and Victoria Wilkinson to the Smithsonian Institution, Washington, DC, together with several other important diamond-set jewels.

Victoria-Transvaal Diamond. Pear-shaped diamond, 67.89 carats, set as necklace pendant. Smithsonian Institution, Washington, DC.

Victorian cut. A style of cutting a diamond during the Victorian era that was a modification of the BRILLIANT CUT, having relatively a smaller TABLE, larger CULET, and greater depth than the standard cut.

Victorian jewelry. Articles of jewelry made in the United Kingdom during the reign of Queen Victoria, but not all of the many varieties produced there during her long reign, 1837–1901, are now generally so classified. The pieces now usually called Victorian include brooches and link bracelets made of gold and decorated with enamelling and inexpensive gemstones (especially garnets) in a wide variety of styles; pendants and brooches decorated with imported coral, tortoise shell, ivory, mosaic, and seed pearls; fans; SPORTING JEWELRY; SCOTTISH JEWELRY; HAIR JEWELRY and other types of sentimental jewelry; ALBERT CHAINS; finger rings; and such special items as REVERSE INTAGLIO CRYSTALS. During the early years of the reign, some jewelry was made in Gothic and Renaissance styles; the middle period saw the vogue for ostentatious jewels decorated with the greatly increased supply of pearls and South African diamonds; and then, after the death of Prince Albert, in 1861, the increased popularity of sombre MOURNING JEWELRY. The 19th century saw a revival of interest in ARCHAEOLOGICAL JEWELRY, influenced by the excavations at Pompeii and the high-quality reproductions made by the Castellanis (*see* CASTELLANI, FORTUNATO PIO), Carlo Giuliano (*see* GIULIANO FAMILY), and GIACINTO MELILLO, and the work of JOHN BROGDEN. Much jewelry was brought back by travellers as souvenirs, especially from India and Japan from *c.* 1850, and this was imitated in England during the 1860s to the 1880s. Gradually large pieces of jewelry were supplanted in the 1880–90s by smaller articles, and the production of inexpensive silver jewelry and novelty COSTUME JEWELRY flourished. Toward the end of the century reaction set in under the influence of the Arts and Crafts Movement, despite which an interest developed in pieces of ART NOUVEAU style. *See* Charlotte Gere, *Victorian Jewellery Design* (1972), and Margaret Flower, *Victorian Jewellery* (1973).

[*Plate XV*]

Viking jewelry. Silver brooches and buckles, 8th/10th centuries. Schleswig-Holsteinisches Landesmuseum, Schleswig.

Viennese turquoise. (1) A misnomer for an imitation of TURQUOISE made by grinding together, heating, and compressing a mixture of MALACHITE, aluminium hydroxide, and phosphoric acid. (2) A misnomer for coloured GLASS in imitation of turquoise.

Viking jewelry. Articles of jewelry made by the Vikings (Norsemen) in Scandinavia during the 5th to 10th centuries, in the Viking Age. The Viking warriors made many raids on the coasts of Europe and the British Isles, and most of the earlier finds of jewelry in Scandinavia are of Greek, Roman or Celtic origin, having been imported by the far-ranging traders. Local work of the 5th/6th centuries shows little artistry except for two gold necklaces of the 6th century (*see* ÅLLEBERG COLLAR). From the 8th century new techniques were developed, including CHIP-CARVING on silver and REPOUSSÉ and NIELLO work on gold. The decoration was often with zoomorphic motifs, sometimes in high relief or IN THE ROUND, sometimes in very stylized form. The extant examples, mostly found in graves, include brooches, TORCS, and BRACTEATES. The main styles of decoration included those known as BORRE, JELLINGE, and RINGERIKE. A number of examples of Viking jewelry have been discovered in the British Isles. *See* David Wilson and O. Klindt-Jensen, *Viking Art* (1966). *See* TORTOISE BROOCH; BOX BROOCH; DISC BROOCH; 'THOR'S HAMMER' BROOCH; HEDEBY TREASURE.

Villanovan fibula. A type of FIBULA of ETRUSCAN JEWELRY from the Villanovan culture that prevailed in northern and central Italy in the 8th/7th centuries BC. At the foot there is a large oval plate set at right angles to the BOW, often with one or two transverse ornaments between the plate and the bow. Some are elaborately decorated with GRANULATED GOLD and REPOUSSÉ work, and some with engraved designs.

vinaigrette. A small receptacle to contain scented vinegar, formerly used by ladies to ward off faintness. The usual type was globular or cuff-shaped, made of gold, silver or porcelain, with a metal grille (of gold, silver or PINCHBECK) under the stopper or hinged lid to hold a sponge saturated with the scented substance; often they had an attached chain so as to be suspended from a bracelet, CHATELAINE or finger ring (such as one worn by Queen Victoria). Some examples have a LOCKET at the bottom, and rare examples are in the form of a small powder horn (sometimes called a 'bugle') with a built-in whistle. Vinaigrettes were made in France, Switzerland, and England.

vinaigrette. Gold, with enamelled decoration. W. 2.5 cm. City Museums and Art Gallery, Birmingham, England.

Virgin Mary's Ring. Onyx bangle, suspended from jewelled crown. Cathedral of San Lorenzo, Perugia.

violan(e). A variety of DIOPSIDE that is translucent to opaque, and violet-blue. It is used for beads, but seldom in jewelry.

Virgin Mary's Ring. A finger ring made of ONYX that is venerated at the Cathedral of Perugia, Italy, as having been worn by the Virgin Mary at her marriage to St Joseph. The ring, said to have been brought to the Cathedral in 1472, is kept suspended from a jewelled crown that hangs in a gilded silver tabernacle made in the early 16th century. A ring at the Ashmolean Museum, Oxford, has an attached sealed certificate dated 1764 attesting that it is a true replica.

'virtuous' stone. Any gemstone (or the TOADSTONE) that was formerly regarded as having protective or curative powers, either medically or psychologically, by reason of its alleged magical powers as a stone, without regard to the stone being a precious stone or even a rare stone, or to the setting (some inferior stones of this kind were set in superior-quality finger rings). Various stones were considered to be efficacious against certain specific ailments or types of accident. Such beliefs were especially prevalent during the Middle Ages. *See* MAGICAL STONES; MAGICAL JEWELRY; CHARM RING.

vitreous lustre. The type of glassy LUSTRE shown by most transparent stones, e.g. RUBY, SAPPHIRE, PERIDOT, and GLASS, etc., where the refractive index is about 1.3 to 1.8.

Vix Treasure. A TREASURE excavated in 1929 at Vix, near Châtillon-sur-Seine, France, that included, along with other bronze and gold objects, some jewelry on the skeleton of a young woman thought to have been a Hallstatt princess who died *c.* 500 BC. The jewelry included a gold diadem, a bronze anklet and TORC, bracelets and necklace of amber beads, and iron brooches.

vorobyevite. A variety of BERYL that is rose-coloured or colourless, found in Madagascar, and so named by A. Lacroix, but the name had been previously given by V. I. Vernadsky, in memory of V. I. Vorobyev (1875–1906), to colourless beryl from the Urals.

votive crown. A CROWN given, usually by a Sovereign or a Pope, to a church in fulfilment of a religious vow, such as is sometimes seen hung before an altar or above a statue of the Virgin Mary or a saint. The crowns were usually modelled in the form of contemporary regal crowns and were generally suspended by gold chains. *See* GUARRAZAR TREASURE.

W

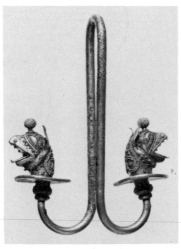

W-shaped ear-ring. Gold with griffin heads. Melos, late 7th century BC. Staatliche Museen, West Berlin.

W-shaped ear-ring. A type of ear-ring in the general shape of the letter W, formed by a splayed, coiled rod or by a wire bent with two descending loops of which the inner arms rise to form a high narrow central loop. Examples are known from *c.* 800 BC–600 BC, mainly from Rhodes and Melos. Decorated versions have the outer ends topped with small horizontal discs, and others have superimposed on the discs the heads of griffins or a pomegranate ornament; on some the ornamented discs are turned outward. On later examples the apex of the central curve is masked by an embossed rosette. Such ear-rings were worn suspended from a thin wire passing through the ear-lobe.

Wagner, Karl (1799–1841). A German jeweller and silversmith, born in Berlin, who revived the technique of NIELLO decoration after settling in Paris in 1830 and obtaining a patent. His company, Mention & Wagner, was patronized by Louis Philippe.

Waldalgesheim style. A style of metal decoration named after Waldalgesheim, on the Middle Rhine, and appearing on some jewelry of early Celtic art. It was probably developed on the mainland of Europe north of the Alps in the latter part of the 4th century BC and continued to the 3rd century BC. The style was derived from the floral patterns of Classical art in the Mediterranean region and has been noted on some TORCS and brooches of the Early La Téne culture, 4th/3rd centuries BC, found in eastern France, and on some articles buried in the 4th century BC at Waldalgesheim.

Walderite. A trade-name for a SYNTHETIC CORUNDUM that is colourless and simulates the white SAPPHIRE.

Wales's, Prince of, Investiture Coronet. The CORONET worn by Prince Charles at his investiture as Prince of Wales at Caernarvon Castle in 1969. It is made of gold by ELECTROFORMING, was designed and executed by LOUIS OSMAN, and was the gift of the Worshipful Company of Goldsmiths. Although in modern style, it preserves the traditional symbols but in stylized form, being a band with four CROSSES FORMÉE and four fleurs-de-lis, surmounted by a single arch topped by an engraved MONDE and a cross formée; it has an ermine head-band. The only jewels are small, square-cut diamonds at the intersections and the arm-ends of the crosses, small emeralds on the fleurs-de-lis, and small diamonds on the monde. The earlier Prince of Wales's Crown, kept in the Jewel House, London, was made for Frederick Louis, son of George II and father of George III, on his creation as Prince of Wales in 1729.

wallet bead. A type of bead that is of semi-oval shape, with a curved bottom rim and across the top a straight or scalloped rim. Such beads were originally of EGYPTIAN JEWELRY, but later of MYCENAEAN JEWELRY, *c.* 1450 BC–1150 BC.

walrus ivory. A variety of IVORY from the outside portion of the tusks (canine teeth) of the walrus. It has a dense texture and a core that is coarser than ELEPHANT IVORY and HIPPOPOTAMUS IVORY. Also called 'morse ivory'. A somewhat similar ivory is obtained from the sperm (cachalot) whale and wart-hog. *See* NARWHAL IVORY.

wampum. A type of bead made of quahog SHELL and strung on thongs used to decorate woven belts, sashes, and bandoliers, for bracelets and necklaces, and also for currency between the North American Indians and early settlers. They were made by the Indians of north-eastern United States (who called them *wampumpeag*, hence the term *wampum* often still used as slang for money). The beads were highly polished and were of two varieties, either black (or dark purple) or white, and were used in contrasting designs. Imitation wampum was made of white porcelain for sale to the Indians.

wardite. A mineral that occurs in bluish-green masses and that resembles TURQUOISE but is softer. Wardite also occurs as spherical growths in VARISCITE, with concentric markings that resemble an eye; the eyes are sometimes cut from the MATRIX and set as CABOCHONS. It was named after Henry A. Ward (1834–1906), an American mineralogist, and is found in Utah (USA). When in its MATRIX of QUARTZ it is called 'amatrix'.

wart pearl. The same as a BLISTER PEARL.

watch. A small timepiece to be carried or worn on the person. Watches were probably made from *c.* 1500. A watch is worn in several ways: (1) a POCKET WATCH, attached to a watch fob or a WATCH CHAIN; (2) a bracelet watch or WRIST WATCH, attached to a bracelet or band around the wrist;

Waldalgesheim style. Torc, hollow gold with repoussé relief. Early La Tène culture, 4th/3rd centuries BC. W. 14.8 cm. British Museum, London.

Wales's, Prince of, Investiture coronet. Designed and made by Louis Osman, 1969. Reproduced by gracious permission of Her Majesty the Queen.

watch bracelet. Gold bracelet set with gemstones and pearls and incorporating a watch. 1960. Patek Philippe, Geneva.

watch-case. Gold, silver, diamonds, and enamel. Pierre Viala, Geneva, *c.* 1770. W. 6 cm. Schmuckmuseum, Pforzheim, Germany.

(3) a PENDANT WATCH worn by a woman suspended from a brooch or chain; (4) a LAPEL WATCH; and (5) a finger-ring watch (*see* WATCH RING). The various types of watches and their movements are in the field of horology rather than of jewelry, and so are beyond the scope of this book. *See* WATCH-CASE; FAUSSE MONTRE; NUREMBERG EGG. *See* T. P. Camerer Cuss, *Antique Watches* (1976).

watch bracelet. A type of bracelet that is flexible and made to include an integrated WRIST WATCH. Such pieces are usually made as luxury jewelry for a woman, being of gold or platinum, set with gemstones, and having the hinged lid completely jewelled so as to conceal the watch and appear as a continuation of the bracelet.

watch-case. The metal case enclosing the works of a watch. They have been made mainly of GOLD, PLATINUM or SILVER, but some were made of ORMOLU, GILDED BRONZE, PINCHBECK, or ROCK CRYSTAL, and recent examples are of chrome. Although usually circular, some are oval, triangular, hexagonal, octagonal, square or of fantasy shapes (known as a 'form watch'). Cases of an open-face watch cover only the back, with the dial exposed through a glass; the front cover of a closed-face watch is attached by a hinge which is usually released by pressure on a button. Sometimes there is a fixed back cover and also a hinged outer cover, and sometimes there is a hinged front cover protecting the glass ('hunter watch' or 'half hunter'). Some cases are ornately decorated, with ENAMEL or ENGRAVING, some have decoration of CLOISONNÉ, CHAMPLEVÉ, REPOUSSÉ, NIELLO, or PIQUÉ, and luxury examples are decorated with gemstones or are made from a gold coin (*see* COIN WATCH). Some cases, especially of a 'clock watch' or a 'repeater', are pierced. A 'pair-case watch' has two cases, the outer case being usually ornately decorated and the inner case (called the 'box') plain. The first portable watch is said to have been made soon after 1500 by Peter Henlein of Nuremberg, and within the century watch-cases were being decorated with gemstones and worn as articles of jewelry.

watch-case. Form watch. Silver depicting lion couchant. Geneva, *c.* 1625. Ashmolean Museum, Oxford.

watch chain. An ornamental CHAIN, of various styles, attached to a man's POCKET WATCH to safeguard it from loss and worn extended across a waistcoat (vest) to a watch-pocket, with the watch on one end and a WATCH CHARM on the other end, and often with a SEAL, CHARM or watch key suspended from the centre of the chain. During the 18th century in England watch chains were often worn with attached suspended ornaments, such as a LOCKET, seal or miniature portrait. *See* ALBERT CHAIN.

watch charm. A small ornament designed to be suspended from a WATCH CHAIN, sometimes known as a BRELOQUE.

watch-hook. A device for holding a man's POCKET WATCH, in the form of a short bar to slide behind the belt and curve over the top and downward, the front with a decorative ornament, sometimes in the form of a band with a snap to hold the watch. Some also had a loop to be attached for security to a WATCH CHAIN.

watch-case. Pair-case. Foiled hollow moss agate with gold mounts. London, *c.* 1735. Ashmolean Museum, Oxford.

watch-case. Jewelled. Gold with enamelling. Paris, 1762. Ashmolean Museum, Oxford.

watch key. A small instrument for winding a POCKET WATCH, used before the invention, *c.* 1680-1700, of the keyless watch. Some examples, especially those made of gold as ornaments in the 19th century, have an ornately decorated or jewelled shank or handle, sometimes with a figured head, and usually have a swivelled bow for suspension from a WATCH CHAIN or a CHATELAINE.

watch ring. A type of finger ring that has a miniature watch set in the BEZEL. Some have a hinged crystal lid, and in one rare example from Augsburg, *c.* 1580, the movement is also hinged to fold within the bezel, and the hinged lid is in the form of a TRIPTYCH. The watch sometimes has, in addition to the main dial, a seconds dial and a date dial. Watch rings were made in the 17th century in Germany and 18th century in England (some by John Arnold, 1730-99, the celebrated horologist), France, and Switzerland; some are inscribed with the name of the maker of the watch. Such watches are being made today, usually as luxury articles with decoration of gemstones; some have a hinged jewelled lid to conceal the dial.

water. (1) A vague, non-gemmological term meant to indicate the limpidity and lustre of a PRECIOUS STONE, especially a diamond. The 'first water' signifies a diamond perfectly transparent as water and free from flaws; the 'second water' and 'third water' signify decreased transparency. The term 'water-white' refers to the clearest and preferred colour for a diamond. (2) The degree of translucency of the surface layer of a pearl (*see* ORIENT).

water opal. A transparent colourless (or nearly so) variety of PRECIOUS OPAL with interior floating flashes of colour. Also called 'iris opal'. *See* HYALITE.

water sapphire. A misnomer applied to: (1) the colourless TOPAZ found in Sri Lanka (formerly Ceylon); and (2) the light-blue CORDIERITE (IOLITE) found there.

watermelon tourmaline. A variety of TOURMALINE that has zoned pink and green segments separated by planes at right angles to the length of the crystal. In the Brazilian variety the inner segment at the core is sometimes red or deep pink, the next white, and the outer green, and the boundaries between the segments are sharp. In the California variety, the core is green and the outer segment is pink. A related variety of tourmaline has separated zones of pink and green at the extremities of the elongated crystal, due to crystal polarity.

Watkins, David (1940-). An English sculptor and also a DESIGNER-MAKER of contemporary jewelry, much of whose work is in acrylic (sometimes steel) combined with gold or silver, all (especially large neckpieces) in highly original and extremely radical designs. He is the husband of WENDY RAMSHAW. *See* ACRYLIC JEWELRY.

wavellite. A mineral, used as a gemstone in some modern jewelry, composed of crystals that radiate like sun-rays. Its colour ranges from white to yellow, green, and black, the coloured specimens being dichroic. It was named after William Wavell (d. 1929), an English physician.

waz-lily bead. A type of bead that is a variation of the LILY BEAD, having a small projecting arc connecting the two volutes of the lily. It was named by Sir Arthur Evans, combining the Egyptian *waz* (papyrus) with lily. Such beads are from the Middle Minoan III Period, *c.* 1700 BC-1600 BC, and also the Late Minoan and Mycenaean Period, *c.* 1600 BC-1100 BC. Occasionally two lily forms are connected adjacently into a 'double waz-lily'.

Weckström, Björn (1935-). A Finnish DESIGNER-MAKER of contemporary jewelry whose work features abstract designs executed in textured gold, occasionally set with uncut and unpolished gemstones or a BAROQUE PEARL. Much of his work is executed by Lapponia, a Helsinki firm that engages many craftsmen to mass produce work of various designers.

watch-case. Engraved. Gilt metal case. Late 16th century. W 8.7 cm. Ashmolean Museum, Oxford.

watch-case. Enamelled. Gold case. French, *c.* 1640. Ashmolean Museum, Oxford.

watch-key. Heraldic brooch with watch key and seal; gold set with diamonds. Courtesy of Wartski, London.

watch ring. Gold with alarm movement and enamelled Crucifixion scene on inside of triptych lid. Augsburg or Munich, *c.* 1580. Schatzkammer, Residenz, Munich.

Wedgwood jewelry. Buckle with jasper cameo and frame, with cut steel and crystal and jasper beads, *c.* 1786. Courtesy of Wedgwood, London.

wedding ring. A finger ring that is given upon marriage (usually as a part of the wedding ceremony) by a man to the bride, and sometimes also by her to the groom. In Roman days and the Middle Ages the wedding ring was indistinguishable from a BETROTHAL RING or an ENGAGEMENT RING, but since the 16th century it has become customary to use a simple gold (or recently PLATINUM or PALLADIUM) band, albeit in recent years some have been engraved on the outside or inside with a sentimental inscription or names, or have been decorated with faceting, DIAMOND-MILLING, or several varicoloured metals, or occasionally (for the bride) set with gemstones, usually a band of small diamonds. A recent development is a matching engagement ring and wedding ring. A wedding ring has conventionally been placed since Roman days on the left hand, except for a short interval in the Middle Ages when it was placed on the right hand. *See* JEWISH MARRIAGE RING; GIMMEL RING; ETERNITY RING.

Wedgwood jewelry. Various articles of personal adornment decorated with plaques of ceramic ware made by Josiah Wedgwood & Sons Ltd. Such articles (including finger rings, MEDALLIONS, brooches, pendants, BUCKLES, CLASPS, ear-rings) were often made by Josiah Wedgwood (1730-95) of JASPER or black basaltes earthenware, sometimes as a CAMEO or INTAGLIO set in a metal mount. The mounts were of gold, silver or MARCASITE, or of cut steel frequently made by MATTHEW BOULTON of Birmingham, *c.* 1790. Other articles which have been made of, or decorated with, Wedgwood jasper include beads, COMBS, CHATELAINES, and scent bottles. The ground of the jasper ware is of various colours, e.g. pale blue, lilac, sage-green, yellow, and black. Josiah Wedgwood II made, *c.* 1812-22, some medallions of bone china that were mounted as brooches.

weights. (1) Gemstones. The unit of weight since 1913 is the metric CARAT, with fractions expressed decimally in POINTS (rarely now in GRAINS), except that (a) less valuable stones are sold by the metric gram; (b) SYNTHETIC GEMSTONES by the size in millimetres; (c) pearls by carats and grains (1 carat = 4 grains); and (d) CULTURED PEARLS formerly by the momme. As a diamond that is BRILLIANT CUT is of a prescribed shape, its weight can be closely estimated (as is usually done if it is in a setting) by its diameter at the GIRDLE, e.g. a stone with a diameter of 6 mm (about ¼-inch) weighs approximately 1 carat, and there are standard schedules for other sizes. (2) Precious metals. The unit of weight now is the metric gram or the kilogram (1,000 grams), replacing the use of the Troy ounce (oz) which equalled 20 pennyweights or 480 grains.

wesselton. A colour grading term formerly used for a diamond of white colour with very faint yellowish tinge, ranking just below RIVER. The name is derived from the Wesselton Mine at Kimberley, South Africa. *See* DIAMOND COLOURS.

West African jewelry. Articles of jewelry that have been made in the region of West Africa bordering the Gulf of Guinea, mainly the Gold Coast (now Ghana) (*see* ASHANTI JEWELRY) and Nigeria (*see* BENIN JEWELRY), and the area along the upper Niger River to Timbuktu. *See* J. B. Donne, 'West African Goldwork', in *Connoisseur*, February 1977, p. 100.

Westminster Torc. A gold TORC large enough to be worn around the waist, being 127 cm long and 35.5 cm in diameter. It is in the form of a circular cruciform flange, spirally twisted, with recurved solid terminals hooking into each other. It is attributed to the Middle Bronze Age, 12th century BC. It was found in a quarry in 1816 by a miner near Holywell, Wales, and acquired by the Marquess of Westminster, and in 1966 by Partridge (Fine Arts), London, by whom it was sold to a private collector. *See* HARLECH TORC.

wheat-ear style. A style of decoration in the form of ears of wheat. It was introduced in France in the 18th century, following the PEAPOD style, and was used for brooches with single sprays or elaborate sheaves, usually of silver set with small diamonds.

wheel brooch. A type of brooch in the form of a circle with ribs crossing the central space as spokes in a wheel, sometimes having the ribs decorated with gemstones. Such brooches followed the RING BROOCH when it was no longer necessary to keep the open space in the centre for fastening by means of pulling up the fabric to be pierced by the pin; such brooches were fastened by the pin and a CATCH-PLATE.

whistle. An instrument that produces, by having air (or steam) blown through it, a shrill sound. Air-whistles were made in ornamental form from the 16th century, to be hung as a pendant or from a girdle or CHATELAINE (sometimes used for calling domestics), and are shown in Renaissance paintings and DÜRER engravings. Some were made of gold or silver, with CHASING or enamelled decoration, and some carved of BOXWOOD. One made for Henry VIII, set in a finger ring, was decorated with diamonds and a RUBY. Examples were hung with silver bells to ward off the 'evil eye', and some were in the form of a case to hold TOOTHPICKS and EAR-PICKS. *See* HANS BROSAMER.

white gemstone. Any transparent gemstone that is colourless.

white gold. An ALLOY of GOLD with a high percentage of SILVER or any of several other white metals, the percentage of gold varying depending on the other metal used. It is of a pale gold colour. The term is sometimes applied to the ancient ELECTRUM. Before the use of PLATINUM or PALLADIUM, white gold was often used as a setting for diamonds, being highly reflective and, unlike silver, not subject to TARNISH.

white opal. A variety of PRECIOUS OPAL that is transparent and colourless (or nearly so), with flashes of colour. Also called 'iris opal'. *See* ANDAMOOKA OPAL.

White Rose Jewel. A pendant in the form of a gold open rose with white enamelled petals and having in the centre a large BALAS RUBY (SPINEL). It was given by Edward IV of England to his sister, Margaret of York, upon her marriage in 1475 to Charles the Bold (1433-77), last Duke of Burgundy, from whose tent it was stolen (together with the THREE BROTHERS JEWEL) after his defeat by the Swiss at the battle of Grandson, 1476. It is depicted in a watercolour painted on vellum, *c*. 1500.

widow's ring. A type of English finger ring received by a widow who took a vow of chastity that prevented her from making a second marriage which would confer on her second husband the property she had received from her first husband; but in rare instances the vow could be set aside, e.g. by Eleanor, sister of Henry III, whose first husband was William, Earl of Pembroke, and who later married Simon de Montfort, Earl of Leicester (1208-65).

Wièse, Jules (1818-90). A Parisian jeweller who studied under F.-D. FROMENT-MEURICE, and worked for him and his son, Émile, until 1860 when he opened his own workshop and exhibited in 1862. He made jewelry in ARCHITECTURAL STYLE, often making gold brooches with openwork patterns and small figures IN THE ROUND. Shortly before his retirement in 1880 he made pieces with Japanese motifs.

Wild Jewel. A pendant decorated with a CAMEO carved in TURQUOISE with a portrait of Elizabeth I. It is said to have been a christening gift from the Queen to a member of the Wild family, a descendant of which subsequently lent it to the Victoria & Albert Museum.

willemite. A mineral that is an ore of zinc, but from which some pale-yellow crystals have been found that are used as gemstones, sometimes cut as a BRILLIANT. If pure it would be colourless but it is often stained various shades by the colouring agents present. The MASSIVE variety is sometimes cut EN CABOCHON or as BEADS. It fluoresces brightly in ultraviolet light. It was named in 1830 after William I, King of the Netherlands, 1815-1840.

williamsite. A variety of SERPENTINE that is yellow to dark green, sometimes with black patches. It is used more for ornamental purposes than for jewelry, but some translucent specimens are faceted or cut EN CABOCHON.

Westminster Torc (detail below). Gold girdle torc, spirally twisted with recurved terminals; Middle Bronze Age, 12th century BC. L. 127 cm. Private collection. Courtesy of Partridge (Fine Arts), London.

White Rose Jewel. White-enamelled, with spinel, as depicted *c*. 1500 on vellum, in the Historisches Museum, Basle.

Wilton Cross. Pendant cross mounted with gold solidus and set with *cloisonné* garnets. Anglo-Saxon, 7th century, found at Wilton, Norfolk, L. 4.5 cm. British Museum, London.

Williamson Diamond. A rose-coloured diamond weighing 54 carats rough that was found in 1947 in the Tanganyika mine of Dr John T. Williamson and was given by him to Princess Elizabeth upon her marriage in 1947. She had it cut by Briefel & Lemer, of London, to its present weight of 23.60 carats and set in a brooch made as a stylized Alpine rose with five diamond petals. It is the most famous pink diamond, and is sometimes called the 'Queen Elizabeth Pink'.

Wilson, Henry (1864–1934). An English architect, metalworker, silversmith, and sculptor who was also a jeweller and who was a leader in the Arts and Crafts Movement. The designs for his jewelry were very original, and his techniques are discussed in his book, *Silverwork and Jewellery* (2nd ed. 1912). Much of his work featured REPOUSSÉ and PLIQUE À JOUR decoration, emphasizing ART NOUVEAU motifs from nature, but he is known also for his religious and allegorical designs.

Wilton Cross. A gold PECTORAL CROSS with four arms of equal length and having rounded extremities, all extending from a large central ring enclosing a solidus (a gold coin). The arms and the ring are decorated with rectangular, step-shaped, and mushroom-shaped cells formed by prominent CLOISONS filled with enamel and GARNETS. At the top there is a horizontal FILIGREE bead, of BUGLE BEAD shape, for a suspensory cord. The solidus is a coin of Heraclius, Byzantine Emperor 610–41, mounted to show its reverse which depicts a cross potent on a four-step base, being mounted upside down; the reverse of the solidus depicts an effigy in proper position. The cross is Anglo-Saxon from the 7th century, and was found at Wilton, Norfolk, England. *See* IXWORTH CROSS.

window. (1) A facet on the side of a native-cut, partly-coloured gemstone (usually a SAPPHIRE) that is cut so that the strongest colour is at the base and the stone consequently appears to have a uniform colour when viewed through the TABLE but appears clear when viewed from the side. (2) A facet cut on a diamond with a rough or coated surface to permit a visual examination of the interior. The process is called 'opening the diamond'. (3) A facet on some square-cut emeralds or other so cut gemstone that permits light to escape and through which an object can be seen when viewed from the table.

Winston, Harry. Platinum necklace with marquise, pear-shaped, and round diamonds; designed and made by Harry Winston, Inc., New York.

Winston, Harry (1896–1978). The world's largest individual dealer in, and a leading connoisseur of, diamonds, noted for the famous stones that he handled or owned (60 of the 303 listed major diamonds) and for the extensive business of his firm, Harry Winston, Inc., as a wholesaler, retailer, and cutter of diamonds, as well as a maker and designer of important jewelry set with diamonds, emeralds, rubies or sapphires. He was born in New York City where the firm still has its principal business and workshop at 718 5th Ave., but also with workrooms and offices in several foreign countries. Among the major diamonds that he handled are the ARCOT, BRIOLETTE OF INDIA, CARTIER, DEEPDENE, EUGÉNIE BLUE, IDOL'S EYE, JONKER, LESOTHO, LIBERATOR, NEPAL, NIARCHOS, POHL, SHAH OF PERSIA, STAR OF INDEPENDENCE, STAR OF SIERRA LEONE, STAR OF THE EAST, VARGAS, WINSTON, Vitoria, and Queen of Belgium, and also the HOPE DIAMOND, the NASSAK DIAMOND, and the OPPENHEIMER DIAMOND that he donated to the Smithsonian Institution, Washington, DC. Since his death in 1978 the firm has been directed by his son, Ronald Winston (b. 1941). *See* FARAH DIBA TIARA. *[Plate XVI]*

Winston Diamond. A colourless diamond, originally called the 'Jagersfontein' after the mine in South Africa where it was found in 1952, weighing rough 154.50 carats. It was bought in 1953 by HARRY WINSTON who had it cut into a 62.50-carat heart-shaped stone and sold it, it has been said, to King Ibn Saud of Saudi Arabia who returned it 18 months later in exchange for other diamonds; it was then resold to a private Canadian owner.

wire. Metal in the form of a thread or a very slender rod, usually flexible and circular in section. Wire of gold has been used in jewelry from ancient times, as surface or openwork decoration (*see* FILIGREE) or for joining the elements of an article. Originally it was made by rolling a hammered strip of SHEET METAL between two very hard surfaces (e.g. stone or bronze) until circular in section, or by twisting a thin strip of

wire enamelling. Reliquary pendant, silver gilt, with blue and green enamel frame encircling Resurrection scene; and, on the reverse, a central cabochon crystal. Transylvania, 1451. W. 11.5 cm. Hungarian National Museum, Budapest.

metal into a spiral. Later, in the Roman era and the Middle Ages, the draw-plate was used to reduce the thickness of the wire and to stretch it. Thick wire was made by CASTING, and hollow wire (tubing) by hammering strips into grooves in wood or metal or by wrapping it around a mandrel and hammering it into shape. Beaded wire was formerly made by pressing wire into a beading tool on which depressions had been engraved. Today wire manufactured in many gauges is available to jewellers from rolling mills and metal refiners. *See* SPECTACLE BEAD; SPECTACLE FIBULA.

wire enamelling. A technique of decoration in ENAMELLING by which the outline of the design is formed by twisted wire, not fixed to the base by soldering (as in FILIGREE enamel) but held in place by the opaque coloured enamels that fill in the spaces. It was developed in Transylvania and the neighbouring regions in the 15th century, and spread in the late Middle Ages to Venice, thence to the Abruzzi and Campagna regions of Italy. *See* TRANSYLVANIAN ENAMEL.

wire ring. A type of finger ring made as a hoop of WIRE. The earliest rings of precious metal were so made of gold in the third millennium BC. In England Saxon rings of the 9th/11th centuries were made of gold wire, some having the wire twisted, others plaited, in each case flattened at the back of the hoop.

wirework mesh jewelry. Articles of jewelry made of fine iron wirework mesh. Examples were made of extremely thin wire in the form of brooches, necklaces, and handbags, and also pendants in the form of a Gothic cross, attributed possibly to Silesia in the 18th century. Some such pieces were decorated with polished steel *paillettes* (sequins). Related articles of BERLIN IRON JEWELRY were made in the early 19th century of fine plaited iron wire.

Witham Pins. A PIN SUITE composed of three PINS linked together by short bars at the head ornaments, which are discs of gilt bronze decorated with CHIP-CARVING depicting in minute size animal motifs mingled with ornamentation in RIBBON STYLE and with the small eyes of the animals originally inlaid with blue glass. The suite is Anglo-Saxon, 8th century, and was found in 1826 in the River Witham near Fiskerton, Lincolnshire, England.   [Plate I]

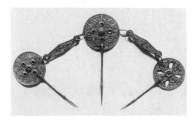

Witham Pins. Pin suite, gilt bronze. Anglo-Saxon, 8th century. L. 12 cm. British Museum, London.

Wittelsbach Diamond. A blue diamond, weighing 35.32 carats rough, of Indian origin, first recorded when it was part of a gift from Philip IV of Spain to his daughter upon her marriage in 1664 to Leopold I of Austria. It was inherited by Maria Amalia of Austria from her grandmother, and passed to Charles Albert of Bavaria (later Charles VII, Holy Roman Emperor, 1742-5) upon their betrothal in 1722. It remained in the Wittelsbach family (which included the first dukes, later kings, of Bavaria) until 1931 when Bavaria offered it unsuccessfully for sale at Christie's, London. It disappeared until offered in Belgium in 1961 and was bought by a group headed by the Antwerp dealer I. Komkommer. It was exhibited in Europe and in 1964 was acquired in Germany by a private collector.

Wolfers Frères. Pendant 'Charmeuse' with ivory figure, iris wings, and suspended opal. Designed by Philippe Wolfers, *c.* 1894-1903. H. 8.5 cm. Courtesy of Wolfers Frères, Brussels.

wreath. Gold ivy leaves, *c.* 3rd century BC. British Museum, London.

wreath. Gold oak leaves, Classical period, *c.* 475 BC-323 BC. Museo Nazionale, Taranto, Italy.

Woeiriot, Pierre (1532-96). A designer of RENAISSANCE JEWELRY, born in Lorraine. He moved in 1555 to Lyons where he made a large number of engravings for jewelry of great variety, which were published in Lyons in 1555 and 1561. His work influenced the designs of English jewelry. His designs often featured a cartouche with upturned edges and motifs of nude figures. His greatest work is the *Livre d'Anneaux d'Orfèvrerie*, published in Lyons in 1561 (of which a copy is at the Bodleian Library, Oxford, and a facsimile, with an Introduction by Diana Scarisbrick, was published at Oxford in 1978), which includes 40 plates showing 96 designs for rings; many of the actual rings from his designs are in the Victoria & Albert Museum, the Ashmolean Museum, Oxford, and the British Museum.

Wolfers Frères. The leading Belgian jewelry firm and the Belgian Court Jeweller. The firm dates back to Guillaume Wolfers, a journeyman jeweller from Vienna who came to Brussels in 1841. His son Louis Wolfers established in 1850 a workshop of craftsmen from twenty guilds; it designed and created gold and silver jewelry. His sons Philippe (1858-1929), Max (1859-1953), and Robert (1867-1959) joined the family business and started their retail store in 1890; it was moved in 1911 to Rue d'Arenberg and later to its present address at 82 Avenue Louise. Philippe became interested in Japanese ware in 1873, and in 1890 started his own workshop; from 1893 he started to make articles with IVORY imported from the Belgian Congo (now Zaïre). He became a leading exponent of the ART NOUVEAU style; his pieces were usually dated and signed. After 1905 he became occupied with sculpture and silverware, and by 1910 he ceased making jewelry. The next generation that carried on the jewelry business included several cousins: Marcel (1886-1976), Lucien (1891-1969), Raymond (1893-1975), Willy (1895-   ), and Gustave-Louis (1905-44), and they have been succeeded by the following generation, Freddy (b. 1920) and Jean (b. 1922), sons of Willy Wolfers.

wood. A material that (except when petrified) has seldom been used for jewelry, despite the attractive grain and colour that occurs in many varieties; but some articles of jewelry have been made of BOGWOOD, ebony, sycamore, and some fruit woods. Wood has been used in some INDIAN (UNITED STATES) JEWELRY, and in some fashionable modern jewelry, e.g. pieces designed by Angela Cummings for TIFFANY & CO., New York.

Woodstock jewelry. A type of CUT STEEL jewelry made in the small town of Woodstock, near Oxford, England, possibly from the Elizabethan era, but well regarded *c.* 1750 owing to its skilled craftsmanship, intricate designs, and ability to be disassembled for cleaning. The articles then included CHATELAINES, WATCH CHAINS, BUCKLES, etc., and later, *c.* 1850, the work became popularized and included bracelets, necklaces, brooches, etc. The pieces were ornamented with cut steel studs fastened by rivets and closely packed, creating a sparkling effect from the reflection from the facets.

worry beads. Beads usually made of AMBER or a synthetic imitation, which are strung together and carried by men in Turkey and Greece, who use them as a tranquillizer by handling and sliding the loosely-spaced beads with the fingers.

Woyie River Diamond. *See* SIERRA LEONE DIAMONDS.

wreath. An ornamental band in the form of naturalistic or stylized leaves, worn on the head on festive occasions or by victors at the ancient games. Early Greek examples, from the Classical period, *c.* 475 BC-330 BC, were made of gold, silver, gold-plated metal or gilded wood, and simulated the leaves of myrtle, oak, olive or ivy. Such wreaths were also an article of ETRUSCAN JEWELRY; they were awarded as prizes, worn in processions, dedicated in sanctuaries, and buried with the dead. They were also made in Byzantium, and worn there on festive occasions, especially at weddings when the bride and groom wore them, mingled with real flowers, as crowns, returning them later (as in some Scandinavian countries today; *see* BRIDAL CROWN) to the owning church. Roman examples featured stylized leaves. In the Middle Ages young women wore a wreath of gold; it was a forerunner of the CHAPLET.

wrist clasp. A sleeve ornament for fastening the cuff of a leather or home-spun tunic. Some examples of Anglo-Saxon make, 6th century, found in East Anglia, are rectangular, others have a pyramidal upper half; they are made of cast bronze, brightened by a graver and then gilded, and have holes for being sewn to the garment. *See* SLEEVE FASTENER.

wrist clasps. Gilt bronze. Anglo-Saxon, late 6th century. L. 8.5 cm. Museum of Archaeology, Cambridge University.

wrist watch. A type of small WATCH worn on a wristband by a man or woman. The first example was made by CARTIER in 1904 for the aviator Alberto Santos-Dumont who found use of his fob watch difficult; it was a round-cornered, square watch, and the design is still copied. Such watches became popular after World War I owing to the practicality in wearing and referring to them while the wearer's hands were otherwise engaged. They are now made is various styles, sizes, and qualities, with hands or moving digits to show the time, and activated by traditional movements or by quartz. Although basically utilitarian, examples that may be classified as jewelry have been made with cases of gold or platinum, set with gemstones. The case of some such watches for men's use is made of a hollowed gold coin. *See* WATCH BRACELET; COCKTAIL WATCH; COIN WATCH.

Wykeham, William of, Jewels. Several jewelled articles that were bequeathed to New College, Oxford, by William of Wykeham (1324-1404), Bishop of Winchester and Lord High Chancellor of England, entombed at Winchester. They include the FOUNDER'S JEWEL, the FOUNDER'S RING, and some fragments that originally decorated his mitre, including jewelled hinged bands, two rosettes, and two quatrefoil badges of silver gilt. The bands are silver gilt plates decorated with BASSE TAILLE enamel representing grotesques and animals, alternating with white crystals and dark-blue PASTES, and having a border set with irregular pearls. The rosettes, square with concave sides, are decorated with Gothic foliation and are set with white crystals. The badges are quatrefoil ornaments, each set with a gemstone. All are of English make from the late 14th century.

Wyoming jade. A misnomer for JADE MATRIX. Sometimes sold as 'snowflake jade'.

X

X-Group Treasure. A TREASURE of ancient articles, including some jewelry, discovered in tombs in cemeteries and tumuli in the Qustul and Ballana regions of northern Nubia (now part of Egypt), between Abu Simbel and Sudan, excavated in anticipation of the flooding by the Aswan Dam. The tombs are from the little-known X-Group (or Ballana) culture of the 3rd/6th centuries AD, between the Meroitic and Christian eras. The first excavations (apart from ancient tomb plundering) were by Walter Emery between 1931 and 1933 and later by Shafiq Farid, and then in 1963-4 by Prof. Keith C. Seele, of the Oriental Institute of the University of Chicago (which was given ownership of 95% of its finds). The finds included pottery, bronze vessels, and metal tools, and also many articles of jewelry, such as a silver wreath and gold and silver bracelets, finger rings, ear-rings, hair-rings, and necklaces with suspended amulets and pendants, as well as numerous beads and ornamental objects of EGYPTIAN FAIENCE, bone, shell, ivory, glass, and CORNELIAN. *See Journal of Near Eastern Studies*, vol. 33, no. 1 (January 1974).

xanthite. A variety of IDOCRASE that is transparent and yellowish-brown.

Y

Yalalag cross. Silver. San Juan Yalalag, Oaxaca, Mexico. Photo by Marcos Ortiz.

Yalalag Cross. A popular article of Mexican PEASANT JEWELRY in the form of a pendant cross, made only in the town of San Juan Yalalag, east of Oaxaca, from before the 16th century and possibly derived from a Spanish prototype. It is made of cast silver, with hammered and embossed decoration, and from its foot and side arms hang small crosses or other ornaments, e.g. coins, medals, crowns, hearts or figures, with sometimes a winged heart or other design at the intersection of the arms. Some such pendants are up to 15 cm wide. They are usually presented, attached to a necklace, by a mother to her daughter on her wedding day. *See* MEXICAN JEWELRY.

Yanhuitlán Brooch. A Mexican gold brooch (in the form of a miniature war shield, called a *chimalli*) that has a central ornament of interlocked symbols made of gold and turquoise mosaic, said to be the only known surviving example of stone inlaid with gold. Projecting from each side of the circular shield are the heads and ends of four horizontal spears (or arrows) and suspended from the feathery cast gold FILIGREE frame are 11 (originally 13) CASCABELES. It has been ascribed to the Mixtec-Zapotec culture (*c.* 1200-1540) and was found in 1903 on a skeleton near the village of Yanhuitlán in Oaxaca, Mexico. A replica was given by President Alemán to Princess Elizabeth upon her marriage in 1947, and many modern copies have been made, some of silver with a variety of local stones. *See* MIXTEC JEWELRY.

yellow-belly. A variety of TORTOISE SHELL that is from the plastron (underside) of the turtle. It is of a uniform yellow colour, and is less valuable than the marbled brownish plates from its carapace (upper side). It is preferred for women's hair combs, especially in Spain and Japan, to contrast with dark hair.

yellow gold. An ALLOY of GOLD with SILVER and COPPER, with the copper in increased proportions producing a reddish gold. Yellow gold is the type most frequently used.

yttrium–aluminium–garnet. A SYNTHETIC GEMSTONE that has a structure the same as that of a GARNET, but has no chemical counterpart in nature. It has been produced since 1969 in a range of colours, but especially as a colourless stone to simulate a diamond; but it has much more FIRE. A comparable synthetic stone is 'yttrium-iron-garnet' which is opaque, black, and metallic, examples of which have been polished to imitate HEMATITE without its red streak. These are usually called, respectively, by the trade-names YAG and YIG; other trade-names are, in England, Diamolaire and Cirolite and, in the United States, Diamonair.

Yanhuitlán Brooch. Gold frame with gold and turquoise mosaic; dangling *cascabeles.* Mixtec-Zapotec. W. 8.5 cm. Museo Nacional de Antropología, Mexico.

Z

Zapotec jewelry. Articles of PRE-COLUMBIAN JEWELRY possibly made by the Zapotec Indians of Mexico who inhabited southern Oaxaca and the Isthmus of Tehuantepec, near Monte Albán. They were closely affiliated with the neighbouring Mayan Indians of the Old Empire, *c.* 317–987, and after *c.* 1300 with the Toltec Indians who followed them in the region and to whom much of the jewelry of the MONTE ALBÁN TREASURE has been attributed.

zibellino (Italian). Literally, sable. The Italian term for FUR JEWELRY.

zircon. A variety of gemstone of which the common natural colour is reddish-brown but stones exhibiting green and several other natural colours are found. However, most marketed specimens are brown stones that have been subjected to HEAT TREATMENT which produces a colourless stone or stones of a wide range of colours, especially blue, bluish-green, purple, deep red, and golden-yellow. When the stones are heated in a closed container, they become colourless or blue; when a flow of air is permitted to enter the container, they become golden-yellow or red. Such converted colours are fairly stable, but sometimes revert in time to greenish- or brownish-blue. Certain coloured varieties have been given special names (e.g. HYACINTH, JACINTH, JARGOON) which have been recommended to be discarded in favour of merely prefixes of the particular colour. The zircon has ADAMANTINE LUSTRE and high colour dispersion, so that a colourless stone often resembles a diamond, but with less FIRE and BRILLIANCE. All zircons are brittle and tend to chip at the facet edges. They are classified as (1) 'high' or 'normal' (which are CRYSTALLINE), (2) 'low' or metamict (which are AMORPHOUS or nearly so), and (3) intermediate (which can be converted by heat to 'high'). Zircons are faceted usually in the MIXED CUT or ZIRCON CUT style. Most zircons are treated and cut in Bangkok, Thailand. Misnomers that have been applied to zircon are 'Siam aquamarine', 'Matara diamond', and 'Ceylon diamond'. Synthetic zircons have been produced but not commercially; a blue SYNTHETIC SPINEL has been miscalled a 'synthetic zircon'. *See* STARLITE.

zircon cut. A style of cutting a transparent gemstone (often used in cutting a ZIRCON, owing to its brilliance) in a manner similar to the BRILLIANT CUT but with an extra row of 16 small FACETS between the PAVILION FACETS and the CULET.

zircon cut
side view

Ziwiye Treasure. A TREASURE of articles of gold, silver, and ivory jewelry said to have been found in 1947, between Kurdistan and Azerbaijan, in Iran, in an Assyrian bronze 'container' (later referred to as a 'coffin') and which has been attributed to the late 7th century BC. Many pieces now in the Iran Baston Museum, Tehran, and other leading world-wide museums have been attributed to this source, especially as a consequence of the book, *Le Trésor de Ziwiyé*, written in 1954 by André Godard who claimed to have recovered some of the pieces (through a Tehran dealer, Ayoub Rabenou) from the pillaging natives, and also the writings of Roman Ghirshman, a French scholar. However, as the number of pieces now attributed to this source has greatly increased beyond the early reports, the authenticity of many of them has been seriously questioned, particularly by Oscar Muscarella, an American archaeological authority, who has based his contention on the fact tht no example was excavated under controlled methods and that many pieces were looted, or possibly even faked, by local villagers to sell to antiquarians. Some of the museum

Ziwiye Treasure. Gold bracelet decorated with lions, 8th century BC. W. 9 cm. Iran Bastan Museum, Tehran.

pieces show motifs, including animals heads, usually ascribed to the Assyrians and the Scythians who inhabited the surrounding territories, thus supporting the claims to authenticity. *See The Sunday Times* (London, 7 May 1978); R. D. Barnett, 'The Treasure of Ziwiyé', *Iraq*, xviii (1956), 111-16.

zoomorphic jewelry. *See* ANIMAL JEWELRY.

Zündt, Matthias (1498-1586). A German designer of jewelry, formerly known as the 'Master of 1551'. He became a citizen of Nuremberg in 1566 as a recognized goldsmith and lapidary, but is now known for his engraved designs which exemplify the Mannerist style of Nuremberg.

Zuñi jewelry. Articles of silver jewelry made by the Zuñi Indians of western New Mexico since *c.* 1870 when they first made silver pieces resembling NAVAJO JEWELRY, but mainly since *c.* 1890 when they developed the cutting and inlay setting of turquoise. In 1935 they began the making of multicoloured articles, using with small pieces of turquoise some inlays of jet and shell, and their work is now characterized by emphasis on the stones rather than on the silver. They also make fetish necklaces with many small pendants in the form of animals, birds, and grubs. Since the 1940s they have developed the process of decorating with CHANNEL WORK.

Addenda

Thetford Treasure. An important TREASURE of Roman gold pieces found in England on a building site at Thetford, Norfolk, in November 1979, including jewelry consisting of 22 gem-set gold rings, 5 gold necklaces, 4 gold bracelets, and a gold belt buckle, all said to have been part of a jeweller's stock of unused items made somewhere in the Roman Empire. The treasure has been declared treasure trove and awarded to the Crown; it is now at the British Museum, London.

WITHDRAWAL